Sharīʿa Scripts

SHARĪʿA SCRIPTS

A Historical Anthropology

BRINKLEY MESSICK

COLUMBIA UNIVERSITY PRESS *NEW YORK*

Columbia University Press
Publishers Since 1893
New York Chichester, West Sussex
cup.columbia.edu

Paperback edition, 2022

Library of Congress Cataloging-in-Publication Data

Names: Messick, Brinkley Morris, author.
Title: Sharīa scripts : a historical anthropology / Brinkley Messick.
Description: New York : Columbia University Press, 2017. | Includes bibliographical references and index.
Identifiers: LCCN 2017003801 | ISBN 9780231178747 (cloth) | ISBN 9780231178754 (pbk.) | ISBN 9780231541909 (e-book)
Subjects: LCSH: Justice, Administration of—Yemen (Republic)—History—20th century. | Law reform—Yemen (Republic)—History—20th century. | Islamic law—Yemen (Republic)—History—20th century. | Zaydīyah—Yemen (Republic)—History—20th century. | Legal documents (Islamic law)—Yemen (Republic)—History—20th century. | Legal documents—Yemen (Republic)—History—20th century.
Classification: LCC KMX1046.8 .M47 2017 | DDC 349.533—dc23
LC record available at https://lccn.loc.gov/2017003801

Cover image: Ahmad Muhammad al-Ḥaddād, Judge of Ibb, reading a rolled court judgment, 1976. Photo provided by the author.

Contents

Map of Upper and Lower Yemen

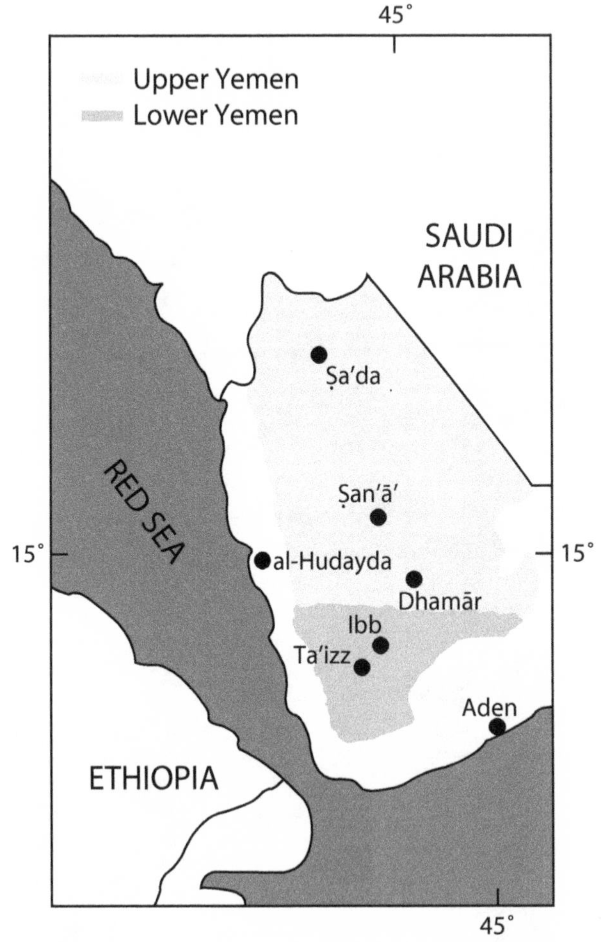

Sharīʿa Scripts

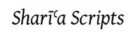

Ibb, 1976.

Introduction

> Law is for me a kind of writing, at its heart less an interpretive process than a compositional one.
>
> —James Boyd White, *The Legal Imagination*

AS IN MUCH of the historical Muslim world, in early twentieth-century highland Yemen a hallmark of academic formation in a madrasa was the study of the sharīʿa. This took the concrete form of instruction in the doctrinal literature known as the *fiqh*, the shrunken presence of which in the contemporary era makes it difficult to appreciate its centrality in former times. Educated individuals of the older generation—including not only jurists but also individuals who went on to become governors, functionaries, and merchants, as well as literati and historians—virtually all received training in the *fiqh* works of a particular school of sharīʿa interpretation.

For trained jurists not cut out for the rough and tumble of the sharīʿa court, a suitable alternative post was at the Endowments Office, an administration that collected revenues from urban and rural properties for the support of mosques, madrasa instruction, and related institutions including, in the old days, water systems. After completing his studies, an earnest young man named Muhammad ʿAli al-Ghurbānī obtained an Endowments post, initially in his native Yarīm, a district seat located over the Sumāra mountain pass to the north, and then in Ibb, the provincial capital. Following the 1962 Revolution, he would continue on as the head of the Accounting

Section. In scholarly *ʿimāma* turban, tinted glasses, and close-trimmed salt-and-pepper beard, al-Ghurbānī received me in the Ibb office in 1975. He offered to help in what was then my dissertation research.

One afternoon at his house, as he fielded the disparate questions I had accumulated since my previous visit, al-Ghurbānī remarked that I should not attempt to approach the sharīʿa piecemeal. Five years later, during my second extended stay in Ibb, as I began to concentrate on judicial processes, he led me through the main points of the standard doctrinal chapters on the judgeship and court claims. Open in his lap as he instructed me was the fourth volume of an authoritative commentary on a classic text he had studied in his youth, *The Book of Flowers*, a basic work of *fiqh* according to the Zaydī school of interpretation.[1]

I also frequented the afternoon sitting room of a second man as he received pieces of paper bearing written questions. People approached Muhammad al-Wahhābī, the Muftī of Ibb, to get his juridical opinions. Prior to the 1962 Revolution, al-Wahhābī had been a teacher at the Madrasa of the Great Mosque, and prior to that he had been a student at the same school. Provided food and lodging at the endowment-supported residence located near the Great Mosque, al-Wahhābī rose from a humble background to become one of the town's leading sharīʿa specialists.

Tall and physically strong, the Muftī had become hard of hearing and did not see well by the time I knew him. He sat on a cushion at floor level wearing a skullcap and a vest over a full-length white gown. As he chewed the mildly stimulating, alkaloid-rich leaves of the *qat* plant, he took turns with others smoking the tall Yemeni water pipe. When the Muftī received a question he held the paper up close to his face before dipping his old-fashioned carved reed pen into the inkwell on the chest in front of him. Then, without hesitation, holding the paper up in his hands, his fingers on the back meeting the pressure of his pen on the front, the Muftī wrote out his response, which he placed in the vacant space purposely left above the question. Such a written response by a muftī is termed a fatwā, a distinctive, nonbinding genre of sharīʿa opinion. When he was finished, he handed the paper, now bearing both the question and his fatwā, back to the questioner, who took it and left, although a few individuals paused to ask someone in the room to read or interpret what the Muftī had written. Since no copies were made, the evidence of this everyday interpretive work departed with his questioners. With the Muftī's permission, I hired a man to sit with him to make copies of this traffic in questions and answers.[2]

It was at the house of a third man that I first encountered a judicial archive. Ahmad Muhammad al-Ḥaddād had been the town muftī during part of the pre-revolutionary period, and he still was known to locals of the older generation as Muftī al-Ḥaddād. By the mid-1970s, however, he occupied a new position and signed himself as the "Judge of Ibb." At the time, Judge al-Ḥaddād resided on the alley that descends along the west wall of the Great Mosque of Ibb, just down from the high stone archway of the town's former water-lift tower and not far from where the rear gate to the town had stood. He held his morning court sessions on the other side of the walled part of the town, near the location of the old main gate. Like most of the town's rear gate, which led out to the mountain towering immediately to the east, the impressive main gate, from which a steep street descended down into what later became the new market area, was torn down following the Revolution. Navigating the stone-paved streets of old Ibb, the judge used a cane to make his way to and from the sharīʿa court. He, too, wore an *ʿimāma* and, during the cooler months, a long black formal overcoat.

Judge al-Ḥaddād had me sit near him when I attended his morning court. This he convened with an ordinary table and a few chairs in what otherwise would have been a room in a new-style residential apartment. At his house in the afternoons, as his lounging soldier-retainers chewed *qat* and monitored the ground floor entrance, disputants and petitioners went up a flight of stairs to a semi-public sitting room furnished in rough mats and floor cushions, with ankle irons hanging from pegs on the wall. On any given afternoon the judge would come and go, but his court secretary, who was his son-in-law, took an accustomed place at the head of the room to chew *qat*. He listened to people who came to see the judge or occupied himself copying out court documents. When the secretary worked on one of the judgment rolls the court issued to litigants, coils of paper spilled out of his lap.

One afternoon I came up the alley to a surprise: the old judge had moved out. Like many others in those years, Judge al-Ḥaddād's family had relocated from the walled town to a house in one of the more spacious outlying new quarters, from which he was driven to court in the family's Toyota Land Cruiser. At his just-vacated house I encountered one of his soldier-retainers, a man I knew named Mustafa, who carried a rifle and wore crossed cartridge belts. We went upstairs and in the hallway across from the now-empty sitting room I noticed that a door stood ajar to a small, windowless storeroom. A rubbish pile of documents had been left behind, the remnants of some sort of archive. There were fragments of judgment rolls and various legal instruments, mostly faded copies made on the older type of wet-process photocopier. Among the discarded documents, however, was an old sharīʿa court register. Water-damaged and containing only a few case entries, it pertained to a local judge who had served in the 1950s, the decade before the Revolution. I photographed the few pages that contained court record entries. Mustafa's fingers holding the pages down appear in the corners of the images.

A fourth man, the slight and elegant ʿAbd al-Karim al-Akwaʿ, also an employee at the Endowments Office, was the first of several individuals in the town to allow me access to their personal archives of legal documents (figure 0.1). His son Ahmad, then a primary school teacher, worked as my occasional assistant. Unlike al-Ghurbānī, whose training had been in the *Flowers* literature of Zaydī *fiqh*, but like Muftī al-Wahhābī and Judge al-Ḥaddād, both of whom also grew up in Ibb, ʿAbd al-Karim in his youth was formed in the Shāfiʿī tradition, having studied such standard works as *The Cream*, an introductory *fiqh* text in rhymed verse by the Palestinian jurist Ibn Raslān (d. 1440).[3]

Before the Revolution, ʿAbd al-Karim led a life of refinement and leisure, although he engaged in seasonal tax-collection work for the provincial government during the fall harvest and later supervised the endowments for students at the Madrasa of the Great Mosque. He spent his afternoons with local literati and other friends chewing *qat* in his fifth-floor reception room atop Dār al-Thajja, one of the massive named houses of old Ibb, where the assembled men looked out across the rooftops as the light slowly changed on the surrounding mountainsides. By the time I arrived on the scene in Ibb, what remained of Dār al-Thajja was a mound of stone rubble in the lot east of the Jalāliyya Mosque. A couple of years earlier, following a series of loud warning creaks, the great house had collapsed. ʿAbd al-Karim now could be found in the afternoons in his small personal room in the new house he built around the corner. The items of his everyday outdoor attire—suit jacket, shawl, sheathed dagger in its embroidered belt, and his ʿ*imāma*—hung from pegs on the wall.

Figure 0.1 ʿAbd al-Karim al-Akwaʿ, endowments functionary.

We were talking one day about inheritance. To illustrate what he was telling me ʿAbd al-Karim lifted down a white cloth bag in which he kept family property documents. These were either rolled or tightly folded, and some were tied together in bunches. My document photo no. 1, in a numbered series that eventually extended into the thousands, is a contract of sale dated 1298 AH (1881 CE) for fractional parts of certain rooms in an Ibb house purchased by ʿAbd al-Karim's grandfather for the sum of five silver *riyāls*. Next is an individual inheritance document, dated 1265 (1849), pertaining to a female ancestor, and following that a family endowment instrument, by another al-Akwaʿ, that man's two sisters, and their mother, concerning the old house, Dār al-Thajja. Dated 1278 (1861), this document bears an added note, dated 1311 (1893), by a local judge, prohibiting an attempted sale of the house. I shot the remainder of this initial roll of film at the Endowments Office, where I posed a large register on one of the deep windowsills, holding the pages down with the old-style, hand-forged key to my rented Ibb house. The third roll includes photos of ʿAbd al-Karim's mother's lengthy document of inheritance from her father, dated 1328 (1910), listing landed properties that later became the principal source of his own wealth.

ʿAbd al-Karim and others in Ibb allowed me to photograph selections of their family documents and often were able to provide supporting information. Far from being either anonymous or publicly held, such holdings were personalized and private. I sent the initial rolls of film home to my father, a retired ad man in Ohio, who sent back eight-by-ten-inch glossy prints, but this soon became impractical, and I turned to developing in Ibb studios.

* * *

This book examines the Islamic sharīʿa as a formation of local texts. In my early fieldwork, sketched above, such a conception was not in my mind, but a number of the research activities initiated then opened lines of inquiry that, brought together, eventually led to this study. Returning to Ibb over the years, I assembled a diverse corpus of written work that pertains to the town society and its contingent of jurists and practitioners. Yemen, mountainous and agrarian, remains the setting and the Zaydī and Shāfiʿī schools, rooted in the highlands for a thousand years, the juridical traditions.

Understood to be divine in origin and human in interpretation, the sharīʿa comprises a character both transcendent and immanent, a reality at once timeless and historical.[4] Yet beyond the twin formal senses of the term—as a revealed law and as the humanly created jurisprudence of the *fiqh*—a colloquial term will serve to indicate the further range of the lived phenomenon to be addressed in this book. In a down-to-earth sense, dropping the definite article, "sharīʿa" refers to litigation, to conducting a lawsuit before a judge. "Me and you, sharīʿa!" is an age-old challenge to an adversary to take a matter to court.

Although my research in and on Yemen has spanned the last several decades, the readings I carry out here center on a prior moment. This is the first half of the twentieth century (up to the republican Revolution of 1962), during which time the town of Ibb and its region of Lower Yemen were under Zaydī administration. I concentrate on this recent historical era rather than, more conventionally for an anthropologist, on the years of my research residence because of the significant opportunities that this earlier period affords. These are to study a set of sharīʿa writings in a context apart from direct western colonial control, and thus at a remove from the decisive legal changes wrought by such regimes; in an interval just prior to the advent of the Yemeni nation-state, and thus before the onset of the equally transformative changes associated with such modern political orders; and, not least, in the final half-century of the classically styled, sharīʿa-based Islamic polity of the Zaydī imams.

Through a localized history of a civilization-wide tradition I engage the still elusive question of how the sharīʿa functioned in specific settings. While limited in scale, my text-focused inquiry is comprehensive in perspective. In terms of genres, the assembled writings offer a representative inventory. With an emphasis on the Zaydī tradition and on the late period of imamic rule in the Ibb region, these sources are of four broad types: (1) *fiqh* works of literary jurisprudence, notably *The Book of Flowers* and its major commentaries, plus selected works in collateral academic fields and several types of minor doctrinal writings; (2) free-standing formal opinions in two varieties, one (the fatwā) known to all historical Muslim societies, the other (the *ikhtiyār*, or "choice," of a ruling imam) specific to Yemen; (3) transcript-based case records issued by the sharīʿa courts of Ibb town in the twentieth-century imamic period; and, from the same town and its hinterland in that period, (4) private notarial documents embodying acts such as land sales, sharecropping leases, and marriage contracts. The main law books became available in print editions in the early decades of the century, but the bulk of these writings, including the court records, are handwritten and were obtained from private individuals. In the range of genres, their collective association with a particular time and place, and their ethnographic sourcing, this corpus of writings offers an unprecedented set of objects for a situated study of the historical sharīʿa as a textual tradition.

I read these variegated Arabic texts as a historical anthropologist. My general premise is that a given sharīʿa system may be instructively approached through an analysis of its written acts, from the literary to the documentary. To inquire into what kind of writings these are is also to ask what kind of law this was. In more specific terms, I suggest that a grasp of textual relations in the sharīʿa is a prerequisite for understanding both how it operated in concrete situations and how it moved over time. "Genre" in this book refers not only to elements of form and types of texts—the familiar senses of the term—but also to institutions of human thought and action.[5] To the extent that the sharīʿa may be conceived of as "saying" or "doing" things, it spoke and acted in specific genres. Texts of the various types provided the differently patterned vehicles for linking fact and rule while at the same time serving to define the principal judicial roles.

Considering writing to be a social fact with its own significance, I treat written texts, from the law book to the common contract, not simply as the means for an inquiry—that is, as conventional sources—but also as ends. Reversing the normal order of the source, I address writings to learn about their production and reception. I distinguish between acts and artifacts, between the fleeting historical events of writing and their persisting material objects. I read the latter, the extant artifacts, for evidence of the earlier acts of writing. The general strategy of this book (and its basic conceit) is to isolate this textual dimension for separate study and to then sustain an analysis of what Hayden White refers to as "the content of the form." This is a conception according to which form "already possesses a content prior to any given actualization of it in speech or writing."[6]

In addition to what can be learned in this way about the overall shape and the detailed working of the sharīʿa, I maintain that close attention to textual form ought to be a precondition for wider research, for properly assessing the import of the various sorts of source materials—doctrinal passages, formal opinions, litigation transcripts, contracts, etc.—for the writing of history. Here, I venture into the rich substantive concerns of such writings only insofar as the topical emphasis is on textual matters. Together with limiting the scope of the inquiry to a specific spatial-temporal instance, this determined focus on textual form describes the circumscribed history I have attempted in these pages.

My analysis of the diverse textual deployments of sharīʿa-based knowledge tracks relations of power rather than a pursuit of hollow or neutral formal abstractions. Connecting genres of texts with forms of authority, I understand writing, reading, and interpreting as specific moments in such relations. In the historical period in question, a key part of the authoritative character of textual events derived from the interpretive presence of a ruling imam. Such texts, in short, are "facts of power."[7]

Rather than an ideal or generalized Muslim, my concern in this book is with the particular people of this local textual order—that is, with the individuals who taught, studied, wrote, copied, memorized, commented on, and interpreted works of *fiqh*, some of whom from time to time issued formal opinions or delivered court judgments and others of whom drafted the various types of routine instruments. This also includes the individuals who retained caches of such documents in their homes or who were merely among the documented, the countless persons whose names—or those of their relatives or ancestors, not to mention their adversaries—figured in these locally placed writings as questioners and petitioners, litigants and witnesses, owners and agents, landlords and sharecroppers, heirs and beneficiaries, spouses and children.

In my ethnographic research, which commenced a decade and a half after the demise of the old imamic polity and which has continued, intermittently, into the present century, I read with jurists, practitioners, and nonspecialists and I observed diverse scenes of writing. My fellow readers assisted me in explicating issues of doctrine and custom, understanding genre constraints, and identifying local written usages. They also exposed me to techniques of textual implementation and analysis, including how a compound undertaking or a complex dispute could be broken down into a series of written acts, or how a single text could be dismantled into its component clauses. Closely related was my research on instances of writing and reading in the varied contexts of text production. In connection with disputes and settlements I focused on transitions from spoken words and quotidian realities to written documents and juristic expression. I examined written documents in situ and archives at their points of creation. In this manner, I began to learn what to read for and how one did things with these sorts of written texts. I draw here on these ethnographic experiences in participatory reading and in observation of the drafting, use, and preservation of texts for the purposes of historical reconstruction.

I also take cues from the textual imaginations of the historical jurists. These highly reflective scholars thought deeply about textual matters, from the constitution of authoritative knowledge in written books to the status of ordinary written instruments as evidence in court, and they did so over many centuries. I am interested here in their views as to how the textual universe behind the interpretive act was configured as well as in the model texts and the instructions they created for the preparation of routine records and documents. A distinct thread of their thought was motivated by the perceived evidentiary dilemmas of ordinary sharīʿa writings such as contracts. Concerns about forgery, error, ambiguity, uncertainty, and so on were part of broader debates focused on a long-standing juridical problem, that of basing action on writing or, simply, "practice with writing" (*al-ʿamal bi-l-khaṭṭ*). It may be remarked that in one respect the textual approaches of these jurists parallel mine in this book. For certain of their own analyses they, too, separated form—that is, writing itself—from any particular content. Regarding their worries about such matters as the falsification of written evidence, the court transcripts of the period, with their accusations, contestations, and findings, demonstrate that these were not unfounded.

This thread of the jurists' thought figures as a topical theme in the following chapters, in a two-sided approach that is characteristic of this study. On the one hand, I follow this doctrinal thinking across its formal instantiations in multiple written formats of the period, including books, freestanding opinions, and model texts. On the other hand, I offer parallel coverage of the indicated types of local documents, again across a detailed roster of written genres, including items prepared by the period courts and by private notarial writers. Taken together, these conceptual and applied perspectives on written practice permit a dialectical understanding of the textual relations in play. In this way, via readings that commence within specific genres but then traverse, and ultimately comprise, the entire corpus, I elucidate the statuses and the roles of the differing categories of writings in what may be thought of as a textual formation.

Imamic Yemen

Characterized by its implementation of the sharīʿa, the highland polity of the first half of the twentieth century was headed by a jurist-leader known as an *imām*. This type of Muslim leader cum ideal moral subject may be referred to as the "great" (or "original," etc.) imam so as to distinguish his role from that of the ordinary imam, the prayer leader at a mosque. The usage also is distinct from the same term when employed as an honorific for a prominent jurist of the past. A synonym, especially among Sunnīs, but instanced as well among the Shīʿīs, is "caliph" (*khalīfa*), whence the old state form of the caliphate, referenced in our day by some Islamist groups and by extremists.[8] Representing the fundamental Islamic institution of sovereignty and legitimate rule, conceptions of the imamate (*imāma*) are an integral part of the jurisprudence of the sharīʿa and figure as such in the authoritative law books of the juridical schools, Sunnī and Shīʿī alike.[9] In *The Book of Flowers*, the work of Zaydī *fiqh*, the relevant chapter opens by stating, "The Muslims are required, according to the sharīʿa, to designate an imam."[10]

As one of the branches of the Shīʿa, the Zaydīs are generally distinguished from the Sunnīs by their view of the special legitimacy and authority of the descendants of ʿAli bin Abī Ṭālib (d. 661), the cousin and son-in-law of the Prophet Muhammad. Where the Sunnīs respect ʿAli as the fourth of the four "Rightly Guided" leaders who immediately succeeded the Prophet, the Shīʿīs honor him as the first imam. While, again, all schools of sharīʿa jurisprudence conceived of Islamic governance in terms of the leadership of an imam, the Shīʿīs stood apart from the Sunnīs in holding narrower views of the eligibility for this position that focused on the person of Imam ʿAli. As is expressed in the *Flowers*, the Zaydīs adhered to the condition that an imam must be, more specifically, a lineal descendant of the union of ʿAli and the Prophet Muhammad's daughter Fāṭima.[11]

While sharing an essential core of ideas regarding the centrality of Imam ʿAli and the authority of his descendants through Fāṭima, in other elements of their doctrine on the imamate and in its institutional history the Zaydīs differed significantly from the other Shīʿīs. Many of the conceptual differences were set forth in the separate literature of theology,[12] but the Zaydī jurists also offered their own pragmatic definitions of the distinctive features of the Shīʿī imamates.[13] Concerning the descent-defined eligibility for the imamate, the Zaydīs opposed conceptions of a hereditary position, as among the much better-known Twelver (or Imāmī) Shīʿīs of contemporary Iran, Iraq, and Lebanon; they instead envisioned any adult male descendant of ʿAli and Fāṭima, through the lines of their sons Hasan and Husayn, as a possible candidate. Likewise, it was not required that the Zaydī imam be "the most learned in the Muslim community," as was the case for the Twelvers.[14] And where conceptions of infallibility were axiomatic for other types of Shīʿī imams, the Zaydīs conceived of a highly accomplished but still quite worldly leader, to the extent of explicitly anticipating the possibility of an "error by the imam" or of an action leading to "censuring the justness of the imam."[15] Unlike the other Shīʿī traditions, no elaborate cosmology surrounded the figure of the Zaydī imam, and there was a relative lack of cult and related notions of miracles. In fact, on the continuum of Islamic thought about the imamate, the location of the Zaydī institution has been understood to approach that of the Sunnī schools.[16]

This ideally exemplary, but also potentially fallible, Zaydī leader was to be both a fully qualified jurist and a capable commander, a this-worldly master of both the pen and the sword. Concerning the latter, the Zaydīs honor the story of the eighth-century rebellion of their eponym, Zayd bin ʿAli (a great-grandson of Imam ʿAli), against the unjust rule of his day. This historical event would leave a distinctive mark on their juridical doctrine of the imamate, specifically in the conditions that the imam must be a capable and undaunted leader in war and must also be prepared to rise against injustice. Concerning the former sphere, the realm of the pen, which is the focus of this study, the central condition was his capacity for *ijtihād*, a demonstrated aptitude for independent sharīʿa reasoning and interpretation, based on an acute intellect, an upright moral character, and acquired knowledge. According to the doctrine, the knowledge in question was mainly the *fiqh* itself, the humanly authored jurisprudence derived from the divine text and the example of the Prophet Muhammad and based on interpretive reasoning, inasmuch as this body of knowledge "pertains to the general and detailed understanding of the licit and the illicit (*al-ḥalāl wa-l-ḥarām).*"[17] With respect to the textual order of the sharīʿa, in this type of polity an actively ruling and qualified imam represented the final reader, the apical interpreter.

The differences in institutional history are as significant. In contrast, again, with the Twelver Shīʿīs, for whom the last of their line of twelve recognized imams is thought to be in a many centuries-long "occultation" or "absence" (*ghayba*), the history of the Zaydī imamate in Yemen is one of a presence, of a roughly continuous, sometimes contentious, but always squarely feet-on-the-ground series of approximately one hundred imams, from Imam al-Hādī (d. 911), who was the first to come to the highlands and who ruled in the late ninth century, down to Imams Yahya and Ahmad in the early to mid-twentieth century.

There are few documented instances of rule by such a textbook type of great imam, much less the specifics of such a leader's administrative and interpretive efforts in implementing the sharīʿa.[18] To the extent that its *fiqh*-based conception of the imamate was realized in this centuries-long history of rule, the Zaydī institution also offers a significant counterexample to prevailing western understandings, not only concerning Islamic governance but also regarding how the sharīʿa functioned in historical states.

Joseph Schacht, the leading mid-twentieth-century western student of Islamic law, categorically asserted, "The state as envisaged by the theory of Islamic law is a fiction which has never existed in reality."[19] A leading scholar of our time, Wael Hallaq, has expressed a similar view. He states that, as opposed to the "will-to-power" characteristic of the modern nation-state, "in Islamic law such a will-to-power could not exist except at the level of the abstract and theoretical."[20]

It is true, to be sure, that the pattern of rule in most historical Muslim states involved a split between sharīʿa and temporal authorities, between the jurist-interpreters (the *fuqahāʾ* or *ʿulamāʾ*), on the one hand, and the sultans, kings, shahs, etc., on the other. Referring to this predominant pattern, Schacht writes, "Islamic law provides the unique phenomenon of legal science and not the state playing the part of legislator, of scholarly handbooks having the force of law." This situation obtained since "the place of the state was taken by another authority," a purely "political authority." In equivalent terms, Hallaq describes the typical historical circumstance in which the schools of Islamic jurisprudence "act as a substitute for the absent legal power of the sovereign." In premodern states headed by such primarily temporal figures, with the doctrinally envisioned sovereign, the imam, "absent," Hallaq describes the historical sharīʿa as operating "horizontally," its authority anchored not in the ruling stratum but in that of the socially embedded jurists and their schools of law.[21]

These views are closely associated with two venerable, and related, understandings regarding what Schacht refers to as the essential "nature" of Islamic law.[22] First, the issue of "theory and practice." Identifying what he describes as the "discordance between the sacred law and the reality of actual practice," Schacht concludes that the "contrast between theory and practice" constituted the "perpetual problem" of Islamic law.[23] While subsequent research has strongly criticized this depiction with respect to other domains, Schacht's prime example of the "discordance," in what he termed "constitutional law," remains unchallenged. As noted, he understood this domain of legitimate Islamic governance, represented by the doctrine of the imamate, as a "fiction." Second, the concept of a "jurists' law," which refers to the role of "private" specialists. Max Weber famously wrote, "the sacred law of Islam is throughout specifically a 'jurists' law' "; following him, Schacht states, "Islamic law represents an extreme case of a jurists' law."[24] But his conception of a "jurists' law" is precisely that of the "horizontal" interpretive authority of Muslim jurists under a temporal state authority—that is, in the absence of the sharīʿa-based governance of an imam.

In the Yemeni highlands, the sharīʿa vision of legitimate rule articulated in Zaydī jurisprudence found concrete exemplifications in a long series of imam-led polities. Rather than "fictions," these polities were historical facts. It then may be asked what these facts have to say about the "nature" of Islamic law? In its conceptualization and its centuries-long implementation the living imamate of the Zaydī tradition offers an alternative, if admittedly minor, history of Islamic governance and, by extension, of the sharīʿa itself. In this alternative history, when qualified ruling jurists presided over the legitimate administration and interpretation of the law, the theory and practice of the sharīʿa converged.[25] In such a Zaydī polity, including that of the first half of the twentieth century, the sharīʿa may be described as operating vertically.

Imam-led polities in the Yemeni highlands existed for a full millennium, their fortunes ebbing and flowing.[26] In the late eighteenth and early nineteenth centuries—that is, in the era prior to the return of the Ottomans

(1872–1918)—a series of three imams failed to meet the interpretive criterion of *ijtihād*.[27] The incapacity on the part of the ruling imams of this period coincided with the intellectual and political ascendancy of Muhammad ʿAli al-Shawkānī (d. 1834), an ardent, in-house critic of Zaydī school positions, notably including their *fiqh* doctrine of the imamate. In his commentary on the *Flowers*, Shawkānī argued for a Sunnī-style imamate, which, as opposed to the narrower lines of Zaydī-stipulated descent through ʿAli and Fāṭima, would admit a wider range of possible incumbents. He also held that such an imam should focus on the governing tasks of defense, security, and the maintenance of order rather than on sharīʿa interpretation. He criticized the too exacting requirement that the imam be capable of *ijtihād* and argued that these less than fully qualified leaders ought to rely instead on the advice of jurists capable of interpretation.[28] Shawkānī himself was one of the leading jurists of his time, and he also served as the head judge under the three imams in question. Together with other qualified jurists in the rulers' circles, Shawkānī advised these imams in a sharīʿa system that nevertheless remained vertical in orientation.

The ruling imams of the first half of the twentieth century, in contrast, were qualified interpreters. They were from the Ḥamīd al-Dīn family line: Imam Yahya, who declared himself imam in 1904 and ruled 1918–48, followed by his son Imam Ahmad, who ruled from 1948 until just before the Revolution of 1962. Imam Yahya reigned in patrimonial fashion, with his sons posted as the governors of key provinces, including Ibb.[29] The circumstances of these twentieth-century leaders were in many respects unlike those of the imams from prior centuries, however. Among other newly introduced technologies, Imam Yahya adopted the telegraph, which had been put in place under the turn-of-the-century provincial administration of the Ottomans, and he also made use of the printing press they left behind. For his part, Imam Ahmad screened films in his mid-century residence and traveled to Rome for medical treatment. The formula of rule in their late imamic polity also began to shift. While Imam Yahya retained the old rubrics of imamic rule, he also permitted the use of "caliph," the more familiar and politically current term of the era.[30] He additionally began to refer to his state as a "kingdom" and introduced a novel (and contested) dynastic principle.[31]

Yet, much like their predecessors, the twentieth-century imams intervened in many aspects of conflict resolution, an activity that provided a central rationale for these polities from their advent in the ninth century.[32] Imams Yahya and Ahmad devoted a significant part of their routine work time to responding to the daily volume of written petitions that arrived from near and far, many of which concerned disputes. In terms of his formal capacity, an imam was a judge (and a muftī) writ large, while at the same time he presided over the work of the regular court judges that he appointed to the various highland jurisdictions.[33] The attention of these imams to the administration of formal justice also involved seeing to the proper academic training of qualified jurists to ensure the necessary manpower for the courts. They also authorized the printing of selected works of Zaydī school jurisprudence, with a ruling imam from an earlier era figuring prominently among the newly published authors. Both imams reviewed appeal rulings and selected regular court decisions, notably in capital cases. In his day, Imam Yahya would return drafts of appellate decisions with the errors marked in red.

Like some of their predecessors from previous centuries, the twentieth-century imams issued formal juridical opinions. While these personal doctrinal "choices" (*ikhtiyārāt*), or "interpretations" (*ijtihādāt*), originated in the imam's responses to particular interpretive difficulties encountered by their appointed judges in specific litigations, these authoritative opinions subsequently were used, much like a form of precedent, to guide the judges of the realm in deciding related cases. I analyze this distinctive institution of opinion giving, including both their genesis and later implementation, through readings in the behind-the-scenes correspondence between the ruling imam and the presiding court judges. Rather than their military, political, or diplomatic initiatives, it is this intramural dimension of the practice of imamic governance that concerns me in this book. I thus attend to this Islamic form of leadership from the perspective of the textual relations that surrounded an imam's role in sharīʿa applications. This is to focus on the place of discursive form in the exercise of interpretive authority and to address an essential institution in a historically specific regime of truth.

Zaydī control of Ibb and Lower Yemen dated from the early seventeenth-century rise of the Qāsimī dynasty, which coincided with the end of the first Ottoman occupation. During the following two and a half centuries, relatives of the Qāsimī imams and individuals from various Upper Yemen descent groups, including Zaydī jurists, tribesmen, and craftsmen, settled in the local society.[34] In 1918, at the end of the nearly half-century-long second Ottoman occupation, as Imam Yahya extended his dominion to the whole of the former Province of Yemen, Zaydī jurisprudence returned to official status in Ibb and the movements of northerners into the local society resumed. In addition, from 1948 to 1962, Imam Ahmad made his capital in the city of Taʿizz, now an hour's drive south of Ibb. To approach the sharīʿa regime of the period from the vantage point of Ibb and Lower Yemen is to view it off-center with respect to the home districts of the Zaydīs in Upper Yemen and yet squarely within a long-standing and, in the first half of the twentieth century, closely administered territorial realm.

Independent from 1918, this Zaydī polity stood apart from the pressures and changes associated with direct western colonial rule. From the Dutch in Southeast Asia to the English in India, South Arabia, and Northeast and sub-Saharan Africa and the Italians and the French in North and West Africa, western colonial regimes elsewhere decisively altered the political, societal, and epistemic existence of the sharīʿa. Colonial administrations typically acted to replace its procedural, criminal, commercial, and real estate provisions with western law, effectively narrowing its sphere of jurisdictional relevance to matters of personal status and family law while also transforming the character of court processes. Roughly the same results emerged from the efforts of the nineteenth-century reformers in the Ottoman Empire and in Egypt. In contrast, under the twentieth-century imams, the highland sharīʿa court maintained a broad and unified competence. Madrasa-trained judges formed on the *Flowers* and related doctrinal works heard the gamut of justiciable lawsuits, including landed property disputes, criminal matters, and the occasional commercial contract case, and they did so employing sharīʿa-based rules of procedure, evidence, and substantive law. The handwritten techniques of the local archives of sharīʿa court records and notarial documentation likewise had yet to be replaced by modern standards of file keeping and the use of typed, printed, and, eventually, computer-based forms.

Highland Yemen thus was on the cusp of a local modernity. To the south, in the bustling international port of the British colony of Aden, another variety of sharīʿa law was applied within the framework of a colonial legal system. The highland north (comprising Upper and Lower Yemen), as noted, had been under Ottoman provincial administration from 1872 to 1918, during which time Yemenis were exposed in a limited fashion to the partial late nineteenth-century Ottoman codification of the sharīʿa known as the Majalla. The new-style first-instance courts introduced in other parts of the empire, which assumed much of the former jurisdiction of the sharīʿa courts, likewise made only a brief appearance in the Province of Yemen, but the two succeeding imams retained and adapted a version of the equally new Ottoman institution of judicial appeal.[35]

Although the highlands were not colonized by a western power and did not experience anything like the full brunt of late Ottoman reforms, the impacts of both the nearby colonial enclave in Aden and the almost fifty-year period of provincial rule as part of a modernizing empire strongly condition the view of this early to mid-twentieth-century legal system as a surviving remnant of the classical sharīʿa. Yet the fateful confrontation with the epistemic universe of the nation-state remained on the horizon. In these final decades prior to the legislative restatement, repositioning, and selective re-institutionalization of the sharīʿa as a nation-state "law," under a constitution, the old jurisprudence remained in authoritative application.

In readings at once particular and general in intent, I treat this instance from the first half of the twentieth century on its own terms, in its detailed specificity, and as a platform for broader reflection on patterns of textuality in the history of the sharīʿa. While the sharīʿa regime of the period highlands bore a family resemblance to other such historical instances, especially to those of the Arab heartlands of which Yemen was an integral part, every such instance differed in its societal relations, political history, geographical circumstances, etc. In this study, I explore the specific and comparative implications of a pair of context-specific institutions with reference to their textual manifestations. Both bore singular relationships of relative conformity to the doctrinal worldview of the sharīʿa.

First, as I have discussed (and analyze further in chapter 4), in its lengthy history and in twentieth-century practice, the imamate tradition of the Zaydīs was relatively closely attuned to the vision of sharīʿa authority and governance articulated in their jurisprudence. Despite the complicating vicissitudes of the final two centuries of its history, I suggest that, in comparative terms, this enacted institution of legitimate rule by qualified interpreters sheds light on how premodern Muslim societies could relate to the interpretive demands of sharīʿa application.

Second, I explore (mainly in chapter 10) an equally fundamental institutional feature of this highland instance, namely the on-the-ground structures of property relations. I likewise approach this other side of the "political economy," as it were, from the perspective of an associated range of textual forms.

Chronologically part of the twentieth century, but still entirely agrarian, highland society of the era was based primarily on settled plow cultivation using animal traction. In its physical setting—mountainous, elaborately terraced, and watered by variable summer rains generated by the monsoon system—highland Yemen differed from the Muslim-majority societies where plains cultivation, riverine irrigation, or nomadic pastoralism predominated. The associated highland property system—not only in and around the towns but also in the cultivated areas of rural districts—was largely private, based more or less explicitly on the foundational sharīʿa category of *milk*, or individual ownership.[36] In this basic feature, the property relations of highland Yemen were decidedly unlike the historical conditions that obtained elsewhere in the larger region, where ultimate title was vested in the state, as in the *mīrī* system that prevailed in much of the Ottoman Empire, including Egypt, or where customary forms of collective rights were significant at the village or tribal level.[37]

In comparative terms, while Muslim jurists in these other historical settings (and, for that matter, western scholars studying those settings) struggled to interpret existing land tenure practices using the categories available to them in the doctrine of the sharīʿa, their Yemeni colleagues found the implemented property system in the highlands to be legible in terms of those same categories.[38] Divergent types of regional land tenure systems meant dissimilar patterns of conflict, which resulted in differing types of cases being handled by the sharīʿa courts and reported in litigation records. Such contrasts in terms of the standard types of landed property transactions also resulted in important differences in the applied genres of notarial instruments.

In the late agrarian-age highlands, with truck transport only beginning after mid-century to replace mountain-going camel caravans, and amid many other harbingers of advancing commercialization, older conceptions of property remained in place. Anchored in agrarian production and with closely adapted relations of trade and governance, this distinctive property system was expressed, applied, and contested in a spectrum of sharīʿa texts.

To that underpinning the imamate, then, I add this second, but equally foundational, unusual, and therefore interesting historical fit, or compatibility, as the individually oriented property scheme that prevailed in practice approximated the structures of landed property relations envisioned in the *fiqh*.

Library and Archive

This book offers a case study in the working textual architecture of the historical sharīʿa. In sorting a specific version of this discursive tradition into its component genres, the following chapters highlight an elaborate division of textual labor. While I treat the key types of texts—law books, opinions, judgments, and instruments—as distinct and historically particular forms, I also inquire into their interconnections. The central conundrum of this study concerns this last issue, the nature and the import of the relations that obtained between the differing types of texts. Did these imamic-period writings constitute a more or less integrated textual "formation," as I phrased it earlier? How might an understanding of the various written genres and their linkages illuminate the concrete operations and the overall character of the sharīʿa? In order to pursue these questions about the coordination and interaction of this textual world, I first introduce a broad distinction.

While the conceptual thought elaborated in doctrinal treatises and formal opinions may be considered among the greatest intellectual achievements of Islamic civilization, the judgment records of sharīʿa courts and related archives of legal documents are among the most important sources for its social history. Connections between an accumulated corpus of doctrine and the ongoing tasks of judgment giving and notarial drafting, between an academic tradition of the law and the rulings and other acts that pertain to concrete human endeavors, are at the crux of any working legal system. Across this gulf between sharīʿa writings, from the lofty books of jurisprudence to the routine records of proceedings and transactions, the energy and ingenuity of the literary jurist is as striking as the tenacity and resourcefulness of the litigant in court.

While *The Book of Flowers* dates from the late fourteenth century, in the early twentieth it remained a focus of instruction, reference, and interpretation. Since it also was the object of a four-volume commentary work, *The Gilded Crown*, written and published in the 1930s and 1940s,[39] this body of doctrinal thought may be considered fully contemporary with the court case materials and the notarial documents that I also examine. These last, the records of lawsuits and the gamut of ordinary legal acts, represent the other end of the law. Put in writing by Yemeni jurists and practitioners of the era, some of them noted scholars for whom entries may be found in the biographical histories of the period, lawsuit and instrument documentation reported on the acts and rights of ordinary men and women, individuals who went unnoticed in the biographical literature. Doctrinal works, formal opinions, court judgments, and routine instruments, again, are distinct genres of legal writing. To extend the floral metaphor, if authoritative doctrinal works such as the *Flowers* were the textual perennials of particular sharīʿa traditions, the court judgments and notarial documents were their equally significant annuals.

To begin to parse this written tradition, I refer to these major clusters of sharīʿa texts as the "library" and the "archive," terms that indicate separate yet interdependent textual realms that respectively encompassed the book and the document. In their contrasting discursive horizons these major groupings of texts may be thought of as cosmopolitan as opposed to contingent writings, a distinction that I suggest has important implications for situated histories of the sharīʿa. While the library was associated with the disciplines and the activities of academic learning, including the madrasa as the formal site, the early to mid-century archive had primary links to the *maḥkama*, the judge's court, and its larger surround, which included the private notarial writer. Although the writings of the library and the archive exhibited separate discursive dynamics, their histories were intertwined.

Placing a period library and a local archive together at the center of the inquiry is integral to my examination of the sharīʿa as a "written law." Extending this old notion beyond a narrow reference to the law on the books or the legal literature—here, the *fiqh*—I also take into account sharīʿa writing at the less exalted, but hard-working levels of both court litigation records and ordinary contract documents. This more holistic approach to what Raymond Williams termed the "multiplicity" of writing is designed to bring the complex interactions among doctrine, opinions, judgments, and instruments into view.[40] To put the prestige texts of the library into conversation with the humble documents of the archive is to treat the latter as integral to what Talal Asad has referred to as a "discursive tradition."[41]

I employ these library and archive constructs to summarize contrasting discursive modalities within an overarching juridical culture. Sharīʿa traditions operated on the basis of a textual partition between doctrinal genres that were relatively context-free, atemporal, and strictly technical-formal in expression versus a spectrum of richly circumstantial applied genres that were context-engaged, historically particular, and linguistically stratified. As opposed to the consistently general phrasing of doctrinal discourse, the practical acts of the courts and the notarial writers were resolutely specific. A defining feature of library texts is their reference to actors and objects using the noun *fulān* and its variations and extensions—the "so and so" and the "such and such" of formal Arabic. In premodern sharīʿa regimes, this generalizing library discourse of *fulān* was the discourse of theory and law.

Archival texts, in contrast, equally characteristically named proper names. Where the doctrinal literature and related texts assumed a nonreferential guise, consistently avoiding particular coordinates in time and space, court rulings and notarial instruments carefully attended to matters of dates and locations.[42] Where doctrinal works engaged formal logical arguments, archival texts, while including some of the results of this thought, additionally embodied varieties of informal logic.[43] And where the literary jurists commonly distinguished between formal Arabic (the *lugha*, "language") and their own specialized linguistic usages, in archival writings such as court transcripts these registers of tutored discourse were joined by expression, some of it colloquial, excerpted from primary texts both oral and written. Adopting all manner of regional and locale-specific vocabularies and terminologies, archival texts brimmed over not only with the names of people, places, and things but also with precise indications of amounts and quantities, using named currencies and the variety of existing measures. In sharīʿa regimes, this particularizing archival discourse of the name was the discourse of practice and custom.

The contrast between library and archive also may be thought of as one between authored and written texts. Referring to the western tradition, Michel Foucault states, "the name of an author is a variable that accompanies only certain texts to the exclusion of others."[44] A related distinction may be made within a formation of sharīʿa texts, with the relevant textual "others" being the range of archival writings. Where library discourse embodied a set of culturally and historically specific "author-functions," archival discourse comprised distinct writer-functions.[45] I adopt the plural for Foucault's well-known term and for my proposed archival counterpart to account for the distinct genres that existed within both the library and the archive. Following Foucault, such conceptions should be understood as defining functions that provide a basis for what he termed "a typology of discourse."[46]

Such usage separates a named author or writer from a discursive function, historical agency from textual form. For library texts, the intention is to distinguish attributions to (and also in-text citations of) specific authors from the patterned avoidance of the proper name. By the same token, the possibility of dating a book or an opinion is distinct from the atemporal nature of its textual discourse. Among archival texts, in contrast, we enter a realm defined by the identifiable handwritten scripts and the signed names of the court or notarial writers together with, in certain periods, a personal seal. But the discourse of the proper name that was characteristic of archival texts pertained not to such secretaries or notaries, who in fact wrote and signed them, but rather to the parties who entered litigation or a contractual undertaking and who usually did not sign the resulting documentation.

While named genres and sub-genres populated both the library and the archive, these two higher-level categories themselves were not labeled as such. Library and archive, again, are my terms for the clusters of genres marked by the just-described discursive differences exemplified by the utilization of the generic term *fulān* versus the proper name, and the work of "authors" versus "writers." I maintain, however, that my higher-level rubrics give expression to an important but implicit pattern of opposed features and, in this sense, represent a constituent aspect of the "traditional order" of sharīʿa texts.[47]

To suggest that these library and archive constructs might have wider comparative potential, I would point to two very different anthropological studies, one pertaining to a modern western legal system and the other to a different institutional branch of the Islamic tradition. In his ethnography of the French Conseil d'État, Bruno Latour foregrounds the analysis of the relations between established doctrine and ongoing case decisions, while

Charles Hirschkind's readings of mosque sermons in late twentieth-century Cairo likewise fall into two categories: one, the doctrinal works and specialized treatises on sermon-giving, and the other, the sermons themselves.[48]

In the highlands, the imamic-period library and archive shared the medium of paper and ink as well as the means of handwritten Arabic script, but their materialities otherwise diverged.[49] A successful book or a significant opinion was apt to be reproduced and multiplied. It could be copied, taught, commented on, and possibly memorized. An important archival writing, by contrast, typically remained a solitary original with, at most, a single copy. A resulting feature of their respective materialities is that while library works were relatively few in number and highly restricted in terms of their social placement, among texts they were the mostly likely to be preserved over time. In contrast, while archival documents were very numerous and relatively widely dispersed in society, as texts they were vulnerable and perishable, most likely to be lost or destroyed.

Written artifacts embodying the library discourse of *fulān* or its equivalents frequently had exchange value as commodities. Copyists labored for a wage; manuscript books were bought and sold and also could figure as the objects of endowments, although books prepared as a pious activity or as the by-product of instruction usually were not intended for circulation. In contrast, a paid writer of a different type normally drafted the artifacts embodying the proper name of archival discourse. Such instruments did not circulate as commodities but, in contrast, typically referred to commodities, notably to landed property rights. Aside from their standard roles of residing in an archive and of being brought forward in disputes or in subsequent transactions, and despite the considerable efforts made to guard them, the different value of ordinary documents made them susceptible to forms of aggression. In addition to the possibility of being lost or accidently destroyed, documents also were intentionally forged, stolen, burned, and even, in one case I learned of, eaten.

With technological modernity and the onset of mechanical reproduction, the writings of the library and the archive were differently affected. In the first half of the last century, selected old manuscript books were converted into print editions, and new authors began to write with print publication in mind. Archival documents, in contrast, remained exclusively manual products throughout the period. Laboriously prepared, the handwritten document copy did not look like its original in the modern photo-identical sense, nor was it so readily multiplied. Depending on the labor of reproduction by the pen, the derived authority of the period archival copy instead passed through the fallible medium of human script, usually in a hand different from that of the original. The first typewriters at court offices and the first printed forms for judgments and contracts did not appear in Ibb until well after the Revolution of 1962.

Lest my paired library and archive constructs and their posited cosmopolitan and contingent qualities (see below) seem overly rigid, some previews of later-to-be-examined qualifications are in order. Certain genres, notably freestanding opinions such as the muftī's fatwā and the imam's "choice," straddled the two discursive categories, as both of these library forms had roots in the archive. Movements back and forth between the library and the archive also occurred, both through modeling relations and by means of genre flexibilities. In addition, in lower-level library texts, such as the contract models I read at the end of this book, a degree of contingency was mixed in with the formal doctrinal stipulations, specifically in the use, albeit infrequent, of highland-specific terminology. Conversely, among the archival writings I note a limited cosmopolitan quality of an interregional sort, especially in the instruments that pertained to property relations.

I should add that these library and archive constructs do not represent a return to the analysis of the "great" and "little" traditions, a conceptual pair developed in the 1950s.[50] In that era, anthropologists, who had been exclusively concerned with even smaller-scale and more remote tribal societies, had just started to work in peasant villages where they began to encounter the written texts of literate societies. This research imagined a scholarly divide between the historians and students of literature and the fieldwork-conducting anthropologists. The first type of scholar would handle the history and the written materials while the anthropologist contributed information on the societal context. There was no notion at the time of an anthropologist as a reader of written source texts.

As opposed to this old conception of the high and low, the literate versus the nonliterate strata or versions of a civilizational tradition, both library and archive refer to clusters of written texts, each consisting of a distinct set of genres. Library and archive thus represent the complementary textual domains that together constituted the range of written expression in a given tradition or, as here, a central discipline of such a tradition. Where the old conceptual opposition typically identified the high tradition with urban centers and the low with rural districts, a given library and a period archive should be understood as co-present in, and co-constitutive of, particular locales.

Local Texts

Taking the sharīʿa as one of his examples, anthropologist Clifford Geertz describes law as a form of "local knowledge."[51] In this book on the sharīʿa as a system of local texts I examine how such knowledge was constituted in and through its written forms. I am interested in the different ways that the various writings were rooted in a specific setting and connected to the depth and breadth of an intellectual tradition.

For matters of location and reach with respect to particular library-and-archive tandems, I turn to conceptualizations of the "cosmopolitan," especially as this term might apply to premodern and non-western instances.[52] With such historical circumstances in mind, Sheldon Pollock describes a cosmopolitan text as one that "thinks of itself as unbounded, unobstructed, unlocated."[53] Library texts were in this sense cosmopolitan: their characteristically non-contextually referential discourse enabled such texts to travel, to relocate. By means of their distinctive discursive horizons, such generalizing genres thought beyond any local frame. While in this sense not limited to particular settings, library texts nevertheless also pertained to historically specific locales. I thus address the transportable nature of cosmopolitan library texts together with the less apparent, approximately inverse problematic of their localization.

The lens of micro-history reveals the differing connections between the extant types of writings and the given locality. When the question of the "production of the local" is posed with respect to this range of active writings, contrasts of chronology and spatiality become salient.[54] Where, as noted, library texts were phrased in the timeless and placeless language of theory, archival texts employing the grounded language of practice exhibited defining attachments to time and place. In an order of sharīʿa texts, this cosmopolitan character of the library contrasted with, yet also depended on, the contingent character of the archive. However, expression in the archival genres blended elements of library discourse with that of the proper name. Such defining combinations involved sourcing both in the mobile literary formulations of the *fiqh* and in the immobile nomenclature and fact-terms of the local world. The contingent quality of archival writings hinged not only on such expected features as the particulars of evidence presented in court rulings or the negotiated terms set down in notarial instruments but equally on the inconspicuous textual routines of naming, dating, and placing.

Whereas archival texts were connected to particulars by their genre constraints, unconnected library texts had to be made local. How were such "translocational" library texts localized? How, by extension, were the related dimensions of formal knowledge established and engaged? Responses to these questions entail library-specific considerations, and they also concern the interface of a particular library with a specific archive. Cosmopolitan library works thus may be examined both in terms of the local incidence of their own bookish practices and for a variety of possible intertextual relations with a particular array of practical documentation. A study of their local-level reception and application thus involves a close look, on the one hand, at the activities of instruction, memorization, commentary, copying, etc. and, on the other, at the possible forms of structuring of court judgments and the various types of notarial instruments.

A virtue of the old approach to the "great" and "little" traditions was the attention given to their dialectical relation. An echo of this is found in the referenced conceptions of the cosmopolitan, where the relevant pairing is with the "vernacular." Thus Pollock speaks of the "vernacularization of a great tradition and the amplification of a *petit récit*."[55] In his own work on the *longue durée* in South Asia, however, the cosmopolitan-vernacular relation is more a matter of transformation and historical succession within a literary tradition, events entirely within the book-sphere that I am calling the library. He nevertheless conceives of a "dialectic between cosmopolitan and vernacular that creates them both." In the course of this complex process of mutual constitution, "if the vernacular localizes the cosmopolitan as part of its own self-constitution, it is often unwittingly relocalizing what the cosmopolitan borrowed from it in the first place." Such suggestive thinking about the dialogues between texts in connection with issues of localization may be adapted for the different perspective of the library-and-archive relation.

Still, the history of vernacularization with respect to Arabic—if such a history can be said to exist—would be fundamentally different from that with respect to, in Pollock's case, Sanskrit (or Latin). As noted, his terms refer to changes and exchanges within the same or similar literary genres, whereas mine refer to textual discourses in fundamentally different genres. Pollock's focus on literary texts specifically excludes consideration of the "documentary," the genres of what I term the archive.[56] As opposed to treating an exclusively literary landscape, I give equal thought to the other, more modest, registers of written language that were simultaneously associated with this historical instance of the sharīʿa. As a consequence, rather than the horizontal spread of the given written tradition—the phenomenon that interests Pollock—I explore what may be thought of as its vertical integration.

The cited work on cosmopolitanism additionally recommends considering the plural of the term. It suggests that we focus on the resultant "affiliations," or the interpretive communities indexed by the creation and circulation of cosmopolitan texts.[57] As I have indicated in passing, two such communities or schools of sharīʿa interpretation, known as *madhhabs*, were current in pre-revolutionary Ibb. The Zaydī *madhhab* was official under the imams, while the Shāfiʿī was indigenous to the region of Lower Yemen. Coexistences of interpretive schools, including this type of official precedence of one over the other under the regime of a particular polity, were important to many regional histories of the sharīʿa, but the textual dimensions of these encounters have not been closely studied.[58] A collateral problem for the present study thus is to be attentive to the discursive articulations of these schools within Lower Yemen during the rule of the twentieth-century Zaydī imams.

A sharīʿa jurist resident or posted in a place may be thought of as what Engseng Ho terms a "local cosmopolitan."[59] But part of what it meant to be a jurist was to be aware of similarities and differences between one's own and other schools of interpretation. This sort of knowledge could take on a heightened significance within particular polities or given physical proximity. In their library thought, the highland exponents of the Zaydī and the Shāfiʿī schools displayed a marked sharing, both in terms of substantive juristic provisions and also in the works considered authoritative in the several allied literatures. As I detail later, in their doctrinal works and opinions, Zaydī jurists routinely referenced the jurists of the four Sunnī schools.

But in their respective patterns of affiliation and dissemination the two schools embodied contrasting cosmopolitanisms. Zaydī and Shāfiʿī thought flowed in separate scholarly channels that exhibited different degrees of historical extension in the wider Islamic ecumene. While the Zaydīs in the later centuries were largely confined to Upper Yemen, the Shāfiʿīs, in addition to their presence in Lower Yemen and in the regions to the south and east—that is, in the former sultanates surrounding Aden and in the Hadramawt—also predominated around the perimeter of the Indian Ocean littoral, from the East Africa coast to island Southeast Asia, and they figured importantly as well in Egypt and the Levant.

The differing historical geographies of these cosmopolitan *madhhabs* form part of the backdrop for their contrasting localizations in Upper and Lower Yemen, informing both the situations of scholarly reception and production and the various aspects of implementation. In Ibb, the relevant textual relations of the first half of the twentieth century comprised interactions between the two interpretive communities in terms of their cosmopolitan libraries and also in their respective relations to the locally documented archive. Under the Zaydī administration, the ruling imams redirected local endowment revenues to the support of instruction in the *Flowers* literature in the town madrasa while the judges they appointed decided court cases according to the official *madhhab* and applicable imamic opinions, or "choices." At the levels of the routine local fatwā and the mundane archival documentation of property relations, however, *madhhab* distinctions were less marked.

Contingency in sharīʿa texts was intimately tied to custom (*ʿurf*, *ʿāda*), an essential ingredient in particular histories of the sharīʿa.[60] According to Schacht, custom "coexisted with the ideal theory of Islamic law, while remaining outside its system."[61] This view of custom is confined to the level of the library—or, in his terms, "the ideal theory." It also restates a simple association, and opposition, between sharīʿa and custom that is enshrined in folk and scholarly categories alike. My contrasting view of custom is based, in the first place, on a different conception of a sharīʿa "system," as one that consists of both library and archive. In the second, it emphasizes the role of custom not only "outside" but also *inside* such a system. I stress the active dependence of a sharīʿa system thus conceived on receptions of local usages and conventions.

What is known as "tribal custom" (*ʿurf al-qabīlī*) is largely separate and specialized, however. Anthropologists Paul Dresch, Martha Mundy, and Shelagh Weir have focused attention on the rich local documentation of such custom among sedentary cultivators in rural Upper Yemen.[62] As Schacht noted on the basis of research in the highlands by an earlier generation of scholars such as E. Rossi, C. Rathjens, and R. B. Serjeant, highland Yemen is unusual in that the elaborated general principles of tribal custom as well as specific undertakings and settlements typically were placed in writing.[63] Also in written form, but proximate to the sharīʿa, is customary urban market law, notably that for Ṣanʿāʾ, studied by Serjeant and by the anthropologist Franck Mermier.[64]

Islamic Legal Studies

While the sharīʿa may be viewed as a complex edifice of writings, western accounts of its premodern history developed bifurcated approaches. On the one hand, there was the long-standing emphasis on books and formal opinions—that is, on the high-level doctrinal literatures of the sharīʿa. Now conducted by Islamicist historians, work of this type has a legacy in Orientalist scholarship, with its roots in colonization and empire. On the other, there emerged a body of research based mainly on routine documents, including court records, estate inventories, title registries, leases, etc. This comparatively recent work dates to the rise in the second half of the twentieth century of the new field of social history. How might a historical anthropology of sharīʿa texts relate to this fractured field?

Colonial-era research by Orientalists held that the jurisprudence of the sharīʿa was largely "ideal," in the negative sense that it was seen as having only a tenuous relationship to the actual conduct of affairs.[65] Assessments of this sort culminated in Schacht's authoritative *Introduction to Islamic Law* (1964), cited earlier. A towering figure in late Orientalist thought, Schacht (d. 1969) addressed his topic in admirable terms—as "a remarkable example of the possibilities of legal thought and of human thought in general" and also as offering "a key to understanding the essence of one of the great world religions."[66] Yet, as noted, a major thrust of his work was to emphasize the "discordance" between theory and practice. The purportedly ideal character of the sharīʿa was associated with his view that, at the conclusion of its "formative period"—that is, by about 900 CE—the doctrine was a largely finished work that would be unable thereafter to properly adapt to changing circumstances. Such views about the early closure and the theoretical rigidity of sharīʿa jurisprudence impeded understandings of its later vigor, including how this corpus of formal thought related to institutions of mundane implementation.

Such pronouncements about the supposedly flawed relation of theory and practice in the sharīʿa were based exclusively on literary, or what I term "library," materials. This, of course, had to do with the nature of the sources available for the early centuries, but the pattern continued in Schacht's work on practice in the post-formative period. This he studied, in part, through newly arising concerns in the later commentaries. He writes, "Hostile references to practice in works of Islamic law are an important source of information on it for the Middle Ages." He also sought to learn about later practice through the application-oriented doctrinal subliteratures that he brought to the attention of western scholarship (the *ḥiyal* and *shurūṭ* works). He states, for example, that a treatise on the legal stratagems (*ḥiyal*) "enables us to discern, through the thin veil of its legally unobjectionable forms, the realities of practice in that place and time."[67] However ingenious the scholarly method, from a genre perspective this remained a practice represented in doctrine, a practice known only from the works of theory rather than also from the texts of application. The underlying assumption remained one of a fundamental impracticality, which was construed as a failure, as a flawed "gap" or disconnect between the library of the sharīʿa and the archive of its written acts.

Schacht's *Introduction* appeared just prior to the onset of intensive research based on sharīʿa court records and related archives, and thus before many questions about the textual aspects of practice could be properly posed. For their part, social historians have concentrated mainly on the territories of the Ottoman Empire in the sixteenth to the late nineteenth centuries.[68] The topics of this voluminous research have ranged from aspects of economic history to family structure and gender relations. An important feature of this scholarship, however, is a continual struggle with the limitations of the principle source, the court record. Although the sheer quantity of the extant records from Ottoman jurisdictions is astounding, the individual entries in the court registers, including those produced in connection with litigation, tended to be sparse in nature. Taking the form of summaries, these premodern case records are not explicit about procedures and legal arguments, and provide a limited view of the court as a legal institution. In this social historical scholarship it is rare to find sustained attention to the specifically textual character of the judgments, transcripts, and instruments prepared or recorded by the courts.[69] In addition, social historians have evinced only a minimal interest in the relevant jurisprudence. Inasmuch as these studies based on court documents have lacked an equivalent concern for the relevant doctrinal texts, the result is approximately the reverse of the pattern that obtained in the Orientalist tradition (i.e., inquiries into sharīʿa practice absent an attention to its theory). While Islamicists tended to depict a sharīʿa without moorings in particular times and places, social historians have been apt to detail a phenomenon of strictly local character. In textual terms, this has meant the utilization of a contingent archive without corresponding attention to the relevant cosmopolitan library.

Innovative students of the sharīʿa took steps toward more integrated approaches. In a work critical of Orientalist views concerning the absence of doctrinal change, Baber Johansen writes that researchers "should pay more attention than in the past to the relationship between the different levels of the legal literature." His study considers the basic manuals and the commentary genres of the *fiqh* together with the fatwās of muftīs, and he concludes, "A systematic comparison of the results obtained from these layers of the legal literature with the *qāḍīs*ʾ *sijillāt* [judges' court registers] seems highly desirable."[70] Fully realized, such a project would unite an analysis of the interrelated "layers" of the library with readings in the various modalities of archival documentation.

Where Johansen's inquiries cover a vast geographic and temporal expanse, Zouhair Ghazzal's work by comparison is relatively tightly focused. In his study of Ottoman judicial thought and practice in Greater Syria during the first part of the nineteenth century, Ghazzal focuses on matters of textuality. Reading at the two ends of the library-archive continuum, he analyzes doctrinal chapters, such as that on the judgeship (*al-qaḍāʾ*) in the important *fiqh* work of the Damascene jurist Ibn ʿĀbidīn, together with a "typical contract of sale" concerning a house in the same city.[71] Readings of treatises, fatwās, and court decisions fill in the middle range of the continuum. Ghazzal's method involves "the deep analysis of individual texts, and their juxtaposition with other texts," which then "leads to the discovery of broader discursive formations." He seeks to understand both the "inner logic" of discrete texts and the "overall logic of such discursive practices."[72] In his commitment to both the library and the archive (in my terms) Ghazzal's work offers an exemplary prototype for an anthropological history of sharīʿa texts.

The Anthropologist as Reader

Before proceeding further, it should be noted that the western study of the specifically textual aspects of the sharīʿa also has involved a clutch of additional fields, beginning with the venerable discipline of philology,[73] but also including epigraphy, paleography, papyrology, codicology, bibliography, and diplomatics (or diplomatic).[74] These are the specialized forms of inquiry devoted to identifying, dating, deciphering, and reading scripts and manuscripts; they also consider writings, including some printed works, as material and cultural objects. Many such studies attend to form rather than content, an approach I adopt here, and to the literary rather than the documentary, which I do not.[75] Together with scholarship in such additional fields as the history of the book and the specialized studies of the oral and written,[76] these are the established modes of textual inquiry from which a nascent anthropology of the written text has much to learn, and to which, perhaps, something to contribute.

I admit that I only learned of the existence of the field of diplomatics after completing my first book, *The Calligraphic State*, when my publisher notified me about the decisions of the Library of Congress regarding the cataloging information that would appear in the forthcoming book. The identifying rubrics provided by these librarians included "2. Manuscripts, Arabic," and also "5. Diplomatics, Arabic." Diplomacy, I initially wondered? As it turned out, like Molière's prose-speaking bourgeois gentleman, I had unknowingly stumbled upon something that approximated an established type of textual analysis.

Anthropology, indeed, may seem an unlikely discipline from which to mount a study of written texts. In the early years of the last century, Franz Boas, a founder of the modern American branch, defined anthropology as the study of people "without written languages" and "without historical records."[77] At the time, the relation of anthropologists to written sources seemed simple: they did not work on such texts because the people they studied were not literate. But the reality, even then, was more complex. Research by founding fathers such as Boas and Bronislaw Malinowski, the equivalent figure in the British branch, resulted in the publication of grammars and corpuses of oral texts, including stories and myths. As later observers would remark, this was philology in all but the name.[78] By mid-century, however, this sophisticated early form of textual inquiry in the discipline was contested, and a break with such philological methods ensued in the name of an advancing social science.[79]

In recent decades, however, as reliance on written source materials has become routine, anthropologists have emerged as unabashed analytic readers. Yet it is not at all clear that this crossing of a disciplinary threshold has been accompanied by an adequate stocktaking, not to mention the specification of suitable methods. A basic argument of this book is that a maturing historical anthropology of the sharīʿa must attend to its complex textual manifestations. I thus confront the fact that, due to its long-standing and deeply engrained reliance on the colloquial and the observational, anthropology lacks a developed disciplinary capacity in the use of written sources and in the requisite reading techniques, Jack Goody's sociology of literacy and Clifford Geertz's conception of "textual" interpretation notwithstanding.[80] In addition to providing a newly conceived textual and contextual history of the sharīʿa, a parallel aim of this book is to extend the humanistic social sciences to accommodate a further type of analytic reader: the anthropological student of written traditions.

Will an anthropologist be a distinctive kind of reader? How will disciplinary history—that is, the weight of the anthropologist's own academic tradition—figure in the character of his or her readings? To retrace some of the steps in the emergence of a "literate" anthropology, I turn briefly to the work of Talal Asad. In addition to his renown for the comparative study of religion and secularism, and also to the fact that he was a pioneer in historical inquiries by anthropologists,[81] Asad is an accomplished student of the sharīʿa and has been a quiet innovator in the requisite reading practices.

Let me start in the 1980s, at what amounts to his mid-career. Anthropologists at the time found themselves in the throes of the discipline's "historical turn." They also had begun to reflect critically on their own writing and on related questions of representation. I would note two key interventions made by Asad at this juncture, both of which show a lingering reference to the former specialization of the discipline in the study of nonliterate societies. Thus, first, in a chapter from 1986, he explores the foundational question of translation.[82] Critically examining the power relations surrounding the rendering of indigenous concepts and categories, Asad highlights the distortions associated with what he refers to as the "inequality" of languages. He presents, but also begins to move away from, the then-existing holistic anthropological conception of "cultural translation," a disciplinary metaphor for the aims and the products of research. Unlike the work of the early twentieth-century anthropological philologists of the oral text, this was a form of "translation" without quotation. Consisting of "reading other cultures," this form of translation resulted in generalizing representations of "modes of thought" or "worldview" in nonliterate societies. At the same time, however, Asad appears to envision a more literary type of translation. This is suggested, for example, when he states that in certain instances the anthropologist "should retain what may be a discomforting—even scandalous—presence within the receiving language."[83] He also at this point differentiates between the inquiries of historians and anthropologists, identified respectively as specialists in written versus spoken sources. In a statement that acknowledges the onset of historical studies by anthropologists, but that does not yet conceive of the anthropologist as a reader, he maintains that "the historian is *given* a text and the anthropologist has to *construct* one."[84]

In a second paper from the same year, "The Idea of an Anthropology of Islam," Asad introduces his concept of a "discursive tradition," which I cited in passing earlier.[85] Here we find what I take to be the beginning of an explicit mandate for textual inquires, but, once again, with a limitation characteristic of the discipline. "If one wants to write an anthropology of Islam," he states, "one should begin, as Muslims do, from the concept of a discursive tradition that includes and relates itself to the founding texts of the Qurʾan and the Hadith."[86] This is a step toward anthropological engagements with the sorts of written textual materials that had been the exclusive domain of historians, area specialists, and the students of literature and religion. He goes on to explain that, far from being either "homogeneous" or simply "imitative of what was done in the past," a discursive tradition is characterized by its selectivity and adaptability. The basic guidelines for such research—versions of which I adopt in this book—are to focus on forms of reasoning and topics of debate and to attend to the related "instituted practices."[87] His qualification, however, is that the intended practices are those pertaining to "unlettered Muslims." "A tradition," he explains, "consists essentially of discourses that seek to instruct practitioners regarding the correct form and purpose of a given practice." To illustrate this broadly pedagogical conception, he mentions scenarios in which a scholar-jurist, a sermon-giver, the head of a Sufi order, or a family member offers guidance to, again, "unlettered" individuals.[88] Even though his example interchanges imply an underlying dynamic of the written and the spoken, and while they also represent distinct forms, or genres, of discursive transmission, he does not raise questions regarding writers and the status of written texts, nor does he refer to the task of reading.

But when Asad later turns his attention to the sharīʿa, he begins to write as a reader. In the first of two chapter-length studies, that from 1993 (in a book section labeled "Translations"), his topic is a named "genre," *naṣīḥa*, a centuries-old Islamic form of written public advice to the ruler.[89] He brilliantly compares the *naṣīḥa* tradition with the European Enlightenment form of critical public reasoning, as represented by Kant, observing, for example, that whereas the western form of criticism is understood to be a "right," the Islamic one is considered a "duty." *Naṣīḥa*, he states, is "something called for by the sharīʿa as a precondition of moral rectitude."[90] His specific examples involve Saudi *ʿulamāʾ* who address the late twentieth-century king. His close reading of one such advice text is accompanied by his translations, which appear in extended passages of quotation.[91] In an instance of a potentially "scandalous" translation he renders the Arabic word *ʿabd*, which describes the relation of the Muslim to God, as "slave," rather than, more conventionally, as "servant." Building on this translation decision, he contrasts the "metaphor of slavery" in Islamic theology with constructs of the Jewish and Christian traditions.[92]

In passing remarks in his readings in the *naṣīḥa* genre, Asad elaborates on his notion of a "discursive tradition." In 1986 he had emphasized the fundamentally historical and dynamic character of this concept, which engages questions of the past, the future, and the present.[93] Now, from the perspective of a reader, he emphasizes the "temporal situatedness of all texts," which I take as a foundational principle for my readings.[94] In a related formulation, he conceives of approaching a discursive tradition as a composite whole, historically situated. This is to understand "the way a particular discursive tradition, and its associated disciplines, are articulated at a particular point in time."[95] In this study, I detail "articulations" at several levels. First, there are the historically specific articulations *within* the sharīʿa "library" of the imamic period—that is, among Zaydī school works of *fiqh* and related genres and disciplines. I am equally interested, second, in the articulations *within* the period "archive," among a set of local genres from the particular setting. Third, at the higher or encompassing level, I study the articulations of these broad categories of writings in a textual formation.

In a chapter from 2003, Asad focuses directly on the sharīʿa.[96] He offers a richly technical exposition of thought by jurists in colonial-era Egypt around the turn of the twentieth century, with the *fiqh* as the discipline in question. With the larger aim of illuminating the historical preconditions and the processes of secularization through examinations of the associated "reconfigurations of law, ethics, and religious authority," he reads his Arabic sources for their arguments and conceptual work, especially as these "reflect" new discursive and institutional "spaces."[97] An example of these readings is that of the 1899 report on sharīʿa court reform by Muhammad ʿAbduh, the recently appointed Grand Muftī of Egypt.[98] Translating and also strategically transliterating the Arabic, he quotes the report to pinpoint the introduction of unfamiliar terminology.[99] A key instance is a passage in which ʿAbduh refers to "households that are called families." Asad argues that ʿAbduh's notion of "the family" represented a novel usage that appeared within a context of both accumulated social change and new limitations on the jurisdictions of the Egyptian sharīʿa courts. He also argues that this new category of "the family" would be linked to other emergent conceptions, notably those defining "society" and the "nation." He thus understands ʿAbduh's analysis to be part of a local process of reform and transformation that, in Egypt and a number of other modern states (not including Yemen), "eventually translates the sharīʿa as 'family law.' "[100]

I conclude this slice of disciplinary history on the emergence of the anthropological reader with some notes on how Asad's work relates to the project of the present book. First, I want to take up Asad's early statement that one should strive "to understand the historical conditions that enable the production and maintenance of specific discursive traditions, or their transformation."[101] In an analysis focused on the sharīʿa, what are the relevant "historical conditions"? In approaching the sharīʿa as a formation of cosmopolitan and contingent writings, the immediate conditions pertain to the institutional milieus corresponding to the genres in question, from madrasa culture to notarial practice. Further conditions arise in connection with archival writings, the contingent features of which particularized the civilizational reach of the sharīʿa.

Asad also refers more specifically to "the constraints of political and economic conditions in which traditions are placed." In studying the sharīʿa, what are the dictates, or the desiderata, of this wider contextual and historical specificity? Between the two instances he has treated—late twentieth-century Saudi Arabia and turn-of-the-twentieth-century Egypt—and between them and highland Yemen, the differences extend well beyond their respective institutionalizations of the sharīʿa and the doctrinal footprints of their particular schools of jurisprudence to include substantial contrasts in political histories, economic structures, geographies, etc. The bearing of such wider ranges of "conditions" on our understandings of the historical sharīʿa is rarely treated, and never in systemic terms. In this book, to reiterate, I extend my attention to the textual aspects of both the imamic polity of the period and the relations of late agrarian age property, a pair of institutional complexes foundational to the broader "political economy" of the era. I argue that in their historical enactments of key doctrinal scripts these collateral institutions of the highland instance challenge prevailing assumptions concerning the sharīʿa in history.

Second, regarding Asad's "genealogical" method—that is, his approach, following Michel Foucault, to writing the "history of the present"—I would begin by mentioning a similarity—his robust analytic interest in secularism aside—to the historical method of my earlier work on Yemen.[102] *The Calligraphic State* examines discursive ruptures dating from the turn-of-the twentieth-century Ottoman period; the ensuing "hybrid" institutions of the following decades of imamic rule; and the further discontinuities of the late twentieth-century republican-era nation-state. Adapting a concept from Marcel Mauss, I characterized the historical sharīʿa as a "total" discourse. This was meant to contrast with what replaced it under the succeeding Yemeni nation-state, following selective restatement, codification, and legislation, and also the promulgation of a national constitution, namely a modern form of "law." Despite the many contextual differences, what happened in Yemen was analogous to the discursive shift that took place in Egypt, where chapters of the old doctrine were "translated," as Asad puts it, into personal status and "family law."

In *Sharīʿa Scripts*, however, I have turned away from anthropological efforts (including my own previous book) to locate the sharīʿa, or its discursive remains, in a colonial setting or in the time of a specific nation-state. I have turned away, in other words, from assessing the fate of a specific instance of this tradition as it has been "reconstituted by modern forces."[103] As a consequence, rather than to the predicaments of modernity—the typical application by anthropologists—the concept of a "discursive tradition" mainly refers here to situations prior to their rise.

Rather than a genealogical approach, this study embodies a text-focused anthropological history of the past. While concentrating on the specific instance of the early to mid-twentieth century in the highlands, my analysis also works backward from that historical present. Although my efforts are primarily directed toward the elucidation of the discursive relations that obtained at a "particular point in time," I think with the specifics of this instance as I pursue comparative textual perspectives on the premodern sharīʿa. These I develop by means of selected sondages in the research of scholars whose methods I at the same time distinguish from those of historical anthropology.

Third, Asad has referred to the sharīʿa as having "parts."[104] These comprise, on the one hand, the more conventionally recognizable sphere of justiciable legal rules and related reasoning and argumentation and, on the other, the realm of ethical and moral dispositions. The latter are cultivated and embodied by individual Muslims and may be enacted in interpersonal relations that involve advice, persuasion, exhortation, warning, etc. Asad differentiates these "parts" in commenting on the book by Hussein Agrama on the personal status courts and on what is known as the Fatwa Council of twenty-first-century Egypt.[105] Asad states that whereas the courts enact a version of the former part, based on a transformed body of justiciable rules in the guise of personal status "law," the Fatwa Council engages the latter, which is not "law" but rather a distinct "tradition" of "the premodern, pre-state sharīʿa."[106]

Asad's own studies of the sharīʿa have gravitated to this less understood moral and ethical part, which he associates conceptually with Foucault's work on the ethical structures of "the care of the self."[107] In his 1993 study, in addition to treating the advice genre as a sharīʿa-based duty of "moral rectitude" vis-à-vis the ruler, Asad refers to another institution in this category, the virtuous public or interpersonal form of "commanding right and forbidding wrong" (*al-amr bi-l-maʿrūf wa-l-nahy ʿan al-munkar*), which, in turn, is related to the duty of *ḥisba*, originally the public or personal upholding of proper marketplace practices and morality.[108] All three named institutions of sharīʿa-based moral intervention were integral to the *fiqh*, and, as such, their respective rules and conditions and related discussions appear in doctrinal works. In the Zaydī tradition, two of the three are treated in the *Flowers* literature chapter on the imamate—that is, under the doctrine of sharīʿa governance—while an early imam was the author of a treatise focused on the third.[109]

In his 2003 study, Asad analyzes sharīʿa reform as a general process of "reordering" that involved "a new distinction being drawn between law and morality," which likewise produced new subjectivities.[110] In this connection, he elaborates on the sharīʿa-based ritual practices (*ʿibādāt*), including prayer, fasting, etc., which are covered in the opening chapters of *fiqh* books, and also on the possible connections to Sufism, or Islamic mysticism (*tasawwuf*), which might be viewed as a distinct "discipline" within the larger discursive tradition.[111] Both of these major institutional corpora offered jurists and practitioners, including judges, resources and frames for the cultivation and embodiment of proper ethical dispositions.

In these pages I hold to a basic assumption of my earlier characterization of the historical sharīʿa as a "total" discourse, namely that it consisted of rules suffused with premodern ethical and moral concerns. This, it must be emphasized, was the case across the spectrum of the historical *fiqh*, including not only the ritual coverage but, equally, the "transactions" and other such matters—that is, both the *ʿibādāt* and the *muʿāmalāt*. Focused throughout on questions of textuality, this book addresses the various discursive modalities of the sharīʿa rule together with the period ethics of sharīʿa writing.[112]

Composition

> We are interested primarily in concrete forms of texts and concrete conditions of the life of texts, their interrelations, and their interactions.
>
> —M. M. Bakhtin, *Speech Genres and Other Late Essays*

I now provide an overview of the interrelated reading methods on which this historical anthropology of sharīʿa texts depends. These bring together discrete elements: conceptual leads from the thought of the Muslim jurists in the traditions in question on the topics of writing and texts; approaches adapted from the analyses of western-trained Islamicist scholarship; concepts derived from the usages of linguistic anthropologists (the intellectual descendants of the former philologists of the oral text); and oral history and retrospective ethnographic insights into the formal and informal aspects of sharīʿa textuality.

To approach the spectrum of writings at hand I thus far have introduced the library and the archive as general textual categories. Delimiting my period history, I then presented a conception of the local as a discursive space opened at the meeting points of these cosmopolitan and contingent texts. What I have described as the central concern of this book—the relationship between a given library and a specific archive—may now be restated as a series of analytic initiatives. Focusing on the dynamics of texts in a formation, these approaches are tailored to the disciplinary interests and the research possibilities of a still relatively new figure: the anthropological reader.

Simply stated, my method is to read related texts together, to read across genres, and to read for discursive system. A principal inspiration is the work of M. M. Bakhtin, the twentieth-century Russian literary critic and philosopher of language. Bakhtin and his circle criticized the tendency in philology and related textual studies to view texts in isolation, as individual "monuments." They advocated an approach to texts as "generative" elements within particular traditions. In their "dialogic" conception they examined how individual writings could be understood as responding to and as anticipating responses from other texts.[113] An important context for a given text thus is other texts, including those not only of the same but also of different genres. When I turn to detailing the structure and history of this local formation of texts, my further concern is with how the several types of writings acted as interlocutors.

Bakhtin's work has for some time informed research in the subfield of linguistic anthropology, but with a constraint characteristic of the discipline. Anthropological appropriations of his ideas have been restricted mainly to studies of spoken texts, whereas Bakhtin, a student of the novel, among other genres, was concerned with texts both spoken and written, and especially with their interrelations, including the representations of the former in the latter—approaches that are essential to the textual study of the historical sharīʿa. I also join anthropologists such as Annelise Riles, Ann Stoler, Ilana Feldman, Penelope Papailias, and Matthew Hull, who place analytic emphasis on matters of written form and who foreground the material qualities of texts, especially in studies of documents, archives, and files.[114] This book differs from such studies in that it views genres of these types as active elements in an overarching system, a formation of writings that, in this instance, simultaneously included sacred texts, doctrinal books and formal juridical opinions.

Composition is central to my interests. When I characterize the humanist-social scientist as an "analytic" reader, I have in mind various techniques for studying the composition of writings. From Raymond Williams and Bruno Latour I take the basic perspective that composition refers to a "process" in which "things have to be put together."[115] To reconstruct the work of composition in the imamic-period highlands I read extant artifacts—from books to documents—for indications of prior acts of writing. Such reconstructive readings address form, both conceptual and material. Composition differs according to genre, of course, yet the regularities across genres are as significant. The more or less established conventions of composition defined the specific genres that, in turn, accomplished the range of existing discursive tasks of the time and place. Relations between texts begin with the apparently simple act of writing in genre. At the elementary level, to write in genre is to quote form itself. By extension, it is to reference a given order of texts. Inasmuch as it represented an implicit acknowledgment of an existing formation of writings, composition initiated a fundamental dimension of the intertextual.

What is the compositional role of what Bakhtin termed "authoritative" discourse?[116] He noted that special framing or quotation devices (see below) typically guard the integrity of the words in question. In the study of sharīʿa regimes it is common to emphasize the roles of the "sources," the texts of divine revelation and prophetic example—thus Asad's invitation to anthropologists to attend to such texts. I look closely at the Zaydī jurists' techniques for handling these "sources," at the guidelines for their mobilization in interpretation, and at the transmutations of their original forms of expression into the rules-and-stipulations language of the *fiqh*. I note that the jurists distinguished between the ordinary meanings of Arabic words and the technical usage of the same words as juridical terms. I take pains throughout to underline the historical specificity of the authoritative doctrinal language of this period. Since it permitted distinctive flexibilities of quotation and paraphrase, and the use of versification, this period discourse is distinct from the types of legal language that, a few decades later, would be utilized in nation-state codification and the legislation of modern law. I am especially interested in the circulation of such formal language between the library and the archive, and I have a parallel interest in the less understood authorities specific to archival language. Jurists and practitioners alike recognized the special weight of the wording that appeared in court testimony, in the expressions of contractual intent or consent, and even in customary stipulations.

It was a commonplace for jurists and others to refer to named genres of sharīʿa texts. The literary specialists among them employed a variety of terms to speak of the "authoring" of writings, including a form of "compilation" based on already existing texts. The jurists additionally found occasion to consider both the material attributes and the epistemic statuses of written and oral texts, including the sonic qualities of the latter. Behind the various interests in and capacities for textual analysis among these Muslim lawyers lay the specialized studies of the grammarians and their colleagues in the several additional branches of the "language sciences," fields that typically figured in the basic madrasa training.

To learn about composition, the pertinent thought of these historical jurists is essential. The required readings amount to thinking with the various types of specialist writers while also rethinking, connecting, and extending their ideas. I make no claims of mastery in my readings, nor do I exhaust the sources in question. Using a variety of strategies, I follow texts closely, translating and transliterating as need be. At different points in this book, I adhere to written presentations, including works of commentary, in a manner analogous to a commentator; or I select particular aspects that interest me and bring together and sample what I take to be relevant passages; or I read different texts, or different genres, together, side-by-side. Rather than pushing these varied sources off my page and into my notes or references, I attempt to write with them.

Linguistic anthropologists have addressed how people think about and refer to language, but the conceptual tools, such as linguistic "reflexivity," "metapragmatics," and "language ideology," mainly have been applied to speech.[117] Hull proposes the term "graphic ideology" to refer to conceptions specific to writing.[118] I prefer "textual ideology," which encompasses ideas about both the oral and the written. Explicit juridical ideas about writing and about topics such as oral testimony or the value of documentary evidence are an integral part of sharīʿa discourse. As elements of an academic discourse, however, these ideas were subject to elaboration, as well as to challenge. Rather than as timeless ideals, I address such conceptions as understandings and debates with histories, and I treat them as having potential rather than assumed implications for what happened on the ground.

Formal textual ideation of this sort is a mainstay of Islamicist inquiry. Norman Calder, to mention a prominent example, analyzed Nawawī's "typologies of *fiqh* writing," and he also studied the same jurist's treatise on the muftī, which largely concerns the fatwā as a genre.[119] In contrast, at least until recently this type of thought represented unfamiliar terrain for mainstream anthropologists, researchers more attuned to the study of unconscious structures (Lévi-Strauss), commonsense assumptions (Geertz) or implicit dispositions (Bourdieu). From Boas's time forward, "native theory," as it later would be termed, has been viewed askance, as unreliable "secondary" material, even as positively "dangerous."[120] The written status of the juridical conceptions in question only compounds this unfamiliarity, underscoring the need for new disciplinary protocols for analytic readings.

Modeling

A subset of the jurists' conceptions took the form of models. This specialized "library" discourse involved established scripts for the drafting of "archival" texts. Modeling of this type is part and parcel of the jurists' theories of composition. To understand textual modeling as a relationship, I read and juxtapose the two types of imamic-period writings: models and modeled texts. Models are elaborated types of meta-texts—that is, texts about texts. In its dual dictionary meaning, "meta" refers to phenomena of a "higher logical type" and also to the sequential status of "occurring later."[121] The models in question had related features: they offered an abstraction, or reduction, to pure textual "form" and their appearance on the historical scene followed that of the indicated types of applied writings. While predicated in this sense on the prior existence of the archival text, the modeling relationship per se commenced with the composition of the model text.

Approaching this dialectical scripting of written practice, I think of these specialized library texts as models in two senses: as both models *of* and *for* particular archival genres.[122] The historical existence of a given model text thus comprised an initial construction stage (or stages) with a pronounced model *of* aspect and a later implementation stage (or stages) in which it served mainly as a model *for*. In reading the period models together with the indicated genres of local documents from Ibb, however, I hold open the two related questions, namely whether the existing models were in fact built from the archival writings and whether they subsequently figured in the drafting of such writings.

Modeling relations represent an important aspect of the wider ties between a library and an archive, one that highlights the intertextual production and circulation of rules and related language. In this larger dialectical sense, such relations pertained both to how practice entered into theory and to how theory entered into practice. The model *of* dimension emphasizes how practice informed theory; the model *for* dimension foregrounds the reverse: how theory informed practice. These reciprocal movements are vitally important for any living legal system, but neither has been properly understood with reference to a historical instance of the sharīʿa.

Regarding the library as a model *of* the archive (the practice-into-theory side), the key question is the extent to which, and the specific ways that, significant but otherwise transitory developments at the archival level could make an impact on the permanent corpus of the library. In textual terms, the problem is one of understanding how certain types of writings oriented to particulars could be modified for incorporation into the more general discursive formats of the doctrine. To this end, I adapt and extend the notion of textual "stripping" proposed by historian of the sharīʿa Wael Hallaq.[123] Little noticed as such, the indicated editing techniques relied on the behind-the-scenes services of the flexible textual form of the *masʾala*, a "problem," "issue," or "case." The changeability of this basic textual vehicle permitted the re-scripting shifts of genre that enabled the movement of substantive materials between different levels of sharīʿa texts, notably, from the archive to the library.

Regarding the reverse, the library as a model *for* the archive (the theory-into-practice side), the key question concerns the mechanics of implementation. What happened when an element of existing doctrinal thought, a rule or a concept, or specific technical language was implemented in an applied text? The obvious aspect of implementation involves the apparent reproduction of doctrinal discourse. My qualifier, "apparent," points to the fact that, in the archival writings, any utilized formal language found itself in the altered discursive context of the name and its many practical entailments. But even in what might be considered a situation of full or strict implementation part of the directly relevant doctrinal discourse would be left unstated, which points up an underlying difference between library and archive texts. A comparable difference—to make my title metaphor explicit—is that between a theater script and a particular performance. Discursive elements such as the stage directions elaborated in the former guided the enactment of the latter, but without being mentioned as such.

Other genres of "texts about texts" figured at both the library and archive levels. Thus the major institution of the written commentary and the several types of marginalia were integral to the culture of the library book, while incidental added remarks and annotations by practitioners such as judges, court secretaries, and notarial writers likewise augmented the main texts of litigation records and ordinary instruments. In both situations, a subset of this meta-discourse directly concerned matters of writing and textuality. Furthermore, speaking now just of the archive, in lawsuits, handwriting itself or the formulations of particular written instruments could become a focus of contention. In such circumstances, the anthropological reader also is apt to encounter a much more accustomed body of material, albeit in written transcripts. I refer to a vibrant substratum of popular ideas about matters such as falsification and forgery and related stratagems that surfaced regularly in the court records of the period, both in the assertions and arguments of litigants and in the testimonies of witnesses. Very interesting in its own right, such contentious discourse about writing and writings in the course of litigation also provides an instructive counterpoint to the formal discussions of textuality by the literary jurists.[124]

Textual Habitus

All such readings stress the significance of explicit textual perspectives. These, to repeat, ranged from formally argued, mandated, or modeled doctrinal ideas to the written remarks of court personnel or notarial writers in the court or documentary record to the just-mentioned, and also transcribed, statements of litigants and the testimonies of witnesses. In contrast, the complementary realm of what I term the "textual habitus" consists of a spectrum of largely implicit discursive patterns and informal textual logics.[125] This is the sphere of elementary textual forms and minor discursive institutions that figured among the mundane modes and methods of composition. Rather than through formal acquisition in academic instruction, a local writer achieved mastery in these routines of drafting and reading through repeated contact with the genres in question, in direct personal experience or informal apprenticeship. Where readings for explicit textual perspectives may follow written prompts or formal models or the relevant passages in court transcripts an analysis concerned with the textual habitus might appear to have less to go on. To clarify the obvious and therefore unremarked upon roles of such forms and techniques, I reconstruct compositional processes together with their immediate contexts and ambient institutions. I focus, in particular, on (1) the recurrence at various discursive levels of the earlier-mentioned mutable form of the "problem" or "case" (*masʾala*); (2) the basic relations and institutions of the original and the copy; (3) the types of oral-written (and written-oral) synapses that punctuated the textual order; and (4) the functions of the adaptable minor institution of "dictation" (*imlāʾ*).[126]

Among the unassuming techniques of composition, I read for methods of quotation. Such genre-specific methods were quietly essential to text building, to putting sharīʿa discourse together. Quotation begins by identifying and then "taking" an appropriate excerpt from an existing text. At the other end of the process, equally implicit compositional determinations and methods guided the insertion of the excerpted passage into the text being created. Such movements between texts were material processes that led to the creation of new ranges of meaning. An excerpted passage came with its original grammar and other, still resonant, connections to the lines left behind. Insertion in a book or document usually required some form of linguistic marking, equivalent to our quotation marks, and also involved other less pronounced adjustments to, and reverberations in, the textual stem it was made to join. More or less securely tied to the new textual location, the quoted passage, even a single word, actively recalled other scenes of writing and/or speaking.

Latour refers to "the almost physical work of intertextuality."[127] Among linguistic anthropologists, the phenomenon of quotation goes to the basic definition of a "text," which refers to language that may be cited or reiterated, to language that, in a conceptual-material sense, may be "detached."[128] While Muslim specialists in the rhetorical arts theorized quotation, their concepts (e.g., *taḍmīn, iqtibās*) were elaborated with poetry and the Qurʾan in mind.[129] In research on ordinary language use, anthropological linguists have followed Bakhtin in focusing on the phenomenon of "reported speech."[130] This includes the general situation of "speech in speech," and the more markedly reflexive circumstance of "speech about speech." Closely related to this conception would be that of reported writing, including instances of writing that appears in another writing and, again, more pointedly reflexive in nature, writing about writing. Attention to what may be comprehensively termed "reported texts"—that is, the reporting of texts spoken, written, and mixed—places an emphasis on the constitutive and continuing relations.

Bakhtin also identified what he referred to as "incorporative" genres: types of written texts that, as he put it, characteristically "absorb and digest" other texts.[131] Critical theorists have repeatedly stressed the significance and the two-part (absorb *and* digest) nature of this key textual event.[132] For his part, Bakhtin refers to the "double-voiced" quality of utterances of such types, a notion that includes written works in which an author or writer uses the text of another.[133]

Beyond the conventional genre-specific forms, other types of "quotation" may be thought of as quietly underpinning a variety of further intergenre relations, from commentary, to modeling, to dictation. When the scope of the inquiry is extended to the entire textual formation, unnoticed parallels surface. Thus, for example, the earlier-mentioned form of editorial "stripping," carried out when certain types of writings were modified for inclusion in doctrinal works, may be compared with the processes of excerpting and inserting that occurred in the selective citation of oral testimonies or written instruments in a court transcript. In this comparison, a significant difference between the two comes to the fore. Whereas quoting a stripped text in a doctrinal work (a type of a library text) depended on the elimination of the prior genre-markings, notably including the identifications established in the archive, quotation in a court transcript (a type of archival text) required the opposite: the retention of the genre-markings of the incorporated text, including the language of the proper name and the indications of location, time, amount, etc. Whereas the former discursive operation may be largely imperceptible to the anthropological reader, the latter is clearly evident.

Temporality

Temporality is a factor throughout these readings. Texts that might otherwise be taken to be spatially isolated and temporally flat may be read for their synchronic and diachronic connections.[134] Such readings move beyond the association of a text with the contours of the finished page. They also move beyond analyses constrained by the biographical coordinates of specific authors or writers. Readings sensitive to temporality focus on "the life of texts." They are attuned to process and duration, the indicators of which may be found within (and without) texts, starting, in this instance, with the tenses of Arabic verbs. I have characterized *fulān*-oriented library texts as atemporal in their discursive horizons and name-based archival writings as concerned with the timing of acts. I also have noted that models and meta-texts entail specific historical chronologies in relation to the texts they are "about." Oral-to-written and written-to-oral acts (including those based on different forms of "dictation") involved sequential steps, and the same was true in the making of copies from originals. Similar reading attitudes may be brought to forms of quotation, in noting the prior time frames of the incorporated texts; to marginalia in the library and annotations in the archive, the presence of which tracked histories of subsequent textual interventions; and to the doctrinally envisioned technique of reading an evidential document aloud in court, which indexed an earlier moment of composition.

Such readings attend to processes of composition and to the later fortunes of written artifacts. From books to documents, the potentials of the latter included physical retention, displacement, duplication, alteration, erasure, destruction, loss, etc., as well as, across these and other such possibilities, evidence of being read and further written on. The conventional outcome, of course, was to be located on a shelf or in a document bag—that is, in a physical library or archive. In such open-ended circumstances we may speak of stopped time and of a stationary inactivity, although the simple knowledge of the availability of a book or a cached document could be weighty in and of itself. In preservation, however, there also were possibilities of returns, of exits from such conditions of textual liminality. A book was taken down from the shelf, or its passages recalled from memory; a document was removed from a cloth bag, or its copy retrieved from a register. Consulting, referencing, checking, citing, interpreting, etc. ensued. These and other such textual events amount to varieties of what may be thought of as an "actualization."[135] Actualizations brought a return from the textual shadows to the light of day, from suspension and mere potential to ordinary time and ongoing engagements. While the creation of such texts centered on acts of writing, the later actualizations of their extant artifacts depended on acts of reading.

Paper Language

Finally, this book may be thought of as offering a local history of a "paper" language. I take this conception of the objects of composition from a passing reference by Bakhtin, whose usage may be generalized. Bakhtin depicts an encounter between an illiterate Slavic peasant and a writer of petitions. He explains that the peasant "lived in" several "language systems," including those of prayer, song, and colloquial familial expression, and that, in dictating to the scribe, he tried to speak in an "official-literate" or "paper" language.[136] Later, in considering a similar (and perhaps historically related) dictation-based institution of writing petitions to the authorities in Ibb, I mention a type addressed to a judge as a pre-text to court litigation.

The oral-written interchange depicted by Bakhtin also may be seen as part of a wider phenomenon, as a type of societal event in which particular affairs of the world went into writing and, specifically for this study, into sharīʿa discourse. As hitherto unscripted matters took written form, such events characteristically were transformative. Questions posed to muftīs, formal claims made in court, and instruments drafted by notarial writers were among the institutions predicated on the reframing of everyday realities. Such elementary moments in the onset of the paper discourse of the sharīʿa typically entailed the translation of modes of expression and the overwriting of quotidian actualities.

Perspectives on such transitions to paper may be difficult to recover from the historical record, but they may be illustrated ethnographically. An example from Ibb concerns a type of wife-initiated divorce. At the conclusion of one I observed, with the husband and the wife's father facing each other on opposite sides of a narrow sitting room in a private residence that had been made available by a helpful intermediary, the man who eventually would write the divorce instrument stood up and went to the door of the room. From there he could see the wife, who had just appeared in the hallway outside the room. He spoke to her so that all could hear. There was a pause, and he put his hand to his throat, indicating she was unable to speak. Then she was heard to blurt out, "no, no, no," a delayed response to the three questions he had posed to her. The man at the door then turned to the husband sitting in the room, expecting a response. The husband said, "That ends it." The man at the door looked back at the woman in the hall and said, "good-bye," and returned and sat down. The following day, this same man, the notarial writer, prepared an instrument in which he converted the binding words he had heard from the wife and the husband into the proper clauses and stipulations of a divorce document.

In another Ibb example, families in my neighborhood in the old part of town fell into conflict over a plan to add a new room atop one of their physically adjoined residences. An issue in the conflict concerned the leaving of a space between the new room and the neighbor's wall. The popular notion related to me by Muhammad, a young man on the side that intended to build, was that one had to allow enough room for "a bird to pass" (*murūr aṭ-ṭāʾir*, i.e., not enough for a human). He also told me, "The sharīʿa says that if you leave 30 centimeters between you and your neighbor it is okay to build." Building stone was delivered and the initial dressing work began. Soon, however, the other side managed to get soldiers to stop the construction. In the following days there was fighting in the alley between Muhammad and a man from the other side and Muhammad's mother jostled with the neighbor woman. According to a document that identifies Muhammad's father as the "claimant," a building expert and another respected man, chosen by the two sides, were dispatched to the site by a mediator. These men found that Muhammad's father should leave a "sharīʿa space" (*ḥāʾil sharʿī*) on his rooftop and then should be permitted to "build above his property."[137]

From the "no, no, no" uttered in the hallway to the requisite formulae of the ensuing divorce document, and from the popular conception of room for "a bird to pass" to the technical rendition as "sharīʿa space," writing conveyed and yet also altered colloquial words and ideas. Such changes associated with the drafting of paper language texts underscore the fact that the resulting writings were not simply representations of acts but further acts in their own right.[138]

Beyond such initiating inscriptions, any subsequent textual movements and their discursive changes would entail the re-scripting of the already written, this within the world of the given paper language. Such further historical events of composition, which would be more amenable to the previously discussed methods for analytic reading, take us back to the broader dynamics of the written sharīʿa, to the basic distinctions and dialogues between the library and the archive, the deployments of authoritative discourse, the roles of models and other meta-texts, and the informal patterns of text-building, including those involving orality, the techniques of quotation, and matters of textual temporality.

Chapters

The following chapters disassemble this specific historical instance of a sharīʿa tradition into a series of types of writing. In the process, I connect each of the component genres to particular local institutions—of study, interpretation, judgment, and documentation. Part I introduces books and freestanding opinions, the main types of "library" texts. It also includes alternating chapters that examine how such doctrinal works conceptualized the status of their counterpart texts, the archival writings. Part II introduces the "archive" per se, which comprises both court-based genres and a range of privately written instruments. It also brings in the conceptual perspectives of further specialized types of library-form texts. Throughout, my analysis highlights the genre-specific yet always intertextual work of composition. This work started at the level of the unremarked-upon discursive building blocks and culminated in the broader patterns of cohesion and interdependence that structured the textual formation as a whole.

Library

Using *The Book of Flowers* as the main example, chapter 1 addresses the past, the historical present, and the future of the sharīʿa book. Against the backdrop of the long history of the Zaydī *madhhab* as a community of interpretation, the chapter examines the imamic-period discourse of literary-juridical authorship. It concludes with a discussion of the localization of this discourse in Ibb through instruction in the town madrasa and appointments of *Flowers*-trained Zaydī jurists to the courts. In chapter 2, I read a short text on interpretation that commonly appears at the front of *Flowers*-tradition books. This allows me to step back to survey the place of the sharīʿa in the wider landscape of the discursive tradition, with a particular emphasis on the accessing of the "source" texts of the Qurʾan and the *ḥadīth*. Chapter 3 takes closer looks at Qurʾan exegesis (*tafsīr*) and *fiqh* commentary. It represents an initial installment in my analysis of how particular types of library texts modeled the requirements and addressed the perceived problems of archival writings. Chapter 4 considers two genres of freestanding opinions, the fatwā of the muftī and the "choice" of the ruling imam, as vehicles for the articulation of rules. I also begin my analysis of textual "stripping," which involves genre-to-genre, archive-to-library shifts. Chapter 5 gives extended readings of two specific opinions, a c. 1920 "choice" by Imam Yahya and a fatwā-like "investigation" from the first half of the nineteenth century, both of which concern the status of archival writings, specifically the issue of basing of action on writing, or "practice with writing" (*al-ʿamal bi-l-khaṭṭ*).

Archive

I transition from the library to the archive in chapter 6, "Intermission," in which I first pause to elaborate on "script" as a metaphor for my object of inquiry. After a schematic overview of the archive, and after raising issues concerning the "textual surround" of archival writings and their "ethnographic sourcing," I address questions of historical specificity, including the key role of custom. For purposes of comparison with the highland instance, I engage with the work of selected historians whose findings and methods I contrast with those of a historical anthropologist. Chapter 7 examines the textual domain of the sharīʿa court, centering on the judgment issued by a judge. I read five example Ibb judgments from the era together with Imam Yahya's "Instructions" for the courts, which were adapted from late nineteenth-century Ottoman guidelines. The chapter concludes with a typology of contrasting forms of oral "dictation," including its use in petitions and in connection with the court record. Chapter 8 returns to the beginning of the litigation process to consider the register-based composition of the court minutes. I refer, comparatively, to Jeremy Bentham's study of minutes in the Common Law and, again, to the imam's "Instructions." I highlight the use of proper names and the modalities of text building through quotation. I conclude with an excursus on "false writing." Chapter 9 initiates my analysis of ordinary documents and their writers by concentrating on a locally written "stipulations" (*shurūṭ*) treatise, notably its sections on the "science of writing" and on the etiquette and morality (*adab*) of the writer. This analysis continues in chapter 10, where I present three genres from Ibb: the land sale instrument, the agrarian lease, and the marriage contract. Juxtaposing treatise models and historical documents, I further explore the "stripping" hypothesis. To comprehend the articulations of library and archive discourse, I invoke Durkheim's opposition between the regularities of "contract-law" versus the negotiated particulars of "contract."

PART I

Library

If I were asked to name the chief event of my life, I should say my father's library. In fact, I sometimes think that I have never strayed outside that library.

—Jorge Luis Borges, *The Aleph and Other Stories, 1933–1969*

ONE

Books

> The frontiers of a book are never clear-cut . . . it is caught up in a system of references to other books, other texts, other sentences: it is a node within a network.
>
> —Michel Foucault, *The Archaeology of Knowledge*

AS AN ESSENTIAL feature of its mature historical existence the sharīʿa was articulated in a number of schools or traditions of interpretation known as *madhhabs*.[1] The Zaydī jurists of highland Yemen represent one such school, a tradition among the traditions that together constituted Islamic law as a historical phenomenon.[2] Each of these schools of reception was distinguished by its own intellectual genealogies and juridical literature. Consisting of important juristic ancestors and their works and also of their living descendants—including madrasa-based teachers and authors, muftīs and independent scholars—and informing the work of practicing court judges and notarial writers, a *madhhab* was a type of interpretive community. Internally, such communities were as much about argument as they were about agreement, their histories as marked by factionalism as by allegiance. Some contemporary Muslim jurists would explicitly throw off such school-based identities, but prior to the onset of colonial and national changes, to encounter the sharīʿa in local history was to encounter one or more such interpretive traditions.

In a living *madhhab*, much of the juristic interchange turned around a received corpus of texts. My main concern in this chapter is with the leading genres of the later Zaydī *madhhab*, the official juridical school of the period Islamic polity, and the interpretive community associated with basic works such as *The Book of Flowers*. But the library, as I term it, also was an arena of practice, of literary and doctrinal-theoretical acts. Beyond composition itself, which employed detailed sub-forms and distinctive modes of citation and quotation, these acts ranged from the multifaceted work of instruction to the reading and writing that took place in such supporting professions as the handwritten reproduction of books by copyists. Such an active world of literary jurisprudence implied the existence of an elaborated scholarly craft, and it depended on a variety of explicit and implicit techniques associated with studying, teaching, memorizing, commenting, debating, referencing, and many other types of text-related efforts. A growth point of a *madhhab* was the lesson circle of teacher and students, which was an interpretive community in microcosm.[3]

Madhhabs existed in larger interpretive worlds constituted by other such communities of interpretation. At various levels inside and outside their cosmopolitan juristic traditions scholars engaged in direct borrowing, cross-citation, polemics, and other forms of intellectual interchange. Rather than cross-referencing their intellectual counterparts in the other Shīʿī traditions, however, the Zaydī jurists built their most active juridical connections with the several Sunnī schools. To further locate their own doctrinal positions, *Flowers*-tradition authors routinely cited the jurists of these four *madhhabs*.

When, as in imamic Yemen, one school was associated with the polity as the official school of interpretation, inter-school relations could be hegemonic. As I have indicated, the representatives of two *madhhabs* were resident in Ibb. In addition to Zaydī jurists educated in Upper Yemen and posted to town judgeships and to other positions by the ruling imams, there were Shāfiʿī-trained scholars of the school indigenous to Lower Yemen, including individuals who actively adapted themselves to the textual world of imamic rule. At the end of this chapter I discuss the roles of texts and men in the localization of the *Flowers* tradition in Lower Yemen.

In the eighteenth and nineteenth centuries, leading Muslim intellectuals began to advocate for significant sharīʿa reform, which involved challenges to existing *madhhabs*. Prominent among these figures was Muhammad ʿAli al-Shawkānī (d. 1834) of Yemen.[4] Shawkānī critically addressed an authoritative *madhhab* text, in his case the *Flowers*, which he had memorized as a youth. Elsewhere in the second half of the nineteenth century, in dialogue with colonial modernity, a legal *nahḍa* would closely parallel the better-known "renaissance" in Arabic literature. One eventual result was a pragmatic eclecticism that involved new crossings and borrowings between the several old schools of sharīʿa interpretation. By the turn of the twentieth century, Muhammad ʿAbduh and Muhammad Rashīd Riḍā, based in Cairo, were carrying out a program of systematic rethinking and publication. A few decades later, also in Egypt, ʿAbd al-Razzāq al-Sanhūrī would draft widely influential new codified laws that were sharīʿa-derived but western-influenced. Yemen stood largely apart from these developments, but less dramatic changes were under way there as well.

From the vantage point of the period library in the highlands it is possible to reflect on both the past and the future of the sharīʿa book. Classical forms of text building persisted into the twentieth century, and these represent a major interest of this chapter. Notable among them were established institutions of textual commentary as well as the diverse minor mechanisms of quotation and citation. I also examine some literary structures associated with the generalizing, or *fulān* ("so-and-so"), language characteristic of the library. In *fiqh* books this name-less discourse mainly appears in the guise of numerous role-terms (e.g., witness, contractor, agent, heir, murderer, etc.), whereas in archival texts such terms acquired substantive implications through associations with named persons.

All such old forms must be examined through or in conjunction with a number of important discursive developments. Literary jurisprudence remained vibrant in this era, but it was enacted on the verge of a regional modernity. Tentative steps toward the adoption of new forms of the sharīʿa text registered more dramatically in the law book than in the less well-known genres I treat in later chapters. In connection with the period law book—specifically in reading *The Gilded Crown*, the four-volume commentary on the *Flowers* published in the 1930s and 1940s—we may also study the advent of print technology and a newly emergent type of authorship. These and other discursive initiatives may be thought of as preparing the *fiqh* corpus for the exigencies of the modern code.

Late in the last century, during the years of my research residence, the principal fate of the *fiqh* was to be selectively appropriated and reframed as the numbered articles of nation-state law.[5] Other types of new writings also appeared, and these, too, stand in instructive contrast to the old-style sharīᶜa law book. Muhammad Yahya al-Muṭahhar wrote a two-volume comparative work devoted to the sharīᶜa-derived law of "personal status," itself a distinctly modern legal category.[6] An imamic-era judge born in Upper Yemen and trained in Zaydī jurisprudence, al-Muṭahhar moved to Lower Yemen in the 1950s in the service of Imam Ahmad and took up residence in the capital at the time, Taᶜizz. When I met him in the 1990s, al-Muṭahhar represented that city in the National Consultative Assembly. His former colleague, the Muftī of the Republic and historian Ahmad Zabāra, who had served in imamic Taᶜizz as the presiding justice of the Sharīᶜa Panel (*al-hay'a al-sharᶜiyya*), the highest-level appellate group, described al-Muṭahhar's new book as "modern in style" and "the first of its type by a Yemeni scholar."[7] Another new author of late twentieth century, the Zaydī scholar Muhammad al-Ghurbānī, relocated to Ibb in the 1950s, and, as I noted at the outset, introduced me to selected chapters of the *Book of Flowers*. In later years, al-Ghurbānī wrote a monograph in the collateral science of *ḥadīth*, the traditions of the Prophet. Written for university and secondary school students, his book chapters conclude with the modern textbook device of review questions.[8]

Al-Muṭahhar and al-Ghurbānī separately characterized their new books to me in the same terms. The main innovative feature, both authors explained, was that they intended their works to be read on one's own, "without a teacher"—that is, through a form of direct knowledge acquisition in private, presumably silent, readings. What does such a remark indicate about the nature of the prior textual world in which both men had been formed? What earlier conceptions of knowledge and institutions of instruction served as the foils for the anticipated utilizations of their new-style writings? What was the discursive role of the lesson-circle teacher in the creation and transmission of the authoritative texts of the past? What kinds of law books were the old works of *fiqh*, and, by extension, what sort of law did they embody and convey? Ethnographic work in the present thus led me to questions concerning the past of the sharīʿa book.

Madhhab

As jurists, the Zaydīs have a lengthy and distinguished, if lesser-known, history. Early segments of this history involved individuals active in Madīna and Kūfa (Iraq), and a branch that flourished in the Caspian region of Iran, but the bulk of the school's juridical and related political history unfolded in the northern highlands of Yemen.[9] As is the case for the four well-known Sunnī *madhhabs* (the Mālikī, Ḥanafī, Ḥanbalī, and Shāfiʿī), the Zaydī school is named for a prominent early figure, Zayd bin ʿAli (d. 740). Zayd was a great-grandson of ʿAli bin Abī Ṭālib and Fāṭima, the daughter of the Prophet Muhammad, through their son Husayn. Within this tradition, Zayd figures as an exemplar of the worldly imamic virtues of both the pen and the sword. Attributed to him is a treatise some western scholars called the first compilation of sharīʿa law. He also led and was martyred in a revolt in Kūfa against what he perceived as the unjust Muslim leader of his time. But Zayd bin ʿAli's juridical oeuvre was not comprehensive, and the positions he set forth were not consistently adopted. In the next chapter, I discuss the character of this early work, the *Majmūʿ*, and its place in the textual universe of the later Zaydī interpreter and the twentieth-century sharīʿa library.

With Zayd as their eponym, the Zaydīs are commonly thought of as constituting a *madhhab*. Yet Bernard Haykel and Aron Zysow argue that a current of internal contestation marked the status and identity of the *madhhab* idea in the Zaydī tradition.[10] The interesting sidelight to this meta-discourse about their own school is that both critics and partisans alike exhibited a well-informed comparative awareness of the *madhhab* phenomenon, notably concerning the detailed features of the several schools established by the Sunnī jurists. Beyond the issues specific to the role of Zayd bin ʿAli, the "formative period" of this community of interpretation was distinctive in other ways. A number of the early Zaydī imams were highly reputed for their sharīʿa scholarship, and five of them, al-Hādī (who brought the school to highland Yemen), his grandfather, uncle, and two sons, are collectively known in the juridical tradition as the *ahl al-nuṣūṣ*, the foundational "people of the texts."[11] The writings of these five, rather than the early treatise attributed to Zayd bin ʿAli, are understood to have initiated the Zaydī *madhhab*. The interpretive project of this group of related jurists later was fleshed out by two subsequent (and also named) generations of jurists, who elaborated the conceptual bases and extended the substantive coverage of the school, thereby contributing to its systematization and consolidation. Given the efforts of these discrete sets of contributors, the "formative period" of the Zaydī *madhhab* may be considered "tripartite."[12]

The Book of Flowers

A learned Yemeni imam of a later period was the author of *The Book of Flowers*, a work that became a standard text of the Zaydī *madhhab*. Although his tenure in office turned out to be brief, as he was not suitably qualified for the martial aspect of the position, Imam al-Mahdī Ahmad bin Yahya al-Murtaḍā (r. 1391–92, d. 1437) was a consummate sharīʿa jurist.[13] His law book appeared centuries after the beginning of doctrinal inquiry in the school, but its synthesis of Zaydī juridical thought became authoritative. From the fifteenth century forward, this new work set many of the terms of debate in the school's applied jurisprudence, and reference to it became a hallmark of Zaydī rulings. A concise and therefore memorizable text, the *Flowers* came to serve as the introductory manual for generations of students, and it also launched the school's most extensive and celebrated commentary literature. Writing in the first part of the nineteenth century, Shawkānī describes the *Flowers* as "the pillar of the Zaydīs in all regions of Yemen."[14] My account of textual relations in the later Zaydī tradition commences with this seminal work of doctrinal *fiqh*.

Yemeni historians recount a story of the prison composition of the *Flowers*. Deposed and confined, Imam al-Mahdī al-Murtaḍā also had been deprived of access to his books and writing materials. In this story, authorship is complemented and materially realized in the feat of a student. We learn in passing that the *Flowers* represented an abridgement of a prior work by the imam.

> Since he was in prison, Imam al-Mahdī feared that his scholarship in the *fiqh* would be neglected.[15] But God Almighty inspired him to abridge the book that

> he had composed in the *fiqh*, in which he went deeply into the disputes and all that had been written in the school of [Imam] al-Hādī, in an expressive form that was succinct and clear in meaning.
>
> The method of composition (*jamᶜ*) of it was that he would orally recite (*yulqī*)[16] its formulations to [his also imprisoned companion] Sayyid ᶜAli bin al-Hādī who would write them on the nailed doors of the cell. His "ink" was white plaster that he took from the walls, up to the pottery ceiling, and he wrote with a stick. When the door was covered he [Sayyid ᶜAli] would repeat all that was upon it until he had it exactly, then he would clean it off and write more. He did this until the book was finished and it was completely memorized.
>
> It would not take the form of a written book and be placed on paper for two full years, until Sayyid ᶜAli bin al-Hādī, who had memorized it, wrote it out and named it "The Flowers in the *Fiqh* of the Pure Imams."[17]

Despite the unusual circumstances, the authorship of this key library text was enacted in a characteristic interchange of the spoken and the written, in a historically specific form of "writing aloud."[18] Authorship that took the oral form of "recitation" or "dictation" was accompanied by and achieved in the companion work of writing and memorization (or, more exactly, listening, writing, memorization, erasure, and writing). The format was that of teacher and student in lesson-circle instruction.

As in western academic disciplines, *madhhab*s typically comprised divergent or minority positions and even separate subgroups, each of which could amount to a distinct community of interpretation in its own right. The *Flowers* commonly is identified with the Zaydī school's older mainstream branch, which is known as the Hādawī, after Imam al-Hādī, the mentioned first imam to appear on the highland scene in the late ninth-century. In these more specific terms, the *Flowers* is considered the representative Zaydī-Hādawī text, the elaborated later literary tradition of which would be brought into the twentieth century in printed pages, including those of a new work of commentary.

Just as the rubric "Zaydī" did not necessarily indicate blanket acceptance of the views articulated by the school's eponym, Zayd bin ᶜAli, so this identification with the school's Hādawī mainstream did not necessarily mean approval of all of al-Hādī's legal stances. Of what, then, did a *madhhab*, or a branch of one named for a particular jurist, consist? A question exactly along these lines was posed to the famous imam al-Qasim bin Muhammad

(d. 1620), the initiator of the Qasimī dynasty, mentioned earlier in connection with the end of the first Ottoman occupation and the beginning of an extended period of Zaydī rule in Ibb and Lower Yemen. The question to Imam al-Qasim is phrased in terms of the relationship of the text of the *Flowers* to a particular *madhhab*. The questioner requested that the imam give "a determination as to what the text (*matn*) of the *Flowers* contains. Is it according to the *madhhab* of a specific imam, such as al-Hādī or Zayd bin ʿAli, or [someone] other than them? Did Imam al-Mahdī [al-Murtaḍā, the author] elaborate the *madhhab* of this imam?"[19]

The questioner continues, asking if Imam al-Qasim's response is "yes"—that is, if the *Flowers* does convey the *madhhab* of a specific jurist—then why does the author al-Murtaḍā criticize the views of al-Hādī in some matters as "weak," for example, and then state that the "*madhhab*" position is otherwise. The questioner also asks why the opposing positions of other authors or imams are mentioned.

Imam al-Qasim responds that the "*madhhab*" contained in the *Flowers* represents a selected and evaluated composite of the expressed views of the five early imams, including al-Hādī, and also those of certain prior imams, including Zayd bin ʿAli. Drawing on such figures, he continues, the jurists of the succeeding generation made the *madhhab* out of what would be applicable. Their construction of this set of active *madhhab* positions was based on their elaboration of "general rules and basic principles."[20] In relation to these higher-level concepts they identified the "applicable substantive issues (*masāʾil al-furūʿ*) in each of the chapters [of the *fiqh*]."[21] As was generally true of law book discourse in the historical sharīʿa, the applicable *madhhab* positions were complemented and specified by the mention of the opposing or alternative views of other recognized jurists. Since such differences of opinion were not erased, these juristic discussions retained an open quality.

Muslim interpretive communities involve great historical depth, and the Hādawī mainstream of the Zaydī school persisted into the twentieth century. But from the fifteenth century a vigorous "neo-Sunnī" school contested its authority.[22] An outgrowth of the Zaydī *madhhab*, these "Sunnīs," as they were known in Yemen, are not to be confused with the adherents of the four Sunnī *madhhabs*, including the Shāfiʿī school, which, as noted, had a majority following among jurists in the southern highlands, including Ibb and elsewhere in Lower Yemen. Represented by a series of important intellectual figures and culminating in the late eighteen and early nineteenth century with the formidable Shawkānī, these "Sunnīs" took positions against the Hādawī mainstream and represented the most significant manifestation of critical positions with respect to the Zaydī *madhhab*. At the same time, however, several of these influential jurists, including al-Hasan bin Ahmad al-Jalāl (d. 1673), Muhammad bin Ismaʿil al-Amīr al-Ṣanʿānī (Ibn al-Amīr, d. 1769), and Shawkānī himself, authored important commentaries or glosses based on the key Hādawī text, *The Book of Flowers*.[23]

A trademark of the "Sunnīs," as Haykel has shown, was their turn away from the Zaydī school's own *ḥadīth* sources and toward those relied on by the four Sunnī schools. These "Sunnīs" of Upper Yemen advocated the basing of doctrinal positions on Qurʾanic texts and these *ḥadīth* sources. They criticized the accumulated doctrinal thought of the Zaydī-Hādawīs, represented by *The Book of Flowers* and much of its commentary literature, which they found not properly anchored in these fundamental "sources" of the law.

Commentary

In the sharīʿa literature, basic treatises (*mutūn*, sing. *matn*) such as the *Flowers* and commentary works (*shurūḥ*, sing. *sharḥ*) based on them represent two distinct genres, but their relationship could not be closer. Although normally composed by different authors at different times and places, the two nevertheless appeared together in a single physical book. According to the basic formula, the commented-on basic treatise was quoted in its entirety within the given commentary work. A commentary thus offered a literally comprehensive reading of the basic treatise. In one compositional format, the commentary author inserted commentary passages of varying length, from single words to lengthy statements, between gradually introduced words and phrases of the basic text. Within the encompassing text of the commentary the quoted language of the basic text was set off by a marking device, typically red ink or over-lining in manuscripts and parentheses or boldface in modern print editions. This overt and carefully maintained physical encounter between what Bakhtin might have termed the incorporating and the incorporated text went to the heart of commentary as a genre. Rather than being collapsed in or obscured by the commentator's composition, the "double-voiced" quality that resulted from this utilization of another's text was fully apparent throughout.

Each of these two doctrinal genres depended on the existence of the other: the radically succinct basic text on the commentary for its necessary elucidation; the commentary on the basic text for the material and conceptual framework of its presentation. A commentator's contributions were cued by segments of the basic text, which quite mechanically determined both the order and the initiating language of the presentation. As a function of this constraint inherent in the commentary genre, the evolution of new interpretive thought was predicated on the persistence of the old. In the relation of these two doctrinal genres we thus find an instantiation of the dilemma of continuity and change in the sharīʿa library.

Pronounced stylistic differences figured in the densely intertextual relations between the *matn* and *sharḥ* genres. Where basic works such as the *Flowers* were typically concise and implicit in expression, features that, again, facilitated their study and memorization but at the same time required interpretation, commentaries were just the opposite: expansive in scale, explicit in character, and devoted to the ramifying tasks of elucidation.

In elementary terms, a commentator read, formulated a comment, and then wrote. In composing a commentary, this second writer endeavored to produce regular sentences and regular sense out of the radically condensed language and conception of the *matn*, all the while remaining wholly dependent on this target text for its given vocabulary and its constraining grammar. Through a variety of basic interpretive acts a commentator sought to make the implicit explicit while also beginning to augment and qualify. The standard tools of this process were a set of small inserted words, word fragments, and conjunctions, such as "that is" (*ay*), "as" or "like" (*ka-*), "and" (*wa*), and "or" (*aw*). These initiated simple glosses and definitions for *matn* terminology or introduced illustrations and examples. Modifications of *matn* words by commentator-added adjectives and adverbs contributed to this effort. Such close-in textual work began to explicate the *matn* and extend its meaning.

However, commentators could, at least momentarily, leave the language of the *matn* behind to develop a point. As a result of such digressions, words that appear side by side in the *matn* could end up lines or even pages apart in the commentary. The commentator could, for example, insert one of several types of specialized sub-genres that inhabit the *fiqh* literature in this tradition. Notable among these is the earlier-mentioned *masʾala*, the fact situation and associated rule, found here in one of its literary incarnations.[24] In another type of intervention, the commentator might utilize the schematic language given in the *matn* to build up a more elaborate analytic frame, thereby extending the issue in question. This could occur by means of a commentator-introduced series of "conditions" (*shurūṭ*) or "types" (*ṣuwar*, sing. *ṣūra*). Such a new framework might also concretize or institutionalize a notion that had remained un- or underspecified in the *matn*.

Despite such efforts on the part of the commentator, the commentary text itself would not be viable, or even readable, were it to be extracted to stand alone, the *matn* deleted. If such a thing could be imagined at all, the "commentary" would be a text full of holes, a fragment of writing lacking both subject matter and predicate.

It was by means of full-text commentary and the related genres associated with the margins and the spaces between the lines that the sharīʿa literature grew. The *Flowers*, for example, is a one-volume work in manuscript and in its twentieth-century print editions, but commentaries based on it (and therefore also including it) typically extend to four. More important was the fact that the commentaries themselves multiplied. It was in this sense that a significant *matn* was generative. The number of commentaries and other responsive works elicited by such a text was one measure of its significance. In the case of the *Flowers*, these numerous works began with an auto-commentary by the author himself and a commentary by his learned sister Dahmāʾ bint al-Murtaḍā (d. 1433).[25] In this particular textual lineage of the Zaydī sharīʿa tradition, the commentators commonly open their presentations and introduce sections of the *Flowers* text with the phrase "the Imam said" (*qāla al-imām*), words that identify the author commented on and that also return us to the earlier depicted scene of composition, inscription, and memorization, with Imam al-Murtaḍā, deposed and in prison, reciting his book.

To study *fiqh* doctrine at a given point in time and space is to study an accumulated literature and its discursive relations—that is, the world of a particular sharīʿa library. Three commentaries on *The Book of Flowers* mainly concern me here. First, one of the earliest, the fifteenth-century work that came to be known simply as the *Commentary on the Flowers*, by ʿAbd Allah Ibn Miftāḥ (d. 1472), a student of *Flowers* author Imam al-Murtaḍā, remains, to this day, the most authoritative.[26] When he instructed me about the chapters on the judgeship and claims, Muhammad al-Ghurbānī had volume four of the *Commentary on the Flowers* open in his lap (figure 1.1).

Second, and somewhat unusual for the genre, at least outside the highland context, is the previously mentioned *Flowers* commentary by Shawkānī,

Figure 1.1 Muhammad ʿAli al-Ghurbānī, reading the *Commentary on the Flowers*.

the dominant intellectual figure, jurist, reformer, and head judge in the late eighteenth- and early nineteenth-century imamic polity. In his autobiography, Shawkānī tells of beginning his post-Qurʾanic school studies by memorizing the *matn* of the *Flowers*.[27] According to his personal notes (in the third person), Shawkānī "studied the *Flowers* and mastered it with a number of teachers, and he [also] taught it to his students."[28] Shawkānī's commentary, called *The Raging Torrent*, also in four volumes, is relatively unusual in that it is predominantly critical. As such, it is representative of the distinct subtradition in *Flowers* commentaries associated with the jurists known as the highland "Sunnīs," discussed above.[29] In addition, rather than using the style of fully embedded quotations, Shawkānī uses an alternative "He said" / "I say" (*qāla/aqūl*) commentary format. This employs block quotations of text from the *Flowers* followed by selected comments by the commentator. As he rejects one after the other of Imam al-Murtaḍā's late fourteenth-century positions, the furious critical flow of Shawkānī's commentary eventually inundates (in his work's pointed subtitle) "*the Garden of the Flowers*."[30]

Finally, third, and my principal point of entry into the juristic tradition of *The Book of Flowers*, is the doctrinal work produced in the same era as the archival materials I examine later in this book: the twentieth-century *Gilded Crown*. Destined, perhaps, to be the last of the classically styled commentaries, the four volumes of this work were published by Ahmad bin Qasim al-ʿAnsī (d. 1970) between 1938 and 1947.[31] Unlike Shawkānī, but like Ibn al-Miftāḥ, al-ʿAnsī mainly carried out a positive elaboration of positions in the *Flowers*, yet he also introduced some modifications.[32]

After my early introduction to the *Flowers* literature in Ibb by al-Ghurbānī, it was mainly through the medium of this last commentary that I later studied it on my own. In approaching the late fourteenth-century *Flowers* through *The Gilded Crown*, one reads, on every page, the authoritative past of Zaydī doctrinal thought together with its twentieth-century present. According to the rule of full quotation, which is the constitutional principle of all such commentaries, every word of the *Flowers* is repeated by al-ʿAnsī. As the target-text for the new commentary, *The Book of Flowers* was thus materially brought whole into the new century.

But even before the publication of *The Gilded Crown*, the twentieth-century presence of the five-hundred-year-old work already was assured. In the madrasas of the independent imamic state, students continued to hear, write, read, and memorize this basic book at the outset of their higher studies.

Many earlier commentaries (each, again, containing the complete text of the *Flowers*) also were extant, and at least one, the *Commentary on the Flowers*, already had been issued in a print edition. For the ruling imams and for their appointed judges, even as they implemented revisions or reversals of its directives, the *Flowers* remained the default reference for sharīʿa applications. At the same time, the four volumes of *The Gilded Crown* represented a significant new statement, an important update in the sharīʿa library of mid-century Yemen.

The Gilded Crown

As his subtitle indicates, al-ʿAnsī's twentieth-century work was intended, in a new manner, to convey the "rules (*aḥkām*) of the school (*madhhab*)" while at the same time taking the centuries-old form of a "commentary (*sharḥ*) on the *matn* of the *Flowers*." In his brief preface, al-ʿAnsī speaks, in rhymed prose, about his rationale. He begins with general laudatory statements about *fiqh*, the humanly authored doctrine of the sharīʿa, and then turns to Yemeni contributions based on the *Flowers*:

> Since the science of the *fiqh* is the greatest of the sciences in esteem and also the most significant in terms of instruction and writing, the fruit of the arts and their core, the end result of the religious sciences and their entryway, our noted scholars' writings in it increased, exhaustively covering the opinion of every jurist, especially the commentators on the *matn* of the *Flowers*, may God thank [them for] their efforts. They have elaborated its methods, and they have differed in contraction and expansion, between an abridgment—which we do not hear about except for its [genre] name—and a long work, which the beginner has difficulty understanding.

While not entirely unknown, certainly not as a genre, abridgments were not readily available in the large literature that had grown up around the text of the *Flowers*. This mainstream Zaydī school literature instead consisted mainly of the genre of "long" works.[33] Al-ʿAnsī continues:

> Best known among them [viz., the long works] for the instruction of the beginner, and for the inquiry of the intermediate and the advanced, is the [fifteenth-

century] commentary of the learned ʿAbd Allah bin Qasim bin Miftāḥ, may God have mercy on him, titled « *al-Muntazaʿ al-mukhtār min al-ghayth al-midrār* » [known as the *Commentary on the Flowers*], together with explanatory remarks on it and what has been added as its glosses. But since it encompasses many schools and differences [of opinion], and that which would be expected to occur [only] in the rarest of potentialities, it absorbs the student for a long time. Except for a few, it is not possible to complete it.[34]

In the sharīʿa literature, one rationale for a new book was that the great bulk of a key text posed a problem for study. The normal solution was the abridgment genre. In the specific literary tradition generated by the *Flowers*, however, the problem was, first, that the large authoritative text in question was itself a commentary and, second, that it was not simply its size that was a problem but also something newly perceived, namely its superfluous and extraneous contents. The solution offered by al-ʿAnsī thus takes the form of a hybrid genre, an "abridged commentary" (*sharḥ mukhtasar*). He writes that he had "heard from those of understanding . . . concerning the urgent need among students for a good abridged commentary to be utilized in their studies of the noble knowledge." He continues that the new work should be "important in its benefits and approachable in its aims, neither overly succinct nor tediously long."

Al-ʿAnsī states that he has divided his new work into two parts, under the conventional topical headings "ritual practices" (*ʿibādāt*) and "transactions" (*muʿāmalāt*). The former is contained in volume 1, and the latter, which includes the standard wide range of subject matter, in volumes 2 through 4. He also writes, "I identified a number of sections (*fuṣūl*; sing. *faṣl*) in the two parts as an aid to the beginner." There traditionally were "sections" in the *Flowers* chapters as well, to which al-ʿAnsī adds a numbering system. This makes possible a more precise form of cross-reference, facilitating a new form of reading internal to the newly ordered text. At various points in his commentary, al-ʿAnsī provides references to relevant numbered sections in other chapters. His book also contains other innovative minor structures such as quotation marks, sentence-defining periods, and paragraphing, none of which receive mention as such. Such fundamental spatial devices first appeared in the Arabic texts of the Yemeni legal literature in conjunction with the twentieth-century transition to print (see figure 1.2).

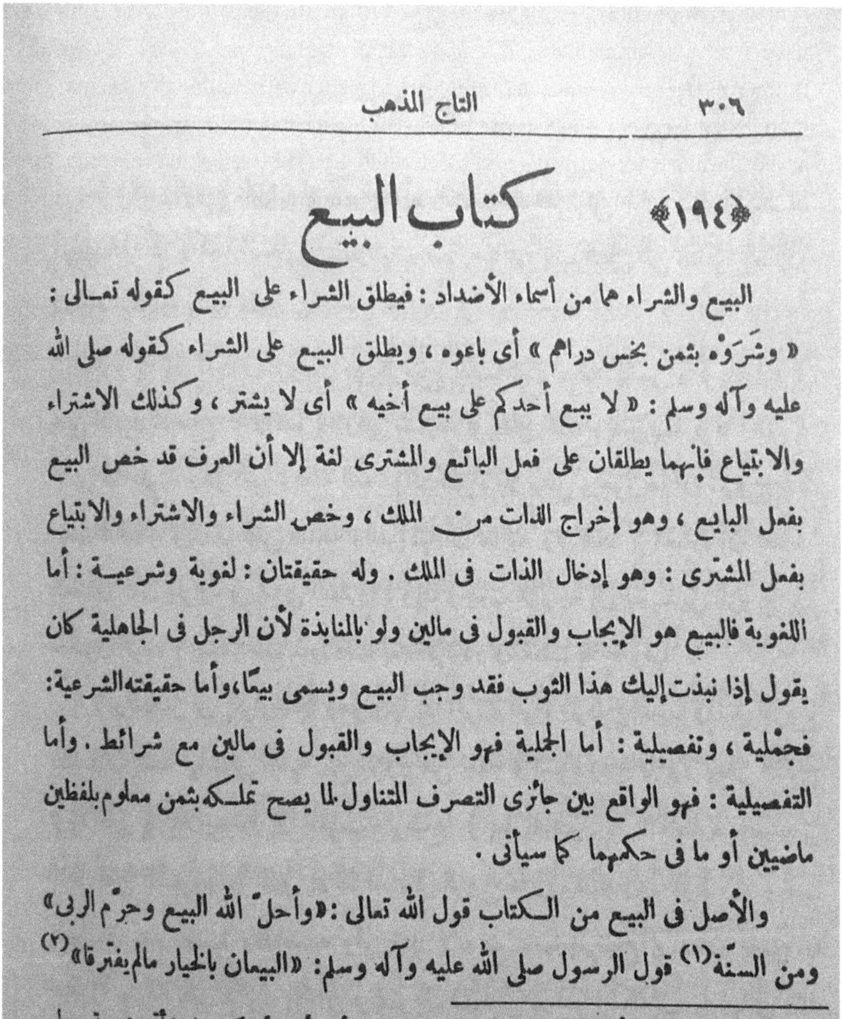

٣٠٦ التاج المذهب

﴿١٩٤﴾ كتاب البيع

البيع والشراء هما من أسماء الأضداد : فيطلق الشراء على البيع كقوله تعالى : « وشروه بثمن بخس دراهم » أى باعوه ، ويطلق البيع على الشراء كقوله صلى الله عليه وآله وسلم : « لا يبع أحدكم على بيع أخيه » أى لا يشتر ، وكذلك الاشتراء والابتياع فإنهما يطلقان على فعل البائع والمشترى لغة إلا أن العرف قد خص البيع بفعل البايع ، وهو إخراج الذات من الملك ، وخص الشراء والاشتراء والابتياع بفعل المشترى : وهو إدخال الذات فى الملك . وله حقيقتان : لغوية وشرعية : أما اللغوية فالبيع هو الإيجاب والقبول فى مالين ولو بالمنابذة لأن الرجل فى الجاهلية كان يقول إذا نبذت إليك هذا الثوب فقد وجب البيع ويسمى بيعًا، وأما حقيقته الشرعية: فجملية ، وتفصيلية : أما الجملية فهو الإيجاب والقبول فى مالين مع شرائط . وأما التفصيلية : فهو الواقع بين جائزى التصرف المتناول لما يصح تملكه بثمن معلوم بلفظين ماضيين أو ما فى حكمهما كما سيأتى .

والأصل فى البيع من الكتاب قول الله تعالى :«وأحلّ الله البيع وحرّم الربى» ومن السنّة(١) قول الرسول صلى الله عليه وآله وسلم: «البيعان بالخيار مالم يفترقا»(٢)

(١) ومن السنة أيضا قوله صلى الله عليه وسلم « لأن يأخذ أحدكم حبله فيأتى بحزمة حطب على ظهره فيبيعها فيكف بها وجهه خير له من أن يسأل الناس أعطوه أم منعوه » رواه البخارى ، وفى هذا الحديث إشارة إلى ما يجب على الإنسان من العمل فى هذه الحياة فلا يحل له أن يهمل طلب

Figure 1.2 "Sale" chapter of *The Gilded Crown*, twentieth-century commentary on *The Book of Flowers*.

Footnotes were another minor innovation introduced in *The Gilded Crown*. One group of these notes provides the brief texts of the interpretive "choices" (*ikhtiyārāt*) issued by Imam Yahya. As I discuss in detail later (chapters 4, 5), these were the concisely stated doctrinal positions formulated by the ruling imams to guide their appointed court judges in a limited number of recurrent or emergent types of problem cases. In *The Gilded Crown*, the footnotes containing the current ruling imam's choices are placed throughout the text. Their physical locations precisely indicate—in a new spatial and material sense—where the imam had intervened in the standard doctrine.[35]

In addition to its status as a *Flowers* commentary, *The Gilded Crown* also represents a selective reading of the authoritative mediating text, the *Commentary on the Flowers*. This fifteenth-century work, in addition to its principal contents—the *Flowers* text and the commentary by Ibn Miftāḥ—also includes extensive later marginalia. These appear in two genres: explanatory remarks (*taʿālīq*, sing. *taʿlīq*) and glosses (*ḥawāshī*, sing. *ḥāshiya*). When they consisted of repeated interventions by a single jurist, both of these genres could be considered independent works.[36] But the marginalia added to the *Commentary on the Flowers* represented accumulated reactions and added citations by various jurist-readers, known and unknown. In handwritten manuscripts of the *Commentary on the Flowers*, these two types of augmentation were arrayed between the lines of the main text and in the surrounding margins. In the twentieth-century printed versions of the *Commentary*, however, both of these forms of marginalia were repositioned as footnotes.[37]

Al-ʿAnsī states that for his twentieth-century commentary he deleted, as superfluous, most of the corpus of marginalia attached to the *Commentary on the Flowers*. However, he absorbed selected items of this marginal material directly into his own commentary text. His selections mainly adhere to the established pattern of significance marking found in the old text. In cases of differences of opinion, this marking served to identify the opinion that represented the authoritative position of the school. Known as marks of *tadhhīb* (from the same root as *madhhab*), these indicators were written either as superscripts above or at the end of the line of the opinion in question.[38] As Eirik Hovden has shown with specific reference to the chapter on endowment (*waqf*), these "validation signs" represent further distinct textual levels within the multi-genre architecture of the *Commentary on the Flowers.*[39] While *tadhhīb* marks do not appear in the printed text of *The Gilded Crown*, al-ʿAnsī makes occasional use of explicit in-text expressions such as "this is our *madhhab*" (*hadhā madhhabunā*).[40]

Al-ʿAnsī explains that his new work "brings together—despite the smallness of its size—what is contained in the *Commentary on the Flowers* and its numerous glosses in the way of substantive positions designated as those of the school (*al-masāʾil al-muqarrara li-l-madhhab*)."[41] As is stated clearly in his book's subtitle, the emphasis in streamlining the doctrinal presentation is to focus narrowly on the positions of this single school of sharīʿa interpretation. It may not seem surprising that a *madhhab* text would focus mainly on the positions of that school, but this is represented as something new in the Zaydī literature.

Cross-citation

Medieval western manuscripts were "turgid with abbreviations," Walter Ong notes.[42] Zaydī manuscript books of *fiqh* had a similar appearance. For their most frequent citations, they used conventional symbols (*rumūz*).[43] This old device employed one or more letters of the alphabet to stand for the full names of repeatedly referenced jurists. A few key books had their own symbols as well, beginning with the *Book of Flowers*. The book's formal Arabic title, which begins *Kitāb al-azhār*, is abbreviated to the two-letter symbol *az*. Such minimalist citations were intended to save space (lit. "to shorten the writing"), but their standardization also sketched out the recurrently significant referential world of the Zaydī jurists.

In an inter-cosmopolitan fashion, sharīʿa *madhhab*s paid attention to the doctrinal views of other schools. Beyond their own leading jurists, including the five prominent "people of the texts" and the important authors in the following generations, the eponyms of the four Sunnī schools are notable among the jurists mentioned so regularly by the Zaydīs as to necessitate the use of symbols. While intellectually vigorous and highly productive in their own right, the Zaydīs regularly situated their doctrinal positions with respect to those of leading Sunnī jurists. It also should be noted that this referential practice both obtained before and continued after the rise of the contesting "Sunnī" jurists who distanced themselves from the mainstream Zaydīs. While the chosen interlocutors of Zaydī jurists were the representatives of the four Sunnī *madhhabs*, the extent to which their communicative efforts were reciprocated is unclear.

In the abbreviation scheme of older Zaydī manuscripts, and also in the first print edition of the *Commentary on the Flowers*, the Sunnī eponyms could be referred to collectively as the "four imams" or simply as the "jurists" (*fuqahāʾ*). More often, since their views differed, they were cited individually, using abbreviated symbols. The four eponyms and their respective symbols are as follows: al-Shāfiʿī (*sh*), Abū Ḥanīfa (*ḥ*), Mālik (*k*), and Ahmad ibn Ḥanbal (*md*). More specialized abbreviations in these cross-*madhhab* citations refer to the "associates of al-Shāfiʿī" (*aṣsh*) and to the "associates of Abū Ḥanīfa" (*aṣḥ*), while still others indicate that a given view is one of several held by al-Shāfiʿī (*ʿsh*), or Abū Ḥanīfa (*ʿḥ*).[44] An aside in the book section that introduces these symbols cautions that a given "text" (*naṣṣ*) of one of these major Sunnī jurists may differ from the currently prevailing or implemented position (*al-maʿmūl ʿalayhi*) in the school bearing his name. There also were conventional symbols for selected early individual Shāfiʿīs and Ḥanafis such as al-Muzanī (*nī*) and Abū Yūsuf (*f*).

A further token of this systematic inter-*madhhab* thinking on the part of premodern Zaydī jurists is another major work by Imam al-Murtaḍā, the author of the *Flowers*. His comparative study, *The Overflowing Sea*, comprises six volumes in its print edition. The *Sea*, as it is known, carefully cross-references Zaydī positions with respect to those of the leading jurists of the four Sunnī schools.[45] Although not an expressly comparative work, the *Commentary on the Flowers* also contains a considerable volume of cross-citation using such abbreviations. In the more streamlined design of al-ʿAnsī's "abridged commentary," however, the great bulk of this citational material was cut, and the use of the conventional symbols discontinued. Nevertheless, in the twentieth-century *Gilded Crown*, al-ʿAnsī continued to mention key jurists, including both Zaydīs and leading Sunnīs, but he did so by name. At the turn of the twenty-first century, the editor of the new print edition of the *Commentary on the Flowers* noted the "great difficulty" such symbols cause the nonspecialist reader, and he, too, elected to spell out selected book titles and authors' names.

Husayn al-Sayāghī, a leading twentieth-century Yemeni jurist, writes that in the early period, "as the Zaydī literature became extensive and multiplied and [as] the thought developed with the changing times, they [viz., the Zaydī jurists] appropriated a huge amount from the books of the four

[Sunnī] schools."[46] In the view of an early twentieth-century western authority on the school, the juristic interchanges were such that "we find individual Zaydīs appearing with individual Sunnīs against other Zaydīs and other Sunnīs in changing combinations, so that the Zaydī madhhab in practice is a fifth alongside of the four."[47] Bernard Haykel argues, however, that this "fifth school" notion was "deliberately contrived" by Imam Yahya in an effort to claim "an identity of interests and ideology with a wider, pan-Islam movement of reform."[48] Haykel, in contrast, would emphasize the important conceptual differences, especially in theology, ritual law (*ʿibādāt*), and the institution of the imamate.

Reported Texts

Quotation in al-ʿAnsī's commentary occurs in four major formats. Each implements a specific strand of intertextuality that highlights a particular relation between texts. As was described earlier, there is, first, the necessary, genre-defining, global quotation of the *matn*, the basic text of the *Flowers*, the single words or longer passages of which appear in the printed commentary text within small ornate brackets. In this style of commentary, the embedded segments of the *Flowers* are to be read as integral parts of the encompassing commentary text. The commentator's language therefore had to accommodate the grammar and syntax of the incorporated text, which occasionally posed compositional challenges at the sentence level.[49] At one point, al-ʿAnsī explicitly mentions a difficulty in fitting the two genres together, a gesture that implicitly respects the authority and detailed integrity of the quoted *matn*, a text likely to have been separately memorized by some of his readers.[50]

Second, there are direct quotations of verses from the Qurʾan, individual *ḥadīths* and language from other works of *fiqh*, mainly other *Flowers* commentaries. These typically are introduced by versions of the *qāla* ("he said") formula, and then are further marked by a print-era innovation: French-style, guillemet quotation marks (« . . . »), the first instance of which appeared in the passage from al-ʿAnsī's preface cited above, where they enclose a book title. Accompanying these quotation devices are in-text citations of the standard formulas for each level of authoritative text. Thus, "the Almighty said," precedes a Qurʾan passage, while a named oral transmitter or the *ḥadīth*-compiler appears with the citation of a Prophetic *ḥadīth*, and a book title or an author's name with that of a specific *fiqh* doctrine.[51]

A third type utilizes the introduced footnotes. Beyond the novelty of the footnote form itself, these quotations are new to the *Flowers* literature inasmuch as they are author-compositions by commentator al-ʿAnsī. Among these footnotes, one variety gives detail as to his methods of textual appropriation, which include but are not limited to indications of direct quotation: e.g., "Stated in (*qāla fī*) *al-Athmār*"; "From (*min*) *Ḥāshiyat al-Saḥūlī*"; "Formulation (*ʿibāra*) of *al-Fatḥ* and its commentary"; "Quoted (*naqlan*) from *al-Baḥr*"; "*Masʾala* [case, problem] quoted from *al-Bayān*"; "Understood from (*yustafādu min*) *al-Zuhūr wa-l-Bayān*"; etc. Some of these footnotes fill in blind references in the *matn* of the *Flowers*. When the *Flowers* uses *qīl*, the passive of "he said," which refers, in this discursive context, to an alternative position or doctrine, a footnote by al-ʿAnsī may explain, for example, "This statement is by Ibn al-ʿAbbās al-Ṣanʿānī. He mentioned it in his *Kifāya*."

Beyond these three explicit forms, however, there is, fourth, the pervasive use of quotation and paraphrasing without any marking devices or overt citations. As indicated by the term "abridgment" he uses to describe his work, al-ʿAnsī routinely and liberally appropriates language from the fifteenth-century *Commentary on the Flowers* and, selectively, from its extensive marginalia. The result, which constitutes the basic fabric of his commentary, is a montage of phrases from the earlier work by Ibn Miftāḥ.

Authorship

We do not have a history of the author function for the sharīʿa law book. For the early period we have the brilliant but controversial work of Norman Calder. Calder argues that, despite their standard identifications with named authors, the initial works of the formative period were not conventionally authored but were instead "organic" or "school" texts, consolidated at some point after the authors' lifetimes. "Books," he writes, "were originally the product of followers, not masters."[52] We also have seen that a *mukhtaṣar* work such as the *Flowers*—that is, a specialized genre of abbreviated law book—also could be authored in a lesson-circle format, and, if well received, it could continue to flourish through the receptive efforts of later commentators and glossators. In the first half of the twentieth century in Yemen, however, we are concerned with the late history of this textual tradition. In reaching a local end point in the long pre-modern history of the sharīʿa book, we witness the opening moments in a local transition to modern forms of individual authorship and the entailed legal rights.

As a symptom of its precocious but still only partial modernity, *The Gilded Crown* would be given an unusual reception, part of which centered on questions about the author and his authorship. Discussions of this work both utilized and strained against the available vocabulary of literary composition. On the title page, Ahmad Qasim al-ʿAnsī is designated the "author" of his book, using the standard terminology for author and authorship (*muʾallif, taʾlīf*). Al-ʿAnsī himself identifies his authorship of the work in the literal, "by the pen (*qalam*)" sense and at several points identifies it as "my book" (*kitābī*). At the same time, he also refers to his work of "collection" or "compilation" (*jamʿ*), another classical usage.[53]

Some Yemeni scholars have pointed to a mid-nineteenth-century work as a textual antecedent. The work in question, which is not acknowledged in *The Gilded Crown*, is by another member of the al-ʿAnsī family, ʿAbd Allah bin ʿAli (d. 1883).[54] In his *History of Islamic Thought in Yemen*, Ahmad Husayn Sharaf al-Dīn states that the author of *The Gilded Crown* "summarized" a larger work identified as *The Compilation of al-ʿAnsī*. Sharaf al-Dīn also states that al-ʿAnsī simply "compiled" school opinions.[55] This same antecedent work also is mentioned in the biographical entry for Ahmad Qasim al-ʿAnsī by Ahmad Zabāra, the historian and Muftī of the Republic who headed the Sharīʿa Panel in the 1950s. Zabāra begins by saying that al-ʿAnsī "was the author (*muʾallif*) of *The Gilded Crown*, a commentary on the *Flowers*."[56] He goes on to describe al-ʿAnsī's achievement by saying that he "compiled the entire *madhhab* from the *Commentary* [on the *Flowers*], the glosses [on the *Commentary on the Flowers*], the *Bayān* [by Ibn al-Muẓaffar], and the *Big Compilation of al-ʿAnsī*."[57]

In his *Culture and the Revolution in Yemen*, ʿAbd Allah al-Baradūnī, the eminent Yemeni poet, historian, critic, and, in his youth, student of *fiqh*, also takes up the question of this author and his book.[58] Al-Baradūnī does not directly address the issue of an intermediate text by an al-ʿAnsī from the nineteenth century. For him, the crux is that although al-ʿAnsī certainly was a jurist (*faqīh*), he "was not reputed for juristic achievement." As a consequence, he writes, "the appearance of the book *The Crown* was surprising due to its being issued by a man not known for juristic mastery." Soon thereafter, he reports, "rumors circulated about the author and his work." According to one rumor, al-ʿAnsī had "inherited the book, as a manuscript, from his father, and he presented it to Imam Yahya Ḥamid al-Dīn for print publication under the name of Ahmad Qasim al-ʿAnsī." Other rumors suggested that the real author was al-ʿAnsī's famous brother, the nationalist Muḥy al-Dīn, or that al-ʿAnsī had simply "stumbled upon" the work of an unknown author. The assumption of all such rumors was that al-ʿAnsī could not have been the author of such a book, based on what people knew of him from his days as a student, from his work record, and from interactions with him. There were those who affirmed and those who denied the attribution of the book to him.

Al-Baradūnī turned to the view of a judge from the town of Dhamār, a man he considered especially well positioned to decide the matter. In this connection further reference is made to the available ideas concerning authorship and book-creation. According to the jurist from Dhamār, *The Gilded Crown* involves "neither authorship (*taʾlīf*) nor composition (*taṣnīf*); instead it is an 'extraction' (*intizāʿ*) of the [Zaydī] school from the other schools, the principles of which are established in two books [by Imam al-Murtaḍā], *the Overflowing Sea* and the *Flowers*."[59] Al-Baradūnī comments that the judge's response involves distinctions between, on the one hand, "composition and the abbreviation of compositions" and, on the other, "extraction from a book or books, and summarization (*talkhīs*) as a commentary in book form." Composition per se aside, these other indicated categories of book creation—abbreviation, extraction, and summarization—shared the characteristic of working from already existing book-length sources.

Al-Baradūnī notes that the "doubt" that in the late 1930s surrounded the authorship of the book "still continues" (i.e., in the 1990s). At least in part, however, the rumors concerning the book and its author must be attributed to the fact that *The Gilded Crown* did not come into existence in the recognized manner and thus did not exhibit the recognized form of textual authority. Unlike most prior works of *fiqh*, a well-known teacher did not produce *The Gilded Crown* in an instructional setting. Was *The Gilded Crown* a forerunner of the shift in the function of the author and the relations of reading? Could it have been meant for use in the lesson circle? Or was this a book to be read "without a teacher," as late twentieth-century authors al-Muṭahhar and al-Ghurbānī would later put it to me?

According to al-Baradūnī, the controversy about its authorship does not detract from the value of the book itself. He therefore takes his own stab at describing the literary nature of *The Gilded Crown*. "It represents," he writes, "an abridged, simplified (*mubassaṭ*) commentary on the *matn* of the *Flowers*." He then poses the question, "What distinguishes this book from all other commentaries on this *matn*?" His answer is that "its distinguishing feature lies in its restriction to the meaning of the text established in the *matn*." He says that this feature separates *The Gilded Crown* from all prior commentaries, which always brought in "the rules of all five schools"—that is, the Zaydī and the four Sunnī schools.

Al-Baradūnī and Zabāra—the former a literary-historian and the latter a juridical-historian—give different portraits of Ahmad Qasim al-ʿAnsī. In support of his presentation of al-ʿAnsī's alleged incapacity as an author, al-Baradūnī simply notes a non-specific series of employments in the judiciary (*al-qaḍāʾ*), "transferring from place to place in the subdistricts of Yemen." Al-Baradūnī points out that while a thorough knowledge of the *fiqh* and related sciences was required for the judgeship, authorship was not. Such men adjudicated on the basis of what they had learned from their teachers, and he also says that individuals with less academic training in the law would be appointed as court *kātib*s—writers or secretaries. In contrast to this image of a modest career in the imamic judiciary, Zabāra tells us that among the scholars al-ʿAnsī studied with in Sanʿāʾ was the very distinguished Husayn al-ʿAmrī (d. 1942), the first Yemeni chief justice of the (Ottoman) Appeal Court,[60] and it seems that al-ʿAnsī also served the great man as a secretary and special assistant. Later, Zabāra informs us, al-ʿAnsī was appointed to posts in the Red Sea port town of al-Ḥudayda and then to a series of positions in Taʿizz under the then governor and heir to the throne, Ahmad bin Yahya Ḥamid al-Dīn. After the coup of 1948, as Imam Ahmad succeeded his assassinated father, al-ʿAnsī served as head of the municipality of Taʿizz, which had become the capital city. After the Revolution of 1962, he would become the governor of Taʿizz Province and, later still, the minister of endowments (*awqāf*) and then the governor of Ṣanʿāʾ Province.

There is an important interruption in this career story, however. This occurs the year after the publication of the fourth and final volume of *The Gilded Crown*. A short biographical notice in a publication of the ministry he later headed states that in the years prior to 1962 al-ʿAnsī had been "imprisoned."[61] While al-Baradūnī does not mention what would appear to be a significant nationalist credential, Zabāra does. He goes on to state that al-ʿAnsī played "a major role" in the brief and unsuccessful "Constitutional" (*dustūriyya*) coup and government of 1948 and that he eventually was arrested in a group of some thirty men that included most of the prominent early nationalist leaders. "He had knowledge of the Constitutional Movement before it began, together with his martyred brother Muhy al-Din."[62] Monitoring Sanʿāʾ radio on the fateful Thursday night, al-ʿAnsī heard the report that Imam Yahya had been assassinated. He immediately changed from his turban and robes into a khakhi uniform, cartridge belt, and rifle and is portrayed as having taken a series of decisive actions to support the short-lived nationalist coup. Captured some days later, the prisoners, including al-ʿAnsī, were taken to a prison in the northeastern town of Ḥajja.[63] Those who were not executed (such as the claimant to the imamate, ʿAbd Allah al-Wazīr, and al-ʿAnsī's brother) famously turned their prison into an academy. A number of the 1948 conspirators were scholars and literary figures and, upon their release a few years later, nationalists such as al-ʿAnsī were returned to judgeships and other positions of responsibility.

At the most general level, then, in its appearance and its reception *The Gilded Crown* signals an important event of the history of the book in Yemen. But this quasi-classical commentary also exemplifies the ambivalence that commonly attended important changes in the texts of the sharīʿa. In the difficult-to-label identity of this commentary work and in the questions surrounding its authorship we also may locate part of the related fate of *The Book of Flowers*, the venerable authoritative text it contained, as it entered a local modernity.

Blurbs

It was a different part of the reception given *The Gilded Crown* that actually sparked the interest of literary critic al-Baradūnī. When the book was published, a coterie of nineteen short texts, many in poetry and some in prose, appeared with it. A select group of individuals penned these accompanying texts, including some of the highest officials in the imamate plus some leading independent jurists and several of the foremost Yemeni poets.[64] The genre in question was *taqrīẓ*, a form that conveyed a learned and artistically refined appreciation of the work thus accompanied, in this case into print.[65] When classic works such as *The Commentary on the Flowers* or the commentary by al-Sayāghī on the *Majmūʿ* of Zayd bin ʿAli were first published, the Yemeni scholars who saw them through the presses in Cairo and elsewhere sought poetic testimonials in this genre from Egyptian and other jurists.[66] These book endorsements, or "blurbs" of the era, appeared on pages inside the hard covers. In the case of *The Gilded Crown* they are found just before the index of the fourth and final volume of the first edition. Like the modern blurb, the *taqrīẓ* of the era was a specialized type of meta-text that involved discourse about the book in question. Added at the end of the publishing process, but often read first, these book testimonials were structurally similar to library marginalia and also to the added notes placed on ordinary legal documents.

Al-Baradūnī dates a noteworthy moment in the history of this little genre in Yemen to the late 1930s, a period he describes as "charged with anxiety." He states that this form of "poetic art" contributed to expressing the growing "nationalist fervor." In the case of *The Gilded Crown*, the supporting *taqrīẓ* texts also provided a strongly legitimizing local reception for the work and its new aims. The participation of the imam's son Ahmad, the then Heir to the Imamate, and other high level officials suggested the approval of Imam Yahya himself.

One of the *taqrīẓ* poets speaks of *The Gilded Crown* as a "constitution" (*dustūr*), using the newly current idiom of the quintessential nationalist text to refer to this work focused on the legal school of the ruling imam.[67] Applauding the work's steps toward concision and accessibility, and especially noting benefits for instruction and reference, these accompanying texts express a pervasive new and characteristically modern dissatisfaction with the unwieldy massiveness of the old Zaydī *fiqh* literature with its excessive qualifications and cross-citations. Al-Baradūnī also senses a general desire among such blurb writers for access to contemporary literary culture and education, for new forms of instruction that would go well beyond the innovations of the hybrid madrasa established by Imam Yahya in the 1920s. Al-Zubayrī, the famous young poet and later a leading nationalist, seized the occasion to push the genre of *taqrīẓ* toward a nationalist and revolutionary agenda, stressing the need among the youth for new forms of knowledge. Al-Baradūnī ends his discussion with a question concerning the group of poetic endorsements in *The Gilded Crown* that took the classical *qaṣīda* form. He asks, do they represent "a new chapter in [the history of] Yemeni poetry?"

Context and Custom

Where the older library texts of the *fiqh* were characteristically devoid of specific references to context, al-ʿAnsī's new commentary begins to connect with its time and place. A number of concrete aspects of the modern era are pointed to in *The Gilded Crown*. This occurs in locutions such as, in the chapter on the imamate, a reference to "Islamic society" and to the Qurʾan as its "constitution" (*dustūr*).[68] This indexing of the author's era also occurs in his isolated mentions of contemporary phenomena such as colonial regimes and modern technologies, including airplanes and execution by electrocution, although this last did not exist in Yemen. Also expressed in *The Gilded Crown* is the very up-to-date theme of modern efficiency. The classical goal concerning the desired general "benefit" of a book now is linked to a design intended to "guard time against waste."[69] Efficiency, the characteristic cheaper-by-the-dozen mentality that was emergent in the western Fordist economies of the period, is tied to features of the work such as its reduced overall volume and its cross-referenced subject matter.

A footnote refers to "colonial laws" (*al-qawānīn al-istiʿmāriyya*). Al-ʿAnsī knew, for example, of the suppression the sharīʿa rules regarding theft in other Muslim societies. In this connection he expresses the hope that contemporary Muslim "reformers" (*rijāl al-iṣlāḥ*) will seek a return to the Islamic "constitution." This "divine constitution," he writes, "sent down by a Wise One, All-Knowing about the welfare of His servants," is "suitable for every time and place." He refers to the métier of the literary jurist when he states, "our forefathers have left to us a great wealth in jurisprudence (*fiqh*)." He also poses a general question concerning this corpus of law. This underscores the nature of his own effort and takes into consideration the views of a non-Muslim audience: "why aren't we taking care to refine it," he writes, "making it accessible and prominent for the Islamic world in attractive dress so that it appeals to the perceiver and its good qualities are recognized by the non-believer (*kāfir*)?"[70]

A different form of contextualization occurs in a set of footnotes devoted to prevailing "custom" in the highlands, some of which ran counter to existing doctrine.[71] As with the equally innovative footnotes conveying the imamic "choices," the physical placement of these citations highlights specific points of contact between the doctrine and custom. Al-ʿAnsī's recognition of current custom also extends to some passages in his main commentary text. As I mention in chapter 10, he refers to a problematic sharecropping arrangement as "the custom in our times and our Yemen."[72] In these explicit terms, al-ʿAnsī's new *Flowers* commentary was putting down temporally specific local roots.

In older works of Zaydī *fiqh*, various substantive passages explicitly stated that certain of the relevant details of particular legal acts should be determined according to standards set locally. Chapters on the marriage contract, for example, identify a dower payment to be made, but state that the actual amount should be determined by local custom.[73] Likewise, the specific wording to be used in sale contracts is to be determined "according to custom" (*ḥasaba al-ʿurfi*).[74] In such passages the literary jurists pointed to the assumed existence of parallel normative regimes current in given locales.

These jurists also conceptualized the authority of custom. This is to speak of custom in general, apart from any particular instantiation. One of the broad maxims of the Zaydī school held that "custom is enacted (*al-ʿurfu maʿmūlun bihi*) . . . insofar as it does not conflict with a text (*mā lam yuṣādif naṣṣān*)"—that is, an explicit authoritative text, beginning with the Qurʾan or the Sunna.[75] A kindred maxim from the Ḥanafī tradition entered Yemeni discourse via the late nineteenth-century *Majalla*, the Ottoman code. Judge al-Ḥaddād quoted it to me in Ibb: "That which is accepted in custom is equivalent to that which is formally stipulated" (*al-maʿrūf ʿurfān ka-l-mashrūṭ sharṭān*).[76]

These doctrinal jurists even conceived of a form of "custom" that pertained to their own work. Such writers commonly made a distinction between the specialist meanings of their juridical discourse as opposed to the ordinary or "dictionary" meanings of the same words in "the language," or formal Arabic, it being understood that the latter served as the general linguistic medium of their writings. The conceptual conventions of *fiqh* discourse depended on these specialist definitions, which the jurists characterized as their "technical uses" (*iṣṭilāḥāt*). Collectively, such linguistic conventions could be thought of as representing the "custom of the sharīʿa" (*ʿurf al-sharīʿa*).[77]

There also were limits. The main one, mentioned earlier, concerned what is known as "tribal custom" (*ʿurf al-qabīlī*). In the sedentary societies of rural Upper Yemen, tribal custom often held sway without regard to the sharīʿa. The jurists polemically classified custom they considered entirely pagan and beyond the pale as *ṭāghūt*. But in a large number of such rural locations resident jurists were available to actively represent the alternative legitimacy of the sharīʿa. Part of this phenomenon involved the existence of numerous and widely spread institutions called *hijras*, village-based communities of scholars protected by local tribesmen.[78] The *hijras* of Upper Yemen have been compared, as teaching institutions, to the rural madrasas found across Lower Yemen, including those in the Ibb region.[79] Beyond these *hijras*, another part of the presence of the Zaydī library in the domain of tribal custom involved individual jurists who attached themselves to specific tribal groups. For example, due to their close association with the tribal people of Banī Jabr, one line of scholars came to be known as the "al-Jabrīs." Of the first jurist in this line, a man who died in 1855, it is reported that "he occasionally ruled, when necessary, with a customary judgment (*ḥukm ʿurfī*), so long as it was not in conflict with the sharīʿa." This man's great-grandson, who lived in the same tribal setting in the twentieth century, is identified as "a scholar knowledgeable in the *fiqh* and inheritance."[80] Such men were qualified jurists who also were capable of producing written texts wearing an *ʿurfī* hat—that is, following the established "scripts" of custom.

For its part, the imamic polity of the first part of the twentieth century posted judges to many subdistrict seats in the Yemeni countryside. According to their appointment letters, the imam charged these men "to enliven the sharīʿa" in those quarters. Beyond the incidence of the stationary scholarly communities in rural districts, the individual lines of jurists resident among specific tribal groups, and these regular judicial postings, scholars also circulated through the rural districts. This mainly occurred in individual pursuits of knowledge and instruction, but on occasion it took the form of a progression of the imamic retinue. A different sort of movement, one specifically associated with conflict resolution, brought disputants in from the countryside to approach town-based jurists, or the imam himself. This not infrequently resulted in a reverse flow of jurists traveling out the rural districts in question to investigate and hear evidence.

Figure 1.3 "Book" (*kitāb*). Title design of *The Book of Flowers*, printed edition (Cairo: Tamaddun Press, 1332 AH [1913]).

Printing the Library

> This book concerns the *fiqh* of the people of Yemen affiliated with Imam Zayd ibn ʿAli, bin al-Husayn, bin ʿAli bin Abī Ṭālib, may God be pleased with them. None of its substantive issues diverge from [those of] the four [Sunnī] *madhhabs*. . . . This is the *madhhab* of the descendants of the Prophet, the prayers of God upon him and his family and peace, and those who agree with them among the imams.
>
> —*The Book of Flowers* (Cairo ed., 1332 AH [1913])

If the main classical features of *The Gilded Crown* are that it situates itself with respect to the doctrinal literature of a specific interpretive community and that it takes the genre form of a commentary on an authoritative text, the foundation of its simultaneous, but less pronounced, modernity is the fact that it appeared first in print, at the time still a relatively new technology in Yemen. Unlike all of the numerous Zaydī commentaries before it, *The Gilded Crown* did not initially circulate as a manuscript text but instead was directly prepared for print publication. Although the *Flowers* itself and the fifteenth-century *Commentary on the Flowers*, among other works, already had appeared in published editions, such texts had not been composed with the new possibilities of print in mind.[81] My earlier work on the advent of "print culture" in highland Yemen examined the historical circumstances and the detailed discursive shifts involved in the introduction of this new technology.[82] To describe the decisive alteration of form in the movement from manuscript to print in late nineteenth-century works of *fiqh* in Morocco, Jacques Berque spoke of a "change of optic."[83]

The transition to the new technology elicited interesting reflections both on the technology itself and on the shift from manuscripts to printed books. In 1928, the press at the imam's palace produced the *matn* of a work titled *al-Kāfil*, the introductory Zaydī *usūl al-fiqh* text by Muhammad bin Yahya Bahrān (d. 1550), embedded in a well-known commentary known as *al-Kāshif*, by Ibn Luqmān (d. 1622).[84] Two notices at the end of the publication provide information about the circumstances of its printing. The first, located before the *fihrist*, or table of contents, explains how the text came to be printed: "Since this book is an introduction to the art of *usūl* [*al-fiqh*], and is among the works people are interested in due to its reputation for quality, the generality of its benefit, and the perfect asceticism of its author, the Commander of the Faithful [Imam Yahya] . . . ordered its publication." Continuing, the notice comments on some problems in the process. The notice focuses in a novel fashion on the language of the manuscript, underscoring how print technology immediately began to alter the ways manuscript works would be read. In preparing the print edition, some weaknesses in the available manuscripts also became apparent. The notice anticipates a reader comparing the manuscript and print versions of "the book."

The imam had ordered

> the correction of shortcomings in some copies of the book regarding insignificant words in a number of formulations. This is rare, and the reader should not think, if he encounters a word or words at variance with some handwritten copies, that this is an instance of typographic error. No, associated with print

> publication, investigation and interpretation have taken place, together with a review of some [manuscript] copies we believe to be accurate and of some authoritative glosses.[85]

The second notice, which appears as the last lines of the printed edition, after a brief biography of the commentator, further addresses weaknesses in the source manuscripts and also the deficiencies of the available printing machine (after nearly a half century of use). Of the source text in question this notice states, "There are to be found an expression (*lafẓ*) or two which are ungrammatical (*malḥūna*), not following the rule of Arabic." Turning to the equipment and the printed text, the notice continues, "there also will be found a letter without a dot or with part [of it] not appearing, and this is due to [the fact that] the ink did not reach the letter, as occurs in many publications. Or a letter without a *hamza* when it should have a *hamza*, and this is due to the non-availability of this letter. Or the absence of some dots or parts of letters is to be excused in view of the age of the type."[86] In this early moment in Yemeni printing history, as in the historical introductions of the typographic format elsewhere in the Middle East, a novel human mechanism was engaged to guarantee authenticity and textual authority in the technological transition. This notice concludes by identifying two well-known Yemeni scholars who were responsible for the final "correction" (*taṣḥīḥ*) of the proofs prior to printing.

Such "correctors" had been envisioned as a key element of the 1727 fatwā that first authorized printing in the Ottoman Empire. The fatwā was issued in response to a question about whether an individual may engage in printing certain specific categories of works, including dictionaries and treatises of logic, philosophy, and astronomy. The responding Ottoman muftī stated:

> Supposing that one had found the art of printing correctly, with type characters of metal . . . furnishing a means of reducing work, of multiplying copies at low expense, thereby rendering acquisition easier and less costly. I decide that this art, by reason of its great advantages, ought to be encouraged, and its execution not be deferred, provided that one chooses some capable and intelligent men who, before the works leave the press, correct them and verify them using the best originals.[87]

This institution of correction proved to be essential to initial transitions to print. In Tunisia, for example, such "correctors" were drawn from the local community of scholars. These individuals "offer[ed] the desired cultural guarantee" to the early generation of Muslim typographic works.[88] For Muhsin Mahdi, "the *muṣaḥḥiḥ*—literally the person in charge of producing a 'correct' printed version—performed a task similar to that of the scribe in the manuscript age, that is, he corrected and sometimes revised the language of the manuscript copy before it was sent to the printer, and the same person contributed to assuring the proofs were properly corrected and a list of errata was appended to the printed book."[89] As agents in the transition from manuscripts to books printed in moveable type, "correctors" applied old scholarly skills to two new necessities of the print era: the standardization of language and the certification of accuracy in published works.

By the 1930s, when the first volume of *The Gilded Crown* appeared, the once-new technology appeared relatively routinized. As an ancillary part of the progress of local print culture, a full page "announcement" (*iʿlān*) for volume 1 of *The Gilded Crown* appeared in the official Yemeni literary monthly of the period, *al-Ḥikma*.[90] This advertisement represented something still very new in the history of the book in highland Yemen, namely commercialized publicity. The associated legal status of the book as a literary property, with copyright pertaining to its author and publisher, was not as yet clear. By the 1993 edition, however, all rights to *The Gilded Crown* were reserved and the publisher's name is given on the title page, together with that of the author.[91] In the 1941 announcement of volume 1, by contrast, those wanting to obtain a copy are directed to named individuals in three specific towns, Ṣanʿāʾ and Yarīm, in Upper Yemen, and al-Ḥudayda, on the Red Sea coast. Booksellers existed at the time, but modern bookstores would not begin to appear until after the Revolution.

At the level of the madrasa lesson circle, however, many techniques of manuscript culture continued to prevail.[92] Ismāʿīl al-Akwaʿ describes the situation in the Upper Yemen town of Dhamār, a center of Zaydī instruction: "Most of the students studied without one of them owning a book. They borrowed books from private owners or from their teachers and copied the section for study from them every day. By the time he had finished a book, a student had his own manuscript copy of what he had studied. In a few years he had all of the books of instruction."[93]

Codification

The Gilded Crown offered an important response to the newly felt need for a more concise corpus of law for the twentieth-century imamate, an old-style polity that found itself in a challenging global environment of emerging and established nation-states. This multivolume book reduced the open-ended argument and the examination of many different opinions that had characterized sharīʿa doctrine in general, and it also began to suppress the inter-school comparativism that had long distinguished Zaydī legal thought in particular. It instead stressed the univocality of the official *madhhab* while providing new textual orderings, efficiencies, and attention to accessibility. This still quite traditional Yemeni law book thus participated in its own modest way in broader regional movements of sharīʿa transformation. While adhering to the old constraints of the commentary genre, *The Gilded Crown* also foreshadowed the coming paradigm shift in Yemeni sharīʿa discourse.

This new law book laid groundwork for later efforts at codification. Highland movements toward codified law would not be fully realized until after the birth of the nation-state with the 1962 Revolution, following the promulgation of a national constitution. In the new order of the nation-state the sharīʿa would be subjected to restatements in which the authority of the old *fiqh* texts was repositioned.[94] Thus the constitution of the Yemen Arab Republic (in the North) proclaimed (art. 3), "The Islamic sharīʿa is the source (*maṣdar*) of all laws." By contrast, in the new southern regime after its Revolution in 1967, laws were adapted from Soviet bloc socialist countries. When the two nations were joined in 1990, the initial constitution of the unified Republic of Yemen stated (art. 3), "The Islamic sharīʿa is the main source of all laws," with the added word "main" reflecting the different legal history of the southern regime. But after the southern socialists were vanquished in the Civil War of 1994, article 3 was amended to state, once again, "The Islamic sharīʿa is the source of all laws."

The Gilded Crown would be followed, in the 1950s, by a codification project patronized by Imam Ahmad, but the resulting text circulated only in manuscript and would not be published until the 1980s, well after the Revolution.[95] Like the innovative nineteenth-century Ottoman *Majalla*, this mid-twentieth-century Yemeni project rendered the *fiqh*, in this case the Zaydī doctrine of the official *madhhab*, into the form of numbered articles. Prior to the 1950s code, however, and just prior also to the appearance of al-ʿAnsī's new commentary on the *Flowers*, Imam Yahya had taken an important, but thus far unrecognized, step toward codification. In 1937, he assigned regular study of the Ottoman *Majalla* to the justices serving on the Appeal Court. The envisioned eventual result of this labor would be a published code.

The imam required his appointed justices to "undertake the study of two pages every day from the printed text of the *Majalla*, and to correct, revise, and refine it according to what is set forth in the principles of our *madhhab*, and to arrange it according to this order and these rubrics so as to print it and publish it and communicate it to the judges."[96]

The *Flowers* in Lower Yemen

How was the cosmopolitan Zaydī tradition localized in Ibb? Here I address the general circulation and transmission of the *Flowers* and its related literature. Later chapters consider local fatwās, receptions of imamic "choices," applications in court rulings, and the impacts of Zaydī models in the drafting of local notarial instruments. In 1919, after the demise of the Ottoman Empire and the extension of rule by Imam Yahya to the whole of the highlands, this quintessential Zaydī text of Upper Yemen returned to official status in Lower Yemen.[97] In the past, when Zaydī scholars were assigned to positions in Ibb, some eventually settled there permanently, and their descendants adopted the Shāfiʿī *madhhab* as a result of instruction by local teachers. Others posted in the town, however, notably those who did not intend to settle, sought to avoid this outcome by sending their sons back up north for instruction in Zaydī centers such as Dhamār.

Under the Islamic polity of the first half of the twentieth century, the *fiqh* text retained its classical role as the centerpiece of instruction. In this era, study of the "sharīʿa sciences" still represented not an advanced specialization but a cornerstone of intellectual life. The engineer, the PhD, and the medical doctor would not appear on the highland scene until after the Revolution of 1962.[98] Nationalists and reformers of the late imamic period came to see this centrality of *fiqh* as a flaw. One stated, "[W]e define ignorance as a lack of knowledge of Islamic jurisprudence, grammar, morphology. . . . [Our] institutions over the past centuries produced hundreds of notable judges. . . . However, it is not possible to find a doctor, . . . there are no experts in agriculture, . . . and no industries."[99]

From the mid-1920s onward, a significant segment of the Zaydī interpretive community was shaped in the instructional institutions of the imamic state, mainly in Imam Yahya's new *madrasa ʿilmiyya*, founded in Ṣanʿāʾ in 1924,[100] but also in smaller institutions modeled on it in other towns, including Ṣaʿda in the far north. I review the curriculum of the imam's new school in chapter 2. Under Provincial Governor and then Imam Ahmad, a similarly conceived school known as the Ahmadiyya, operated in Taʿizz, the important Lower Yemen town that became his capital.

At the Madrasa of the Great Mosque in Ibb, the advent of the new regime meant that endowment stipends for students, which provided for the acquisition of the "noble knowledge" (*al-ʿilm al-sharīf*), now would be earmarked for the study of the *Commentary on the Flowers*. The Ibb academic community included both day students from town families and stipend-supported rural students who lived in the endowment-run dormitory.[101] An orphan by the name of Muhammad Zayn al-ʿAwdī was one of those who received a stipend for his studies. Al-ʿAwdī, who became a post-revolutionary educator and a writer of sharp-edged political skits, joked that the four thick volumes of the *Commentary on the Flowers* provided a good armrest for floor-level sitting. As in other highland towns, jurists also continued to be trained beyond state and formal madrasa auspices in lesson circles at other mosques and in private residential sitting rooms.[102] In Upper Yemen, as noted, Zaydī scholars also studied *Flowers*-tradition texts in numerous rural *hijras*, protected enclaves in tribal territories. In addition, biographies record that many jurists from scholarly lineages began their studies in home schooling with their learned fathers or other relatives.

Shāfiʿī jurists in Ibb and elsewhere in Lower Yemen, and a contingent in Zabīd on the Tihāma coastal plain,[103] studied the same basic *fiqh* treatises that were standard and authoritative for Shāfiʿīs elsewhere, including those in Egypt, the Levant, East Africa, and Southeast Asia, as well as, closer to home, in the Yemeni sultanates to the south and east. These books included the famous *Minhāj al-ṭālibin* by the Syrian al-Nawawī (d. 1277), and its commentary literature; the *Mukhtaṣar* ("Abbreviation") of Abu Shujāʿ (11th–12th century), a much briefer work with its own commentary literature, including the influential late nineteenth-century gloss (*ḥāshiya*) by the Egyptian al-Bājūrī;[104] and the *Zubad* ("Cream"), the earlier-mentioned concise and rhymed law manual by the fifteenth-century Palestinian jurist Ibn Raslān (see figure 1.4). That a nineteenth-century Ibb jurist wrote a commentary on this work speaks to the vitality of the local Shāfiʿī community.[105]

Aside from the separate, *madhhab*-marking character of their *fiqh* texts, the intellectual cultures of the Shāfiʿīs and Zaydīs of Yemen, especially the "Sunnī" stream of the latter, exhibited a considerable overlap. In addition to their convergence in the Qurʾan, the sharing extended to many specific principal texts in the collateral academic fields. This may be illustrated in a brief comparison of the academic profiles of two late Ottoman Yemenis, the prominent Ibb Shāfiʿī, ʿAbd al-Raḥman al-Ḥaddād (d. 1922),[106] and his contemporary, the leading Zaydī scholar Husayn bin ʿAli al-ʿAmrī (d. 1942), the mentor of Ahmad bin Qasim al-ʿAnsī, author of *The Gilded Crown*. Al-Ḥaddād had been the Muftī of Ibb and later served as a judge and a high Ottoman official in Lower Yemen, based in Taʿizz, while in Upper Yemen al-ʿAmrī was the first Yemeni Chief Justice of the Ottoman Appeal Court.

Regarding the *fiqh* discipline, while al-Ḥaddād's Shāfiʿī training included the school texts mentioned above, in his autobiography al-ʿAmrī states that, among other works, he studied the Zaydī-Hādawī *Commentary on the Flowers* with no fewer than six teachers.[107] Historian Muhammad Zabāra writes that al-ʿAmrī continued his studies "until he excelled in all of the sharīʿa sciences."[108] Yemeni historians have referred to al-ʿAmrī as "Shaykh al-Islam," the highest honorific for a jurist, and also as "shaykh of shaykhs," "teacher of teachers," or "scholar of scholars."[109] His formation is detailed in his autobiographical account of his teachers, which mentions the books he studied with each of them.

While their *fiqh* programs diverged, the related academic studies of these leading figures ran parallel. In Qurʾanic exegesis both al-Ḥaddād in Ibb and al-ʿAmrī in Sanʿāʾ studied the *Kashshāf* of Zamakhsharī. In grammar, Ibn Ḥishām and the thousand verses (*alfiyya*) by Ibn Mālik were standard for both the Shāfiʿīs and the Zaydīs, as was the *Talkhīṣ*, by Qazwīnī, in rhetoric.[110] In the field of *ḥadīth*, both men read the *Ṣaḥīḥ* of al-Bukhārī, the *Ṣaḥīḥ* of Muslim, and the *Sunan* of Abu Dāʾūd—that is, three of the "Six Mothers" of the Sunnī discipline. Regarding this last discipline, while al-ʿAmrī's concentrated study of the *Flowers* literature established his Hādawī credentials as a Zaydī jurist, that of the Sunnī *Ḥadīth* works indicates that he was of the "Sunnī" persuasion that traced its intellectual lineage back through Shawkānī.

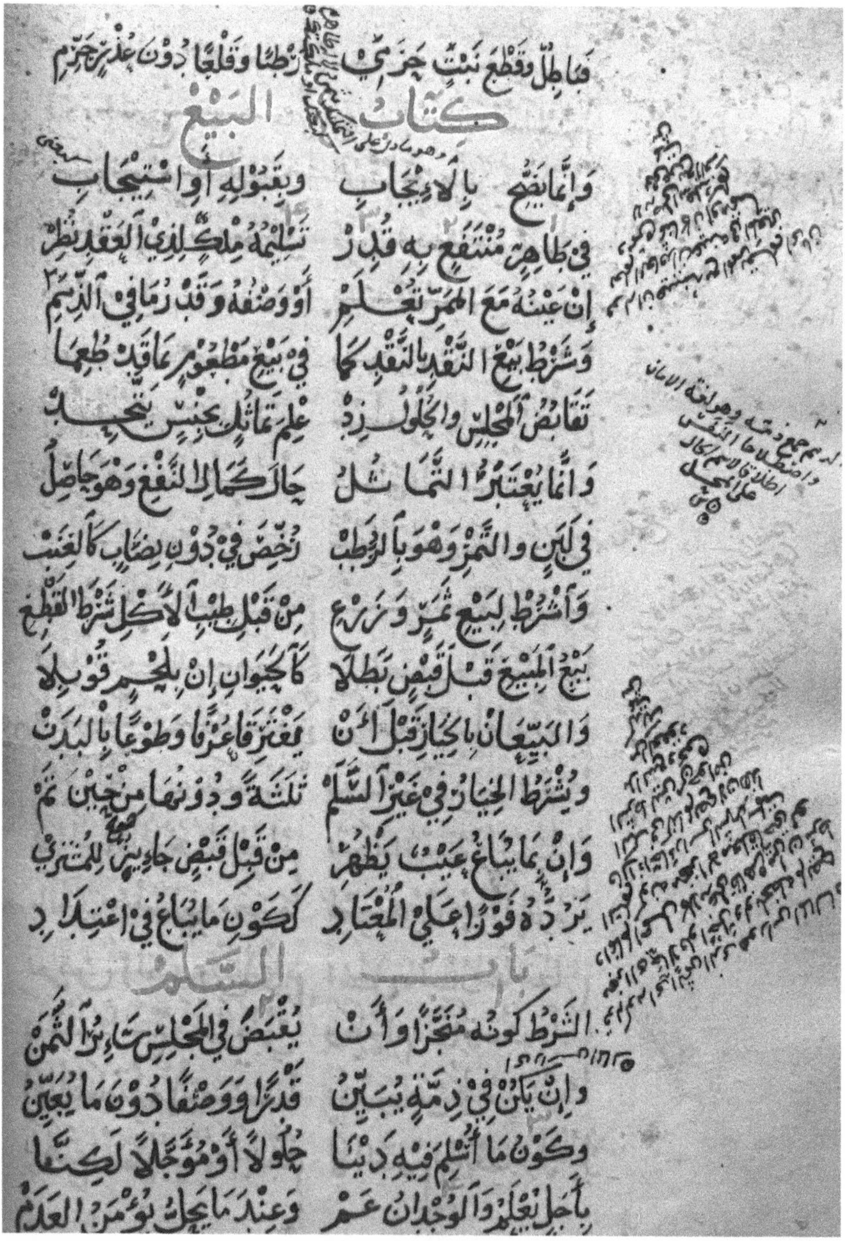
فباطل وقطع نبت حرمي رطبا وقلعا دون عذر حرم

كتاب البيع

وإنما البيع بالإيجاب وبقبوله أو استيجاب
في طاهر منتفع به قدر تسليمه ملك للذي العقد نظر
إن عينه مع الثمن يعلم أو وصفه وقدرا ما في الذمم
وشرط بيع النقد بالنقد كما في بيع مطعوم بما قد طعما
تقابض المجلس والحلول زد علم تماثل بجنس يتحد
وإنما يعتبر التماثل حال كمال النفع وهو حاصل
في لبن والتمر وهو بالرطب رخص في دون نصاب كالعنب
واشرط لبيع ثمر وزرع من قبل طيب لا لأكل شرط القطع
بيع المبيع قبل قبض بطلا كالحيوان إن بلحم قوبلا
والبيعان بالخيار قبل أن يفترقا عرفا وطوعا بالبدن
ويشرط الخيار في غير السلم ثلاثة ودونها من حين تم
وإن بما باع عيب يظهر من قبل قبض جاز للمشتري
يرده فورا على المختار ككون ما باع في اعتبار

باب السلم

الشرط كونه منجزا وأن يقبض في المجلس رأس الثمن
وإن يكن في ذمة يبين قدرا ووصفا دون ما يعين
وكون ما أسلم فيه دينا حالا أو موجلا لكنما
بأجل يعلم والوجدان عم وعند ما يحل يؤمن العدم

Figure 1.4 “Sale” chapter of the *Zubad* (“Cream”), with marginalia, from *Majmūʿa ʿAzīz* MS (Ibb, n.d.).

The Shāfiʿī-educated al-Ḥaddād siblings of Ibb successfully transitioned to function as jurists in the Zaydī state. They actively adapted themselves to the regime of the imams by becoming versed in the details of the ruler's doctrinal thought. In chapter 4, I discuss how ʿAbd al-Rahman al-Ḥaddād and another member of his family in the next generation, the man I knew as the "Judge of Ibb," responded to the Zaydī legal order by penning commentaries on imamic opinions, or doctrinal "choices." Another dimension of such relations concerned the established highland practice of cross-*madhhab* certifications.[111] Al-Ḥaddād's also distinguished and much younger brother, Yahya bin ʿAli (d. 1955),[112] requested a "general diploma" (*ijāza ʿāmma*) from Husayn al-ʿAmrī. This al-ʿAmrī issued, but only after al-Ḥaddād had agreed to give similar licenses to al-ʿAmrī's sons. This same younger brother, Yahya bin ʿAli, who served as an Ibb court secretary, and occasionally as an acting judge (see chapter 7), taught at the main town *madrasa* and authored a book-length biography (*sīra*) of Imam Yahya, offering a portrait of the "Imam of our Age."[113] Al-Ḥaddād's biography also provides a description of the imam's new school, the *madrasa ʿilmiyya*, in which he notes that the *Flowers* was a set text for the beginning classes and that the study of the *Commentary on the Flowers* was repeated in the curriculum of the later years.[114]

Sharīʿa court judges were prominent among the twentieth-century postings of Zaydī tradition scholars to the key towns of Ibb and Taʿizz. Specific careers in the judiciary further indexed the presence of the *Flowers* in Lower Yemen. This localization mainly occurred through court case rulings (chapter 7), but these jurists also wrote and taught. Under Imam Ahmad the highest ranked judge was Ahmad bin Muhammad Zabāra (d. 2000), the presiding justice of the Sharīʿa Panel in Taʿizz during the 1950s. Zabāra studied Zaydī *fiqh* with, among others, an Ibb judge mentioned below.[115] He also taught *fiqh* to, among others, the young Muhammad Yahya bin ʿAli al-Ḥaddād from Ibb, the son of the Ibb sharīʿa court secretary and biographer of Imam Yahya. Muhammad (whose marriage contract I read in chapter 10) was a secretary for Imam Ahmad at the time and a student at the Ahmadiyya madrasa. He went on to a career as a government minister and republican-era historian.[116]

Seeking further information about the judges assigned to Ibb in the 1950s, I visited Ahmad Zabāra at his house in old Ṣanʿāʾ. In his eighties, tall, stout and vigorous when I knew him, Zabāra served as the Muftī of the Republic and taught *fiqh* and the specialized sub-topic of inheritance law at the College of Sharīʿa and Law at Ṣanʿāʾ University, which opened in 1965.[117]

He also had become a historian. I have cited his assessments of al-Muṭahhar's new book on personal status law and of al-ʿAnsī's commentary, *The Gilded Crown*. I also have cited the *Entertainment of the Gaze*, the last of several major biographical histories by his father, the prominent historian Muhammad Zabāra (d. 1961). Published posthumously, in 1979, the father's book is indispensible for this study since it surveys the prominent Yemeni jurists and literati of the then just completed fourteenth Hijrī century.

When I asked Muftī Zabāra about particular judges who had been posted to Ibb during his time as the Presiding Judge under Imam Ahmad, he rose from his corner seat next to glass-windowed book cabinets, crossed the carpeted floor of his spacious residential sitting room in stocking feet, and disappeared upstairs. When he came back down he was carrying some loose pages of handwritten biographical text on the individuals in question, which he told me were from his father's *Entertainment of the Gaze*. I was confused. I knew this book as a printed volume that I had consulted from the library of the University of Michigan, where I then taught. But I also knew that when I had acquired my own copy of the book from the Center for Yemeni Studies, in Ṣanʿāʾ, my purchased book had been crudely censored. Republican authorities had cut out entries on leading figures in the prerevolutionary imamic state.

This treatment of his father's book had enraged the muftī, and his response was remarkable. He returned the book from print to manuscript, painstakingly writing it out in his lucid script while also significantly augmenting it with new materials and further biographies based on his own knowledge and further inquiries.[118] Only a man of his generation and facility with the pen could have contemplated such an enormous manual task. It was a few pages of this much expanded and now dual-authored, father-and-son work that Zabāra brought downstairs to provide answers to my questions. He later permitted me to photocopy the complete expanded work, which consists of four thick handwritten volumes. Retaining the father's original title (with a slight revision of subtitle), the new manuscript book states, on the title page, that it is "written in the script of the author's son."

Judges in Ibb

Imam Yahya's first appointment to the judgeship of the Ibb District (*qaḍāʾ*) around 1920 was the very learned Yahya bin Muhammad al-Iryānī (d. 1943).[119]

The Iryanīs hail from a village not far to the north of Ibb town (and west of Yarim), but they are Zaydī in jurisprudence. The judge's paternal uncle was the author of the treatise of models for notaries that I read in chapter 9. Among several other members of the extended family, Hasan bin Ahmad al-Iryānī (d. 1968) served in the town as the late-imamic and early republican Judge of the [provincial] Seat (*maqām*).[120] I obtained two of Hasan bin Ahmad's mid-century court registers from his son Muhammad, a republican-era Ibb judge I knew from sitting in his court.

Yahya bin Muhammad was a *ḥāfiẓ*, one of the individuals in his place and time to have memorized the entire Qurʾan. He is referred to in the same exalted terms as Husayn al-ʿAmrī, that is, as a "shaykh of shaykhs." There also was an instructional connection between the two great men: al-Iryānī asked for and received a diploma from al-ʿAmrī. In Ibb, al-Iryānī's "work in the judgeship did not inhibit his teaching those who desired to acquire knowledge."[121] After he was appointed to and then headed the Appeal Court in Ṣanʿāʾ, al-Iryānī continued his lifelong instructional work, teaching at the imam's *madrasa ʿilmiyya*, at the al-Filayḥī Mosque, where early nationalist discussions were beginning to occur, and in private homes. Although it is recorded that he was trained in *fiqh* and later taught works such as *The Light of Day*, the important commentary on the *Flowers* by al-Jalāl (d. 1673), his special expertise was in *ḥadīth*, a field in which he also was an author (see chapter 2).[122]

Al-Iryānī was followed in the principal Ibb judgeship by Sayyid Hasan bin ʿAbd al-Wahhab al-Warīth, who died in the post in 1934.[123] Born in the upper plateau town of Dhamār, al-Warīth is described by his biographers as a specialist in *fiqh*. It is reported that when he moved to the capital early in his career, Husayn al-ʿAmrī taught him *The Overflowing Sea*, the cross-school comparative *fiqh* work by Imam al-Murtaḍā, the author of the *Flowers*. Next to occupy this Ibb town judgeship was Sayyid Ismaʿil ʿAbd al-Rahman al-Manṣūr (d. 1963), a Zaydī jurist from near al-Shuhāra in Upper Yemen. Judge al-Manṣūr later became Judge of the Province (*liwāʾ*), when Ibb was elevated to this administrative status.[124] During his many years in Ibb as a sharīʿa court judge, al-Manṣūr "taught whenever he was free and his house was open to all who arrived." I obtained two of his 1950s court registers, also from Judge Muhammad al-Iryānī. In the next generation, Sayyid ʿAbd Allah bin Muhammad bin Isḥāq (b. 1902) received training at the imam's new madrasa where he taught before taking up his Ibb appointment as Judge of the Ibb Sub-district (*nāḥiya*). As I noted at the outset, a damaged register from Judge Isḥāq's court was left behind at the house when Judge al-Haddād moved out.[125]

As for the community of jurists in nearby Taʿizz, the post-1948 seat of Imam Ahmad, I have noted that Ahmad Qasim al-ʿAnsī, the author of *The Gilded Crown*, held several positions there. Among the Zaydī jurists appointed as court judges in Taʿizz, the most notable was ʿAbd Allah bin ʿAli al-Yamānī (d.1972), the Judge of the [provincial and then imamic] Seat.[126] Like his esteemed father (and teacher) before him, Judge al-Yamānī represented the highest caliber of Zaydī juridical knowledge. Imam Yahya's father, Imam al-Manṣūr (d. 1904), had honored the father, ʿAli bin ʿAli al-Yamānī, with the title "Shaykh al-Islam."[127] Where Ibb judges al-Manṣūr and H. al-Iryānī are described by biographer I. al-Akwaʿ as "verified in the branches (*furūʿ*)" and as a "scholar of the *fiqh*," Judge of the Seat al-Yamānī is identified as "a scholar verified in the branches of the *fiqh* and its roots"—that is, as one also qualified in the higher-level methodological and theoretical literature of *uṣūl al-fiqh* (see chapter 2). Historian Muhammad Zabāra says that Judge al-Yamānī was "one of the greatest scholars of the era." His profile thus is comparable to such already-mentioned leading early twentieth-century Yemeni jurists as Husayn al-ʿAmrī, Yahya bin Muhammad al-Iryānī, and, among the Shāfiʿīs, ʿAbd al-Rahman al-Ḥaddād. Biographer al-Jirāfī says of the senior al-Yamānī that "many were his memorized works (*maḥfūẓāt*)."[128] In addition to the Qurʾan, of which he was a *ḥāfiẓ*, the senior al-Yamānī "memorized abridged works in his youth and did not omit their study in his adulthood." This detailing of the memorization of specified *mutūn* (sing. *matn*) or *mukhtaṣarāt*, "abridged works," in a scholar's post-Qurʾanic school training is characteristic only of the biographies of the major intellectual figures, such as al-ʿAmrī, al-Yamānī's father ʿAli bin ʿAli, and earlier, Muhammad ʿAli al-Shawkānī (in his autobiography).[129] In the list of titles of al-Yamānī's father's memorized works, the *Flowers* appears first, and it occupies the same prominent position on the similar list that is given for his son, the mid-century Judge of the Seat in Taʿizz.

The connections of the al-Yamānīs, father and son, with the Ḥamīd al-Dīn imams, father Yahya and son Ahmad, were close.[130] In his youth, the future imam Yahya studied with the senior al-Yamānī. Years later, this same teacher also issued a diploma for the future imam Ahmad. In addition to these important instructional relationships, which helped establish and certify the interpretive capacities of the two twentieth-century rulers, the al-Yamānīs also served the imams as troubleshooting emissaries to handle important legal matters. Such interventions on behalf of the imams include that by the senior al-Yamānī in Lower Yemen. "In the year 1921," M. Zabāra writes, "Imam Yahya commissioned him to go to the town of Taʿizz to settle some of its problems, and he resolved lawsuits among its people concerning property and water systems endowed for mosques and schools."[131] Under Ahmad, serving as the Judge of the Seat, the junior al-Yamānī would be dispatched for similar tasks, including, in the late 1940s and then again in 1958 (at age seventy-four), the resolution through sharīʿa litigation of two thorny Ibb town disputes, the original judgments of which were retained in private holdings.[132]

Originally from Ṣanʿāʾ, Judge of the Seat al-Yamānī remained in Taʿizz for more than twenty years, during which time he built a house and took up full residence. A similar career story, but in the next generation, is that of Sayyid Muhammad Yahya Muṭahhar, the earlier-mentioned author of the late twentieth-century work on personal status law, whom I stayed with in 1995. Born in 1922 in the mountainous redoubt of Shuhāra, an old center of Zaydī scholarship, in his early post-Qurʾanic school training al-Muṭahhar studied *fiqh*, inheritance, and Arabic.[133] At age eighteen, he traveled further north to the town of Ṣaʿda where, nine years later, he graduated from the Madrasa of the Mosque of Imam al-Hādī, named for the first Zaydī imam in Yemen and eponym of the Hādawī branch of the juristic school. Al-Muṭahhar's studies there comprised *fiqh*, the two *uṣūls* (of *fiqh* and religion), the language sciences, *ḥadīth*, and Qurʾan exegesis. Coming to Ṣanʿāʾ after the coup of 1948, al-Muṭahhar studied in the afternoons with the new Presiding Judge of the Appeal Court, the learned Muhammad bin Hasan al-Wādaʿī. Some years later, al-Muṭahhar had an occasion to read aloud the *Ṣaḥīḥ* of al-Bukhārī, the authoritative Sunnī *ḥadīth* collection, together with Judge al-Yamānī while the two men sojourned in Ibb on assignments from Imam Ahmad.[134]

TWO

Pre-text

Five Sciences

HOW WAS SHARĪʿA interpretation conceived? How was the textual universe behind the interpretive act configured? In this chapter I sample the Zaydī theory of the interpreter and sketch the location of the *fiqh*—the central academic discipline—with respect to the closely related fields of inquiry within the larger discursive tradition. A key question concerns the jurist's interpretive relation to the twin corpuses of authoritative rule-bearing texts, the Qurʾan and the Sunna of the Prophet Muhammad, the two recognized "sources" for the sharīʿa. In this connection, I am mindful of Talal Asad's seminal suggestion, mentioned at the outset, that studying the transmission of these "founding texts" should be part and parcel of "an anthropology of Islam." Equally apropos is Asad's aim, also cited earlier, to understand how "a particular discursive tradition, and its associated disciplines are articulated at a particular point in time."

Interpretation in all its conceptual complexity and textual range is the focus of a rich literature in Islamic studies.[1] The justification for further treatment here, again, is a situational perspective. I thus seek to ground interpretation in a particular intellectual, institutional, and discursive world, to locate these high-level textual arts with respect to a specific formation of sharīʿa texts, to an arc of genres that ultimately comprised both a library and an archive.

In this chapter I read a brief theoretical discussion devoted to interpretation and its textual resources. In the preceding chapter, I skipped over a distinctive feature of this particular lineage of juridical literature. What I skipped, and return to now as a frame for the present chapter, is a diminutive text placed at the front of books in the *Flowers* literature. In my printed edition of *The Book of Flowers*, the three pages in question appear following the title page (and after the opening *Basmala*) and before the standard first chapter, which is on ritual cleanliness. In an apparently routine manner, these same three pages, which share the concise stylistic demeanor of the following *matn*, are incorporated in the *Flowers* literature commentary works, including the fifteenth-century *Commentary* by Ibn Miftāḥ and the twentieth-century *Gilded Crown*.[2] In the latter work, the comments inserted by al-ʿAnsī extend the combined text to thirteen and a half pages. Yet this little text has an ambiguous relation to the book it physically precedes. While it often appears attached to the *Flowers* literature, as in the mentioned instances, it also is detachable. In the first printed edition of the *Flowers* in 1913–14, for example, it is absent.[3] Meanwhile, the independent significance and the separate existence of these opening pages are signaled by the fact that they elicited their own standalone works of commentary.[4] Part of the ambiguity of the connection between these three pages and the following *matn* of the *Flowers* rests on the simple fact that the two texts are by same author: Imam al-Murtaḍā.

I refer to the three pages as a "pre-text," rather than as an introduction or a preface. In doing so I am drawn into a skirmish among the commentators that centers on Imam al-Murtaḍā's initial word in his little text. It remains unclear to me whether the word I have translated as "pre-text" is a title, a label for a genre, or a term for a text-unit, such as "chapter" (*bāb*) or "part" (*faṣl*). In his *Flowers* commentary, Shawkānī calls this an argument about "naming" or "title giving" (*tasmiyya*).[5] In any event, the word in question seems to hold a key to understanding the relation of these pages to the following textual unit, the book *matn*. In the commentaries, the word in question normally appears without the vowel marks indicated—that is, as an unpointed written consonant string: *m-q-d-m* (*mīm-qāf-dāl-mīm*), with the letter *d*, or *dāl*, understood to be doubled. Engaging their craft at this elementary, intra-lexemic level, the commentators discuss the alternative possibilities for the key vowel that should follow the doubled *dāl*. Is the correct vowel an *a* or an *i*? Is the opening word *muqaddama* or *muqaddima*? The latter, of course, is known as the title of Ibn Khaldun's introduction to his ten-volume history.

In his *Commentary*, Ibn Miftāḥ, a student of Imam al-Murtaḍā, states that, grammatically, the *a* version of the word has the meaning of something that is presented before the intended object (*al-maqṣūd*), whereas the *i* version has the meaning of something presented before the intended object that is also a part (*faṣl*) of it.[6] Both Ibn Miftāḥ and Shawkānī, in commentaries written some four centuries apart, also refer to an alternate distinction, that between an "introduction" to knowledge (*ʿilm*), i.e., the knowledge associated with the sharīʿa, versus an "introduction" to a book (for Shawkānī, at least, the little text is neither).[7] While arguments were made for the *a* as opposed to the *i*, the *a*, and therefore *muqaddama*, seemed to prevail. A contemporary Zaydī scholar who studied the *Flowers* in his youth told me his teacher "always emphasized, *muqaddama* not *muqaddima*."[8] In the later printed editions of the *Flowers* alone (without commentary) in which the *matn* is preceded by the little text, both the *matn* and the three pages are fully pointed, with the vowel at issue marked accordingly, as an *a*, or *fatḥa*.[9] In the *Gilded Crown*, the word remains an unmarked consonantal string and al-ʿAnsī does not take up the issue.

Let me summarize what I take from this curious opening debate. First, the prevailing view is that the *Muqaddama*, the preceding pre-text, and the following book, *The Flowers*, are not, at least conceptually, parts of the same text. Second, however, when they appear bound together in the same physical book, in material terms they are parts of the same text. Third, as noted, the small text commonly was placed before the big one, and in this position it was commented on together with the following book. Fourth, when they appear together between the same covers, a specific relation exists, although this is not the conventional one that would be translated as that of an "introduction" or "preface." Finally, fifth, when the two texts are juxtaposed it is evident that the sharīʿa discourse of the initial three pages is conducted at a higher level of abstraction.

Recall that the *Flowers* is correctly considered a book in what is known as the "branches," or *furūʿ* literature, of the *fiqh*—that is, the *fiqh* proper. In contrast, theoretical and methodological discussions related to interpretation, such as in this small preceding text (albeit briefly and partially), normally were the domain of a separate juridical literature known as the "roots," or *uṣūl al-fiqh*.[10] In the previous chapter, I mentioned that a limited number of jurists of the first half of the twentieth century, including individuals resident in Lower Yemen, were singled out for their qualification in this specialized register of juridical thought. While the "branches" works (i.e., the *fiqh* per se) represents a theoretical literature in its own right it is, more precisely, a theory of practice. It is therefore often referred to in western scholarship as the "positive" or "applied" law. In relation to this "branches" corpus of practice-oriented doctrine, the "roots" literature represents a theory of theory.

In an alternative conceptualization, the *uṣūl al-fiqh* works may be seen as a type of meta-literature. This refers to a type of textual discourse with two previously mentioned basic features: it operates at a higher conceptual level, and it comes into existence at a later point in time. Thus the *uṣūl al-fiqh* literature emerged as a distinct literature some two centuries after the "branches." Schacht therefore characterizes these works as "a retrospective systematizing and justification of the existing positive doctrines."[11] This captures only one side of a historical dialectic, however. It concerns only the initial or construction stage of this theoretical and methodological discourse, ignoring its subsequent history. This one-sided characterization did accord, however, with Schacht's view of the early interpretive closure of the sharīʿa. We, in contrast, may understand the presence of the pre-text before the *matn* of the *Flowers* as a tradition-specific moment in the long history of dialogues between these distinct levels of juridical thought.

In giving attention to these opening pages, I return, as it were, to the beginning of the *Flowers* tradition literature, to recommence and also broaden my account of the sharīʿa library. I introduce additional textual materials on the period library of the Zaydī *madhhab*, and I also refer to related textual activities in the interpretive communities resident in imamic-era Ibb. I rely on the research of Ismaʿil al-Akwaʿ, a Zaydī-trained scholar and a one-time resident of Ibb, whose detailed studies of highland instruction include the curriculum particulars of the *madrasa ʿilmiyya*, the advanced school established in the 1920s in Ṣanʿāʾ by Imam Yahya. I rely as well on the biographical history of the late imamic period published by Muhammad Zabāra, the work that his son Ahmad, the Muftī of the Republic in my day, later augmented as he returned his father's book to a handwritten manuscript.[12]

In the curricula of the era, in addition to Zaydī school standards, the doctrinal texts set for study included works that originated in other textual communities. I therefore need to refine my earlier point concerning the relationship of the library to locality. Initially, I argued that since doctrinal texts were created without specific discursive coordinates in any particular space and time, they had to be actively made local. These curricula, however, reveal the more complex circumstance of academic disciplines that, in addition to the utilization of texts produced within the *madhhab* community, also relied on non-Zaydī authored texts. This reliance was either direct or by means of receptions in Yemeni-authored commentaries, glosses, and annotations. I suggest that such features of textual provenance also inform the contrasting cosmopolitanisms of the Zaydī and the Shāfiʿī *madhhabs*.

While I frame this chapter as a partial reading of the pre-text, there is a further textual twist. While the three pages provide the overall structure for my reading, in approaching this text through the more expansive commentaries I immediately encounter an extended digression, which I then interrupt my reading of the pre-text to pursue. This commentators' digression, which in fact occupies me for most of the first half of this chapter, details, in a classical manner, the discrete, textually constituted bodies of knowledge, the "five sciences" that must be mastered by the interpreter. The digression offers a concise view of the immediate disciplinary surround of the *fiqh*, the interconnected fields sometimes referred to as the "sharīʿa sciences." Pondering what I understand to be premodern forms of disciplinarity and interdisciplinarity, I consider the established techniques of textual appropriation and construction, the detailed methods of citation and quotation, and, again, the work of orality. These textual aspects of sharīʿa interpretation bear not only on the activities of authorship in the *fiqh* literature but also on the roles of a ruling imam, a muftī, and a judge, figures whose written interpretive acts I examine in chapters 4, 5, 7, and 8.

Finally, I note that the little text I read below has another appellation, used by early *Flowers* commentator Ibn Miftāḥ. Toward the end of his authoritative, four-volume work, in the chapter on the imamate, when he introduces two of the requirements for an imam—those of being a qualified interpreter (*mujtahid*) and of justness (*ʿadāla*)—he states that these topics have been covered earlier in what he terms the "*dībāja* of the book" (*dībājat al-kitāb*).[13] From a root that can mean to embellish, decorate, etc., and also to compose or put in writing, the *dībāja* of a manuscript could refer to an illuminated (painted) frontispiece, or, as here, to a written preamble.[14] Anticipating the two-part breakdown of my discussion in this chapter, Ibn Miftāḥ explains that the *dībāja* of the book (evidentially including the digression) contains a "presentation of the sciences of interpretation" (*bayān al-ʿulūm al-ijtihād*) and a "specification of justness" (*taḥqīq al-ʿadāla*) in the interpreter.

"An Interpreter . . ."

Two key roles figure in this small text. They represent opposed positions in the human relations of sharīʿa interpretation. The discussion specifically addresses the circumstance of the individual who, in endeavoring to know the position of the sharīʿa on an issue, whether to act accordingly or as a point of information, must seek out and follow the guidance of another, a qualified interpreter. The doctrinal "follower" is known as a *muqallid*, one who engages in (from the same trilateral root) *taqlīd*. The qualified interpreter is known as a *mujtahid*, an individual who engages in (from the same root) *ijtihād*. These actor-types and their respective roles in the interpretive relationship represent stock topics in the higher-level *uṣūl al-fiqh* works. There is an interesting ambiguity, or tension in these roles, however. The interpretive predicament of the "follower," in particular, requires elucidation. This jurists' perspective on the interpretive dyad of follower and interpreter also could be generalized. This results in an image of the Muslim social order as a hierarchy of the few and the many predicated on the social prestige and the limited social distribution of the requisite knowledge.[15]

Who is the intended reader of these pages? This issue is joined in the first line of the pre-text: "*Muqaddama* [on] what the *muqallid* cannot be ignorant of."[16] Who is this "follower?" Is this individual one of the "many" in society, an ordinary Muslim, an untutored commoner (*ʿāmmī*)?[17] The pre-text does speak to the situation of such an individual, but only further along (see below). Otherwise, considering the soon-to-be-elaborated detail regarding the conditions of entering into an interpretive relationship, it is apparent that the initially targeted individual is not the ordinary Muslim. Since the untutored commoner did not read, much less comprehend, technical topics, who was being addressed?

The discussion proper in the pre-text commences with a simple affirmation: "*taqlīd* is permitted." This permission immediately is qualified using the ubiquitous textual form of the *masʾala*, which refers to a fact situation associated with, or to be associated with, a rule—that is, to a "case" or an "issue."[18] The permission to engage in *taqlīd* extends to "issues" that are qualified as falling within (1) the doctrinal "branches" of the law, specifically within (2) the areas of application, and in the spheres of either (3) probable or (4) certain knowledge.[19] A key point that is not explicitly developed here but that I want to underscore is that human interpretation is understood to operate primarily in the realm of probable knowledge (*ẓann*), which provides a positive basis for action.[20] In chapter 5, I give an extended illustration of an opinion underpinned by an orientation to probable knowledge, with the applied "issue" in question the evidential status of written documents in court practice.

Meanwhile, Shawkānī, the critical commentator, attacks this opening line of the pre-text (viz., "what the muqallid cannot be ignorant of"). He does so by reading just ahead to the above-mentioned line that states that the permission to engage in *taqlīd* is limited to "branches" issues. He notes that, rather than dealing with "branches" issues, the pre-text mainly concerns "roots" issues. How, he then asks, can the "follower" be held responsible for not being "ignorant of" issues the "following" of which is not permitted for one of his knowledge status? Imam al-Murtaḍā, he concludes, "has contradicted himself," and this even "before his pen dries" (i.e., within the space of the first few lines of his text). Shawkānī mischievously suggests that the only thing the imam got right in these lines was the neutral word "part" (*faṣl*), which simply marks the pre-text's first text-section.

With this mention of the term *taqlīd*, commentator al-ʿAnsī, who here and throughout closely follows the earlier *Commentary on the Flowers* in his treatment of the pre-text, inserts a definition. *Taqlīd*, he states, is "acting on the basis of the opinion (*qawl*) of another, or [holding] the belief or [the view as to] the probability of his veracity."[21] This, in turn, leads al-ʿAnsī to a defining point of institutional difference: while acceptable for the follower, this posture of *taqlīd* is not permitted for the interpreter.[22]

Coupled with a determined openness to interpretive *ijtihād*, this rejection of *taqlīd* for the capable jurist commonly is taken as a leitmotif of the Zaydī school. In contrast, in what amounts to a stereotype, the Sunnī schools have been characterized as accepting of *taqlīd* at the highest interpretive levels and, by extension, as closed to the possibility of *ijtihād*. I heard these sorts of contrasting portrayals of the Zaydī and the Shāfiʿī *madh-*

habs from al-Ghurbānī, the *Flowers*-trained jurist. Yet this twentieth-century depiction of the "Zaydī" school obscures its deeper history, notably the contestations of Hadawī positions, including those set forth in the *Book of Flowers*, by the highland "Sunnīs," such as Shawkānī. Part of the twentieth-century highland reality, and thus part of the backdrop for al-Ghurbānī's experience and perspective, was the instituted success of Shawkānī's "Sunnī" views in the polity of the era. Central among these views were his systematic advocacy of *ijtihād* and his thoroughgoing rejection of *taqlīd*. It may be noted, parenthetically, that Shawkānī's strong position on and practice of interpretation has served as important evidence for the western scholarly refutation of the notion that the "gate of *ijtihād*" had been closed.[23]

After some further qualifications, the next phrase in the pre-text states that a *muqallid* should "follow an interpreter (*mujtahid*) who is just." Al-ʿAnsī here inserts a definition of the *mujtahid*, as "he who is capable of the deduction of sharīʿa rules (*aḥkām*; sing. *ḥukm*) from their indications and signs"—that is, from source texts in the Qurʾan and the Sunna. At this precise point, still focused on the first half of the pre-text phrase "a *mujtahid*," and leaving the second half, "who is just," for later (see below), al-ʿAnsī opens the aforementioned digression. He states, "[A]n individual who is capable of this"—that is, capable of the deduction of rules—"masters five sciences (*ʿulūm*)." The digression that I now follow takes the form of an annotated listing of these "sciences."[24] Lists such as this one are well known in the Islamic juridical tradition, and they also have received attention in western studies, but as mainly as lists, without historical contextualization.[25] The lists provided by *Flowers* commentators Ibn Miftāḥ in the fifteenth century and al-ʿAnsī in the twentieth are typical in that they provide concise coverage of a relatively small number of academic fields. In contrast to these commentators' lists, the always demanding and exacting Shawkānī penned a separate treatise on this topic that offers lengthy and detailed lists of fields of inquiry appropriate for several distinct levels of jurists.[26]

As he proceeds to enumerate and discuss the indicated "sciences," al-ʿAnsī quotes directly, with minor alterations to be noted, from the fifteenth-century *Commentary on the Flowers*. Entering this digression, the perspective shifts from the "follower" to that of the interpreter.

Five Sciences

The first item in this program for the interpreter comprises the several academic subfields concerned with the Arabic language. This requirement is obvious, al-ʿAnsī states, "since the indications (*adilla*; sing. *dalīl*) from the Book and the Sunna are in Arabic." To carry out the derivation of sharīʿa rules the qualified interpreter must sufficiently understand the "language of the Arabs in vocabulary and structure." In line with his more detailed requirements, Shawkānī enumerates a full list of the language sciences, including grammar, morphology, rhetoric, (aspects of) logic, semiology, and the figures of speech. At the advanced madrasa established by Imam Yahya, the language curriculum was subdivided into separate lists of titles that covered grammar (*naḥw*), morphology (*ṣarf*), rhetoric (*balāgha*), and logic (*manṭiq*).[27]

The second academic field concerns knowledge of the Qurʾan, the first of the two primary textual "sources" (*uṣūl*) for deriving the law. While Shawkānī holds the interpreter responsible for the whole of the Qurʾan, al-ʿAnsī follows his fifteenth-century colleague in stating that complete mastery of the Book is not a condition for interpretation. The required knowledge is limited and specific, namely "the discipline of the verses containing sharīʿa rules." As he notes, the accepted number of verses in this rule-bearing subset of the Qurʾanic text, known as the *ayāt al-aḥkām*, is five hundred.[28] Expertise in these five hundred verses is a sub-specialization of the wider meta-textual discipline of *tafsīr*, or Qurʾan exegesis. At the imam's advanced madrasa in Ṣanʿāʾ, under the subject heading "Exegesis and Rules," students studied three Yemeni-authored works of *tafsīr* focused on these rule-bearing verses, notably the *Thamarāt* of al-Faqīh Yūsuf (d. 1429), plus the renowned general work of Qurʾan exegesis studied throughout the Muslim world, the *Kashshāf*, by the Persian exegete, al-Zamakhsharī (d. 1144).[29]

Regarding the rules contained in this subset of the five hundred Qurʾanic verses, al-ʿAnsī explains that the requirement for the interpreter is to be informed as to their manifest and unambiguous meanings. Recognized problems of the esoteric and the ambiguous in the verses thus were set aside. Although there was great societal value placed on the memorization of the Qurʾan, the interpreter is not required to have memorized these rule-bearing verses. Instead, this qualified jurist is meant to be a skilled finder of this "source" of the law. Al-ʿAnsī explains that an interpreter who is properly informed as to the general locations of the relevant verses in particular *sūras* should not need to search through the entire Qurʾan every time an appropriate verse is sought.

In another of his works, the comparative legal compendium known as *The Overflowing Sea*, the author of the *Flowers* presents a listing of these five hundred verses as one of several preliminary texts.[30] In lines that introduce this separately titled sub-book preceding the *Sea*, Imam al-Murtaḍā anticipates the remarks of the *Flowers* commentators when he states, "[T]he scholars have agreed that the recognized standard in interpretation (*ijtihād*) from the Book of God is knowledge only of the rule-bearing verses." To analyze a "verse," the sub-genre of text in question, the jurists drew on the language sciences. Imam al-Murtaḍā explains that the conveyance of a rule within a verse entailed considerations of both semantic and syntactic coherence. He additionally mentions the possibility of combinations of rules and verses with respect to the textual unit of the sentence, or clause (*jumla*). For his part, repeating a gloss on the fifteenth-century *Commentary on the Flowers*, al-ʿAnsī defines a verse as consisting of "connected language" (*kalām murtabiṭ*).[31]

In this sub-book that appears at the front of the *Sea*, the listed verses are numbered from one to five hundred, and their order of presentation is that of the Qurʾan. Grouped in their *sūras*, the verses also retain their intra-*sūra* verse numbers. The result is two numbering systems. For example, the verse fragment that states, "God made sale lawful" appears as number 82 in the list of the five hundred rule-bearing verses. At the same time, these lines of *sūra* 2, "The Cow," are grouped with other rule-bearing verses from the same *sūra*, and they also are marked, at the end, with their intra-*sūra* verse number, 275. Not all of *sūra* 2, verse 275, was taken over to the new list, however, as only part of it was considered rule-bearing.

Thus, in the creation of this specialized sub-literature on the five hundred verses, the Qurʾan was read for its isolable rule content. Referring to the five hundred verses and to the *Sea* and the preceding sub-book, Imam al-Murtaḍā states, "[W]e have extracted (*n-z-ʿ*) them and transferred (*w-r-d*) them to our book."[32] In these terms he depicts the process of quotation that underpinned this specialized genre of library discourse. The textual movement, which embodies a form of interpretation in its own right, begins with the identification and the excerpting of the relevant verses or verse fragments from the source-text, the Qurʾan. It concludes with their insertion in the new textual location, here the sub-book that precedes the *Sea*. The intended reader for such an extracted collection of rule-verses is the interpreter. Imam al-Murtaḍā states that this sub-book is intended as "a facilitation for the *mujtahid*." Specifically, he states that this collection of rule-bearing verses will be of use for the interpreter "when he searches for a rule from them, or [when] he wants to copy (*n-q-l*) them to present them." Al-Murtaḍā again describes a form of quotation, now one that occurs in the giving of an opinion or a ruling. The interpreter locates the proper verse in the specialized textual corpus presented at the front of the *Sea* and then excerpts it for redeployment—whether as quotation or as gloss—in his own presentation—that is, in the new textual site, the different genre used to express the opinion or ruling.

In such interpretive acts, quotation materially accompanies deduction. With a specific fact-configuration, problem, issue, or case-type—that is, a *masʾala*—in mind, the interpreter considers the corpus of rule-bearing verses in search of a relevant "indication." If the initial stage of the simple type of deduction was to identify a specific rule-verse as the appropriate "indication," the next was to bring the rule out, to extract it from its verse-discourse, and then, finally, to quote it, cite it, or restate it, and to thereby associate it with the problem or case it was meant to regulate.

In chapter 3, I consider how the exegetical literature of *tafsīr* treated the specific Qurʾanic verses concerned with the substantive topic of archival writing. Later still, in chapter 5, in the course of reading a jurist's opinion on the substantive question of "basing action on writing," or "practice with writing," I illustrate how selections of the same verses were mobilized in an argument.

The third academic field mentioned by al-ʿAnsī concerns the Sunna, the practice or custom of the Prophet, the other authoritative textual "source" of the law. The Sunna consists of *ḥadīth*s. An individual *ḥadīth* (lit. a "report" or "narrative") is composed of two parts: an opening chain (*isnād*) of named transmitters followed by the basic "text" (*matn*), typically a sentence or two in length. While the chain of transmission offers evidence as to authority and reliability, the basic text is the potentially ruling-bearing part. The links in the chain ideally index an accurate person-to-person (retention-citation-retention) transmission of the basic text while the texts themselves frequently incorporate a statement made by or about the Prophet, often in direct quotation. The specialized field of *ḥadīth* criticism, which is not mentioned in this context, focuses mainly on the soundness of the chains of transmitters, including whether these chains are complete or incomplete.

Al-ʿAnsī, still following the fifteenth-century *Commentary*, states that the requirements that apply to the *ḥadīth* corpus are similar to those concerning the five hundred Qurʾanic verses. Again, the interpreter need not memorize *ḥadīths*: "sufficient is the ability to find the *ḥadīth*" in an authoritative collection.[33] As with the Qurʾan and its *sura*-organization, the interpreter should know which chapter of a given collection to look in if, as al-ʿAnsī remarks, the *ḥadīth* book in question is structured in chapters. Paralleling what he said concerning the Qurʾan, al-ʿAnsī states that the suitably prepared interpreter should not need to look through an entire volume every time a rule-bearing *ḥadīth* is sought.

For this search al-ʿAnsī recommends any of the well-reputed *sunan* works. This generic title refers to a particular category of *ḥadīth* books, but he also singles out a specific book that he identifies by title and author: the *Sunan* of Abū Dāwūd (d. 889). This is one of the "Six Mothers," the authoritative *ḥadīth* books of Sunnī Islam. The *sunan* collections are distinguished by their concentration on the rule-bearing *ḥadīths*, the *aḥādīth al-aḥkām*.[34] Abū Dāwūd himself confirms this specialization in his introduction (a separate work), where he states that the 4,800 (actually some 5,274) *ḥadīths* he included "all pertain to rules (*aḥkām*)."[35] "As for the numerous *ḥadīths* on asceticism, the virtues, etc.," he adds, "I did not select them." Other types of specialized *ḥadīth* collections that dealt with such matters did not have a rule-bearing focus. An example from the Yemeni *ḥadīth* literature is a book by the Judge of Ibb of the 1920s, Yahya Muhammad al-Iryānī, which concerns rituals (viz., *adhkār* and *daʿawāt*) rather than rules.[36] Ninth-century author Abū Dāwūd explains that he selected his rule-bearing *ḥadīths* out of some 500,000 texts that he personally gathered. Some estimates of the total number of *ḥadīths* range as high as "a thousand thousand," or a million items.[37] Christopher Melchert notes that Abū Dāwūd adds his own comments on about a fifth of the *ḥadīths* presented in his *Sunan*, and that he frequently "ventures his own explicit comment on the legal application of a particular *ḥadīth* report."[38]

As with a Qurʾanic verse, the rule embedded in a given *ḥadīth* did not necessarily present itself as such; it had to be extracted. With both of the "sources" the emphasis, for the purposes of the jurist, was on the narrower subset of rule-bearing texts. In their overall scale, however, the approximately five thousand rule-bearing *ḥadīths* represent a corpus of texts roughly ten times the size of the rule-bearing Qur᾽anic verses. However, unlike the rule-bearing verses, which in their separate collections retained the textual order of the Qur᾽an, the relevant *ḥadīth* collections were organized according to the chapter structure of the *fiqh* works so that, although larger, this second corpus was easier for the jurist to search.

Al-ʿAnsī's explicit identification of the *Sunan* of Abū Dāwūd marks a small, but perhaps significant, departure from the script he had been following in the fifteenth-century *Commentary on the Flowers.*[39] The *Commentary* likewise begins by requiring of an interpreter the knowledgeable use of "a book containing most of the *ḥadīths* on the rules, such as one of the *sunan* books." A gloss on this sentence names books by "al-Bukhārī, Muslim, al-Tirmidhī, al-Nasā᾽ī, the *Muwaṭṭa᾽* of Mālik ibn Anas, and the *Sunan* of Abū Dāwūd"—that is, five of the "Six Mothers" of the Sunnī tradition, with the *Sunan* of Ibn Māja omitted and the early law book of Mālik added.[40] A second gloss, on the latter part of the sentence ("such as one of the *sunan* books"), adds "in the *madhhab* or in other than it," which broaches the issue of a Zaydī Hādawī-specific *ḥadīth* literature, an issue not raised by al-ʿAnsī in the twentieth century.

As the *Commentary* continues, a specific title is mentioned: "or *al-Shifā᾽* in our *madhhab*, or others."[41] The named book, *al-Shifā᾽*, a work on the rule-bearing *ḥadīths* by the Yemeni al-Husayn bin Badr al-Dīn (d. 1263),[42] is to the fifteenth-century *Commentary* what the *Sunan* of Abū Dāwūd is to the twentieth-century *Gilded Crown*, namely the single specialized *ḥadīth* work recommended by title in the main commentary text. It is notable that where the earlier commentator suggests a locally standard Shīʿī *ḥadīth* collection as the proper reference work for the prospective interpreter, the modern commentator identifies an authoritative Sunnī one. This switch in recommended titles may represent a detailed piece of evidence for the success of the "Sunnī" trend that had emerged from within Zaydī Islam.

As analyzed by Haykel, a main critical tenet of this historical movement was the rejection of reliance on the Zaydī *ḥadīth* works in favor of the authoritative Sunnī collections, including the *Sunan* of Abū Dāwūd and others of the "Six Mothers."[43] On the one hand, use of the Sunnī corpus meant drawing on a much wider community of transmitters. On the other, these oppositional jurists advocated the better securing of *fiqh* doctrine in the "sources" of law, notably in the rule-bearing *ḥadīths*. According to their intellectual biographies, discussed in the previous chapter, both ʿAbd al-Rahman al-Ḥaddād, in Ibb, and Husayn al-ʿAmrī, his early twentieth-century (and late Ottoman) contemporary in Ṣanʿāʾ—that is, leading jurist-intellectuals (and political actors) from Lower and Upper Yemen—studied the thousand-year-old book by Abū Dāwūd as part of their respective academic formations.

Other well-known works also focused on this rule-bearing subset of the ḥadīth corpus. One of these, *Bulūgh al-marām*, by the famous Egyptian Ibn Ḥajar (d. 1449), was commented on by the Yemeni Muhammad bin Ismaʿil al-Ṣanʿānī, known as Ibn al-Amīr (d. 1769), in his *Subul al-salām*.[44] This highland jurist and *ḥadīth* specialist was far from a passive local recipient of the Sunnī *ḥadīth* tradition, however. As Jonathan Brown notes, "al-Ṣanʿānī stands out as one of the most fearlessly iconoclastic *ḥadīth* scholars in Islamic history."[45] The Shāfiʿī-trained Ibb judge of my day, Ahmad bin Muhammad al-Ḥaddad, ʿAbd al-Rahman's nephew and son-in-law, told me that during his years in the 1940s as the Ibb Muftī he read *Subul al-salām*. This book, which also has been considered authoritative by jurists in places as far removed from the highlands as Java and Nigeria, appears among the listed *ḥadīth* works on the curriculum at the imam's advanced madrasa in Ṣanʿāʾ.[46] A second such work, similarly centered on the rule-bearing *ḥadīths*, is by Ibn Taymiyya (d. 1254), the grandfather of the famous jurist of the same name, and was commented on by Shawkānī in his monumental *Nayl al-awṭār*, a work that would later achieve wide recognition across the Muslim world after its print publication in Cairo in 1928.[47] At the advanced madrasa in the capital, Shawkānī's important work was included, together with the "Six Mothers," on the reading list for the final year, which was known—in a new academic conception—as the "Ijtihād Class." These two widely reputed and consulted works, *Subul al-salām* and *Nayl al-awṭār*, shared a basic textual identity as receptions of Sunnī collections of rule-bearing *ḥadīths* via commentaries penned by leading Zaydī-tradition "Sunnīs" of highland Yemen.

In Ibb and elsewhere in Lower Yemen during the month of Rajab, Shāfiʿī scholars customarily interrupted their studies to devote themselves to reading aloud the leading general *ḥadīth* compilation, the *Ṣaḥīḥ* of al-Bukhārī.[48] There also is evidence of the study of this and other Sunnī *ḥadīth* works by Zaydī tradition, "Sunnī" jurists connected with Ibb. Thus, in the nineteenth century, the posting of one of Shawkānī's students to Ibb gave rise to the local branch of the al-ʿAnsī family. As his student's biographer, Shawkānī writes that Ṣāliḥ al-ʿAnsī "studied under me the two *Ṣaḥīḥs* [al-Bukhārī and Muslim], the *Sunan* of Abū Dāwūd and some of my own writings."[49] For the twentieth century, as I noted at the end of the preceding chapter, ʿAbd Allāh ʿAli al-Yamānī and Muhammad Yahya al-Muṭahhar, two Taʿizz-based court judges trained in the *Flowers* tradition in different locales in Upper Yemen, occupied their spare hours while on assignment in Ibb reading aloud together the famous *Ṣaḥīḥ* of al-Bukhārī.[50]

The predominance of the Sunnī *ḥadīth* works advocated by the highland "Sunnīs" who branched off from the later Zaydī tradition was by no means complete in twentieth-century Yemen. The venerable *Shifāʾ*, the recommended Zaydī-Hādawī work on the rule-bearing *ḥadīths*, retained a secure place in the *ḥadīth* curriculum at the advanced madrasa in Ṣanʿāʾ. Meanwhile, it may be noted that to parallel his critical commentary on the *Flowers*, the basic Hādawī *fiqh* text, Shawkānī also wrote a commentary on *al-Shifāʾ*, as the basic rule-bearing Hādawī *ḥadīth* text.[51] It also is notable that the fifteenth-century *Commentary on the Flowers*, the work that recommended the *Shifāʾ* by title, remained authoritative in the twentieth-century highlands. The *Commentary on the Flowers* appeared, as a matter of course, on the *fiqh* curriculum of the Imam's Madrasa, and, as I have noted, its study was mandated for endowment-supported students in imamic-period Ibb. It appeared in a print edition some years before al-ʿAnsī's newly conceived *Gilded Crown*. While the *Gilded Crown* expressed the elements of some more recent thought, the *Commentary on the Flowers*, on which it was based, continued to be far more widely studied and consulted. Thus the long-standing and contentious conversation between the Hādawīs and the "Sunnīs" was both preserved in, and also further played out through, the academic program instituted in the Imam's Madrasa.

Still concerning this collateral discipline of *ḥadīth*, let me return to the previously mentioned fact that the *Muwaṭṭaʾ* of Mālik (d. 795), which is commonly recognized as one of the earliest works of *fiqh*, appeared in the list of *ḥadīth* books (in the referenced gloss to the *Commentary on the Flowers*). The *Muwaṭṭaʾ* has been described in western scholarship as "a treatise of *fiqh* based on *ḥadīth* which plays the role of judicial argument."[52] In the *Muwaṭṭaʾ*, according to Schacht, "the legal thought of Islam has not yet become jurisprudence." He also states that this work "represents the transition from the simple *fiqh* of the earliest period to the pure science of *ḥadīth* of the later period." In passing, Schacht notes that the other candidate for the honor of the "the oldest surviving Muslim law book" is the *Majmūʿ al-fiqh*, the work attributed to the eponym of the Zaydī school, Zayd bin ʿAli (d. 740).[53]

For its part, the *Majmūʿ* attracted the attention of a series of colonial-era Italian and French scholars interested in the Mālikī (named after Mālik) school of Sunnī jurisprudence that predominated in North and West Africa.[54] As in the *Muwaṭṭaʾ*, a large portion of Zayd's work consists of *ḥadīth* texts. On this basis, Bousquet and Berque remark that the two books share a similar "archaism." Although a majority of the *ḥadīth*s presented in the *Majmūʿ* are traced to the Prophet, a substantial subset are transmissions by Zayd (via the links of his father and grandfather) from his great-grandfather, ʿAli bin Abī Ṭālib (d. 661), the Prophet's cousin and son-in-law, and, as noted, an early leader of the Muslim community. *Ḥadīth*s traced back to Imam ʿAli are considered the hallmark of Shīʿī *ḥadīth* collections. Bousquet and Berque find the "figure of ʿAli" already delineated in some of the substantive treatments in the *Majmūʿ*. They additionally note that a large proportion of the text is devoted to ritual matters, the *ʿibādāt*.[55] In the law books of later centuries the chapters on ritual matters would constitute a much smaller proportion of the typical whole (e.g., one volume out of four in the *Flowers*-tradition commentaries.) Despite its *ḥadīth*-heavy content, however, the *Majmūʿ* is structured according to a *fiqh* chapter scheme.

Although the early genre-type of the *Majmūʿ* would be superseded by the developed and differentiated forms of the later *fiqh* books and *ḥadīth* collections, this old-form text continued to occupy an important place in the Zaydī library. Commentary further assured that this text from the distant past would be continually present. As arguably the first Muslim law book, and also as an initiating work in the field of Zaydī *ḥadīth*, the *Majmūʿ* was brought forward in time in the pages of the eighteenth-century commentary by al-Husayn bin Ahmad al-Sayāghī (d. 1806), in a work he titled—again the floral metaphor—*The Blooming Meadows*.[56] Al-Sayāghī's multi-volume work was still widely read in the twentieth century. It appears first among the list of books studied by Husayn al-ʿAmrī, and it also was a set text in the curriculum of the imam's advanced madrasa, where it appeared in the list of *ḥadīth* works.

The fourth academic field out of the five, although not a discipline like the others, required the interpreter to know those *masāʾil* (sing. *masʾala*)—issues, problems, or cases—concerning which there existed a widely held juristic "consensus" (*ijmāʿ*), specifically among the Prophet's "Companions and Successors, and others"—that is, in the early Muslim community. Al-ʿAnsī refers to the view of the *Flowers* when he says that these widely recognized areas of agreement are "extremely few" in number. A gloss to the *Commentary on the Flowers*, which al-ʿAnsī follows, fills in some detail at this juncture, stating that "there are fourteen *masʾala*s, [or] it is said, sixty, [or] twenty, [or] fifteen." Fourteen items are then specified. They are the consensus concerning the invalidation of one's pilgrimage by having sexual intercourse during it; the violation that pertains to drinking wine; two matters concerning blood-money; the prohibition on sale transactions by slave-mothers; the definitions of the term "the land of the Arabs" and also that of "the land of Iraq"; and six matters concerning inheritance. The *Commentary* indicates that the interpreter should simply memorize these matters so as to avoid the possibility of issuing an opinion counter to the consensus of the Muslim community.[57] In this sketch of the "five sciences," consensus, which is normally considered one of the two foundational methods of Islamic jurisprudence, appears much reduced in sway.[58] It is not that the method itself is criticized but that virtually all of the later results of its application, including the accepted views enshrined in the "branches" literature, receive no recognition as such.

The term *masʾala* refers, in general, to either a settled or an unsettled matter, issue, problem or case, always oriented to a specific configuration of facts. The fourteen items detailed in this section are examples of settled *masʾala*s, but there also is an example provided of an unsettled matter. I return in chapter 4 to the phrase employed in this connection, "a current case" (*masʾala ḥāditha*), which refers to something that has come to the attention of a jurist and for which an interpretive intervention is pending. In a settled matter, the fact situation in question has been given a rule; in an unsettled matter, the facts either have yet to be subjected to interpretation or are susceptible to being reopened to it. Normally, a set of facts previously associated with a rule could be considered anew. The indicated exceptions would be the fourteen *masʾala*s (or some other finite number) that even the perfectly competent ideal interpreter should not disturb. Otherwise, according to this construct of the ideal interpreter, all matters of fact must be considered de novo.

In *ijtihād*, a jurist carried out interpretation with respect to a particular *masʾala*. In terms of their proper rule, the facts in question were considered unsettled (or unsatisfactorily settled) prior to the interpretive act. Following it, to the extent that the opinion carried weight, they were deemed settled (or differently settled). In my later discussion of the fatwa, additional institutional meanings of this quietly essential and multivocal term come into play. In asking for a fatwa, the questioner sought the correct rule for the *masʾala* presented in his or her question. To prepare the question, the *masʾala* itself had to be created. That is, the fact situation described for the purpose of eliciting a muftī's opinion as to the relevant rule was itself composed, not simply found already existing as such. At the other end of the process, an important opinion by a muftī could be edited for inclusion as an item in a "branches" law book—in a unit also referred to as a "*masʾala*," among other terms. As a named literary sub-genre, a *masʾala* comprised a fact situation associated with a rule, or an opinion, or, in the accompanying law book discussion, perhaps more than one alternative position. In addition to an origin in a fatwā, a law book *masʾala* also could be formulated in exploratory but still substantive legal thought, or in response to other such formulations. When I later give examples of such literary *masʾala*s, it will become clear that the jurists strategically arranged and characterized their facts as part of the process of expressing their opinions. At the still higher level of the "roots" literature, a *masʾala* was a conceptual problem or theoretical issue.[59]

Later still, moving in the direction of the archive, I cite the procedural doctrine concerning whether a jurist who had previously acted as a muftī may address the same *masʾala* in the role of court judge. This view of the "sameness" of a particular *masʾala* refers to it as a given fact configuration. Finally, at the ethnographic level in Ibb, I saw the origins of *masʾala*s in the uncertain facts of the everyday world. These colloquial *masʾala*s were the mundane "matters," "issues," and "disputes" that one encountered percolating, but as yet unformulated, much less addressed or resolved, in the morning streets of the town.

The fifth and final field for the interpreter to master is the meta-discipline of *uṣūl al-fiqh*. The focus of the *uṣūl al-fiqh* works, again, is *ijtihād*, interpretation itself, and its sources and methods, including "consensus," and also the features of the interpreter's status and role. As with the language sciences, the Qurʾanic rule-bearing verses, and the rule-bearing *ḥadīth*s, the reference here is to a named literature, one that, as I have noted, emerged some two centuries after the applied "branches."

In addition to such leading early twentieth-century jurists as Husayn al-ʿAmrī and, among the Shāfiʿīs, ʿAbd al-Rahman al-Ḥaddād, whose intellectual profiles I compared in the last chapter, certain judges of the first half of the century were considered qualified in *uṣūl-al-fiqh*. Notable among them were the first Judge of Ibb appointed by Imam Yahya, Yahya Muhammad al-Iryānī, the earlier-mentioned *ḥadīth* specialist who later headed the Appeal Court in Ṣanʿāʾ, and also ʿAbd Allah bin ʿAli al-Yamānī (d.1972), the Judge of the (provincial and then imamic) Seat, who was assigned to two Ibb court cases I have studied.[60] Like his father before him, Judge al-Yamānī was said to be qualified in both the branches and the roots of the *fiqh*. In my day in Ibb, however, the principal of a new institute (*maʿhad*) in Ibb that specialized in Islamic instruction was of the opinion that no one in the town was knowledgeable in *uṣūl*. He kindly presented me with a copy of a famous short treatise in this field, the *Waraqāt*, or "Pages," by the prominent Shāfiʿī jurist Imam al-Ḥaramayn al-Juwaynī (d. 1085).

At the Imam's Madrasa, *uṣūl al-fiqh* figured as a separately categorized academic subject comprising seven titles, beginning with *al-Kāfil* by Ibn Bahrān as the introductory text. I mentioned this work in the previous chapter as one of the books printed (in the commentary known as *al-Kāshif*) in Yemen in 1928. If one reads chapter 9 on "*al-ijtihād wa-l-taqlīd*" in this introductory *matn* by Ibn Bahrān, one finds, in virtually the same language, a technical outline that parallels the material I am presenting in this chapter.[61] While I have fleshed out my presentation using the digression of the fifteenth- and twentieth-century *Flowers* commentators, Ibn Bahrān renders the required five "sciences" in a single line: "Arabic, the *uṣūl*, the Book, the Sunna, and the *masāʾil* of consensus."

The set *uṣūl* texts at the Imam's Madrasa are listed in order of advancing difficulty. They comprise six Yemeni titles, including works by *Flowers* author Imam al-Murtaḍā and by al-Shawkānī, and a single non-Yemeni work. The listed *uṣūl* text by Ibn al-Murtaḍā also appears among the preliminary texts in the *Sea*, his comparative work.[62] The non-Yemeni text, listed last, is the abbreviation by the Mālikī jurist Ibn al-Ḥājib (d. 1249) of his longer *uṣūl* work, an abbreviation studied at the Imam's Madrasa in a famous commentary.[63] While they were not on the curriculum, it may be noted that there also were a number of Yemeni commentaries on Ibn al-Ḥājib's abbreviation, including one by *Flowers* commentator Dahmaʾ bint Yahya al-Murtaḍā, the sister of the *Flowers*' author.[64]

In addition to the *uṣūl al-fiqh* subject listing, other texts were listed for the "*Ijtihād* class," the last level of the three-year curriculum at the Imam's Madrasa. These included both further *uṣūl al-fiqh* treatises together with, as I mentioned above, a large component of *ḥadīth* works, the centerpiece of the highland "Sunnī" program, including the books known as the "Six Mothers" and Shawkānī's *Nayl al-awṭār.* The *uṣūl* works listed at this top level of the curriculum are another work by Shawkānī and an additional non-Yemeni book, the *Bidāyat al-mujtahid* by the remarkable Andalusian Ibn Rushd (d. 1198), a man famous in the East as a leading Mālikī school jurist and an important philosopher, and in the West as Averroes, the commentator on Aristotle.[65]

As for the topical specifics of this last of the disciplines covered in the digression, al-ʿAnsī gives two concept-filled sentences, the first of which begins, "It comprises an understanding (*maʿrifa*) of . . . " In the fifteenth-century *Commentary*, which al-ʿAnsī in the twentieth follows word-for-word, these two sentences are encumbered with no fewer than thirteen footnotes to elucidating glosses.[66] Another way to read these heavily laden sentences, however, is with reference to the tables of contents of *uṣūl al-fiqh* treatises, since the rapidly listed analytic topics coincide with the chapter titles in the standard Zaydī *uṣūl* works, starting with the elementary book, *al-Kāfil* by Ibn Bahrān. Thus the first mentioned topic, concerning the "general and the specific," is the subject of chapter 6 in *al-Kāfil*; those that follow on the "ambiguous and the clear," chapter 7; and the "stipulations of [Qurʾanic verse] abrogation," chapter 8; and the issues of "commanding and forbidding" (and two sub-terms), chapter 5. The "rules of consensus (*ijmāʿ*) and the stipulations of analogic reasoning (*qiyās*)"—which, following the Qurʾan and the Sunna as the two textual "sources," represent the two means of establishing the "indications" (*dalīl*s) of the sharīʿa—are treated in chapter 2.[67] Al-ʿAnsī concludes his two-sentence passage on the *uṣūl* science as follows: "except with the understanding of all this, the deduction of the rule (*istinbat al-ḥukm*) is not mastered" (lit. "completed").

Al-ʿAnsī then concludes the entire digression in a parallel phrase: "when these five sciences are not mastered, *ijtihād* cannot be mastered." He also states, "[O]ther than these [sciences] have been stipulated [by others], but they are not a stipulation for us."[68] Thus, in sum, according to both the modern commentator al-ʿAnsī and his fifteenth-century predecessor, the model sharīʿa interpreter required a technical knowledge of Arabic; should be capable of informed access to the rule-bearing texts of the Qur'an and the Sunna; must avoid contradicting the handful of consensus opinions that date from the era of the early Muslim community; and should have competence in the conceptual tools of interpretation set forth in the treatises of *uṣūl al-fiqh*.

Before concluding my reading of the three pages of the pre-text by taking up the second half of the phrase "an interpreter who is just," I pause here to pose a set of questions related to the just discussed "sciences."

Orality

Although routinely, as here, addressed as written texts, each of the two foundational "sources" for the interpretive act retained a vibrant "oral" character.[69] Qur'anic verses and *ḥadīths* are distinct genres, which were received and transmitted in different oral-aural formats. As is well known, the two corpuses of what were originally oral scripts reached separate historical watersheds of collection, editing, ordering, and presentation in written form. These processes resulted in the advent of the definitive written version of the Qur'an and, somewhat later, the authoritative *ḥadīth* collections, also written books. For the Qur'an, we have the history of the creation of the authoritative redaction on the order of the Caliph ʿUthmān.[70] For the *ḥadīth* corpus, the efforts of indefatigable men like Abū Dāwūd defined the process of "recording" (*tadwīn, taqyīd*). While the Qur'an maintained its principal identity as an oral recitation, books of *ḥadīth* typically were taught and studied in a special recitational-auditory mode. An early local example of the latter is the teaching of the *Ṣaḥīḥ* of Muslim (d. 875) by a twelfth-century Ibb man known as "Sword of the Sunna."[71] A mid-twentieth-century example is the already-mentioned instance of the two Zaydī-trained jurists sojourning in the town reading aloud the *Ṣaḥīḥ* of al-Bukhārī.

These two momentous oral-to-written transitions were occasioned by controversy within the early Muslim community, however, most acutely in connection with the writing down of *ḥadīths*.[72] At issue was the proper form to be taken by the essential knowledge these texts contained. In his republican-era book on the science of *ḥadīth*, Muhammad al-Ghurbānī, the Zaydī-trained Ibb resident I worked with, includes a section on the historical process of "recording" in which he reviews the early "aversion (*karāha*) to the writing of *ḥadīth*."[73]

If the histories and identities of the two "sources" established authoritative textual templates, what were the impacts of these models on the other types of texts in the discursive tradition? I suggest that the momentous transitions from oral originals to written transcriptions found resonances across the sharīʿa, library, and archive. Thus, in madrasa lesson circles, the teacher "recited" or "dictated" a doctrinal *matn* while students listened and also took the text down in writing; in courts, spoken testimony was converted into written minutes; and, in a contract session, the notarial writer reduced (as we say) an oral agreement to a documented instrument. Across the period formation of sharīʿa texts, in patterned and analogous textual movements, oralities were anchored and, in more or less evident ways, altered in writing.

At the same time, words considered divine or prophetic provided expressive forms for a range of authoritative human utterances. Thus the basic "oral" rubrics of the *qawl* and the *qāla*—the "word" or "statement" and the "he said" or "he stated"—recurred at multiple levels of sharīʿa discourse. Such inconspicuously shared usage connected the form of the speech of God and that of the *Shāriʿ*, the "legislator," the Prophet Muhammad, to the opinions of jurists in their law books, the legal dicta of muftīs and interpreting imams, the rulings of judges, and, finally, the binding utterances of individuals such as testators and contracting parties.

Disciplinarity

Concerning the several specialized sciences stipulated in the commentators' digression might we speak of a premodern type of interdisciplinarity? A few of the greatest scholars studied, gained mastery, wrote, and taught across many fields of inquiry. Writing as their biographer, Shawkānī states, for example, that Imam Yahya bin Ḥamza (d. 1346) "mastered all of the sciences" and that Imam al-Murtaḍā, author of the *Flowers*, was an "author in all of the sciences."[74] Shawkānī's own range was as broad.

Specific textual relations between these fields facilitated a jurist's interpretive act. Beyond the basic analytic tools provided by the language sciences and the meta-role played by the *uṣūl al-fiqh* discipline, the connections with the collateral fields of Qurʾan exegesis and *ḥadīth* studies were close. As noted, both of these disciplines generated specialized sub-literatures designed to accommodate the narrower, rule-oriented interests of the jurists. In addition, in the sub-literature devoted to the Qurʾanic rules, a second numbering system (1–500) complemented the *sūra* order and the verse-numbering system of the Book itself, while in *ḥadīth* studies the close relationship to the *fiqh* was further facilitated by the use of the latter discipline's chapter scheme.[75]

Other aspects of the connectedness between these fields were conceptual and terminological. These involved the sharing of a variety of approaches, albeit with modifications and with applications to different sorts of materials. Essential elementary concepts, such as *ḥukm*, which among the jurists referred to the sharīʿa "rule," also figured centrally in other disciplinary projects. The relation between the disciplines of grammar and *fiqh* has been a focus of western attention by scholars such as Michael G. Carter, and Aria Nakissa recently has emphasized their shared analytic orientations to rules.[76] Linguists and jurists, among others, utilized a variety of paired analytic terms, such as "expression" versus "meaning," and "clear" versus "figurative" language (*lafẓ* and *maʿnā*, and *ṣarīḥ* and *kināya*), which I discuss in chapter 3. Among the jurists, such contrasting technical conceptions were utilized in the analysis of contracts, etc. An example of a different type of cross-discipline sharing is the compound analytic of *jarḥ wa-l-taʿdīl*, a procedure of negative and positive evaluation, which was applied by *ḥadīth* specialists to the assessment of individual *ḥadīth* transmitters and by the jurists to that of court witnesses.

Fiqh

A question remains with respect to this five-science plan about the status of the *fiqh* itself, that is, the "branches" literature. In the digression, the "roots" (*uṣūl*) literature is referred to as one of the required "sciences" to be mastered by the interpreter, but the *fiqh* is not mentioned per se. Should it simply be presumed that the *fiqh* was the central discipline around which the others revolved?

Before addressing this question, I first must briefly specify what the study of the *fiqh* entailed at the Imam's Madrasa. According to al-Akwaʿ, the curriculum listed under the subheading "*fiqh*" consisted of four items. In this built-in order of study for the discipline, item one is the first quarter of a book, namely the "ritual" or *ʿibādāt* section of the *Flowers*. This section, which was to be studied in both "meaning and expression," includes the standard chapters on ablutions, prayer (including the special types for funerals, solar and lunar eclipses, etc.), fasting, the pilgrimage, and the tithe. (It is not clear whether the immediately preceding pages that I have referred to as the pre-text also were to be studied at this juncture.) Item two on the madrasa *fiqh* list is the authoritative *Commentary on the Flowers*, "with its glosses." Item three is another important and massive work of *fiqh* that, like some of the pre-*Flowers* works in the Zaydī tradition, is arranged in chapters composed entirely of *masʾalas*. This is the *Bayān* of Ibn Muẓaffar (d. 1470), another student of *Flowers* author Imam al-Murtaḍā.[77] The fourth and final item is the aforementioned *Sea*, also by Imam al-Murtaḍā, although it is not clear whether students also were responsible for the several small books that preceded the multivolume main work.[78]

As for my question about the centrality of the *fiqh*, its privileged place among the classical academic disciplines commonly is assumed. In his authoritative study of Islamic education, George Makdisi speaks of the *fiqh* as the "ideal religious science" among the madrasa subjects.[79] Recall also al-ʿAnsī's preface to his *Flowers* commentary (cited in the last chapter) in which he states, admittedly with a vested interest, "The science of the *fiqh* is the greatest of the sciences in esteem and also the most significant in terms of instruction and writing. It is the fruit of the arts and their core, the end result of the religious sciences and their entryway."

And yet, as noted, the digression concerning the five required sciences for the interpreter does not mention the *fiqh* per se. To pose a seemingly obvious question, what is the relation of the interpreter to the *fiqh*? Should the *fiqh* be considered the interpreter's home discipline? Interesting light on this question is shed in a contrarian gloss that appears in the fifteenth-century *Commentary*.[80] As opposed to the positively stated position of both the *Flowers* and the main commentary text on the question of the "justness" of the interpreter (see below), this contrarian gloss maintains that this is not a condition for the individual who interprets. The same gloss goes on to identify a series of other nonconditions, all of which, unlike that of "justness," involve issues that are not brought up in either the *matn* or the *sharḥ*. One of these is "knowledge of the branches of the *fiqh*." In this contrarian view, knowledge of the *fiqh* is not a condition for interpretation. The noncontrarian or default view, which, again, is not positively stated as such, would be the opposite: that such knowledge is expected, even required.

Could it be argued that the interpreter need not know the *fiqh*? In a technical sense, if the "branches" literature of the *fiqh* is understood to be the product of deductive interpretation, then the ideal interpreter is barred from relying on it by the rule against *taqlīd*, since the *mujtahid* may not "follow" the interpretations of another. In this ideal sense every interpretive act starts afresh. All such acts return to and carry out an original analysis that involves a deduction from source texts located in the Qurʾan and the Sunna, and the result defines the new (or affirmed) sharīʿa rule. As for the accumulated rules and conditions (concerning contracts such as sale, and a host of other topics) found in the existing doctrine, "on the books," we might say, all—in a strict sense—were to be sidestepped. Another way of saying the same thing is that the results of later "consensus"—the rules associated with the settled issues or cases (*masāʾil*) mentioned in the "branches" literature of a particular interpretive community—are to be ignored. For the ideal *mujtahid* the only proper postures with respect to the *fiqh* literature are those of author and critical commentator. One thinks here of the work of Imam al-Murtaḍā, who wrote his own *fiqh* work, the *Flowers*, and then commented on it, and centuries later, that of Shawkānī, who, in addition to writing an extended commentary-cum-critique of his distinguished predecessor's *matn*, did the same.[81]

Such high-level interpreters were initiated and then matured in the *fiqh*. They began by internalizing its texts. Shawkānī, as I have noted, memorized the *Flowers* in his youth. In an important sense, however, the most accomplished jurists eventually left such formative texts behind in order to create their own. *Fiqh* was the "entryway," as al-ʿAnsī put it, and it also was the "end result," but for the great *mujtahid*s the initial and the final texts were not the same.

On this question of the status of the *fiqh* in the premodern disciplinary scheme I conclude by citing a view of the interpreter that is expressed elsewhere in the fifteenth-century *Commentary on the Flowers*. In the final chapter, which is on the rules that pertain to the imamate, a footnote/gloss is attached to the key condition that the imam be a *mujtahid*, a qualified interpreter.[82] The gloss states that "most of his knowledge"—that is, most of the knowledge required of the interpreting imam as a *mujtahid*—"is *fiqh*." This focus on *fiqh* is appropriate, the gloss continues, since the knowledge in question "pertains to the understanding of the licit and the illicit (*al-ḥalāl wa-l-ḥarām*)." Up in the main commentary text at this same point, following the term *mujtahid*, Ibn Miftāḥ adds, "in the religious sciences." In indicating what he means by this last formulation, Ibn Miftāḥ also characterizes the subject matter of the pre-text (seemingly including the digression). "Earlier," he writes, "in the *dībāja* of the book, an enumeration of the sciences of interpretation was provided."

The Follower

If this is the interpreter, then who is the *muqallid*?[83] In the strict sense presented thus far, the ideal "follower" is not the uneducated Muslim on the street but an educated individual who possesses basic competence in the "branches" literature. This individual is the ordinary jurist, the student of the *fiqh*, a scholar unprepared, however, for the highest levels of interpretation. Further along in the pre-text we read that the *muqallid* is the individual who "adheres" to a *madhhab*. "Adherence" (*iltizām*) itself, as the pre-text notes, requires considerable knowledge.[84] A threshold of competence in the *fiqh* permits the intellectual commitment that is at the heart of a relationship of *taqlīd*. In contrast, and by definition, in this juridical tradition and in those of the Sunnīs, an uneducated individual cannot formally associate with a *madhhab*.[85] A technical perspective on *taqlīd* thus is mainly at issue in the pre-text. In this sense, the discussion is located entirely within the world of jurisprudence and its expert practitioners. With the possible exception of an issue raised further along (again, see below), this discussion has little to do with commoners in need of guidance. It has nothing at all to do with individuals who asserted geopolitical identities employing superficial *madhhab* labels, as occurred in the highlands and in other historical Muslim societies. The social order implied thus is not the wider one of the few and the many but rather the much narrower hierarchy of roles based on interpretive authority among the specialists in the sharīʿa. The targeted individual of the pre-text is this *muqallid*, the non-*mujtahid* jurist, who, likewise, is the intended reader, as a student or as a teacher, of the immediately following text of the *Flowers*.

While this five sciences view stresses an attainability, an overall reasonableness and practicality concerning the requisite knowledge for engaging in interpretation, the ideal interpreter at the same time emerges as an impossible figure, or nearly so. The great "independent" or "unlimited" *mujtahids*—the discourse-setting interpreters of the caliber of Imam al-Murtaḍā or Shawkānī—were very few in number.[86] In addition to these rare and indispensable talents, Muslim societies also required jurists prepared to offer more mundane and readily available forms of interpretation. In the highlands and elsewhere, commoners in search of routine sharīʿa guidance made decisions to approach particular scholars for their opinions, and we shall see that this, too, is modeled in the pre-text. The giving of guidance as an everyday occupation would be the task of a local community's most respected scholar. Assuming the role of muftī, these *muqallid* jurists offered opinions within the frames of reference established by the particular *madhhab* of their training.[87] Despite their reputation for an unwavering valuing of *ijtihad*, the Zaydī Hadawīs also acknowledged *taqlid* and detailed its circumstances, and in this respect at least appear very much like their fellow jurists in the Sunnī *madhhabs*.

Within the larger divine to human continuum, in which the sharīʿa scholars, the muftīs and other *mujtahids*, were considered the mediating "heirs" of the prophets (according to a famous *ḥadīth*), we find a further, more detailed ranking. Everyday acts of opinion giving should be thought of not as dyads but rather as interpretive triads—of questioner, *muqallid*, and *mujtahid*. The middle role was that of the respondent with respect to the questioner and, at the same time, a "follower" with respect to the *mujtahid*. While socially vital and therefore honored, was this middle position also inevitably marked, beyond the wider awe of the divinity, by a particular anxiety of knowledge lodged in these human relations of interpretation?

Cosmopolitantism

I have characterized library works as cosmopolitan in a pre-modern and non-western sense, as texts that were discursively transportable, that "thought" beyond local frames of reference. Yet I also identified the reciprocal problem of their localization, their adaptation to and application in particular settings. Part of this phenomenon concerns the archive, and is discussed later, but the other part concerns the discursive world of the madrasa and interpretive communities. Based on the foregoing survey of the five sciences and the specific books set for the formation of the Zaydī jurist, some further observations are necessary. Jurisprudence itself and the wider fields of the sharīʿa sciences together demonstrate that part of the technical knowledge that came to be adopted locally had non-local origins.

Beyond the paradigmatic, everywhere-local and everywhere-present qualities of the Qurʾan and Sunna, the two "sources" whose advent and existence indexed those of Islam itself, a further range of the knowledge considered local was articulated in region-specific *madhhabs*. But these interpretive communities also thought across discursive schools and geographic boundaries. In addition to their internal deliberations, *madhhab* scholars commonly related to (and also theorized relating to) the texts of other similarly constituted interpretive communities.[88] While each school of interpretation necessarily focused primarily on its own authoritative "branches" *fiqh* books—the *Flowers* literature, for example, in the case of the Zaydīs—*madhhab* thought commonly also sampled the thought of the neighboring schools. Such inter-*madhhab* readings were not confined to the specialized literature on points of doctrinal "differences" (*ikhtilāf*). For the Zaydīs, rather than the other schools of Shīʿī jurisprudence, the further scholarly communities addressed in the wider vision of their juridical project started with the leading jurists of the four Sunnī *madhhabs*. The character of this long-standing cross-*madhhab* address within the Zaydī school is concretely evidenced in the patterns of the conventional symbols (*rumūz*) for jurists' names and a few book titles that were regularly cited in their doctrinal literature (see chapter 1).

Other dimensions of what may be described as a historical form of cosmopolitan thought are reflected in the broader sharīʿa library of the Zaydī scholar. The discipline of *fiqh* aside, two patterns persisted in the twentieth-century curriculum of the Imam's Madrasa. One, mentioned at the beginning of this chapter, was the direct reliance by highland scholars on texts authored outside the highlands by individuals affiliated with the Sunnī intellectual traditions. The other was the reception of additional "outside" texts through highland works of commentary, gloss, annotation, etc. In these two ways—that is, either through direct study and teaching, or through the further engagements of incorporative or responsive authorship—important non-highland texts were domesticated in the historical highlands. Texts that had been rendered local in these ways also were made present in the twentieth-century curriculum of the Imam's Madrasa. The examples given above are, by discipline: Ibn al-Ḥājib, and several others in language studies; Zamakhsharī in Qurʾan exegesis; the Six Mothers, including the *Sunan* of Abū Dāwūd, plus works such as that by Ibn Ḥajar, as commented on by Ibn al-Amīr, and Ibn Taymiyya, as commented on by Shawkānī, with, as a special exception, Mālik's *Muwaṭṭaʾ*, in *ḥadīth* studies; and, finally, Ibn al-Ḥājib again, who was read both directly and in Yemeni commentaries, plus, in the terminal year, Ibn Rushd, in connection with *uṣūl al-fiqh*.

A contrasting form of cosmopolitanism existed among the Zaydīs' immediate Sunnī interlocutors, the highland Shāfiʿīs, whose *madhhab* colleagues also flourished elsewhere in this corner of Arabia, notably just to the south and to the east, in the Hadramawt, from which a diaspora reached every shore of the Indian Ocean.[89] Unlike the Zaydīs, whose own doctrinal literature was largely native to the highlands (or received from the Caspian Zaydīs), for the local adherents of the Shāfiʿī *madhhab* the centers of textual gravity in the discipline of *fiqh* lay elsewhere. Beyond such key highland Shāfiʿī figures as al-ʿImrānī,[90] their authoritative basic texts were written by jurists from outside the highlands, specifically by men from Iraq (Abū Shujāʿ, d. 12th century), Syria (Nawawī, d. 1277), and Palestine (Ibn Raslān, d. 1440), and the same was true of the authoritative commentaries on these works. According to ʿAbd Allah al-Ḥibshī, the tireless Yemeni bibliographer who has compiled information on the numerous, now mostly forgotten works produced over the centuries by the local adherents of both schools, Yemeni Shāfiʿīs composed a versification of the "abridgment" by Abū Shujāʿ; some fifteen commentaries, glosses or annotations on Nawawī's *Minhāj*; and at least three works concerning the already-versified *Cream* by Ibn Raslān.[91] The *Cream*, as I have mentioned, also was the focus of a (now published, and edited by al-Ḥibshī) commentary by an Ibb jurist by the name of al-Muftī, who died in 1866.[92]

In addition, there were at least six works of Yemeni response to the important commentary on Nawawī's *Minhāj* by the Egyptian Ibn Ḥajar (d. 1567), including one by a jurist from Ibb.[93] In earlier centuries, local Shāfiʿīs paid close attention to two esteemed works of *fiqh* by the great al-Shirāzī (d. 1083). Yemeni students of the eras in question frequented the lesson circles of both Ibn Ḥajar in Cairo and al-Shirāzī in Baghdad. An Ibb jurist of the twelfth century used to say that "between him and the author [al-Shirāzī] were two men," which meant that he had been taught one of Shirāzī's works by the student of another Yemeni jurist who had studied with the master at the famous Niẓamiyya Madrasa.[94] According to bibliographer al-Ḥibshī, this book (the *Muhadhdhab*) was the focus of ten Yemeni works, while al-Shirāzī's equally renowned summary treatise (the *Tanbīh*) attracted sixteen highland receptions in various genres.

As in the past, local Shāfiʿīs in recent times also interacted with local Zaydīs, especially those of the "Sunnī" offshoot. As I discussed in the last chapter, the resident interpretive community of Ibb in the first half of the twentieth century was a mix of local Shāfiʿīs, some of them of distant Zaydī descent, and a number of recently appointed Zaydīs. Their interactions were particular to the highlands context, involving experiences not shared with communities of Shāfiʿīs in other lands, who had their own particular histories of *madhhab* interactions. In the early nineteenth century, the major "Sunnī" jurist al-Shawkānī taught in a number of locales in the Shāfiʿī districts of Lower Yemen. In the twentieth, as I have mentioned and will detail later, men from the Shāfiʿī-trained al-Ḥaddād lineage of Ibb were active commentators on the interpretive choices issued by imams Yahya and Ahmad, while another of the al-Ḥaddāds, a scholarly sharīʿa court secretary in the town and an occasional acting judge, wrote a book-length biography (*sīra*) of Imam Yahya. As I noted above, however, the fact that the then muftī and later court judge Ahmad bin Muhammad al-Ḥaddād was a reader of the *ḥadīth* treatise *Subul al-salām*, Ibn al-Amīr's commentary on a non-highland Sunnī work, was not an experience exclusive to the highland Shāfiʿīs.

"... Who Is Just"

To round out the profile of the interpreter, I return now to Imam al-Murtaḍā's pre-text (*Muqaddama*), specifically to the second part of the phrase "an interpreter who is just." To recapitulate, the "follower" should seek interpretive guidance from an individual who satisfies two conditions, being a *mujtahid* and being "just." This second condition prompts comments about justness (*ʿadāla*) in general and about how its existence in an individual may be ascertained. As I mentioned earlier, however, a contrary view on this issue held that "justness" was not strictly a condition for interpretation, although the "follower" nevertheless should endeavor to select a just person.[95] This same dissenting gloss, which also maintained that knowledge of the branches of the *fiqh* was not a condition, additionally identifies two further non-conditions of a social nature, namely being male and being free. At this juncture, in sum, the contested social issues related to interpretation concern the individual's justness, gender, and free as opposed to slave status.

In this discussion of the interpreter's justness, the practical needs of the ordinary Muslim seeking advice appear to be acknowledged. For such individuals, access to the law begins with finding an interpreter. Whereas an interpreter's academic qualifications would prove difficult for an uneducated potential questioner to assess, justness was easier. Al-ʿAnsī opens with the view that the requisite justness in the potential interpreter is indicated by a religious conservatism summarized as God-fearing and virtuous, and that also avoids "[illicit] innovation." Al-ʿAnsī goes on to cite the view that while the justness of an imam who would head the Muslim community, or a judge, or a prospective witness, must be "verified," this higher standard is not applied to the interpreter. The approach to justness in an interpreter should instead be the lower standard for assessing the suitability of a potential imam to lead the prayer. This is defined as a record of the noncommission of the great sins and of noninclination toward the commission of the lesser ones. The related point is that for both the imam of prayer and the interpreter no formal examination of the individual's justness is required.

A more street-level or marketplace-type of approach to locating a suitable interpreter then is suggested. This solution builds on the simple but important fact that this form of sharīʿa interpretation had a social character anchored in popular acceptance. The interpretive activity in question is that carried out by a muftī and that takes the discursive form of a fatwā. In this context, the "follower" (*muqallid*) is equated with the "questioner" (*mustaftī*),[96] and the interpretive relation reverts to a more popular type of dyad. Al-ʿAnsī writes, concerning this second condition of justness,

> Sufficient for one who wants to practice *taqlīd* and is uncertain as to the quality of the individual with whom he seeks to engage in *taqlīd*, with respect to knowledge of [this potential interpreter's] suitability, is that he look at his activity

> (*intisāb*),[97] that is, the activity of this scholar in the giving of fatwas, such that he sees people "taking [fatwās]" from him. This is a method for probability [as opposed to certainty] regarding his suitability.[98]

Beyond the interpreter's recognized activity, a further contextual guarantee and an additional basis for probability regarding the interpreter's justness concerns a muftī active in a polity presided over by a legitimate imam. In basing one's decision to approach an interpreter on that individual's social reputation as a muftī, it is also probable that one will avoid encountering and following an interpreter who holds dangerously wrong views. Technical terms exist for such interpreters, and the commentators also provide specific examples of groups advocating objectionable doctrinal perspectives.[99]

Next in the pre-text is a phrase that bears on the status of informed juridical opinions and on the significance of interpretative acts to the Muslim community. The phrase is, "every mujtahid is accurate (*muṣīb*)." In indicating that this formulation is the "most valid" Imam al-Murtaḍā acknowledges that there are other positions on the issue. According to Schacht, writing in an encyclopedia entry on the topic of "error," there are three such positions.[100] The widely held different position is that where there are opposed views, only one can be "right," which introduces the possibility of error. The second position is the one asserted in the pre-text. Schacht states that the view that every *mujtahid* is "right" is the Muʿtazilī position, which would include the Zaydīs. He notes it also was held by some of the most prominent Ḥanafīs and Shāfiʿīs. The third position, said to be a middle view, is that of Abū Hanīfa himself.

Translating *muṣīb* as "right" implies a zero-sum activity. In contrast, a translation such as "every *mujtahid* is accurate" shifts from the issue of right and wrong to that of the legitimacy and importance of a properly qualified act of interpretation. The commentators connect the idea that "every mujtahid is accurate" to the "will (*irāda*) of God Almighty" rather than to the status of the specific resulting opinion. The reference is to interpretive exertion by the suitably skilled jurist and to arriving at an opinion as to "the acceptance of a matter, or its forbiddance, or its recommended [status], or its permissibility."[101] When the competent interpreter "makes every effort to find the strongest signs that indicate the rule," such an exercise of *ijtihād*, in and of itself, represents the will of God.[102]

There were well-known divine rewards associated with engaging in sharīʿa interpretation, whether the outcome proved right or wrong. A formulation attributed to ʿAli, the apical Shīʿī authority, is quoted in a gloss to the *Commentary on the Flowers*: "if you carry out *ijtihād* and are right you receive ten rewards, and if you are wrong you receive five." Versions not attributed to ʿAli use the same proportions, "two rewards and one."[103] The historical consequence was a "plurality of opinion" in the sharīʿa, which Hallaq describes as its "defining feature par excellence."[104]

Three pieces of advice then are given to the prospective "follower" who seeks a suitable interpreter. The first two of these involve opposed categories. Referring to possible interpreters, the first is phrased: "the living is more suitable than the dead."[105] Where a "living" interpreter, a muftī, a person to "take [a fatwā] from" and to otherwise "follow," could be located using the just-discussed socially available information about that individual's activity, reliance on a dead interpreter necessitated the mediation of a written text. The *taqlīd* of a deceased *mujtahid* thus was a literary act. Shawkānī remarked, however, that the basic idea regarding sharīʿa knowledge was "not simply to preserve it in the bodies of pages and registers but rather to have actual individuals available to represent it to the people at all times and in every necessity."[106] Presumably, a living interpreter would be more attuned to the concrete circumstances of the questioner's time and place. But at the same time, those who gave opinions often would be transmitting rules that had been established in their *madhhab* by generations of deceased jurists.

An interesting sub-point in this discussion states that the preference for the living over the dead presumes that the interpreters in question are equal as regards their knowledge (*ʿilm*) and their piety (*waraʿ*). This distinction then becomes the basis for the second bit of advice—that is, a preference for "the most learned over the most pious." The explanation given for this trumping principle is that, as opposed to the qualification or the motivation of piety, the more technically knowledgeable individual "is better guided to the truth (*al-ḥaqq*) and better informed in the attainment of the indications (*adilla*) and in their demonstration (*istiẓhār*)."

The third piece of advice takes us into conceptual terrain particular to the Zaydīs. An opposing category is not named in stating a preference, among deceased interpreters, for following "the famous imams of *ahl al-bayt*." The imams in question are specifically the "people of the house"—that is, the lineal descendants of the Prophet. The major recognized interpreters among these descendants of the Prophet are said to be notable for the "completeness of their *ijtihād* and their justness." According to the commentators, these distinguished descendant imams divide into those who arose and claimed the imamate, the leadership of the Islamic polity, such as Imam al-Hādī (d. 911) and Imam al-Qasim (d. 1620), and those who did not. Al-Murtaḍā, who is of this lineage and who also served, very briefly, as a ruling imam, writes that following these imams is "more suitable." The commentators add that this preference for such particular interpreters is justified by the "closeness of their descent to the Prophet of God"; by certain *ḥadīths* concerning the *ahl al-bayt*; by the widely accepted sense of the validness of these imams' beliefs; and by their unblemished character.

As with the earlier-mentioned use of abbreviations for citations of the key figures of Sunnī juridical thought, a larger set of conventional symbols—from Zayd bin ʿAli (*z*), to al-Hādī (*h*), to *Flowers* author al-Murtaḍā (*taḍā*)—indexed the frequency and the citational significance of these jurist-imams of the *ahl al-bayt* in Zaydī doctrinal discussions. In chapter 5, I read a nineteenth-century Zaydī analysis that illustrates this foregrounding of the views of imams representing the *ahl al-bayt*. A closely related ideology of righteous rule was continuous into the twentieth century.[107]

THREE

Commentaries

"Write It Down"

HOW DID the late imamic-period library, specifically the *Flowers* literature law books and commentaries, conceive of the archive? How did this elevated category of written juridical expression address the ordinary types of sharīʿa writings? In this chapter I string together selections from several standard doctrinal chapters as elements of a formally stated set of ideas, or ideology, concerning archival writing. Referring to the various archival genres, this doctrinal thought consisted of concepts and associated minor institutions, and it is marked by differences of opinion among the jurists.

Informing these technical discussions was the jurists' preoccupation with the perils of meaning and evidential truth in written form. Later, I consider materials complementary to these dispersed law book treatments. In chapter 5, I read freestanding opinions focused on the question of "basing practice on writing," or, simply, "practice with writing," *al-ʿamal bi-l-khaṭṭ*. Rather than the piecemeal approach of the law books, these opinions phrased the issues associated with archival writing in sustained and comprehensive terms. Complementary in a different sense are the colloquial accusations of falsification and forgery recorded in the archival transcripts of period litigation that I examine in chapter 8. This substratum of informal thought and popular sayings about texts indicates the existence of a grassroots counterpoint to the formal ideas of the jurists.

In discussing the *fiqh* selections, I illustrate in passing some characteristic forms of *madhhab* discourse—specifically, aspects of the text work of literary-juridical commentary. My interest in sharīʿa textuality at this juncture thus is double: I examine the form of an argument (in the law book nexus of *matn* and commentary genres) in order to understand an argument about a form (the archival document genre). Alternatively phrased, how did the meta-texts of the *fiqh* literature model the practical genres? In this discussion, library models figure both as ends, as textual types that are interesting in their own right, and also as a means, among others, for understanding the textual practices of the archive. Such literary modeling is differently motivated, however, than that found in the local "stipulations" (*shurūṭ*) treatise that I read alongside Ibb documents from the period (chapters 9, 10). Where the objective of a "stipulations" work was to present model document texts in a clause-by-clause format to provide guidance for notarial writers, the variety of doctrinal thought I survey in this chapter was concerned not with the drafting of instruments but with the conceptualization of their evidence value.

Before addressing the law book formulations, I first consider a key passage from the Qurʾan, *Sūra* 2, verses 282–83. This historically and discursively prior "source" text on the question launched an institution of archival writing specific to the Islamic tradition. What was the relationship of this seventh-century template from the Qurʾan to the treatments of such writings in the later literature of the *fiqh*? I reflect first on the analyses of these verses carried out in locally studied works of *tafsīr*, the earlier-discussed specialized literature of Qurʾan exegesis. *Tafsīr*, again, is a kind of commentary. To elucidate the meanings and implications of the Qurʾan, the Muslim exegetes inventoried the verses phrase by phrase, and word by word, and they debated the vocalization of the consonantal text.

The jurists, in turn, drew on these specialized works. As I discussed in the last chapter, exegesis represented one of the five "sciences" to be mastered by the sharīʿa interpreter. Works in this separate field, notably those in the sub-literature devoted to the rule-bearing verses (*ayāt al-aḥkām*), together with lists of five hundred of these verses, were among the basic textual resources in the sharīʿa library. Here I read the treatment of 2:282–83 by Faqīh Yūsuf (d. 1429), the leading Zaydī exegete, and by al-Zamakhsharī, whose interregionally famous twelfth-century work also was on the curriculum at Imam Yahya's Madrasa. I refer as well to the nineteenth-century work in this discipline by Muhammad ʿAli al-Shawkānī.[1] Later, in chapter 5, I look closely at how passages from these specific Qurʾanic verses were deployed as proof texts in an extended opinion on the question of "practice with writing."

The general point in what follows—to restate a principle theme of this book—is to analyze a particular textual formation in terms of the relations that obtained between the different types of constituent writings. The step I take in this chapter focuses on one side of the equation. I read formal conceptions about practical documents found in the Qurʾan and related *tafsīr* discussions and in the books and commentaries of the *fiqh* literature. This is to explore the contours of existing doctrinal thought about the evidential status of archival writings separately from the corpus of historical documents from the same period. The materials I present here thus foreshadow my discussion from the other side of the equation, that of twentieth-century archival usages, which is presented in the second half of this book.

Tafsīr

As the exegetes note, verse 282 of *sūra* 2 is the longest in the Qurʾan. Its opening lines mandate a form of documentation:

> O believers, when you contract a debt
> one upon another for a stated term,
> write it down, and let a writer
> write it down between you justly,
> and let not any writer refuse
> to write it down, as God taught him;
> so let him write, and let the debtor dictate . . .[2]

With other Muslim students of the Qurʾan, the Zaydī exegetes recognized that these lines convey a divine "order" (*amr*) concerning the writing of a document. The order is substantive and particular rather than abstract or general (e.g., "contracts, or transactions must be placed in written form," etc.). It refers to a single type of undertaking and an associated sub-genre. As Faqīh Yūsuf notes, the exegetes also identified two other orders in these opening lines. Thus, in addition to the mandate for the transacting parties to have the appropriate document prepared, they identified a second order to the writer to write, and a third to the debtor in the transaction to "dictate" the terms. Concerning this repetition of the order to write, Faqīh Yūsuf comments: "This was due to the fact that the written document among them in the era of the Prophet of God was a rarity, and so He [God] confirmed the order."[3]

A later passage in the same verse connects this form of writing and the role of the writer to witnessing and the role of the witness, and it includes a significant gender distinction. This further divine order states, "[A]nd call into witness two witnesses, men; or if the two be not men, then one man and two women." Later still, the verse provides a set of rationales for this type of archival writing. The indicated practice of having a document written and witnessed is deemed "more equitable in God's sight." More specifically, the existence of such a document is described as "more upright for testimony" and will mean that it is "likelier that you will not be in doubt."

Normally, an explicit order in the Qurʾan translated into a requirement. Differences of opinion existed about the implications of these passages, however. In agreement with the majority of Qurʾan interpreters in other schools, the Zaydī exegetes reduced the force of the order connected with this institution of writing. Rather than "required," they qualified it as "recommended," or "advisory."[4] How might we understand the exegetes' hesitation in this instance?

As an aside, let me note the very different take on this verse by the author of the local "stipulations" (*shurūṭ*) treatise, the work examined in chapters 9 and 10. In the first place, al-Iryānī (d. 1905) reads the divine "order" to write as a clear-cut requirement. In the second, while the exegetes reflected on the general import of this order for purposes of application, the "stipulations" writers analogized. Thus al-Iryānī states, "It is known that God Almighty textually specified in the precision (*muḥkam*) of his Book the requirement (*wujūb*) of writing down debts." And then, indexing the topical coverage in his treatise for notarial writers, he states, "[T]his was extended by analogy to the other types of transactions."[5]

The open disagreement among the exegetes over 2:282–83, in contrast, sheds light on the textual transition from a divine order to an applicable rule, and on the role of human interpretive agency with respect to the sacred text. This is not the common type of exegetical situation in which the meaning of a passage is open or uncertain, leading to the presentation and assessment of alternative possibilities. Nor is this one of the recognized "ambiguous" verses of the Qurʾan, which might necessitate an allegorical or metaphorical reading.[6] In 2:282–83, the meaning appears straightforward, and a different sort of engagement takes place. The upshot is a highlighting of the distinction, normally collapsed and unproblematic, between a divine order (*amr*) and an applicable rule (*ḥukm*).

This awareness also complicates our understanding of the rule-bearing verses. As I pointed out in the previous chapter, after the basic interpretive work of identifying the appropriate "indication" for a given case (*masʾala*) in the "source" text, the rule had to be materially extracted from the language of the verse so that it could be quoted or glossed in an applicable fashion. Beyond this movement from the isolation of a discrete "order" to the extraction and articulation of the associated "rule," we now see the possibility of an additional interpretive act. We see that the resulting rule could be subject to further specification, notably including, as in this instance, a qualification and reduction in its status for application. Such human exegetical interventions not only led to the worldly modulation of the sharīʿa rule but also appeared to reach into the realm of divine authority and intention.

Beyond what the contested reception of 2:282–83 may directly or indirectly indicate about perceived problems associated with archival writing, these complex verses also open the way to other types of analytic readings relevant to the study of sharīʿa texts. One concerns recurrent textual structures, or what I think of as minor institutions. The main example in these lines is that translated as "dictation," which is at the crux of the third of the mentioned divine "orders" identified in these opening lines, and which refers to a basic means for the authoritative oral production of a text. In passing, the exegetes remark that the Qurʾan uses words from two different Arabic "dialects" to convey the same meaning of "dictation," which grounds this minor discursive institution in the linguistic specificities of the Arab past.[7] For my analytic purposes, the transition from "dictation" to document envisioned in these lines may be related to several other types of "dictation" that figure in the larger textual formation, as well as to further types of authoritative linkages and transitions between oral and written texts. As I discuss in the section below on *fiqh*, the jurists adopted the kindred technique of an "oral reading" for use in presenting written documents as evidence in court.

Dictation also is associated with the activity of witnessing. Linked together, the two exemplify an authoritative form of oral-aural transmission.

The wider models for this sort of authority include the transmission of the Qurʾan to the Prophet, and that of teacher to student. Here, however, a single speaker communicates with two types of listeners. As a consequence, a unitary dictation leads to differing outcomes. Uttered by the dictating party to the contract, here the debtor, the spoken terms are heard—that is, perceived and then retained in the memories of the listening witnesses. Shawkānī states that what the witnesses witness is the "acknowledgment" (*iqrār*) of the debt as conveyed in the party's dictation.[8] The witnesses "carry," as the evidence doctrine has it, what they hear, and this consists of the "same" text that the party dictated. Meanwhile, the writer, to whom the dictation is directed, also is listening. The writer thus hears this "same" text. But he then converts it into the requisite stipulations, the formally expressed paper language of a proper sharīʿa instrument. This form of "dictation" thus leads both to the (more or less complete) retention of the dictated text in memory and to the inscription of a transformed version in writing. The former is taken to be a form of "knowledge" and therefore is suitable as evidence and may be reproduced as testimony in court. The latter, the evidential status of which may be suspect, nevertheless also could find its way into court. The differing material authorities framed are those of authentic but fleeting speech and questionably authentic but more permanent writing.

Another type of wider reading strategy suggested by these verses would attend to the related textual temporalities, and on this I would make three interconnected points. The first is to observe that time is built into the foundation of this divinely ordered archival writing. The debt transaction that is the substantive focus of the verse is meant to comprise, in the language of the Qurʾan, a "stated term."[9] The exegetes differed, however, about how the duration and due date of the debt agreement should be expressed. Among the possibilities were statements such as at the "harvest," or at the "return of the pilgrims [from Mecca]," which, although they might have the authority of custom, were rejected by most jurists.[10] The majority preferred the precision of a specific number of days, months, or years. Since debt agreements foreground the relation of time and money, at least one interpreter thought the verse actually applied to the *salam*, the licit future delivery contract. At the same time, the discussion in 2:282–83 stands in contrast to the ban on illicit "interest" (*ribā*), another time and money institution, which, as the exegetes remark, is treated in the just prior verses. The strong "economic" undercurrent in these verses also includes the situation of traveling parties who are unable find a notarial writer, for whom the solution provided in 2:283 is a pledge (*rahn*), still another type of financial relation over time. Finally, the marked association of temporality and writing is confirmed negatively: 2:282 states that the exception to the otherwise mandated documentation is that of "present trade" (*tijāra ḥāḍira*)—that is, a face-to-face transaction concluded in the moment, which need not be placed in writing.

Second, the verses underscore the anticipated roles for the archive going forward. Among the rationales given in the Qurʾan is that of fending off doubt. In also mentioning a document's use in connection with testimony, the possibility of a conflict situation is envisioned. Among the related rationales that Shawkānī supplies is that a written instrument is "more defensible in dispute and more decisive in conflict."[11] But for subsequent trouble to be remedied by the existence of an earlier written document implies both an initial preservation and a subsequent retrieval of the text in question, that is, both a form of archivization and a later activation, or what de Certeau referred to as an "actualization."[12] Separated by an interval of time, distinct varieties of witnessing and related evidential moments are indicated: the one associated with the act, agreement and writing; the other with the artifact, disagreement and reading.[13]

Third, in a summary sense, since the Qurʾan both recognized and regulated archival writing, the implied temporalities extend into the past and the future. The verses thus have the basic features of a model and therefore may be read dialectically. The 2:282–83 passage represents both a model *of* the documentary practices already in existence at the dawn of Islam and a model *for* this variety of practical writing in the new era of the Prophet's message. The verses thus index a prior and ongoing reality while also providing a legitimating template for times to come.

Referring to the writer simply as the *kātib*, verse 282 of *sūra* 2 further specifies that the individual in question must not refuse to write, must write "justly," and that, in so doing, will engage "what God taught him." Elaborating on this role, the exegetes outline an institution of notarial writing. Al-Zamakhsharī gives a "description" of a "trustworthy writer" (*kātib maʾmūn*): "In what he writes he writes with equality and circumspection; he does not exceed what it is required that he write, nor fall short. In it, the writer is a jurist knowledgeable about the stipulations (*shurūṭ*) such that his writing accords with the sharīʿa."[14] Shawkānī says much the same and continues that this writer "should not favor either of the parties. . . . There should not be in his heart or in his pen an indulgence (*hawāda*) for one of them to the disadvantage of the other."[15] Since the verse orders the debt contractors to choose a third party writer, one imagines a task similar to that of the questioner looking for a muftī (see chapter 2). Rather than attempting to assess scholarly credentials, the parties would be more apt to rely on an individual's locally established reputation for this type of writing. But in the sense that any qualified jurist could be suitable, it was not absolutely necessary to find a professional writer.

How might we understand the exegetes' reduction of the divine order from a requirement to a recommendation? Was there a relation between the resistance, or "aversion," to writing down the "source" texts of the Qurʾan and the *ḥadīth*, mentioned in the previous chapter, and the issues associated with ordinary documents and the archive, explored here? Faqīh Yūsuf makes the connection explicit when he mentions the "aversion to the writing of knowledge (*ʿilm*)" (i.e., Qurʾan and *ḥadīth*), as part of his explication of his position on the verses on archival writing.[16]

We may differentiate textual questions proper to the "sources" themselves from the authoritative views expressed in these same "sources" about archival texts. Unlike the relatively settled nature of the former questions—inasmuch as both the Qurʾan and the *ḥadīth* corpus took accepted book forms early on—those surrounding the latter involved intractable problems that continued to generate concern and debate down to the twentieth-century era of this study. Also, unlike the relatively unelaborated, if forceful, expressions of opposition to written forms in the early histories of the two "source" texts, the conceptualizations associated with archival writings were comparatively complex.

Faqīh Yūsuf, the leading exegete, and Imam al-Murtaḍā, the jurist-author of the *Flowers*, were contemporaries. What sort of interdisciplinarity existed between the scholars of *tafsīr* and their *madhhab* colleagues, the scholars of *fiqh*? In his pages on 2:282–83, Faqīh Yūsuf mentions the views of numerous jurists, including both the eponyms of Sunnī schools such as Mālik, Abū Ḥanīfa, and al-Shāfiʿī and also Zaydīs from Zayd bin ʿAli to al-Hādī and al-Manṣūr Billāh. He also indicates that certain positions were those of the *madhhab*. Just as Shawkānī, for example, wrote in the fields of both *tafsīr* and *fiqh*, so we know from the biography of Faqīh Yūsuf that students came to him to study "all of the sharīʿa sciences."[17] Shawkānī, as his biographer, refers to Faqīh Yūsuf as a "Zaydī" and as a "famous author." In addition to his respected book, *The Fruits* (*Al-Thamarāt*), on the exegesis of the rule-bearing Qurʾanic verses, which I have repeatedly cited, he also wrote in *fiqh*, and in such specialized fields as inheritance.

Fiqh

Relevant passages on the status of archival documents are dispersed in various chapters of the *Flowers* literature. In the following inventory, I group my selected readings under the rubrics of oral reading, memory, material trace, and expression, which approximate the jurists' categories. As might be expected, the most important and sustained treatment of the topic of writing occurs in the standard chapter on evidence. But as its title "Testimonies" (*shahādāt*) indicates, the emphasis throughout the chapter is on oral evidence produced by witnesses as testimony before the judge.[18]

As a feature of their expansive character, commentary chapters often open their topical presentations with mentions of the relevant "source" texts from the Qurʾan or the Sunna, or both, and relevant matters of consensus. In the fifteenth-century *Commentary on the Flowers* chapter "Testimonies," for example, there are initial references to a verse from the Qurʾan and to a *ḥadīth*. The cited text from the Qurʾan is from *sūra* 2:282, the lines that include the just discussed passages on writing. But only an excerpt from the phrase concerned with bearing witness ("and have two of your men act as witnesses") is quoted.[19] Al-ʿAnsī's somewhat abbreviated twentieth-century commentary chapter on "Testimonies" provides no such initial references to relevant "source" texts. I mention these simple facts to note a silence: neither commentary invokes the available and, in the case of the *Commentary on the Flowers*, textually adjacent mandates, namely the Qurʾan passages that require, or recommend, that the parties contracting a debt have a document prepared and that a writer write.

Oral Reading

Although written forms are acknowledged in al-ʿAnsī's chapter on "Testimonies," they remain hedged about with concerns and restrictions. The first passage I want to consider focuses on the relation of writing and speech. At issue is the dependence of written evidence on the normative form of oral testimony. The jurists permitted writings such as contract instruments prepared by notarial writers to enter the realm of court evidence, but only by means of accompanying testimony. In this juridical depiction of the court forum documentary evidence does not stand by itself.

Witnesses present at an original event, such as a contract session, could be summoned to appear in court to testify to the document's contents. As the important detailed feature of this institutional mechanism, these witnesses were required to "complete" their testimony by means of an "oral reading" (*qirāʾa*) of the document in question. Beyond the general resonance with the practice of Qurʾan "recitation," this *qirāʾa* construct also subtly links this courtroom plan for the introduction of documentary evidence to a basic instructional method of the madrasa lesson circle.[20] In an opinion discussed in chapter 5, this type of "oral reading" is interchangeable with an act of "dictation."

The relevant fragment from the *Flowers* on this mechanism appears embedded in the commentator's surrounding wording. (As noted, the printed text of al-ʿAnsī's commentary uses special parentheses to set off the *matn* text, and in the following examples I use italics.) Out of concise *Flowers* language (in italics) the commentator manufactures a list of ten types of testimony requiring "completion" (*takmīl*), of which the following is the seventh: "And, the seventh type: it is required that the witnesses complete their testimony about the document of *a will, or* [about] *the document of a judge to his counterpart, and like these*, such as transaction instruments, *by an oral reading*, by the maker of that [document] *to them* [the witnesses]."[21]

Concerned with ordinary legal documents such as a will or a contract, this "oral reading" of the text in question was to be carried out in court, typically by a third-party notarial writer. The reading was to be directed "to" the witnesses to the contract or disposition. According to al-ʿAnsī, in their eventual testimony the witnesses must be able to say, "[H]e [the notarial writer] read it aloud to us and we listened," or, the other way around, "[W]e read it aloud and he listened to our reading." According to this theory, to have evidential value archival writings first must be converted to, and checked in, the auditory medium of the court, this for the purpose of subsequent testimony as to the substantive contents.

This oralization method may be understood as the specifically juridical template for the "actualization" of an existing archival text. This involves a return from the stopped time of the archive to the in-time process of the court. In a temporal perspective, again, two different evidential moments are separated in time. The first is a witnessing act that occurred in the past, at the moment of the act of writing; the second, a form of testifying that occurs at some subsequent present, in a moment associated with a reading of the archival artifact. What draws the jurists' attention is the key underlying change regarding the transaction in question, which is from the uncontested to the contested. This change engages the rules of court evidence. It also triggers a juridical question about memory, discussed further below.

Ibb case records from the mid-twentieth century are replete with quoted excerpts from documents placed in evidence (chapter 8). Each such evidential presentation involved some form of actualization. These presentations also resulted in the admitted documents being written out once again, usually in excerpted form, for insertion in the ongoing minutes of the litigation. Added remarks in the minutes would cover any relevant authentications or other significant notes appearing on such documents. However, it was only when an opponent challenged a document presented in evidence that the mechanism of summoning the document writer and witnesses to testify occurred. We know from the court records that writers and witnesses in Ibb did testify to the authenticity of such "questioned documents."[22] But there are no explicit indications that they carried out the full doctrinal script that provided for the "completion" of testimony by means of an "oral reading," although this may have occurred. Here, as elsewhere in sharīʿa applications, we should not expect to find the reproduction of the stage directions that appear in the doctrine at the level of the archival performance.

The types of archival writings pointed to in this passage on "completed testimony" are standard unilateral instruments, such as wills and endowments, and the bilateral transaction documents, such as land transfer contracts. The quoted passage also mentions a further genre, however. The phrase, "or the document of a judge to his counterpart," refers to judge-to-judge communications.[23] In addition to this passing mention in the "Testimonies" chapter, the same topic is treated in the "Judgeship" *(al-qaḍāʾ)* chapter. Using the cross-referencing tool al-ʿAnsī installed in his twentieth-century commentary to enhance the internal ordering of his text and to enable a newly efficient form of study, the reader may note the section number (406) provided and elect to proceed to this other textual location.

Following this in-text reference—switching chapter and institutional frames from witnessing and evidence to the judgeship and procedure—the reader arrives at the second passage I want to consider.[24] In this new textual location we join a discussion that is, again, already in progress—here concerning the general topic of the judge's rulings against an absent party. The next point to be raised is the issue characterized in the *Flowers* as the "implementation of the judgment of other than him" (*tanfīdh ḥukm ghayrihi*)—that is, a judge's implementation of a ruling by another judge. The background assumptions here include the geographic distribution or mobility of litigants and the stationary quality of judges, inasmuch as they were appointed to specific territorial jurisdictions. The basic scenarios are two. One is that the other judge has completed the litigation proper, which consisted of hearing the claim and the response and, usually, a presentation of evidence, and then followed this process with his ruling in the case. The second is that the litigation process has been completed before the other judge but his judgment has not been issued. In either actuality, the basic aim is to avoid having to conduct the now completed litigation all over again, and at this juncture judge-to-judge writing intervenes. The dangers associated with writing in this context are equivalent to those in others, including forgery, etc.

Out of the discursive rudiments provided by the *Flowers* text, commentator al-ʿAnsī once again has created an itemized list, here of ten conditions. The first is that there must be a written communication from the other judge, and the second, that it is witnessed. The third provides for a reading of this written communication and provides a cross-reference back to the "Testimonies" chapter. This states that the first judge's writing is "read aloud to them [the witnesses] as previously given in the seventh type, section 378 of [the chapter on] Testimonies." Due to the constraints particular to the judge-to-judge genre, there are two differences in this instance of oral reading: (1) it involves what I have referred to as "mobile witnesses," individuals who are witnesses not to the case but to the document, and who accompany this text in its travels and attest to its authenticity; and (2) that the oral reading is carried out by the receiving judge and is addressed "to" these document witnesses.[25]

The proper detailing of the case in the first judge's letter is exemplified in a parenthetical model text al-ʿAnsī provides that uses the characteristic *fulān* discourse of the sharīʿa library. Thus the first judge should write: "Testimony has been presented against Fulān bin Fulān al-Fulānī that he unlawfully seized from Fulān bin Fulān al-Fulānī the house that is in Such and such district in Such and such location, bounded Such and such."[26]

Al-ʿAnsī describes the general textual situation here as "acting upon the document" (*al-ʿamal bi-l-kitāb*) of another judge.[27] Commenting on the same passage in the *Flowers* at the turn of the nineteenth century, Shawkānī associates the specific issues of judge-to-judge communications with the wider problem (*masʾala*) of "practice with writing" (*al-ʿamal b-ʾl-khaṭṭ*), the general framework for the jurists' preoccupation with the perils of meaning in written form.[28]

Memory

Rule 612. Writing Used to Refresh a Witness's Memory.

—*Federal Rules of Evidence* (United States)

Returning to the "Testimonies" chapter, and recalling my earlier discussion of the topic in the *tafsīr* works, the third doctrinal passage I want to address conceptualizes the relationship between the archive and memory.[29] Both the archive and memory index the passage of time. In ordinary Arabic, the processes of archivization and memorization share a vocabulary derived from the trilateral root *ḥ-f-ẓ*, which has the basic meaning of "to store, preserve, safeguard." To place or enter a document in an archive is terminologically equivalent to memorizing a text. But where retention in an archive and in memory could be analogous in ordinary language, in the tutored view of the law book distinctions were necessary.

In this connection, the Zaydī jurists consider the evidential value of what is contained in the judge's archive. Linking writing and memory, the late fourteenth-century *Flowers* asserts the primacy of the latter. The basic rule is that a judge must not act upon what he later finds in his archive "if he does not remember."[30] The full phrase is "and not on the basis of what he found in his archive if he does not remember." Using the emphatic word "only," al-ʿAnsī expands this language from the *matn* (in italics) to read as follows in his twentieth-century commentary: "*and* it is *not* permitted that a witness testify or that a judge rule only *on the basis of what he found in his archive (dīwān)*, among papers written in his handwriting and under his seal or signature, [whether in] a document (*sijill*) or other than it, *if he does not remember.*"[31]

Thus the old rule-bearing phrase is transported into the twentieth century. To do so al-ʿAnsī draws on prior commentaries, first, to specify that autograph writings are at issue and, second, to extend the applicability of the rule to the witness. He relies on, but in this instance does not copy, a similar passage in the fifteenth-century *Commentary on the Flowers*: "*and* it is *not* permitted for the judge to rule *on the basis of what he found in his archive*, written in his script and his seal, [whether in] a document (*sijill*) or court minutes (*maḥḍar*), *if he does not remember.*" Referring to the Zaydīs and to the eponyms of two of the Sunnī schools, fifteenth-century commentator Ibn Miftāḥ notes that "this is [the position of] our *madhhab*, and it is [also] the position of Abū Ḥanīfa, and al-Shāfiʿī."[32]

It is now common to translate the Arabic term *dīwān* as "archive."[33] In classical Arabic, *dīwān* generally meant either an official register or an office, without particular reference to the sharīʿa court.[34] In twentieth-century imamic Yemen, the *dīwān* was the highest-level administrative unit. In the Ottoman Empire, the sultan and other senior leaders operated with organs of the same name.[35] In Yemen, a circle of prominent men and talented younger scholars surrounded the imam as his secretaries, literally as his "writers" (*kuttāb*, sing. *kātib*). ʿAbd al-Qadir bin ʿAbd Allāh, later the presiding justice of the republican-era Supreme Court, for example, started his career as a young writer in the circle of Imam Yahya.[36] Governors, in Ibb and other provincial centers, functioned with similar small circles of local secretaries, as did the sharīʿa judge. There also were structural similarities between these groupings of administrative writers and the lesson circles of students that gathered around teachers.

A *dīwān* also referred to the everyday administrative workroom, located in an official's personal residence. The Sharīʿa Panel, which handled appeals, operated out of one of the sitting rooms in Imam Ahmad's residence in Taʿizz. Its seal, which was affixed to court documents, refers to its administrative location in the *dīwān* of the imam.[37] In provincial Ibb, *dīwān* was the colloquial name for a standard type of room in the larger, multistory stone houses. In the vertical orientations of such residences, the *dīwān* was located one flight of stairs up from the ground floor and the street-level storage area inside the main door, which usually stood open during the day.

Furnished in rough and minimal fashion for floor-level sitting, the *dīwān* was the semi-public afternoon space for everyday male gathering and *qat* chewing, the place where a landlord received agents and tenants and where the judge or the muftī received disputants, petitioners, and questioners.

To my knowledge, there was no colloquial term for "archive" in the highlands, at least not until very recent times when the French-derived *irshīf* was introduced. In the *Gilded Crown*, it is necessary to define the term *dīwān* for the reader, and al-ʿAnsī does so in a footnote. It is, he writes, "a site (*mawḍiʿ*) where the circumstances of the people (*aḥwāl al-nas̄*) are entered and recorded."[38] He continues that the word "refers to the register (*daftar*), and to its place, and to the book." This last, the *dīwān* as a book, as al-ʿAnsī explains, mainly or customarily refers to volumes of poetry.

His footnote also mentions related terms for court materials. Both *sijill* and *qimaṭr* (or *qimṭar*) appear in the main text of the old *Commentary on the Flowers* and are defined in its glosses, the former as "a piece of paper (*waraqa*) that is written upon" and the latter as "a container for papers." For his part, al-ʿAnsī defines *sijill* as "a document" (*kitāb*), although he must have known the standard Ottoman meaning of court "register." The word *qimaṭr* does not actually appear in al-ʿAnsī's commentary, but he defines it nevertheless, demonstrating his connection to the fifteenth-century commentary. *Maḥḍar*, the term for process notes or "court minutes," also is not found in al-ʿAnsī, but, as noted, it does appear in the *Commentary* and is defined there in a gloss.[39] The definition provided takes the form of a sample entry rendered in the impersonal *fulān*-language of library discourse: "the *maḥḍar* [is, for example], 'Fulān ibn Fulān and Fulān ibn Fulān appeared [from the same root, *ḥaḍara*] and thus and so happened.'" The term "seal" (*khatm*), which appears in al-ʿAnsī's main text but is not defined, also is the subject of a gloss in the earlier *Commentary*. This states that the judge applies his seal to clay or wax on a piece of paper "such that a trace of the seal is manifest." Also according to this gloss, this usage was a practice of the Prophet Muhammad. The same gloss continues that "as for the custom of the people at this time [the fifteenth century], the seal is simply that the judge places his signature (*ʿalāma*) on the judgment paper."[40] In the twentieth century, to the extent that they were used, Yemeni seals were inked.

Among the intervening commentators on the *Flowers* passage "if he does not remember," al-Jalāl (d. 1673) affirms the basic rule and adds the possibility that the archival document in question may have been written by the judge's secretary, his *kātib*.[41] But Shawkānī, a scathing critic of the formulations of the *Flowers* throughout his commentary, rejects the whole topic (in the "he said" / "I say" format):

> He [the author of the *Flowers*] said: "and not on the basis of what is found in his archive if he does not remember."
>
> I say: The Judge is charged with judging according to the rule (*ḥukm*) of God Almighty. And this must not occur except on the basis of acknowledgment, testimony, or oath. How could it enter into the mind of one who would write a book [viz., the author of the *Flowers*] that he [viz., a judge] could judge on the basis of what he found in his archive without remembering the cause (*sabab*) for what he found? . . . What is the use of mentioning something like this?[42]

So much for an uncontested rule . . .

A fourth set of passages, also from the "Testimonies" chapter, further pursues the issue of writing and memory. They bring into play conceptual distinctions regarding the nature of memory. According to the exegetes, a basic rationale for the use of documents mandated in verse 2:282 was that they served to "re-inform the mind." The jurists understood that both a document writer and the witnesses to a document could forget some or all of what had happened, and they had analytic language for such eventualities. Employing a well-known conceptual pair that also underpinned many other types of analyses, al-ʿAnsī states that writers and witnesses might forget the precise "expression" (*lafẓ*), the detailed wording or terms of the contract, while retaining its gist, or general meaning (*maʿnā*).[43] He additionally discusses memory issues in the situation of giving testimony with reference to one's autograph documents held in a personal archive. Now using a different concept-pair, he states that the associated remembering need not be of the detail (*tafṣīl*) but only of the general (*jumla*).[44]

Memory issues also extend to the recognition of handwriting. "Customary now," al-ʿAnsī states, referring to the practice of his own time, "is that the judge or his secretary places his signature (*ʿalāma*) on what he writes." This signature should consist, he continues, of three features: "his name, the name of his father and his lineage (*nasab*) or agnomen (*laqab*)." With such a signature, the document may be relied on, provided the writer remembers its contents generally, even if the details are forgotten. But if the document is not remembered beyond the writer's simple recognition of his own script, neither reliance on it nor reference to it in testimony is permitted (cf. chapter 5).

Memory remains the concern at the end of the *Flowers* chapter "Testimonies," where "writing" (*khaṭṭ*) appears as, literally, the last word.[45] Al-ʿAnsī places a footnote at this location to indicate that this passage is the doctrinal site for Imam Yahya's intervention in an interpretive "choice," an opinion discussed in chapter 5. Earlier in the "Testimonies" chapter, writings remained securely buttressed with the spoken words of witnesses, but here at the end it is suggested that certain types of authoritative writings, in certain situations, might stand alone as evidence. Having introduced the concepts of detailed versus general memory, the jurists at this juncture present the all-too-human figure of the "forgetter," one of many such small analytic constructs.[46] This is the fallible witness whose failing may be redressed by reference to writing. I quote the chapter-concluding passage from the *Flowers* as prefaced by the lines of al-ʿAnsī's commentary. Again, it is the temporally determined situation of a witness to an earlier act, such as a contract, who now appears in court as a litigation witness. "The witness [in court], if his [prior] witnessing [act] is written in his writing or in the writing of one trusted by a judge, or other than him, but he forgets the detail of what he bore witness to on the matter, then *sufficient for the forgetter, where he knows the general but is in doubt about the detail, is writing*."[47]

Testimony in court, conveyed in the spoken words of present individuals, remains the emphasis. But predicated on the general memory of a prior legal act, questions of detail may be established by, as al-ʿAnsī goes on to say, the witness's "consulting of" (*rujūʿ ilā*, lit. "return to") a written text. Referring in this manner to a document that meets other requirements, such as bearing an upstanding third-party's recognized signature, a witness to a prior undertaking may testify, in the example given, to the details of a sale, such as the amounts, prices, and boundaries of the property in question. Using a further term for a "document" (*ṣakk*)—whence the English "check"—al-ʿAnsī notes that writings presented in court must be materially free of evidence of alterations, whether additions or deletions, and must not be blotted or effaced.[48]

With his coverage of the *Flowers* chapter completed, al-ʿAnsī goes on to conclude his commentary chapter with an excursus he takes from a gloss to the *Commentary on the Flowers*.[49] As the prime example of the sort of document that is in question, the jurists, both early and late, mention by its colloquial or customary name the Yemeni sale-purchase contract instrument, the *baṣīra*. As detailed in chapter 10, the *baṣīra* is the ubiquitous highland instrument for the sale and purchase of immovable, landed property, whether residential or agrarian. By virtue of being mentioned by these commentators, this common name for an essential document type entered into doctrinal discourse. Representing a rare instance of contingency in such library texts, this usage at the same time would be a potential locus for noncomprehension by cosmopolitan readers outside the highlands.

Speaking of this specific type of sale-purchase instrument, al-ʿAnsī states that if the document's witnesses and its writer are known for their "religious character and trustworthiness" (*diyāna wa-amāna*), then the document may be relied on in sharīʿa terms. This scenario immediately is qualified, however, with reference to the real-world situation in which the writer and the witnesses, the potential givers of testimony in subsequent litigation, are deceased. With the passage of time, as writers and witnesses either forget or die, a text is gradually, then decisively, deprived of the legitimation provided by human memory. When such a document has been held in a private archive, it is a matter of whether the individual presenting the document as evidence also has possession (*yad*) of the property in question or not. The first possibility is that "weak" is joined to "strong," as the evidence of the written document, although diminished in its evidential potential by the deaths of writer and witnesses, is joined to that of possession, one of the highest levels of support for a property claim. Together, they produce evidence that is stronger still. The second possibility is that "weak" is joined to "weak," as the documentary evidence is paired with the fact that the presenter does not have possession, resulting, in theory, in no evidential value at all.

Material Trace

For my fifth doctrinal passage I turn from "Testimonies" to another chapter of the *Flowers* tradition *fiqh* literature. "Repudiation" (*ṭalāq*), or unilateral divorce by a husband, may seem an unlikely topical location to expect to find thinking about the legal status of writing.[50] The jurists mainly envisioned spoken repudiation, but they also took the occasion to address the possibility of one in writing (*al-kitāba*). When they speak of writing here they consider it as a form with characteristics that are analytically prior to and apart from the specific content. As with spoken repudiation, the jurists' main concern in connection with writing is to establish the husband's intent to repudiate. In reflecting on the question of the authoritative registering of intent in the husband's autograph writing, they utilize a conception of a "trace" (*athār*) that they then connect to the different physical qualities of possible writing materials. For his part, Derrida approaches the connection between the archive and memory through the shared phenomenon of a (differently conceived) "trace," and he also examines what he terms differences of "impression." The archival trace, he writes, involves an "inscription . . . that leaves a mark at the surface or in the thickness of a substrate." As an aside, he asks what is known about "the history of substrates."[51]

Concerning the husband's expressing his intention to repudiate in written form, the jurists drew an analytic contrast between distinct kinds of writing, only one of which constitutes part of the sharīʿa archive. Although both types of writing are understood to involve a "trace," in only one does this remain manifest, and thus legible. The *Flowers* text refers to "inscribed writing" (*al-kitāba al-murtasima*), but in the commentator's hands this phrase is broken apart, such that "writing," which comes first in the Arabic word order, appears in the commentary text a few lines prior to "inscribed." The elaboration of the distinct types of writing is built around the commentator's discussion of this second word in the *Flowers* text.[52]

For it to be effectively authoritative, al-ʿAnsī states (the *Flowers* in italics), "it is necessary that the writing leave a trace which may be seen externally, and this does not occur unless it is *inscribed* writing, as in writings on paper, or boards, or stone, etc., on which the letters of the writing remain inscribed. [This could even include] writing with earth or flour, or upon them." Given such a writing by the husband, together with his intent (*niyya*), the divorce occurs. Equally recognized by these jurists as a type of "writing," but one that does not meet the criterion of leaving a legible inscription, is that which occurs "in the air, or on water, or stone, on a surface not manifesting the trace of the writing and which is impossible to read, either immediately or [because] the first part of a letter disappears before the second part is begun." With this type of writing the divorce does not occur, even if he intended it. Thus the possibility of a subsequent reading is the condition for a written act to figure as a part of the archive of sharīʿa practice. As Baber Johansen notes, the Ḥanafī jurists presented the same material dichotomy. In their terminology, the key factor is that the written trace remains "visible" (*mustabīn*).[53]

For different analytic purposes Derrida speaks of "separating the impression from the imprint."[54] In the Zaydī jurists' classification scheme and in their quick survey of the possible materialities, the analysis yields one act of writing in which an "impression" results in an artifact and another in which it does not. This last, which also is an act of writing, but one that takes the form of a "trace" without an "imprint," shares the ephemeral quality of an act of speech.

Expression

For my sixth and final law book reading, I consider a passage that develops a further distinction regarding writing. Remaining in the "Repudiation" chapter, just a few lines earlier in the same section on "inscribed writing," al-ʿAnsī connects the *Flowers* word "writing" to the concept of "indirect" or figurative expression.[55] *Kināya*, the *Flowers* term that is used here, appears in this discussion together with its conceptual pair, the term *ṣarīḥ*, which refers to "direct" or unambiguous expression. This further set of contrasting terms are better known as technical tools in the language sciences, but they also figure in the "tropology" of the higher-level "roots" literature of the *fiqh*.[56] In the language sciences, *kināya* refers to a specific figure of speech, metonymy, but in these "branches" legal contexts it refers to allusive or figurative language of several types, although metaphor is treated separately. Al-Jalāl, the seventeenth-century *Flowers* commentator, remarks, "[T]he intention in [the use of the term] *kināya* here [that is, in the *Flowers*, the text he is commenting on] is not the *kināya* of the science of rhetoric (*ʿilm al-bayān*)."[57] This less-specialized use of a technical term by the jurists illustrates their conceptual borrowing from the collateral disciplines of the language sciences, discussed in the preceding chapter. It also underscores the practically oriented nature of the linguistic tool kit employed by these lawyers of the *fiqh*.

The main application of this pair of concepts is to the analysis of spoken repudiation, with writing mentioned as an exception. The jurists explain that, as compared with its role in connection with many other types of legal acts, writing—that is, written documentation—in the context of repudiation is different. In repudiation, writing takes the form of unilateral expression (by the husband), whereas in the contractual domains, for example, it is connected with the complexities of bilateral expression. If the unilateral situation is that of the singly acting individual's proper or autograph writing, the bilateral is one of writing between the self and the other, in the space between two parties, which frequently involves a third-party notarial presence.

The jurists mainly were interested in questions of binding intent, which they considered easier to ascertain in unilateral as opposed to bilateral acts. In the context of repudiation, which is a unilateral act (and is similar in this respect to an oath), a written text is permitted to contain expression that is "indirect," or figurative, whereas in the bilateral contractual domain writing must be "direct." In his chapter on the bilateral contract of "Marriage" (*nikāḥ*), al-ʿAnsī explains the issue as follows: in the unilateral act of repudiation, it is permissible for an "*inscribed writing*" to contain "indirect" expression because it involves "expression between him [the writer] and his self (*nafs*)." By contrast, in bilateral acts such as marriage or sale, a written text must contain "direct" expression "since it is a contract between him and other than him."[58]

* * *

What do we learn from this survey of *Flowers*-tradition exegetical and law book thought concerning the humbler genres of legal writing? What do we learn about the related rule-making and model discourses? It is important, first, to note the great age of some of the key conceptions. Whereas the "source" text of Qurʾan 2:282–83 dates to the lifetime of the Prophet in the seventh century, the *fiqh* doctrines date back, at the least, to the late fourteenth-century *Flowers*. The repetition of many of the key concepts was a function not only of continuing debate but also of commentary, which carried key ideas of the *matn* forward, eventually into the twentieth century. While the interpretation of the divine "order" to write as a "recommendation" was relatively stable, the conceptions elaborated in the *fiqh* were subject to revision and restatement, and sometimes to outright challenge, as illustrated by Shawkānī's dismissive view of one conceptual point.

At this literary level, in addition to their elaboration of applicable models, rules, and stipulations, there was scope for wider exercises of the imagination, for hypothetical and logical explorations. Thus the jurists could conceive of a category of "writing" absent a visible trace. In these passages, as throughout the doctrine, the jurists refer to their own technical "usages" (*iṣṭilāḥāt*), which they contrast with the meanings of the same words in the standard "language," the *lugha*. But many of the terminologies, including the three mentioned pairs of opposed concepts—*lafẓ* and *maʿnā*, *tafṣīl* and *jumla*, *kināya* and *ṣarīḥ*—were conceptual crossovers shared with or adapted from other disciplines. In these selections we also found instances of the use of the generic "so-and-so" *fulān*-discourse that, in library works, stands in for references to particular persons and things. Mainly, however, we encountered a variety of generic role-terms—writer, judge, witness, husband—as well as the occasional lesser, analytic figure, such as the "forgetter."

What do we learn about the genres of sharīʿa application? These doctrinal passages certainly, if cautiously, recognize the existence and the potential significance of these diverse and routine writings. We learn that the jurists relied on the trusted oralizing, or recitational technique of "oral reading" to create a formal mechanism for the introduction of written documents as court evidence. We learn that they perceived a vital connection between memory and writing, and that this entailed primary versus derived authority. We learn, moreover, that memory has its limitations and different dimensions, and that these influence the possibility or the necessity of recourse to an associated written document. We additionally learn that these jurists contemplated the status of a document without the support of memory, whether of the writer or of the witnesses, but also that the value of this inherently "weak" form of evidence depended on the contextual features of the litigants' property relations. We learn that the jurists at one point recognized two distinct and opposed types of "writing" and used the concept of a "trace" to rule one out as a form of evidence. We learn, finally, that the jurists made practical, lawyerly use of technical semiotic conceptions of plain and figurative language to make distinctions regarding autograph as opposed to either bilateral or third-party notarial texts.

In these passages, writing is analyzed as a form apart from any specific content.[59] Rather than learning about such primary writings directly (the task, again, of chapters 9 and 10), what we have here instead are the components of a textual ideology. If a judge of the late imamic period sought to implement aspects of the thinking set forth in these law book scripts, would we find a sign of this aim in the texts he issued? Or would the result be similar to many other applications of doctrine, where, for example, a particular entry of recorded testimony did not necessitate a restating of the rules of evidence. May we assume, moreover, that despite the lack of an explicit citation in a work such as the twentieth-century *Gilded Crown*, the Qurʾanic injunction to write down the terms of a debt hovered over these literary discussions, even though the jurists may have understood this verse as only a "recommendation?" Might we additionally expect that such literary discussions were informed by the jurists' own day-to-day experiences with documents? Among the notarial writers in Ibb, some were madrasa-based teachers who conducted lesson circles in the mornings and then made themselves available to write contracts and other instruments in the afternoons. Among the documents these and other local writers prepared were *baṣīras*, the land sale instruments mentioned by name in the commentaries. We are left to wonder, however, whether a jurist somewhere in the Yemeni highlands actually encountered a "document" written in or with earth or flour, or whether a litigant in court had argued that he had written his repudiation of his wife in the air or on water?

FOUR

Opinions

ALTHOUGH BASED ON an ongoing process of literary accumulation, the temporality of the library also was manifested in a textual simultaneity, a co-presence of works of differing chronological ages. This available doctrinal corpus of sharīʿa texts—enacted and elaborated by teachers, students, and other scholars through the cloistered pursuits of reading, copy making, reciting, dictation, audition, memorization, debate, citation, etc.—also could be mobilized to respond to an emergent issue. The occasions for such responses were many and varied, including queries presented by individuals or problems raised by perplexing court cases. Directed in these situations toward the formulation of a new rule, or the rearticulation of an existing one, library discourse issued forth into the world in the form of an interpreter's opinion.

How did new sharīʿa rules arise?[1] Beyond the body of rules already in existence at a given point in time—that is, beyond the law "on the books" (discussed in chapter 3)—how were appropriate rules identified or newly established in response to the needs of ongoing human activity? This chapter considers the activities of two types of interpreters who functioned outside the confines of madrasa instruction, and who wrote in further specialized sharīʿa genres linked to the imamic-period library. These interpreters are the muftī and the imam, and their respective interpretive acts are the fatwā, a considered opinion, and the *ikhtiyār*, the ruling imam's doctrinal "choice." In institutional terms, the fatwā and the "choice" bridged the discursive categories of library and archive. As formal opinions, both genres adhered to the cosmopolitan discourse of the library, but inasmuch as they were issued in response to inquiries, their origins may be traced to the contingent circumstantiality of the archive. While bearing the discursive markings of the library, both genres offered mechanisms for addressing (in the fatwā) and adjudicating (in the choice) the practical affairs of the world. In fatwās, which were issued to individual questioners, muftīs ascertained or created rules in a nonbinding manner. In choices, ruling imams established binding rules meant to guide their appointed judges in deciding certain types of court cases. Set within institutionally specific relations of interpretation, writings in both genres were facts of power.

Whenever and wherever Muslim societies sought to adhere to the sharīʿa, the role of the interpreting muftī was integral to the scene, while over the course of ten centuries interpreting imams headed the distinctive Islamic polities of highland Yemen. In recent years, the work of muftīs has become better known, both to scholarship and in the popular press, but the figure of the actively interpreting (great) imam remains largely unknown, and this despite the dramatic new currency given the role (known by the term "caliph") in the ideologies of contemporary Islamists and extremists.

This chapter extends my account of library discourse. The understandings I pursue of the forms of worldly interpretation carried out by muftīs and imams are bracketed by the textual articulations of the sharīʿa rule discussed in the preceding and in later chapters. Behind us now are the literary jurists, with their patterns of authorship, position taking, and debate concerning doctrinal rules in the library discourse of the law book. Waiting in the wings are the judges, their court judgments, and the varied archival expressions and applications of the rule.

To properly locate the muftīship and the imamate as institutions of the new or rearticulated rule requires a sense of the complex textual forms of the existing law. Consistent with the overall focus of this book, however, my examination of these active interpreters and their rule-conveying genres emphasizes matters of textual form. Attention to the content side of rules—whether those existing "on the books" or the newly issued, procedural as well as substantive—must be the project of another study. It is useful, nevertheless, to offer a quick illustration of the scope of the existing rule content in the *fiqh*, since the highly specific rule material within a given juridical tradition placed constraints on the possibilities of the "new." "Sale," the fundamental bilateral transaction, is the title and topic of the longest of a total of twenty-eight chapters in *Flowers*-tradition law books. This chapter begins with sixteen conditions or stipulations (*shurūṭ*)—four dealing with the contracting parties, seven with the contract form, and five with the sale object—and each of these is subject to further considerations, qualifications, and exceptions. These basic stipulations represent merely the opening section of a lengthy discussion of numerous other rules pertaining to the many aspects, variations, and potential circumstances of this contract form.[2]

Regarding these institutional loci of rule production, some potential assumptions of western readers also may be anticipated. These expectations attach to the creation of law either by means of legislation or through the institution of case law and the formation of precedent. Regarding the latter, it might be assumed that the Muslim court judge likewise would play a key role in the creation of new rules. For a premodern Islamic setting, however, this would be misleading. Although judges were understood to be interpreters, their activity was not defined as rule creation. They might be better described as rule finders who applied the law. Although it may be argued that since every sharīʿa court case is different in its details the rule applied is always in a sense "new," this was not the existing conception. The significance of this comparative fact for the form of the sharīʿa court ruling is taken up in chapter 7. Its significance for the activity of Muslim interpreters other than the court judge is the task of the present chapter.

Here I compare the fatwā and the choice as textual forms. By extension, I analyze the specific interpretive roles of the highland muftī and the twentieth-century Zaydī imam. I also locate the lesser-known institution of the choice with respect to the wider spectrum of responses by a ruling imam. I then examine the receptions of the sets of choices issued by Imams Yahya (r. 1919–48) and Ahmad (r. 1948–62) by jurists in the interpretive communities of the two periods, including, in both instances, leading Shāfiʿī jurists from Ibb. Finally, the imam's intramural correspondence with active court judges provides important perspectives on the related interpretive labor, shedding light on both the issuance of new choices to adjudicate specific hard cases and on the later application of existing choices to similar cases. Together with an imam's personal involvement in the settlement of major conflicts, the institution of the doctrinal choice was central to imamic governance.

Interpretive acts by muftīs and imams represented important elements in this historical regime of the sharīʿa rule and its human agents. The "rule," or *ḥukm*, is encountered in a spectrum of textual sites. Closely associated with these textual locations are different locutions of the *qawl* ("word," "statement," "opinion"). In addition to these conceptions of the rule and the opinion, I continue to follow the ubiquitous third term, *masʾala* (pl. *masāʾil*), literally, again, a "question," and also a "matter," "issue," "problem," or "case," which likewise recurs at many levels of sharīʿa discourse (see chapter 2). In tracking this basic language of *ḥukm*, *qawl*, and *masʾala* I seek to understand how, through particular textual institutions of opinion giving, the imamic-period sharīʿa rule entered into dialogue with the local culture of the fact.

Fatwās and choices offered distinct channels for the ascent of new facts into relation with the rule-discourse of the *fiqh*. Viewed the other way around—since the process was dialectical—the same channels also enabled the descent of newly expressed or restated rules into everyday life situations. In this chapter, I am particularly interested in how, in the hands of a muftī or an imam, a given and undecided configuration of fact, a *masʾala*, acquired a rule through an interpretive act.

To address the textual movements involved, I explore the "stripping" hypothesis put forward by Wael Hallaq.[3] With specific reference to the textual shift from fatwā to law book doctrine, Hallaq examines how a factual issue posed and a response given by a muftī could be edited for placement as a discursive element in the legal literature. After presenting some suggested revisions to his analysis of "stripping" as applied to fatwās, I then extend the analysis to the genre of the imamic choice. I show how particular choices emerged out of the imam's engagement with court case materials. The implication of this extension of the stripping analysis is that while court judgments, as noted, did not constitute precedents in the western manner, their essential materials, their stripped facts and the associated rulings, could find their way into doctrinal discourse. The wider theme—also pursued in later chapters in connection with local instruments and the models provided in the period *shurūṭ* treatise—is to focus on how edited versions of writings that captured concrete local realities could be absorbed into the cosmopolitan library of the sharīʿa.

Sourcing

My ethnographic work on local fatwās in Ibb started with the Shāfiʿī scholar, Muftī Muhammad al-Wahhābī, whose activity in his afternoon sitting room I depicted at the opening of this book (figure 4.1).[4] In that early research I also interviewed Judge Ahmad al-Ḥaddād concerning his previous service as the town muftī during the imamic era. In his later years, the Zaydī scholar Muhammad al-Ghurbānī (d. 1991), the man who introduced me to the *Flowers* literature, moved to Ṣanʿāʾ to assume a new position and took up responding to listeners' questions for the national radio service, together with Muftī of the Republic Ahmad Zabāra and one or two others. While Zabāra's official position had only a symbolic or ceremonial place in the legal order of the nation-state, he still carried out the routine work of writing ordinary fatwās from his old city residence. Small children brought written queries up from the street to his sitting room and, later, his fatwā-answers could be retrieved from where he had them placed: in a slot in the stonework outside his front door. I photocopied some four hundred of al-Ghurbānī's broadcast fatwās, and I compared their modified discourse and topical coverage to the more traditional style and content of al-Wahhābī's fatwās in Ibb.[5] When al-Ghurbānī learned that I also was engaged in a general project on muftīs and fatwās,[6] he made me a present of a booklet by the Shāfiʿī jurist al-Nawawī (d. 1277) on *adab al-fatwā*, the etiquette or conceptual culture of the muftīship.[7] Returning to Ibb in 2008, I found that al-Ghurbānī's old friend and Ibb neighbor, Yahya al-ʿAnsī, a former judge and notarial writer I had known from the mid-1970s, had assumed the work of giving local fatwās (figure 4.2). Individuals with written questions approached him as he sat in a regular morning spot in front of a friend's shop.

I will not forget my last visit with Muftī al-Wahhābī, who died in 1993. He no longer came down to his second-floor sitting room to receive questions and give fatwās, and I had never before gone upstairs to the more private floors in his large old house. I found him up there sitting in a small room where a man cared for him. As I used to, I wrote out a question on a piece of notebook paper and gave it to him for a response. He took my pen and, as he used to, immediately commenced to write. But this time the paper did not move in his hands as he wrote. Instead, the letters piled up futilely in a blot of ink that, for me, marked the end of the old writing.

Figure 4.1 Mufti Muhammad Naji al-Wahhābī. Ibb, 1976.

Figure 4.2 Mufti Yahya bin Ahmad al-ʿAnsī. Ibb, 2008.

In the section below on the fatwā, I draw on ethnographic insights to pose retrospective questions about the textual practices of muftīs. Reliance on ethnography is especially important in connection with the routine type of local fatwā, as these ephemeral writings tend not to survive. For the pre-revolutionary period, I also consider the place of this widely known and essential Islamic institution of fatwā-giving in an interpretive environment structured by the active interventions of a *mujtahid* imam.

A particularly important objective of my later research trips was to obtain detailed lists of the choices issued by the two twentieth-century imams. In *The Calligraphic State* I took account of some important local connections concerning the imamic choices, notably the responses by Shāfiʿī jurists from the al-Ḥaddād line.[8] I also obtained the 1937 booklet printed in Ṣanʿāʾ of Abd Allāh al-Shamāḥī's versification of and commentary on a set of Imam Yahya's choices.[9] In addition, Rashād al-ʿAlīmī published a list of Imam Yahya's choices in an appendix to his book on legal traditionalism and modernism, while Bernard Haykel transcribed a list of

Imam Ahmad's choices in his doctoral thesis.[10] There also were republican-period inventories of such choices, but without attribution to the Ḥamīd al-Dīn imams.[11]

To augment these materials in hand, I turned to Zaydī jurists who had been active in the imamic era. Muhammad Yahya Muṭahhar, the former judge and modern law book author provided me with his personal list of Imam Yahya's choices. As an eighteen-year-old attending the madrasa in the northern town of Ṣaʿda, Muṭahhar wrote out the imam's choices in a tiny volume of miscellaneous texts that he carried in his breast pocket.[12] Since the little volume was so small and tightly bound, my photocopy of the two and a half pages came out poorly, but Muhammad kindly made me a fresh transcription (figure 4.3). He also asked the son of a former Sharīʿa Panel secretary to bring over an appellate register, and this turned out to have a copy of an individually issued choice by Imam Ahmad written on its inside cover. When I later showed Muhammad the photocopy I'd made of this solitary choice, he surprised me by crossing out some of the words to make corrections. As a consequence of this simple act on his part, a question gelled in my mind about the status of this type of authoritative language.

I obtained a text of Imam Ahmad's early choices from ʿAbd al-Qadir bin ʿAbd Allah, in Ṣanʿāʾ.[13] Years earlier, at the outset of my research, when he was serving as the Presiding Justice of the republican-era Supreme Court, ʿAbd al-Qadir had provided me with a letter of introduction to the authorities in Ibb. Decades before that, as a young man, he had been a "writer" (*kātib*) in the circle (*dīwān*) around Imam Yahya. I interviewed him about the role of such secretaries, especially in the important former system for responding to petitions (*shakāwā*, sing. *shakwā*).[14]

At my behest ʿAbd al-Qadir searched for and, a few weeks later, turned up what he described as some "marvels" (*ʿajāʾib*). These included the short manuscript of Imam Ahmad's thirteen original choices and also a versification of the choices by a jurist from the Red Sea coastal town of al-Ḥudayda. The manuscript of the choices also had interesting marginal notes and a few appended texts. The latter, concerning difficult court cases brought to the attention of the imam, figure centrally in my analysis of the choice as a genre. With these materials I am able to document the genesis of choices and examine the related process of textual "stripping."

Regarding the imamic opinions from the perspective of Ibb, my friend and occasional co-reader Dr. Muhammad Aziz recalled something his

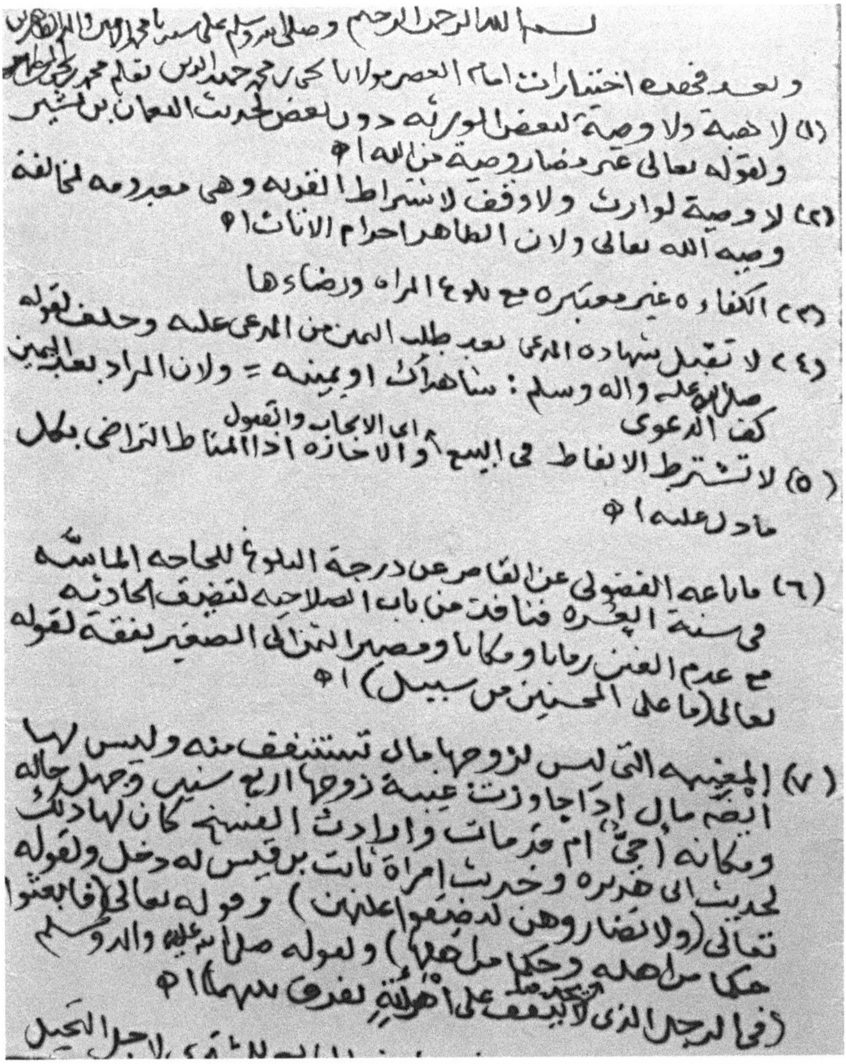

بسم الله الرحمن الرحيم وصلى الله وسلم على سيدنا محمد وآله الطاهرين

وبعد فهذه اختيارات امام العصر مولانا [illegible] يحيى بن محمد حميد الدين [illegible]

(١) لا هبة ولا وصية لبعض الورثة دون بعض لحديث النعمان بن بشير

ولقوله تعالى غير مضار وصية من الله اهـ

(٢) لا وصية لوارث ولا وقف لاشتراط القربة وهي معدومة لمخالفة

وصية الله تعالى ولان الظاهر احرام الاناث اهـ

(٣) الكفاءة غير معتبرة مع بلوغ المرأة ورضاها

(٤) لا تقبل شهادة المدعى بعد طلب اليمين من المدعى عليه وحلف لقوله

صلى الله عليه وآله وسلم: شاهداك او يمينه = ولان المراد بعد اليمين

كف الدعوى

اي الايجاب والقبول

(٥) لا تشترط الالفاظ في البيع والاجازة اذا انما [illegible] التراضي بكل

ما دل عليه اهـ

(٦) ما باعه الفضولي عن القاصر عن درجة البلوغ للحاجة الماسة

في سنة [illegible] فما [illegible] من باب الصلاحية لتضييق الحادثة

مع عدم الغبن زمانا ومكانا ومصير [illegible] الصغير بنفقة لقوله

تعالى (ما على المحسنين من سبيل) اهـ

(٧) المغيبة التي ليس لزوجها مال تستنفق منه وليس لها

ايضا مال اذا جاوزت غيبة زوجها اربع سنين وجهل حاله

ومكانه (حي) ام قد مات وارادت الفسخ كان لها ذلك

لحديث ابي هريرة وخبر امرأة ثابت بن قيس له دخل ولقوله

تعالى (ولا تضاروهن لتضيقوا عليهن) وقوله تعالى (فابعثوا

حكما من اهله وحكما من اهلها) ولقوله صلى الله عليه وآله وسلم

(في الرجل الذي لا ينفق على اهله يفرق بينهما) اهـ

[illegible] لا اجل التحيل

Figure 4.3 "Choices" (*Ikhtiyārāt*) of Imam Yahya (recopied by Muhammad Yahya Muṭahhar, Taʿizz).

grandmother used to say. When she wanted to tell a family member who was hurrying unnecessarily to "slow down," that there was "no need to rush," she would say, "The choices (*al-mukhtārāt*) have not yet flown."[15] What sorts of local knowledge and experience might have given rise to her metaphor? It seems this particular grandmother had reason to know whereof

Figure 4.4 Imam Ahmad Ḥamīd al-Dīn.

she spoke. As Muhammad remembers, and as my kinship materials collected from the al-Ḥaddād family also show, before her marriage to his grandfather, Sayyida bint Ahmad al-Burayhī had been married to Ahmad bin Muhammad al-Ḥaddād, the former Ibb muftī and the republican-era "Judge of Ibb." Pursuing her metaphor, we may ask, how did the imam's choices "fly"? When and how did they arrive in localities and circulate to the judges who were meant to apply them, not to mention to litigants and their savvy advocates (*wukalāʾ*, sing. *wakīl*)?

Fatwā

A fatwā is a considered sharīʿa opinion issued by a muftī. It takes the specific discursive form of an answer to a question. A venerable and distinctively Islamic genre of formal response, fatwās have been essential to the functioning of historical Muslim communities across time and place, and while heavily modified in modern media and institutional contexts, remain so to the present.[16] The fatwā is among the key genres, or textual vehicles, of the *qawl*, the juridical opinion. A typical question posed to a muftī asked, "What is your opinion (*mā qawlkum*)," and the muftī's response often began, "My opinion . . . " (lit. "I say," *aqūl*). In the spectrum of sharīʿa discourse, the fatwā hovered on the border between the contextless universal address of the juridical literature and the context-rich character of archival writings. Behind the interpretive act of the muftī was the textual universe of the "sources" and the *fiqh*; before it the (also textualized) facts of the world. Doctrine and circumstance, the cosmopolitan and the contingent, intersected in the fatwā genre.

The sharīʿa division of judicial labor between the roles of the judge and the muftī also informed the textual qualities of the fatwā. Unlike the situation before the judge, which involved two-party litigation that could terminate in an enforceable decision, the muftī received a single party and the resulting fatwā was nonbinding. Where the judge conducted an evidential proceeding, the muftī took the facts presented in the question as given. But where the judge's ruling was particular to the case at hand, the muftī's fatwā was generalizable. Court judgments were not reported or otherwise cited, while important fatwās could become part of the expanding doctrinal corpus of the law, as discussed below. In terms of substantive purview, while the judge was restricted to litigable and justiciable matters, which excluded the *ʿibādāt*, or ritual topics, the muftī was competent in all chapters of the *fiqh*.[17]

Only men could serve as judges, but either a man or a woman could act as a muftī. Among the conceptions behind this further distinction separating the two interpretive roles is the difference between the "private" qualities of a muftī's response to an individual questioner and the "public" nature of a lawsuit before the judge. According to Shawkānī, where the muftī's interpretive act pertained to a finding with respect to the law, the court judge had to make a determination not only of law but also of "justness." This last necessitated concrete circumstantial knowledge and an associated capacity, as he puts it, for "clear-sightedness in human affairs (*al-umūr*), and [for] the comprehension of their realities."[18] In this sense, the male requirement for the judgeship focused not on the typical woman's intelligence or her potential for scholarly capacities but rather on her different range of experience and resulting practical knowledge, the consequence of the sorts of gender segregation documented in Muslim societies. In particular, it was elite women of the era, those most apt to be educated, who were the most likely to remain secluded and to avoid everyday contacts in the marketplace and other "public" places. "Public" experience and practical knowledge figured differently in an institution that took presented facts as given versus one oriented to litigation to establish the facts.

In passing, the standard *fiqh* chapter on the judgeship and court procedure sets forth a doctrinal rule relevant to acting as a muftī. This states that it is forbidden (or, in other opinions, simply not permitted) for an individual to act as a judge after having previously acted in the same matter as a muftī. Al-ʿAnsī quotes the *Flowers*: "Among the acts forbidden for the judge is *a judgment after a fatwā* from him in that [same] matter (*masʾala*)."[19] While this rule underscores the basic division between the two key types of interpreters, it also envisions the possibility of the same individual acting in both capacities. The rule specifically holds that a jurist cannot later hear evidence and give a binding court judgment in a matter in which he has already given a nonbinding legal opinion—that is, a fatwā. The rationale provided is that issuing a court judgment after an earlier fatwā gives rise to a "suspicion" of partiality or favoritism, inasmuch as the jurist in question previously had "become involved" in one party's case. "Involvement" (*khawḍ*) by the judge with one litigant to the disadvantage of the other is prohibited.[20] In giving a fatwā, it is understood, the jurist in question had not examined the facts of the matter the way a judge who hears evidence would in a forum that requires the presence of the opposing litigant. Acting as a muftī, he gave a formal opinion as to the relevant law, and did so on the basis of the questioner's unexamined and uncontested rendition of the facts.[21]

Did the presence of a third major interpretive role—that of a qualified imam—complicate the standard Islamic institutional arrangement consisting of judges and muftīs? To be sure, Zaydī doctrine recognized that not all individuals who served as the legitimate heads of the Muslim polity were *mujtahids*. Thus the conceptual category of the "caretaker" imam, a purely temporal leader not qualified to interpret, and who could be appointed in the absence of a qualified interpreter.[22] Aside from this technical distinction, it also was recognized that some historical imams were not up to the task of interpretion. As I noted above, during the reigns of the three less-than-competent imams of the late eighteenth and early nineteenth centuries, the formidable Muhammad ʿAli al-Shawkānī, serving as the head judge, issued personal opinions and "became the ultimate legal reference in the imamate."[23]

However, with capable jurists as the incumbent imams—as in the first half of the twentieth century up to the Revolution of 1962—the field of action of regular muftīs and judges was altered. A qualified imam was a muftī and a judge writ large, a figure institutionally capable of issuing both fatwās and court judgments. (Below, I examine an instance of a ruling imam issuing a fatwā, and I contrast this type of imamic act with the issuance of a doctrinal choice.) A legitimate imam also appointed court judges and retained the right of final review of their judgments. Aside from this feature of interpretive hierarchy, an imam could, and the twentieth-century imams occasionally did, directly hear "first instance" court litigation. Commonly, however, as in two major Ibb disputes I have studied, the imams delegated or assigned the handling of difficult or important cases to experienced judges, but they also offered their own auspices for final settlements. In addition, it was technically possible for a ruling imam to be a litigant party in a lawsuit. This, in fact, happened during the rule of Imam Yahya, who, in the event, lost his case.[24]

In other historical settings, an important institutional link typically existed between fatwās and court judgments. The former were sought to provide technical doctrinal guidance regarding the legal issues at play in the latter. To cite just two examples of this well-known phenomenon, Haim Gerber describes his Ottoman sharīʿa court records as "replete" with fatwās, including those requested by judges and others sought by the parties, while in his studies of several centuries of North African and Andalusian fatwās collected by al-Wansharīsī (d. 1508), David Powers focuses on questions posed by judges in connection with difficult court cases.[25] In contrast, my early ethnographic observation was that there was no such direct connection between local fatwā-giving and court processes. While an individual contemplating legal action before the sharīʿa judge certainly might test the legal waters by means of a question posed to the Ibb muftī, fatwās obtained by the parties to a lawsuit were not cited in case records, and judges did not obtain fatwās as aids in reaching their decisions.[26]

That fatwās did not figure in the post-revolutionary republican sharīʿa court practice I observed is not surprising inasmuch as the muftīship had little legislative purchase in the modern legal order of the nation-state. But some of the republican judges I knew also had served in the imamic-era sharīʿa courts, and it was possible that the lack of a connection between fatwās and judges' rulings also represented a carryover from prior practice. Court records for the first half of the twentieth century are more conclusive on this issue. These case documents, which tend to be lengthy and detailed, do not cite fatwās, and I have found no other evidence of fatwās being presented by litigants or obtained by courts.

To what should this comparative difference be attributed? In my view, this lack of a direct connection between fatwās and court activity in the highland setting should be attributed to the presence of an interpreting imam, specifically to the existence of the imamic choices, which were intended to guide court judges in certain types of difficult cases (see below). As opposed to the frequently instanced horizontal interventions of muftīs in the court processes of a variety of types of historical Muslim polities, this sort of vertical interpretive role of a qualified jurist-imam has not been studied.[27]

Stripping

As a consequence of its compound and literally dialogic—answer-in-response-to-a-question—textual format, the fatwā institution straddles the realms of the library and the archive. In their fatwās, muftīs spoke of the law and its indications, but they were prompted to do so by the facts of particular worldly situations. In his discussion of how certain fatwās—that is, texts originally consisting of both questions and answers—later made their way either into specialized books of collected fatwās or into the pages of standard law books, Hallaq hypothesizes a process of textual "stripping."[28] In general terms, this transformative reproduction involved the removal from the original fatwā text of "a number of elements" that were not "necessary to" the new literary genres. Hallaq characterizes another such instance of stripping (see below, chapters 9 and 10) as "a drastic process of editing."[29] He also states that the stripping of a fatwā rendered the resulting new text "abstract." This was accomplished by the "omission" of a variety of "details" that would be found in the original, including certain formulas and phrases that marked the fatwā genre. At the end of the process, placed now in a new textual location, such as in a book of the "branches" literature of the *fiqh*, the stripped text appeared under headings such as the sub-genre rubric "*masʾala*." The process Hallaq identifies is one that involved a movement from genre to genre, specifically from "fatwā to *furūʿ*," and that entailed a form of quotation or citational reproduction, a rescripting marked by editing. Bakhtin might have described the overall process as one in which the law books "absorb and digest" fatwās.

For my suggested revision of Hallaq's analysis it is necessary to distinguish two moments of "stripping." The first occurred prior to the issuance of the fatwā, in the formulation of the question. "The questioner (*al-mustaftī*)," according to a general principle of Zaydī *fiqh*, "is the one who asks about the rule (*ḥukm*) of a current matter (*ḥāditha*)."[30] A presented question was an already "stripped" text. In the drafting of the question, personal names and other particulars typically were replaced by an abstract or generalized form of expression. A question thus referred, in hypothetical terms (although the questioner's motive should not be purely hypothetical), to "a man" or "a woman" (or, in Ottoman and alternative Zaydī usage, to standard names—Zayd and ʿAmr, and Hind for a woman) and to generically posed facts. In Ibb usage, the only remaining link to an actual person was the name entered below the question text as that of the "presenter." In the making of a question to be submitted to a muftī, a transition occurred from the discursive universe characteristic of the archive, which was preoccupied with proper names, specific locales and particular temporalities, to that of the "library," characterized by the use of *fulān* ("so-and-so") and its equivalents ("a man," etc.), a discourse devoid of actual names, times, and places.[31] This first moment of "stripping" contributed to masking how the concrete realities of human affairs made impacts on the law, the *fiqh*.

In substantive terms, the initial going-into-writing that occurred in the formulation of a question necessitated the "editing" of an unwritten worldly context for the purpose of the presentation. Facts, as Geertz reminded us, are made rather than simply given as such in reality.[32] The possibly cluttered and perhaps uncertain circumstances at issue had to be focused and framed—that is, composed—in the relatively concise and clarified substantive form of a query that could be responded to by a jurist. Questions also were motivated. I saw questioners redraft and resubmit their questions in an effort to achieve the desired response from a muftī. The "stripping" of unnecessary detail and specificity aside, a question typically posed a more or less interested identification of a factual matter as a legal problem. A question thus was based on a lay (or sometimes expert) construction of the facts, and it often referred, in colloquial (or sometimes technical) terms, to a named legal category or institution. In this sense, a question posed to a muftī already included an "interpretation," of both fact and law, although this was not recognized as such.

Question formulation, the scripting of a *masʾala*, represented the delimiting opening moment in the fatwā institution.[33] This constraining of the muftī's interpretive scope by the terms of a question may be compared across institutional settings to the different constraining of the judge by the initiating court claim (*daʿwā*). But, again, while the muftī accepted the questioner's representation of the facts for the purpose of the fatwā-answer, the court judge heard litigation over the facts as the basis for his decision.

The muftī's response to a given question completed this compound textual event. In Ibb, as I indicated at the outset, the two textual elements were joined together on the same piece of paper, as the fatwā response was written in the space left atop the question. Although all fatwās were by their genre nature generalizing, certain fatwās by certain muftīs—fatwās notable for their analytic significance and for the authority of the interpreter—could have an enduring importance. Some of these found their way either into fatwā collections or, as Hallaq argues, into law books—that is, into the "branches" literature of the *fiqh*. In the former situation the texts retained their identities as fatwās, and sometimes also included the questions posed, whereas in the latter the edited remains were relabeled as *masāʾil*, among other terms. In this second step in the process a further textual transformation occurred, one that may be understood as a shift of genre within the library, from freestanding opinion to book entry. Whether it merely extracted the gist of the fatwā or included its specific language of fact and rule, the authorial act of retrieval and reproduction in the new textual location in the law book required an additional form of "stripping." Carried out for such law book placements, this further textual act involved editing away the characteristic features of the fatwā genre itself, including the question, the formulas of the fatwā request, the qualifying remarks of the muftī prior to responding, etc. Combined with the first, this second moment of "stripping" was so effective that what had occurred, namely the reporting of question-generated fatwā material in the "branches" literature—had gone unnoticed until Hallaq's insightful analysis.

Local Fatwās

The interpretive work of a number of the great muftīs of Islam is known either from collections of their fatwās in book form or from the central records of the major public muftīships, such as the Ottoman Shaykh al-Islam. In contrast, since their fatwās left little or no documentary trace, the activities of the many unheralded muftīs who labored in the provinces, small towns, and neighborhoods remain largely unknown.[34] If the major opinions of the former may be understood as instances of interpretive lawmaking, the responses of the latter were mainly citational exercises in law finding. But even great muftīs issued routine fatwās. In the late eighteenth- and early nineteenth-century highlands, Shawkānī gave both significant and often lengthy fatwās, which remain extant in published and unpublished collections, and also ordinary and brief fatwās so numerous, he remarked, "they could never be counted."[35] For the twentieth century, I will give the example of an ordinary fatwā given by none other than Imam Yahya.

Elementary forms of the fatwā institution could be enacted without labels or fanfare. Taken as a mandate for the seeking and giving of fatwās, the Qurʾanic injunction to "ask those who know" envisioned interpretive relations based on a restricted social distribution of knowledge.[36] Any scholar (*ʿālim*) could be approached and would be obligated to respond. ʿAbd al-Karim al-Akwaʿ, the Ibb Endowments Office functionary introduced at the outset, a man with training in the *fiqh* but not known as a muftī, would answer when a neighbor came to him with a query. Even the humblest responses that resulted from such interactions replicated the basic profile of library discourse specific to the fatwā genre. Typically concerned with an unambiguous point of law, an unassuming fatwā remained an advisory opinion delivered by an individual approached for a response. Based on a more or less abstracted statement of a fact situation presented in the scripted form of a question, the response identified a relevant sharīʿa rule.

Among those identified as muftīs, Ahmad Muhammad al-Ḥaddād—the "Judge of Ibb" in later life—in the 1940s gave fatwās from the afternoon sitting room of his house, but he also could be approached when he was out in the mornings. "If anyone came up to us with a matter, we used to answer him in any place he found us, in the street or in any other place."[37] As noted, questioners in my day carried away the town muftī's written responses without any copies or records being left behind. Some routine fatwās were preserved in private hands, at least for the short term, as I have seen in a few instances. Dispersed in personal caches, such retained fatwās were bundled together with any other documents pertinent to the matter in question. The example I give later of a locally archived fatwā concerns a routine topic, but, again, the muftī was the ruling imam.

What was the technical status of the modest fatwā? This depended, in part, on the status of the issuing muftī. Sunnī jurists elaborated various hierarchies and typologies of muftīs, from the all-empowered "independent" or "unrestricted" interpreter to jurists of limited interpretive reach, including a type confined to reporting the established rules of a particular *madhhab* and another restricted in competence to particular chapters of the *fiqh*.[38] While the interpretive conduct of the highest-level muftī, the *mujtahid*, was a standard topic in their theoretical jurisprudence, the Zaydīs also countenanced a less-accomplished type of interpreter (see chapter 2). Another of the general principles of Zaydī *fiqh* legitimated the latter's interpretive agency. It begins, "fatwā-giving is permitted for the non-*mujtahid*. . . ."[39]

Among western students, the initial wave of interest in the muftīship was tied to the general issue of interpretive dynamism in the sharīʿa. Studies of leading muftīs and their major fatwās helped refute the colonial-era assumption that independent reasoning had ceased and that the doctrinal corpus therefore was "closed" at an early date. Recent work on muftīs, however, has inquired further into the range and variety of their interpretive acts. Ethnographic research, meanwhile, has pointed up the significance of the otherwise unnoticed type of mundane fatwā in the everyday life of Muslim societies. In connection with his study of the ordinary questions posed in person to Egyptian muftīs of the Fatwā Council of al-Azhar in Cairo, Hussein Agrama has advocated an "anthropology of the fatwā."[40]

In the absence of existing local distinctions, I compared al-Wahhābī's routine and spontaneously delivered Ibb fatwās to acts of "recitation"—that is, to a form of authoritative textual reproduction known from the madrasa setting. Rather than instances of full-blown *ijtihād*, such fatwās carried out the "creative matching of comprehended practice with an identified and then transmitted segment of existing text."[41] The categories of muftīs developed by Muslim interpretive communities identified the lowest type in similar terms, as a simple "transmitter or informant" (*rāwī* or *mukhbir*),[42] or as one who on the basis of textual acquisition through memorization (*al-iftāʾ biʾl-ḥifẓ*), another madrasa-based method, "reproduced earlier opinions on the same facts."[43] Concerning this last type of response, however, Hallaq wonders whether "they can properly be called fatwās." In his analysis and partial translation of the same *adab al-fatwā* treatise that al-Ghurbānī gave to me in Ibb, Norman Calder covers a total of eight grades of muftīs, the last three of which were deemed "deficient."[44] Calder later would distinguish between what he termed the "judicial fatwā" and the "basic fatwā."[45]

Ranging from reasoned arguments at the highest levels of discursive interchange to straightforward answers provided to the untutored, the fatwā genre was (and is) a remarkably flexible textual form essential to the localization of the sharīʿa. As I noted earlier, however, an analysis of unrecorded routine fatwās is impeded by the absence of extant sources. Had such sources existed for the period in question, my later ethnographic work suggests giving attention to two related features: a particular horizon of custom and a historically specific configuration of *madhhabs*. As for custom, questioners with a customary view or solution in mind approached the muftī of my day to learn the view of the sharīʿa. Traces of locally conventional understandings, marked and unmarked, thus found their way into many of the questions posed. Rather than explicitly noticing and rejecting the mentioned customary practices, the muftī instead usually indicated the correct practice according to the sharīʿa. At the same time, on certain topics, such as the amount of a dower or the level of child support, the muftī responded that the details of correct practice should be determined "according to custom" (*bi-ḥasab al-ʿurf*).

As for schools of jurisprudence, rarely did the questions posed in Ibb rise to a level of complexity that would engage doctrinal differences within or between *madhhabs*.[46] There were few topical differences between applied Zaydī and Shāfiʿī doctrine that might have figured in the concerns of the typical questioner, a well-known exception being the rules of preemption (*shufʿa*) in connection with sales of landed property. Despite the geopolitical differences summarized in the colloquial labels "Zaydī" and "Shāfiʿī," the jurists of both schools agreed that the "commoner has no school of law."[47]

In his position of giving fatwās as the town muftī of the 1940s, Ahmad al-Ḥaddād succeeded two of his uncles and his grandfather, Shāfiʿī jurists all.[48] With the advent of imamic rule in Ibb in 1919, several in the al-Ḥaddād lineage purposefully engaged with Zaydī *fiqh* and specific imamic doctrines, as I detail in the next section of this chapter. It also may be presumed that the Zaydī-trained jurists posted to Ibb also were asked to give fatwās. But did the discourse of the *Book of Flowers* find one of its limits of applicability in the local giving of mundane fatwās?

Choice

Authoritative interpretations given by qualified imams were fundamental to the highland system of rule. Given the active presence of such a great imam in these polities, the sharīʿa regime was oriented vertically. As I suggested at the outset of this book, the long career of these imamic polities in the highlands challenges assumptions about the status of the sharīʿa in historical Muslim states. While this vertical aspect of interpretive relations was the distinctive and contrasting feature of their system of rule, the Zaydī imams also represent a counterexample to a further general pattern of premodern Muslim leadership with respect to the sharīʿa. As Arabic speakers (and writers) the form of leadership by the imams of Yemen was different from the widespread pattern that joined a "Turco-Persianate political culture" to an "Arabicate legal tradition."[49]

From its advent in the ninth century CE, the resolution of disputes was a key rationale for the existence of this form of imamic governance. Choices delivered by imams helped regulate that part of the volume of the dispute traffic handled by sharīʿa court judges. Known formally as *ikhtiyārāt* (sing. *ikhtiyār*, lit. "choice"), and sometimes simply as "interpretations" (*ijtihādāt*), these concise personal doctrines were issued by both Imam Yahya (d. 1948) and Imam Ahmad (d. 1962). Collections of such imamic choices also are known from earlier centuries.[50]

Choices dealt with a finite number of substantive issues and were designed, in the twentieth century at least, to guide court judges in their rulings in these particular areas of the law. None of the legal topics was altogether new to sharīʿa doctrine—that is, to existing discussions in the *fiqh* literature.[51] A given choice often amounted to a selection of one of several existing alternative positions on a matter as the rule to be followed by court judges. As a mechanism for the expression of doctrinal preference, the *ikhtiyār* was known to Islamic legal usage beyond the important applied elaboration given to it by the Zaydī imams of Yemen.[52] As in other *madhhabs*, a conception from the same root referred to the doctrinal position "chosen" by an individual jurist, or by the school as a whole (*mukhtār al-madhhab*).

The twentieth-century choices I consider here, however, existed outside of the books of law as a separate textual form. Grouped together in a numbered list, the initial sets of twentieth-century choices were posted at the appellate court and circulated to the judiciary. As one of his innovations in the *Gilded Crown*, his printed commentary work, al-ʿAnsī employed footnotes to physically mark the interventions of Imam Yahya's choices with respect to the *Flowers* text.

Representing a limited sphere of personally issued rules in relation to the broader backdrop of Zaydī doctrine as the official school of law, choices were doctrinal acts. While such acts associated an imam with his juridical tradition and identified him as a jurist-leader, they mainly permitted him to regulate problems either endemic or emergent in his realm. Although always relatively few in number, an imam's choices indicated the specific domains of his doctrinal concerns. Both twentieth-century imams issued initial sets of choices upon accession to the imamate, and both later issued further individual choices. In his first recorded list, from about 1920, Imam Yahya's choices numbered thirteen; according to a list transcribed in 1930, he had issued fifteen; the tiny volume Muhammad Yahya Muṭahhar carried in his breast pocket gives twenty-five; and a 1934 list kept on hand at the Appeal Court records twenty-eight.[53] Imam Yahya also is known to have issued at least five more choices.[54] Beyond his original thirteen of 1949, Imam Ahmad also issued additional choices during the following decade of his rule.[55]

As I noted in chapter 2, a principle of interpretive theory held that "the living individual [i.e., interpreter] is given precedence over the dead." Did this principle extend to the interpretive work of imams in their choices? Did the new choices of the current imam replace those of the former ruler? Were the choices of the ruling Zaydī imams applicable only during the issuer's reign? I have not seen this specific question addressed by highland jurists, but certain topics, such as the dissolution (*faskh*) of a marriage contract by reason of the husband's absence (or other causes), were addressed in the choices of both father and son. Although the two imams generally agreed when their choices touched on the same topic, there also were different emphases and minor changes of position. Al-Muṭahhar, the Taʿizz-based judge of the late imamic period noted, generally, that "choices change according to what suits the era, but do not differ from the sharīʿa."[56]

The issuance of choices may be understood within the wider domain of imamic responses. A central activity of this form of rule, an imam's *ajwiba* (also *jawābāt*, *ijābāt*, sing. *jawāb*, lit. his "answers") took many forms, some of which occurred in named sub-genres. Broadest in scope and everyday significance as an instrument of rule was his routine work of replying to the large volume of written petitions, the earlier-mentioned *shakāwā* (sing. *shakwā*), an institution known in diverse historical political entities, notably including the Ottoman Empire as well as in post-revolutionary republican Yemen. In his service as one of Imam Yahya's secretaries, a youthful ʿAbd al-Qadir bin ʿAbd Allah handled part of this everyday work (see chapter 7).

Also among the forms of twentieth-century imamic responses was the occasional fatwā, although this specific activity is little known.[57] An imam-as-muftī represents a special type, as this giver of fatwās was the head of the polity. Carrying an efficacy unique to the genre, an imamic fatwā did not so much advise a potential litigant or guide a judge in his ruling as decisively decide and terminate a matter before litigation commenced. Al-Ghurbānī suggested to me that Imam Yahya's formal fatwā-giving activity was confined to the early years of his rule. If this is true, his giving of individualized opinions in the form of fatwās may have been largely superseded by his issuance of generalized opinions, his choices.

One such fatwā document, which was retained by the questioner-recipient, a resident of Ibb, is dated 1342 AH (1924), or six years after the end of the Ottoman Empire and the extension of Imam Yahya's rule to Lower Yemen.[58] The question text opens with a lengthy section of honorifics, beginning with a reference to the imam as the "general authority" (*al-marjiʿ al-ʿāmm*) in interpretation.[59] The main text utilizes the conventional formulas of the fatwā-request: *ma qawlkum*, "what is your opinion," and at the end, *aftūnā*, "give us a fatwā." The substantive matter is generically stated as concerning "a woman who made a legacy for the son of her brother," a routine topic. The fatwā itself is contained in the answer, the *jawāb*, which is written on the same question-bearing document, at the top to the left side and at an angle. Under a separate *Basmala*, and also under the circular, red-ink imamic seal bearing Imam Yahya's name and titles, this brief response text, like the question, is expressed in general terms. There is no naming of people or properties, no referencing of evidential texts, no specific dates, sums, or terms. The remaining link with the particular, the archival, is the questioner's name, which appears below the query. An added phrase (at the bottom) mentions the intermediacy of another individual who must have handled the physical delivery and the receipt at the imam's residence. The ultimate destination of this compound artifact, the place of deposit of this text bearing the calligraphic seal of the imam, was in a personal document cache in the provinces. Nothing is known about what prompted the question or what use was made of the response.

As genres of sharīʿa discourse, the fatwā and the choice were similar in some respects, but their differences are instructive. Fatwās and choices represent separate types of juristic responses to the concrete affairs of a particular society. As statements of sharīʿa rules, both were generalized and generalizable. They were issued in response to given fact situations, and they were applicable, in turn, to similar fact situations. Technically, for a given matter, a fatwā sought to determine the relevant indication (*dalīl*, or *ḥujja*) in the "source" texts of the law. A choice likewise was articulated with respect to such indications, and it usually also made a selection among preexisting doctrinal positions. In scale and formulation, many choices looked something like brief fatwās.

But where fatwās were generated, and also constrained, by the questions posed, choices emerged from a different type of institutional nexus, as I discuss below. When compiled in a list and circulated, the choices represented the imam's interpretive responses, not to particular queries but to general types of fact situations, to patterns of events or varieties of cases. Fatwās and choices also differed in substantive coverage. Choices addressed the topical area of the *muʿāmalāt*, the general category of the premodern justiciable, extending beyond the types of contracts and dispositions to include criminal and also procedural matters. Like the judge's judgment, with which it was linked in purpose, and unlike a muftī's fatwā, choices did not address the other major topical area, the non-justiciable *ʿibādāt*, or ritual matters.

While fatwās varied widely in scale, from single word answers such as "yes" or "no" to small treatises, and also in degrees of explicitness regarding the interpretive reasoning employed, most choices were brief texts, sometimes one-liners. They were compact statements of a rule, although of a distinctly premodern or pre-legislative sort. As in certain fatwās, some choices included a mention of a supporting "source" (*aṣl*) text—that is, a citation of Qurʾan or *ḥadīth*. As was also technically possible with a fatwā, the issuing imam could retract a choice, such as in an instance mentioned below.

As opposed to the nonbinding status of fatwās, choices were intended for enforcement, through the ruling of a judge in a court case. In his appointment letters, Imam Yayha ordered judges to make their rulings accord with the "texts of the scholars of the imamic school of law" and with "our well-known choices."[60] The imam's court "Instructions" (*taʿlīmāt*) of 1937 state that a judge's judgment must conform with the "texts stipulated by the imamic school, except in matters where there is a choice of the imam."[61] Court records from Ibb mention when a given case ruling by the judge is based on an imamic choice, using such language as "applying the honored choice of the imam of the age" (*ʿamalan bi-l-ikhtiyār al-sharīf li-imām al-ʿaṣr*). In some lawsuits, however, it was not the judge but litigants who invoked an imamic choice. Although choices took precedence over the existing doctrine "on the books," since they were relatively few in number and covered specific points of law, the background or default rule system applied in the courts remained that of the *fiqh*.

Lists of choices were kept at the Appeal Court.[62] An indication of how some of an imam's later issued choices were communicated to the judiciary is found in the note from 1960 written on the inside front cover of a register of the Sharīʿa Panel, the high judicial review organ.[63] The opening lines read: "Copy of an imamic choice from our master, Commander of the Faithful, may God strengthen him, sent by telegraph to his Honor the Judge of the Seat. This is its text." In the twentieth century, the choices sometimes "flew" by means of modern technology.

The lines that follow in this telegraphed copy show that choices were subject to review and revision: "From the Imam to the Judge of the Seat, the learned Qāḍī ʿAbd Allah b. ʿAli al-Yamānī, God protect him. After further consideration and examination of a previous choice . . ." The text goes on to revise a rule—specifically, number two of the original set of choices from 1949—concerning permissions from heirs in matters of legacies. It is unclear, however, if this retraction resulted from a query to the imam by Judge al-Yamānī. In the manuscript I obtained of Imam Ahmad's thirteen original choices, a marginal note added next to choice number two states, "This choice was retracted."

Choices and the Interpretive Community

When the twentieth-century imams made their initial sets of choices known, their efforts drew learned reactions from highland jurists of the period. One type of reaction was to restate the texts of the imam's choices in rhymed verse; another took the form of prose commentary. The first type, versification, was not at all exceptional in this intellectual culture. It was common across the sharīʿa genres as well as in key texts of the other academic disciplines. Among the Shāfiʿī school jurists of Ibb, the law book *The Cream*, a standard *matn*, was in verse. Excerpts of a jurist's *qaṣīda* poetry, which was different in genre from simple versification (*naẓm*), were a mainstay of the biographical literature.[64] In the legal instruments of the period one reads passages in rhymed prose (*sajʿ*), a style similar to literary devices that date back to the early Arabic papyri.

Rephrasings of an imam's choices in verse form facilitated retention through memorization, as one such versification explicitly states. In addition to its attraction for scholars as a pleasurably challenging exercise for the intellect—something on the order of a crossword puzzle—versification also represented a modality of interpretation and commentary in its own right. Renderings in verse additionally point up a distinctive flexibility with respect to the wording of an imam's original prose formulations.[65] As I noted, this question arose for me when Muhammad Yahya Muṭahhar startled me by "correcting" the apparent language of a choice by Imam Ahmad. In the published collection of versification and commentary on the imamic choices of Imam Yahya (discussed below), it is notable that the original prose versions of the choices—that is, the imam's own wording—are not included. Yet for the purposes of court applications, there could be relatively strict adherence to the imam's stated position (also discussed below). In any event, it is clear that the attitude toward the language of the applicable rule was not like that in the following republican era, whether in a legislated code text or a text published in the official gazette (*jarīda rasmiyya*). Ottoman versions of both of these modern genres had existed in the era of the provincial administration around the turn of the twentieth century but would not reappear in highland Yemen until after the Revolution of 1962. As for the numbering found in the initial sets of imamic choices, this, too, was not of the type found in modern legislation, such that the number alone may refer to the rule.

Such versifications represent a specific form of juridical-literary ingenuity. For the first half of the twentieth century we have three exhibits, two of which concern Imam Yahya's choices. ʿAbd al-Rahman bin ʿAli al-Ḥaddād (d. 1922), the Ibb muftī and former Ottoman official, whose scholarly profile has been discussed, versified Imam Yahya's thirteen initial choices.[66] He converted the imam's original prose list into eighty-seven rhymed couplets, capturing the gist of the positions in a different, poetic phrasing. Aside from the significant interpretive effort represented by this rephrasing, some lines of al-Ḥaddād's verses specifically located the Zaydī imam's choices with reference to the legal idiom of Lower Yemen. Al-Ḥaddād makes two direct references to the views of Muhammad bin Idris al-Shāfiʿī (d. 820), the eponymous jurist of his school, one in connection with the imam's position on the dissolution of marriage contracts due to the long absence of the husband, and the other the non-legality of endowments for heirs.

At the time, in 1920, Imam Yahya's rule was still new to Lower Yemen, and this versification by one of the leading lights of the region, an individual who in 1904 had led the successful defense of Ottoman Ibb against besieging imamic forces, helped legitimate the new imamic state. Al-Ḥaddād speaks of, and thus recognizes, Imam Yahya as the "Imam of the Age" and characterizes his "choices" as representing an exercise in *ijtihād*. Appended to the manuscript of al-Ḥaddād's versification is a related instance of *madhhab*-crossing gestures. ʿAli bin ʿAli al-Yamānī (al-Yadūmī), the leading Zaydī jurist, penned seven couplets of "appreciation" (*taqrīẓ*) of al-Ḥaddād's versification of what he refers to as the imam's "chosen issues" (*masāʾil al-mukhtāra*).[67]

Some years later, in 1937, ʿAbd Allah al-Shamāḥī, a leading Zaydī scholar, published the mentioned printed book presenting a selection of Imam Yahya's choices. This included a second rendering in verse, but, as noted, the imam's own language was not published as such. Al-Shamāḥī's work, fifty-five lines in *rajaz* meter, like those of al-Ḥaddād, opens by identifying its mnemonic intent: "among the most important of requirements [is] / memorization of the choices of the Imam of the Arabs." In his preface, al-Shamāḥī explains that he initially presented his completed versification to the imam, who approved it and ordered that it be commented on in prose, a task to which al-Shamāḥī then turned.

Representing a further type of response from the community of jurists, prose commentaries on choices reversed the interpretive process engaged by the imam.[68] If the imam's main interpretive effort was to extract clear and applicable principles from the "sources," the commentators recontextualized and re-anchored the chosen principles with respect to these texts and the broader doctrine. Al-Shamāḥī's seventy-eight-page book, printed at the Ministry of Education in Ṣanʿāʾ, contains both his versification and this second interpretive register, in which he provides extended treatments of a total of twenty-three choices. In the following chapter, I draw on al-Shamāḥī's commentary to discuss a choice by Imam Yahya that is of substantive import for this book. This is the imam's choice on "the basing of action on writing," or "practice with writing."

Imam Ahmad's thirteen initial choices, issued at mid-century shortly after he succeeded his assassinated father, in 1948, were versified by a scholar and man of letters named Muhammad bin ʿAbd Allah bin ʿAli ʿĀmuwa, who identified himself as a muftī and as an adherent of another Sunnī school of law in the principal Red Sea coast town: "the Muftī of the Ḥanafīs of al-Ḥudayda." Like the treatment of the choices of Imam Yahya in 1920 by the Shāfiʿī jurist al-Ḥaddād, this versification of Imam Ahmad's choices circulated only in handwritten form.[69] I also know of prose commentaries on Imam Ahmad's choices, both penned by two other members of the al-Ḥaddād family in Ibb. These efforts, contained in letters sent to the capital, explicated the textual referents of the choices issued by the new imam upon his accession.

For his commentary, Ahmad bin Muhammad bin ʿAli al-Ḥaddād, then muftī and later republican "Judge of Ibb," received a seal-bearing personal letter of appreciation from the imam dated August 26, 1950.[70] The imam wrote, "[Y]our letter of commentary (*sharḥ*) on our honored choices arrived clothed in eloquence and originality in the derivation of the Qurʾanic indications and the Prophetic *ḥadīths*, and we thank you for that." This letter also suggests that what al-Ḥaddād initially had received, and had used as the basis for his commentary, was a versified form of the choices. The imam further states in his letter to al-Ḥaddād that he had also received a commentary from "your paternal uncle." That would be Yahya bin ʿAli al-Ḥaddād (d. 1955), the much younger brother of ʿAbd al-Rahman, mentioned earlier as a biographer of Imam Yahya, who also was a court secretary and an occasional acting judge in Ibb. Finally in this letter, on the model of al-Shamāḥī's printed volume on the choices of his father, the imam indicates that he hoped to have his choices and the selected commentaries published, which did not happen. As with ʿAbd al-Rahman al-Ḥaddād's earlier versification of Imam Yahya's choices, the commentaries offered by his nephew and his younger brother expressed their fealty to the newly installed ruler while also demonstrating their mastery of this technical form of juridical reasoning and their specific understanding of his applied doctrinal rules. Not long after his exchange of letters with the imam, Ahmad bin Muhammad al-Ḥaddād received his first appointment as a sharīʿa court judge, in a sub-district in the western mountains of Ibb Province.

Choice Applications

In the mid-twentieth-century Ibb court records we find references to decisions in the relevant types of cases being based on an indicated imamic choice. The main examples of such applications include conflicts in the topical areas of marriage contract dissolution (*faskh*) and land sale contract preemption (*shufʿa*). The anchoring of part of a case ruling in an existing imamic choice also occurred in a relatively rare type of litigation that concerns the sale of the assets of a minor by a fiduciary in a time of famine (*majāʿa*).[71] In addition to citations by presiding judges, choices occasionally were referenced in the claims and arguments of local litigants. Examples include the mention of a choice in a claim for compensation for damage (*ḍarar*) caused to a house by the operation of a mill next door,[72] and, in a marriage case, the dueling citations of the claimant and defendant—the former citing a choice-rule on limiting the "substantive focus" (*jawhar*) of a judgment, the latter referencing a choice on marriage contract dissolution (quoted below).[73]

An instructive instance of choice application occurs in the record of a long-running and high-stakes conflict that tore apart one of the leading families of Ibb.[74] It may be noted that the losing defendant in the first part of the case, a local *adīb*, or literary figure, served as an influential secretary in the Ibb governor's *dīwān*. At issue were two types of "private" or family endowments (sing. *waqf*). After years without a resolution, Imam Yahya assigned Judge ʿAbd Allah bin ʿAli al-Yamānī to the case. I have mentioned the al-Yamānīs, father and son, as leading Zaydī jurists who served the twentieth-century imams, father and son, as troubleshooters in such intractable major conflicts. About a year later, Judge al-Yamānī would become the Judge of the Seat under Imam Ahmad, who, as noted above, had an occasion to send him a telegram about a choice.

The sharīʿa court transcript from 1947 records that Judge al-Yamānī asked for and received guidance from Imam Yahya regarding the choice(s) to be implemented in his ruling (spacing and indentation added):

> I consulted with Our Lord the Commander of the Faithful [Imam Yahya], may God protect him, about these two endowments and others because the judgment will be in conformity with the honored choice (*ikhtiyār*). The honored response (*jawāb*) was:
>
> > The crux of the validity of an endowment is the establishment of [its being] a work pleasing to God (*thubūt al-qurba*). With the retraction by Muhammad bin ʿAbd Allah al- . . . of the recitation endowment and the exclusion of the descendants of the daughters from the descendants' endowment established, so in the absence of a work pleasing to God, [there is] no endowment, due to its absence. This is the formulation (*manṭūq*) of our choices. That endowment which is for a mosque or for students of religious learning [i.e., a "public" endowment] is acceptable for implementation from the third [of the estate].

> This is the summary contents of the response of Our Lord the Commander of the Faithful, including most of his wording.

After carefully reporting his communication with the imam, Judge al-Yamānī continues to his own ruling, which begins, "On this basis I judged . . ." He recapitulates the specific invalidity of each of the two endowments and then concludes by reiterating that his judgment is in accord

> with the choice of Our Lord the Commander of the Faithful, al-Mutawakkil ʿalā Allah [title of Imam Yahya], the judge of the invalidity of all involved that either excludes an heir or is a legal stratagem (*ḥila*). This is what is correct to me and on this [basis] I have judged the two endowments. God is the bringer of good fortune. Written on the 26th of the month of Dhū al-Ḥijja, the year 1366 [November 10, 1947].[75]

It is unusual to find such a passage in a court transcript. The reporting of this high-level exchange in what would become the final judgment document in the case did not have to do with the conceptual difficulties posed by a "hard case," as facts such as these had been addressed in existing imamic choices. I believe it had to do with the need to decisively settle a disruptive conflict in an important family and that it was to this end that the imam's incisive words were quoted.

The imam's response and the judge's ruling invoke specific well-known choices, but without quoting them as such. Implicit referencing of this sort was standard in the judicial culture of the court. Rather than re-citing the existing language of these rule-choices—not to mention a modern style of reference to a numbered code, rule, etc.—the imam's "formulation" consists of a case-specific gloss on and confirmation of his opinions. If we look at the various lists of Imam Yahya's early choices (c. 1920), we see that the first and second are relevant to the rulings in this case. It also may be mentioned that the "authoritative language" of the two choices is consistent across these lists.[76] I hope to further explore these choices elsewhere as their substantive content is unusually rich in both juridical terms and societal implications.[77] Here, in accord with my focus on textual form, I simply quote the two choices, which serves to highlight the distance between their actual language and how they are invoked and glossed in connection with this court case. This distance provides further evidence—added to the patterns of versification and the incident of al-Muṭahhar casually "correcting" a choice—that this is not the sort of "authoritative language" that demands precise quotation, as per Bakhtin. Choice one states, "No gift and no legacy (*waṣiyya*) to some of the heirs without the others, following the *ḥadīth* of Nuʿmān bin Bashīr, and according to His, the Almighty's statement, 'Not harmful: a legacy from God.'" Choice two states, "No legacy to an heir, and no endowment, due to the [required] stipulation of *al-qurba* [a work pleasing to God], which is absent, due to its [viz., a legacy's or an endowment to an heir's] inconsistency with a legacy from God Almighty, and because the manifest [intent] is to disqualify females." Although its role is not invoked in the cited exchange between the judge and the imam, a third choice also concerned with what we might term "estate planning" figures in the backdrop of the reasoning in the case. Concerning the "donative transactions of commoners" (*taṣarrufāt al-ʿawāmm al-tabarruʿiyya*), this choice provides the basis for permitting the retraction of the recitation endowment.[78] Although some of their rule terminology is reproduced in passing, none of these three choices is directly quoted as such in the case transcript.

Further examples of such intramural exchanges between the imam and the members of his judiciary regarding existing choices are found among the eight short texts appended to the ʿAbd al-Qadir bin ʿAbd Allah manuscript of Imam Ahmad's thirteen original choices. A question posed to the imam by the Appeal Court in 1370 AH (1951), for example, asks about the intended meaning (*al-maqṣūd*) in his use of a specific word, "excuse" (*ʿudhr*), which appears in the seventh of his initial choices, on a woman's right to sexual intercourse as a factor in marriage contract dissolution. The appended text records "the answer, in his words, from the Imam, to the brother Yahya b. Muhammad [al-Mutawakkil]," the head of the Appeal Court, which provides two examples of the "excuses" intended. Another of the appended texts concerns a "raised question" (*marfūʿ*), also from the Appeal Court, dated 1368 AH (1949), conveyed to Muhammad Hasan al-Wādaʿī, the head of the imamic *dīwān*, for him to present to the imam. This question comprises several short queries concerning the imam's choices numbers two, five, and thirteen, which concern legacies (sing. *waṣiyya*) to heirs, marriage contract dissolution due to the lengthy absence of the husband, and the substantive focus in judgments. The imam's concise response to each of these queries is quoted. A third question, dated 1369 AH (1949–50), again conveyed by the head of the *dīwān*, concerns a choice on the dissolution of a marriage contract due to the husband's poverty (*iʿsār*), and again the imam's reply is quoted.[79]

Unlike the earlier discussed versifications and commentaries by highland jurists, these queries by judges represent a practice-oriented category of response to existing imamic choices. Such questions issued from that segment of the period interpretive community actively engaged in service as trial and appellate judges, individuals motivated by the pressing demands of decision making in particular cases. These direct interrogations of the imam regarding the details of his earlier issued choices underscore the highly personalized nature of the interpretive mechanism at the apex of this system of sharīʿa rule.

Stripping

Others of the appended texts on subsequent interchanges with Imam Ahmad are of a different type. These lead me to consider again the phenomenon of textual "stripping" and to extend the analysis to the genre of the imamic choice. Unlike the instances of judges querying the imam concerning an existing choice, these interchanges involved topics without an existing choice. They concern what later would be recognized as imamic choices but at a point in time when the choices were still under construction. While the texts in question express authoritative opinions of Imam Ahmad, the rules remain attached to their archival roots. These texts thus do not have the stand-alone form of the imam's thirteen numbered choices (or of his later, individually issued choices), nor have they fully adopted the general language required in the choice genre.

These choices-in-the-making, I suggest, are not as yet "stripped." This further variety of "stripping" occurred as a movement between the genre of the court case judgment and that of the imamic choice. In a "finished" choice that had originated in a response to a difficult decision, the recorded specifics of the originating case were edited away in a rescripting process that resulted in the creation of the independent choice. Like the earlier discussed transit, from the posing of a question to the muftī's fatwā to the literary *masʾala* in a law book, this process of isolating an imamic choice entailed a shift from the archive to the library, from the particular to the general, and from the discourse of the proper name to that of *fulān* and its variants.

As a modeling dialectic, the passage from case ruling to imamic choice may be thought of as the model *of* side. In this aspect of the modeling relationship archival materials were edited in the construction of a library text. The established-choice-to-new-case ruling, or model *for* side, would be engaged in later applications in rulings by judges in similar cases. In this aspect of modeling, the library text was used in the interpretation of other archival materials. Further moments and patterns in these dialectical relations also were possible, as is demonstrated by Imam Ahmad's review, revision, and retraction of one of his previously issued choices.

The factual features of a case emerged in the course of sharīʿa litigation, which typically involved a more or less formally phrased and substantively detailed claim, evidence presentation by one or both sides, and the possibility of other assertions by the two parties. The litigants' efforts to establish the facts and the legal issues in the case culminated in a ruling by the trial judge. Judges, however, often introduced their own technical language to evaluate the facts and to frame the issues.

To illustrate this stripping process, I start with a text appended to the manuscript of Imam Ahmad's initial choices. The text in question concerns a 1952 case of marriage dissolution (*faskh*) on the grounds of "strong hatred" between the spouses, complicated by "timidity" on the part of the wife. It is further characterized as pertaining to a "current case" (*qaḍiyya ḥāditha*—an equivalent term, used in other examples, being *masʾala ḥāditha*). Written by an appellate court judge, the text in question begins by mentioning the names of a wife and a husband, and a previous lower court ruling:

> In a current case [involving] the wife, Fatima bint Ahmad Qasim, and her [court] adversary, her husband, Salih Husayn Khalil, from . . . , the litigation is before me. The woman claimed, first, that the [marriage] contractor (*al-ʿāqid*) for her was other than her guardian, and a [trial] judge gave a judgment for the dissolution of the marriage [contract]. [But] then the appeal [by the husband] was sustained and it was ruled that the contractor for her was among her male-line relatives (*ʿaṣaba*), [specifically] the paternal cousin, following testimony concerning the descent, and this was confirmed by the Sharifian Majesty, our Master the martyred Imam [Yahya, assassinated 1948], may God be pleased with him.
>
> During this lengthy period, extreme timidity was manifested on the part of the woman, and there were many mediation efforts between them [the wife and the husband] for a good outcome, but the husband did not help. The woman is

young and claims that her husband is impotent and she asks for dissolution [of the marriage contract.]

I referred the situation to the Sharifian Majesty, the Victorious for the Religion of God [Imam Ahmad], and the response from the palace was, in the honored pen, God support him, in his wording:

> Greetings of God Almighty. If extreme timidity [in the wife] and hatred of the husband are established before you, then in the sharīʿa of Muhammad bin ʿAbd Allah [the Prophet], prayers of God upon him, the clear solution [is found] in the case of the wife of Thabit bin Qays. The woman must return what she received as dower (*mahr*), and [then] either repudiation by the husband or dissolution by the judge. Greetings to you, 4 Ramadan [1]371 [May 28, 1952].

On this is the [imamic] signature with the expression "Commander of the Faithful," God forgive him.[80]

As presented in this appended text, what would later be considered an imamic choice is not yet "stripped." The rule conveyed had not yet fully emerged from the chrysalis of a particular case. It remains embedded in and associated with the court case it initially regulated, in a text that includes the names of the litigants, information on prior rulings, etc. Had theirs been a common law system, subsequent highland judges and litigants might have cited the 1952 precedent case as "Fatima bint Ahmad Qasim v. Salih Husayn Khalil."

Through the imam's interpretive intervention, the matter finds its "solution" in a "source" text, a prophetic *ḥadīth*. In the correspondence between the imam and the judge, citational detail was unnecessary since the *ḥadīth* was well known to the members of the judiciary. The imam references the Islamic "case" of the wife of Thabit bin Qays, which is commonly taken to be the main early instance of the *khulʿ* type of wife-initiated divorce (see chapter 10).[81] In his interpretive act the imam succinctly links the past and present cases.

Such intramural messages between the ruling imam and one of his sitting judges concerning a specific case disclose a further dimension of the detailed mechanics of sharīʿa decision making in this Islamic polity. Such exchanges focus on the imam's language, which is directly quoted. Quotation here iterates the presence and the active engagement of the ruler. His opinion is given in "his answer," sent from his palace, written with "the honored pen," with his title and "signature," and, most important, "in his words."

Thereafter, but in stripped form, Imam Ahmad's decisive opinion in this 1952 case would be taken to be a generally applicable imamic choice. That is, the imam's language would begin to circulate and function as rubrics of reference for decisions by practicing court judges. That this particular newly minted rule could figure in other cases found to raise similar issues and to be based on similar facts is illustrated by a sharīʿa court trial conducted six years later in Ibb.[82] According to the litigation record from 1958, a party addressing the court referred to the existing choice, and he did so in a manner that demonstrates his precise knowledge of its language (quoted above). The choice clearly had "flown," not just to the judiciary but to the subjects of the imamic polity as well.

The Ibb transcript reproduces the litigant's statement addressing the Judge as follows:

> The Judge is aware of that which is in the clear statement of the honored choice of [Imam] Ahmad, the Victorious, concerning the non-necessity [i.e., non-viability] of hatred in marriage. Rather, it is clear that [for] the married woman, if the judge verifies her hatred and her inability to be patient and to remain with her husband, due to hatred of being married, then it is required to make the husband repudiate and, if he does not repudiate, then dissolution [of the marriage contract is to be ordered] for her by the judge.[83]

What does a "finished" choice look like? Such a rule is one fully detached from case particulars. It is expressed not in terms of archival names and other such detail but in the more generic discourse of the library. An example, which refers to "women" in general, is the first of Imam Ahmad's initial thirteen choices (numbering in original):

> (1) All transactions by women with their close relatives and their children regarding what is in their possession among their properties, or under their influence, have no enforceability,[84] whether the disposition was in the form of a gift, pledge (*nadhr*), transfer of ownership (*tamlīk*), or endowment, inasmuch as this [transaction] would not have occurred except due to fear, shyness, or desperation connected with the greedy taking advantage of them and seizing their property, except if it is a transaction by sale to their relatives without alteration or deceit against them [the women] from them [their relatives], or from others, and with no fear or fraud against them, in which case it is legal.[85]

بسم الله الرحمن الرحيم

يقول عبد الله امير المؤمنين احمد بن امير المؤمنين المتوكل على الله يحيى
بن امير المؤمنين المنصور بالله محمد بن يحيى حميد الدين غفر الله لهم
جميعاً وسامحهم وشملهم بعفوه وتولاهم بالطافه انه ترجح لديه
واختاره بحسب الادلة الشرعية والنظر الصحيح

(١) ان كل تصرفات النساء لاقاربهن واولادهم فيما هو تحت أيديهم
من املاكهن او تحت نفوذهم لا نفوذ لها سواء كان التصرف بهبة
او نذر او تمليك او وقف اذ لا يكون ذلك الا لخوف او حياء
او يأس من تمكنهن وقبضهن لما لهن اللهم الا اذا كان التصرف
بالبيع الى اقاربهن بدون تغرير ولا تدليس عليهن منهم او من
غيرهم ولا خوف ولا غبن عليهن فذلك صحيح

(٢) والله اعلم الوصية للوارث غير معتبرة مطلقا ولو من الثلث لوجوب التسوية
بين الاولاد لحديث النعمان بن بشير وحديث اتقوا الله وساووا
بين اولادكم وفي الوارث من غير الاولاد بالاولى لحديث لا وصية
لوارث الا ان يجيز الورثة والوارث الضعيف لابد ان يعرف
قدر الموصى به وانه من الثلث او زائد عليه واعلامه ان نفوذ
ذلك في حصته متوقف على اجازته وانه لا بأس عليه اذا لم يجز

وان يكون

Figure 4.5 No. 1, on the "transactions of women," in "Choices" (*Ikhtiyārāt*) of Imam Ahmad MS (c. 1950, copy in the possession of ʿAbd al-Qādir bin ʿAbd Allāh, Ṣanʿāʾ).

My argument, in sum, is that several of the texts appended to the manuscript of the imam's thirteen initial choices contain unfinished or embryonic choices, choices not yet fully extracted from their archival building materials, which were the specific factual features of current court cases.[86] I understand this extractive process as a further variety of textual "stripping," editing, or rescripting to achieve a change of genre. When completed, this process resulted in additional "finished" choices. Since the process remained incomplete at the time these texts were added to the ʿAbd al-Qadir bin ʿAbd Allah manuscript, we are better able to understand the nature of both the building materials and the editing process.

In this specific historical instance, the creation of generalized formal opinions embodying doctrinal rules occurred in response to and on the factual basis of particular sharīʿa court cases. This twentieth-century mode of rule creation was associated with a specific doctrinal genre, the imamic choice; a specific type of Islamic polity, based on the rule of a *mujtahid* imam; and a specific hybrid mechanism of appeal, adapted from an institution originally introduced by the Ottomans. It is unknown whether the choices of imams from previous eras—that is, before the introduction of the Ottoman appellate mechanism—also were built out of the particulars of court case materials.

My larger point concerns the sharīʿa court as a locus for the development of doctrine. While I am able to demonstrate that this occurred in the highland setting, it is normally assumed that sharīʿa court decisions had few, if any, implications for doctrine. At most, courts have been understood as sites for application. Hallaq expresses the received understanding when he states that "the decisions of the *qāḍīs* do not appear to have been taken into account in *furūʿ* [viz., doctrinal] works."[87]

Another view would build on an understanding of the flexible and shifting nature of the *masʾala*, as a fact and rule conception. I would first recall the Zaydī jurists' rule against an individual acting as a muftī and then later as a judge in the same "matter," which assumes the relevance of the *masʾala* conception to both institutional venues. Different dimensions of a *masʾala* were foregrounded in a fatwā as opposed to in a court judgment, however—the one emphasizing the generalizable, the other not. In a fatwā, the process focused on determining the rule side, with the facts presented by the questioner taken by the muftī as the uninterrogated point of departure. In a court judgment, in contrast, the procedural emphasis was on establishing the facts, with the corpus of rules normally taken as unproblematically ready and available for application.

Based on the first type of "stripping" analysis, it may now be clear how, through editing, a rule-emphasizing *mas'ala* in a fatwā could be converted into an item of literary doctrine. But perhaps something parallel was possible starting with the different genre of the court judgment and utilizing a version of this just demonstrated second type of "stripping." The question is this: Were the types of *masā'il* that figured in difficult or otherwise significant court cases also adaptable for the purposes of doctrinal discussion and position taking? In short, were there stripped court materials behind some of the *masā'il* that appeared in law books?

As is well known, Anglo-American jurisprudence formalized analysis in terms of cases. Although it remained comparatively informal, that carried out by these Muslim jurists in the language of the *mas'ala* and related terms was equally integral to their intellectual habitus and practice. Both legal traditions were oriented to fact and rule combinations, and both traced the origins of these basic combinations to events in the world.

FIVE

"Practice with Writing"

CONSIDERED ESSENTIAL TO civilized society, but known to be potentially dangerous, archival writings posed a dilemma of long standing. This predicament of the ordinary evidential document animated a problem that reverberated through the history of the sharīʿa library. The jurists' reflections on the proof value of these ordinary sharīʿa writings contributed to the range of textual modeling provided by the doctrinal genres. Augmenting my earlier discussion of the exegetical and the law book commentary versions of such discourse (chapter 3) and following upon my treatment in the last chapter of the key interpretive institutions in question, I turn now to a pair of freestanding opinions, a twentieth-century imamic choice and a nineteenth-century fatwā-style inquiry. Both tackle the substantive topic, the applied issue or *masʾala*, of "basing action on writing" or "practice with writing" (*al-ʿamal bi-l-khaṭṭ*).

Once again, my interest in writing is double. In chapter 2 I discussed the literary resources ideally available to the sharīʿa interpreter; here, I illustrate how this textual universe could be mobilized to articulate particular opinions. At the same time, I am interested in the opinions themselves as instances of topical reasoning within the scope of the shariʿa. That is, on the one hand, I track the deployment of the "source" genres and the references to the *fiqh* literature, and on the other, I seek to understand how the primary genres, the types of routine instruments, are dealt with conceptually in the opinion-discourses of the choice and the fatwā-response. With respect to the overall trajectory of this book, the following paragraphs conclude my chapters on the "library" and provide a segue to those on the "archive."

I start with the c. 1920 choice on writing by Imam Yahya, which I review together with the versification and commentary on this opinion published in 1937.[1] I then work backward to an extended inquiry on the same topic by a Zaydī jurist from the first half of the nineteenth century.[2] Taking the form of a response to a question, this earlier analysis offers a more explicit genealogy of the sorts of thinking and, especially interesting for the purposes of this book, the types of texts that went into the making of a juridical opinion in this interpretive tradition while at the same time providing a more integrated view of written court evidence as a problem. Both the choice and the fatwā treat archival forms of writing analytically, which is to say apart from any examples of such writings, and thus separate from any particular content or context. Despite the topical focus on this level of writing, we nevertheless remain within the *fulān*-contoured realm of the library rather than in the archive, a realm structured by grounded temporalities and the proper name.

Choice

Imam Yahya's choice addresses the venerable juridical problem by focusing on the evidential status of archival writings. In the concision characteristic of the genre, the imam states, "Basing action on [or practice with] writing (*al-ʿamal bi-l-khaṭṭ*) is acceptable (*muʿtabar*) if the writing is known and its writer is known for justness."[3] The rule mandated in this choice may be understood as an updated contribution to the local theory of archival practice. Where the law book treatments of these issues remained embedded in the weave of text and commentary, imamic choices such as this appeared as items on numbered lists or as individually issued doctrinal rules intended to guide court judges. This opinion on writing figures in the early list of choices that ʿAbd al-Rahman al-Ḥaddād (d. 1922), the Shāfiʿī jurist from Ibb, versified. In 1937, it appeared in the set of choices re-versified and commented on by al-Shamāḥī, whose rendering is: "Just writing, we know, is accepted / its indication (*dalīl*) is humanly transmitted, linked in a chain [of transmission]."[4] This rhymed (in Arabic) rephrasing is different from the earlier prose and the initial verse rendering, and its obvious strategy is to graft an understanding of sound archival writing onto established conceptions associated with the reporting of an authoritative *ḥadīth*. Al-Shamāḥī's terms "humanly transmitted" (*muʿanʿan*) and "linked in a chain" (*musalsal*) connect the written domain of the primary instrument with mechanisms identified with the secure oral transmission of the paradigmatic "source" text.

According to al-Shamāḥī's following prose commentary on the imam's choice, archival writings are recognized as both vital and hazardous. Documents are portrayed, positively, as the "pillars of human undertakings (*muʿāmalāt*)" and as specifically important for protecting "the wealth of the community," including its "rights and properties." Numerous but unspecified texts of the Sunna are said to authorize the reliance on forms of writing. Writing in general is eulogized for its many crucial societal roles—notably for preserving the Sunna itself, and thus essential rules, rights, knowledge, and history; for its use in conveying the academic disciplines; and as the medium of fatwās and court judgments. Archival "documents" (*awrāq*) are referenced in general, as is the "basing of action on" (*al-ʿamal bi-*) the writings of judges and notarial writers (*umanāʾ*, sing. *amīn*). In this connection, al-Shamāḥī names a particular archival genre, the same document type mentioned in the *Flowers* commentaries, culminating in the contemporaneous *Gilded Crown* of al-ʿAnsī. The genre in question is the fundamental highland real estate sale contract, the *baṣīra* (pl. *baṣāʾir*), to which I devote close attention in chapter 10. Al-Shamāḥī additionally develops the theme of the equivalence between the reliance on such writings and the reception of authoritative oral texts. He asserts that the status of an individual's writing is like that of "taking his dictation or valuing his testimony." But he also portrays documentary usage negatively, as attracting the "practitioners of forgery" and leading to the illicit "temptation of pens and geniuses."

Then he briefly identifies and criticizes the polar positions concerning the status of archival texts—namely the total abandonment of writing versus the unquestioning reliance on it—after which he reintroduces the imam's choice as the mediating solution. Blanket acceptance or rejection concerning the basing of legal action of writings thus gives way to an opinion that upholds a measured reliance on sound archival instruments. The imam's choice is asserted to be "what accords with the sharīʿa, and what is called for to maintain order and protect civilization."

Older documents whose writers and witnesses were deceased posed a special problem. Commentator al-Shamāḥī refers here to the situation of sound documents, those "well known among the old writings for which there is no suspicion of falsehood or forgery." "If we were to give up the basing of action on (*al-ʿamal bi-*) such [documents]," he states, "this would entail the loss of rights and properties whose records these old documents are, their writers unknown and unknowable." These are documents that could not be validated through the basic mechanism established in the *Flowers* literature—that of summoning the notarial writer to court to read the text aloud before the document witnesses, who then give testimony (chapter 3). These truthful and indispensable "old writings" thus raise the more troubling issue of writing standing alone as evidence.

According to al-Shamāḥī, the imam's opinion envisions charging the presiding judge with the required task of evaluation. The judge thus served as the pivotal archival practitioner. His decisive reading occurred in a conflict situation in which the document in question has been presented as evidence in litigation. In analytic terms, his reading may be separated into his consideration of the document's formal integrity and his consideration of its substantive contents. There must be a prior determination of its outward status as an evidential writing before a presented document may be inventoried for its internal evidential import. The determination by the judge about the writing as a writing depended not only on his academic formation but also on his familiarity with a particular world of documentation and its notarial practitioners. His exposure over time to locally held documents would include an acquired knowledge of well-reputed notarial writers who had been active before his appointment to the jurisdiction. The judge's determination specifically required a subtle appreciation of handwriting (*al-khaṭṭ*) itself as a material sign.

Unlike the earlier discussed twentieth-century choices with documented origins in specific cases, the impetus for Imam Yahya's choice on writing is unknown. We are left to imagine the sort of litigation-based quandary that might have triggered a question from the presiding judge to the imam. Since we do know that this opinion was among the initial set of the imam's choices that al-Ḥaddād versified by about 1920, the immediately preceding context of late Ottoman documentary practices may be relevant to its issuance.[5] What, in turn, was the history of this choice being used in regulating ongoing affairs? How was it applied? Unlike a number of the choices issued by the twentieth-century imams, I have not encountered an application of Imam Yahya's choice on writing in a court case.

Inquiry

To situate Imam Yahya's twentieth-century opinion with respect to the wider arc and the deeper interpretive past of this discursive tradition, I now consider a more comprehensive earlier opinion. Taking the form of an "inquiry" (*baḥth*) in response to a question posed, and dating from the first half of the nineteenth century, this fatwā-like opinion issued from a noted Zaydī school jurist, Ahmad bin Zayd al-Kibsī (d. 1855).[6] A student of al-Shawkānī, among other leading scholars in Ṣanʿāʾ, and subsequently a highly reputed teacher in his own right, al-Kibsī was known for his fatwās and inquiries.

Al-Kibsī's response is more comprehensive in that, in addition to sampling the positions of a range of jurists, he devotes attention to the "source" texts of the Qurʾan and the Sunna. As I am equally interested in the form of his argument, I read for how the jurist works through his problem. Although al-Kibsī's passages can be dense with citations and ramifying arguments both explicit and implied, I make observations about his order of presentation, preferences in authorities referenced, and decisions about quotation.[7] As he mentions the names of many jurists and *ḥadīth* specialists, as well as the titles of some of their works, we are exposed to the contours of a large citational library. We can only wonder about his access to the numerous and often multivolume works in question—that is, about the nature of his physical library. In actuality, as a result of his madrasa formation, many of the texts may have been "filed in his memory."[8] In the late manuscript era, in which al-Kibsī wrote, handwritten copies differed in pagination so detailed references were not given. I have provided cross-references to some of the works now available in printed publications.

In closing, al-Kibsī addresses his questioner, although the print edition version I have at hand does not mention the individual's name or provide the question text. We thus miss the potentially instructive opening gambit in the textual exchange. We do not know, for example, whether the query was posed as a technical academic issue about writing in general or evidence in particular, or whether it was instead phrased as a practical matter that concerned the documents in a "current case." Given the length and formal precision of the response, it should be assumed that the intended recipient was well educated.

The inquiry opens with a general statement: "To act on the basis of writing, with certain or probable knowledge concerning it, having arrived at trust regarding it, the imams who are members of the family (*ahl al-bayt*), peace be upon them, chose." He thus asserts that while technically distinct as preconditions for action, certain and probable knowledge (*ẓann*) both justify reliance on a written document. The interpreters identified as holding this opinion are of a specific category that marks this inquiry as Shīʿī. By the opinions of imams who are "members of the family," al-Kibsī refers to lineal descendants of the Prophet Muhammad through his nephew and son-in-law ʿAli bin Abī Ṭālib. I touched previously on this special category of interpreter in my reading of comments on the second part of the phrase "an interpreter who is just" (chapter 2).

"Among them"—that is, among the indicated imams—al-Kibsī then mentions four individuals, which establishes a specifically Zaydī frame for his inquiry: Imam al-Ḥujja al-Manṣūr billāh ʿAbd Allah bin Hamza (d. 1217), Imam Yahya bin Hamza (d. 1348), and Imam Ahmad bin Sulaymān (d. 1170), whose position is related by Imam Muhammad bin al-Muṭahhar (d. 1327).[9] All four were "imams" in the two major senses of the term: they were prominent Zaydī school literary jurists, and they ruled over highland Islamic polities. In stating that these imams are among the jurists who "chose" this view, al-Kibsī uses the terminology of the "choice" in its broader (and conventional) sense that includes statements made and positions taken in an individual's juridical writings. Such an indicated "choice" referred to a jurist's preferred view.

Despite the specificity of this opening, a thrust of the immediately following lines and of the inquiry as a whole is that, despite detailed differences of opinion, this generally stated position on the acceptance of trustworthy writings was widely shared beyond the confines of the school. Al-Kibsī quotes a Zaydī jurist who states that a number of "the associates of al-Shāfiʿī affirmed the requirement of acting on its basis when there is trust."[10] In this connection, al-Kibsī also mentions the names of such prominent Shāfiʿī school jurists as al-Juwaynī (d. 1085) and Nawawī (d. 1277), both of whom were studied in Ibb.[11] The immediate conclusion is that the position stated at the outset was one "decided upon for action by the imams of the members of the family and their party, and by the famous imams, jurists and judges in all quarters and ages, according to the schools of the members of the family and others."

Al-Kibsī also speaks at this early point in practical, archival terms, referencing both institutional roles and specific primary genres. He states that this position "would not be opposed by a judge, or a muftī, or others, inasmuch as real estate sale documents (*baṣāʾir*, sing. *baṣīra*) and inheritance instruments (*fuṣūl*, sing. *faṣl*) and the documents useful for establishing debts and their amounts, and the registers (*musawwadāt*) of endowments (*awqāf*), etc.—all of these represented a proof (*ḥujja*) and a record (*mustanad*) acted upon, and all involved acting upon the basis of writing, where it was not opposed by something stronger than it [in evidential terms]."

Qurʾan

As the main discussion commences, al-Kibsī implements a conventional textual prioritization for such juridical thinking. He presents, first, Qurʾanic texts and, second, Sunna (*ḥadīth*) texts on his topic. He asserts that both types of source texts authoritatively "indicate"—that is, as proof texts support—"the acting on the basis of it [writing]." He proceeds to quote three excerpts from the key verse 282 of *sūra* 2, "The Cow." In this interpretive act, the jurist selects rule-bearing texts from the Qurʾan to serve in his analysis.

In this longest of all Qurʾanic verses, al-Kibsī isolates passages that mention writing. He begins each of his back-to-back quotations from 2:282 with the standard *qawl* frame for the divinity: "the Almighty said (*qāla*) . . ." followed by special brackets (in the printed edition) to mark the quoted words (spacing added):

> The Almighty said: {O believers, when you contract a debt one upon another for a stated term, write it down, and let a just writer write it down between you justly, and let not any writer refuse to write it down, as God has taught him; so let him write, and let the debtor dictate, and let him fear God his Lord and not diminish aught of it.}

> And the Almighty said: {And be not loth to write it down, whether it be small or great, with its term; that is more equitable in God's sight, more upright for testimony, and likelier that you will not be in doubt. Unless it be merchandise present that you give and take between you; then it shall be no fault in you if you do not write it down.}
>
> And the Almighty said: {And let not either writer or witness be pressed.}[12]

To better understand al-Kibsī's citation choices we may refer to the text of the five hundred rule-bearing Qur'anic verses that appears before Imam al-Murtaḍā's *Overflowing Sea* (see chapter 2). According to this reference work, the verse in question includes a total of eight distinct rule-texts, which are numbered 85 through 92.[13] This is not to suggest that al-Kibsī consulted this listing, although he may have, as he cites the *Sea* itself further along in his inquiry. Concerned only with the recognized rule-bearing passages in the Qur'an, this reference work listing leaves aside the many non-rule-bearing passages.

Using this breakdown of the rule-text structure of verse 2:282, we may identify the rules al-Kibsī selected for quotation in this argument and those he did not select. He begins with rule number 85, the opening lines of the verse, which he quotes as it is presented in the listing of the five hundred rule-verses. He then adds his versions of rule-texts 89 and 90, in both instances omitting some final words that appear in the pre-text to the *Sea*. Al-Kibsī does not mention the five other rule-texts identified in this rule-laden verse. The interspersed texts that he does not cite concern the following topics: 86—the debtor who lacks full legal capacity; 87—that two men or one man and two women should serve as witnesses; 88—that people should not refuse to witness; 91—the situation of contracting when traveling; 92—that individuals should not conceal testimony. Rule-texts 86 and 91 both concern special circumstances for archival writing—namely the debtor unable to dictate to the writer, and the nonavailability of a writer while the contractor is traveling—so al-Kibsī did not exhaustively mine the available references on the topic in this Qur'anic verse.[14]

At the outset, al-Kibsī referred to al-Zamakhsharī (d. 1144), the famous Qur'an exegete, who was mentioned as the oral transmission source for the view of the third of the imams as reported by the fourth. In this section on the Qur'anic indications supporting his opinion, however, al-Kibsī does not mention exegetes or venture into how his selected passages were handled in the *tafsīr* literature (see chapter 3). Rather than extracting or glossing the indicated rules, and without engaging with exegetical arguments, he simply quotes the three selected passages one after the other without intervening elucidations. His is a jurist's pragmatic utilization of Qurʾanic passages to support an argument, with the import of the cited texts taken as self-evident. After his three quotations from the Qurʾan, al-Kibsī draws a straightforward conclusion: "Were it [writing] not to be acted upon, what would be the use of the order (*al-amr*) concerning it?"[15] He thus bypasses the long-established exegetical conception of this divine order (or orders) as having the lesser status of a "recommendation" rather than being "required."

Sunna

Moving to the Sunna, the textual corpus mentioned only in passing in the twentieth-century commentary on the imam's choice, al-Kibsī considers specific *ḥadīth*s. I should note that, unlike the situation regarding his Qurʾan citations, for which I was able to refer to the listing of the five hundred rule-bearing verses, I know of no equivalent tool to provide a perspective on his *ḥadīth* selections.

"Among them," he writes, is a *ḥadīth* he treats at some length but does not actually quote as such. This concerns a "document" (*kitāb*) the Prophet had a man named ʿAmrū bin Ḥazm write to record the prescribed scales of *zakāt* [the tithe mandated in the sharīʿa] and the amounts of the compensations for injuries (*diyāt*, sing. *diya*).[16] This document later was consulted and relied on by the Prophet's Companions, who are said to have "placed aside (*tarakū*) their opinions." That is, instead of referencing and holding to their own views and memories on these topics, the Companions depended on the written document. Al-Kibsī refers to an early eighth-century jurist named Ibn al-Musayyib, known as one of "the seven lawyers of Madina."[17] According to this authority, the writing in question was consulted in the presence of a number of the Companions by ʿUmar (the second caliph). He sought to determine the correct amount of compensation in a case of severed fingers. ʿUmar likewise is reported to have "placed his opinion aside" in favor of the written text.

The issue at this juncture is the proof-value of this first *ḥadīth*, which al-Kibsī explores at some length. Remarking that the historical occurrence involving ʿUmar is "well known in the books of *fiqh* and in other [literatures]," he proceeds to quote the later historian and *ḥadīth* specialist Ibn Kathīr (d. 1373) as follows: "[T]his *ḥadīth* has been related with [both] an uninterrupted and an interrupted chain of transmitters." For the "uninterrupted" reports of the *ḥadīth*, which indicate the soundness of the proof text inasmuch as its chain of reliable transmitters is intact, al-Kibsī lists the names and a few book titles of some fourteen Sunnī *ḥadīth* writers. This list begins with al-Nasāʾī and Abu Dāwud, indicating two of the six "mother" texts of the Sunnī *ḥadīth* tradition. As I noted earlier, Abu Dāwūd's *Sunan* is the single *ḥadīth* work explicitly recommended for use by the sharīʿa interpreter according to al-ʿAnsī's twentieth-century *Flowers* commentary (see chapter 2). For this particular book al-Kibsī also provides a more specific citation to "the chapter on written communications (*al-marāsīl*)." He then quotes the estimation of al-Bayhaqī (d. 1066), another respected authority: "[I]t is a *ḥadīth* with an uninterrupted chain (*mawṣūl al-isnād*), [and its status is] very good (*ḥasanun jiddan*)."[18] For the "interrupted" reports of the *ḥadīth*, which place its proof value in question, al-Kibsī returns to Ibn Kathīr and to what is referred to as a lengthy discussion of "contention concerning the validity of its chain of transmitters."

After surveying these standard Sunnī treatments, al-Kibsī concludes his handling of this *ḥadīth* with references specific to the Zaydī tradition. Among those who reported it he names two individuals. The first is the famous jurist-imam al-Muʾayyad billāh Ahmad bin al-Husayn (d. 1020), who resided in the Caspian region of Iran, the other historical stronghold of the Zaydīs, and whose *Sharḥ al-tajrīd* is cited by title.[19] The second is the highland jurist al-Amir al-Husayn bin Badr al-Dīn (d. 1263) whose *al-Shifāʾ* also is identified. I previously mentioned this last work as the single *ḥadīth* work explicitly recommended for the sharīʿa interpreter in Ibn Miftāḥ's fifteenth-century *Commentary on the Flowers*.

Although some of the details differ, the early writing he now discusses remains a document that contains information on *zakāt*. The further authorities referred to are the foundational figures of the school. Transmitted by the first Zaydī imam in highland Yemen, al-Hādī ilā al-Ḥaqq Yahya bin al-Husayn (d. 910), this report quotes a statement attributed to the original Shīʿī figure, Imam ʿAli (d. 661). Al-Kibsī presents this report from Imam al-Hādī as follows: "from the Commander of the Faithful [Imam ʿAli], peace be upon him, that he said: 'in the sheath of the sword of the Prophet of God

I found a sheet (*ṣaḥīfa*) with the prescribed *zakāt* of camels, cows, and sheep.'"[20] Referring then to the eponym of the Zaydī tradition, al-Kibsī states: "[I]t was related thus by Zayd bin ʿAli [d. 740], peace be upon him, from his fathers [i.e., his father and his grandfather], from [Imam] ʿAli, peace be upon him."

After quickly presenting a second *ḥadīth*, which concerns a different writing received from the Prophet about the use of carrion for hides,[21] al-Kibsī pauses to summarize:

> These are a sufficient indication of what the Sunna has in it concerning acting on the basis of writing (*kitāba*). If we exhaustively treated the received *ḥadīths* on this we would depart from the main point. In general, if the basing of action on writing were eliminated, rights, properties, and endowments would be impeded, and the people unjustly consuming each other's property would ensue.[22] Likewise, benefiting from knowledge would be impeded in the later eras, which would be the cause of ignorance of the sharīʿa.

Not yet finished with this topic, al-Kibsī introduces an additional *ḥadīth*, which provides a different perspective. Where his previous citations referred to the status and reception of written texts loosely associated with the Prophet Muhammad, this one centers on an explicit order to have a document written. Characterized broadly as an "order to write to preserve knowledge," the specific writing was connected with a sermon given by the Prophet. The story in question concerns an interlocutor named Abū Shāh. Where al-Kibsī omits the circumstantial detail, my friend Muhammad al-Ghurbānī, writing in the 1980s, explains that Abu Shāh was from Yemen and that he was present at the Prophet's sermon on the occasion of the Muslim conquest of Mecca.[23] According to the report, Abu Shāh said, "O Prophet, have [it] written for me." Al-Ghurbānī comments, "the intended was the writing down of the sermon that he had heard from the Prophet of God." The Prophet's reply, the authoritative passage in the *ḥadīth*, was, as some report, "Write for Abī Fulān"—that is, using the generic name for the man's actual name, Abu Shāh. Al-Kibsī and al-Ghurbānī both mention that this *ḥadīth* was reported by al-Bukhārī, Muslim, and al-Tirmidhī, three of the six "mother" collections of the Sunnī tradition.

Concluding his section on the Sunna, al-Kibsī makes a series of quick conceptual points. He states, first, that the "abundance" of the related *ḥadīth* reports about writing is such that the technical status of *tawātur* applies. In the usage of the *ḥadīth* specialists, the reference is to "reports so massively transmitted that they could not possibly have been forged and thus conveyed epistemological certainty."[24] Al-Kibsī argues, second, that the acceptance of writing in the early Muslim community was a matter of "consensus" (*ijmāʿ*), again a technical term, in this instance one specific to the jurists, as noted in chapter 2. The reference, again, is to the well-known fundamental principle of epistemic authority. Al-Kibsī explains that what he has presented from the Sunna "indicates that the acting on the basis of writing was a consensus of the Companions and the Followers." That is, writing was an accepted practice for the two named categories of authoritative individuals in the early community. Finally, third, he again raises the technical issue of *ẓann*, or probable knowledge, which always stands in contrast to the foil of certain knowledge. Ambiguously repeating his earlier transitional formula "among them," al-Kibsī writes, "Among them is that it [writing] conveys probable knowledge."[25] While it is understood that probable knowledge can involve different degrees, the principle here is "that which conveys probable knowledge must be acted upon." By extension to the topic at hand, "trusted writing must be acted upon."

Fiqh

Al-Kibsī now turns to the discourse of the jurists, his own field of specialization. Unlike his citations from the Sunna, which are about writing in general, and more in line with those from the Qurʾan, which refer to documenting a debt, the concern here is with the evidential status of archival writings. Al-Kibsī starts with a dense set of seven unannotated references. Rather than attempting to paraphrase, summarize, or narrate these shorthand citations, I will quote him in full, adding punctuation. Al-Kibsī begins with works and positions that depend on the language of the *Flowers* text and then moves on to further positions that are reported in the self-contained, fact-and-rule unit of the *masʾala*, here in one of its literary forms. In sampling these specific developments in what amounts to a centuries-long argument, he also notes some disagreements.

The first of the rapid-fire quotations rejoins a theme and the specific language I examined in chapter 3:

> As for what Imam al-Mahdi [al-Murtaḍā (d. 1437)] mentioned in [his book] the *Flowers*: in his statement (*qawl*): "*and not on the basis of what he found in his archive if he does not remember*,"

As I have discussed, this key passage from the *matn* of the *Flowers* connects archival writing and the authority of memory (*dhikr*). The reference is to the judge and the judgment act, and in these specific terms it restricts acting on the basis of writing. This initial quotation serves to anchor al-Kibsī's opening presentation of related positions in the *fiqh* literature.

> he said in *al-Kawākib*, [in] his sentence, "like the witness,"

This cited phrase extends the *Flowers* rule to the situation of the witness. The author is not mentioned by name. There are numerous works with this popular title ("The Stars") and al-Kibsī assumes the reader knows the correct reference. It could be *al-Kawākib fī-l-fiqh* by al-Amīr ʿAli bin al-Husayn, "one of the most famous of Yemeni Zaydī jurists," a work I do not have at hand.[26]

> and he said in *Ḍawʾ al-nahār*, "the circumstance of the writings,"

The book cited, again without naming its author, is the well-known commentary on the *Flowers* by the prominent Zaydī-tradition "Sunnī," Hasan al-Jalāl (d. 1673). Quoting this phrase is clarifying only in that it evokes the larger passage that it concludes.[27] Also added in this passage of al-Jalāl's commentary, but not noted by al-Kibsī, is the writing role of the court secretary.

> and what Imam Sharaf al-Dīn mentioned in *al-Athmār*, in his statement, "and he must not judge only (*bi-mujarrad*) on the basis of what he found in his archive,"[28]

Both the author and the book title are named. The jurist is *Flowers* author Imam al-Mahdī al-Murtaḍā's grandson, Imam Yahya Sharaf al-Dīn (d. 1558), a man known to highland political history as the first ruling Zaydī imam to militarily confront the occupying Ottomans. *Al-Athmār*, which I do not have, is an abbreviation of the *Flowers*.[29] This later authority reiterates the basic point expressed in the word "only": writing must not stand alone—that is, independently, as evidence. Al-Kibsī will return to this wording, which also appears in al-ʿAnsī's twentieth-century *Flowers* commentary as well as in earlier writings by the Ḥanafīs.[30]

> and what Imam al-Mahdī [al-Murtaḍā, the *Flowers* author] mentioned in *The Overflowing Sea*, in his statement, "*Masʾala* of the [Zaydī] school (*madhhab*) and of Abū Ḥanīfa and al-Shāfiʿī: the judge may not judge on the basis of what he finds in his archive if he does not remember,"

This seemingly redundant quotation from the *Sea*, al-Murtaḍā's cross-school comparative work, enables al-Kibsī to reassert a point that runs through his inquiry. Here it is noted that the eponyms of two Sunnī schools also held the same restrictive position concerning evidential writing. As I mentioned earlier, Ibn Miftāḥ (d. 1427) pointed this out in his *Commentary on the Flowers*.

> and what Ibn Muẓaffar [d. 1470] mentioned in *al-Bayān*, in his statement, "*Masʾala*: if in his archive, or in a container for papers, the judge found a document (*sijill*)[31] written in his handwriting and under his seal, if he remembers it, he rules on the basis of it; if he does not remember it, he does not rule on the basis of it, [which is] contrary to Abū Yūsuf and Muhammad"[32]

Here al-Kibsī is citing the prominent student of the *Flowers* author. Ibn Muẓaffar's important four-volume work, which I mentioned earlier as one of the set texts in the *fiqh* curriculum at Imam Yahya's twentieth-century madrasa in Ṣanʿāʾ, is not a commentary on the *Flowers*. It is instead organized in chapters that consist entirely of *masāʾil* and equivalent units. While Ibn Muẓaffar's position gives some further substantive detail—container, document name, seal—it also concludes with a significant phrase. This acknowledges, but does not further specify through citation or paraphrase, the opposing view held by two leading Ḥanafī school jurists, Abū Yusuf (d. 798) and Muhammad al-Shaybānī (d. 805), the prominent students of the eponym Abū Ḥanīfa (d. 767).[33] The implied opposing position—that the judge may act on the basis of such a document even if he does not remember it—rested on a determination as to the security of his archive.[34]

> and what al-Muʾayyad billāh mentioned in *Sharḥ al-tajrīd*, in his statement, "*Masʾala*: If a man knows his own handwriting and forgets the act of witnessing, he should not testify until he remembers the witnessing act and is certain about it."[35]

As the seventh and final item in this initial cluster of *fiqh* references, al-Kibsī quotes the pre-*Flowers* view of the eleventh-century Caspian imam, whose book he also cited in his section on *ḥadīth*. Like his second *fiqh* citation above (from *al-Kawākib*), this one poses the issue from the viewpoint of the witness. The substantive addition here is the reference to the individual's handwriting on the written instrument.[36] It is considered possible to recognize one's own script while forgetting the witnessing act of which it was a part. Between the uncontested past and the contested present, writing offers a temporal continuity, but its evidential authority depends on memory. According to this passage, remembering remains possible, but the standard is certainty, not probability.[37]

What interpretive conclusions does al-Kibsī draw from this collection of bare-bones *fiqh* citations? How do they pertain to his argument? "All of this," he writes,

> does not negate the opinion for acting on the basis of writing, since the intent in all of these formulations (*ʿibārāt*) is that, if he found his own writing and did not remember the witnessed or adjudicated matter, either in general or in detail, where it is only writing (*mujarrad al-khaṭṭ*, i.e., writing unsupported by memory), he should not testify about it or give a judgment using it.

"This," he continues, is

> due to the frequency of the occurrence in writings of dubiousness, forgeries, additions, and omissions. With his non-remembering, either in general or in detail, the uncertainty strengthens and the inference (*al-istidlāl*) [provided by writing] is invalidated, whereas with his remembering of it [the matter in question], this uncertainty is not strengthened.

In using the word "only" al-Kibsī returns to the language he quoted from Imam Sharaf al-Dīn. Regarding memory itself, he references the earlier-mentioned conceptual distinction between general and specific recall.[38] With his acknowledgment here of the distinct types of dangers commonly associated with the use of documents, he also introduces the key conception of "uncertainty" (*al-iḥtimāl*), which in this and in other schools points to a basic attribute of archival writing.[39] In reducing or balancing this inherent uncertainty, remembering permits reliance on an otherwise trusted writing for its evidential "inference." The lack of such remembering, in contrast, foregrounds or enhances the intrinsic uncertainty, and the result is the invalidation of the evidential worth of the writing in question. A century later, in al-Shamāḥī's commentary on Imam Yahya's choice, the potential dangers of archival documents would be expressed in this same conceptual idiom of the "uncertain" nature of writing.[40]

To further detail a negative conception of "untrusted writing,"[41] al-Kibsī employs more active notions of doubt (*shakk*, *shubha*). After stating, "With doubt and non-remembrance it is forbidden to undertake testimony or judgment," he pauses to back this assertion up with further "source" texts (three Qurʾanic verses, one *ḥadīth*). These convey the fundamental idea that testimony must be based on secure "knowledge" (*ʿilm*). Thus, for example, according to the Prophet Muhammad, "pointing to the sun, 'if you know [something] like [you know] that sun, then bear witness, otherwise, no.'"

Al-Kibsī then circles back to the already cited set of *fiqh* passages and recapitulates the book titles. He again quotes Imam Sharaf al-Dīn's rendering of the *Flowers* position on the judge and the archive—the passage with the phrase I have translated as "only"—that is, exclusively. Pursuing his interest in this specific wording, he quotes still another *Flowers*-tradition text, namely the commentary on Imam Sharaf al-Dīn's abridgment by Muhammad bin Yahya Ibn Bahrān (d. 1550).[42] Al-Kibsī reproduces the passage in this commentary that singles out the wording in question:

> Ibn Bahrān stated in the *Sharḥ al-Ithmār* [*sic*], in his commentary: "he [Imam Sharaf al-Dīn] stated 'only' because if he added to that [i.e., to the written document] the remembering of the circumstance, in general or in detail, or [if] he reached probability (*ẓann*) which permits judgment, he gives judgment on the basis of it."

"This," al-Kibsī summarily asserts, "is the intent of his [Imam al-Murtaḍā's] statement in the *Flowers*, '*if he does not remember.*'" He continues:

> This is the [position of] the school of the family of the Prophet (*madhhab al-ʿitra*), it is the position of Abū Ḥanīfa and al-Shāfiʿī, and it also was the position of [the Caspian imam] al-Muʾayyad billāh in the *Tajrīd*, "until he remembers what it comprises, and as for if he remembers, [then] it is permitted for him to bear witness."

His main point is that "the formulations (*ʿibārāt*) in these books convey, all of them, the acting on the basis of writing with remembrance." The cited passages, he continues, concern the "particular situation" of non-recall, and they lead to a "particular interdiction," which does not restrict the reliance on writing in other circumstances. He notes that he draws his conclusion despite the linguistic differences in these law book "formulations," differences he glosses, in technical terms, as contrasts between the "expressed," or "literal," and the "understood" (*manṭūq* versus *mafhūm*).[43] Advancing the positive "presumption" (*aṣl*) that individuals will remember the circumstances associated with their own written documents, at least in general terms, he characterizes the situation of non-recall in encountering one's own writing as "rare."

In the remainder of his inquiry, al-Kibsī ventures beyond the scope of these initial *fiqh* citations, with their special relevance to autograph writings and the rule of recollection, to resume a broader analysis buttressed by further arguments and citations. In these later sections he touches on the problems that motivated Imam Yahya's twentieth-century choice. Thus he covers the evidential status of archival documents written or signed not by the "self"—whether the judge, the court secretary, or a witness—but by an "other," a third party, which establishes the standard scenario of the notarial writer. Anticipating the twentieth-century issue of the "old writings," those privately held documents considered both sound and indispensible, he also mentions the problem posed by the deceased writer. Imam Yahya's solution, which depends on a finding by the presiding judge, represents an innovation, although it does accord with the general orientation of al-Kibsī's inquiry, which is to affirm acting upon the basis of writing "when there is trust regarding it."

In his later lines al-Kibsī returns substantively to the land sale instrument and the individual inheritance document, and he adds a mention of the will (*waṣiyya*). He additionally names other categories of archival writings, such as the judgment (*ḥukm*), minutes (*maḥḍar*), and register (*sijill*), all of which pertain to the sharīʿa court, and also the imamic opinion (*raʾy*). At the same time, he references some material accoutrements of the archival world, such as the paper container (*qimṭar*), as well as basics such as "his pen" and "his ink," the distinctive or personalized manifestations of which may or may not be recognized or, more formally, acknowledged in a particular writing.

In a selective manner, he quotes the Caspian imam further:

> As for what al-Muʾayyad billāh mentioned in *Sharḥ al-tajrīd*, in his statement, "*Masʾala*: [As for] one who testified against (*ʿalā*) a person on the basis of handwriting he saw, his testimony is invalid and the judge should not give judgment on the basis of the handwriting . . ."[44] This is predicated upon the fact that he [the witness] testified about a writing that he was not certain was the writing of the writer. The end of this passage [from al-Muʾayyad billāh] indicates this when he states, "and this [opinion] is valid because writing can be similar to writing, and forgery can occur in it." He also mentioned earlier that something could be written for a purpose (*gharaḍ*).[45]

"Writing can be similar to writing" (*al-khaṭṭ qad yashtabihu bi-l-khaṭṭ*): versions of this realistic but also somewhat ominous statement were articulated by other Zaydīs and by the jurists of different schools.[46] Al-Kibsī also notes but does not develop the theme of possible ulterior motives on the part of particular writers. Re-quoting the same *masʾala* a few lines later, he comments that "this formulation indicates that the basis (*sabab*) of his [the witness's] testimony is the seeing of the writing, [and] no more, without remembering the case borne witness to, without a reading of it, without observing the writer writing, and without dictation to him by the writer." In this listing, al-Kibsī includes an interesting conceptual distinction between a simple "seeing" (*ruʾya*) of a given writing and a silent "reading" (*iṭilāʿ*) of it. This mere seeing, but "no more," restates the basic idea of writing standing alone, which is the troubling evidential situation that consisted "only" of a written document.

Among the possible reinforcements enumerated (memory, reading, observation), al-Kibsī mentions a further modality of dictation (*imlāʾ*). This, again, is the minor institution that has figured in the conceptualization of the notarial craft at least since its identification in verse 2:282 of the Qurʾan. However, rather than the familiar Qurʾanic model of the debtor dictating to the writer, which involves a movement from speech to writing, in this situation the writer dictates to the witness, a movement from writing to speech. While the former mode of dictation is understood to be transformative, since the writer must reformulate the orally expressed colloquial terms in the proper technical language of a specific type of instrument, the latter is understood as an exact reproduction of the text for the purpose of confirmation.[47]

In passing, al-Kibsī notices some lesser remedies for the general insecurity of writing as evidence. One involves the relative certainty provided to a document by its being "safeguarded" or "protected" (*maḥfūẓ*) in a personal archive, which included the *dīwān* of the judge.[48] Another focuses on the situation of a short time interval between the original writing and the later testimony. Such remedies specifically reduce the likelihood of additions or omissions. However, the dominant evidential strategy remains that of carrying out an oral reading (*qirāʾa*) of a questioned document (cf. chapter 3). For this, another Caspian imam, al-Nātiq Abū Ṭālib (d. 1032), the brother of al-Muʾayyad billāh, provided the pivotal language.[49] Again using the juridical notion of an opinion "chosen," or preferred, by the interpretive community, while also glossing the key conception of "uncertainty," al-Kibsī writes: "The people of the school chose the wording (*kalām*) of Abī Ṭālib. He stated in *al-Bustān*... 'If it is not orally read to them [the witnesses] it is uncertain whether it contains irregularities (*taraddud*), whereas with an oral reading the uncertainty is eliminated.'"

An oral performance of the text overrides the potential danger, the "uncertainty" ingrained in the written archive. What is the temporal moment of this reading to the witnesses? Is this the law book institution discussed earlier in which, with an elapse of time and in a situation of conflict, memory issues were engaged and the oralization of the written instrument occurred as part of a court process? Or is this a reading to the witnesses at the time of the writing—that is, in the original context of the agreed-upon act? This last possibility, which would be equivalent to a "dictation" by the writer, also is recommended as a precaution by the author of the local manual for notaries, as discussed in the following chapters on the archive. Was the application of this mechanism of oral reading limited to primary instruments such as contracts and wills? Al-Kibsī's discussion suggests a wider usage. He mentions the "custom" of a particular Ṣanʿāʾ judge in connection with the witnessing of his judgments, although it is noted that this practice was criticized.

Regarding this technique of carrying out an oral reading of a written evidential text, al-Kibsī returns near the end of his inquiry to Imam al-Mahdi al-Murtaḍā. This time he quotes the imam's own commentary on the *Flowers* (that is, *al-Ghayth al-midrār*): "He said, 'The rationale for the oral reading is [that of] a precaution against an addition that is not insignificant, such that it would be known to he who remembered the general meaning. An example is the addition of an option regarding the sale object [in a sale contract instrument].'" Were it not for the writing, the imam continues, a witness would not be aware of any added expressions (*alfāẓ*).

I want to conclude my reading of al-Kibsī's inquiry by taking note of his passing reference to a further technical concept. This occurs just after his introduction of Abū Ṭālib's pivotal language on the oral reading of a written text, and it represents an additional analytic specification for the recurring notion of archival "uncertainty." The technical term in question is *ʿilla*, which points to the underlying crux of a given legal formulation, matter, issue, or case.[50] Al-Kibsī identifies the *ʿilla* that underpins Abū Ṭālib's notion of "uncertainty" as "the non-permissibility of testimony," and he also states that the *ʿilla* is not "the non-permissibility of basing [practice] on writing." His point is that in Abū Ṭālib's language the thrust is a question of evidence rather than of writing per se.

Where an *ʿilla* may be identified as the analytic underpinning of a particular matter, issue, or case at hand, it also could be a generative tool. It could serve as the conceptual means for interpretive extensions to other such matters, which then may be thought of in terms of their shared relation to this common *ʿilla*. In this type of casuistic thinking, the materials are *masʾala*s, and the associated form of reasoning is by analogy.

In the course of this extended "inquiry" al-Kibsī presents numerous distinct *masʾala*s, or issue "formulations," each of which conveys a distinctively expressed fact and rule situation. The *ʿilla* concept surfaces here in a narrow sense, in reference to the specific wording of Abū Ṭālib. As such, it is merely an isolated token of a characteristic mode of analytic thought, one that may be applied both within and across instances of circumstantial variation. Its use does suggest, however, that al-Kibsī saw at least part of his cited corpus of juridical thought through this lens of shared meaning.

PART II

Archive

SIX

Intermission

> The printed script of a play is hardly more than an architect's blueprint of a house not yet built or built and destroyed.
>
> —Tennessee Williams, *Camino Real*

IN ACTIVE TRADITIONS of written law neither the library nor the archive stood alone. Dialogues between these broad categories of necessarily "complicit" texts were fundamental to local histories of the sharīʿa, and their divisions of discursive labor provided cohesion to particular textual formations.[1] As I begin now to inquire into the various archival forms, I pose again the question earlier addressed to the texts of the library: what sorts of writings are these, and, by extension, what kind of law was this?

To transition from the library to the archive is to shift attention along the spectrum of writings from the esteemed book and the formal opinion to the varieties of ordinary documents, including court records (chapters 7–8) and selected genres of contracts (chapters 9–10). It is also to shift from authors to writers, from the productions of literary jurists, muftīs, and ruling imams to the work of others in the local interpretive community, those who served as court judges and secretaries, independent sharīʿa advocates, and private notarial writers.

Yet the line between the individuals concerned with library/theory and those engaged in archive/practice was fluid. Recall that Ahmad Qasim al-ʿAnsī, author of *The Gilded Crown*, the twentieth-century commentary on the *Flowers*, pursued a lengthy career of service in the imamic-era judiciary, while the imam himself, the head of the polity and the giver of formal opinions, actively immersed himself in archival paperwork. Aside from receiving petitions concerning disputes that he either handled himself or transferred to others, the ruler read capital cases and marked up the drafts of appellate rulings. In provincial Ibb, a number of the court judges, men responsible for an important segment of the local archive, also contributed in their own right to the period library, as authors or teachers or both, while the town's madrasa-based scholars, men who taught doctrine in lesson circles in the early mornings, supplemented their incomes by drafting legal documents in the afternoons.

In transiting to the practical genres and their specialized writers, library conceptions are by no means left behind. The strands of library thought focused on the archive, notably the general thematic of "basing practice on writing," plus such envisioned techniques as the "dictation" or "oral reading" of documents in court, now may be viewed from the perspectives and contexts of application. In addition, I consider two further modeling genres, both closely attuned to the realities of the period archive. In the next two chapters, I analyze the textual forms of the sharīʿa court judgment in conjunction with the set of formal "Instructions" for court organization issued by Imam Yahya in 1937. In the final two, I read historical documents from Ibb in tandem with the models provided in an early twentieth-century "stipulations" (*shurūṭ*) treatise.

In addition to being informed by such tutored approaches, the drafting of court and notarial documents also depended on the writers' untutored standards of composition. These standards derived not from formal lesson-circle instruction or explicit models but from informal apprenticeships and practical experiences in the indicated archival routines. While there were, of course, many parallels and influences from across the literary and spoken arts, the discursive methods in question also were specific to the sharīʿa archive. While I draw on ethnographic insights in studying the local modes of archival composition, my main task is to read this written work.

I have relied thus far on the basic distinction between the generalizing or *fulān*-oriented discourse of the library and the archival emphasis on particulars associated with the proper name. In the exclusively handwritten medium of the archive the message was one of specific human actors and their acts, and in the following chapters I examine how writers anchored their work in the particulars of people, places, and things. I also have distinguished between the atemporal and non-located modes of expression characteristic of cosmopolitan authorship and the efforts to date and place their work on the part of the writers of contingent texts. The forms of archival temporality modeled in the doctrine now may be viewed in terms of specific enactments. Beyond the relatively straightforward archival conventions for dating and placing, I also seek to understand the marking of intervals and sequences in the textual work. I read for indications of duration in the time of the text and for the traces of different temporalities that are indexed in the connections established with other texts.

Beyond these defining archival features associated with naming and temporal-spatial specificity, I follow other continuing themes. Regarding the basic methods of text building, I look closely at the diverse archival techniques for quotation and citation; regarding textual materialities, I consider the distinctive physical forms of the rolled or folded document and the bound register; and regarding discursive orality, I examine archival varieties of spoken "dictation" and their contrasting written outcomes in either exact transcription or transformative restatement.

Scripts

As a metaphor for the objects of this study, "script" serves to point up the statuses of the discursive phenomena that I have categorized as the library and the archive. This metaphor also serves to acknowledge the inherent distinction between sharīʿa writings of the various types and their indicated "performances."

Both library and archive texts may be thought of as scripts, but in different senses. With their highly elaborated templates and models, juridical stage directions, and even the occasional suggested dialogue, library writings provided complex scripts for archival acts, whereas the archival genres, with their commitments to proper names and other local identifiers, conventionally are thought of as the texts of practice and application. Consisting of entries compiled in one or more sessions, court records had their distinct enactment rhythms, as did the more condensed notarial acts. In addition to these roles as written performances with respect to the library, however, archival writings also should be understood as scripts in their own right, and this in a dual sense. Temporally, such documents represented both the written scripts *of* preceding oral testimonies, verbalized contracts, expressed or implied intent, achieved understandings, etc., and the scripts *for* subsequent enactments. In the case of a written contract, the following performance, the unfolding human experience of the contracted relationship, included the possibility that, with a dispute, the written document in question might be brought forward as evidence in a trial or, in the event of a complete breakdown between the parties, that what was "built" in the agreement script could be "destroyed." To study the lives of such archival texts thus requires thinking beyond their dated points in time, not only to processes of composition but also to textual pasts and futures.

I have shown in the preceding chapters that *fiqh* scripts were dialogic in construction. On the one hand, the doctrine may be seen (or represents itself) as a highly developed corpus of discrete receptions of and elaborations on the rule-bearing passages of the "sources," the oral/written texts of the Qur'an and the Sunna. On the other hand, in composing their books and opinions, literary authors quietly incorporated adapted versions of certain types of writings that had originated at the archival level—in the questions posed to muftīs, in the facts of significant court cases, and, as I examine later, in the stipulations of contractual undertakings. In the following chapters, I show that the composition of archival scripts was equally dialogic. While notarial writers could rely on the compositional models elaborated by the doctrinal jurists (or the ruling imam), their drafting efforts at the same time responded to the concrete demands of rendering spoken or lived arrangements in written form, as documented acts.

My archival readings compare lower-level library scripts—that is, locally tailored late-imamic-period models for court and notarial writings—with the varieties of coexisting historical documents they were intended to model. I additionally suggest that there were further modeling possibilities, though these are difficult to examine as such. First, rather than relying on the textual mediation provided by the lower-level models, archival writers may have bypassed these available scripts to engage directly with the higher-level body of script material found in the relevant doctrinal chapters of the *fiqh*. Second, experienced court and notarial writers necessarily, but in a lateral fashion, drew on established but nowhere formalized paper language conventions. Representing the known and accepted forms of documentation in the various genres in question, these implicit scripts of and for archival practice were inculcated as the textual habitus of the seasoned practitioners and reproduced in the routines of their written acts.

As for contrasts between scripts and performances, the differences to be understood do not represent the failing or flawed gap commonly associated with Orientalist dichotomies of theory and practice in the sharīʿa. In those positivist readings, written sources were thought to provide direct access to social realities and to justify judgments regarding the societies in question. Since the texts of what I have termed the library and the archive did not appear to match up, the former were deemed "ideal" and the latter taken as the evidence of "discordance." In such readings, however, written sources provided access to social realities in which the sources themselves, the acts of writing, were not included. Writing itself remained without qualities, and without agency.

In this book, the important differences to be acknowledged between scripts and performances resulted, in part, from the constraints of genre, which, in the relation between the writings of the library and the archive writings, informed their distinct but complementary discursive roles. In the theater analogy, every dated, placed, and name-filled archival text represented a particular performance with respect to an existing doctrinal (or lateral) script. In part, however, the differences between scripts and their performances pertain to the limitations of a study centered on writing and relations of form, and thus of my chosen mode of textual analysis. And this is not to mention what took place behind the scenes or offstage—action recoverable only by oral historical or retrospective ethnographic means. Yet when writing itself is taken to be an act, and composition a type of "performance," and when, rather than consisting of an empty formalism, the analytic project is to explore the "content of the form," the opposition between script and performance begins to break down. As differing types of scripts, then, and, to an interesting extent, as distinct varieties of "performances," the library and archive texts of the era may be studied as the sharīʿa "art" of highland jurists and practitioners.[2]

* * *

In the remainder of this "intermission" I offer some preliminary thoughts on what I refer to as "elementary forms" of the local sharīʿa archive. I follow this schematic discussion with comments on the "textual surrounds" of archival texts and on matters of "ethnographic sourcing." I then turn to questions of historical specificity, which I pursue through a series of forays into existing studies of pre- and early modern archival textuality in the sharīʿa. One purpose in these forays is to raise some basic comparative questions. At the same time these comparisons help to clarify the specificity of the highland instance, for which I also fill in some necessary background detail. Another purpose is to underscore the methodological differences between existing historical scholarship and the project of this book. The chapter concludes with a preview of the role of custom as an indispensible archival component of historical specificity in the sharīʿa.

Elementary Forms

In the following schematic survey of the sharīʿa archive, I sketch three pairs of rudimentary distinctions: *genres*, produced either by the courts or by notarial writers; *holdings*, either public or private; and *status*, either originals or copies.

In accord with the genre-based organization throughout this book, the chapters of the second half align with the distinction between writings issued by the court and those prepared by notarial writers. The major genre groups of archival texts I focus on are the transcript-based texts of court-contested lawsuits and three types of written contracts, which are examples of the primary instruments that pertained to uncontested acts. Judges and the courts were responsible for the issuance of the former while private individuals, usually third parties, including both established and occasional notarial writers, prepared the latter. These two groups of writings interacted when court minutes and, later, final case records quoted excerpts of instruments and other writings presented as evidence. Following Bakhtin, I examine this basic event of composition as one involving incorporating and incorporated, or narrating and narrated, texts.[3] In addition to the written notarial genres, I am equally interested in the incorporations in the written transcripts of oral texts such as witness testimonies and litigant responses, as well as oaths and spoken acknowledgments.

Crosscutting these basic types of genres were two archival formats or categories of holdings. Public registers pertained to the courts and were controlled by judges or their secretaries, while private individuals held personal or family collections of documents, which they kept in cloth bags, tubes, or chests. However, since the categories public and private properly pertain to the liberal order of a nation-state, in a polity such as that of the Zaydī imams the applicability of the distinction must remain an open question.[4] In connection with archival holdings and related matters of textuality, I will cautiously refer to the opposition of "public" and "private." On the "public" side, the indicated holdings were not "archives" in the modern sense. These collections were not established by nation-state institutions or colonial administrations nor were they maintained by modern professional archivists. On the "private" side, the important institutional caveat, discussed further below, is that the local notarial writers wrote without formalized state recognition or court approval. Their archival writings also were not assembled using the material and conceptual means of the typical modern transmission and storage device, namely the bureaucratic "file."[5] As a consequence, neither the "public" nor the "private" holdings fit the profile of what we conventionally think of as "documents," the writings that Annelise Riles refers to as the characteristic "artifacts of modern knowledge."[6]

Augmenting these basic contrasts of genres and holdings, I factor in an elementary archival distinction between an original and its copy. As intimately related texts, originals and copies were at once the "same" and different, with the difference being one not only of conceptual status but also of visual and material qualities, given a handwritten archive based on manual rather than photographic reproduction. The creation of such a textual double was a separate act, a further event of writing predicated on a complete reading and a reproduction of the original. In addition to what the culture of the copy reveals about that of the original regarding themes of primacy, authenticity, and authority, the relations of original and copy indexed the physical existences of archives of different types.

Court judgments involved both originals and copies. A pair of originals (sing. *aṣl*), which bore the signature of the judge, were issued to and kept by the litigant parties; a version with the status of a copy (*ṣūra*), usually without a signature, was entered in the designated type of court register. Notarial documents, the focus of the final two chapters, mainly consisted of individually held originals, without copies. Some notarial writers made and retained copies, however, and in some instances, normally at the initiative of the client, a copy of an instrument was entered in a court register. Under the Ottoman administration, however, the recording of copies was more formalized. This is indicated on some privately held documents from that era by revenue stamps and entry notes that mention the payment of a recording fee (*rasmiyya*).

For all original documents of the imamic period—that is, for both court-issued judgments and the variety of "privately" prepared notarial instruments, the archival pattern was one of dispersal rather than of centralization, of holdings distributed in diverse "private" hands rather than collected in a "public," central or state archive or record place.[7] However, in both the issuance of the original judgment documents and in the keeping of the register copies, there was a degree of centralization. Regarding the latter, the retention of copies, centralization consisted in the fact that records of litigated cases and selected instrument copies were entered in designated types of court registers (with sequential entry numbers and separately numbered pages); moreover, the keeping of such registers was a recognized administrative function. What made this centralization of the copy less pronounced—underscoring the limited extent of the "public" realm in the pre-revolutionary imamic polity—was that these register archives were not kept in designated official places but rather dispersed in the houses of judges or their principal secretaries. The procedural complement to this archival situation was that judges commonly heard cases in front of their personal residences. Such were the practices, it must be added, even though, in the years of the Ottoman Province of Yemen and also according to the "Instructions" later issued by the imam, the court was meant to be an "official" (*rasmī*) place where hearings were held and registers kept. Despite the advent of these new ideas, the arrangement that obtained in pre-revolutionary Ibb bore a resemblance to the premodern history of the sharīʿa, during which "the Muslim *qāḍī* had no specific place in which to hold court sessions" and court archives "were in the possession of private individuals, not institutions."[8]

When these elementary forms are combined, the anthropological historian of such a judicial system confronts contrasting archival series. Whereas "public" court registers contained the records of disparate cases and other matters (e.g., murder, inheritance, sale, etc.), entered in earmarked types of registers on the basis of their common genre identities—as (1) initial claims and ensuing case minutes, (2) final judgments in decided cases, and (3) instrument copies—"private" archival holdings, in contrast, typically brought together disparate genres united by their substantive relevance to particular properties or issues of concern to the individual or family in question. Adding in the distinction between original and copy, the clusters of written sources consist of, on the one hand, genre-related copies representing different cases or matters entered in "public" court registers and, on the other, genre-unrelated (or not necessarily related) original documents pertaining to particular cases or matters retained in "private" hands. In material terms, these were the contrasting series of the bound and the loose.

While it is instructive to break down the wider network of the sharīʿa archive in the indicated ways, it is equally important to recombine the discrete types, locations, and identities of the writings. Bringing these differing forms and features together in the inquiry enables an understanding of the various determinants of intertextuality and its binding force within the archive. The method here thus is equivalent to that pursued in the preceding chapters on the interrelations of the several library genres. The larger project of this book depends, in turn, upon joining these inquiries conducted internally to both the library and the archive. To then think across these major discursive categories is to consider such interrelations at the level of the textual formation as a whole.

Textual Surrounds

Like the books and opinions of the library, the documents of the sharīʿa archive were not isolates and should not be read as individual "monuments." Other writings, of the same and of different types, constituted their significant written contexts, and they did so in locally specific ways. Attention to these textual environments, to other writings temporally prior, co-present and post, helps position the main genres to be examined with respect to the processes and institutional structures of the local archive. Some such textual surrounds are evident in the historical sources. Others may be clarified through ethnographic means.

Antecedent texts ranged from extant writings of the same genre focused on the same substantive matter, a previous sale instrument, for example, to preceding writings in different genres. Final court judgments, as I detail in chapter 8, routinely included excerpts of written instruments and oral testimonies. In the overall construction of the judgment, however, the materially and conceptually distinct transcript of the litigation minutes provided the foundation. Other types of preceding genres include, for the court, a complaint or petition (*shakwā*) that led to a trial (chapter 7), and the summons issued prior to the hearing. For the notarial sphere, an example is an agency contract that would be referenced in the subsequent transaction instrument. In estate matters, several types of working documents (inventories and division preliminaries) figured in the preparation of individual inheritance documents.

Some of these writings, including drafts of the various kinds, were ephemeral or disposable. Prior texts also could be entirely informal, including writings devoid of technical discourse that nevertheless paved the way for the sharīʿa scripting. In a marriage negotiation I followed, in the weeks leading up to the drafting of the formal marriage contract, there was an exchange of polite written messages that served to establish the necessary intentions of the parties, without any mention of specifics. At a later social event, men briefly stepped outside the afternoon sitting room to orally agree to the final terms, and the contract itself was written the following morning.

Concurrent writings were a common phenomenon, especially in complex settlements and compound undertakings. In the wife-initiated divorce that I sketched in the introduction, for which the main resulting genre was a divorce instrument, three additional simple documents were prepared on the spot by the parties themselves. These concerned the further financial terms of an overall settlement, which were set down in (1) a receipt for the money paid as part of the necessary inducement to the husband; (2) a promissory note for the balance; and (3) a document canceling a separately written injury award—as it seems the husband had attacked and injured his wife's father, who was also his paternal uncle. Similarly, in a land sale transaction I observed, the final contract was predicated on a separate loan agreement written at the same session, although the loan was not mentioned in the sale instrument.

Although they pertained, collectively, to a single settlement or transaction event, the multiple documents produced in such circumstances usually did not reference their sibling texts, even when their own existence and terms depended on those of the other writings. Clusters of technically separate acts also could be associated with identifiable legal stratagems.[9] A reconstructive textual analysis may stress the interdependence of such documents, but notarial writers in Ibb purposely drafted them as self-sufficient and blinkered texts. While observable by an ethnographer, such textual practices are likely to be obscured in the historical record.

In the mentioned divorce settlement, the participants divided the resulting documents into holdings in separate residences. The husband's side retained the promissory note and the injury award cancelation while the receipt for the payment made to the husband and the divorce instrument itself went to the wife's side. The same two residential caches also were the repositories for the prior documentation, including the original marriage contract and the wound evaluation. An effort to reconstruct what had transpired at such an out-of-court settlement on the basis of these written sources would depend on locating the relevant archival holdings and bringing the dispersed texts together.

Subsequent texts, which typically necessitated readings of what had already been written, brought further developments. In the aftermath of a court judgment, a formal appeal and an appellate ruling were possible in this period, as was an additional settlement. Such later texts reframed the outcome set forth in the prior judgment. Appeal rulings were written directly on the original judgment documents held by the litigant parties while, minus the signatures, seals, and related entry notes, the same appellate text was added to the copy of the judgment already entered in the court register. In out-of-court settlements, in contrast, the written texts would be found only in the hands of the parties. For notarial documents, later annotations of several types were common, as I discuss in detail in chapter 10. Seemingly minor in import, such added notes were predicated on a reading of the main document text and embodied a range of possible further written acts. Circulating in locally patterned ways and perhaps accumulating further readings and written interventions along the way, such original court judgments and archival instruments served as the premodern equivalents of the dossier or file.

Ethnographic Sourcing

As with certain of my chapters on the library, those on the archive are characterized by their reliance on ethnographic sourcing. In the absence of central archives, the challenge was to locate and seek access to the dispersed private holdings of documentation for the first half of the twentieth century. Individuals I came to know in Ibb and elsewhere in Yemen gave me selective access to their holdings of records and documents, written materials that had been retained either by reason of a personal or family connection or as a result of a profession. The individuals in question decided what to show me based, in part, on their understandings of my research interests. In no instance did I see the totality of a personal holding. Although the documents I have accessed mainly date from the first half of the twentieth century (and earlier), they often were mixed in with contemporary papers, in active holdings otherwise engaged in ongoing affairs. In only one instance, involving some 112 historical documents, did I receive access to a self-contained and, in this sense, "completed" collection (the Burayhī-ʿAzīz collection in Ibb).

Ethnographic sourcing requires extended commitments to people and place, and its basic contributions are to the certainty and specificity of provenance and to relevant contextual information. Such sourcing entails knowing the archive in person, as it were. While the contextual information I obtained extended to local history, social relations, and political economy, my purposes here are not those of general ethnography. I should note, however, that my early efforts on the topic of kinship, for example, resulted in detailed family trees that later helped me to understand who was who in complex court cases.

I learned to be circumspect about putting the copies I had made before other local readers, even members of the same family. I learned, for example, that a pre-revolutionary murder case could stir sentiment among present-day descendants. Likewise, access to the details of an old property case might threaten to reopen the conflict, or those of a hard-fought court struggle among relatives in the past could be seen as harming the family's current reputation.

Ibb, of course, is by no means unique in the keeping of records and documents. Referring to a rural location near Ṣanʿāʾ, Martha Mundy remarks that documents of ownership and inheritance were "stored in the trunks of most every home." Paul Dresch observes generally that the documentary sources for the pre-revolutionary period in the highlands "remain in private hands."[10] From the mid-century efforts of S. D. Goitein and from Isaac Hollander's social history of villages near Ibb we know that the Jewish communities of Yemen likewise kept all manner of documents.[11] Work by anthropologists mainly has focused on the documentation of tribal custom in

Upper Yemen,[12] but Mundy, whose village lies within the active region of the capital and its courts, mentions the existence of local documents of sale, lease, marriage, endowment, and inheritance—that is, a representative series of the primary notarial genres in the highland sharīʿa archive. These, she adds, were "penned in the formulae of the *fiqh*."[13] Shelagh Weir's collection of local documents from a rural district in the far north opens with four seventeenth-century land sale contracts, the paradigmatic sharīʿa instrument of the agrarian-age highlands.[14] As for the "public" side, during his residence in Yemen, Jon Mandaville, a pathbreaker in the study of sharīʿa court records in the central Middle East, traveled in Lower Yemen and elsewhere to collect extant late Ottoman court registers.[15] And in his innovative *Wathāʾiq yamaniyya* [Yemeni documents], Sayyid Muṣṭafa Sālim published part of a corpus of urban and state writings that he obtained from "private" individuals.[16]

Yemen, for that matter, is not alone in its extensive family-held archives. In Morocco, Jacques Berque, the leading French Arabist, conducted mid-twentieth-century field research in a village in the Atlas Mountains south of Marrakesh. Having found that most individuals in this rural district retained at least a few important documents and that among the leading families the holdings were in the thousands, Berque remarked, "This society is enamored of the written."[17]

Historical Specificity

An analysis of the features of a given instance of the sharīʿa in history should be accompanied by an awareness of their significance in comparative terms. To extend the schematic identifications presented thus far of the principal archival writings to be read in the following chapters, I now explore a series of comparative issues by reference to a selection of existing studies of historical sharīʿa archives. In such work, archives have been treated in opposed ways: either from the top-down perspectives of various types of doctrine, through what I refer to as theories of archival practice, or from the bottom-up perspectives of particular archival configurations. I comment on such research from the perspective of the integrated, top-down *and* bottom-up approach of the historical anthropology pursued in this book.

The bottom-up perspective is characteristic of social history. Viewed locally, particular historical instances of the sharīʿa entailed particular arrangements of archival genres. Given a requisite institutional apparatus (e.g., formal instruction, opinion-giving interpreters, sharīʿa courts, and notarial writers) significant instance-to-instance archival continuities may be expected, with two qualifications: the use of standard genre terms could mask important differences and, conversely, variations in genre terminology could obscure important similarities.

In the introduction I raised a contextual issue regarding land tenure regimes. What are the connections between the givens of political economies and the coexisting forms of written archival usage? In each historical-geographical setting, the prevailing land tenure system involved particular tensions or contradictions, and it may be expected that these would be manifested, directly or indirectly, in the patterns of conflicts that arose. To the extent that certain of these disputes were settled or adjudicated in the sharīʿa courts, the result would be recorded entries in court transcripts, the social historian's principal source. The indicated landed tenure relations also would be manifested, again more or less directly, in the patterns of the principal types of contractual undertakings, and thus in the genres in use at the notarial level, another key source.

To return to the illustration I mentioned at the outset, I would first make the simple observation that the general textual forms of the court judgment and the notarial document from late-imamic-period Yemen broadly parallel the *iʿlām* and the *ḥujja*, the court decision and the evidentiary instrument of nineteenth-century Ottoman usage.[18] This correspondence in text types obtains despite the use of differing genre labels and the various administrative differences. But how might this apparent correspondence be complicated by contextual differences with respect to property relations? As I have noted, the old "public" form of *mīrī* property predominant in the Ottoman heartlands, and in Egypt, which assigned ultimate title to the state, the sultan, or the treasury, and which was not a sharīʿa conception, was virtually unknown in the world of highland Yemen, where agrarian property relations mainly took the form of "private" ownership rights (including endowments), based on the sharīʿa conception of *milk*. This property form (Turkish, *mülk*), of course, was of importance in the empire, but mainly in the towns.

Limited historical comparisons with respect to litigation patterns thus would be possible, at least up until the points in the nineteenth century when a series of important institutional changes occurred in both land tenure and in the courts of the empire.[19] Wider comparisons using the written records of disputes arising from property forms such as *mīrī* as opposed to those connected to individual *milk* holdings would seem difficult, however. In his research on mid-nineteenth-century records from Damascus and Beirut, Zouhair Ghazzal found that a number of types of court cases were resolved using procedural and other types of "fictions."[20] Was the incidence of, or the resort to, such "fictions" the result of the encounters of sharīʿa jurisdictions with conceptually unrecognizable property types such as *mīrī*—that is, forms unknown to the *fiqh*? Ghazzal indicates as much in stating that the jurists of those places and that time found the existing property forms to be "incongruent with their own conceptions and beliefs."[21]

A related comparative quandary exists at the level of notarial documentation. The basic Ottoman land transfer instrument was known as the *tapu*, a document that embodied usufruct rights in *mīrī* land. This genre of notarial writing was unknown in Yemen, where (inheritance aside) the typical land transfer occurred by means of the contract of sale, which established *milk* ownership rights. This contract was embodied in the instrument known as a *baṣīra*, which I have mentioned in terms of the passing references to it found in Zaydī doctrinal discussions. The sale contract itself was a standard of the doctrinal *fiqh* and was recognized as such across the *madhhab*s, although its application to land transactions appears to have been variable across historical instances. As a context-specific archival genre, the *baṣīra* was known throughout the highlands but nowhere else. For the same reason of the differing underlying property statuses of the land, the agrarian lease (*ijāra*) contract, nominally fundamental to both the Ottoman and highland settings, amounted in each to quite different bundles of rights and obligations.[22]

Since the Ottoman case was the best known example of the historical sharīʿa, one wonders whether this specific impasse between the law on the books and the main patterns of land tenure played a role in the wider Orientalist assumption of, to quote Schacht again, a "discordance between the sacred law and actual practice."[23] In the present book, in demonstrations that depend on readings that cross between a library and an archive and that address the contextual circumstances of both governance and property relations, I provide further refutations of the already broadly discredited notion of an ingrained disjuncture between sharīʿa theory and practice. As these contextual materials also offer clear contrasts with the more familiar Ottoman institutions, they additionally help us to understand the Ottoman instance—however thoroughly studied, widely relevant and interesting in its own right—for what it is, namely a historical instance (or set of instances) among others rather than an embodiment of the timeless and essential character, or "nature," of the sharīʿa.

"Public" and "Private"

Different comparative questions arise from what I have referred to as the "public" versus "private" distinction. Existing research on the sharīʿa archive has emphasized its "public" face. In the following chapters, I complement the study of this "public" aspect of the local archive with equivalent attention to its "private" dimension. As I noted earlier, my conception of the "private" archive in late-imamic Ibb refers both to court-produced, but individually retained, original judgment documents and to unofficially produced and also residentially held notarial writings. As I also noted, the distinction between originals and copies crosscuts that between "public" and "private," in a perhaps unexpected way, inasmuch as it was the "public" authority that held the copy.[24]

Absent a perspective on the "private" dimension and on the related patterning of originals and copies, an understanding of the overall structure of the sharīʿa archive is blocked, especially the archive-wide relations of intertextuality. An exploration of the phenomenon of "private" archival holdings completes an understanding of the material and conceptual connections of individuals to a particular sharīʿa regime. Beyond the range of links documented in the "public" court registers lies the hitherto largely unexamined documentary terrain of individually held original writings, notably including the gamut of genres not issued by the court.

A view of the sharīʿa archive restricted to its "public" face is characteristic of Ottomanist research, but there are exceptions. Beshara Doumani's historical sources, for example, comprise both registers from the local courts and also collections of family "papers" from the same Palestinian town.[25] For family "papers," however, there is a question about the sharīʿa-specificity of the documentation in question. Typically, locally utilized genres of sharīʿa instruments represented an identifiable subset of the retained practical writings. There are remarkable early examples of such mixes in the massive corpuses of the Arabic papyri from Egypt and, within a different institutional framework, the huge trove of documents from the Cairo Geniza.[26] An example of such a mix of strictly sharīʿa and other genres in a near-modern historical setting is Rudolph Peters's recent study of a "family archive" from Dākhila Oasis in Egypt.[27] In contrast, research by Mikhail Rodionov and Hanne Schönig on a twentieth-century archive from southern Yemen concerns a "private" corpus devoid of sharīʿa writings.[28]

As for the "public" identity of sharīʿa court registers, I would repeat the earlier quoted remark of twentieth-century *Flowers* commentator al-ʿAnsī on the technical term *dīwān*, or the judge's "archive." This he defines as "a site where the circumstances (*aḥwāl*) of the people are entered and recorded," adding that the term "refers to the register (*daftar*), and to its place."[29] The notion of "the people" (*al-nās*) and the indicated activity of register keeping point to separate dimensions of a period-specific "public" function. Considered collectively, "private" individuals constituted "the people," a particular kind of "public." Court registers were associated with this "public" sphere in the highlands both as repositories of records of concern to "the people" and as a key material implement of the imam-appointed judge and his secretary. By the turn of the twentieth century, at least in the earlier noted Ottoman conception, this activity was beginning to be associated with the new domain of the "official," the *rasmī*. Under the following imams, however, this "public" quality would be modified by the fact that the registers typically were kept in "private" residences.

Registers

Bound records of various sorts figured centrally in the institutional apparatuses of many complex premodern states with the Ottomans among the great keepers of registers.[30] Their tradition likely was introduced in the Yemeni highlands during the first occupation of the highlands (sixteenth–seventeenth centuries), and we know it was updated and extended in the second (1872–1918). In the following chapters, I refer to three types of registers kept by the post-Ottoman highland courts, two devoted to litigation and one to contracts and other instrument copies.

Of particular comparative interest for the meta-textual aspect of my inquiry is the fact that the Ottoman-era jurists thought conceptually about registers. That is, together with many other categories of written texts—from the "sources" of the sharīʿa and the books of jurisprudence to the common instrument—the register also was subjected to reflective juridical analysis. Guy Burak has shown that Ḥanafī jurists addressed the "evidentiary status" of the "imperial register."[31] The issues at stake ran parallel to the Zaydī jurists' thinking about the written document, notably their concern with forgery, and some of the conceptual language employed is identical. Two examples of the latter are the basic question of whether registers could stand alone (*bi-mujarrad khuṭūṭihim faqaṭ*) as evidence—that is, independent of supporting witnesses—and the larger question of "practice with" or "based on" imperial registers (*al-ʿamal bi-l-dafātir al-sulṭaniyya*).[32]

Ottoman arguments about the integrity and evidential value of registers also referred to the related but much older topic of commercial registers. Concerning the evidence value of these writings, Baber Johansen cites the views of Central Asian Ḥanafī jurists from as early as the eleventh century and from Syria as late as the nineteenth, which involved three factors.[33] First, the physical circulation of these commercial registers was strictly limited, a feature that they were seen as sharing with state registers and that was understood to significantly reduce the possibility of forgery. However, while a commercial register was "private," controlled by the individual merchant, those of the state were "public." It may be noted, in passing, that approximately the reverse rationale was applied to accepting the authority of the knowledge found in books, although this was not a matter of evidence. Very wide circulation and their well-known (*mashhūr*) identities made certain noted cosmopolitan books virtually unimpeachable. Second, the merchant writings were autograph texts, involving entries kept in the merchant's own hand, without third-party or notarial intervention. Something equivalent, involving designated scribal functionaries and their professional commitments, structured the maintenance of a state register. Third, "custom" (*ʿāda*) provided the decisive basis for accepting a commercial register as evidence. Wielded by the jurists, custom here validated power and legitimated privilege. By providing a conceptual language for the assumption of the general integrity of their practices, the jurists buttressed the interests of the commercial elites, and, by extension, those of high state officials.

Commercial registers also appeared as a topic of juridical discussions in pre-revolutionary Yemen. In 1950, Imam Ahmad issued a doctrinal choice (*ikhtiyār*) on this theme, specifically, on the evidence value of "the registers of the merchants" (*dafātir al-tujjār*).[34] It states, "The registers of merchants are accepted and trusted if the merchant is reputed for truthfulness and good conduct, and nothing [untoward] is discovered about him, and [in this there is] no difference between the Muslim and the *dhimmī*" (the Jew or Christian). While I have no information about the context in which this choice originated (i.e., whether it arose from a quandary in a litigated case), I do have an example of its influence in a later case. In the following chapter, I treat an Ibb sharīʿa court case from 1956 (case 3) that was decided, in part, on the basis of reports of entries in the register of an Aden-based commercial agent. After an affirmation of this agent's good reputation, the relevant transaction evidence was sourced as follows: "The accounts for the purchase were transcribed from the register (*daftar*) of the agent al-Hajj ʿAbd Allāh bin ʿAli Sālim al-ʿAwlaqī."[35]

Official register keeping in Ibb was not confined to the sharīʿa courts.[36] This keeping of other types of "public" registers represents a cross-institutional backdrop for those maintained by the court. According to a 1916 accounting document for the Ottoman District (*qaḍāʾ*) of Ibb, the existing local offices in the final years of the empire included that of the district officer (*qaʾim maqām*), the court (*al-ʿilmiyya*),[37] the Treasury, the Education Office, and the Gendarme Unit. Other local records show that a Municipality (*baladiyya*) Administration existed as well. Across these administrative units, the Ottomans introduced a version of their empire-wide standards of recordkeeping.[38] Only the local Endowments (*awqāf*) Administration stood apart from these reforms.[39]

"Private" registers also were in use in Ibb. Landlords of a certain scale kept small registers, mainly for leases. One such bound text is mentioned in the court case from 1947 that serves as an example in the following chapter. Leases entered and archived in these "private" registers had the status of originals. In addition to those from an Endowments Office lease register, the corpus of late imamic period agrarian and urban real estate leases that I examine in chapter 10 are from the "private" register of an Ibb landlord. In the same chapter, I also give an example of an Ottoman-era register used for the inventory of properties in a large Ibb estate. Together with the work of an appointed *amīn al-qisma*, revenue stamps give this bound "private" estate register a pronounced "public" quality. Although I mentioned "private" commercial registers above, I have not seen period examples of such account books.[40]

The Judge's Archive

When I went upstairs in Judge al-Ḥaddād's just vacated house, I encountered the remnants of an archive located on the same floor as his semi-"public" afternoon sitting room. On the basis of its physical location and contents, I assumed that what I saw was distinct from whatever personal or family papers the judge retained, which would have been kept on the "private" upper floors of the same residence. As I noted in the opening pages of this book, what I found included not only a damaged register from a late imamic jurisdiction but also fragments of various loose documents, most of them photocopies.

During my time in Ibb I heard from various individuals about the loss of their personal documents when an old judge had died.[41] How should we interpret the fact that judges commonly held loose documents? Did they constitute part of a judge's "public" archive? The schematic introduced earlier in this chapter highlighted the fact that archival accumulation for original documents initially happened in "private" hands. Building on this observation, I want to reflect on the subsequent patterns of document movement and utilization.

Research on the important Mamlūk-era documentary trove found at the Ḥaram al-Sharīf mosque addresses this question.[42] According to the plausible hypothesis advanced by Donald Little, these roughly 900 documents "constitute the remains of archives kept by the Shāfiʿī Court in Jerusalem."[43] Taking up this issue recently, however, Christian Müller makes a different argument.[44] Acknowledging that these documents from the years 1391–95 do, in fact, relate in various ways to the presiding judge, he poses the question of whether the corpus should be considered a "systematic archive" or, rather, a set of documents collected for a specific purpose. He proceeds to ask whether the documents have indications of an intention of "archival storage" as opposed to some more transitory aim. After considering the incidence of filing notations on document versos and also whether or not the paper used was of a standard size, he then asks about the representativeness of the collection. Noting the absences of documents in a number of the expected substantive areas—specifically marriage, sales, and criminal matters—Müller concludes that this was not a judge's archive. He then proposes an alternative hypothesis: that the documents in question were assembled for the particular aim of building "a dossier" for a "corruption case" against the judge in question. He further observes that the status of the collection of documents seems to be connected to the fact that the case may have been interrupted by the judge's death.[45] If this hypothesis is accurate, how had the documents been assembled? Had they been obtained from "private" holdings?

Theories of Archival Practice

> Like people and schools of criticism, ideas and theories travel—from person to person, from situation to situation, from one period to another.
>
> —Edward Said, "Traveling Theory"

Unlike library writings, archival texts were not designed for travel. Where the familiar forms of doctrinal works and opinions were recognizable across Arabic-reading settings, the same would not necessarily be true of the more homespun writings of the archive. Cosmopolitan doctrinal works and opinions, or at least those of consequence, were able to move across regions and were apt to be addressed in receptions that ranged from instruction in lesson circles to written commentaries to simple citations (chapters 2, 5). Facilitated by the generic, or *fulān*, structure of their discourse with its relative absence of attachments to specific locales, the displacements of such texts nevertheless were modulated by their *madhhab*-specific identities. Contingent archival writings, in contrast, with their orientations to proper names, careful specifications of dates and locations, and complex ties to local custom, were largely stay-at-home texts.[46]

Further perspectives on the judge's *dīwān* derive from the textual categories and related logics set forth in the top-down perspective of doctrinal sources. Elaborated in various genres, including both standard *fiqh* chapters, such as that on the "judgeship" (*al-qaḍāʾ*), and in specialized doctrinal treatises, such as those on the "culture of the judge" (*adab al-qāḍī*), the jurists' practice-oriented depictions of the judge's archive necessarily had model qualities. Discursively cosmopolitan and by design comprehensive, these conceptual presentations identify the writings appropriate to each of the analytically recognized intervals and tasks in the court process and in the duties of the judge. As opposed to written archival practice itself, grounded as it was by multiple attachments to particulars, theories of archival practice also could travel as part of the wider journeys of sharīʿa doctrine.

Theories of these types are central both to general histories of the sharīʿa and to the present anthropological history. In *Sharīʿa*, the authoritative general history by Wael Hallaq, theories of practice serve as essential source materials for determining, according to the focus of his study, the "systemic components" of the historical sharīʿa. These were the structural "constants" that "did not change over time and place"—that is, over the many centuries prior to the colonial era.[47] General history and historical anthropology share an interest in these "systemic" aspects of the sharīʿa, but they do so from different vantage points. While the genres of the doctrinal sources drawn on are identical, and while both macro and micro readings may value, translate, and analytically extend the thought of the historical Muslim jurists in question, the implications of the inquiries differ. In a macro-history the identified structural consistencies apply *across* historical instances, whereas in a micro-history they figure *within* a particular instance.

The approaches to practice differ accordingly. Hallaq's overall aim is to "map out the system of knowledge and practice that is Islamic law."[48] Regarding practice, this is to determine its regularities as an integral part of the larger systemic unity of the historical sharīʿa. As a domain, practice includes what he refers to as standard institutional "functions" and "functionaries," among them the familiar archival personnel—the judge, the court secretary, and the notarial writer—whose functions represent "constants insofar as their *structural* performances were concerned."[49] A historical anthropology is equally interested in this systemic dimension of practice, but practice consisted of more than these regularities. While Hallaq's *Sharīʿa* both recognizes and illustrates the significance of local variations in practice in the historical sharīʿa, this book treats the phenomenon of archive-level contingency as an analytic problem.

Patterns of variability in the practice of the sharīʿa are a defining but little studied feature of its history, and the archive the site of variation par excellence. In the absence of the requisite archival sources, or, with their presence but without reading these sources together with their doctrinal counterparts, such patterns cannot be properly understood. While cosmopolitan theories of practice were unlocated by discursive orientation, and therefore, as sources, tend to obscure the specificities of particular instances, a historical anthropology shows how specific library writings of these types were made local by being brought into dialogue with a coexisting archive. Marshaling both categories of source texts in separate and then conjoined readings, this type of inquiry disentangles the theory of textual practice from practice itself.

An important resulting finding is that practical writings typically contained both doctrinal and non-doctrinal elements. In a mix on display in every archival document, cross-instance terminology appears on the same page and in the same lines with instance-only language. In this way, the discursive "constants" of the tradition interacted with the particulars of the local. In the absence of the counterweight of archival sources, an analysis based on doctrinal sources alone is liable to see the theory of practice as practice tout court.

The key studies in the theory of archival practice are by Baber Johansen and Wael Hallaq (in a specialized earlier article).[50] While the theories in question are, again, universal in terms of their discursive vistas, they are nevertheless historically and *madhhab*-specific, with Ḥanafī writings predominating in these studies. In addition, since both Johansen and Hallaq utilize multiple doctrinal sources, the resulting surveys can have the character of amalgams. The upshot may be understood as either a maximally detailed or an impossibly complicated view of written practice. However exhaustive their coverage, we should not assume (and Johansen and Hallaq do not assume) that such meta-textual plans were coterminous with the actual institutions of implementation on the ground. On the one hand, as library writings about the archive, such doctrinal sources characteristically recycled earlier doctrinal thought on the topics in question. On the other, these writings presumably also stood in a dialectical (model *for* and model *of*) relation to particular versions of archival practice, although for the early centuries the matching archival writings are unavailable.[51]

From specialized doctrinal works such as the early *adab al-qāḍī* treatise by the Ḥanafī jurist al-Khaṣṣāf (d. 874 or 875),[52] Johansen extracts an inventory of the possible types of writings that may appear in a judge's archive. These he resolves into four categories, which taken together constitute the qāḍī's *dīwān*: (1) documents related to the court process, (2) "notarial documents," (3) administrative documents, and (4) correspondence.[53] The first two, the court process documents and the notarial writings, pertain directly to the genres I examine in the following chapters. Johansen breaks down the first category, the writings involved in the adjudicatory process, into ten subtypes.[54] I comment on several of these document types from the dual standpoints of Zaydī procedural writings and Ibb case records of the first half of the twentieth century, as augmented by cautious retrospection from my ethnographic observations.

Before beginning with the document types, I want to note that Johansen's important article covers a variety of other topics, notably including the institution of court-recognized witnesses, which I hope to treat in a later work devoted to sharīʿa litigation. In some historical setings the precertified "reliable witness" evolved into the "public" notary. This process appears to have been most complete, and historically enduring, in the Islamic West, in the territorial realm of the more doctrinally accommodating Mālikī school.[55] It is, in fact, with reference to this particular region and juridical school that anthropologists have studied the phenomenon of "normative witnessing" and the related authentication of documents.[56] Such witnessing and notarial institutions were particular to certain regional traditions of the sharīʿa, however, rather than essential to all. Suffice it to say here that in imamic-period Ibb there were neither official witnesses nor court certified notarial writers.

First mentioned by Johansen among the court process documents is the *ruqʿa* (lit. "piece of paper"), which issued from two named parties and signaled their desire to engage in litigation, and which the court then used to schedule the case. In Ibb, if both were willing, the parties simply went before the judge, perhaps in the idiom of "you and me, sharīʿa." Status and gender issues complicated the patterns of appearances, as could matters of representation, normally by a "private" *wakīl*, which then implied a supporting agency document (*wakāla*). Closer to the written form of the *ruqʿa*, but involving only a single party, an individual in Ibb could appear and demand that the judge summon the adversary. This also could be based on the written form of a complaint or petition (*shakwā*).[57] Approached in such ways, the Ibb judge could decide to dispatch a soldier-retainer carrying a written summons to the adversary that said (expressed here in model language), "Bring in so-and-so (*fulān*) to give justice to the petitioner."[58] In the written milieu of this judicial process, *shakwās* and summonses were transient and disposable artifacts. Neither left a written trace in the court record, with the possible exception of the mention of a petition having been received. *Shakwas* addressed to the imam or the provincial governor, and that concerned justiciable matters, could be referred to the judge with the relevant jurisdiction. A case that originated elsewhere likewise could be assigned to a specific judge by the imam or by a member of his *dīwān*. In such situations, a transfer order, an *iḥāla*, would be mentioned in the opening line of the ensuing litigation record.

Another item Johansen lists is the *qiṣṣa* (lit. "story"), a text containing a one-sided presentation of the case.[59] What is the degree of formality, and what is the procedural role, of this text? Is this a relatively informal opening gambit in which a party briefly lays out an argument and the supporting evidence? Or is this closer to the nature of a formal claim (*daʿwā*) from the plaintiff to open the litigation? The former is indicated, especially since an overview of the evidence is provided. In litigation, formal evidence would not be required and presented until after the defendant's response to the plaintiff's claim. Johansen mentions the possibility of drafting assistance from a "private" *wakīl* or a court clerk, however, which would indicate a degree of formality. As the term in question suggests, this written document seems to embody a type of narration to the judge to establish the general plausibility of the case in advance of litigation. As such, a *qiṣṣa* might be structurally equivalent to a Yemeni *shakwā*, but more substantively detailed. Johansen notes that in some historical settings the *qiṣṣa* replaced the *ruqʿa* (neither was known in Yemen). He also states that the role of such a written narration could be to prompt initial background inquiries by the judge. It thus could have contributed to the judge's preliminary determination regarding the status quo (the *ẓāhir*) in the conflict and, on this basis, his allocation of the litigation roles of plaintiff and defendant.[60] At the same time, as Johansen suggests, such an uncontested overview of the case could be prejudicial. It also is directly contrary to the dialogic nature of sharīʿa litigation, during which not only the judge but also the opponent must be present, and in which assertions are met by responses, and perhaps by counter-claims and further evidence. On the other hand, the formula of the plaintiff as the presenter of the claim and as the party solely responsible for producing evidence does accord with the less frequently instanced, but normative, single-sided model of litigation set forth in the *fiqh*.[61]

Several of the types of writings that Johansen surveys pertain to evidence, the culminating text being the *maḥḍar*, the minutes transcript (see chapter 8). In the session before the judge, the process unfolds between the two parties, who bring their witnesses. "Of all of this," Johansen states, "the qāḍī takes notes in a dossier." This text (also termed *ruqʿa*) is the judge's own record of the case. It consists of a "word-for-word" account of the parties' statements, and it is kept in the judge's personal control. Following the session before him, the judge sends the parties to the secretary, who prepares the *maḥḍar*, the minutes record. Johansen explains that the secretary enters details on the identities and the physical descriptions of the parties and their witnesses, maintaining a "verbatim" style. He adds that the secretary will at this point "insert in his minutes the copies of documents that the parties had eventually presented to the judge."[62] Extrapolating along the lines of my earlier schema, this means that "private" litigant parties brought original documents to court to present to the judge as evidence, and that the court secretary entered copies of these documents in the "public" minutes transcript.

In the next step in this record-making process, the judge "compares" the secretary's minutes with his personal "dossier." If he finds them in accord, he signs the minutes, "writing thereon that they [the minutes] had been read aloud, in his presence and in the presence of the cited witnesses." Finally, he asks the "witnesses of the court," individuals who are distinct from pre-recognized professional witnesses (whose role I treat elsewhere), to witness and sign, and thus to finalize the minutes of the case, the *maḥḍar*. Later, they did the same for the concluding judgment.[63]

While perfectly correct doctrinally, is this process too complex to have been carried out in practice? An unusual feature, to me, is that of the judge writing his own detailed notes on the process. This separate "dossier" seems to largely parallel, and in fact was used to correct, the case record contained in the minutes, or *maḥḍar*. The judge taking down the statements of parties and witnesses strikes me as unlikely in practice. In the litigation context I study, this was the secretary's function. At most, a judge directed the secretary in this task. If judges took their own notes, have any survived? Or would such a "dossier" be one of the ephemeral writings that did not appear in the final archival record? In my understanding, the sharīʿa judge during litigation was a largely passive listener and observer (unlike the modern judge in Yemen who is an active questioner). Would the demands of "word for word" transcribing have detracted from his attentive presence? As for the step that followed the process before the judge, is it suggested that the parties and their witnesses left his presence for the completion of the minutes with the secretary? Was this a technique associated with urban scale, representing an institutional mechanism for managing a large caseload? In the highlands, all recorded aspects of litigation transpired before the judge, or his presiding delegate. In connection with the case minutes, I would highlight Johansen's mention of a version of the doctrinally mandated oralization technique I discussed earlier (chapter 3). Here, the method of reading a written text aloud helped to confirm the authenticity of the completed minutes record.

The descriptors "word for word" and "verbatim" for this record are interesting to me since a selective mode of exhaustive transcribing also characterized the court process in twentieth-century imamic Yemen (see chapter 8). Concerning the final text comprising the judge's decision, was it understood to include a record of the litigation derived from, or directly based on the approved minutes? The latter was the practice in highland Yemen in the imamic period. Although we know that the final judgment texts entered in the Ottoman *sijill* usually took the form of brief summaries, did a similar type of fulsome recording of litigation minutes also exist? According to Johansen's sources, two versions of the final judgment text were prepared: one was provided to the party who won the case (or to a party requesting it), while the other was kept in the judge's archive.[64] Since it was deemed liable to forgery or alteration, the version obtained by the winning party was not considered a proof-bearing text. This last understanding differs from that up to mid-twentieth-century Yemen, where, as I have noted, a pair of authoritative original judgments signed by the judge went to the parties, while an unsigned copy of the final text was entered in the court register. It may be worth mentioning that a pattern similar to this three-version Yemeni practice regarding final judgment documentation existed in eleventh-century al-Andalus.[65] A final point is that, their detailed differences aside, these scenarios all implied the existence of "private" archival holdings of court-issued judgment documents.

A question remains, however, about the phenomenon of "private" documents—that is, primary evidential instruments—held in the judge's hands. This returns us to the problem of the status of the Ḥaram al-Sharīf collection. Was there a form of deposit with the court that approached the status of a "public" archive? While "deposit" certainly existed as a technical possibility,[66] and while notarial writers in Ibb briefly held personal documents in a fiduciary capacity, my ethnographic work regarding the situation of original documents held by the judge suggests the following understanding. As is envisioned in Johansen's survey, such instruments turned up in an Ibb judge's possession when litigants presented their documents to him in connection with court processes. Imam Yahya's "choice" on written evidence assigned the key task of document (and handwriting) evaluation to the presiding judge (see chapter 5). Judges needed to review such writings both to assess their evidential implications and for related decisions about excerpting them in the minutes. Normally, such presented documents stayed in the Ibb judge's hands only temporarily, since the parties would come to retrieve them. However, people sometimes did not take their documents back for one reason or another, including the fact that a fee might be involved, and in such circumstances a de facto archive of originals could accumulate in the judge's hands.

Regarding the "public" versus the "private" character of notarial writing there appear to be divergent general views, although these may reflect the reliance on doctrinal sources for differing historical periods and circumstances. Johansen writes, "The notarial [function] is assured by professional witnesses, nominated and controlled by the qadi."[67] Hallaq, in contrast, refers to a "notary . . . who did not sit in the qadi's court and whose function was private, not a public one."[68] Minus the formality that may be associated with the term "notary," the latter description fits the situation of the notarial writers in Ibb (see chapters 9 and 10). Yet Johansen also refers to three possibilities: to documents "established by themselves [i.e., the court personnel], by the notaries and by private parties." As I noted earlier, he also alludes to the practice of entering copies of privately submitted, and possibly privately written documents into the court minutes. "Private parties," his third possibility, could designate either professional (but uncertified) or nonprofessional occasional notarial writers, both of which types were found in Ibb. In addition to these sorts of writers and their characteristic third-party discourse, however, "private parties" might also indicate another type of writer, as yet unmentioned. This is the sufficiently educated, but typically nonprofessional, autograph writer, the individual who wrote in the first person. This writer could write, "I sold," "I retracted," "I relinquished," etc. In the idiom of western scholarship, the result was a "subjective" writing, which contrasts with the more conventional "objective," or third-person style.[69]

To conclude this (incomplete) coverage of Johansen's authoritative survey, I want to briefly discuss his second category among the writings that figure in the judge's *dīwān*: the "notarial documents." This refers to writings "for which the *qāḍī* serves as notary, in certifying and authenticating." I understand notarization here to refer to an analytically separate step that follows the drafting of a document, when an already written document is validated by the judge. The genres Johansen mentions include acknowledgments of debt, obligation instruments, contracts, wills, and divisions of property. Something equivalent occurred in Ibb in connection with a similar range of document types, as I detail in chapter 10. In Ibb practice, a primary document typically was written in the script and bore the signature of a locally known (but not in any way certified) writer. The bodies of such instrument texts routinely named at least two ordinary witnesses, who usually did not sign the documents. The drafting work completed, the "private" party in question, the individual who paid the notarial writer for his efforts, might elect to carry the document to a judge, or the muftī or the governor, for a type of certification and authentication. This was known as an *iʿtimād* (or a *taṣdīq*) and would take the form of a note placed in the open space above the main document text. Written in the official's personal script and with his signature, this note usually appeared under a separate *Basmala* and would be dated, although on the official's side there would be no record that this affirming note had been written. Now bearing the *iʿtimād* note, the document was handed back to the party, who carried it home. Taken into the "public" arena to obtain this further level of legitimizing support, but without leaving a bureaucratic trace there, the newly annotated document would be placed in a "private" archive. The other such option was that the party could decide to have a copy of the newly written instrument entered in the court register, with the original, now bearing an entry note, again being retained at home. Many documents, however, bore no certification note and had no entered copy, as neither was required.

Written Custom

A fundamental aspect of historical specificity in a given sharīʿa archive was its anchoring in "custom" (*ʿurf, ʿāda*). As I have noted, archival genres typically made selected use of technical terms from the available library discourse as an integral part of the phrasing of the locally established paper language. This usage was set in conjunction with, and thus was altered by, an encompassing archive-specific discourse of the name, time, and place. Such defining discursive composites in these local written forms were, in their entirety, conventional. Going beyond simple dichotomies of persisting contractual form and ever-changing negotiated content, this is the more complex, dialogic sense in which archival writings should be understood as contingent. The conventions in question comprised the material and stylistic features of the documents, as well as their colloquial names. Thus *baṣīra* was (and is) the standard name for a land sale instrument; *ijāra*, for the several types of land cultivation contracts; and *farz* or *faṣl*, for the individual inheritance instrument. According to the archival practice of the highland judges, the notarial writers and society at large, when applied to real estate, the doctrinal "contract of sale" (*ʿaqd al-bayʿ*) took the written form of a *baṣīra*. In addition, as I have illustrated, highland-wide conventional terms such as *baṣīra* occasionally found their way into Zaydī-tradition literary jurisprudence and formal opinions.

Custom represents an ultimate discursive frontier, the elusive geographic horizon of which extended, in this historical instance, from the heart of the imamic polity to territories beyond its ken and that of the sharīʿa. Let me reprise here a passage from the introduction where I addressed Schacht's statement that custom "coexisted with the ideal theory of Islamic law, while remaining outside its system." The approach I take in this book entails a different conception of the sharīʿa as a "system," namely as a formation of texts that included both a period library and a given archive. My interest is in the place of custom, not outside but inside such a textual formation.

In my examination of the law book in chapter 1, I noted that conceptualizations of custom (as opposed to substantive citations of it) are found in Zaydī *fiqh*. The conceptualizations included such venerable, cross-*madhhab* formulations as "That which is accepted in custom is equivalent to that which is formally stipulated." I also noted that the *Flowers* literature contains place-holding references for the roles of "custom" in specific contracts, such as in sale and in marriage, and that among the small innovations of al-ʿAnsī's twentieth-century *Flowers* commentary was his more expansive attention to the role of custom both in his main text and in the occasional footnote.

In substantive terms, custom mainly figured inside a given sharīʿa formation at the level of the archive, in the recognized paper language of the various genres. To sort out the different possibilities, I make a distinction between marked and unmarked appearances. The marked variety refers to customary content that is recognized and named as such—as *ʿurf*, among other terms. The unmarked variety, in contrast, may be thought of as sharing approximately the same status—that is, as established local usage—but without the content at issue being explicitly understood or labeled as "custom." As for examples of explicit marking, archival sharīʿa texts from Ibb occasionally mention the presence of custom. Thus, a court record from 1956 refers to "commercial custom" (*ʿurf al-tujjār*);[70] the local land sale *baṣīra* typically contains a distinction that is expressed using the adjectives *sharʿī* and *ʿurfī*; and the agrarian lease contract, the local *ijāra*, usually contains one or more stipulations directly identified as pertaining to "custom."[71] Such matters become more complicated in connection with out-of-court settlements, especially those that begin to shade into what amounts to an *ʿurf* system. In his study of villages in the Ibb hinterland, for example, Isaac Hollander provides an example of a type of "judgment" that characterizes itself as "customary with a sharīʿa aspect" (*ḥukm ʿurfī wa-wajh sharʿī*).[72]

As opposed to such explicit archival mentions of "custom," the unmarked or implicit presence of customary content played a broader, but largely unnoticed, role. This unmarked dimension of custom dovetailed subtly with the established conventional forms of archival writing. Most of the richly elaborated archival discourse of the name and the many detailed features of local genre constraints—from the practices pertaining to signatures, seals, witnessing clauses, etc., down to and including the standard techniques regarding the spacing of the writing on the paper surface—should be considered conventional. This thoroughgoing but unremarked on reliance on received usages was part and parcel of the habitus of the sharīʿa archive. Textual custom, in this sense, was everywhere foundational to the historical rooting of particular instances of such discursive formations in specific locales.

SEVEN

Judgments

> It is *not* permitted that a witness testify nor that a judge rule only *on the basis of what is found in his archive*, among papers written in his handwriting and under his seal or signature, [whether in] a register or other than it, *if he does not remember.*
>
> —Gilded Crown, *The Book of Flowers*

WITH LITIGATED CASES that culminated in formal decisions rendered by a judge as the centerpiece, my aim in this and the closely related following chapter is to provide an analysis of the archival production of the local court. Rather than as conventional sources read for other purposes, I examine these records to tease out the principles of their own discursive construction. This is to focus attention, once again, on composition, on the constitutive acts of writing. The textual features in question contribute to my depiction of this historically specific archival culture, and, by extension, to the larger understanding of the sharīʿa as local formation of texts.

The *qāḍī*, the Muslim judge, commonly referred to in Yemen as the *ḥākim*, is a fundamental figure in the sharīʿa dialectic of doctrine and application. The judge's judgment, the *ḥukm*, marks a crucial further installment in the institutional history of the sharīʿa rule (also *ḥukm*). This also is the discursive site for an important additional instantiation of the *qawl*, the individual opinion or statement, which in this arena is another way of referring to the judge's ruling. Also, as I discussed in chapter 4 from the perspective of the imamic "choice," the court was major locus for the *masʾala*, here the "case," also known, in this context, as a *qaḍiyya*. Colloquially, this was the discursive realm known as sharīʿa (the definite article dropped), that of court processes and cases litigated before a judge. Again, the standard challenge was, "You and me, sharīʿa" (*anā wanta, sharīʿa*).[1] Moving their conflict to court, the parties would fight the matter out in a structured formal process.

Litigation has been little studied as such, and the forms of interpretation specific to the sharīʿa court judge remain largely unexamined. I concentrate here on the textual dynamics of completed and decided cases rather than on the writings associated with settlements, whether arrived at inside or outside the court. To work with the records of adjudicated cases permits the study of formal claims, evidence presentations, litigant statements, and final rulings given by judges—textual components and sub-genres that do not figure in most types of settlement documentation. Focusing on completed case records also enables observations regarding the discursive scripting of litigation in late-imamic-period models, which range from Imam Yahya's "Instructions" of 1937 to several standard doctrinal chapters of the *fiqh*, including "Judging" (*qāḍāʾ*), "Testimonies" (*shahādāt*), "Claims" (*daʿāwā*), and others. In addition to examining the important place of litigation texts in the sharīʿa archive and in the larger formation of writings, my further intention in this and the next chapter is to lay the textual groundwork for a later study of formal procedure and judicial interpretation as fundamental components of regimes of truth in the historical sharīʿa.

From the point of view of the common law, a distinctive general feature of the premodern sharīʿa court judgment is the absence of citations to previous rulings, with the possible exception of a continuation of the same case. Court judgments did not constitute precedents and, as I have noted, there was no resulting conception of "case law." No institution of law reporters provided access to such rulings for study by judges or attorneys (a profession that did not exist as such in the premodern era). Thus there was no notion of, or system for, referencing relevant prior rulings in a judgment, which defined the limited "public" nature of such writings. The historical common law, on the other hand, lacked a parallel institution of juridical opinion-giving equivalent to the fatwā (see chapter 4). Generic in their language, fatwās were generalizable. Some had a precedent value that was associated with their collection in book form. Others, "stripped" to their essential facts and rule, were absorbed into works of *fiqh* doctrine. In Ottoman practice, and in some other historical settings, fatwās guided judges in difficult case decisions. But, as I have explained, the situation regarding fatwā-giving in connection with the courts differed in the Zaydī highlands, since opinion-giving ruling imams also occupied the interpretive terrain. As in other Muslim settings, however, individuals commonly obtained fatwās to help them decide whether to go to court in the first place.

Unlike a fatwā, a judgment was phrased in the idiom of the proper name and had no applicability other than to the circumstances of the particular litigants. Regarding the characteristic finality of the sharīʿa court judgment there are two important qualifications, one pertaining to the historical era, the other to the specifics of the textual order. The first involves the continuing existence under the twentieth-century imams of the Ottoman-introduced appeal mechanism, which was concerned with subsequent case reviews and related rulings. The second involves the argument developed in chapter 4 regarding the "stripping" of certain significant or difficult court cases in the process of creating the "choices" of the ruling imam. This resulted in rephrased, doctrinal renderings of such hard cases, which then were cited as such in later lawsuits by judges, as well as by some litigants.

Where the task of a fatwā was to convey a finding as to the law, that of a judgment was to apply it. Distinct routes thus existed for an undecided configuration of facts, a *masʾala*, to acquire a rule. Where a muftī addressed the fact configuration presented by a single party as given, a judge presided over a two-party litigated contest to determine the facts. A consequence of this venerable division of interpretive labor was that, while fatwās were apt to cite doctrine, court decisions rarely referenced the "law on the books." This is unlike the pattern of common law court rulings or, for that matter, the practice of present-day judges in republican Yemen. The court decisions of the Zaydī judges in Ibb are nearly devoid of doctrinal citations, except for statements of conformity to relevant "choices" issued by the ruling imam, which appear frequently in these records. Other than in the specialized form of these imamic "choices," judgments did not reference the apposite *Flowers* tradition *fiqh* literature that implicitly guided their decisions.

After an ethnographic report on my historical sources, this chapter consists of four sections. The first offers a material and discursive overview of the textual process from the perspective of the type of final judgment document the court issued to the litigants. The second surveys the available types of formal models for the drafting of judgments and related records and then begins a close look at the "Instructions" for the courts issued by Imam Yahya in 1937. Continuing with the "Instructions," the third section focuses on textual processes specific to the keeping of court registers and ends with a discussion of the roles of several types of dictation in the court process. The concluding fourth section segues to the dictation-based *shakwā*, or petition, a possible type of pre-text for the textual work of the court. Recalling Bakhtin's depiction of a similar petition-writing event, I proceed to an overview of the discursive relations and outcomes of such oral-to-written or written-to-oral events, and I identify two general types of dictation.

In the closely related analysis of chapter 8, I return to the beginning of the court-based textual process to focus on the onset of writing, and sharīʿa scripting, in the taking of minutes. To elucidate the key role of the minutes transcript in the larger context of the court process, I refer for comparative purposes to Jeremy Bentham (d. 1832), the noted British student of legal evidence (among other topics). In connection with this analytic emphasis on the minutes, I then consider the structure of the proper name in the archival sharīʿa, contrasting how names appear in court records versus in the more informal town charity rolls. Chapter 8 also details the textual work of quotation in the judgments of the period. As I have noted, such text-building techniques are of particular interest in the court genres. How, in Bakhtin's terms, did an incorporative genre such as the judgment "absorb and digest" other types of texts? How did the local court hear, read, and utilize such evidential statements and writings, and what do the resulting patterns of quotation suggest about perceptions of legal significance?

In examining this detailed work of text building, I gravitate to passages that point to how a given litigation record was composed or that otherwise comment on the nature of related spoken or written acts. This is to identify and to learn from reflexive passages, or embedded meta-texts. While the techniques of composition ordinarily went unnoticed in the making of court judgments, recording acts occasionally figured as part of the process recorded. In the much better known genres of Arabic literature, the self-reflexive meta-text "draws attention to narrative art."[2] Focusing on the equivalent usages in the period archive enables an inquiry into the textual mechanics and assumptions that underpinned the art of the authoritative sharīʿa judgment.

Chapter 8 concludes by drawing attention to another type of reflexive passage found in the archive, one that conveys colloquial views about writing, forgery, and falsification. To highlight the existence and to begin to understand the significance of this recorded informal thought, I sample transcript segments on litigant arguments and witness testimonies. Such passages mention and also comment on the sorts of dangers that, at the doctrinal level, had long worried juridical students of "practice with writing."

Sourcing

Late one afternoon during a short return trip to Ibb in the fall of 1995, I stopped by the house of Judge Muhammad bin Hasan al-Iryānī. I had known the judge in the mid-1970s as the head of the Third Sharīʿa Court and later, after a judicial reorganization, as an assistant judge in Judge al-Ḥaddād's Second Court. I sought him out now, however, as the son of one of the principal Ibb judges from the 1950s, the last decade of the imamic state. Experience told me that the most likely places to find court records from the pre-revolutionary period would be in the hands of former judges and court secretaries, or their descendants. Thanks to a number of other local men, I already had in hand a set of privately held original court judgments from the imamic era.[3] But except for the damaged example I photographed with Mustafa's assistance at Judge al-Ḥaddād's just vacated house, I lacked the requisite court registers from the period.

In my previous research, I had been successful in gaining access to republican-era registers, many of which were still kept at personal residences. I also obtained records from the specialized sharīʿa court that existed briefly in the 1960s to hear endowments cases, which were especially numerous in the Ibb area. The former judge (and later muftī), Yahya al-ʿAnsī, had started out as a secretary at the Endowments Office, where he was responsible for entering supporting property documentation in what was known as the *takrīs* register. He told me that, together with the records in the lease registers of the administration, such documentation could be used to counter the occasional ownership claims advanced by tenant cultivators. When I inquired about access to his endowments court registers, al-ʿAnsī told me they were kept at the home of his former secretary. A few days later this man appeared at the door of my house carrying two registers in a shawl over his shoulder.

When I began to look for imamic-period court registers, I inquired at the recently erected, modern-style Ibb Province courthouse, the first local building to be constructed as a dedicated judicial facility. Armed young soldiers in military uniforms initially barred my way at the court complex, but soon I was escorted in by two old acquaintances, Judge al-Haddad's former retainer, Mustafa, and al-ʿIzzī (Muhammad) Fihmī al-Ṣabāḥī, an inveterate jokester and amateur folklore collector who still worked as a court secretary. In my early research, I used to see al-ʿIzzī regularly at court in the mornings, and I sometimes sat with him in the afternoon in his small shop in the old marketplace. I would find him chewing *qat* and either reading a book or engaged in court-related work. When he prepared an original court document, he placed dots down the margin of the draft he was working from to keep from skipping a line.

An imposing curved bench in the main courtroom of the new court building accommodated the panel of appeal justices—the addition of the provincial level of appeals being one of the major innovations of the republican legal system. I was received at this court by Judge Muhammad al-Washalī, who had been appointed to a lower Ibb jurisdiction in 1980 and whom I remembered as the first town judge to come to court carrying a briefcase. The modern court building had a designated room for the judicial *irshīf* (after the French), part of a broader institutional initiative that included the founding of the first national archive in the capital city. As I expected, the court had no case records from before the 1962 Revolution. But in a helpful gesture, using their now-standard in-house technology, they photocopied a case then before the court that had an attached documentary record extending back into that period.

On the mentioned afternoon in the fall of 1995, I had been visiting Yahya al-ʿAnsī, the former Endowments Office functionary, notarial writer, judge, and future muftī, who suggested that Judge al-Iryānī might have some pre-revolutionary registers. On the way back I stopped at al-Iryānī's house where I found a *qat* gathering just breaking up. It had been a decade and a half since we last met, and to reconnect I showed the judge a copy of my recently published book, *The Calligraphic State*. When I turned to explaining my new project on the imamic era and asked the whereabouts of his father's pre-revolutionary court records, he showed me to a shelf of registers in an adjoining storage area. Among the volumes kept there were some that had been passed along to his father after the death of a colleague, Ismaʿil ʿAbd al-Rahman al-Manṣūr, the former Judge of Ibb Province. In the event, he permitted me to take four registers of decided cases, two each for his father and for Judge al-Manṣūr, to be photocopied at a local studio.[4]

Also in the 1990s, I met Muhammad Yahya Muṭahhar, the pre-revolutionary judge mentioned earlier as the author of a new book on the sharīʿa-derived law of personal status. At our initial meeting, which was in Ṣanʿāʾ, where he served as a legislator, Muṭahhar responded to questions I had about pre-revolutionary court cases I had begun to read. A few weeks later he received me at his home in Taʿizz, the former capital of Imam Ahmad in the 1950s, now an hour south of Ibb by car. In the rear of his residential compound, with its windows facing on the tiled pathways of a Ṣanʿāʾ-style interior garden, stood a long, ground-floor sitting room he called his "court" (*maḥkama*). The former "court" was silent now, but during my stay he invited some old cronies to chew *qat*, and, for my benefit, they started the afternoon as they used to, with songs and a round of jokes. In the last decade of the imamic polity Muṭahhar worked as a quasi-independent judge who received cases transferred from the imam's *dīwān*, the ruler's circle, or from a provincial governor.

Next to his garden-style "court" a small storeroom housed the registers in which his secretary had entered archival copies of his judgments. Among the cases I photocopied were Ibb-area matters he had handled, including a case brought against the Ibb Endowments Office and another concerning landed property in Baʿdān, the mountainous sub-district directly east of the town. For the latter case, Muṭahhar went out to see the disputed land and hear testimony, and he made sketches in the case record of the boundaries of the contested terraces. In the register copies of his homicide convictions Muṭahhar later added notes to the effect that an execution had been ordered by Imam Ahmad and carried out. The existence of such subsequent annotations point up a general problem in the historical study of sharīʿa cases. While final rulings in completed court cases may be clear from the record, we lack historical information as to implementation or enforcement. Where possible in selected cases from Ibb, I conducted oral historical interviews to learn about such outcomes. Thus, for example, while I had the original judgment document for a 1961 homicide conviction issued by Judge Hasan al-Iryānī (case 5, below), I was only able to learn what transpired following his ruling by interviewing the advocate, ʿAli Hasan Sāliḥ, who had represented the family of the murdered individual.

Knowing my interest in the Ibb area, Muṭahhar also showed me the documentary aftermath of an extended property dispute he had settled out of court in 1976. This consisted of a set of loose land sale contracts and two related inheritance documents that pertained to individuals in the powerful shaykhly family that controlled the Saturday market in the Saḥūl valley, just north of Ibb town. Muṭahhar's resolution took the written form of a single new sale instrument. Since the two sides had not agreed on who should get them back, he still had all the supporting documents, which were photocopies that he gave to me. These reminded me of the miscellaneous document fragments left behind when Judge al-Ḥaddād moved out of his house in Ibb. The modern use of photocopies obviated having to go through the difficulty or cost of getting personal papers back from a judge.

During my stay, Muṭahhar also contacted the son of a former secretary of Imam Ahmad's high judicial review organ, the Sharīʿa Panel, who brought over one of that institution's appellate registers for me to see. Muṭahhar additionally showed me a different kind of register, called a *safīna* (lit. "ship" or "vessel").[5] This contained handwritten copies of selected texts, including, for example, an admired passage from the eighteenth-century jurist Ibn al-Amīr and, illustrating the detailed linguistic reflexivity of one scholar, a poem on the Ibb dialect. In addition to such items, I photographed an entry containing Imam Yahya's "Instructions" of 1937 for the organization of the courts, the model text that is central to the following analysis.[6]

Judgment

On les roule en *volumen*.

—Jacques Berque, *Structures sociales du haut-atlas*

Ḥukm documents of the late imamic period were handwritten on heavy watermarked bond (*bayāḍ*), one well-known brand of which was imported, with an Istanbul trademark.[7] As opposed to the copies entered on the ordinary paper pages of the court registers, original *ḥukm* documents, especially those of any length, took the striking physical form of vertical rolls. Encountering another tradition of document rolls in private archives in rural Morocco, Jacques Berque was reminded of the classical *volumen*, the rolled predecessor to the codex, the western-tradition book before the advent of print.[8] Like the *volumen*, a Yemeni judgment document was unrolled for reading and rolled up for keeping and storage. As with "scrolling" through a text on a computer screen, one may move up and down in such a document without "leafing," all the while remaining on the same continuous paper surface. To create such a roll, sheets of document paper were glued top-to-bottom.[9] The written words "valid joint" (*waṣl ṣaḥīḥ*), sometimes with an added signature or a seal, appear across the seams on the back of these official documents. The security provided in a rolled document by this vertical physical contiguity was equivalent to that in a court register where the individual pages were sewed or glued together side-to-side.

In this and the following chapter I refer to the original document rolls of five Ibb cases that were heard in the decades leading up to the Revolution of 1962, the period of twentieth-century rule by the Ḥamīd al-Dīn imams. I profiled the presiding judges—al-Ḥaddād, al-Yamānī, al-Manṣūr (two cases), and al-Iryānī—in the final section of chapter 1.

As I note below, I have considered the substantive dimensions of cases 2–5 in separate publications. Also, four of the cases cite or implicity refer to imamic "choices" (*ikhtiyārāt*).

• Case 1. An urban real estate sale litigation ending in a judgment based on the rules of preemption. Heard in 1349 AH (1931) by Acting Judge Yahya bin ʿAli al-Ḥaddād, the author of a biography of Imam Yahya, the younger brother of the famous ʿAbd al-Rahman, and the uncle of the "Judge of Ibb" in my day. The judge cites a choice of Imam Yahya.[10]

• Case 2. An endowment and inheritance case involving landed property in a powerful and wealthy town family. Decided in 1366 AH (1947) by Judge ʿAbd Allah bin ʿAli al-Yamānī (al-Yadūmī), the Taʿizz-based Judge of the Provincial Seat, who was assigned to the case by Imam Yahya. The judge directly and indirectly references three choices of Imam Yahya.[11]

• Case 3. A commercial sale contract case involving damaged coffee sold to the merchant plaintiff by the treasury (*bayt al-māl*) and resold by him in Aden. Decided in 1376 AH (1956) by the Judge of Ibb Province, Ismaʿil ʿAbd al-Rahman al-Manṣūr. There is an implied reference to a choice by Imam Ahmad. [12]

• Case 4. A marriage contract case from 1378 AH (1958) also decided by Judge al-Manṣūr. The litigant sides cite different choices of Imam Ahmad.[13]

• Case 5. A rural murder case from 1380 AH (1961) decided in Ibb by Judge Hasan Ahmad al-Iryānī.[14]

Figure 7.1 Ahmad Muhammad al-Ḥaddād, Judge of Ibb, at home, reading a rolled court judgment, 1976.

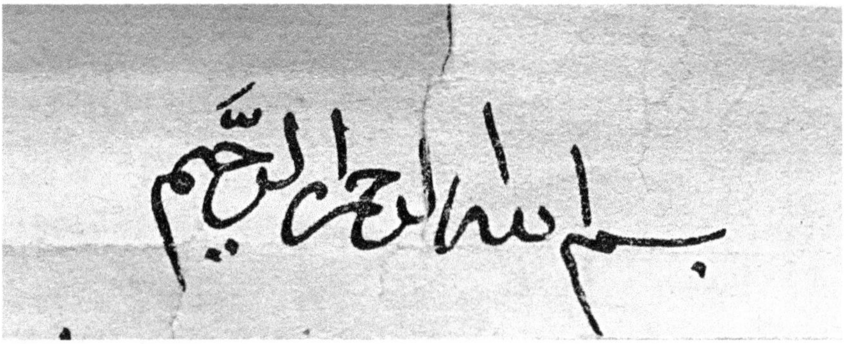
بسم الله الرحمن الرحيم

Figure 7.2 *Basmala* atop rolled original court judgment, case 4, 1378 AH (1958).

بالمحكمة الشرعية بلواء اب

Figure 7.3 Opening line, original court judgment, case 4: "In the Sharīʿa Court of Ibb Province . . ." with court seal dated 1370 AH (1950).

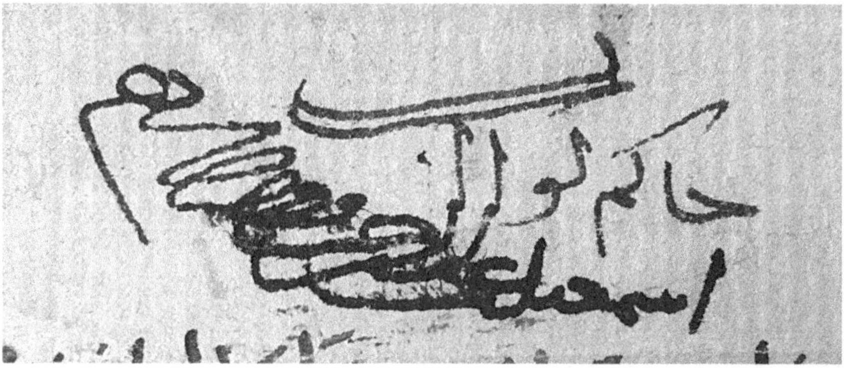

Figure 7.4 Signature of Judge Isma'il 'Abd al-Rahman al-Manṣūr, original court judgment, case 4, top, with title, "Judge of Ibb Province."

Depending on the substantive character and extent of the case, Yemeni judgment rolls could be quite long. The rolled *ḥukm* of case 5, for example, measures eight inches wide by thirteen feet long; that in case 4 is about the same width and seven and a half feet long. As I discuss below, the great length of some such case documents is due to their extensive evidence sections, which often comprised substantial interspersed sections of litigant responses.[15] The relative proportions of the segments in these example cases may be illustrated: case 5 contains a total of 434 lines, of which the opening claim and the initial response together extend for 12 lines and, at the other end of the text, the judge's concluding ruling runs to 20 lines. Case 4 has 365 lines, of which the first 12 are the claim and response while the last 14 are the final ruling. The massive middle sections of both of these texts, approximately 400 lines in case 5 and 339 lines in case 4, record evidence and response statements by the parties.

In the decades after the Revolution of 1962, the length of such final Yemeni judgment documents would become a target for reform. Egyptian advisers attached to the courts in Ibb tried but generally failed to implement a significant shortening of such judgment records. The length of judgment rolls eventually became fodder for criticism. In a dramatic visual metaphor from the year 2000, the cover photo of an issue of the legal monthly *al-Qisṭās* ("The Scales [of Justice]"), published by the lawyers of a Yemeni civil society association, depicts a beleaguered man wrapped head to toe, virtually mummified, in the coils of a court judgment document.[16]

Pre-revolutionary judgment records were handwritten in unpunctuated, continuous, and cursive Arabic script. When such a roll is opened, the writing cascades down the paper unimpeded, without spaces or breaks. The density of the writing, with a small margin to the right, is a feature that renders alterations difficult and thus helps to preserve the integrity of the text.[17] In some judgments, however, the flowing record of the litigation is from time to time interrupted by a tiny inserted word, *batta*, "ended," which is placed slightly above the line and at an angle (and without consonantal points), to indicate the conclusion of a discrete record item or a court session.[18] Together with the infrequent mention of session dates, which occasionally are made explicit in the text in connection with allotted days or an appointment to reappear,[19] and the terminal date of the judgment document itself,[20] such insertions tracked the formal chronos of litigation, the unfolding segments of procedural or court time. Dates referred to in oral testimonies or noted on, or quoted in entered documents marked other, incorporated temporalities—those of undertakings or conflicts in the past, in the time before the parties came to court. A court record routinely was dated (at the end: "written on its date, [date]") and placed (at the beginning: "In the sharīʿa court of Ibb Province . . .").[21]

Rarely, there is an enlargement of a letter or a word in a court record to indicate a section, such as to signal the final lines containing the judge's ruling. Otherwise, pre-revolutionary judgment documents contain no periods or capitalizations to indicate sentences and no other punctuated pauses; no paragraphing, indentation, numbering, or subhead conventions to demarcate subsections; and no abstracting or categorizing devices to state the nature of the case or ruling at the outset or to introduce sections of the document, although the outer flaps of some rolled judgments had simple identifying labels for quick reference in the archive.[22] Spacing and organizing techniques of all these types, similar to those familiar in the West, would be introduced in the decades after the Revolution in conjunction with other legal reforms. In the short-lived Commercial Courts (1976–79), such court documents would for the first time be typed. The different legibility of the sharīʿa court record that resulted from breaking up the continuous old-style text and making its order and substance more apparent through spacing and related devices may be compared to similar watersheds in the histories of western texts.[23]

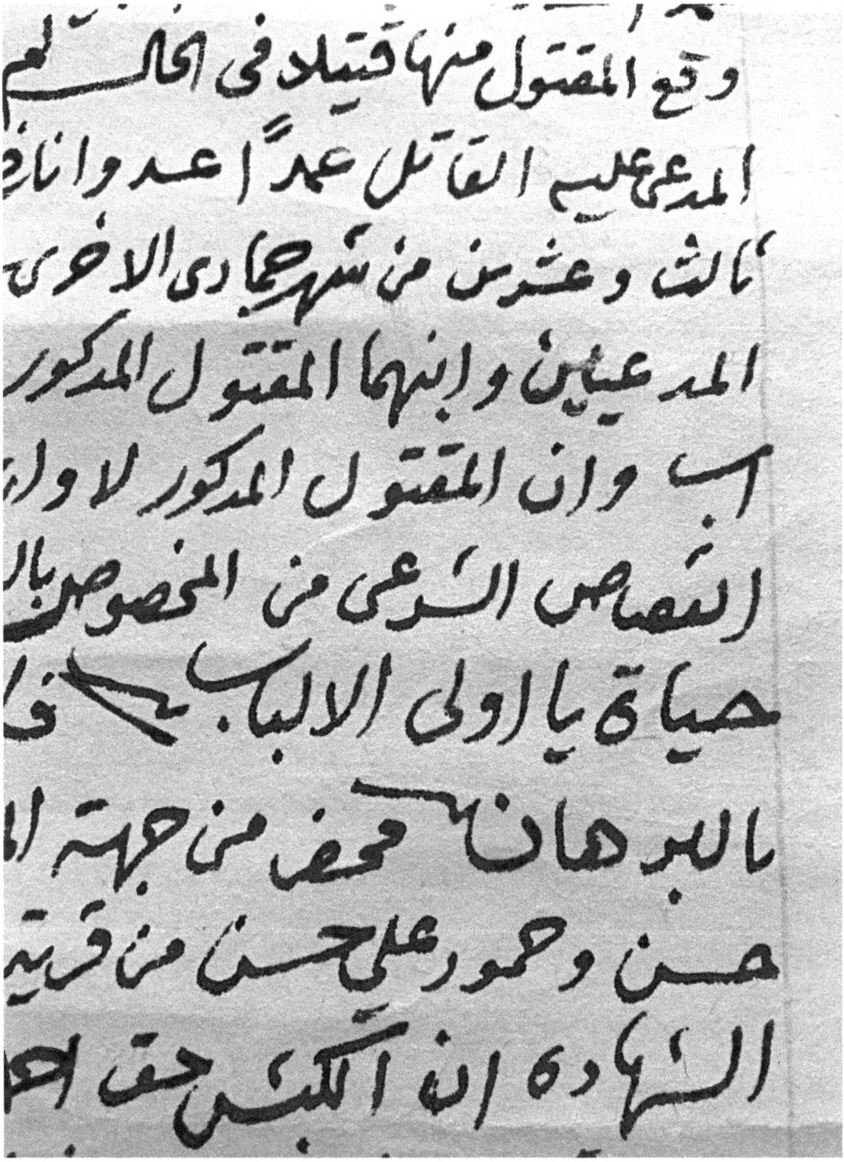

وقع المقتول منها قتيلا في الحال لم
المدعى عليه القاتل عمداً اعدوانا
ثالث وعشرين من شهر جمادى الاخرى
المدعيين وابنهما المقتول المذكور
وان المقتول المذكور لا وا
القصاص الشرعي من المخصوص بال
حياة يا اولي الالباب
بالبرهان محض من جهة ال
حسن وحمود علي حسن من قرية
الشهادة ان الكبش حق

Figure 7.5 Murder retaliation (*qiṣāṣ*) court judgment, showing part of a Qur'an citation and session markers, case 5, 1380 AH (1961).

Discursively, a *ḥukm* of the imamic period had two main parts. The first of these, originating in the minutes transcript, starts with the initial claim and response and then extends through the evidentiary struggle and includes any responses or other submissions from the parties. This main part of the process was known, informally—reversing the English expression—as the "take and give" (*al-akhdh wa al-radd*).[24] Formally, it was known as either the "verbal exchange" (*al-maqāl*) or the "litigation" (*al-muḥākama*),[25] terms that occasionally appear in the records. The typically much smaller second part consisted of the judge's ruling (his *qawl*), generally known as the *ḥukm* or the *jazm*.[26] Transitions between these two main parts of judgment records usually were unmarked and abrupt, but occasionally they were made explicit. In case 5, for example, with the initial word "This" blackened to mark the shift, the text mentions the just completed first part and characterizes the overall transition:

> *This* is what transpired in the way of dispute, difference, and defense (*difāʿ*).[27] The litigation (*muḥākama*) between the two sides ended after signatures were obtained on what was received as testimony. There was an end to the verbal exchange (*al-maqāl*) and a request for the ruling (*al-qawl*) as to what is required according to the sharīʿa.[28]

A passage such as this reflexively articulates the final procedural transition, which is from the judge listening to the parties during their litigation to the parties listening to the judge as he gives his ruling. It is a transition from the open-ended, competing, and undecided plurality of the evidence and argument before the court to the final, decided unity of the ruling. The discursive difference is characterized as that between a dialogic verbal exchange (*al-maqāl*) and a singular statement (*al-qawl*). Where the record of the first part of the proceedings unfolds in an atmosphere of uncertainty and forward-looking anticipation—that is, as a record of differences concerning facts and issues yet to be determined and decided—the judge's ruling in the second part looks back over the completed litigation. In the initial litigation segments, the judge-narrators appear relatively passive, intervening only rarely.[29] But in the final sections the judges turn active as they commence the ruling proper. A parallel shift occurs in the general language of the document, from the third to the first person and also from a standard past-tense framing to selective uses of the present. The judges

Figure 7.6 Muhammad Isma^cil al-Nuzaylī, sharī^ca court secretary, preparing a rolled judgment document in the afternoon sitting room in Judge al-Ḥaddād's house, 1976.

themselves transition from the "We" of their infrequent interventions in the course of the litigation proper to the "I" of judgment.

Behind the textual scenes, in an interval of time and activity unnoticed in the final judgment documents, important preparations enabled this procedural and discursive transition. First, of course, there were the requisite interpretive efforts on the part of the judge to consider the claim(s) and the evidence and formulate his ruling. Second, there was drafting work to be accomplished by the judge together with his court secretary (*kātib*). This latter effort centered on the secretary consulting the accumulated court record of the case, the minutes of the proceedings, in anticipation of their eventual wholesale incorporation, together with the text of the judge's ruling, in the final documents.

The resulting final documents, the two original *ḥukm* documents provided to the parties and the single copy entered in the designated court register, were three versions of the same text. The originals alone bore the judge's signature. In the event of a successful appeal, the signed and sealed response from the high court (or the *hay'a sharʿiyya* in the 1950s), together with a sealed confirmation from the imam's *dīwān*, would be written and affixed to the reverse side of the appellant's original *ḥukm*. Minus the signatures and seals, the same texts would be added to the copy in the court register.

Before the delivery of the final documents to the parties, the local court seal was placed in their top right corners next to small notes. Such notes referred, simultaneously, to the original judgment text written below and to the concurrently existing copy: "recorded in register [number] of the court, number [entry number], page [number]."[30] At the other end of the circuit described by these notes, in the court register of the indicated volume number, in the indicated entry sequence, and on the stated page, the recorded entry begins, "This is a copy (*ṣūra*) of the judgment . . ." After the step of writing out the two original judgment documents, and after that of entering the single copy in the court register, the circuit closed with this return to the originals for the necessary seals and notes. Such notes had to be written last since they contained the relevant details about the register number, entry number, and page number—the information that thereafter tied the two finished originals to their copy. In the process, with links established between the pair of originals and their copy, and between their respective archival sites—two "private," or residential, and one "public"—the overall prospect for the endurance of the case record and thus of the judge's ruling was enhanced through multiple holdings of the "same" judgment text. The court register copies, of course, bore neither the seals nor the notes found on the originals.

Instructions

For the court judgment genre the relevant modeling texts, studied at the imam's advanced *madrasa* in Ṣanʿāʾ and elsewhere, including Ibb, began with the theories of court practice found in the standard *Flowers* literature chapters on *al-qaḍāʾ*, which covers the judgeship and court procedure, and on "claims" (*daʿāwā*). I took notes on these two chapters from Zaydī scholar Muhammad al-Ghurbānī, who, in reading to me from the *Commentary on the Flowers* and adding his own remarks, sought to give me some basic doctrinal background for my ethnographic research.

Commentaries on the chapter on procedure exhort the judge to adhere to the proper textual "form" (*ṣīgha*) for rulings, but nothing further is specified beyond suggested language for the ruling clause itself (see below). Other *fiqh* chapters, especially those on claims and on evidence, provide further standard vocabulary and methods pertaining to litigation.[31] Chapters on the topics of acknowledgment and oath are relevant for textual construction when these acts figured in a case and were reported in its written record, and the same is true of the chapter on agency. None of these *fiqh* chapters give text-models per se.

Two more specialized library sub-genres, the *adab al-qāḍī* and the *shurūṭ* works, offer potential sources of models for the judgment as a text. The first sub-genre elaborates on the general culture, the rules, and etiquette of the judgeship (see chapter 6). Although well known in other schools of interpretation, and a potential future source for the study of Zaydī judicial culture, no such works were available to me.[32] The well-known *adab al-qāḍī* work of the Ḥanafī jurist al-Khaṣṣāf (d. 874 or 875) discusses matters related to the transfer of the archive (*dīwān*) of the outgoing judge to the incoming judge.[33] In this same section, a solitary text model is provided for the judgment, but, as in the basic *fiqh* chapter on procedure, this only concerns the language to be used in the final ruling clause. This model clause is given in standard library discourse: "I have ruled against (*ʿalā*) Fulān bin Fulān for (*li-*) Fulān bin Fulān, for thus and so (*bi-kadhā wa kadhā*)."[34]

As for the *shurūṭ* literature, in her last, unpublished paper, on "The Qāḍī's Archives," Jeanette Wakin discusses chapters on the major categories of court writings (*maḥāḍir* and *sijillāt*)—categories of texts I discuss below—in the formulary of Ṭaḥāwī (d. 933), also a Ḥanafī. Wakin states that, unlike the other chapters of the larger work, which pertain to the work of notarial writers, these two are "addressed squarely to the qāḍī himself."[35] She states that Ṭaḥāwī presents some twenty-five model documents, including eighteen under the heading of *maḥāḍir*, and seven in the chapter on *sijillāt*.[36] Unfortunately, Wakin left both her analysis and her detailing of the models unfinished. For the Yemeni highlands, as I have mentioned, a local *shurūṭ* treatise from the turn of the twentieth century is extant and is closely studied in my final chapters on notarial instruments. Unlike the *shurūṭ* work by Ṭaḥāwī, this Yemeni treatise of the same genre concerns only the types of documents to be prepared by notarial writers.

I focus here on a different type of modeling text, the "Instructions" (*taᶜlīmāt*) for the sharīᶜa court issued by Imam Yahya in 1937. These provide guidelines on the keeping of the written court records of lawsuits. Although we do not as yet have an analysis of an Ottoman equivalent, the imam's guidelines appear to be adapted from a type of text of the same name and coverage that existed in the Arab provinces of the empire.[37] It must be emphasized, however, that the Ottoman "Instructions" texts that date from 1878 and 1884 pertained to a sharīᶜa court system recently and decisively transformed. If versions of the administrative and record-keeping techniques of the nineteenth-century Ottoman "Instructions" made their way into the "Instructions" issued by Imam Yahya, they were grafted onto a highland sharīᶜa system with a decidedly different, if not altogether separate, history. As a model text, the imam's "Instructions" of 1937 thus stands in a less than fully organic relationship to the court documents they were meant to model. In assessing the imam's motivation in issuing these "Instructions," it may be recalled that, as a feature of his second set of these guidelines, which are on the institution of appeals, he assigned the appellate justices the task of reading and adapting the Ottoman *Majalla* "according to what is set forth in the principles of our *madhhab*" (see chapter 1).

As with the nineteenth-century Ottoman judicial reforms, the imam's "Instructions" convey a new spirit of introduced "order" (e.g., art. 12, *tanẓīm*; art. 13, *tartīb*). In addition to the descriptions given in the "Instructions" of the types of archival records that are to be prepared and issued, or

هذه صورة التعليمات الشريفة المطبوعة بمطبعة عاصمة اليمن صنعاء المحمية بالله

بسم الله الرحمن الرحيم

الحكم الشريف

نص التعليمات الشريفة

Figure 7.7 Copy of “Instructions” of Imam Yahya to the courts, 1355 AH (1937).

kept, by the highland sharīʿa court, there also are brief characterizations of the court itself, its personnel, and the judicial process. Although these “Instructions” were designed to model court practices, practice sometimes proceeded differently. Yet in a note located under his seal and in his own pen and that refers to the main text of the “Instructions,” which immediately follows, Imam Yahya indicates that he intended full compliance: “This is what we have ordered and he who contravenes anything of it we will punish." Immediate "oversight" regarding the principles set forth was to be the responsibility of the court judges.

Imam Yahya's "Instructions" are explicitly understood to be different from, and also incomplete with respect to, the higher-level formal doctrine on procedure. The opening statement of the "Instructions" defines their scope as that of "application and implementation" (*taṭbīq* and *tanfīdh*). The relationship of this lower-order meta-text to the higher-order doctrine is made explicit in article 6, where recourse to and reliance on the *fiqh* chapter is mandated: "Required of the Judge is the examination of all that is set down in the chapter on "The Judgeship" (*al-qaḍāʾ*) in the way of sharīʿa issues concerning himself [i.e., the status and role of the judge], concerning the litigants, and the framing of the conflict and its ordering between the litigants. He should not violate any of this."

In many respects, the "Instructions" follow the doctrine, but in simplified form. An important example of the tension between the "Instructions" and judicial practice concerns the location of the court. The term *maḥkama*, or "court," is a concept that refers to the both the session and the physical place—both also known as *majlis* (lit. "sitting" or "sitting place")—with the judge hearing claims, responses, and evidence and issuing rulings. The doctrine on the judgeship considers whether it is proper for a judge to hold court in the mosque,[38] but it does not otherwise locate the court. As I have noted, the Ibb judges commonly held morning "court" in the open air, typically in the partly walled spaces in front of their residences. While not operated or so demarcated in the modern manner, these courts were spatially "public" in terms of their regularity at a specific locale and in their open accessibility to passersby. Thus oral history records that Judge al-Warith (d. 1934) sat in the courtyard (*ḥawsh*) of his rented residence, Dār al-Mulk; that, two decades later, Judge Isḥāq (b. 1902) received litigants in front of his house or in the streets of his neighborhood just north of the Great Mosque of Ibb; and that Judge al-Manṣūr (d. 1963), the Judge of Ibb in his day, worked in the mornings in front of his residence, the elegant four-story house named Dār Daʿfān, which stands across a small square from the porticoed main entrance to the Great Mosque. In the afternoons, judges or their secretaries worked out of their sitting rooms, their residential *dīwāns*.

Diametrically opposed to this actual, residence-based pattern regarding the court, and by extension to the judicial archives of the period, article 3 of the "Instructions" describes the court and the records as properly confined to an "official" (*rasmī*) place: "The place of seeing the claims and settling them is an official and specially designated place. In it are kept the registers of claims and the records of final judgment documents (*marāqim*). The activities of litigation and the giving of judgment must not occur elsewhere, and the registers must not be taken from it to private residences, including those of the judge and his secretary."

As elsewhere in the empire, the late Ottomans in Yemen established such official places, and they may also have managed to confine judicial work to them in their era. For his part, the imam ratified the concept of an official court and its archive in his "Instructions." But the judicial situation in the following imamic period remained split. While the concept of an office was clearly stated in the "Instructions," the mandated separation of the bureau from the residence was incomplete. Judges tended to hold their court sessions and afternoon receptions in front of and inside their residences. Directly counter to the "Instructions," registers were kept in these and their secretaries' private residences (figure 7.8).

Another such issue is formulated in article 13, which states that only the litigant pairs may come before the judge: "In the session (*mawqif*) the judge must receive only the two parties, and others must not be allowed to come before him." The same article mandates correct "order" (*tartīb*) in the hearing of cases, the separation of witnesses from one another, and the elimination of loud voices and other interruptions. While this portrayal of the sharīʿa court may have approximated practice when the judge focused his attention on hearing the litigation in a particular case, by all reports the typical morning scene before the judge's house was one of multiple sets of disputants and occasional jostling and shouting. Judicial order of the type imagined in the "Instructions" later would be built into the specially constructed spaces and elaborated in related modes of conduct for the modern courtrooms of the Yemeni nation-state instituted in the 1980s.

Other articles elaborate on the organization of this official place. Articles 20 and 23 concern the court's administrative workday, which was seven hours, and the role of a caretaker of the court, who was charged with "opening it and locking it at the specified times and cleaning it." Associated with these official places were lists of official judicial employees together with their set salaries. For late Ottoman Ibb we have such a list of the local court personnel.[39] Regarding the two types of registers associated with litigation,

Figure 7.8 Registers kept at home by Ibb endowments functionary ʿAbd al-Wahhāb al-Majdhūb.

article 5 states that "any register of these two [types] that has been filled up should be stored in a special locked place at the court."

Registers

Of the two types of bound sharīʿa court registers associated with Yemeni lawsuits, one was for claims and ongoing entries as the court process unfolded, the other for recording completed case judgments. Identified as the "entering register" (*daftar al-ḍabṭ*) and the "recording register" (*daftar al-qayd*), the two are described in articles 4 and 5 of the imam's "Instructions."[40] The "Instructions" also mention a third type of court register, for recording notarial instruments, which I discuss in chapter 9. The "Entering" register, known in mid-century Ibb as the "claims register" or the "claims and responses register," contained the ongoing minutes of court litigation sessions, including the opening claims and responses, evidence presentations, and any other submissions or statements, oral or written. If a lawsuit continued for more than one session, as many did, the records for the case appeared on different days with intervening entries from other cases. Cases that were dropped, as many were, left incomplete records in this register. In contrast to the open-ended and interspersed method of the "entering" registers, the "recording" registers contained completed and whole texts, consisting of the finished litigation plus the judge's ruling. These were copies of the final judgment records, the issued documents known as *aḥkām* (sing. *ḥukm*).

A similar pattern of using two types of registers was standard in the larger Middle Eastern history of the sharīʿa court.[41] Where the first type of register contained the court "minutes" (*maḥḍar*), the second comprised the overall record of the case, the completed minutes, or a summary of them, and the judge's ruling.[42] In the same terms, Nawawī (d. 1277), a key Shāfiʿī jurist studied in Lower Yemen, made a distinction between the minutes, written in conjunction with court activity that does not necessarily culminate in a judgment, and a second type of register for the recording of judgments rendered. He states that two copies of such final judgments eventually should be produced, "one for them [the party or parties], and one to be retained in the archive (*dīwān*) of the court."[43]

In both the physical and the interpretive senses, the text of the second register was derived from the first. Physically, the minutes of claim, response, evidence, and later responses entered in the first register were gathered together in a unified text and then transferred to the second register, where they were joined with the judge's ruling as the final record text. Interpretively, the minuted record of the litigation, including the original claim and response, the evidence presented, facts established, and any further arguments, provided the substantive basis for the judge's ruling (*ḥukm*).

If the two-register format of early to mid-century Yemen was similar to that of the former Ottoman system, the relatively verbatim style of the final Yemeni judgment record was not. In contrast to the extended final judgment records produced in the highlands, Ottoman records for lawsuits were characteristically brief, even radically summarized, such that one may find entries for more than one case on a single register page. The basic difference between the two recording traditions is that where the Yemenis carried the fullness of the minutes entered in the first register over into the second register (and also into the two original rolls delivered to the litigant parties), the Ottomans did not. This meant that, in Ottoman as opposed to Yemeni practice, the litigants' opening claims typically were restated by the court rather than reproduced verbatim; that there was little room in the final records for transcripts of witness testimonies, which instead were concisely characterized by the court; and that evidence not constituting the basis for the judgment and the often rambling statements from one or both parties (if such statements occurred in Ottoman courts) were cut from the final case record.

The labor carried out by the court staff toward the end of a decided lawsuit involved a textual transfer between the two principal types of court registers. In Yemen this involved a "global" form of quotation. The transfer began with the bringing together of the potentially dispersed entries of separate court sessions into an initial "draft" that represented the first unified record of the litigation process. This draft had to be reviewed, corrected if necessary, and finally approved by the judge before the final records could be written. The judge's monitoring of this unification of the case record followed upon his entry-by-entry monitoring of the minute keeping during the litigation.

These textual preparations involving the court secretary together with the judge are envisioned in Article 11 of the imam's "Instructions," in a passage that begins by checking off a series of procedural steps:

> After the statement of the two sides that the litigation (*muḥākama*) had ended, and after their explicit request for the ruling (*ḥukm*), and their [the parties] refusal of a settlement, and [then with] the availability of the ruling from the judge, the secretary should extract a draft (*muswadda*) of the record (*al-raqm*)[44] from the entering register and show it to the judge for him to correct. After he finishes this correction he places a sign on it indicating that the secretary is permitted to transcribe (*naql*) it from the draft and put it on bond, on the official paper which an imamic order was issued [to the effect] that court documents (*marāqim*) must not be written except on it. And two versions (*nuskhatān*),[45] or more according to need, will be written of it, a version for the party ruled for (*al-maḥkūm lahu*), and a version for the party ruled against (*al-maḥkūm ʿalayhi*). And the judge must write the text of the ruling in his script in the entering register and in the draft.

When the judge was ready to make his decision, the final documentation could be prepared and the ruling placed in final written form. This process of wholesale quotation began, as article 11 states, with the secretary consulting the "entering register" to locate and carry out an "extraction" (*istikhrāj*)[46] of the records of the case so as to bring them together in a unified draft. It ended with these extracted materials, the collected case minutes, being joined with the judge's ruling to create the final text of the case record.

Regarding the language of the judgment clause, the "Instructions" (art. 8) state that the judge must give his decision "with the expression (*lafẓ*) 'I judged,' or 'I required,' or [expressions] like them among the formulations without which it would not be considered a proper written judgment." I noted earlier that *Flowers* commentators refer to the use of correct form (*ṣīgha*) for the judgment.[47] To elaborate on his statement that it is "absolutely necessary for the judge" to adhere to "the [correct] form of the judgment," twentieth-century commentator al-ʿAnsī supplies examples of appropriate language. Thus, "He [the judge] says, 'I ruled' or 'I implemented' or 'I required' or 'established before me' or 'established for me' or 'valid for me' or 'decided' or 'required' or such like, which informs of this."

This model language for the judgment clause is in the first person and the past tense, indicating personal authority and completed action. In the Ibb court records, as I mentioned above, framings in the first person and the present tense are equally common (e.g., *aqūl* ["I rule, or find, or say"]). The fifteenth-century *Commentary* and its glosses cite an early Shāfiʿī school position that holds that the proper "expression" (*lafẓ*) for the judgment is either "I ruled" or "I judged." Some of the language offered by al-ʿAnsī, such as "established for me" and "valid for me," is rejected by some jurists as not constituting a proper "judgment expression." In the different genre of the imamic appointment letters, the requirement is simply for the sharīʿa judge to draft judgment documents "using a solid style (*uslūb matīn*)."[48]

Let me also return to comment on the last line of article 11, "And the judge must write the text of the ruling in his script in the entering register and in the draft." The requirement that the judge write out the text of his ruling in his own handwriting was considered crucial in practice, as his script concretely indexed his judicial presence. But where he should write it was, perhaps, not as suggested by the "Instructions." According to the practice of the period, and persisting after Revolution, the judge wrote out the usually brief lines of his judgment at the end of the originals provided to the parties. Such original lawsuit documents were transcribed by the court secretary, from the opening lines through the evidence section up to where the judge's final ruling would start. I would find al-ʿIzzī al-Ṣabāḥī, the Ibb court secretary, poring over this sort of work in his shop in the late afternoon. The judge later would add the lines of his ruling at the end of the original roll, lines that were equivalent to the text he would then "dictate" to the parties in court. I sat one afternoon with Judge Yahya al-ʿAnsī at the house of his friend and neighbor Muhammad al-Ghurbānī, whom he had just consulted, as the judge wrote his concluding ruling out in his own hand at the end of an unrolled *ḥukm* document.

Article 7 of the imam's "Instructions" provides an overview of the sharīʿa court process, beginning with the claim and ending with the final judgment. As described in this article, the process was to be marked by a series of signatures:

> The secretary takes down the claim, in the presence of the judge, in the designated register, until the judge states that the claim has been validly com-

> pleted. The claimant is required to place his signature at the end of it. And likewise the response: the defendant is required to place his signature under his response. Likewise, the witnesses place their signatures under their testimonies. And [it is] thus until the litigation is ended and the litigants request that the judge rule as to what is required in their dispute, inasmuch as they have no further assertion (*mudāfaʿa*, lit. "defense") other than what has taken place, and no evidence other than what was presented. And they also place their signatures on this last request. The accomplishment of the taking of the signatures is the responsibility of the secretary. At the end of what has been mentioned is the text of the judge's ruling [which is] sealed together with the date. And the signature of the judge is placed in the register.

"The secretary takes down the claim": in many cases, especially in important or complicated ones, a claim was presented in writing to the court and copied into the minutes by the secretary. Otherwise, as described here, the secretary took down the plaintiff's spoken claim statement, possibly with guidance from the judge. In the post-revolutionary courts I sat in, secretaries assisted some individuals to properly phrase their claims.[49] "Likewise the response": unlike some claims, responses were typically very brief. In cases that went on to litigation and the presentation of evidence, the response necessarily consisted of a denial, usually formulaic. Some litigants were unable to respond appropriately, a condition ʿAbd al-Karim al-Akwaʿ described as being "inarticulate" (*ʿayy*), or, simply, as "not knowing how to respond." ʿAbd al-Karim, whose childhood family residence was rented by Judge Hasan al-Warīth, had memories of morning court at the front door during which the judge would supply appropriate responses for such individuals.[50]

Signatures

The placing of signatures at various procedural junctures marked different sub-genres of court transcript writing. Signatures of the parties and their witnesses would be placed in registers of the first type, the "entering" registers. By contrast, in the registers of the second, or "recording," type, and also in the original judgment documents issued to the parties, these signatures are not found, nor are they expected.[51] What is found instead in these final records, but only infrequently, is a report that such signatures had been placed in the minutes transcript—that is, in the first type of register. Basic writing skills seem to be assumed throughout, but some of these "signatures" may have been like the inked fingerprints placed in registers in post-revolutionary courts. As noted, judges signed original judgments. In the case of an appeal ruling, the text would be placed on the back of the original judgment document held by the party making the appeal. Below this text the appellate justices would sign their names. Judges, again, did not sign the copies of judgments entered in the "recording" registers. In the event of an appeal, a copy of the appeal ruling would be added to the entry for the *ḥukm* in the "recording" register, but without the justices' signatures, although their names and the fact that they had signed the original would be noted. To summarize, if the parties and their witnesses signed, this happened in the "entering" register; when judges signed, this was on the court-issued original documents. The copies of final judgments in the "recording" register had no signatures of either category, although they mentioned the placing of signatures in the "entering" register and, in the event of an appellate ruling, those of the justices on the issued originals.

Signatures were the marks, the summary scripts of human presences. Derrida observes, more precisely, that "a written signature implies the actual or empirical nonpresence of the signer," while at the same time it indicates "his having been present in a past now."[52] Much like witnesses before the court, signatures and handwriting were either known or else required supporting identification. A signature, of course, could be read for the actual letters and words of the name, although these often were stylized or otherwise obscure. Depending on the type of writing, a presumption might govern the reading of a signature—namely, that it pertained to an existing judge in a given period or to a known notarial writer. In my day, Judge al-Ḥaddād began his signature in a well-known script and using the rubric the Judge of Ibb, below which he wrote the words of his name, "Ahmad bin Muhammad al-Ḥaddād." In his last years, the shaky but still recognizable version of this same judicial signature at the end of his court documents materially indicated his advanced age. Unlike originals, in the copies of judgments placed in the court register in a court secretary's hand, judges were identified by name at the outset of the record.

The court seal (*khatm*) appeared only on an original sharīʿa judgment, such as on the five example case rolls. If a case had been reviewed on appeal at the higher level, the round blue seal of the Sharīʿa Panel (in the 1950s) appeared as well, above right, together with the signatures of the justices, below. Also in such cases, the larger, round red seal of the imam and a note of confirmation from his *dīwān* would be placed above the review text, to the left.[53] When Judge al-Ḥaddād was retired in 1980 by order of the Ministry of Justice, in addition to penning and circulating a poem in protest, he refused to surrender the court seal. Smaller personal seals, some round, some rectangular, were script-based, like the "public" types, and contained a name and, sometimes, a date. Such seals had been in vogue during the Ottoman period (and earlier) but fell into disuse after about 1930. Seals of notarial writers appear on older legal instruments of all types retained in personal archives. A related formula that appears in the later-added counter-signatures on some documents states that the writer is known in "script, signature and seal" *(khaṭṭan wa ʿalāmatan wa khaṭman)* or, more authoritatively, due to the personal link, but minus the reference to a seal, in "person (*shakhṣan*), script, and signature."

Dictation

As a type of performative quotation, "dictation" (*imlāʾ*) marked several procedural junctures. Mentions of dictation in the record indexed specialized verbal acts that occurred in court. Following oral testimony, dictation was the identified form for reading back to the witness what had been entered in the minutes, which permitted the confirmation of the accuracy of the written transcript. Like the placing of signatures, which could also conclude the process of recording testimony, this form of dictation is envisioned in the imam's "Instructions." Article 13 states, "[A]fter the secretary has written it in the register, the testimony should be dictated to the witness for verification and to guard against addition or deletion, and after that he [the witness] signs."

This seems straightforward. Pivoting on the court secretary's acts of listening, writing, and reading, an initial and authoritative oral-aural communication, from witness to secretary, is reversed, now from secretary to witness. Stated this way, with the communicative roles exchanged, the initial giving of testimony and the taking of minutes appear structurally similar to the following "dictation" relationship. In this discursive synapse, the witness is asked to compare the spoken and written versions of the "same" text. In more precise terms, the witness is to compare a personal memory of what he or she previously had uttered as testimony with a just-heard, oralized version of the written text. As for the "sameness" of the dictated text, I have two questions. Had the minutes taking involved a shift from the colloquial of testimony to the standard, written, or court Arabic of the transcript, and, if so, was the witness capable of understanding and evaluating this shift? Second, if the transcript was not verbatim in form but instead involved summarization, or comprised indirect rather than direct quotation, would the witness be capable of assessing the result of such editorial acts? Following from these detailed discursive questions, should it be concluded that there was an embedded presumption of literate skills on the part of the normative witness?

Like the signatures physically placed in the first type of session register, dictation may have been a standard feature of the litigation process even though it is not regularly mentioned in the final case records. Reports of dictation to witnesses are found in the comparatively full documentation of such measures in the final record of case 5, the murder litigation, but examples exist in the other cases as well. Such archival inscriptions of acts involving the human voice may be compared to institutions associated with the written texts of the library. In both discursive realms, we find emphases on the authority of human presences and the spoken word, together with techniques for the re-oralization of spoken texts that had gone into writing.

In a second court usage, the judge's ruling at the last session was to be pronounced orally, "dictated," as the idiom had it, to the assembled parties. This dictation consisted of reading aloud a prepared written text that had no prior oral existence. This was the "same" text that appeared in writing in the concluding lines of the court-issued judgment document. Law book commentator al-ʿAnsī states that the final judgment, correct in form, should be rendered "in the presence" (lit. "in the face") of the party ruled against.[54] Article 14 of the imam's "Instructions" requires that at the same event at which the final written documents were to be handed out to the litigants, the ruling given should be "dictated" by the judge: "In the court session for the delivery of the judgment record (*raqm*) for the party ruled for and [of that for] the party ruled against, dictation should occur of what the ruling (*ḥukm*) proclaims to the two parties."[55] Unlike that by the court secretary to the witnesses, there would be no mention of the judge's mandated act of "dictation" in the court record.

Petitions

In chapter 8, I look at local court records for indications of archival implementations of the "oral reading" of written texts presented as evidence by litigants. This, again, is the method set forth conceptually in law book doctrine (see chapter 3) that I consider kindred to dictation. While the rationale of this further type of oral-written synapse also appears straightforward, we may ask how what the document witnesses heard in court related to what they remembered. How did the language of the written text read out to them compare to their aural and visual memories of the documented undertaking at some point in the past? Would differences specific to the written versus the aural-visual complicate the impact of the passage of time on memory? Would the jurists' conceptual distinction between a witness's recall of the "gist" versus the "detail" be relevant in this connection as well?

In chapters 9 and 10, I turn to the scene of local notarial writing and consider the faint traces of the form of "dictation" mandated in Qur'an 2:282. Extended by analogy, this divine order to place debts in writing was made to apply to the gamut of primary archival genres prepared by notarial writers. Ideally initiated in a "dictation" from the appropriate party to the undertaking, such writings later could be brought forward as evidence in the event of a dispute, in which circumstances the document would be read aloud in court.

Referencing my preceding treatments of library perspectives and anticipating those on notarial writing, I conclude the present chapter with a typology of dictation and related techniques. To round out this conceptualization, I incorporate a brief discussion of a further genre, the petition (*shakwā*).[56] As I noted in the previous chapter, petitions were occasional pretexts for the court process inasmuch as they sometimes served to initiate the action that led to litigation. In a somewhat unusual example, a petition is mentioned in an Ibb case decided in 1958. This petition had been sent by telegram to Governor al-Sayāghī, who happened to be in the capital, Taʿizz, and who then referred the matter to the judge back in Ibb.[57]

In the introduction, I mentioned Bakhtin's passing reference to the writing of petitions. In describing the scene of an illiterate peasant appearing before a document writer that led to the production of a "paper" language, Bakhtin may have had in mind a related Balkan (i.e., Ottoman) tradition. Prior to the Yemeni Revolution of 1962, responding to the regular influx of hand-delivered, posted, or, for the few who could afford it, telegraphed petitions was an important daily task at all levels of highland government, from the circle of secretaries around the ruling imam, to his governors in the provinces, on down to the district and sub-district officials in their localities. Upon receiving a petition, a secretary in the Ibb governor's circle summarized its gist in a note placed above and to the right of the main petition text. The governor would respond in another added note, placed on the upper left.[58] As in my day, a subset of this routine traffic in petitions represented a recognized step toward the sharīʿa court. In their daily work of textual triage, governors and other officials transferred certain of these petitions (that is, returned them with an added note, to be hand-transferred by the interested parties) to court judges, while other petitions went directly to the judiciary. Whereas the petitions of post-revolutionary citizens were written in the name of "the presenter," in former times the names of the petitioning subjects appeared under the period rubric "your servant" (*mamlūk*, lit. "slave").

When such petitions were written by professionals, including the men who set up box-top desks outside official residences, or simply by the literate for the nonliterate, the situation was much as Bakhtin described. The writer rendered a spoken complaint into the formal terms, the proper paper language, of a written petition. The outcome was a writing that bore the identifiable personal mark of the writer's script, even though his work was "signed" by, or at least bore the name of, his client, the petitioner. Some Yemeni petitions were autographs, written directly by the petitioners themselves. These exhibited varying degrees of competence, from compositions in quasi-dialectical Arabic to others with rhetorical flourishes, rhymed prose, or inserted passages of metered poetry. Such levels of literacy were further indexed in the handwriting of petitions. Beyond the extremely fluid and relatively standardized script of hired writers, the efforts of petitioners ranged from halting, childlike hands to minor calligraphic masterpieces.

Figure 7.9 Public petition writer, Taʿizz, 1980.

In their great variety petitions illustrate the fact that, like spoken language, written language of the era was both socially stratified and highly personalized.[59] On the other side of the interchange, the personal scripts of those who received and responded to petitions were well known among those who regularly read such texts. Governor al-Sayāghī responded to petitions in an aquamarine-colored ink that he alone used. As for the ruling imam, although he did not sign his name as such, an important petition returning from his circle carried his impressive calligraphic seal and a rub of his distinctive red powder.

Petitions prepared for the illiterate by the literate were predicated upon a movement from speech to writing. This interaction between the petitioner and the writer (professional or not) relied on the discursive services of the humble expressive form of dictation. The petitioner "dictated," and the writer wrote. The key point, however, is that in this process the petitioner's spoken words were transformed, rendered into the appropriate paper language of the petition genre. At the imam's residence in the capital, his secretaries allocated time every day for receiving petitioners. "When a petitioner came before the secretaries," explained ʿAbd al-Qadir bin ʿAbd Allah, a former member of Imam Yahya's circle of writers and, later, under the republic, the presiding judge of the Supreme Court, "he dictated, we listened and then we wrote the petition."[60]

A quietly pervasive discursive form, dictation played a role in the composition of a number of genres, but in two distinct varieties. Something similar to the changes made when the spoken complaint became the written petition also occurred in the creation of notarial instruments. Using the idiom that is as old as the Qurʾan and the divine order, "so let him write, and let the debtor dictate," the local "stipulations" treatise explains that, in a sale contract, the terms of the agreement arrived at orally by the parties should be "dictated" by the seller to the notarial writer. Having heard the particulars of an undertaking, the notarial writer set them down in writing, but in so doing he converted the spoken terms into the proper paper language, including the correct legal stipulations for the indicated type of legal instrument.

As opposed to such alterations of spoken expression, the contrasting type of dictation was meant to accomplish an unaltered, word-for-word transmission. This resulted in another form of authoritative written language, one understood to be an exact transcription of speech. In academic instruction, dictation of this type was one of several related modalities, including "oral recitation," that were essential to the secure conveyance of "knowledge" (*ʿilm*). Teachers "dictated" passages from lesson texts to circles of listening students, a prime example of such a text in highland history being *The Book of Flowers*.[61] Some dictated this concise book from memory while others did so either referring to or reading the written text. Dictation of an originary type was a classic way an instruction text such as the *Flowers* came into being in the first place (see chapter 1). Such works were "authored" as dictations to students who, in the process, prepared the first written manuscript versions. Through the centuries, teachers reproduced the text while re-voicing the author's act of composition. As the students listened, the receiving end of the oral-aural link that defined authoritative knowledge transmission was established, but the students also wrote down their own copies of what they heard. Prompted by a written cue and initiating a subsequent inscription, this form of instructional dictation stood between two writings. Reversing this flow made it possible to check the transmission. Thus, in the standard discursive form of *qaraʾa ʿalā*, a student "read back" his written version to the listening teacher-author.

While the judge's concluding "dictation" of his judgment may be grouped with the type of unaltered transmission found in the madrasa lesson circle, that of the court secretary to the witness is more of a mix. It, too, is a dictation from writing, and the desired outcome is the confirmed identity of two texts. Yet the dictation by the secretary may also be related to the altered type of transmission. This would depend on an analytic recognition of the possibility of changes being made in the course of entering the testimony. Such changes could be the results of the techniques of summarization and the choices of person and tense discussed in the next chapter.

EIGHT

Minutes

> It is to the art of writing that testimony is altogether indebted for the quality of permanence.
>
> —Jeremy Bentham, *Rationale of Judicial Evidence*

BRITISH PHILOSOPHER and student of judicial evidence Jeremy Bentham recommended enhancing the quality of court minutes in a manner similar to that set forth in the models for sharīʿa litigation practices in Yemen. In continental, or "Rome-bred law," Bentham notes, "provision is made for obtaining such evidence, as is deemed sufficient, of the authenticity of the minutes."[1] Likewise, the English judge, at the end of a session in which testimony has been given, should "afford [the witness] the faculty of examining into the correctness of the minutes taken of his deposition; and, having done so, to call upon him, in token of his assent, to annex his signature to a short sentence or phrase expressive of such assent." Signatures, Bentham remarks, involve "the best of all instruments of authentication," since they consist of "the name, written by the person whose name it is." As with the "dictation" from the transcript that occurred in the sharīʿa court, Bentham specifically recommends that the record of the minutes be "read aloud" to the witness, or that, with a few precautions, a witness who could read should be allowed to "have a paper in his own hands, that he may peruse it more at leisure."[2]

In Yemen, the minutes taken were dictated back to the court not only to check the transcript with the witnesses but also for the benefit of the parties to the lawsuit, who, as I have noted, sometimes were reported to have then signed their names in the court register. Among the decided cases identified in chapter 7, in case 5, the Ibb murder litigation, a line that immediately follows the entry in the minutes transcript of the full text of a written investigative report introduced by the claimant states that "the dictation to the defendant occurred of the report of the Governor of Ibb."[3] In case 1, which concerns town real estate, a legal representative (*wakīl*) who had been absent is brought up to date: "Then the representative of the claimant, namely, . . . , arrived from Ṣanʿāʾ and the testimony presented [by the defendant] and what he showed [i.e., documents] were dictated [from the minutes]." Later in the same case the record reads, "What was [just] mentioned was dictated to the representative of the claimant."[4] At one juncture in case 4, the marriage conflict, one finds an instance of the minutes of testimony being read aloud in "dictation" to the court: "and when [the defendant] heard the dictation to him of the minutes and the statement by [the claimant] . . . he stated, in his words . . ."[5]

Minutes also could be requested for silent reading. Case 4 records an instance of the parties being provided access to the minutes for their review. Thus the transcript states: "the two parties requested the minutes to read (*liʾl-iṭilāʿ ʿalayhi*)." "After reading," the claimant "returned the minutes" and then presented a memorandum (*raqm*) with a statement in reply, which is entered in the record "letter for letter and in its wording . . ."[6] As we learn from this court record, the minutes were a text that could be requested, perhaps removed, and then read, and finally returned and responded to.

By their nature, until the litigation formally closed on an order from the judge, court minutes were continually under construction. At any given point in time they had recorded what had transpired in litigation sessions up to that moment. In larger terms, the pattern of obtaining extracts from the court record for consultation began, especially in complex cases, with the defendant's initial receipt of a copy of the written text of an entered claim. It ended with the delivery to the parties of the final judgment records, the two rolled *ḥukm*s, which contained the judge-corrected transcript of the litigation minutes. In the final section of this chapter, I note that record keeping by the court also could become a matter of contention.

Technically, again, according to the "Instructions" of Imam Yahya from 1937, the minutes were kept in the "entering register" (*daftar al-ḍabṭ*), a term that there is no reason to expect to find in the court records. In an instance quoted earlier, however, there is a generic mention in the minutes of the placing of signatures "in the register of the court" (*daftar al-maḥkama*). The text of the minutes, as distinct from the register in which it was written, was known in Sunnī doctrine as the *maḥḍar*, a term also known to Zaydī *fiqh*, for instance in the fifteenth-century *Commentary on the Flowers* (cited in chapter 3) but that does not appear in the imam's "Instructions." In quoting passages from these records in the preceding paragraphs I have translated two words as "minutes," both of which suggest the idea of a "summary."[7]

In contrast to the brief summaries characteristic of premodern Ottoman practice the entries in Yemeni court case records are lengthy and relatively verbatim. But how do they compare with an American court transcript? At first glance, these sharīʿa records may seem to have similar features. Like western transcripts, Yemeni court records include introduced written texts, and they also sometimes endeavor to reproduce the colloquial Arabic of spoken statements, especially when language issues are relevant to establishing the facts of the case. An American transcript is different in important respects, however. In the first place, it is an independently authoritative text backed by the certified expertise of a professional "court reporter," and its thoroughness is made possible by an efficient modern technology of mechanical transcribing. Second, where the American transcript purports to contain all the words of the judge, the attorneys, and the witnesses, or at least all those officially "on the record," for pre-revolutionary Yemeni court records we lack information about the three-way interchange (witness-judge-secretary) in which many such minutes were created. In cases I observed, the judge guided the secretary's work.

Focusing on the movement from the spoken to the written, Bentham analyzes "the operation whereby viva voce testimony is converted into minuted testimony."[8] He explains that this process of "notation" or "recordation" is of two types. "What is committed to writing may be either the tenor, the very words of which the testimony was composed," he states, "or no more than the supposed purport of it," which he terms "notation in substance." [9] Recording the tenor, also known as verbatim or literal recording, is "the more accurate," the "standard of reference, from which, without special reason . . . no departure ought ever to be made." Recording the purport or substance, by contrast, is "the looser mode of notation," which is "susceptible" to "infinite degrees of aberration." Properly recording the "tenor" of a testimony meant including not only "the very words" but also "all the words." In the court minutes, he cautions, a judge, lawyer or witness should "speak for himself." "Let not the scribe take upon himself to speak for any one of them." Accordingly, Bentham emphasizes the "impropriety of the grammatical change from the first person to the third."

Bentham also states that the recording of testimony has uses both "to the judge" and "against the judge." The former refers to providing the judge with the correct and complete grounds for his decision, although a record of the "substance" alone may suffice for this. The latter, "against the judge," refers to the protection of the parties "and the interests of truth and justice against any errors (voluntary or involuntary) on the part of the judge," typically in appeal actions. In the sharīʿa courts of early to mid-century Yemen the minutes of lawsuits served both as the basis for the judge to render his decision and, on appeal, as the potential basis for a higher ruling "against the judge." Judges sometimes were rebuked for their conduct,[10] but normally a ruling "against the judge" referred to his decision. During the course of the litigation, sharīʿa court minutes additionally could serve as a reference for the parties in the ongoing construction of their arguments.

Following the standard form of English procedure, the verbatim notation of the "tenor" ought to include not only the "responses," the testimony in the narrow sense, but also the "interrogatories," the eliciting questions. In pre-revolutionary Yemeni sharīʿa courts, however, there was no comparable institution of interrogatories. Witness testimony was neither generated by, nor confronted with, questions. In this historical instance of sharīʿa litigation, the defending party, the party's legal representative or a court-appointed delegate (*manṣūb*) had to be present at the giving of testimony, but there was no concurrent examination or questioning, whether direct or cross. Instead, at a later interval, after the testimony was concluded, the defending party could attack the recorded evidence, perhaps with the advice of a legal representative. A type of special witness (the *jarḥ* witness) also could be brought, separately, to attack the credibility of an opponent's witness. In these sharīʿa processes, an emphasis equivalent to that placed on recording the "tenor" of English interrogatories occurred in recording the "tenor" of the statements made by the parties.

Sharīʿa judges of that era (unlike present-day Yemeni judges) did not direct or otherwise elicit testimony by posing formal questions, as is common in continental European procedure. In the litigation segment of the imamic-period Yemeni lawsuit, sharīʿa court judges were relatively passive. Aside from the necessary overall direction of the proceedings exercised by the judge, which occasionally is noted as such in the record,[11] there are only rare entries containing questions posed by judges to witnesses, and these only for minor clarification. As opposed to the English institution, which involves evidence "extracted by interrogatories," procedure in the Yemeni court appears closer to what Bentham refers to, alternatively, as evidence "spontaneously exhibited."[12] This sharīʿa format, again, was part of a larger system of litigation centered on the evidence-hearing and interpreting role of the judge and otherwise based on the parties' responses to opposing evidence and on the possibility of bringing of special witnesses against (*jarḥ*) the credibility of opposing witnesses and in support (*taʿdīl*) of one's own.[13]

Bentham mentions other important uses of such court writings in English practice.[14] These extend beyond their obvious value with respect to further litigation on the same matter to include their contributions to the "stock of precedents" that have a bearing on other cases. Beyond this there is "the service rendered by the aggregate mass of the facts thus registered," when properly abstracted and publicized, "to the legislator, the guardian of the people, and through him to the people at large," and thereby "to the several ends of justice."[15] Since sharīʿa judgments were not issued under a regime of precedent formation, and were not abstracted or publicized, the keeping of minutes in sharīʿa courts was not motivated or discursively structured by such ends.

Before the advent of machine-assisted transcribing in Anglo-American courts, shorthand was the norm. Bentham remarks, "In the early ages of modern jurisprudence, writing was rare, short-hand writing unexampled." But by his time, "this talent [viz., shorthand] would be regarded as an indispensable qualification in a judicial scribe."[16] An equivalent to the efficiencies of English shorthand did not exist in Arabic writing, although the Ottomans commonly used a somewhat streamlined form of "administrative" (*dīwānī*) script. In this textual universe, however, the longhand transcribing of court minutes was as conceivable, manageable, and, in fact, routine as the act of taking down an entire book in "dictation" from a teacher in a series of sessions in the lesson circle. Since I have not carefully studied examples of the first type of "entering" register (although I have seen some), I cannot speak to whether there were any regular indications of court secretaries being hurried, their work crossed-out, revised, etc.—that is, indications of writing under the pressure of court activity. As opposed to the "entering" register, which was the original site for recording the minutes, both the second, or "recording," type of register and the original documents presented to the litigants were, in major part, records written from—that is, on the fully quoted basis of—these initial transcripts. In examining the "minutes" of the five example cases from Ibb, I refer not to their appearance in the first or "entering" register, but to how they appear, joined with the judge's concluding decision, in the final judgment rolls. Both the texts in the "recording" registers and these rolled originals were prepared in comparative leisure, often at some remove from the bustle of the court—in a secretary's residential sitting room, over *qat*, or in the equivalent of my friend, the court secretary al-ʿIzzi, sitting in his shop in the late afternoon.

The keeping of minutes in the sharīʿa courts of Ibb in the first half of the twentieth century certainly was not the continuous, simultaneous, mechanically assisted, trained, and relatively unguided transcription work of the American court reporter. Article 7 of the imam's "Instructions," cited in the last chapter, refers to the secretary taking down the claim "until the judge states that the claim has been validly completed." The notation of testimony, the segments of which never run on at great length in these proceedings, and which also often appear to have been consolidated, seems to exhibit a form of validating editing. Since the typical written record of viva voce sharīʿa testimony in Ibb extended for a few lines at most (a short paragraph in translation), shorthand skills were not required.

Overall, the "verbatim" or simply prolix character of these records had to do with the aims and ambitions of the judicial processes of the period. The great length of some transcripts reflected the facts that (1) entries were made for every witness, even when the numbers of witnesses greatly exceeded the evidential requirements of the doctrine, and (2) they fully accommodated the occasional lengthy statements made in the course of the trial by one or both of the parties to the case. By design, the process was intended to be exhaustive. Recall the formulation, also in article 7, that says that the litigation will continue until the parties state that the litigation (*muḥākama*) is ended and also formally "request that the judge rule as to what is required in their dispute." By this point the litigants were meant to have made all the arguments and counterarguments they intended to make and to have introduced all of their evidence, to "have no further assertion other than what has taken place, and no evidence other than what they have presented." A by-product of this exhaustive approach to the process and the associated institution of record keeping was that, as noted earlier, in contrast to final Ottoman records, the Yemeni *ḥukm* characteristically contained litigant assertions to which the judge did not respond, and also items of presented testimony and other evidence that did not form the explicit basis for his ruling.

Sharīᶜa Names

What's in a name?

—*Romeo and Juliet* II.2

Archival discourse was a discourse of the cited proper name. A name quoted the existence of a person. As opposed to the several types of doctrinal discourse characterized by the "so-and-so" construct, *fulān*, archival texts equally consistently and carefully mentioned actual names. Attention to the relevant human presences at each of the procedural junctures was a fundamental concern of this system of justice, and the entering of names in the record represented the basic form of implementation. At this level of the law, the many possible categories of status and role set forth in theoretical isolation in the doctrine—the minor, the seller, the heir, the murderer, etc.—were associated with the names of particular people, usually ordinary people. Names thus involve the incumbents of the various possible and locally recognized statuses and roles in the sharīᶜa and in local custom.

Names in the sharīᶜa archive must be understood within the context of Islamic personal name conventions.[17] The more immediate context I want to provide for the sharīᶜa name in these highland texts, however, is ethnographic, but what I have to say is by no means exhaustive. A brief account of informal or practical types of local naming conventions will provide some context for the formal features of name recording in the sharīʿa archive, which covers both court records and the notarial instruments discussed in the following chapters.

In the imamic era people did not carry on their "persons" (which consequently did not exist in this specific sense) the commonplace contemporary pieces of personal documentation such as national identity cards, driver's licenses, military conscription papers, or bank account cards. Such documents now identify the Yemeni individual as a citizen, and by name and also by one or more types of registered numbers. Such individuals now are apt to have a numerical postal address, a telephone number, and a vehicle license number. With print, advancing commercialization, professionalization, bureaucratization, quasi-universal education, and international wage-labor migration, individuals also now are also apt to have entire personal dossiers of documents, including certificates of birth and residence, diplomas of scholastic attainment, employment records, various sorts of attestations of marital, military, or tax status, and, for some, passports.[18] Integral to this familiar modern story of identity construction is the now ubiquitous photo studio, which produces the required photographs to be placed on the various documents and reproduces the necessary multiple copies of the documents themselves. In archival terms, the transition involved was one from entry in one of several old types of registers and placement in a cloth bag or chest of personal holding to the dossier, the portfolio, the personal file.

Imamic Yemen was a society without the proliferating, characteristically modern documents of personal identity, but it was not, to put it mildly, a society without written documents. The old Islamic state of the twentieth-century imams did keep records, including tax (*wājibāt*) and charity (*ṣadaqa*) lists and also simple personnel listings for the military and other administrations. This was not the massively detailed bureaucratic regime of the old Ottoman Empire, although around the turn of the century, under a limited form of Ottoman provincial administration, there had been efforts to institute various local government organs, such as the municipality (*baladiyya*), and to reform existing local bookkeeping practices. Imamic state record keeping, in contrast, was characterized by its informality, both in the concrete sense that its documentation practices predated reliance on printed forms and in the conceptual sense that it was not highly elaborated, rationalized, or standardized.[19] While the state kept records of several types, individuals typically held no personal versions, or certificates, whether originals or copies, to retain and use for themselves.

The Ibb town charity lists of 1962 are organized by quarters, and the personal names that appear on them are instructive in their informality.[20] These charity list names are different from either the formal names found on notarial documents or the several types of honorifics and otherwise extended names common to the entries devoted to notable individuals in the biographical histories. As opposed to the modern legal name, which now includes a permanent, Western-style "family name," which was selected and established when the first identity papers were created in the years after the Revolution, these listed names are practical and local in their everyday style of identification.

One charity list includes, in reference to particular women, "the wife of Muhammad Asad," "the sister of Ahmad Nāgī," "the 'family' [i.e., wife] of Faqīh Ahmad Muḥsin," and "the mother of Muhammad Laṭīf." At the time these lists were compiled, most women were not publicly identified by their first names. At home, but in the presence of guests, an older man in my day still called out to his wife (who was not in the room) using a son's name. When it came time, in 1975, under the nation-state, to conduct the first census, the problem of recording the names of wives, daughters, and sisters arose. Especially in rural districts, a patriarch likely would be offended, and perhaps violent, if a stranger census taker asked for the first names of family women. At least that was the assumption of a humorous skit put on at the time in Ibb town that sought to raise consciousness on this issue. A young actor (my occasional assistant) played the traditional turbaned tribesman smoking his long-stemmed pipe, an individual who was addressed and immediately enraged by the suit-wearing young teacher inquiring about the names of "his" women.[21]

However, on the 1962 charity lists, perhaps indexing differences of status, one also reads, "the free woman Muhsina and her children," "the divorced woman Rabiʿa," and, simply, "Ḥalima daughter of al-Mubayyaḍ." Other recipients' names have pragmatic identifications prefacing their names. These pertain mainly to the various vulnerabilities that made them deserving of charity: "the sick," "the afflicted," "the aged," "the dumb," "the insane," and "the orphans." A further example is an individual identified as "the son of Sinan with the cut-off leg." As opposed to the standardized forms of modern identifications, the local idiosyncratic practicality of the old Ibb charity lists is further indicated by other identifications based on specified residential locations—"in the house of Qasim ʿAli," for example—as part of an identifying one-line entry. Such naming devices indicate a local town community of known individuals, a version of a "face-to-face" society based on gender and other social differences, rather than a modern one of theoretically equivalent citizen-strangers. The character of such lists speaks to the limited degree of control and organization of "private" identities and to the limited "public" bureaucratic reach and rationalization of the imamic polity.

Sharīʿa names, in contrast, exhibit a regular premodern formality. In this era just before family names were chosen, registered, and entered on all manner of personal documents, individuals directly involved in contracts or in litigation were identified, at a minimum, by their tripartite name. This comprised their own "first" name (*ism*), their father's first name, and their grandfather's first name, with "son of" or "daughter of" either stated or implicit. In contrast to the informality and practicality of the names recorded on the local charity lists, the tripartite name constituted an individual's formal identity in the law. Case 5 opens as follows, with the parties to the litigation identified by full sharīʿa names:

> In the sharīʿa court of the government seat of Ibb Province, a claim was entered from Muhammad ʿAzīz Hasan and his wife, the free woman Badriyya, daughter of ʿAli Ahmad Saʿīd, residents of the village of . . . , locality of . . . , after the identification of the aforementioned and the woman by al-Ḥājj Nuʿman bin Muhammad and Ahmad bin Qasim, against the [individual] present with them at the sharīʿa session, Muhammad bin Muqbil Ahmad al-Shamālī, saying in their claim, and indicating the defendant, that he killed their son ʿAbduh Muhammad ʿAzīz, with intent and enmity, by a stab of his dagger, a stab mortal in itself, on the left side of the mentioned killed individual.[22]

The father of the deceased is Muhammad ʿAzīz Hasan. His wife, the mother of the deceased, is Badriyya, and her name is followed by "daughter of," and three male first names, ʿAli Ahmad Saʿīd. The deceased's name is ʿAbduh, which is followed by his father's three names. The three-part name of the accused is followed by a *nisba*, indicating a regional origin, here as al-Shamālī ("the Northerner").[23] *Nisbas* were among the several types of old-style appended names that could be regularized as a "family name" after the Revolution. In this and in other types of sharīʿa documents, women's names appear in full, given the same treatment as men's names. Identity also was firmly territorial: the parties are identified by a named village of residence, in a named region, district, and province—the nonnumerical addresses of the era.

How were the identities of the parties to a case and those of the witnesses established in such a courtroom? In a contemporary Yemeni court, the parties would show their identity cards and the relevant names and numbers would be recorded in the record.[24] Here, "the aforementioned and his woman," the claimants appearing in court, had to be identified by further individuals, ideally persons known to the court. The names of these identifiers are given in the record in two parts, indicating they are not parties to the case or, possibly, that they are familiar to the court. When witnesses appeared for the claimants, the names of these individuals were given in three-part form. Following their testimonies, witnesses themselves sometimes also were identified by a further set of individuals. The passage in the court record of case 5 following the initial set of witnesses states that the identities of "the aforementioned witnesses were made known by [four named individuals], and they also testified to the probity (*ʿadāla*) of the witnesses and that they did not know with respect to any of them any aspersion (*qādiḥ*)."[25] It was through spoken human linkages, rather than any sort of supporting written identification, not to mention bureaucratic numbers or the modern photo ID, that the identity of unknown individuals could be established in court.

In connection with nineteenth-century homicide trials in Egypt, Rudolph Peters notes that errors concerning tripartite names could derail the legal process.[26] In the Yemeni homicide litigation (case 5), mistakes regarding names were given emphasis in the trial record but did not interfere with the process. One witness, for example, referred to the deceased's brother as ʿAbduh, whereas that was the deceased's name. Another witness in the case got the claimant's name wrong, and it is noted that he corrected himself only after being prompted by another witness. Failures of identification also were noted in the court record. Another witness in the same case, who testified that the accused had acknowledged the crime, was asked by the judge to identify him in the courtroom. It is reported in the record that the witness "indicated the father of the murdered man." Then, "Muhammad Muqbil was pointed out to the witness and the witness said, 'that's Muhammad Muqbil.' "[27] In case 1, in a Martin Guerre moment, the identity of the long absent claimant initially was contested.[28]

Human presences were crucial to the authority of sharīʿa court processes and to record them was a basic archival task. Lawsuit records regularly stated of witnesses who had just completed their testimony, "The testimony of the aforementioned witnesses was given in the presence (lit. "in the face," *wajh*) of the defendant," or that it was given "face-to-face" (*muwājahatan*).[29] Mentions of the fact that signatures were placed in the court register indexed the general activity of inscribing and confirming evidence, providing a reflexive view of the creation of the archival record itself. Case 5 is consistently explicit regarding these methods of confirming evidence, perhaps since it concerns a claim of homicide, a matter of the greatest significance. Referring to witnesses in this case, there are repeated lines such as the following: "with the presence (*bi-ḥuḍūr*) of the witnesses who placed their signatures in the register of the court." Referring to the litigants in the case, the same record reads at one point, "[E]ach of the two parties placed his signature below that [in the register]." At another point the record states, "All of the witnesses, and the identifiers, and the claimant, and the defendant placed their signatures on [the record of] this testimony."[30]

Finally, names also represented building blocks for a fundamental mode of technical juridical analysis. Envisioned in the doctrine and carried out in the courts, this focused on patterns of agrarian-age family relations. Anthropologists once prided themselves on kinship studies, which until midcentury represented the core of disciplinary theory. But with the exception of the work of ancestors such as W. Robertson Smith (d. 1894), anthropologists of the Middle East ignored the rich juridical conceptualizations of descent and marriage.[31] Based on discussions in the relevant chapters of the doctrine, this sort of kinship analysis figures in many types of Ibb court cases, where a basic determination centered on the "delimitation" (*ḥaṣr, inḥiṣār*) of the relations of descent relevant to the given claim. Across a variety of agrarian property case types, employing specialized subsets of sharīʿa terminologies, judgments depended on establishing the facts of family relations. While this is perhaps obvious in case 2 (inheritance and endowments) and case 4 (marriage), it is equally true in case 1 (urban real estate) and case 5 (murder). In the "private" pursuit of a murder conviction in these years prior to the advent of a nation-state type of public prosecution, the standing of the claimants was established on a kinship basis, as would be the rights and obligations of the receivers and payers of compensation (*dīya*), if that was the outcome.

Quotation

I read every collection of poetry I see
And I never restrain my bird from quotation.
I quote every verse with meaning
And my poetry is half from the poetry of others.

—Mujir al-Din bin Tamim

I only quote the others the better to quote myself.

—Michel de Montaigne, *Essays* I.26

Quotation structured the texts of the library and the archive. Both the relation of the basic text and the commentary in the library book and the transfers between the two main types of court registers in the court archive involved types of global quotation. In more specific terms, where several types of quotation, including some forms of explicit citation, were crucial to the construction of law book discourse, so the minutes of imamic-period lawsuits depended on detailed mechanisms of quotation. Court register entries included directly reported verbatim texts, initiated by such formulas as "in his words," in the case of speech, or "in its expression," in the case of writing, and also a variety of indirect reports. Rather than consisting exclusively of notation either in "tenor" or in "substance," Yemeni sharīʿa court records were purposeful mixtures of the two, involving strategic shifts between first- and third-person entries. Within the variety of direct and indirect forms of reporting, and across the differences of case types (and the differing judicial styles of the presiding judges), there are certain consistent patterns.

Testimony

Testimony in these court records is framed in the third person, past tense. According to standard word order in Arabic, the entries begin with the verb "bore witness" (*shahada*), although sometimes this is preceded by "appeared" (*ḥaḍara*). The witness's name is then given and this is followed by the crucial marker of indirection, "that" (*anna*). Thus an entry (from case 5) begins, "Ahmad bin Ahmad Muhammad from the town of Ibb appeared and bore witness to God that between the defendant . . . and the [claimants' witnesses] there was preexisting enmity caused by a dispute between them about land."[32]

An entire entry of typical size is the following (from case 4):

> Ahmad Husayn Qasim from the village of . . . bore witness to God that the free woman Bilqis, daughter of ʿAzīz ʿAli Musṭafa, mother of the free woman Arwā, daughter of the aforementioned Muhammad Nājī, went to visit her maternal uncle ʿAli Muhammad Qasim in the month of Jumad II, the year 1362 [1943], and she was pregnant with the free woman Arwā, daughter of Muhammad Nājī. And she stayed with him for two months and then she gave birth to the child she was carrying at the end of Shaʿban, 1362. Then she stayed until the end of Ramadan when she returned to the house of her husband.[33]

Witnesses were witnesses for one of the parties to the case. There were no state's witnesses since there was no institution of public prosecution. Approached and prepared in advance of a session, witnesses were presented in court as part of the unfolding of a side's case. In addition to reports of things seen and heard, testimonies represented efforts to introduce legally relevant facts and language. In court, such "spontaneously exhibited" spoken statements from the witnesses then were "converted into minuted testimony." The spontaneity, again, was associated with the absence of eliciting questions, not with the absence of witness preparation. From the perspective of the court, the resulting entries contain what must be considered the essential information in the testimonies. If some form of editing, selection, or restatement occurred, it would have been the work of the judge and the secretary together, or of one of them alone, and this varied depending on the occupants of these posts. In the republican-era court practice that I observed, judges commonly restated testimony for the record, and this may have occurred in the past as well.

The basic template for the entry of a single individual's testimony could be extended to include a group of witnesses. The entire report on the opening set of three eyewitnesses (each with three-part names, and all from the same village) for the claimants in case 5 is (with a gloss given, in passing, on the colloquial term for a young *qat* plant):

> Each of them bore witness by God, individually, using the expression of the *shahāda*, that a sheep owned by ʿAbduh Muhammad ʿAzīz [the deceased] entered the property of the killer, namely, the defendant Muhammad bin Muqbil Ahmad, a terrace named [name], and on that property were young *qat* plants, known as *ḥadātha*, and when Muhammad Muqbil saw the sheep on his property, he came from his house, took the sheep, and dragged it towards his house. And when ʿAbduh Muhammad ʿAzīz saw him he ran toward him and wanted to take the sheep from the hand of the defendant. Muhammad Muqbil Ahmad simply pulled out his dagger and stabbed ʿAbduh bin Muhammad, a stab that he died from, in his side. The defendant killed ʿAbduh bin Muhammad ʿAzīz with intent and with enmity, and this at noontime, Monday the twenty-third of Jumada II, the year 1380 [1960]. Then the killer fled toward his house. Each of them also bore witness that the killed individual's heirs are limited to his father and his mother and that he has no heir except for them.[34]

Clearly the product of summarization, but quite detailed nevertheless, and attempting to establish both the facts of a murder and the litigation status of the claimants as the victim's only heirs, collective entries such as this covered a set of witnesses who appeared in the same session and who testified to the same facts. These witnesses would have appeared serially and, ideally, according to the doctrine, separately. That they could be represented as having testified to the "same" facts is anticipated in the doctrinal chapter on evidence, where the underlying assumption in the basic doctrine of "differences" is that the testimony of the normative two witnesses on a given side should be the same.[35]

More commonly, such sameness was accounted for in these court records (examples in cases 1–5) by means of the concise formula, "like" (*mithl*), sometimes reinforced by the phrase "without difference" (*sawāʾan sawāʾan*). Following a full-text entry for a preceding witness, the short record of the "same" testimony given by the next named witness would be that he "bore witness to God like the one before him." A subset of these entries of sameness, however, recorded items of divergence, in phrases that begin with "except" or "he added."

First-person direct quotation appears fairly frequently in the records of testimony, but always within a larger third-person frame. Bakhtin, again, maintains that authoritative words tend to be secured by direct quotation.[36]

In the recording of testimony, first-person quotation captures key evidential passages. As there were no quotation marks in the handwritten Arabic of this place and period (unlike some printed doctrinal works of the era, as I noted earlier), the written quotatives, as the linguists term them, the indicators of direct quotation of speech, derive from the verb "to say." Testimony thus should be understood as still another variety and locus of the *qawl*, here as a potentially authoritative evidential statement. In the following example (case 4), the shift from the third-person frame of the entry ("bore witness . . . that") to the first-person, "I said" (*qultu*), occurs via the third-person report "he said" (*qāla*), resulting in the formulation "he said, 'I said. . . .'" In this particular instance, there is direct quotation within the direct quotation. In the report of the statement made in court ("he said"), the witness quotes himself ("I said") about a question he asked at a prior point in time ("Why is that girl crying?"):

> Al-Faqīh ʿAbd al-ʿAzīz al-Baṣīr bore witness to God that he arrived in the village of . . . in the month of al-Qaʿda, in the year 1376 [May 1957], and found al-Ḥājj Ahmad Nājī gripping the daughter of his brother, and she was crying. And he [the witness] said, "And I said to him, 'Why is that girl crying?' And he said, 'We want to contract for her [marriage] with the boy ʿAzīz.'" And he [the claimant] said to the witness, "Come with us into the house to be a witness to the agency and the contract."[37]

To read such an entry is to be confronted with concrete decisions made by the court regarding indirect and direct modes of reporting testimony. Like the choices as to the reporting of substantive detail, we may conclude that such discursive decisions, or habits, also were connected to perceptions of potential legal significance. The final judgments rendered in this and in other cases demonstrate that judges found this level of detail, especially the differences among such details, useful in reaching their judgments. It is also clear that judges explicitly understood, or presumed, that some such testimonies were false, as I discuss below. While relatively fine-grained reporting is characteristic of these mid-century minutes, the reported responses to this type of information by the presiding judges are few.

From the perspective of the larger formation of sharīʿa texts, might this gleaning of facts of potential legal significance from the raw court testimony that occurred in the production of the minutes record be considered in some respects to be analogous to the interpretive extraction of discrete rules from the more voluminous "source" texts of the Qurʾan and the *ḥadīth*?

Isolated testimonies may be better understood, of course, when they are reinserted into the flow of evidence presentation and into the ongoing construction of the presenting party's legal argument and narrative of the facts. Another important view of the significance of testimonies is revealed in critical responses from the opposing party.

Litigant Parties

Reported statements by the parties loom large in these court records. Statements of this type begin with the initial claim and the response. At the opening of a record, after the court itself is identified and the claimant and the defendant are named and, if necessary, their identities verified, another variant of the verb "to say"—"saying" (*qāʾilān*), referring to the claimant—introduces the entry of the formal claim (*daʿwā*). Since the standard phrase "saying in his claim" is in the voice of the court, or of the record itself, and since it typically is followed by the marker of indirection, "that," the speech act indexed in the word "saying" is immediately converted to a third-person report.

Expressed entirely in the third person, a claim could be prepared in advance by the party, or by a legal specialist of some sort, and then submitted in writing to the court. Or the court secretary could create it on the spot, from the claimant's spoken words, with or without the judge's guidance. Occasionally, within reported claims, there are brief switches to the first person, such as, "This is my claim," which appears at the end of a long and otherwise third-person-framed claim that begins, "Saying in his claim . . ."[38] In another case, the claim is mixed, or defectively written: "Saying in his claim that the defendant is holding my share from my father . . ." In the lengthy ensuing detailing of this property claim there also is a brief change to the first person to meet the specific doctrinal requirement of preemption. This part of the claim states that, if it turns out "that the defendant has purchased anything from any of the heirs, then I am preempting."[39]

In many cases the required initial response (*ijāba*) from the defendant is formulaic, consisting of a mechanical denial (*inkār*) of the claim, but it is a denial without which the litigation proper would not have been engaged and the court record created.[40] Initial responses were required and, if necessary, the judge had the adversary brought in by force to respond. In ordinary proceedings, after the claim had been heard, the judge would turn to the defendant and say something like, "What do you respond to that statement?" Slightly more elaborated initial responses consist of a concisely introduced rebuttal or counter argument, or a partial acknowledgment. All initial responses are reported in the third person. The mechanical variety is entered in the record as the defendant "responded with a denial"; those that go further do so employing the marker of indirection, "responded . . . that."

According to the doctrine, there are both "simple" and "compound" sharīʿa proceedings.[41] Case 3, in which only the claimant party presented evidence, is an example of a relatively unusual but doctrinally normative simple proceeding. The other four cases are compound in the sense that evidence was presented by both sides. In such cases, the party that initially responded as the defendant—the side that does not present evidence in the simple case model—later went on to present evidence. While the report of a mechanical denial in case 5 gives no hint of the opposing narrative and evidence later to be presented, in cases 1, 2, and 4 the initial responses introduce capsule counter-arguments. In the simple litigation format of case 3, the following denial, made by the *wakīl* representing the Treasury (*bayt al-māl*), constituted the entire defense case: "When the *wakīl* of the Treasury heard [this, i.e., the claim], he replied by denying the existence of any flaw in the sale object or decrease in the price. The Treasury sold clear to the aforementioned individual, and the buyer was sound in hearing and sight."[42]

After some evidence presentation, further litigant statements sometimes appear in these court records. These, too, were termed "responses." They are different from the first response made by the defendant, however, in that they are reactions to evidence and to subsequent opposing statements rather than to the original claim alone. Such later responses were optional rather than required, and in the compound cases they could come from either party.

These transcripts occasionally attempted to reproduce relevant features of regional dialects in the written minutes. In case 5, some quotations of spoken words mark regional differences. An origin in Upper Yemen was a relevant feature of the defendant's social background in the case, and this was captured in the transcription of his words. After having heard the testimonies of the claimants' initial witnesses, he is reported to have responded, "I am not denying (*mā anā munkir*)."[43] According to Dr. Muhammad Azīz, who is from Ibb town, this rendition of colloquial Arabic indicates a northern ancestry, whereas the statement given in the Ibb dialect would have been *manash munkir*.[44] The entry reads, "The defendant responded, after hearing the testimony, in his statement, 'I am not denying.'" The phrase, "in his statement" (*bi-qawlihi*), uses the noun *qawl* to mark the direct quotation of these significant spoken words, which contain an indirect acknowledgment. Beyond a variety of stock laments and exhortations, such litigant responses could comprise characterizations of the party's own evidence, including that already entered and still to come; arguments as to the relevant legal issues; and detailed critiques of the opposing evidence.

Verbatim quotation of litigant responses underscores their significance in the legal culture of the adjudicators and record keepers. Seemingly without regard to their length, and apparently without editing, extended responses were entered in their entirety, often in the first person. Where entries on witness testimony sometimes quote "the very words" amid otherwise edited or summarized entries, it is especially in connection with reported statements by the litigant parties that these court records enter "all the words." Had these lengthier statements been given orally in court, their simultaneous transcription might have taxed the court secretary. As with some of the more detailed claims, however, we may assume that the lengthier response statements took the form of written submissions to the court. In many instances, the party's legal representative (*wakīl*), or another specialist, must have prepared these submissions. As in American court motions prepared by lawyers, the statements were in the voice of the litigant client.

Based, doctrinally, on the contract of agency, the *wakīl* of this pre-nation-state era was neither formally trained nor admitted for practice before the court nor licensed in any other way.[45] *Wakīl*s sometimes had reputations for preying on their naive clients, and at certain historical junctures there were attempts to ban the unscrupulous among them from the courts. An order issued against such representatives in the early years after the Revolution of 1962 was anticipated by article 22 of the imam's "Instructions" of 1937: "The judge must prohibit those among the representatives he knows for obstinacy and false disputation from representation and

[from] entering the court."[46] Unlike the trained and licensed private lawyers (and, after 1977, public prosecutors)[47] of contemporary Yemen, *wakīl*s did not question witnesses, either their own or those of the opposition, but they could "hear" evidence and "respond" for their clients.

ʿAli Hasan Ṣāliḥ, of Ibb, represented one of the claimants in case 5, and he aided the defendant in case 4. In case 5, his presence in court is noted in the record, but not his spoken interventions, if he made any. However, he must have written the lengthy response by the claimants entered at the end of the proceedings. In case 4, both sides in the litigation clearly had skilled legal advice, although the bearers of this advice are not mentioned in the record. In their dueling responses in this case, each side argued for the applicability of different imamic "choices" (*ikhtiyārat*). (I learned about ʿAli Hasan Ṣāliḥ's roles in these cases through an interview.)

In a number of mid-century court cases I have read that involve the local Endowments Office,[48] and in case 3, which involves the local Treasury Office, a skilled and energetic local man named Muhammad Ghālib al-Muṣannif regularly represented these administrations as their *wakīl*, although he did not have a standing appointment.[49] In case 3, it was al-Muṣannif, appointed by the governor of Ibb, who made the initial negative response to challenge the opening claim. In the opening lines of such case records the appointment of representatives is noted. *Wakīl*s unknown to the court had to show their agency contract document (*wakāla*), and this would be mentioned in the record. Beyond the experienced *wakīl*s there also were individuals who acted for parties on a one-time basis. In case 1, during the claimant's absence from Ibb, another local man began to handle the case as his *wakīl*, a fact noted in the record. Beyond the *wakīl*s who actively heard and responded, there were others who simply stood in for one or more of the principals, often women or minors, usually from their own family, as in case 2.

We correctly think of the lawsuit records issued or retained by the court as the products of court personnel such as judges and secretaries, the men who physically and interpretively managed their construction. But to the extent that verbatim notation appears in these records, an important degree of narrative power pertained to the litigants themselves. Who wrote these court records? In concrete terms, the secretaries and judges. The records were created under the auspices of the courts and court officials. Yet, by design, this style of record keeping provided a relatively open-ended forum for extended expression and, with direct quotation, included the precise language of that expression. If in one sense the final *ḥukm* document was the all-incorporating "utterance" of the presiding and signing judge and, in another, the recording and composition work of the recording secretary, in still another, but less recognized, sense, it was the dialogic creation of the litigant parties and, in many instances, their talented *wakīls*.

There also was variation among the presiding judges, however. In some records the verbatim voices of the litigants are loud and clear, appearing in ample, relatively unrestrained quotation (cases 1, 4, 5), whereas such expression may be relatively curtailed and the judicial voice more predominant, notably in the case record of the specially intervening, Taʿizz-based Judge al-Yamānī (case 2).

Written Documents

Written documents regularly appear in these court records. Among these writings within writings there were two routine types: (1) standard contracts and other such instruments presented as evidence and (2) the written texts of the just-mentioned litigant responses. But other types of written documents also were entered. In the example Ibb cases, these other types include less-standard legal texts, such as a notarial writer's supplementary statement about nonexplicit contract terms (case 1), a writer's admission of written falsehood (case 4), and a patriarch's retraction of an endowment (case 2)—the last two are discussed further below. In addition, some official writings are quoted, such as the report of a killing investigation by the Ibb governor (case 5) and, in the case of the damaged coffee against the Treasury, a letter about a commercial inquiry in Aden, correspondence between the governor and the Ibb Treasury, and telegrams between the imam and the Ibb governor (case 3).

As noted, there are few instances of quotation of the "law on the books" per se. This had to do, in part, with the fact that precedent formation was not involved. Citations of this type over the five selected cases include one phrase each from the *Book of Flowers* and from the Qurʾan, although neither of these source texts is explicitly identified as such. The same is true of the citation of a maxim (*qāʿida*).[50] In contrast, quotations of principles and language from the doctrinal genre of the imamic "choice" are frequent (cases 1, 2, 4).

As we have seen, the doctrine established techniques for the oralization of written documents introduced as evidence in court. In this model, witnesses to the original document later became witnesses in court. In court such witnesses were to "complete" their testimony on the basis of an "oral reading" (*qirāʾa*) of the document in court by the notarial writer. Did this conversion of writings to the spoken word occur in practice? These case records indicate that document witnesses and writers occasionally were summoned to appear, but only in connection with contested documents. One record states, "The remaining witness of the document witnesses testified in the face of its writer, pointing to him in the session, and the document relates that . . ."[51] In another, we read, "He [the defendant] pressed for the summoning of the witnesses and the writer of the first document, the instrument of contract from [name]." The same record continues, "And the summoning of them all took place and they all bore witness to God that the contract occurred from [name], during his lifetime, for his daughter." Later in the same case, the claimant refers back to the fact that

> the judge required us to present witnesses and the contract document together with its writer, and we presented the witnesses to the contract document and its writer to the judge. They were [named individuals]. Their testimony was brought before the face of the opponent [the defendant] in the session. And they all testified in the face of the aforementioned opponent, a unitary testimony, each one of them. And there was not in it [the testimony] any difference in its unitary wording.[52]

However, most documents were entered without a challenge from the opposition, and there are no indications that these uncontested writings were read aloud to the court.

Instruments of standard form that figured in litigation usually were not quoted in their entirety in the minutes. In a manner presumably equivalent to the selection of segments of testimony for recording in the minutes, primary documents placed in evidence were selectively inventoried for their significance by the court. Initiating recording formulas, such as "the gist (*ḥāṣil*) of it" or words from the root *ḥ-k-ā*, "to relate" or "to narrate," opened indirect, paraphrased passages concerning such texts, which likely also included some bits of direct quotation.[53] The standard instrument types entered in the record in this concise manner included the local spectrum of *muʿāmalāt*, including land sale contracts, property leases, marriage contracts, wills, endowment instruments, and individual inheritance documents. Less standard legal documents, or standard ones that were the focus of contention, were more likely to be quoted in full, which again was the treatment regularly given to the extended written responses from the litigant parties.

Mechanisms for the verbatim entry of writings (or parts of writings) included such prefacing formulas as "its expression" (*lafẓihi* or *mā lafẓahu*) and "letter for letter" (*ḥarfiyan*). Alternatively, written documents entered verbatim could be introduced by the phrase "he said in it" (*qāla fīha*): in a response during the litigation, "the defendant presented a written document (*waraqa*). He said in it, 'The defendant responded that . . .' "[54] Various other uses were possible to indicate full quotation: "Here is the text (*naṣṣ*) of the reply, letter for letter. . . . Its expression, after the *Basmala* . . ."[55] Partial quotation also occurred: "[H]e said in it" opens a quoted passage from a document, but then the record reports a skipping: "the remainder of the text continues on until he said, ' . . .' "[56]

Entries of certain written texts were accompanied by recorded remarks from the court about appended writings and signatures. Added writings of this sort usually took the form of notes of various types located in the spaces above or below the main text, a topic I explore further in the following chapters on the notarial documents. Judgments often took note of such annotations. Having completed the entry of a lengthy letter, for example, the transcript of the commercial case states, "Below it is the seal of [name] and [name], and the seal of [name]. On the upper part, in the handwriting and signature of the governor [name], God protect him, in its wording: ' . . .' "[57] Following the entry of a letter in another case the minutes add, "[W]ith the signature of its writer [name] and, under the signature of its writer, the authentication (*taṣdīq*) in the hand and signature of the witnesses [names], and on the upper part of the document [there is] the authentication of the District Officer of [place]."[58] After the partial quotation of an instrument in still another case, the next line states, referring to signatures and a note, "On this is the signature of [name] and [those of] its witnesses, and on the upper part of it, from [name, the same litigant], is that which conveys his satisfaction . . . in his handwriting and signature."[59] In the same case, after an instrument is quoted, the court record continues as follows: "On the lower part [of the document] in the handwriting of his father [is an indication] that he. . . . At the top [of the document] from the Judge of Ibb of the time, the learned Sayyid Hasan bin ʿAbd al-Wahhāb [al-Warīth], may God forgive him [there is a note that states]: ' . . . ' "[60]

In many such passages concerning documents, the third person pronoun, "it" (m. *hu*, f. *ha*), refers to the written text in question, as in "he said in it" or "in its wording." In related ways, the final judgment text itself, the recording *ḥukm*, sometimes also refers to itself in its entirety. A common formula for this, both in lawsuit records and in ordinary legal instruments, appears at the end of the text and involves the passive for "to write." The formula reads, "written on its date [date]," with the possessive pronoun referring reflexively to the whole of the completed text at the conclusion of which this line appears.[61] On rare occasions the judge speaks in the text about the text. I mentioned earlier an instance where, just prior to recording his decision, a judge referenced the past of the litigation, "what had transpired." In some cases the future of the text is indicated. In such instances the judge also speaks as the record's writer. These comments refer not to the past or to the current events of the court process but to what is to come later in the final form of written record itself. Thus the judge of case 2 looks forward to the body of his *ḥukm* document when he states at the outset, "[W]e [will] speak here of the two endowments," with the "here" referring to the remainder of the text of the final judgment record in which he has begun to "speak." Referring to a marriage contract, the judge of case 4 uses the future tense: "and mention will come of this document, letter for letter"—that is, quotation of the contract in question will appear later in the same writing.[62]

False Writing

Given my determined focus on questions of textual form, the only substantive passages I have paid attention to thus far in this book—whether in library or archival writings—are those I have used to examine matters of textuality. In this chapter, as in the last, I refer to the five court cases (chapter 7) to illustrate discursive and material practices. I have refrained from discussing the rich content of these cases, including their topical issues, evidential presentations, and rulings.

An understanding of textual properties remains my analytic purpose as I conclude this chapter with readings of selected passages from these case transcripts. Court writings not only quoted primary texts, oral and written, but also often commented on the incorporated discourse, and it is through a similar lens that I raise, once again, the topic of thought about writing. As opposed to the earlier discussed interventions of the doctrinal jurists, the agency demonstrated here emanates from the archive.

In their purposefully circumstantial yet eloquent manner, these archival records speak to the status of written texts and to the general problem that most worried the doctrinal jurists: forgery and the falsification of evidence. As I discussed in the first half of this book, the main protections or guarantees the jurists proposed to support the otherwise insecure authority of a written document included active recall from memory, oralization in court, and connecting a recognized script to a well-reputed writer. For witness testimony, both the doctrine and Ibb court practice knew the foundational, paired mechanism of *jarḥ* and *taʿdīl*, the attack on and the affirmation of a witness's integrity. This mechanism, however, had both formal (labeled as such) and informal (unlabeled) versions, with the latter illustrated below.[63]

Having lingered earlier over elements of formal textual thought—notably the theory or ideology of evidential writing as expressed in doctrinal works and in the freestanding opinions of Zaydī jurists—I now sample informal ideas and practices that surfaced in the archival records managed by Zaydī judges and their secretaries in Ibb. This is to point up the existence of a little-known substratum of assumptions and strategies related to primary evidential texts, both written and spoken. Dipping here into the heavily populated and turbulent worlds of these unexpurgated case records, I give examples of how such assumptions were articulated and the strategies pursued by litigants through the medium of testifying witnesses. False testimony was a known threat to justice, as was false writing. From a doctrinal position that I have shown is quite close to court practice, Imam Yahya's choice on the integrity of writing was directed at the "practitioners of forgery" (*arbāb al-tazwīr*) of his day. In court cases, forgery and falsification were not theoretical issues but actual, pressing, and at times unresolved problems.

Contestation around writing could begin with the integrity of the court record itself. In case 4, which concerns marriage, the status of the minutes entered in the designated court register came to the fore. As I noted earlier, at one point in this case the claimant requested and was provided a copy of the minutes. On the basis of what he learned from reading this text he then made an argument, presented in writing and itself entered in the minutes. Referring specifically to a section in the minutes that recorded the testimony of a set of his own witnesses and then the immediately following procedural developments, he states, "We did not know at the time about any response to our witnesses from the aforementioned opponent . . . until our reading of the minutes." He continues, "We found in it [viz., the text of the minutes] a response from the opponent which we did not hear in the sharīʿa [court] session, or after it." His main contention is that, upon reading the minutes and finding unknown entries of responses from his opponent (the defendant), "there became apparent to us the assistance of the [court] secretary to the mentioned opponent to transcribe (*naql*) everything he [the defendant] wanted while denying us the possibility of defense, as is required in the sharīʿa."[64] The writing in contention, again, was the minutes transcript prepared by the court secretary. The direct implication of the alleged injustice was that the judge would later use this written record, which the litigant argues was biased, or fraudulent in its construction, as the authoritative basis for his final decision in the case. However, there is no indication in the record that Judge al-Manṣūr took note of the claimant's assertion, either at this juncture in the proceedings or in his final ruling in the case.

Primary written instruments presented in evidence also could be contested in various ways. What was the connection between a given writing and the one who wrote it? While most documents presented as evidence were the work of third-party notarial writers, autograph documents were not uncommon. The treatment of one such autograph text in a local court case engaged practical textual understandings at the archival level. In case 2, the family endowment conflict, the elder brother defendant challenged a key document. Entered into evidence by the claimants, his siblings, this document, which had been written by their now deceased father, carried out his retraction of the endowment he had previously created for the exclusive financial benefit of the elder brother and this individual's line of descendants. Specifically, it was a private "recitation" endowment that involved a responsibility for regular readings from the Qurʾan to the "soul" (*rūḥ*) of the father by the beneficiary (or beneficiaries). The reversal of the father's act of endowment proved to be momentous for the family and appeared to have been wrenching for the patriarch himself. For this act he assembled some consequential local personages as witnesses, inviting them for an afternoon of *qat* in the massive family residence located just across the alley that runs along the west side of the Great Mosque.

The passionate written retraction is entered in the court minutes: "When I saw the hostility and hatred between my sons," the patriarch wrote, "and understood that it would be the cause of the ruin of my free estate, the endowment, and, possibly, some of my descendants, I made myself subservient to God and retracted it. I entrusted myself to God's mercy. I do not want recitation from any of them." He concluded this retraction with a warning: "He among my descendants who violates this, may God bring him adversity and upon him is the hatred of God."[65]

In the court case some years later, the elder brother, the defendant, sought to counter this key piece of evidence presented by the claimants, his younger siblings. To do so he raised the issue of his father's legal capacity at the time of writing. This on the grounds of what is known technically as "the sickness of [i.e., leading to] death," an interval of diminished or non-capacity.[66] The elder brother argued that, due to his impaired capacity caused by the sickness that eventually led to his death, the father's script no longer carried his legal authority and, therefore, that his act of retraction of the recitation endowment was not valid. The unexpressed reciprocal assumption is that, for an individual of full legal capacity, handwriting is authoritative, that it directly conveys the presence, the intention, and thus the act of the autograph writer-subject.

The court record states:

> [The defendant, the elder brother] replied concerning this [viz., the document presented in evidence by the claimants] that his father undertook this [retraction] in the sickness before his death. "He was not fully competent (*annahu fī ḥālatin ghayri muʿtabara*) since he died at about the time of this [document]. He set down what he wrote in a script that is without authority (*lā ḥujjata fīhi*), because the right (*al-ḥaqq*) had commenced to adhere to his [the defendant's] descendants." What he wrote should not be considered a binding document for them.[67]

What is the indicated "authority" or the evidence-value of script? In this argument, the handwriting in question is recognized as the father's, yet it is without the active authority of the self. We may reflect on a double absence: that normal for a document later presented as evidence in court, involving "the actual or empirical non-presence" of the writer, that nevertheless indicates "his having been present in a past now," compounded by the assertion of his lack of capacity, his full presence, at that moment in the past. In this view, while the father was physically able to write, he was not able to act through this writing.

The making of distinctions about writing thus went on at the archival level as well. In chapter 3, we saw that the doctrinal jurists conceived of two types of writing, one that created a legible trace and another, written on water or air, that did not. Here, in the archival transcript, we find a different, and only implied distinction between two types of writing proper to the self, one that contains or transmits the writer's authority and embodies his act and one that does not. In the negative aftermath of these distinctions, we have an analytically identifiable type of "writing" that makes an "impression" but does not leave a persisting trace, and a notion of a document that materially expresses an act in a man's own script but that is not his act. Distinctions presented in the courtroom milieu thus could parallel those developed in academic discussions.

As the case record continues, we read that the defendant lost the capacity argument. Judge al-Yamānī quotes and evaluates a decisive added note—a variety of archival meta-text examined in more detail in the following chapters on the primary instruments. This note takes the form of a sentence, described by the judge as a "line," which was written by another writer and appeared underneath the main text of the father's retraction document and served to verify it. The sentence suggests that the assembled witnesses both observed the moment of composition, therefore, they were able to speak to the physical presence of the writer as he drafted his retraction, and they also heard from him a buttressing oral expression of this act. This seeing and hearing enabled the witnesses to affirm the patriarch's capacity to act. On the basis of this appended note, the judge resolved the contended evidential point.

The judge writes:

> In the document of retraction this line is written at the end, and the signatures of the witnesses are after it, [in] the expression of its writer: "This is in the handwriting and signature of al-Ḥājj . . . [name of the patriarch], and we have

[also] heard this from him speaking in person with soundness of his mind and his body, on its date." Below are their signatures, and they are [five names], and others. This refutes the statement of [the defendant] that his father had entered into a state of severe illness.[68]

Forgery

Although less common than accusations of false witnessing (*shahādat al-zūr*), allegations of forgery (*tazwīr*) by third-party writers appear in these records.[69] The 1958 marriage litigation (case 4) provides an instance that is unusual in that the accusation later eventuates in an admission. At the beginning of the litigation, a marriage contract document was introduced as evidence by the claimant, the young woman's paternal uncle. The defendant in the case, her supporter and her maternal uncle, was present as the contract was introduced in court, as required. The maternal uncle is quoted as responding to this documentary evidence by declaring that the writer of the contract is "well known for forgery."[70] He then exercised his right to demand that his opponent, the claimant, produce the writer and the document witnesses (a passage quoted above). Summoned to court, the writer and the witnesses to the document testified to the authenticity of the contract. Let me note, again, that such document witnesses acted as witnesses in two senses. These distinct senses accord with the different temporal junctures and the changing circumstances of the contractual relation—namely, initial agreement versus later conflict. Whereas they acted as passive, aural, and visual witnesses to the original act of writing at the earlier point in time, they became active, testimony-giving verbal witnesses as to the authenticity of the document later in court.

After a few additional recorded words concerning the document witnesses' estimations of the ages of the boy and the girl in question at the time of the contract, the court transcript passage concludes "and they gave an oath (*ḥalafū*) about this."[71] According to the *Flowers* tradition evidence doctrine, judges have the option of asking witnesses to swear an additional oath "that what they testified to is true."[72] Why did the judge take this step of augmenting the regular formula of swearing by God that always initiates the giving of testimony by also requiring these witnesses to give an oath after their testimony? Was he simply trying to affirm the crucial evidence presented in the written contract of marriage, or did he suspect they were lying?

With the marriage contract introduced by the claimant and authenticated by testimony from the notarial writer and the witnesses to the writing, the defense then endeavors to undermine the status of this evidence. The following record of testimony exemplifies a stratagem that recurs in these court minutes. This involves testimony by witnesses from one side in a case on the basis of a purported encounter with the opponent's witnesses outside of court. In this sort of testimony, the testifying witnesses report either having overheard incriminating statements by individuals who had previously testified for the opponent, or having engaged in brief but significant conversations with them. The pattern thus is one of witness testimony based on chance meetings with the opponent's witnesses including, in the marriage case, the document writer. It is thus a type of testimony that focuses on alleged exchanges of words with other men who had earlier given evidence in court. Both the earlier evidential testimony and the later accusatory testimony appear in the minutes transcript. Since the principals in this particular case were from a rural village west of Ibb, the encounters in question involved men who walked into town.

For the initial individual in a set of four such counter-witnesses appearing for the defense, the transcript uses indirect quotation to record

> that he entered [Ibb] on Saturday, the last day of the month of al-Ḥijja, 1376 [July 1957], with the intention of going to the [town] market. Then he headed back to his house. They [he and some other named men] had arrived part way on the road [back to their village] when they met [three named men, the claimant witnesses to the marriage contract], and these individuals were saying that each of them had received four riyals for testimony from [name, the claimant].

The next phrase in this record, "the witness said," marks a shift to direct quotation which then embeds further reported words, also entered in direct quotation:

> and we said to them, "how could you have sold your responsibility (*dhimma*) and how [could you have given] this testimony of yours?" They said, "We testified that [name, the deceased father of the girl] contracted for his daughter with the son of [name, his brother, the claimant] in the year 1362 [1943]." And we said to

> them, "Were you present [at the contract]?" And they said, "No, we went in and testified for a fee as partisans for [the claimant], and each one of us received four riyals, and by God it was false, and the Judge additionally made us swear an oath. And [the claimant] brought in [as a witness] the writer of the document, [name], and he authenticated it (*qarraraha*) and received ten riyals." [73]

After repeating the names of the three marriage-contract witnesses met on the road, the testimony of this defense witness concludes with his statement, "these [men] are among those for whom the proverb (*mathal*) on false witnessing applies."[74] The proverb referred to here is clarified by its citation in later defense testimony, which I quote and discuss below.

But before considering this passage, I want to briefly demonstrate that this sort of encounter between men who have been and will be witnesses in court is patterned, that the production of such testimony represented a known court stratagem. Two further examples support this characterization. The first is from the same case, but with the situation reversed. In this testimony a claimant's witness responds in kind to the witnesses mounted by the defendant against the contract writer and the document witnesses. It is the same sort of testimony about conspiracy and bribery to obtain false testimony, but now with the defendant and his witnesses as the alleged perpetrators:

> [Named individual, from the claimant side] bore witness to God that he entered [Ibb] Saturday the sixth, or the seventh of the month of Muḥarram, in the year 1377, intending to go to the market, and [name, the defendant] was in the Ẓihār [a location just west of Ibb town], he and six or seven individuals. They [these individuals] said to [name, the defendant], "We will not testify for one riyal for each of us to invalidate writers, witnesses and sharīʿa contracts." And [name, the defendant] said to them, "What do you want from me?" And they said, "We will not testify unless it is for two riyals for each of us, with expenses, and, otherwise, no." And the witness stated that among these men he knew [named individuals].[75]

A second example, which demonstrates the patterned nature of such testimony, is from a different type of case, the murder trial (case 5) that also concerned villagers who lived west of Ibb town. At a stopping place named Mashwara, which is at the crest of a ridge, witnesses for the accused murderer, the defendant in the case, testified that they met witnesses for the claimants who were returning from testifying in court in Ibb. The relevant part of the testimony of the first of these defense witnesses is reported in the minutes as follows:

> The witness asked them [viz., the returning claimants' witnesses, numbers four through seven] about the murdered man [saying] he did not know who he was. They [the returning claimant's witnesses] responded, "We went in [to Ibb] to remove a disaster from over us in [the form of] expenses and soldiers [associated with disputes]. We testified against [name, the accused defendant] that he murdered the son of [name, the claimant father of the killed individual]." And the witness said to them, "How [could you], they will cut off his head based on your testimony!" They said, "He harmed us, he and his mother, for a long time." And he [the witness] stated that he returned to his house, and that this [occurred] next to the warehouse of Mashwara, and that this was the day of the return of the witnesses from [their appearance] before the judge.[76]

The second of the three witnesses for the defendant is reported to have asked the returning witnesses for the claimants, "How could you testify and kill a man (*nafs*)," to which the reply was, "That's what we want." This witness stated, however, that this interchange occurred not next to the warehouse but in a coffeehouse where they were drinking coffee. In such cases, judges confronted dense thickets of back-and-forth testimony, some of it quite outrageous. In this particular case the judge concluded that this set of defense witnesses were lying, and he did so on the basis of the small disparity in their testimonies as to the location of the encounter (i.e., warehouse versus coffeehouse).

My aim in briefly pursing the issue of the patterned quality of such testimony is to underline the fact that evidential struggles around both testimony and written documents employed known techniques of wider import in litigation. To return now to the forgery accusation and the earlier-mentioned "proverb," consider the next passage in the minutes of the marriage case. Adding to the previous testimony about an encounter with the summoned witnesses to the contract (quoted above), the following defense witness reports on an equally incriminating conversation on the same day with the notarial writer of the contract, who, as noted, also had been summoned to testify. Embedded in this passage is an issue of fact about the ages of the boy and the girl. Given their estimated current ages (there were no birth certificates), neither would have been alive when the purported contract was written. There also were various other textual complications in this case that I do not go into here, which include the writing of both an agency contract and a "renewal" (*tajdīd*) of the original contract.

I quote the record of this further testimony concerning the notarial writer to illustrate how practical conceptualizations were deployed in litigation. Unlike the sustained and elaborated formal arguments about textual and related evidential issues enshrined in doctrinal chapters and opinions, these conceptualizations take the humble form of passing bits of folk wisdom that appear scattered in the court records. Anthropologists have thought of common sense as a kind of "cultural system" that offers an "interpretation of the immediacies of experience," while linguistic anthropologists have examined metaphors and proverbs as essential reflexive materials for the study of speech.[77] In his study of highland Jewish perspectives on the sharīʿa regime of this same twentieth-century imamic period, Mark Wagner mobilizes a richly narrated corpus of memoires, anecdotes, and folkore.[78] For their part, scholarly Yemenis, including one of the Ibb court secretaries in my day, were students of proverbs.[79] What was the authority of such everyday knowledge in this setting? What work could its adages do? Regarding the specific project of this book, how did this common thought interact with related formal ideas about evidential texts? I suggest that such ordinary talk about texts, oral and written, should be viewed as an important dimension of a discursive tradition, one providing a complement or counterpoint to the jurists' academic arguments and models.

For the following "proverb" about lying, it is important to keep in mind that it was uttered in the context of agonistic court testimony, specifically, in testimony about the testimony of the opponent's witnesses. This miniature meta-text illustrates the general phenomenon of existing everyday understandings, here concerning false testimony and, by extension, forgery. Within the frame of the earlier described type of patterned testimony that alleges an out-of-court encounter and that seeks to impugn the integrity of the opponent's witnesses, a local conception such as this took the concentrated form of a kernel of popular wisdom.

Actually, there are two such kernels in the following segment of the court record. This passage of reported testimony conveys two subtypes of these colloquial proof-texts: a phrase characterized as a "proverb" and a twisted rendition of an apparent *ḥadīth* (the term is not used) from the Prophet Muhammad.

> On Saturday, the last day of the month of al-Ḥijja, 1376 [July 1957], he [the defense witness] met [name, the document writer] in the marketplace of Ibb and he asked him why he had come in to Ibb. He said, "On account of a document we made for [name, the father of the girl] in the contract for his daughter with the son of his brother [name, the claimant]." And the witness said to him, "Have fear of God, whose prison is the Fire, how could you make a document [dating] from the year 1362 [1943], when now the age of the girl is approximately twelve years and the boy's age is approximately eight or ten years?" And he [the notarial writer] said, "Don't you know my son about what the Prophet of God said to our mother ʿĀʾisha [the Prophet's wife], that if your livelihood (*rizq*) comes to you do not refuse it?" The witness said, "And I said to him, 'How [can you take] this livelihood in the name of falsification (*tazwīr*)? How much did you get?' He said, 'I got ten riyals and [name, the claimant] paid [name, the countersigner, a court secretary in the nearby town of Jibla] to authenticate the document, whereas the document had only been written the week before. And the judge additionally took the oath (*yamīn*) from us. The judge does not know among the proverbs of the Arabs that 'he who fornicates swears, and he who steals swears.'"[80]

Presiding over his court, Judge al-Manṣūr listened to bold but stereotyped witness testimony that included a reference to his purported personal ignorance of an Arab "proverb."[81] Later, in considering his decision in the case, he is likely to have consulted the just quoted passage of testimony from the written transcript. For our part, we may speculate about the veracity and plausibility of the above quoted passages of defense testimony. Would an individual who had just falsely testified and accepted money to that end so readily admit this to others, and in such precisely incriminating detail? How could the serendipitous interlocutor and future witness have had at his conversational disposal such relevant facts as the precise year of the purported contract and the approximate ages of the two children? Or was this precisely elaborated testimony presented on the defendant's behalf simply a necessary strategic and equivalently formulaic response to the dangerous weight of the claimant's systematic falsehoods? Had the proverb about lying been mobilized for telling the truth? The defendant and his niece, the young woman in question, were vindicated in the case, but Judge al-Manṣūr shed no light on the details of these accusations of falsification uttered in his court, except for finding, in general terms, that there was no contract.

There was a late development in the case, however. The minutes state that the young woman, who had reached her majority (by reason of her first period) during the court process, "brought in a written document in the script and signature of [name] and countersigned by its witnesses and by the district officer of Jibla [the nearby town], [name]." This is quoted in full, in "its wording":

> There appeared before me the learned "father" [name, the writer of the contract], from Jibla, and he verified that he was responsible for fraud (*tadlīs*) and deception (*taghrīr*) in connection with the contract document that is in his script and [bears] his signature describing. . . . He had disavowed (*qad tabarra'a min*) this document in its era and . . . he informed [the claimant] of the non-legality of the contract and requested from him the return of the aforementioned document. He [the claimant] continued to promise him [the contract writer] that [i.e., the return of the document]. . . . And when the news now reached him that a dispute was under way on this matter under the auspices of the . . . Judge of the Province, [al-Manṣūr], may God preserve him, the aforementioned "father" [name] hastened to me for the writing of this disavowal of his responsibility (*bara'a li-dhimmatihi*), and to this end it was written for its presentation to Our Master the Judge of the Province, may God protect him, for his view, on its date, Muḥarram, 1378 [July 1958]. Witnessing this was the "son" [name] and the "brother" [name], and God is sufficient witness.[82]

The notarial writer's admission that the marriage contract had been falsified thus was made, in writing, in a text prepared by a third party on his behalf. Identified in this document as "the learned 'father,'" and throughout the case as the sermon-giver (*khatīb*) of Jibla, this was the same contract writer who had earlier testified in the proceedings in support of the instrument when it was challenged after being introduced into evidence. With this document of contract document disavowel entered in the minutes, the young woman immediately "pressed for the writing [i.e., a judgment] of that which is required in the sharīʿa."

Were notarial fraud and false testimony punished? Perhaps not so much by temporal authorities such as sharīʿa judges, who acted in this "world" (*al-dunyā*), as by God, in the "afterlife" (*al-ākhira*). The important caveat is that an individual's worldly reputation for probity (*ʿadāla*) could be damaged and that his or her capacity to engage in undertakings and to give testimony could be altered. Thus the relevant evidence doctrine refers to the judge's knowledge of the probity of witnesses either "by experience or by reputation."[83] In some historical Muslim societies, following the doctrine of *tashhīr*, false witnesses were made known to their communities by public proclamation or by parading the offender.[84] Similarly, the author of the local treatise of model notarial documents examined in the next chapter recommended that the authorities bar unprincipled writers and publicize the names of the perpetrators of fraud in the marketplace.

NINE

Moral Stipulations

Every society is a moral society.

—Émile Durkheim, *The Division of Labor in Society*

EVEN THE SIMPLEST sharīʿa instrument contained the seeds of a world. Written acts such as contracts and bequests helped create, and as artifacts concerned, the individual identities, family structures, and property relations of a place and time. Such societal features must be read, however, in and through the transformative medium of a paper language. Unlike the archival records of litigated conflicts discussed in the previous two chapters, the notarial writings I now consider document the minutiae of uncontested legal acts. I read these quintessentially local sharīʿa writings, these everyday documents, as integral to a discursive tradition.

Such writings must be of particular concern to an archival anthropology. As we have just seen, contracts and other such writings frequently and routinely were presented as evidence in court, especially in property cases. Only in the event of a challenge, however, would document writers and witnesses be called to appear. During the litigation process the courts inventoried such writings and excerpted passages into the minutes transcripts that later would be reproduced in final judgments. My analysis of these acts of written "incorporation" builds on an approach to the relations between what Bakhtin referred to as "primary" and "secondary" genres. In addition to their role in conflicts before the courts, notarial writings also may be considered "primary" with respect to the tertiary superstructure of the texts of the *fiqh*, the doctrinal corpus that was elaborated, in significant part, to regulate the spectrum of rights and obligations recorded in these documentary acts.

In earlier chapters I considered law book positions regarding the evidence value of such written instruments, notably including the late fourteenth-century *Flowers* dictum ("not . . . if he does not remember") that privileged memory over the written archive. Reflecting on the wider phenomenon of writing, the jurists distinguished "inscribed" legal acts from impermanent writings on problematic substrates such as water or air. Among his free-standing opinions, Imam Yahya's early twentieth-century choice on "acting on the basis of writing," or "practice with writing," represented the culmination of a millennium of juridical thought on the problem of such written instruments, and, in the early nineteenth century, the jurist al-Kibsī addressed the same topic in an extended fashion. Despite their specific arguments and positions, and their constant concern with avoiding the perils of evidence in written form, the jurists nevertheless assumed that such common documents were among the mainstays of civilized life.

Notarial Writers

Remaining within the ambit of the sharīʿa archive, I shift now from judgment documents to notarial instruments, from the sphere of the imam-appointed judge to that of the private writer, the *kātib*.[1] Representing another segment of the resident interpretive community, these men were the most organic of sharīʿa writers. As I explained earlier (chapter 6), there were no "notaries" in late-imamic Ibb in either of the technical western senses (Anglo-American or Continental European), as these writers were not certified, licensed, appointed, or otherwise regulated by the state.[2] Nor were these notarial writers, as I refer to them, formally recognized or controlled by the sharīʿa courts, as occurred historically in some large Middle Eastern and North African towns. Portrayed as a standard feature of sharīʿa practice in anthropological accounts focused on modern Morocco, the pre-certified witness-notary, in fact, was an institution restricted to particular times and places.

When I speak of the notarial writer in Ibb, I refer to a well-known and vital institution, one that involved a handful of regulars who derived an important income from their work and many occasional writers, men who prepared documents from time to time but did not consider this work their profession. Perhaps one or more of the regulars of the period sat in marketplace stalls, as a couple of men did in my time in Ibb. Most probably worked from the semi-public afternoon sitting rooms in their own residences, in a pattern similar to the afternoon routines of the muftī and the judges. Unlike those other professionals, however, the writers also would have been available to visit their clients' houses. It would not be until the end of the twentieth century that a state-organized profession would be created by republican legislation and that these newly identified professionals would open offices and begin to put up signs to attract customers.

Among the regulars prior to the Revolution were individuals whose careers were made (and potentially unmade) by the market, by the reputation-sensitive social demand for the knowledge, experience, and personal rectitude that underpinned this form of authoritative writing. Such notarial writers, all of them educated, and some considered scholars, or *ʿulamāʾ*, functioned in the institutional orbits of the madrasa and the *maḥkama*, the school and the court. Among the occasional writers were some of the teachers at the varied levels of instruction, from locally respected shaykhs at the Madrasa of the Great Mosque of Ibb to the humble masters of the town's neighborhood Qurʾanic schools for children. After giving instruction in the mornings, such men could be approached to draft documents in the afternoons. Also among the notarial writers were certain of the secretaries at the sharīʿa court who, likewise, wrote outside of the morning hours of their court service. While some writers thus were tied, in other aspects of their work lives, to the madrasa, the *maḥkama*, or both, when they prepared documents they functioned at a remove from either institution, in separate and "private" spaces of writing.

One did not study to become a notarial writer, at least not in a specialized sense. With some madrasa training—the more, to be sure, the better—one then picked up the rest, the detailed how-to of composition and the requisite local genre determinants, from experience. Ahmad al-Baṣīr (figure 9.1), a former instructor at the Madrasa of the Great Mosque, whom I knew as an old man with black-framed glasses and a hennaed beard, had been a prominent notarial writer in imamic-era Ibb, as was another teacher from that era, the future republican-era muftī Muhammad al-Wahhābī.[3] While the recognized scripts and signatures of these two men appear on

Figure 9.1 Ahmad al-Baṣīr (*left*), imamic-era notarial writer, with his son, 1976.

many documents, the archive also was populated by numerous other writers, only some of whose signed names are legible.

When I first resided in Ibb in the mid-1970s, Yahya al-ʿAnsī, a former and future judge (and, by 2008, the acting town muftī) was a leading notarial writer. A member of one of the scholarly lineages of the town, al-ʿAnsī began his career as a functionary (*kātib*) in the Endowments Office and then served for a time as the special judge for endowments. In his years at the office, part of his work was to enter copies of legal instruments and the occasional court judgment into the designated office register. In pursuit of his "private" notarial work, al-ʿAnsī circulated in the morning in the streets of the new market area where he encountered men and the occasional woman. The scene was one of men in wrapped *fūṭa* skirts, or full-length gowns, with western-style suit jackets, daggers belted at the waist, turbans or scholarly *ʿimāmas*, and shoulder shawls, and women with leggings, dresses, and scarves or headcloths, or the completely covering black *sharshaf.* To draft a routine document al-ʿAnsī would find a place to sit in a nearby shop. He dealt with the more important or difficult assignments in the afternoon at his or his client's residence. His great-grandfather, a student of Shawkānī (and also the great jurist's son-in-law), was a well-known notarial writer in nineteenth-century Ibb.[4] This apical ancestor of the al-ʿAnsī line in the town was remembered in a local saying: "More valuable than gold water: the pen of Salih al-ʿAnsī."[5]

Notarial writers wrote instruments in a spectrum of local genres, documents known generally as *muʿāmalāt* (sing. *muʿāmala*), a term that in the formal sense means "transactions."[6] The local writer of documents thus was known as *kātib al-muʿāmalat*. As I have mentioned, the various types of instruments had particular names. Some of these were derived from the doctrinal term for the category of contract in question (e.g., *ijāra*, lease document), while others were colloquial or customary usages, such as the *baṣīra* (pl. *baṣāʾir*), the real estate sale-purchase document, and the *farz* (pl. *furūz*), the individual inheritance document. Such writings were prepared for and then held by the parties who obtained the rights in question and who compensated the writers for their efforts. Beyond the rights and obligations set forth in them, documents were themselves properties. For the fateful year 1708, when invaders from the region of Yāfiʿ, to the southeast, breached the walls and rampaged and plundered in the town, the historian records the destruction of "property documents" (*baṣāʾir al-amwāl*).[7] During my years in Ibb, there were reported instances of property documents being stolen.[8]

It may be recalled that, according to article 5 of Imam Yahya's court "Instructions" of 1937, two types of registers were referred to: those containing litigation minutes and those for recording final judgments. The same article describes these registers as "the two important ones among the registers of the courts." But it goes on to say that "to these two registers are added what is further required, such as a register for the recording of transaction documents (*muʿāmalāt*)." Such a specially designated "transactions" register existed at the courts in my day in Ibb. At mid-century, to the extent that document copies were recorded, they were either entered in a register of this third type or copied in the main recording register, where contracts may be found interspersed with the finished court judgments.[9] In the Ibb litigation on marriage (case 4) the transcript specifically mentions a "search" in the court register for an entered instrument. When it was located, the marriage contract in question was quoted into the case minutes.[10] Likewise, two documents associated with a dispute I followed were entered in the court's "*muʿāmalāt* register." I learned this not from the court registers but from the originals held by the disputants. These documents had small notes to this effect that had been placed on them by the recording secretary at the court.

"Private" Writing

Where the previous chapters concerned texts produced by the sharīʿa court, which included both the keeping of "public" registers and documents issued to and retained by the litigants, this and the following chapter mainly concern "private" production for, and the content of, "private" archives. The privacy in question entailed both the fact that notarial writers wrote outside the institutional arena of the court and without any formal judicial approval or state licensing, and the additional fact that the main site for keeping the original instruments was in individual hands in personal residences. While personal archives held the originals of all legal-textual categories, the registers of the courts were, again, the place of copies.

The limited "public" quality of this "private" form of writing may be further specified. I have noted that neither the imamic polity of the period nor the local sharīʿa court authorized or oversaw the conduct of this writing activity. Inasmuch as their sharīʿa-based activity was socially recognized in the community, these writers were sought out in a manner analogous to that of seeking an unofficial muftī. Just as the prospective questioner should look to the one from whom people "take" fatwās, as the twentieth-century commentator on the *Flowers* advised, so parties in need of a written document located a known writer. As with fatwās, the other possibility was to approach an educated neighbor or acquaintance, an individual who did not make a regular practice of writing documents but who nevertheless was capable. Thus my friend ʿAbd al-Karim al-Akwaʿ, a functionary at the Endowments Office, wrote an instrument for a man in his quarter, and Muhammad al-Ghurbānī, also an Endowments employee, drafted a marriage contract involving people he knew from a rural district.

This, then, was the relatively or totally informal "public" of "the people" (*al-nās*), the collectivity of individuals that included the persons and the relations of the market, the families and the neighborhoods, and the town and the villages of its hinterland. This was the largely male "public" enacted "before the people" (*quddām al-nās*), as local phrasing had it. These were the same "people" referred to by the *Flowers* commentator, the men and women whose "circumstances" were "entered and recorded" in the "public" registers of the sharīʿa court. To refer to a document written by a third-party writer the same commentator uses the expression, "written [by someone] among the people."[11]

The other possibility, at least for a few, was to write for yourself, or what the commentator refers to as a document written "by its party" (*ʿinda ṣāḥibiha*). As I have mentioned, these two basic types, which involved writing framed in the third versus the first person, resulted in what are known in western scholarship as "objective" versus "subjective" texts. Composition of the third-person type was to be structured by dictation, at least according to the Qurʾanic mandate. In first-person composition, given the absence of a listening notarial writer, is there a remaining role for dictation? Was it simply eliminated from the compositional equation, or should we think, analytically at least, of the writing of an autograph document as prompted by a parallel form of silent "dictation" from the self (*nafs*)?[12]

Histories of the Form(s)

In Yemen, as at varying moments elsewhere across the Muslim world, the advent of a modern system of document registration signaled the onset of a new attitude toward real property, one predicated on the demands of expanding global markets and also on the existence of newly constituted national authorities. Although the placing of instrument copies in court registers probably is as old as the sharīʿa courts themselves,[13] in the late nineteenth century in the highlands, during their nearly fifty years of provincial rule, the Ottomans introduced a more formal and newly motivated procedure, involving the *rasmiyya* fee. The entering of the copy and the payment of the fee were mentioned in an added written note placed in the open space left above the original document text. Not all estate instruments of that era were entered in the court registers, but for those that were, the original documentation held by the families bears revenue stamps and was written on official paper bearing the name of the empire. Such innovations that appeared in turn-of-the-century Ibb were only a small part of what, in the heartlands of the empire, also included institutional elements such as cadastral surveys, formalized title deeds, and the licensing of notaries. These interrelated institutions were part of the fundamentally new regime of land registration and administration introduced in the nineteenth century that has been studied by Martha Mundy and Richard Saumarez-Smith.[14]

In such Ottoman developments in the central Middle East, older forms of land tenure gradually were converted to individual, titled ownership. In colonial settings, such as in French North Africa, introduced systems of registration were central to new patterns of land appropriation by settlers. In British-ruled Aden—which did not involve this form of settler colonialism—the Registration of Deeds and Assurances office was established in 1871, and fees were imposed for drawing up the necessary instruments.[15] As I have indicated, however, the situation in highland (Upper and Lower) Yemen was different. This was due, in part, to the remote and unruly nature of the Ottoman province and the consequent non-introduction of most of the panoply of the empire's new property institutions. But the situation in the highlands also was fundamentally different in that property was already predominantly individually owned. Rather than either state or collective holdings, highland terraces, fields, and gardens were owned by individuals or by several individuals, usually sibling heirs. Rather than the state-titled and leased form known as *mīrī*, which was pervasive in the central provinces of the Ottoman Empire, the major type of holding in highland Yemen was *milk*, the sharīʿa form of individual property. With the demise of the empire in 1918, the formalized document registration system the Ottomans introduced fell largely by the wayside as highland practice reverted to the old system of entering instrument copies on an elective basis. Yet in the sphere of property registration, as in many others, the Ottoman initiative marked the onset of a new institutional direction later hybridized and eventually adopted in highland Yemen.

In previous work, I analyzed the republican-era legislative transition from the sole authority of the document writer, a private figure unrecognized by the state, to the state-backed authority of the officially recorded document.[16] In the late twentieth century, other changes may be charted, including the appearance of, for example, commercial agency contracts typed on letterhead or document forms bearing the printed name of the republican state. The simplest of these printed forms consisted of the printed word "contract" (*ʿaqd*) at the top center, with empty lines to be filled in below. Other printed forms, however, including varieties of marriage contracts and leases, provided uniform legal language with spaces left for the insertion of the archival particulars, names, dates, etc.[17] With the appearance of such templates, the old type of entirely handwritten notarial instruments—my concern in this and the next chapter—began to be replaced by print-era documents with new styles of handwriting suited to straight lines and to the residual task of filling in blanks. Print, type, and standardization thus eventually supplanted the calligraphic arts of the old archive.

To acknowledge another, deeper history, I would note that instruments from Ibb such as the *baṣīra*, the sale-purchase document for landed property, exhibit a lineal relation to medieval and even ancient Middle Eastern contracts. Written contracts phrased in the past tense and the third-person voice, in the "objective" style of a third-party document writer, embody a form that dates back to cuneiform deeds. Early Islamic-era sale documents among the papyri and parchment texts preserved from pre-tenth-century Egypt contain clauses with parallel and sometimes rhymed constructions ("its interior and its exterior, its lower part and its upper part") that are used to describe the sale object.[18] In Yemen, we find similar literary constructions ("continuous and attached, flourishing and in ruins," etc.) both in the model *baṣīra* presented in the *shurūṭ* treatise and in Ibb *baṣīra* documents of the imamic period. Of greater interest, however, are the further striking similarities between the early Egyptian documents and these mid-twentieth-century Yemenī texts, not only in their "objective" style but also in some sharing of terminology, clause order, and overall structure.

Finally, I would reference once again the pivotal historical event that pertains to such written instruments as a specifically Islamic tradition. Distant antecedents of some of these basic documents were either contemporary with, or predated, the appearance of the Qurʾan and its legitimating mandate to "write it down." With the Book came the textual opening of the *Basmala*, "In the Name of God," the phrase that initiates each of the *ṣūra*s just as it (or the *Ḥamdala*, "Praise be to God") opens every document in the sharīʿa archive.

Models

Where the imam's "Instructions," discussed in the previous chapters on judgments and minutes, modeled archival acts in the "public" domain of the sharīʿa court, the *shurūṭ* or "stipulations" treatise to be studied here modeled those in the "private" sphere of the notarial writer. In its complex character as a model, the treatise comprises both introductory and concluding observations, in which the author reflects on the genres to be presented and on the societal role of the writer. These observations bracket the main section, which moves section-by-section through the recognized categories of documents, providing suitable model language for each. A library text focused on the archive, this treatise deploys the faceless and timeless "so-and-so" and "such-and-such" discourse of *fulān* and *kadhā* as it models the writing of legal instruments designed to be filled with the proper names of people, places, and things, as well as relevant dates. Representative of a minor genre of juridical work devoted to a specific type of writing, the treatise is part of a wider field of Islamic diplomatics that includes such major figures as the famous Egyptian al-Qalqashandī (d. 1418).[19]

Unlike the transplanted, Ottoman-derived "Instructions" issued by the imam for the courts, the *shurūṭ* treatise is locally rooted. Rather than a product of recent institutional reform, the treatise was backed by a genre-specific cosmopolitan literary tradition centuries old. Treatises of this type were part of sharīʿa libraries in many Muslim societies. Where we may assume that the imam's court "Instructions" were communicated to local jurisdictions, this type of treatise of notarial models was the creation of "private" scholarship, and there is little information about its circulation or readership, except for the fact that it was twice copied. Developed on the frontier between the accumulated requirements of the *fiqh* and the actual production of legal documents, the provided models may be seen as the products of a dual abstraction. On the one hand, they were the streamlined, application-oriented versions of the rules, stipulations and related discussions found in a given chapter of the *fiqh*; on the other, they were the corrected, theory-compliant versions of the clause structure of actual instruments. With respect to the archive, such library texts thus may be seen as models, both *of* and *for* particular genres of written instruments.

Stripping

In considering this local *shurūṭ* treatise in relation to a range of historical (early to mid-twentieth-century) documents from Ibb, I return to the question of textual "stripping." Thus far I have considered the first variety of "stripping" identified by Hallaq, which concerned entries in doctrinal books constructed out of edited fatwās (see chapter 3). I also have extended this type of analysis into a new domain, that of the composition of imamic "choices" in response to current court cases. I now take up Hallaq's second example, which concerns the *shurūṭ* literature.

Hallaq is interested, as am I, in the "dialectic of doctrine and practice." In this particular form of "stripping," he hypothesizes the editing of actual historical instruments to create the models found in the *shurūṭ* works. This engages a dialectical movement, involving a document-to-model "stripping" process and its reciprocal, the model-to-document drafting process, a movement with complementary model *of* and model *for* moments. The result, he argues, is an ongoing, long-term process of technical refinement, occurring over centuries. Although he carefully surveys a number of *shurūṭ* texts, Hallaq's analysis, like that of Schacht's pioneering work before him,[20] is limited by the lack of an appropriate corpus of historical documents for comparison. But he nevertheless describes an ideal analytic situation. To assess "the extent of conformity between documentary practice and legal doctrine" requires "a model work," a *shurūṭ* text, "of the *very same locale and time* as that of the document in hand."[21]

The Ibb materials satisfy these parameters. With the corpus of texts at hand it is possible to closely compare the models of the pre-revolutionary *shurūṭ* treatise with local documents prepared in the same place and era. In contrast to Hallaq's multiple-century perspective my analysis is micro-historical. I provide a closely focused snapshot of a particular local dialectic.[22] Also, in contrast to an argument conducted comparatively at the level of whole *shurūṭ* works, mine engages at the level of the constitutive model genres in one such work. Further, in addition to comparing models and documents, which is the task of the next chapter, I am equally interested in the *shurūṭ* author's reflexive comments on notarial writing in his time, which I discuss below.

Within this micro-history, I also expand the scope of the dialectical approach. In addition to the *shurūṭ* treatise, other types of modeling texts were in circulation. Most important among these were the substantive chapters in the *Flowers* literature, and also the equivalent books of the Shāfiʿī school. In al-ʿAnsī's twentieth-century commentary, *The Gilded Crown*, the earlier *Commentary on the Flowers*, and other works, the law book genre was equally present and contemporary. Earlier, I drew mainly on evidence-oriented doctrinal discussions on "testimonies" (chapter 3); in the following chapter I draw on the *fiqh* treatments of the several types of examined instruments, the local contracts of sale, lease, and marriage.

I thus triangulate between the historical documents and two levels of models. My simultaneous attention to the standard *fiqh* level of library discourse highlights further inter-genre issues: (1) the connections between specific chapters of *fiqh* doctrine and their counterparts in the *shurūṭ* treatise—that is, the relations between different categories of library texts—and (2) the connections between the library doctrine of the law books and the local archival instruments—that is, the overarching or direct-modeling relations that do not depend on the mediation of a specialized *shurūṭ* treatise.

Sourcing

I obtained the manuscript text of the *shurūṭ* treatise to be read in this and the following chapter from ʿAbd Allah al-Ḥibshī, the indefatigable Yemenī historian. In September 1995, at his Ṣanʿāʾ home, I found ʿAbd Allah in the middle of a large room furnished only with a rug, seated at floor level, surrounded by stacks of books. In addition to his bibliographical works, which are essential reference materials for scholarship on Yemen, al-Ḥibshī has published editions of Yemenī works of various types. Of particular significance for this project is his edition of the commentary by a nineteenth-century Ibb jurist on *The Cream*, the versified Shāfiʿī school *fiqh* manual by Ibn Raslān.[23]

Learning of my interests in notarial writing, al-Ḥibshī kindly offered me the photocopy he had made of what became a crucial text for the present book, *Success of the Student in the Description of What the Writer Writes*, a manuscript copied in 1923.[24] Its author, ʿAli ʿAbd Allah al-Iryānī (d. 1905), was a noted scholar, historian, and poet from the previously mentioned lineage of distinguished jurists that also included several twentieth-century Ibb court judges and secretaries, and whose ancestral home was in Iryān, a village located in the mountains north of the town.[25] Al-Iryānī's biography of Imam al-Manṣūr Billāh Muhammad (d. 1904), the founder of the modern Hamid al-Din line, demonstrates his strong connection to the Zaydī polity.[26] As a jurist, he was a devotee of al-Shawkānī, having penned a 1,530-line versification of one of the master's *fiqh* works.

The Science of Writing

Al-Iryānī opens his treatise with extended introductory remarks (50–56) prior to presenting his model documents, which are grouped in twenty-one short sections (56–86); he closes with a conclusion and twenty-five lines of verse that dedicate the work to "Our Master, the Imam of the Age," the Zaydi leader al-Manṣūr Billāh (86–89). My focus in this chapter is on the meta-discussion that brackets the actual models. His critical and analytic overview of his topic is based, as he notes, on what he has "seen and heard" (57, 87). Throughout, his concern is with the morality of notarial writing.[27]

He begins by identifying a general problem:

> Negligence and rashness have occurred in this area, such that writers acted haphazardly in every "chapter," and did so blindly. They have misled and misguided, and plunged the Muslims into litigation and dispute, with what they illicitly devised in contrived expressions (*alfāẓ*, sing. *lafẓ*), concerning which it is impossible to arrive at an understanding, except after repeated inquiries and careful thought. How much wealth they have lost, and blood wasted! They made the forbidden licit, and the licit forbidden! They made the false valid, and the valid false!
>
> (50)

Here at the outset, as intermittently throughout his treatise, al-Iryānī rails against the subversion of God's rules by notarial writers. In this passage he notices the incidence and also the deleterious consequences of weak instruments. "Expressions" is the standard conceptual terminology used by the jurists to refer to the technical wording of documents. The specific stated concern here is that, rather than being properly applied or utilized, "expressions" were illicitly "devised" and irregularly "contrived," mainly due to writer incompetence. The basic rationale of the "stipulations" literature, the remedy that the models were intended to provide, was to offer suitable documentary language in the form of correct "expressions." Linguistically, "stipulations," or transactional requirements and conditions, were built of "expressions."

According to al-Iryānī, highland writers of documents fall into two groups: "One group grew up in the countryside. They learned the script, but they learned nothing of the rules. They know not the licit and the forbidden (*al-ḥalāl wa al-ḥarām*). They were delinquent in inquiry. They commenced to circulate writings among mankind and they changed the rules" (50–51). "They did not learn," al-Iryānī says of this first type, the rural writers, "that God required the questioning of the learned scholars, and that the Prophet, prayers of God upon him and his people, made the question the remedy for the incapable in all instances." Implicit in this remark is the question-and-answer formula that underpinned the fatwā institution. "I enjoin you, writers," al-Iryānī continues, "not to write anything until you learn what God requires of you." Also significant in these lines is the separate issue of "inquiry," namely the substantive inquiries on the part of the writer that ideally must precede the drafting. An example I explore in the next chapter concerns the need to establish the names and the statuses of the parties to a marriage contract. In this same connection, writers also had to read any relevant prior documents.

"As for the second group," al-Iryānī continues, "they are many among the jurists of the towns, and some of the people of the countryside." These writers,

> [A]llege that they have taken instruction from the masters and have received lofty learning, but on the contrary. By God, they are in the depths of ignorance. They have altered the rules of God and have judged according to other than what God sent down. They have regarded as fair game the property of litigants in a manner God did not permit. And they have set about teaching the people tricks,[28] which have caused the curtailment of sharīʿa rules. And they came to be called, by the commoners, "trusted one" (*maʾmūn*) of the village, or perhaps they refer to him as "al-Qāḍī," untruthfully and falsely. It would be more correct to refer to him as the "Satan of the village." The summit of chaos (*fitna*), without doubt!
>
> (51)

Ending this part of his diatribe, al-Iryānī states (and he will repeat later) that a writer "is responsible for all that he writes, and accountable for all that he earns." He then mentions the specific juridical-literary tradition in which he writes: "among the righteous ancestors in the [Muslim] community this science is called the Science of the Stipulations (*ʿilm al-shurūṭ*) and many of the earlier and later scholars have authored in it," including one individual he mentions by name.[29] If al-Iryānī's treatise may be seen as balanced between the dictates of formal doctrine and the realities of actual documents, it also was attentive to the specific genre constraints of this established specialist literature itself. Ideally, a given *shurūṭ* treatise should be evaluated with respect to other such works produced by jurists within the same *madhhab*. Since I do not have access to other highland treatises of this type, however, it is impossible to assess al-Iryānī's debts or departures within the genre.

This academic subfield, he continues, responds to "the need for it in the transactions (*muʿāmalāt*) of the people." He intends in his treatise to "set forth what is required of writers of documents and papers concerning what is between people." Rather than addressing property as a relation of persons to things, his analytic foregrounds the relations "between people." He states that this "Science of Writing" (*ʿilm al-khaṭṭ*), as he also refers to it, has a sound basis in the Qurʾan, at which point he quotes the opening lines of verse 2:282 (the lines examined in chapter 3):

> O believers, when you contract a debt
> one upon another for a stated term,
> write it down, and let a writer
> write it down between you justly,
> and let not any writer refuse
> to write it down, as God taught him;
> so let him write, and let the debtor dictate, . . .[30]

"All this," the Yemenī *shurūṭ* author observes, referring to the Qurʾanic verse he has just cited and addressing his reader, "[was] out of a desire to protect what you have and to avoid its loss, and as a kindness toward you [against] the occurrence of litigation and dispute" (52). Al-Iryānī goes on to draw other conclusions from the cited Qurʾanic lines, one of which concerns the obligation upon the writer who is asked to write—that is, the second divine order (according to the exegete Faqīh Yūsuf). There is a "requirement not to refuse writing, if the writer is called upon," al-Iryānī states. He repeats that this required work of writing is intended to preserve property and to avoid conflict. Again addressing the reader, he states, "[P]roperty (*māl*) became your greatest concern, and the object of your desire." In passing, we understand that the highland sharīʿa archives al-Iryānī has in mind mainly pertain to property relations.

Picking up the last phrase of the cited Qurʾanic passage, "and let the debtor dictate," al-Iryānī reaffirms a related general point and makes a critical observation. Rather than a specific single term such as "debtor," as in the English translation above, the Qurʾan uses the general phrase *ʿalayhi al-ḥaqq*—literally, the individual "against whom is the right"—to identify the party who is to dictate. Al-Iryānī glosses this dictation mandate, the divinity's "third order," as follows (again, in literal translation): "It is a requirement for every writer that he writes what the one against whom is the right dictates to him" (53). The reciprocal term used to identify the lending party on the other side in the debt contract is *lahu al-ḥaqq*, or, again literally stated, the individual "for whom is the right." Al-Iryānī takes up the latter terminology to make a general point: "It is not permitted that he write according to what is dictated to him by the one for whom is the right." His critical observation here is that this practice occurs among ignorant writers (53).

At this juncture, to extend this transactional logic, he provides a cross-reference to the sale contract. To his gloss on the order specifying that the *ʿalayhi al-ḥaqq* party is to dictate, he adds words of elucidation. He first provides another term for this dictating party, and then mentions the equivalent party in a sale transaction: "I mean the indebted individual (*al-madyūn*), or the seller." Continuing, he employs this further example of the sale contract, in which the seller is to dictate, to illustrate related illicit practices. For this he inserts a sharply worded prefatory remark: "How often we have seen, from a writer of documents, lies and forgeries in order to gain the petty ephemerals of this world." The example he then supplies returns to the issue of who dictates, now within the context of a sale contract. Referring to these corrupt writers, he states, "[Y]ou see them specifying the boundaries of sold land according to what the buyer dictated to them, with the consequence that they invade the individual property (*milk*) of the seller other than the sold [property], and they [also] invade the property of others, and this leads to conflict."[31]

Another typical problem occurs when such a writer records that a seller " 'was observed to have received the price money,' when he had not received any of it." This describes a stratagem I encountered in Ibb (mentioned earlier) in which the contract instrument for a sale of land was kept "clean," or unburdened, by the preparation of a second document that specified the terms of an underpinning loan from the seller for part of the purchase price.

Al-Iryānī states, in summary terms, that certain writers "write counter to reality" (53). Preference in notarial writing therefore should be given to the individual known for "his religion and his trustworthiness." Writers should absolutely avoid writing what was expressly forbidden by the "sharīʿa-giver" (*al-shāriʿ*), the Prophet Muhammad. The example he dwells on in this connection is that of interest taking, which he says is prevalent. He explains that this sometimes involves stipulations concealed from the writer, examples of which he gives. He also states that such a writer and the witnesses to such an instrument place themselves in danger of divine condemnation (86–88).

He maintains that it is incumbent upon the worldly authorities to prevent fraudulent individuals from writing, as they cause harm like that of "highway robbers" (54). In his conclusion, he recommends that these authorities publicize the identities of such falsifiers in the marketplace (87). A different version this oral dissemination of information to the "public" should occur, he states, in the case of a sale ordered by the judge of the property of a minor under a guardianship, or in a judge-monitored sale of estate assets to cover a postponed dower (cf. chapter 10). Both required the giving of a witnessed "call" (*nadāʾ*, *munāda*), or "public" notice, concerning the upcoming sale, this over a period of three days in the locale of the property in question (69, 72).

Al-Iryānī wrote in the era of the late nineteenth-century Ottoman provincial administration, which published an official newspaper among other modern forms of "public" communication. It also was a time of extended conflict between the Ottomans and the Zaydī imam al-Mansur Billāh, to whom the treatise is dedicated. Does the conventional term al-Iryānī uses for the "authorities," the *wulā al-umūr*, recognize the actually existing Ottoman governance of his day, as opposed to that of an imam? Beyond his utilization of the basic category of "the people" (*al-nās*) and that of "the Muslims" (*al-muslimīn*), his language for the "public" includes the incipient modern category of the *jumhūr*, as in the locution "affairs of the public" (*umūr al-jumhūr*) (53).

Also in his introductory pages al-Iryānī comments on the general architecture of his treatise (55–56). As I noted in an earlier chapter, he refers to the work of analogical reasoning, which was basic to fleshing out the doctrine of the *fiqh*. "It is known," he writes, "that God Almighty in the precision of his Book [the Qurʾan] textually specified (*qad naṣṣa fī muḥkam kitābihi ʿalā*) the requirement of writing down debts, and this was extended by analogy to the other types of transactions." In deference to the specificity of the Qurʾanic text, he opens the body of his *shurūṭ* work with a section on the model instrument for the acknowledgment of debt or financial obligation (*dayn*), and he notes that the same pattern was standard among other authors in "this science." Marking this difference of genre, al-Iryānī states that the order of presentation in his treatise is not that of the doctrinal works of *fiqh*, not "the order of the jurists in books"—it being understood that the law books of the *Flowers* tradition contain chapters with many of the same names ("sale," "gift," etc.). He states that he instead arranged the types of document models he covers according to their significance in use among the people, "the most important followed by the next most important." In the order of his treatise, then, the first section is on the acknowledgment of debt, which includes the related, acknowledgment-structured forms of guarantee (*ḍamān*) and pledge (*rahn*). The second section concerns the transfer of debt (*ḥawāla*), which again has an acknowledgment structure; the third, the *salam*, or future delivery contract, likewise is built on an acknowledgment. Sale is the fourth, and by far the lengthiest, section in the treatise. In contrast, the *Flowers* literature "transactions" chapters open with the marriage contract, followed by repudiation, and then sale (also the longest), while that on acknowledgment appears some eleven chapters later.

The *Adab* of the Writer

In the early pages of his treatise (54–55) al-Iryānī quickly covers some basic items that constitute what he refers to as the morality, the proper literary culture and discursive etiquette (*adab*) of the document writer. The first (in my enumeration) is to open and close the text with standard invocations of God. None of his models comprise such openings or closures since they are theoretical rather than actual instruments. The second concerns the identification of each party by means of a three-part name, consisting of the individual's name together with those of his or her father and grandfather, plus any relevant identification by "tribe" (*qabīla*), or craft, or residence, and perhaps also a personal description. In his models, however, the shorthand he uses is either *Fulān bin Fulān al-Fulānī*, or, simply, *Fulān bin Fulān*. He writes that, in general, "the intention is to identify [a party] by that which distinguishes him from other than him, a distinguishing following which no confusion occurs."

This notion of "distinguishing," or "specification" (*tamyīz*) plays a regular role in al-Iryānī's design for notarial writing, although he does not elaborate the term as a concept. *Tamyīz* is crucial to these written instruments not only for the accurate identification of the party or parties to an act but also regarding the property transacted, according to the principle that the object be "known" (*maʿlūm*). As the necessary underpinning for sound contractual conduct, detailed certainty provided the main bulwark against the recognized ethical problems associated with unjustified enrichment and risk, as well as the specific Qurʾanic prohibition on interest taking.[32] As an example, al-Iryānī writes (concerning his first model, on debt), "If the acknowledged thing is dirhems [i.e, currency], he [the writer] mentions their number and he describes them with a description that distinguishes them from other than them, as for example, his [the writer's] statement, 'twenty *qirsh*,' or 'riyals,' or 'silver *ḥurūf*,' from the currency customary (*al-mutaʿāraf*) in the country."

These numbers are written out as words rather than numerals, and to guard against alteration an accompanying technique is to write out half of the indicated amount. Thus, in the model for the debt acknowledgment, he continues, "then he [the writer] halves it." If the debt is in grain, it is to be specified by named type (sorghum, wheat, barley, etc.) and by a unit of measure, whether volume or weight, that is, again, locally "customary." This amount, too, is halved, "as a caution against increase or decrease" (56). In the course of its varied "distinguishing" or "specification" mandates the treatise thus envisages the transition from *fulān* to proper names and the substantive reliance on custom, both of which are distinctive features of the archive.

As mentioned earlier, "gathering information" on the party or parties by the notarial writer was a prerequisite for writing. In connection with this second *adab* principle, Al-Iryānī states, "If the writer does not know him, he must not write until he knows the complete identity." At this historical moment, as I have noted, identification was not a numerical matter. There were no modern addresses, much less digits on an identity card. Gender-specific guidelines for identification are considered in the following chapter in connection with al-Iryānī's model marriage contract.

The third item concerns dating the written instrument with the day, month, and year. As with the invocations of the divinity, actual dates are found only in the historical texts. The fourth, a topic he touched on earlier, concerns the document's "expressions," which constitute its technical language. The notary should "read the writing after it is finished, and distinguish its expressions (*alfāẓ*)." He also suggests that the notarial writer explain the further implications and consequences of the act in question (see below). Such envisioned pedagogical moments associated with notarial writing go to how, in ideal terms, this doctrinal theory entered into practice in human interactions, and specifically to how the technical terminology of a paper language could be introduced into particular application settings. Al-Iryānī mentions in passing the poles of this linguistic horizon: the technical "usages" (*iṣṭilāḥāt*) of the jurists, on the one hand, and the "formulations of the common people" (*ʿibārāt al-ʿawāmm*), in colloquial Arabic, on the other (56, 55). A well-informed and upright writer might have to confront, and perhaps correct, prevailing popular assumptions concerning the language that typically appeared in such ordinary undertakings. It is unlikely, however, that such pedagogical activities would leave a legible trace in the resulting instrument. As a practical matter, Ibb notarial writers often drafted the document the following day rather that at the session.

This explication of the key terms was to occur in the course of the notarial writer reading the draft of his work aloud to the parties, which would represent a significant instance of what I have termed "oralization." In this case, perhaps after listening to dictation from the appropriate party and then writing, the writer reads back the transformed text that he has created. Al-Iryānī notes that this reading serves to check for mistakes and things forgotten, both of which he says may be rectified by lines added at the end of the text. If, as a result, the document requires more space, he says paper may be added, with the making of a joint (*waṣl*). Without actually naming the distinctive vertical shape of lengthy Yemeni documents, al-Iryānī describes the basic step in the making of the traditional highland roll. When added sheets of paper are attached, typically with glue, "the signature (*ʿalāma*) of the writer should be written across the joint"—that is, as in Ibb practice, on the back. At the conclusion of the instrument text, as a security precaution, he says the writer should mention the number of such joints and the total number of lines in the document.

The fifth item in this notarial *adab* is that the writer should make three "versions" (*nusakh*) of the instrument, one each for the contracting parties and one to be kept in his own archive. There is no mention here of a "copy" (*ṣūra*) or of entering such a text in a court register. In contrast to al-Iryānī's three versions, Yemeni notarial practice focused on the single original, which was paid for and kept by the party concerned, such as the buyer in a sale contract, although some writers kept a draft of the text for themselves. According to al-Iryānī, the version remaining in the writer's hands is meant to serve "as a reference (*marjiᶜ*) in case of loss, and as a reminder (*tadhkīr*) to him [the writer] and to the [document] witnesses as needed in the giving of testimony"—vocabulary equivalent to that of the exegetes and the jurists (see chapter 3).[33] Al-Iryānī does not mention a witnessing clause in his introductory remarks, but in connection with the first model contract he pauses to do so (57). There he urges the reliance on "just witnesses" (*shuhūd ᶜudūl*), warning, "He who has unjust individuals witness exposes his property to ruin." The witnesses' names appear in the witnessing clause; there is no mention of witness signatures. It was perhaps too obvious for al-Iryānī to state that it was the writer who normally signed such instruments, not the parties. In this connection he also states, "It is acceptable to put in the hand of the witnesses the like of the writing (*mithl al-maktūb*) to serve as a reminder for them in giving testimony." Thus we see, going forward and, specifically, in anticipation of the possibility of later conflict and court testimony, mechanisms to provide material, written supplements to the writer's and witnesses' memories. The possible existence of such supporting texts complicates the simple distinction between an original and a copy and leads to the potential of further genre subtypes in personal archival holdings.

Other items he briefly enumerates (54–55) may be added to this list. He recommends that writers avoid "mixing things set forth in a single contract." His example clause is the phrase "he gave, dedicated, charitably donated, and made the owner of."[34] He says each of these technical expressions refers to acts with particular rules, and that these conflict. *Flowers*-tradition law books considered similar examples of the use of multiple terms with divergent implications.[35] Al-Iryānī notes that conceptual mixing of this sort was another source of dispute and litigation. Uses of multiple, but not necessarily conflicting, terms occurred in the Ibb endowment instrument (*waqfiyya*) as well as in al-Iryānī's model text for this act, as I indicate in the following chapter. Such multiple usages are exceptions that underscore an underlying contractual or transactional logic that seeks to isolate and specify the act in question. This logic also resonated with the practical analytic that broke down compound undertakings or conflicts into their component parts. In another item, al-Iryānī states that the writer should inform the legal actor or actors about the associated implications of the written act. Thus, in his examples, "it is desirable that the writer inform the donor as to what it is valid for him to retract and what not," and about such things as, in inheritance matters, "what comes out of the estate (*raʾs al-māl*, lit., "capital") and what out of the third [from which it is permitted to make discretionary testaments]," or "what is implemented immediately and what is connected with death." These and other substantive points bear directly on issues litigated in Ibb cases.

Concluding his introductory remarks, al-Iryānī states that in the remainder of his treatise, as he covers "that which needs preservation (*ḥifẓ*) by writings"—that is, "the *muʿāmalāt*," or the various types of transactions and unilateral dispositions—he will give "what the writer should write" in each instance, this "according to a sharīʿa description (*ṣifa*), bringing together the valid stipulations (*shurūṭ*)" (55). As I have noted, in this constitutive language of stipulations, technical "expressions" served as the basic linguistic units. Al-Iryānī's phrase "bringing together the valid stipulations" describes the discursive move that he enacts, a move from the provisions set forth in the *fiqh* books to the terms of the specific model instruments in his treatise. In the following chapter, I sample versions of particular "stipulations" in three distinct instantiations: the *fiqh* book, the *shurūṭ* treatise, and historical documents. Just as it has been possible to track the changing textual locations and locutions of key juridical concepts such as the "rule" (*ḥukm*), so also it is possible to follow the closely related conception of "stipulations" as it, too, crosses genre boundaries.

In one sense, the given stipulations were derived, directly or indirectly, from "the rules of God," the sharīʿa of the Lawgiver (*al-shāriʿ*, the Prophet Muhammad); in another, they arose from ongoing human motivations and interactions. Accordingly, the burden of notarial competence extended from the law on the books to circumstantial knowledge about locally established types of undertakings. For the documentation of a specific act, the notarial writer had to depend on information he obtained from the parties, on what they revealed to him about their undertaking, which may have been "dictated" by one of them. However, he also needed to remain conscious of the fact that some of his clients' stipulations could remain "concealed."

Branching Texts

In cultivating one's disciplinary *adab*—that is, in developing the requisite methods as a reader of writings such as these sharīʿa texts—an anthropologist should pay close attention to this type of formal and informed thinking about writing. This is to learn from those who have reflected on their discursive tradition from within and, in this instance, from an individual who did so from a perspective proximate to the historical writings in question in both place and time. This advice, again, runs counter to the received disciplinary orientations of the anthropologist, notably the venerable conceptions of the unreliability of "native theory."[36] In contrast, an active methodological posture of a willingness (and a trained ability) to learn from a conceptualizing and knowing model builder such as al-Iryānī must be a characteristic of the anthropologist as reader.

Al-Iryānī's treatise is a text about texts, a writing about writings. It is devoted to what I have termed the "theory of practice" of notarial writing. Yet certain aspects of his project remain implicit, or simply pass without mention, notably his techniques for presenting his model documents. While the analytic infrastructure of al-Iryānī's thought about written documents certainly could have affected actual writings and/or reflected their already existing character, the minor organizational devices I turn to now pertain to the textuality of his *shurūṭ* treatise itself, to how it was composed.

Although his instrument models are precise and parsimonious in construction, they are neither simple nor unitary in character. They instead take the complex forms of branching texts. This branching design accommodates a variety of existing circumstances by offering both substantive and conceptual alternatives for the basic clauses, such that the indicated compositions could follow differing paths. At the lowest level, this modeling of the detailed contours of practice provides simple alternatives within the basic models. Such a branch is signaled by the word "or" (*aw*), at which juncture we also may find parenthetical directions from al-Iryānī. In his model sale contract, for example, in a clause that figures as part of the specification of the sale object, the text branches as he gives alternatives, which would be selected by the notarial writer. I indicate these different possibilities of model language with quotation marks: "'that which is his property (*milk*) and in his possession,' or 'came to him as inheritance,' if inherited" (62).

At a slightly higher level, but still within the basic model, al-Iryānī introduces further branching possibilities. These are marked by the boldly inked word "**and**," which is part of the conjunction "and if" (*wa in* or *wa idhā*). Thus, again in the sale contract, he offers model phrases to be used for different types of payment, shown once more using quotation marks. Both of these alternative contract phrases open with his explanatory remarks:

> **And** if the price money was paid under observation, he [the notarial writer] would write, "and the seller received the price in the contract session under observation in the presence of the witnesses." **And** if it remained the financial obligation of the buyer he would write, "and the equivalent of the price became a debt (*dayn*) as the financial obligation (*fī dhimmat*) of the buyer postponed until such and such time," or "indefinitely."

At approximately the same discursive level, but now in his treatment of issues beyond the basic model and its terms, a further type of branching is indicated. For this, both the "and" and the "if" are bold: "**and if**" (**wa in, wa idhā**). Following the conclusion of the standard sale contract, the treatise reads: "**And if** they [dual, viz. the parties] stipulated [the possibility of] rescission (*khiyār*), or if one of them stipulated it, he writes, at the end of the land sale instrument (*baṣīra*), 'They [dual] stipulated a rescission period until such-and-such day,' or 'unlimited,' or '*Fulān* stipulated it.'" Al-Iryānī's extended coverage of the sale contract comprises a total of thirty such mid-level branches.

At the highest level, marked by the rubric "**part**" (*faṣl*), branching involves what amount to distinct sub-genres of models defined by their differing clause structure or in their requirements of related documents or additional procedural steps. Under sale, there are five such indicated sub-genres: buying for one's son, or as an agent; selling the property of an interdicted individual, often a minor, via an appointee from the judge, which involves added procedural steps; sale by a guardian; a sale connected with a woman obtaining her postponed "dower" from the estate of a deceased husband, with three documentary steps;[37] and a technical category of sale reversal (*iqāla*).

Finally, subsuming the textual branches of the various "typological" levels, there is the heading, "**section**" (*bāb*), or treatise chapter, in this instance (using the plural) "sales."

As I have suggested, the double analytic implicit in the treatise's organizational scheme involves a technique of concise selection from the relevant doctrine wedded to an experience-based rendering of prevailing written application. The former can be appreciated by a glance at the topical coverage of the relevant *Flowers*-tradition chapters; the latter by the tenor of some of al-Iryānī's inserted comments. In his treatment of the sale contract variations, for example, he twice digresses to knowingly caution the notarial writer about the properties of the minor (*ṣaghīr*), including the orphan, stating that "his transaction is very dangerous" (*muʿāmalatahu khaṭira jiddan*) (70, 72). The thrust of his criticism centers, once again, on the morality of property relations. He invokes the condemning Qurʾanic, and also colloquial, metaphor of illicitly "eating the property," in this instance of the minor child.

Aside from the various articulations of his subject matter provided by his bold-inked conjunctions and parts, other dimensions of the detailed logic of al-Iryānī's presentation are made evident by a device of decorative punctuation using a plump inverted comma. While there are no capitals or regular punctuation marks in manuscript Arabic, these comma marks appear throughout the treatise to define small segments of text (including the hemistiches of the concluding poetry). Positioned by al-Iryānī (or his copiest) approximately at the level of a dash in English usage, this device breaks down the document model texts into clauses and sub-clauses. An example is the opening lines of the model lease/hire (*ijāra*) contract. I use asterisks to represent al-Iryānī's more robust marks, and I continue to use quotation marks for the indicated model language (74): " '*Fulān* son of *Fulān* appeared * and leased from *Fulān* son of *Fulān* * his house' * or 'his land the *Fulāniyya* * and its boundaries are such and such * and this is his property (*milk*)' * or 'the property of his principal' * or . . ." In the Arabic text, the raised and centered ornamental commas make the structure of al-Iryānī's thought visible. In the just-quoted passage, they show the following sequence of clauses: tenant-lessee identification, including the indicated presence of this individual at the contract session (with the writer); landowner-lessor identification; alternative types for the leased property, which is identified by proper name; boundary specification of the leased property; affirmation of the ownership status of the property. Behind each of these short phrases that together compose the model instrument stood paragraphs of law book prose, whether or not a given notary was fully cognizant of this higher-level literature.

Clusters of four of these commas in a diamond shape mark the end of each of the basic model texts, the last clauses of which are devoted to dating (e.g., for the sale contract, 63). Such diamonds also punctuate the transitions to the "and if" alternatives and sub-genres for the instrument in question. Al-Iryānī's specialized comma marks highlight the building blocks of an instrument's clause sequence, which also dovetails, it may be noted, with the standard mode for the study of such documents in western scholarship.[38] Some such clauses (e.g., witnessing, dating) were relatively standard across the instrument types while others matched up with genre-specific sets of required "stipulations."

My translations of al-Iryānī's models in the next chapter follow his material and spatial representations of their discursive elements, although I replace the asterisks used in the example above with regular commas. As I noted earlier, I also add quotation marks to complement the various levels and types of his markings. The use of quotation marks, again, is intended to make the use of his model language as opposed to his interstitial conjunctions, directions, and observations more evident in the English. Finally, it is important to reemphasize the theoretical and pedagogical status of al-Iryānī's marking devices, which are specific to this modeling genre. This status is clear from the simple fact that, together with the parenthetical instructions and directions provided in these scripts, the many explicit textual segments that he created were not reproduced in the historical documents of the late imamic period.

TEN

Contracts

> A genre lives in the present, but always *remembers* its past, its beginning.
>
> —Mikhail Bakhtin, *Problems of Dostoevsky's Poetics*

INCORPORATING THE FINAL TERMS of what may have been a lengthy process of thought and negotiation, contracts and other types of written instruments gave expression to achieved understandings. In all such texts, what had been mere potential, built of tentative or uncertain motives, became an instance, whatever its effective duration, of relative clarity, certainty, and full knowledge. From the standpoint of a completed instrument, the prior history of unrealized options and false starts, of other understandings or misunderstandings, was definitively edited. Actions, aims, and strategies that bore no fruit were effectively deleted. Such writings then could serve as reference points going forward, as scripts for performances, although the fragility of a mutual agreement or an individual undertaking might be connected to the fate of its material artifact.

The sampling of local notarial writing I provide in this chapter brings us into contact with a significant range of archival vitality, represented here by handwritten instruments of sale, lease, and marriage. Within a given formation of sharīʿa texts, the primary instruments, as Bakhtin might have termed them, constituted a discursive base with respect to the secondary writings of the court and the tertiary doctrine of the *fiqh*. This spectrum of diverse but at the same time interrelated genres of basic instruments populated the broad realm of the established socioeconomic "transactions," to which, in premodern settings, jurists and practitioners alike devoted a major part of their attention.

In this final chapter, I compare a selection of individual model texts presented in the *shurūṭ* treatise (introduced in the last chapter) with examples of the indicated historical documents produced by local archival writers. The method is one of juxtaposition, of reading texts together, rather than in isolation, and of reading across genres. In earlier versions of this strategy, I alternated between the formulations of Imam Yahya's 1937 "Instructions" for the drafting of court records and passages from historical court judgments (chapter 7); compared the doctrine on the "oral reading" of documents presented as evidence (chapter 3) with related implementations mentioned in court transcripts (chapter 8); and analyzed imamic "choices" with respect to their origins in, and subsequent applications to, court decisions (chapter 4). In each of these instances the pairs of genres juxtaposed were representatives of the wider categories of texts I have labeled the "library" and the "archive," the discursive hemispheres, which, in their differences, were mutually dependent.

Such match-ups draw attention to specific modeling relationships. A fundamental determinant of the possibility of integration or cohesion in a textual formation, modeling has been an important analytic thread throughout this book. In this chapter, models of a further specific type confront their possible objects, and vice versa. In placing these counterpart genres side by side, I am interested, once again, in the question of composition. Models serve here both as one of the ends of the analysis and as an important means for cross readings. The reverse is true as well, since the grounded actualities of the historical documents stand in illuminating contrast with the features of the models. Compositional analysis thus involves a two-way street, such that reading the models and the presumptive modeled documents together in the same frame permits insights into both genres.

Émile Durkheim, a founding father of modern social analysis, made a classic distinction between the largely invariant features of "contract-law" and the contingent, negotiated dimensions of "contract."[1] The former may be recognized in the rules and stipulations developed in library discourse, the latter as comprising an essential contribution of the archive. In comparing document models for sale, lease, and marriage with the equivalent historical documents, a distinction of this sort thus is salient. Embodying fitted projections of the doctrinal realm into the practical affairs of the archive, the models of the *shurūṭ* work set forth instrument-scale versions of "contract-law." The features of "contract," in contrast, are found only in the historical instruments. But whereas the models appear single-minded in their "contract-law" purpose, in the contingent instruments locally established versions of "contract-law" and the specific terms of "contract" commingle. In simple textual, substantive terms, while the models consisted of pure form, the historical documents were composites of form and content. When such documents were presented and inventoried in litigation, however, rather than the known language of "contract-law," the court was apt to note and quote the variable names and terms of "contract."

In the dialectical view of Wael Hallaq, historical instruments were mined to create the models, which were then turned back to the task of structuring the writing of future documents.[2] In this understanding, the texts presented in the *shurūṭ* treatises had the dual statuses of models *of* and models *for* actual instruments. In a broader dialectical perspective, however, the instrument models appear suspended between the *fiqh* doctrine, from which they had been extracted, and the historical documents, with respect to which they remained empty shells. In this understanding, the "contract-law" of the models was produced through descending and ascending movements of genre. As opposed to simplistic notions of the relation of theory to practice, seen as one-sided, top-down, and doctrine privileging, such dialectical perspectives take into account the impressive agency of the archive.

From the vantage point of the wider textual formation, we may speak of identifiable levels and aspects of paper language. While we observe that certain technical "expressions" and "stipulations" recur across the *fiqh* doctrine, the *shurūṭ* models and the historical documents, these overlapping usages may be sorted out with reference to genre constraints. In studying the composition of archival instruments, we appreciate how the sense of a given technical term or phrase is altered, literally modified, by its inclusion in a type of document that also comprises the contingent language of "contract." Also in the composition of primary archival genres, explicit or implicit customary terms, which were absent in the tailored models, assumed their recognized places. Viewed as a whole, the entirety of a given document may be considered an "utterance," an instance of conventional composition, a written script in a historically specific and composite paper language.

Composition also may be treated as a process, which is to highlight the taking of discursive steps. Thus the terms of a negotiated "contract" took written form as the third-party notarial writer formulated what he had heard or understood. Were there traces at this juncture of a "dictation" to the writer, vestiges of the initiating act envisioned in the Qurʾan, the *fiqh* doctrine and the local *shurūṭ* treatise (cf. chapters 3, 7, 9)? After listening, the writer wrote. In doing so he replaced the more or less colloquial renderings of the undertaking, converting what he received or perceived from the parties into the terms and clauses appropriate for the type of instrument in question. Enlarging the temporal frame, this core of the composition process may be viewed as bracketed by earlier steps taken to establish the identities and statuses of the parties and also by the possibility of subsequent annotations.

A major objective of this chapter is the presentation of a set of historical instruments, with the genres surveyed comprising three basic types of contracts. How might an anthropologist present such texts? Rather than "editing" the writings in question in the established manner of the philologist (or, for that matter, the early anthropological student of myth), I study them here in several modalities of grounded textual analysis. Translation remains central to this effort, as does the explication of Arabic terminology given in transliteration. For the first genre, the paradigmatic sale contract, I offer an extended version of a clause-by-clause, line-by-line analysis, concluding with attention to the patterns associated with the later annotation of such documents. For the second, the lease, which is associated with the doctrinally problematic but societally normative relationship of sharecropping, I consider the conceptual conundrums and the applied solutions, in which "custom" plays a prominent role, and I then offer a "model" of my own construction. For the third, the marriage contract, I begin by considering ʿAli ʿAbd Allah al-Iryānī's detailed recommendations for the required preliminaries, according to which the writer must ascertain the parties' identities and statuses. I then augment my analysis of his model and the Ibb instruments with reference to an informal, locally prepared "script" for the contract event. I conclude with an excursus on the textual representations associated with the marriage dower.

Figure 10.1 Qasim al-Manṣūb, with property documents, 1976.

In reading these local notarial writings against the relevant *shurūṭ* models I point in passing to a wider context. As I have noted, the general setting may be described as that of a late agrarian-age society, which was in its last decades (1920–60). This agrarian context is of interest since it was in a variety of such circumstances, in the highlands and in many other historical locations, that the sharīʿa flourished for many centuries. In this connection, the texts surveyed in this final chapter may be read for formulations that pertain to a set of essential institutional components of the highland political economy of the late imamic period. That is, with reference to property relations both in land and in persons, specifically in Ibb town and its hinterland, these (and other) archival writings may be approached for their paper language perspectives on the late agrarian order.

Since the various archival genres were recognizable throughout the highlands, we also may speak of a limited form of interregional cosmopolitanism in the period archive. A by-product was the enabling of landlordism, notably in the patterns of documentation associated with the widely dispersed landholdings among leading and governing families, a basic feature of highland power relations in this late agrarian age.[3]

Concerning the place of "law" in another setting (eighteenth-century England), E. P. Thompson famously found it "deeply imbricated within the very basis of productive relations."[4] Something similar was variably true of the historical sharīʿa. At the outset of this book, and then in chapter 6, I suggested that in comparison with the differently structured property relations found elsewhere in the central Middle East, highland Yemen was distinctive in the sense that the doctrinal sharīʿa—always, of course, in articulation with local custom—provided a relevant and active language for the mode of production. While neither the doctrinal details nor even the locally employed notarial stipulations were widely known, "sale," "lease," and "marriage," the substantive topics of the written texts surveyed in this chapter, involved commonly understood acts. Paul Dresch, a leading student of customary law in the northern highlands, provides the appropriate caution. Referring to the use in a "tribal" northern highland setting of the lexeme *milk*, the basic doctrinal term for individual property, Dresch remarks that "one has to be careful not to assume that words carry technical meanings derived from sharīʿa law."[5] From another perspective, I have noted that jurists such as al-Iryānī and Imam Yahya had conceptual views regarding what they referred to as the "formulations of the common people" (*ʿibārāt al-ʿawāmm*).

This political economic dimension noted, in line with the main project of this book the principal contextual thrust of the following presentation of documents concerns the relations among the several written genres. This understanding of the roles of texts as contexts requires attention to intertextual resonances, which play out here in several dimensions.[6] Complementing the technique of studying models and historical documents as paired objects, I am equally interested in their respective textual series. This is to consider the links across the different types of models, on the one hand, and across the several genres of historical instruments, on the other. For the latter, the relevant links also include the serial connections between documents of the same genre, involving patterns of both repetition and difference. Finally, into this textual mix I introduce selected doctrinal materials, mainly from the relevant chapters of the *fiqh* but also including pertinent imamic opinions, or "choices." One motive in these selected references to related library texts is to better locate and specify the paper language found in al-Iryānī's contract models and in the primary contract documents of the period. Another, which again invokes the structures of the agrarian setting, is to call attention to a doctrinal logic that remains implicit in these archival writings. To this end, I conclude the chapter with a succinct analytic statement by twentieth-century *Flowers* commentator al-ʿAnsī in which he connects a set of textual forms with five specific types of transfers of agrarian-age property.

Sale

> God made Sale lawful.
>
> —Qurʾan 2:275

The words of the Qurʾan make sale, or the alienation of property, legitimate for Muslims. In the later elaborated *fiqh*, Muslim jurists would transform this fundamental transaction into an elaborate contract. The result, as I have noted, was the longest of the standard chapters in the *Flowers* and in other such *madhhab* literatures. I mentioned earlier that the commentary chapter on sale (*bayʿ*) in the twentieth-century *Gilded Crown* opens with the

Figure 10.2 Hajj ʿAli ʿAzīz reading a document from his family collection, 1980.

specification of sixteen "stipulations"; four deal with the contracting parties, seven with the contract form, and five with the sale object.[7] The foundational western study of the Islamic sale contract is by Jeanette Wakin, whose work is based on the chapter in the early *shurūṭ* treatise by the Ḥanafī school jurist al-Ṭaḥāwī (d. 933).[8]

Employing a distinction between moveable and immovable forms of property, the contract of sale stood at the base of both the old mercantilism of the sharīʿa and also of its agrarian-age conception of real property. In these two categories of sales, however, written documentation played a very different role. In mid-century Ibb, not only routine retail sales but even wholesale commercial transactions occurred without sale-purchase instruments (or modern receipts), although some supporting documents such as commercial orders were used and other accounts records were kept (e.g., the *dafātir al-tujjār*). The general absence of documentation in the commercial domain finds an antecedent model in the Qurʾanic evidence verses. In the requirement to "write it down," which specifically referred to debt and was then analogized to other transactions, the single explicit exception was in a commercial context: "except if it is present trade (*tijāra ḥāḍira*)."

In contrast to the general absence of documentation in commercial retail practice in Ibb, local real estate sales of immovable property normally took the form of the written contract instrument known as a *baṣīra*, the textual structures of which are my main concern in this section. *Baṣīra* is the colloquial Arabic term used throughout the highlands for the document of sale-purchase. As I noted in earlier chapters, this stalwart of archival usage also made cameo appearances in library texts, both in commentary works in the *Flowers* literature and in the opinions of jurists such as Imam Yahya in the twentieth century and al-Kibsī in the nineteenth.

"Sales" (*buyūʿ*) is by far the longest chapter section in al-Iryānī's treatise.[9] He identifies the primary model as a "*baṣīra*." Although documents of this name were known in both Upper and Lower Yemen, al-Iryānī's model has a touch of Zaydī school and Upper Yemen specificity, representing a degree of contingency in this practice-oriented library text. As I discussed in the previous chapter, this and his other document models take the form of branching texts, with interruptions for alternative wording or for clauses, indicated by the words "or" and "and if," etc., some in bold ink. At these branching points we also find parenthetical remarks and instructions from al-Iryānī. I use quotation marks to differentiate the branching main text of the model from the author's contextual remarks, although some parts of the models, such as those on naming and bounding the property, are indirectly rather than directly stated. As is conventional in all such models, variations on *fulān* stand in for the proper names of people and properties that would appear in an actual document. While the model does not open with the *Basmala* or any other invocation of the divine, as al-Iryānī notes, such openings are required in an actual instrument. In this and the following translations I have added paragraphing and sentence punctuation.

The "Sales" chapter begins as follows:

> If an individual (*shakhṣ*) buys from another individual a house or land, or such like, he [the notarial writer] writes: "*Fulān bin Fulān al-Fulānī* bought, from the seller to him, *Fulān bin Fulān al-Fulānī*, selling for himself, that which is his property (*milk*) and in his possession," or "came to him as inheritance," if inherited, "and it is all of the house," or "the land *al-Fulāniyya*," and he [viz., the document writer] names it and describes it by that which distinguishes it from other than it, and he gives its boundaries in the four directions. Then he writes, "and this with all of its rights, and that which pertains to it, contiguous and detached, flourishing and in ruins, rocks and earth, and irrigation apparatus and canal, and all of that which pertains to it," if a right was attached to the sale object, and, if not, he would write, "and the sale object has no right associated with it," and if the seller excluded something there would be written, in the document, "except the place" or "the land al-*Fulāniyya*," and such like, "which is outside the contract, and the buyer has knowledge of this." Then he writes, "a sale, valid and sharʿī, with the offer and acceptance, in two past-tense expressions (*lafẓayn māḍiyayn*), for a price known in its units and amount, such and such," and then he gives half of it in the currency in use. Then he writes "and when the sale was completed with the stipulations of its legality, the seller surrendered it to the buyer, and the aforementioned sale object became the possession of the buyer, a property (*māl*) among his properties, which he may dispose of as in the disposal of an owner with respect to his property (*milk*), and as those to whom rights pertain with respect to their rights, free and clear, [with] no impediment to him and no challenge to his possession, and this after knowledge of what the two of them had contracted for, and they parted in mutual consent (*tarāḍīn*)."

> And if the price [money] was paid under observation, he would write, "and the seller received the price in the contract session under observation in the presence of the witnesses." And if it remained the financial obligation of the buyer, he would write, "and the equivalent of the price became a debt as the financial obligation of the buyer postponed until such and such time," or "indefinitely."
>
> And he also writes in the *baṣīra*, "a valid sale, with the validity of disposal by the seller and the buyer, and the permissibility of their acts in word and deed." Then he writes the [names of the] just witnesses and dates [the document].

Thus the branching model sale document as it appears in the opening section of al-Iryānī's fourth chapter. The chapter goes on to numerous additional sections marked by "and if," each of which may be matched up with a discussion in the *fiqh* chapter. In the form of the model document, however, we are at some remove from the *fiqh* proper. At this different analytic level the required contract stipulations are pragmatically distilled. Repeated use of the term "sale," however, summons the authority of the wider doctrine. Although we may read this model instrument for its detailed implementations of specific stipulations, the phrase "the sale was completed with the stipulations of its validity" represents a global invocation of and claim to have satisfied the panoply of relevant conditions.

In the model there are traces of two sides in a Zaydī school debate on the relative analytic significance of "expressions" (*alfāẓ*, sing. *lafẓ*), especially concerning the relation of these verbal signs to deeper-seated intent or consent. As I mentioned in the last chapter, "expressions" came up in al-Iryānī's critical remarks in connection with their being "contrived" by ignorant writers, and they also figured in his presentation of the proper *adab* of the notarial writer, who was meant to explicate these technical usages to his clients, the parties to the contract. The doctrinal contention concerned whether or not appropriate "expressions" were necessary to the constitution of contracts, which all agreed are governed, ultimately, by the parties' intentions. In the doctrine, a sale contract is based on a reciprocal "offer and acceptance" between the parties. Representing what I have termed the "linguistic" concerns of the old-line Hādawī jurists, the *Flowers* states that this contract requires an "expression of ownership transfer" and that the valid language in question is to be determined "according to custom" (*ḥasaba al-ʿurfi*).[10] The twentieth-century *Gilded Crown*, which expands the

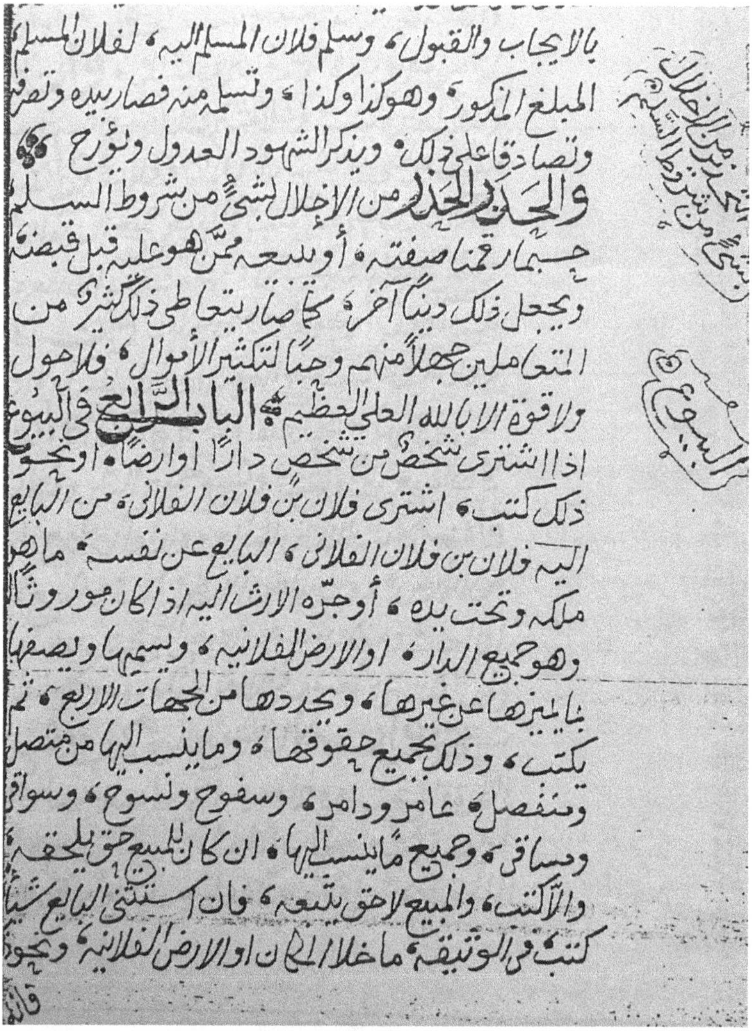
بالايجاب والقبول، وسلم فلان المسلم اليه، لفلان المسلم
المبلغ المذكور، وهو كذا وكذا، وتسلمه منه فصار بيده وتصرف
وتصادقا على ذلك، ويذكر الشهود العدول ويؤرخ
والحذر الحذر من الاخلال لشيء من شروط السلم
[illegible] صفته، أو بيعه ممّن هو عليه قبل قبضه
ويجعل ذلك دينًا آخر، كما صار يتعاطى ذلك كثير من
المتعاملين جهلًا منهم وحبًا لتكثير الأموال، فلا حول
ولا قوة الا بالله العلي العظيم، الباب الرابع في البيوع
اذا اشترى شخص من شخص دارًا او ارضًا او نحو
ذلك كتب، اشترى فلان بن فلان الفلاني، من البائع
اليه فلان بن فلان الفلاني، البائع عن نفسه، ما هو
ملكه وتحت يده، أو جره الارث اليه اذا كان موروثا
وهو جميع الدار، او الارض الفلانية، ويسميها ويصفها
بما يميزها عن غيرها، ويحددها من الجهات الاربع، ثم
يكتب، وذلك بجميع حقوقها، وما ينسب اليها من متصل
ومنفصل، عامر ودامر، وسفوح ونسوح، وسواقي
ومساقي، وجميع ما ينسب اليها، ان كان للمبيع حق يلحقه
والا كتب، والمبيع لاحق يتبعه، فان استثنى البائع شيئا
كتب في الوثيقة، ما خلا المكان او الارض الفلانية ونحوه

Figure 10.3 “Sales” section in a treatise of models for notarial writing by al-Iryānī (d. 1905), MS copy dated 1343 AH (1923).

scheme of these language requirements, further states that for a correct “offer and acceptance” the parties must utter these reciprocally, in the form of “two past-tense expressions.”[11] In al-Iryānī’s model *baṣīra*, following the mention of the “offer and acceptance,” the presence of the phrase “two past-tense expressions” addresses the analytic concern of the Hādawīs about contract language. In contrast, the concluding phrase, "they parted in mutual consent," is a formula that satisfies the strictly intent-based analyses of the opposing jurists, notably the "Sunnīs" of Zaydī extraction, those who followed Shawkānī and others of this offshoot tradition. In one of his twentieth-century opinions, Imam Yahya entered this debate on the intent-based side. Since his opinion took the form of an issued imamic "choice" it was apt to have enforcement implications in the contemporary sharīʿa courts. The imam states, "Expressions are not conditions in sale—that is, in the offer and acceptance, or in lease—since the crux of authority is mutual consent regarding all that is indicated."[12] While the term "mutual consent" and the phrase "they parted in mutual consent" are not particularly distinctive in sharīʿa discourse, the use of the unusual "two past-tense expressions" firmly places this model in the world of Zaydī jurisprudential discourse. Since taking sides in a doctrinal debate was not in the mandate of the *shurūṭ* genre, in his model instrument al-Iryānī endeavored to satisfy both.[13]

We also are at some remove from an actual *baṣīra*. As a model, it is intentionally generic rather than specific in content or context. Doctrinal roles such as the "buyer" and the "seller" have yet to associated with personal names. It is a text timeless by design, rather than historical; it has a dating clause but no date. Yet al-Iryānī explicitly refers to his model document as a *baṣīra*, a term that summarily indexes and locates his model in highland documentary practice.

Local Baṣīras

As examples, I use a selection of documents from Ibb dated 1939, 1941, 1957, and 1958.[14] The first of these concerns parts of a house in Ibb; the other three, agricultural terraces. In contrast to the empty framework of the model, these local Yemeni texts, like their early Egyptian counterparts, are richly circumstantial, with dates, measures, and units of money, and with the names of people and places, all of which attach such documents to specific lives, eras, and regions. These instruments are the archived artifacts of original acts of legal writing. Their scripts and their signatures trace the personal interventions and implicitly invoke the community-established integrities of their writers.

Figure 10.4 Sale document (*baṣīra*), dated 1376 AH (1957), showing added notes.

While such documents are contingent contracts, such that each is different by definition, Ibb *baṣīras* share features as a local genre. The following represents an effort to give the sequential clause structure in such sale-purchase documents, in descending order, from the top down.[15] I postpone until the end my discussion of the physically marginal yet highly significant phenomenon of added notes. This is despite the fact that such notes, although written last, were read first. Moreover, on *baṣīras*, notes are located at the top, in the open space characteristically left above the main instrument text.

1. *Invocation of God.* The *Basmala*, or the *Ḥamdala*, is written first and appears, usually centered, above the document text. This is the ubiquitous and characteristic "opening" of Muslim writing, shared across and thus uniting library and archive.

2. *Signature.* A half-line note, with a personal signature and sometimes with the date, is written last, after the main text of the document is completed. It is located, usually indented to the left, above the main document's first line and below the level of the invocation of God. Its tail end may begin to ascend the page edge. It typically states something like: "What is mentioned [below] occurred under my auspices as written, on its date." The signature itself usually is placed above the note, interlaced in the old style and ascending nearly vertically. These signatures can be hard to decipher, often intentionally so, though they tended to be known in their place and time.[16] An indication of the possible difficulty is found in the 1939 *baṣīra*. Its writer leaves a blank space instead of giving the name of the writer of another *baṣīra* that he mentions he had read. Much less frequently, the writer's note and signature may be placed at the bottom of the document. During the Ottoman period and up to about 1930, the signature note at the top was accompanied by the inked impression of the writer's small seal, bearing his name, descending from the top and, sometimes, the seal date. Seals typically are aligned to the right, just above the opening word, "bought." When such a document later was read, or when it was inventoried as court evidence, the interrelated set of personal calligraphic features that could be remarked on were "script, signature, and seal" (*khaṭṭ wa ʿalāma wa khatm*). Some writers' notes mention the fee paid for the writing, as I discuss below.

3. *"Bought" (ishtarā).* Following the standard word order of Arabic and using the same terminology as the model, this verb appears as the initial word of the main text, often unpointed. It announces the document as an instrument of sale and purchase, and also as a text in the third person, past-tense "objective" style. Most *baṣīras* begin this way, with a few variants.[17]

4. *Buyer.* Still on the first line of the text proper, immediately following the verb "bought," for which it is the subject, the buyer's name usually consists of a three-part identification, including the individual's name (*ism*), the father's name, and either the grandfather's name or an old-style family name of one of several types. In addition, there may be prefacing formalities, such as "the honorable" (*al-ṣadr al-muḥtaram*), or specific titles, such as "Shaykh," "Faqīh," or "Ḥājj," often with the appropriate nickname (e.g., al-ʿIzzī, with Muhammad), and there may be adjectives affirming majority and full capacity.[18] The names of female buyers are commonly preceded with "the free woman" (*al-ḥurra*).

An individual thus is linked to a sharīʿa role. In the remainder of the instrument this archival individual is referred to either as "the buyer" (*al-mushtarī*) or using the appropriate pronoun. It is this individual, the buyer, who compensates the notarial writer and who retains the original written instrument. Further along in the buyer clause any necessary indications of multiple parties or agency appear.[19]

5 . *Property* (generic term: *māl*). Following the buyer's name is the specification of the property (*māl*) involved on the buyer's side of the transaction. In the case of a man buying for himself, his name is followed by the phrase "with his *māl*, for himself" (*bi-mālihi li-nafsihi*), sometimes adding "without others." Later in the contract text, this first *māl* will be referred to more specifically as the "price" (*thaman*). The *Flowers*-tradition jurists give a basic definition of sale as a transaction involving "two *māls*" (*mālayn*), which they also conceptualized as a *māl* and a "counter-value" (*ʿiwaḍ*).[20]

6. *Seller.* Following the preposition "from," the role of "the seller" (*al-bāʾiʿ*) appears before the naming of this individual. This "seller to him," with the preposition and pronoun linking this second party to the first (in the case of a male buyer), and who also may be identified, as in the 1957 *baṣīra*, as "present at the session (*al-mawqif*)," similarly is identified by a tripartite name and potentially also with honorifics. The simple type of text reads that the seller is acting "for himself" (*ʿan nafsihi*).

Multiple parties and agency on this side of the transaction, if any, also are specified at this point. An agency may be based on a document explicitly consulted by the notarial writer, as in the 1957 *baṣīra* (line 8): "and this according to a document of *tawkīl* from them [the principals] to the aforementioned seller [the agent] in the handwriting and signature of Ahmad bin Hasan bin

Husayn al-Barīrī, which was read [and is] dated, month of Rajab al-Fard [epithet of the month], 1376, which was read [*sic*]."

7. *Sale object* (*mabī*ʿ). The more specific term for the second of the two *māl*s exchanged.

(a) Maximally correct documents specify how what is being sold came to be the property of the seller. Such a specification phrase either follows the seller's name or appears after the identification of the property as the sale object. As with some agencies, when such a specification occurs it may be accompanied by a reference to the notarial writer having carried out a preparatory examination or reading (*iṭṭilā*ʾ) of another, earlier *baṣīra* or an individual's inheritance document (*farz*, *qur*ʿ*a*, or *faṣl*). Such preceding texts also may be described in terms of their script, signature, date, and, especially in late Ottoman usage, seal. Sometimes there is mention of the earlier writer's name or of a significant countersignature. Unlike agency documents, however, which were only read, the notarial writer also may indicate that he has canceled the prior instrument by means of the appropriate annotation (*tanbīh*), a brief statement that would have been written in that document's vacant upper space or in its margin.[21] Canceling notes of this type figured among the distinctive conventions of erasure. I discuss other types of notes later.

Instances of this placing of canceling annotations on the relevant prior documents are reported as follows in the example *baṣīra*s:

1939 (line 7), referring to another sale document: "according to a *baṣīra shar*ʿ*iyya* in the handwriting and signature of [left blank—notarial writer's name probably not legible] which was read and annotated."

1941 (line 6), concerning an inheritance document: "according to a *farz* in the handwriting and signature of al-Faqīh Sinna [coll., Qurʾan school master] Muhammad al-Yamānī, which was read and annotated."

1957 (line 16), concerning an inheritance instrument, with a parenthetical mention of a previous note of a different type found on it: "according to the *qur*ʿ*a* of inheritance written with the pen and signature of Ḥayy [i.e., deceased] al-Qāḍī al-ʿIzzī Muhammad bin Muhammad al-Muftī, God forgive him—which is authenticated above, under the signature of the judge of the Ibb District in his era, the learned Qāḍī Yahya bin Muhammad al-Iryānī, God forgive him, dated month of Rajab, 1340, thirteen forty Hijrī which was read and annotated on the [property] item (*maktab*)."

1958 (line 10), referring to two sale documents: "according to a *baṣīra* in the handwriting of Ahmad bin Hasan al-Barīrī dated Rabīᶜ II 1375, which I read and annotated, and it is in the possession of the buyer, and his share by purchase from the free woman Wasīᶜa Bint ᶜAbd Allah bin Naṣr in the handwriting of the Faqīh Ahmad Muhammad ᶜAbd Allah ᶜAbd al-Mughnī al-Ḥammāsh, which I read and annotated."

On the receiving end of this annotation—that is, on the prior instruments—the notes in question were placed above the main text of a *baṣīra*, while on an inheritance document they were placed in the margin, next to the relevant property item. In referring to the property in question, such notes use the passive "was transferred" (*nuqila*).

Instruments of this type anticipated such canceling notes in the sense that the possibility of repeated alienation was in the nature of sale. Necessitated by the new acts, such annotations also created material links in document chains. Such notes placed on old documents often explicitly mention the existence of the new. Despite their deactivation, annotated old documents were still kept, although they switched archives. Delivered at the new contract session, such old documents passed from the archive of the seller to that of the new owner. If a property was repeatedly sold, a series could emerge.

(b) Most sale objects are identified by their proper names, measurements, regional or village locations, and boundaries in the four directions.[22] Each of the myriad terraces that surrounded the town, crossed the valley floor, or rose up the mountainsides had a name. Documents from the Ibb region are distinguished by their use of a specific term of the land surface measurement, the *qaṣaba*, a unit of approximately sixteen square cubits.[23] The equivalent term for Upper Yemen is *libna*. Al-Iryānī's use of the latter term in another of his models indicates a sphere of reference and application in Upper Yemen, which points up a degree of substantive contingency in his cosmopolitan doctrinal text.[24] Both regions, again, utilize the same document name, *baṣīra*, and both employ the same term for the smaller unit, the *dhirāᶜ*, or cubit, which mainly is used for the measurement of rooms in buildings.

The boundary directions, which could include the mention of other named properties, or physical features such as a footpath, a prominent rock, or a saint's tomb, begin with "on the north" (*qibliyyan*)—that is, the direction of prayer (*qibla*), toward Mecca, which, in contrast, is "south" in the early documents from Egypt. The Yemeni documents continue with east, south (*ʿadaniyyan*, the direction of the port-city, Aden) and, finally, west.[25]

(c) Agricultural terraces or buildings may be further identified in terms of the standard rights (*ḥuqūq*, sing. *ḥaqq*), including physical parts and other rights, which typically pertain to such types of properties. An agricultural terrace thus includes, in formulaic terms, "its earth and its stones and its trees and its . . ." A building comprises, the 1939 *baṣīra* reads, "its earth and its stones and its wooden boards and its windows and its passages, and all that is related to it and for it in the sharīʿa and in custom (*sharʿan wa ʿurfan*)." This last formulation, specifically referencing custom, appears also in descriptions of the landed properties in the 1941 and 1957 *baṣīras*. Phrases such as, in the 1958 instrument, "with its vital parts and its ruined parts" (*ʿāmirha wa dāmirha*)—referring to a sale object comprising village buildings and land—recall the parallel and rhymed constructions in both the early Islamic sale documents from Egypt and al-Iryānī's model. However, the model, as we saw, goes on to offer the possibilities of there being "no [further] right associated with it," and also of something being specifically excluded by the seller.

8. *Offer and acceptance.* In several variations, this key clause employs language close to that in al-Iryānī's treatise for notarial writers, which is also that of the *fiqh* itself. Thus, the 1939 contract states, "a sale and purchase, valid in the sharīʿa, complete and definitive, with the expression of the offer and the acceptance, with past form." This last phrase, "past form (*ṣīgha māḍiyya*)," represents a direct reflection of what I described earlier as the Hādawī-Zaydī "linguistic" approach found in al-Iryānī's model. The 1941 *baṣīra* reads, "a valid sharīʿa sale, definitive and complete, with the expression of the offer and acceptance, with the statement of the seller, 'I sold,' and the buyer, 'I bought.'"

Provision of the parties' purported words is unusual. In general, the binding "offer and acceptance" phrase is in itself a prime example of how the discourse of the jurists overwrites any actual contract utterances. The 1957 *baṣīra* gives "a sale and purchase, both valid in the sharīʿa, implemented and complete; with an offer and an acceptance, both [of them] unambiguous (*ṣarīḥ*); immediate and comprehensive of sharīʿa considerations, including stipulations and principles, [and] devoid of what might be judged corrupt or invalid." This lengthy formulation is notable for employing the technical term "unambiguous" (discussed in chapter 3). The 1958 *baṣīra* states, simply, "with the offer and acceptance, and a proper sharīʿa form."

Beyond my four example instruments, a 1955 *baṣīra* recorded the special sale of a normally inalienable *waqf* lot.[26] This substantively unusual contract is further distinguished by its quotation of a telegraphed authorization from the imam, which references an imamic choice on the topic, and also by the fact that its writer was Ibb judge al-Manṣūr. For his clause, this Zaydī-trained scholar wrote, simply, "[T]he sale occurred with the expression of the offer from the seller and of the acceptance from the buyer in the session."

I return below to the "offer and acceptance" clause in remarks concerning the question of the Qurʾanic mandate of "dictation."

9. *Price* (*thaman*). The more specific term for the first of the two values or *māls* exchanged. With respect to its "amount, number, type, and description," and possibly also "form" and "kind," the price, which may also be generally characterized as "known" (*maʿlūm*), is written out in words. As a further precaution, one also mentioned in the notarial treatise, half of this sum then is written out. Prices are given in named currencies. Indexing both the long-standing connections of the highlands with broader spheres of circulation and also the limited institutional development of the indigenous polities, the principal coin of the highlands was the Maria Theresa thaler, the international but unofficial currency minted in Vienna (and elsewhere) from the late eighteenth century onward. The twentieth-century highland contract currency, the riyal, is characterized in early instruments as "stone, silver, French," indicating the Maria Theresa thaler. Later, the currency simply is described as "stone," indicating the imamic period silver riyal minted in Yemen from 1906 to 1963. After the Revolution of 1962, contracts began to speak of the riyal as "republican, paper." Prior to the turn of the twentieth century the common term for the thaler was *qirsh* (pl. *qurūsh*), which also was further described as "stone, silver, French."[27] In his first model, which is for the acknowledgment of a debt, al-Iryānī mentions *qirsh*, riyal, and *ḥurūf* currencies, and silver versus gold money (56).

10. *Receipt of the price*. Using the third-person, past-tense verb *qabaḍa*, the typical instrument then reports that "the seller received" (or "took possession of") the price money. Possible additional phrases may indicate that this occurred with the "permission" of the buyer, "from the hand of the

buyer," or "in the contract session" (*majlis*); that it was "complete"; that the seller "acknowledged" this receipt; and that, as a consequence, "the buyer's obligation was satisfied regarding all of the price."

11. *Transfer of the sale object to the buyer.* The reciprocal act is the receipt of the sale object, using the same verb, *qabaḍa*, sometimes with the reported "permission" of the seller. This transfer may begin, however, with a report of the vacating (*al-takhliyya al-sharʿiyya*) of the sale object and the statement that the seller guarantees against any default in ownership (*al-darak*). Then, usually by means of the pivotal verb of alienation, *ṣār*, "became," the verb also of the model, the sale object becomes the buyer's individual property, or *milk*, in ownership and sometimes explicitly also in "possession" (*yad*). The newly established property right also may be characterized in terms similar to the model, as in an Ibb *baṣīra* from 1913: "And he [the seller] gave permission to the buyer to take possession of the aforementioned sale object among the group of his *milk* [properties], which he may dispose of how he wishes, when he wishes, and where he wishes, as in the disposal by [other] owners of property with respect to their properties, and those with rights with respect to their rights."[28]

12. *Witnessing.* A reflexive bridge phrase, such as "concerning all that has been mentioned, there occurred the writing (*taḥrīr*) and the witnessing (*ishhād*)" or "built upon what has been mentioned, and for it, there occurred the writing and the witnessing," usually marks the transition from the record of the legal act proper to the concluding meta-clauses. The witnessing clause itself typically names the names of at least two male witnesses, sometimes specifying their villages of residence if they are not from Ibb town. A bit of Ottoman usage is found in some late nineteenth- and early twentieth-century instruments that refer to the witnesses as the *shuhūd al-ḥāl*.[29] Witnessing clauses always conclude with "and God is sufficient witness," a Qurʾanic phrase not found in al-Iryānī's models.

Although he is not categorized as a witness unless he later appeared in court in the event of litigation, the notarial writer was the linchpin of the human support for the written instrument.

13. *Writing and dating.* In the passive and thus reflexive voice of the verb "to write" (*ḥurrira*) usually with a pronoun referring, at once, to the finished and being-finished text, the next and final standard clause is "written on its date," after which the date is given. This might include the day but always includes the month and the year, usually written both in numbers and then

in words. The date given is that of the writing. (A few decades later, with the transition to the intensifying international relations of the post-revolutionary republican era, the dual recording of the *Hijrī* and *Milādī*, or Christian, date became common, together with a new linking phrase, "corresponding to," between the two dates.)

Notes

Added notes were the marginalia of the archive. Placed in the blank space purposely left above the main instrument text, small notes marked distinct moments in the archival chronos and introduced further forms of intertextual complexity. A single document could exhibit a growth of notes of different types, but not all *baṣīras* had them. Archived in the space above, notes were further acts of writing, each of which, however minor, was predicated on a reading, however cursory, of the main text appearing below. As demonstrated in chapter 8, courts scrutinized notes on documents and sometimes quoted their contents in case transcripts.

As opposed to the undated non-time of the document model, the dating of the notarial writing of the instrument established the baseline present for the text. Other points in the textual past could be mentioned in passages referring to earlier instruments that the notarial writer had read and annotated before this present writing and the small notes added later designated points in the textual future. With the exception of an autograph note placed on a document by its writer, added notes also charted the movements of the text. A document had to be delivered and physically presented to a countersigner, the court, a later writer, etc. Notes thus recorded departures from, and returns to, particular personal archives. In the case of cancellations, as I mentioned, they also indexed transfers from one holding to another. In these annotated circulations of a text we also follow a partial history of its being read. Documents laden with annotations were the non-bureaucratic "files" of this particular pre-modernity.

The Ibb *baṣīra* written in 1957 offers an example consisting of four installments. As I mentioned earlier, the main text of this instrument contains a report of the notarial writer's having read and annotated an earlier inheritance instrument, a document that, as he states, already bore a significant affirmation note from the Ibb judge of the 1920s. Both of these notes (early and late) on the consulted inheritance instrument are mentioned in the body of the new *baṣīra* of 1957, a document that during its own archival existence acquired notes of its own. Soon after it was written, this contract instrument received a buttressing countersignature or affirmation (*iʿtimād*; also *taṣdīq*, *taqrīr*), in this instance by an Ibb judge. He wrote, "[A]ffirmed is the issuance of the sale from the one mentioned, as is written below this [note] in the script and signature of the learned Faqīh al-ʿIzzī Muhammad Naji al-Wahhābī [later the muftī of Ibb], God protect him." The same note continues, "and it [the document] was entered in the Transactions Register of the Court of the Ibb Subdistrict, on its date, Shaʿbān, year 1376." Above the note is the judge's signature, and above that the legend "Judge of Ibb," and, higher still, the note's own *Basmala*. Such countersignatures also could be obtained from the local governor or from a noted scholar. Second, at the top and to the right on the same 1957 *baṣīra*, a related note specifies the link of this original to its copy. Written by a court secretary, it states that the document was "entered in the Register for Recording Transactions (*daftar qayd al-muʿāmalāt*) of the Ibb Court, on page 185, as item number [5?]66."

This did not end the annotation history of the 1957 document. Third, a further type of possible note concerns transaction expenses. Such notes were added to a *baṣīra* as a precaution against a claim of sale preemption (*shufʿa*). This was to insure that, in addition to the purchase price, the preempted buyer also would be compensated for any paid commissions associated with the original transaction and for the writing fee paid to the notarial writer. Rather than appearing as a separate note, on the 1957 instrument this information is included in the notarial writer's signature statement in the line above the main text (what I refer to as line 2). This statement begins: "What is mentioned [below] occurred as it is written," which is standard. It goes on to say, "and the buyer incurred a commission (*siʿāya*) and a [document writing] fee (*ujra*) of seven riyals, only" [signature above, no date]. Finally, fourth, on this *baṣīra* of 1957 there is an example of the type of transformative note that alters the original act recorded in the main text below. Written high and at an angle above the original *Basmala*, and under its own *Basmala*, this last note speaks of what was purchased "in the *baṣīra*"—that is, the sale object indicated in the main document below, as having been transferred to another party. This last of the four notes served to cancel the 1957 document. But, as in the transformative additions to other categories of texts, from abrogating verses in the Qurʾan to negating commentary in a work of *fiqh*, with the addition of this final note, the decisively altered original instrument text continued to be legible. Transferred to the new owner, it also continued to be archived.

* * *

The foregoing schematic of clauses, lines, and added notes concludes a partial reading of a particular genre of Ibb document. Versions of many of these basic features, from the invocations of the divinity to the witnessing and dating clauses, also are found in other local primary genres. In contrast to the singular and purposely sterile world of the *fulān*-structured model, in these local texts we encounter the endless multiplicity and fecundity of the archive. In terms of their "contract" dimensions, the names alone, of people, places, and things, could launch an entire social history. As for the "contract-law" features, there are variations from document to document. We remain at a handwritten moment prior to the installation of the regularities that would be introduced and concretized with the printed forms of the twenty-first-century regime of the nation-state. Although the overall convergence of "contract-law" categories and language between the model and the Ibb instrument is striking, with an exception noted, these Ibb documents do not reference the small indicators of juridical concerns specific to Zaydī *fiqh* that are found in al-Iryānī's model (i.e., the phrase "two past expressions" and the notion of parting with "mutual consent").

Some points may be made concerning other differences between the model and the historical documents. One is that this genre of Ibb document typically references "custom," whereas the model does not. It does so using the phrase "in sharīʿa and custom," specifically in connection with the rights associated with the sale object. I pursue the issue of the explicit referencing of custom further in connection with the next contract types: lease and marriage. A second point, for which the contrast only becomes explicit in one of al-Iryānī's later models, is that the local documents are linked to the Ibb region of Lower Yemen through their regular use of the *qaṣaba* unit of surface measurement. A third concerns the many forms of textual reflexivity exhibited in this type of Ibb instrument. These include internal reports on readings and annotations of other writings; bridging and passive language at the end of the instrument; a witnessing clause; a signature line that refers to "what is below"; and the variety of added notes. With the exception of the witnessing clause, none of these features have counterparts in al-Iryānī's preliminary discussion or in his "sale" model.

What the layperson might perceive as a single act or event—in this case, a sale of land—the jurists understood and the notarial writers realized as a series of steps, which lent an internal duration to the act. This analytic perspective and the related chronos are associated with a paper language and composition. Thus the "offer and the acceptance" is preceded by clauses for identifying the parties, the buyer and the seller, and for specifying the two *māls*, the sale object and the price. Then the exchange itself is carried out, but it too is broken down into the transfer and receipt of the price money, and then the transfer and receipt of the sale object. If earlier documents are cited, these introduce internal ties to other temporal settings. If background efforts had been necessary to ascertain personal identities or to read prior documentation, the overall work also included a period of effort prior to the drafting.

Traces of spoken interactions at the contract session are faint in these archival instruments. All that is left of whatever words might have passed between the parties is the record of the satisfaction of the technical requirement for an "offer and acceptance." An exception that proves the rule is the unusual *baṣīra* that also reported "I sold" and "I bought," words that may or may not have been heard as such by the writer. Shāfiʿī *fiqh* books give these and other past-tense wordings as the suggested contract language; the *Flowers*, as noted, requires only that the binding language of ownership transfer be determined "according to custom." Except for the recorded details of the properties themselves, there is no evidence of a spoken exchange that may have occurred between the seller and the notarial writer—that is, following the form of the Qurʾan-mandated "dictation." For his part, al-Iryānī references this mandate in a discussion that is separate from his models. There is no reason to expect an explicit mention of such speech acts in a primary document genre, whether or not such acts occurred. Another perspective, however, is that the "offer and acceptance" formula itself, specifically the "offer" side, may be seen as comprising an act equivalent to a "dictation." Yet the "offer" phrase is not an utterance but rather a technical representation of one. As for the requisite detail concerning the transferred property—its name, dimensions, boundaries, etc.—these could just as well have been copied from a previous contract instrument read by the notarial writer.

Lease

Give the hired man his wage before his sweat dries.

—*Ḥadīth* cited in the *Flowers*

Like sale, which structured transfers of both (moveable) commercial goods and (immoveable) real estate, such as cultivable land, the doctrinal *ijāra* contract also carried a dual significance. It covered both the hire of services, from tailoring to construction labor, and the lease of agrarian land and buildings, including residences and commercial establishments. As with sale, a parallel difference existed regarding the pattern of documentation: where most hires of service were not placed in writing, agricultural and other leases typically were set down in contract instruments. The foundational western study of the hire/lease *ijāra* and the related sharecropping contract, the *muzāraʿa*, is the earlier referenced work by Baber Johansen, based on Ḥanafī texts.[30] A recent study by William J. Donaldson pertains specifically to leases and sharecropping in Yemen.[31]

The lease texts I focus on in this section are known locally and throughout the highlands as *ijāra* contracts, but their relation to the doctrinal contract of the same name is a complex question. The corpus of late imamic period contracts at hand comes from Ibb landlords and from a register at the Ibb Endowments Office.[32] In both sets, agricultural land contracts are mixed with leases of residential rooms, floors and whole houses, and also marketplace shops, warehouses, and other miscellaneous buildings located both in Ibb town and in the surrounding villages.[33] I limit the discussion here to contracts concerning productive land.

At elevations of 6,000 to 7,000 feet and higher, cultivated terraces in the nearby Ibb countryside follow the contours of the high valley and the surrounding mountainsides, with stone walls buttressing those on sloping land. Land is of two general types: rain-fed and irrigated, the latter by small springs and runoff streams. Rain-fed, grain-producing land was the predominant form in the Ibb region, representing about 70 percent of the agrarian contracts in my corpus, with sorghum being the principal crop.

As a consequence of the documented undertakings, donkeys completed an annual circuit between the town and the terraces in the surrounding countryside. Traveling the network of old stone-paved roads and the innumerable small footpaths, in the late winter months in advance of plowing the animals delivered pack baskets of night soil from catchment bins in Ibb houses to be spread on the terraces. At the end of the fall harvest, the donkeys returned from threshing floors with bags of grain, representing the measured-out harvest shares to be delivered in the town. A month or so later, they brought dried sorghum stalks for cooking fires. Landlords stored the received grain in lined and sealed underground pits (*madfan*, pl. *madāfin*) located below their tall stone residences and under the town's several warehouses. Houses and other buildings were equipped with low exterior buttresses to direct rainwater away from their foundations and the storage pits that honeycombed the town's substratum.

For productive land in Ibb, there were two types of local *ijāra* contracts, which I term conventional tenancies and sharecropping leases. In the Ibb corpus, both "private" and institutional, all irrigated land was covered by conventional leases, while rain-fed land was equally divided between conventional and sharecropping contracts. Like other documents, leases could be written on individual pieces of document paper, but landlords with multiple holdings tended to keep small personal registers for their leases, which were entered two or three to the page. Larger landlords sometimes used the services of a regular writer, whose script and signature repeated in such records.

Concerned as they were with a widespread type of socioeconomic relation, these simple contracts were perhaps the most numerous type of sharīʿa instrument. In a sense, they also were the most "democratic" of documents. In them we read the names of ordinary people, tenants of all types, rural and urban, agrarian, residential, and commercial. Where *baṣīra* contracts documented the relations between buyers and sellers—that is, transactions between those of sufficient means to own property—and where inheritance and other estate matters required a threshold of wherewithal to necessitate documentation, *ijāra*s reached into the wider world of those engaged in the use of agrarian property. Only marriage contracts, if consistently documented, would compete with the written *ijāra* in social reach. While the names of tenants appeared in the written text, however, the landlords retained the documents. The "democratic" nature of the local *ijāra* thus was limited by the fact that landowners (and the Endowments as an institution) controlled this range of the agrarian archive. As was the case for other local instruments in this period, neither party to the contract signed an *ijāra* instrument.

Ijāras for cultivation were the written manifestations, the facts of power, of an institution foundational to the old social order and to the broader political economy of the highlands.[34] Documenting the relationship of landlord and cultivating tenant, these instruments addressed the combining of the premodern factors of land and labor for agrarian production. The landowner-tenant relationship, and the sharecropping bond in particular, may be thought of as the agrarian-age equivalent of Marx's industrial-era relationship between the capitalist and the wage laborer. Although a high-status or otherwise resourceful tenant was not unknown, the landlord-tenant relation usually was one of dominance and subordination. However, in a fashion analogous to Engels's remark about the capitalist wage-labor contract, a written *ijāra* contract made "both parties equal on *paper*."[35]

Such documents could figure in the defense of property rights. For a private landlord (as for the Endowments Administration), especially in the case of a property relatively distant from the town, or in another region, a document of this type could be valuable as supplementary evidence of ownership (or of endowment status), since a sound lease was predicated on such ownership (or status). In mentioning the tenant's name and village, a lease identified the active disposition of the property. Sharīʿa court cases show that *ijāra* documentation was used as evidence, for example, to counter a tenant who asserted an ownership claim, or in struggles between joint owners.[36] On the other hand, in the person of the identified tenant, the owner had a potential witness against outside claims.

I begin by presenting the first of two model instruments provided in the *ijārāt* (pl.) section of the *shurūṭ* treatise, which concerns the lease of real estate. "One writes," al-Iryānī states, "something like":

> "*Fulān* son of *Fulān* appeared and leased (*istaʾjara*) from *Fulān* son of *Fulān*, his house," or "his land the *Fulāniyya*, and its boundaries are such and such, and this is his individual property (*milk*)," or "the property of his principal," or "is a guardianship, to use it (*liyantafiʿa bihā*), as a residence and inhabitation, and he

permitted him this, for a period of a year" or "a month, from the date of month such and such, for a known rent (*ujra maʿlūma*) in the amount of such and such, every day such and such" or "every month such and such, after [the establishment of] knowledge of what was being contracted for, and they parted mutually consenting." Then it is witnessed and dated.

(74–75)

Al-Iryānī's text models the real estate lease side of the doctrinal *ijāra* contract. Its features, beyond identifying the parties and the property, are that the property in question is explicitly characterized as *milk*; that it provides what is characterized as a "known rent," which then is specified, rather than a future harvest share, which is the hallmark of a sharecropping contract; that it names a terminal date for the contract, which sets it apart from some historical Ibb contracts; that it employs the verb of "use," which is the language of the use right, or usufruct (*manfaʿa*);[37] that it indicates the anticipated use (which is feature of local republican-era contracts); and that, finally, as in the model *baṣīra*, it records the contracting parties' "mutual consent." This last feature illustrates a consistency of Zaydī school technical usage across al-Iryānī's model texts.

Beyond its general local identity as an *ijāra*, the conventional lease in Ibb sometimes is referred to more specifically as a *ḍamān*, which indicates a guaranteed payment. This term may or may not appear in the documents, but in some instances it replaces the term for "rent" (*ujra*). The basic identity of this type of Ibb lease is established, as in al-Iryānī's model, by the specification in the contract of a stipulated payment amount. In the Ibb instruments, this amount usually is in-kind—that is, in grain, using the dry measure unit, the *qadāḥ* (pl. *aqdāḥ*), known throughout the highlands. The relevant clause of such local leases reads, for example, "for a known *ujra* every year of three *aqdāḥ* of sorghum (*ṭaʿām*)."

Differing local measures followed the general pattern of regional and subregional variation in agrarian practices and terminologies. Many local leases further specify that the *qadāḥ* unit must be according to the "Ibb measure" (*mikyāl al-ibbī*), sometimes further described as the "old" or "prior," while others refer to the "local" (*maḥallī*) or "country" (*baladī*) measure or, in one lease, to the "measure of the aforementioned village," indicating the existence of measures of even more restricted use than those pertaining to the Ibb region. In this period, however, perhaps marking the incipient forces of commercialization, a new standard measure had been introduced by the imamic polity. This slightly smaller "Prophet's measure" (*mikyāl al-nabawī*), is mentioned in a number of local lease instruments, and in some this introduced unit is referred to as the "now customary."[38]

Ibb leases of both types, conventional and sharecropping, refer to the appearance of the tenant before the notarial writer. When the Ibb writer did not know this individual, a sub-clause followed the name indicating that the necessary establishment of legal identification (*ta*ʿ*rīf shar*ʿ*ī*) had occurred, a process I take up further in the following section on the marriage contract. When the property in question was extremely well known, the names of the bounding terraces might be omitted and a phrase added, such as "renown (*al-shuhra*) makes it possible to dispense with boundaries."

According to the doctrinal chapter, an *ijāra* is based on an "offer and an acceptance" between the lessor and lessee, which exemplifies the paradigmatic nature of the sale contract with respect to this and the other types of bilateral acts in the *fiqh*.[39] As opposed to the *baṣīra*, however, there is no mention of an "offer and acceptance," or of any related representations of utterances from the parties, either in al-Iryānī's model text in or in the Ibb instruments. Finally, I note but cannot explain why both the treatise model and the Ibb contract documents give only two-part names for the parties, unlike the more complete three-part names in *baṣīras* and other instruments.

Sharecropping

Does al-Iryānī offer a model *for* (and thus also *of*) the sharecropping contract in his *shurūṭ* treatise? Not in this seventh section devoted to *ijārāt*, for which his two models include the just-quoted model lease and a specific type of hire of services—that of an individual paid to undertake the Islamic pilgrimage on behalf of a party. However, in the eighth section of the treatise (75–76), al-Iryānī provides a model instrument that is similar in conception to a sharecropping contract. This is a watering contract, which refers specifically to the cultivation of the date palm. The palm, it should be noted, is not cultivated in the Ibb valley system, nor at the still higher altitudes of the author's native Iryān or elsewhere in Upper Yemen, although it is found in the lower altitude *wādī* systems that cut into the highlands from the West. This watering contract provides for future harvest shares for the owner of the palm and for the watering party. The wording of al-Iryānī's model asserts a sharīʿa identity for the contract and identifies God as the creator of the harvest return. The instrument concludes, "[W]hatever God Almighty causes to be the yield is between them [the two parties] half each."

Given the restricted mandate of the genre in which he writes, al-Iryānī does not notice a further set of partly sound and partly defective contracts mulled over by generations of doctrinal jurists. These specialized contracts, including that for sharecropping, were meant, but usually failed, to remedy a key problem of such contracts, namely their unspecifiable, or unknown rent terms. The jurists staunchly opposed "uncertainty" (*gharar*) in all types of sharīʿa acts, mainly since this introduced the possibility of forms of interest taking, which was forbidden.[40] As a result, while the venerable sharecropping relation and its several related forms remained indispensible on the ground, the discourse of the jurists, itself centuries old, became tied in knots.

Shāfiʿī works of *fiqh* discuss three subtypes of contracts for the letting of agricultural land. These are presented together in a separate doctrinal chapter that appears just before that on the *ijāra*. The contract specific to the watering of palm trees, also applied by analogy to the cultivation of grapes, is considered sound, while the other two, which approximate the contractual relation of landlord and sharecropping tenant in the Ibb area, are deemed defective (*fāsid*) by authorities such as Abu Shujāʿ, Nawawī, and Ibn Raslān. As for the applicability of the *ijāra* contract itself to such circumstances, the last of these jurists, the fifteenth-century Palestinian whose versified *fiqh* work was commented upon by the nineteenth-century Ibb jurist al-Muftī, states, in definitive terms, "The leasing (*ijāra*) of land for part of what is produced from it in the contracted-for harvest the Best of Men [i.e., the Prophet] forbade."[41]

Why, then, is the similarly structured watering contract permitted? The simple answer is that it is supported by the authoritative weight of a specific "source" text. This is the *ḥadīth* of the Jews of Khaybar, which is cited by the Shāfiʿī commentator from Ibb, as well as by the Zaydī jurists.[42] The seventh-century Jewish community in question lived in the Khaybar oasis, some 90 kilometers north of Medina. According to the *ḥadīth*, once the people of this oasis submitted to his rule, the Prophet stipulated an arrangement whereby their palms would be cultivated with a share of the resulting harvest coming to him. Whether this constituted a model for sharecropping in general or only for the watering contract is contested.

Some jurists, meanwhile, read this "source" text as a precedent for the tax established for non-Muslim communities of "the Book" under Muslim rule.

In his review of the watering contract, the local Shāfiʿī jurist thinks substantively, casuistically, about the application implications. First, as noted, he associates palm and vine cultivation, noting that they fall into the same tithe category; he then distinguishes these two and their fruit from "others, including the grains, vegetables, and all the trees such as the fig, apple and apricot, since these last produce fruit without being cared for," which is an analysis according to the indicated type of labor. That this is a discourse of cosmopolitan commentary rather than a locally directed inquiry is demonstrated by the fact that al-Muftī does not mention the cultivation of either coffee or *qat*, the relevant crops of the Ibb region where he resides. Beyond the basic and evidently sufficient justification provided by the "source" text, his assessment of the watering contract includes two additional general features. He refers to (1) the pressing "necessity" (*al-ḥāja*)—presumably socioeconomic—to make the contract permissible, and (2) the decisive role of "custom" in permitting these contracts and in setting their detailed terms.[43] He notes in passing, but without explaining how the issue might pertain to the watering contract, that the problem of contractual "uncertainty" bars the related contracts.

The second and third types are the *mukhābara* and the *muzāraʿa*, the sharecropping contract. Al-Muftī states that the *mukhābara*, which he defines, following Nawawī, as the "*ijāra* of land for part of what is produced by it, [with] the seed grain from the worker," is "absolutely invalid" (*bāṭila muṭlaqan*).[44] This definition nonetheless roughly approximates the actual agrarian leases of his native region, perhaps even including holdings in his own family. Both for the *mukhābara* and for the closely related *muzāraʿa*, this local commentator goes on to suggest a "way" (*ṭarīq*) to licitly "provide the yield (*ghilla*) to them both [i.e., both parties], without an *ujra*," that is, without the specification of a known rent at the time of the contract. The somewhat complicated and, to my knowledge, never practically attempted solution is similar to that described by Zaydī commentator al-ʿAnsī involving conceptual halves of the land and of the seed grain together with inputs of the worker's labor and the use of his animals and his tools.

Thinking across the *fiqh* transaction types, the Shāfiʿī and the Zaydī jurists saw an analogy between sharecropping contracts and the arrangement of another characteristic institution of the agrarian age. This was the mercantile relation known in the West as the commenda, which brought together merchant capital and labor for trade. In the simple versions of both the sharecropping contract and the commenda, an individual with capital but unprepared to work joined with a willing worker without capital, entering an agreement that involved specified shares of the proceeds.[45]

Among the Zaydīs, following the text of the *Flowers*, the jurists gave attention to five subtypes of agrarian contracts, one of which was considered strictly defective.[46] Once again, the root of the negative assessment was a firm opposition to contractual undertakings embodying "uncertainty." Twentieth-century commentator al-ʿAnsī surveys the five contractual subtypes introduced or implied in the *Flowers*, including the strictly defective *mukhābara*.[47] The other four sub-forms—the sharecropping *muzāraʿa*, a planting contract (*mughārasa*), a watering contract, and a lesser-known contract between a landowner and the owner of seed grain (*mubādhara*)—had both valid and defective varieties according to whether they met the governing conditions of the *ijāra* form. The many ramifications the jurists take up involved evaluating aspects and versions of these suspect forms, and finding ways around the related problems.

The solutions finally arrived at combine the dual contractual dimensions built into the *ijāra* form, that is, the hire of labor and the lease of land. Yet the object of these theoretical exercises remained the cultivation of a single plot of land. In the marvelously complex Zaydī version of a legal *muzāraʿa*, for example, an individual leases one part of the piece of land, entering into a relationship of joint ownership of the crop with the land owner while at the same time working for a wage on the other part of the property, utilizing seed grain contributed by each of the two parties in fractions related to their eventual harvest shares. The revenue received by the landlord in the (first) lease stage of this compound contract is used to employ the same tenant as a worker in the (second) hire stage.[48] Needless to say, the beautiful architecture of this technically valid contract never saw the light of day in the routine notarial documentation prepared for highland landlords and sharecroppers.

Meanwhile, of the strictly defective *mukhābara* contract, al-ʿAnsī remarks that in Yemen it is "customary in many regions."[49] He describes this contract as follows: "It is where the owner gives over the land to the cultivator such that its crop will be between them according to what they agreed to." If there is conflict between the two parties, however, the jurist's strong reservations about this contract come to the fore. Al-ʿAnsī remarks, "In our view, if they [viz., the parties] litigate, it is defective (*fāsida*) regarding the future [i.e., regarding still to be completed aspects of the undertaking], but legal concerning what has [already] transpired of it." Al-ʿAnsī additionally treats the issue of cash versus in-kind payments. In the sharecropping contract, with its halves of the land and inputs of seed, etc., he says that if the wage of the cultivator or the rent of the land is customarily expressed in money terms, then matters are clear and sound. But if custom dictates, "as is the custom in our times and our Yemen, a requirement of half of the crop, or less, or more, at the time of its harvest," then the value of such shares of the harvest cannot be known at the time the contract is entered into.

Following a *Flowers* dictum, however, such defective contracts for future shares of the harvest return were rendered permissible by the decisive intentional force of the parties' "mutual consent" (*tarāḍīn*).[50] Criticizing this passage in the *Flowers*, Shawkānī comments, "[T]his is obvious, and need not be recorded, since mutual consent renders valid every transaction except that which is inherently forbidden."[51] As I have noted, in his *shurūṭ* treatise al-Iryānī uses the term "mutual consent" to conclude both his model *baṣīra* instrument and his model *ijāra*. In the Ḥanafī school, an equivalent move was made to accept such problematic contracts based on the general principle of *istiḥsān*, which Johansen defines as "admitting for practical purposes legal solutions that openly contradicted conclusions drawn on the basis of analogical reasoning."[52] Thus both juridical traditions suspended the strict requirements of juristic principle, reason, and systemic regularity. While these suspensions were phrased in quite different conceptual terms, the ultimate sanctioning force of custom (*ʿurf*) underpinned both.[53] Regarding the sharecropping contract, according to commentator al-ʿAnsī, "custom is equivalent to the formally stipulated."[54]

Sharecropping Ijāra

Both the conventional and sharecropping leases written in Ibb for the properties of "private" landlords violated the doctrinal rule—and al-Iryānī's distillation of this rule in his model *ijāra*—according to which a terminal date for the contract must be specified. While this feature rendered them technically invalid, the fact that these arrangements continued year after year without necessitating acts of renewal reflected the local social reality of these durable relationships, which frequently extended over generations.[55] Contractual custom again trumped a *fiqh* rule. Like other types of instruments, these contracts employed past-tense verbs, referencing thereby what were conceived of as concluded acts. Yet, at the same time, these *ijāras* embodied a yet-to-be-concluded character.

While the two types of local leases shared this temporal feature, they diverged regarding the rent specification. The conventional leases adhered to the *ijāra* requirement of a rent specified in cash or in kind at the time of the contract while the sharecropping leases did not. Instead, as noted, these contracts specified a future harvest share for the landlord, and thus also, by implication, for the tenant. From a doctrinal perspective, as well as from that of al-Iryānī's model instrument, this amounted to an intractable problem. It, again, introduced a fundamental "uncertainty" that the jurists staunchly opposed in all types of transactions.

Both the concept of a harvest share itself and the actual fraction designated for the landlord were anchored in the authority of local custom. For the rain-fed cultivation of grains, the one-quarter share due to the landlord was standard throughout the Ibb valley system and was not subject to "contract" negotiation. Different fractions were customary, however, in other regions of the highlands. While the jurists were concerned about "uncertainty" inasmuch as it opened the door to problems associated with the prohibition on interest, a range of material uncertainties existed regarding the harvest returns. Aside from the problems that could arise in connection with the envisioned work itself, the natural factors that loomed over the outcomes of these contracts included the chances of partial or complete failure of the crop due to flooding, drought, damaging winds, insect spoliation, and plant diseases.

In addition to this central customary provision regarding the harvest share, sharecropping contracts in Ibb comprised a further set of explicitly stipulated provisions regarding the tenant's obligations and conduct, all also determined by custom. We have seen that the Ibb sale instruments referenced custom, albeit in minimal terms, in the conceptual couple "in sharīʿa and in custom." In contrast, as a distinctive feature of both types of local *ijāra* contracts, custom-based stipulations accounted for a substantial portion of the written text. The fact that al-Iryānī makes no mention of custom represents a major (but not surprising) divergence between his model and the historical documents. As opposed to the earlier-mentioned abstract identifications of custom as a decisive constructive force in the doctrinal library, we encounter it here, in the notarial writings of the archive, as a fleshed out, implemented presence.

At this juncture, I present a rendering of the Ibb sharecropping *ijāra*, a contract that again applies only to rain-fed cultivation. Instead of the clause-by-clause approach I used for the sale instrument, I resort here to an integral model *of* the local document, a text, or "script" of *my own construction*, using *Fulān*, and X, Y, etc. As opposed to the *shurūṭ* literature model discussed earlier, my model offers a summary representation of the basic features of the locally existing sharecropping contract, customary provisions included. It thus represents the type of document prepared by notarial writers in Ibb in the 1950s. As such, it endeavors to make explicit the normally implicit script of what I have termed the "lateral" model.

> Praise be to God
>
> *Fulān* son of *Fulān* from the village of X in the subdistrict of Y appeared before me and leased (*istaʾjara*) from *Fulān* son of *Fulān*, and this the terrace [named] the *Fulāniyya* in the cultivated area of the mentioned village, bounded on the north [terrace name and owner], on the east [terrace name and owner], on the west [terrace name and owner], and on the south [terrace name and owner], for a known rent (*ujra maʿlūma*), its amount, every year, a quarter of the return (*rubʿ al-ḥāṣil*), and a pound of clarified butter [as] *ʿiwāda*[56] and a laborer [as] assistance (*ʿawn*). The lessee is obligated (*yaltazimu al-mustʾajir*) for upkeep and fertilizer [night soil], to not be negligent, to protect the boundaries, to bring the yield to the place of receipt in the town of Ibb, and everything required of tenants. With the presence of [two named witnesses], and God is sufficient witness, on its date [date] [signature of the writer].

This model of the sharecropping *ijāra* shares the standard, third-person, and past-tense "objective style" of al-Iryānī's models. The first section of my version of an Ibb text through to the mention of the terrace boundaries is comparable to the opening of the model instrument in al-Iryānī's *shurūṭ* treatise, but from the specification of the "rent" (*ujra*) to the witnessing clauses, at which point it returns to approximate his model form, the document is Ibb-specific in its detailed formulae. While this local sharecropping contract uses standard *ijāra* language—namely, the verb "to lease" and the nouns "lessee" and "rent"—the key conceit of these historical instruments is to forcibly connect the notion of a "known rent" to that of the "quarter of the return." Beyond the simple indication of the fraction to be applied, the actual amount is unknown at the time of the contract. Where the notarial model explicitly states that the property leased is the *milk* property of the lessor, this fact remains implicit in the Ibb contracts, although some local documents add the phrase "that which is his/hers in," referring to the lessor, before naming the terrace(s) in question. Several other explicit formulae used by al-Iryānī—"he permitted this," referring to the lessor; the "[establishment of] knowledge of what was being contracted for"; and the characteristic statement that the parties parted with "mutual consent"—do not appear in the Ibb contracts.[57]

Looking closer at the further custom-based "clauses" of my model let me first repeat that such lines are relatively standard in both the conventional and the sharecropping leases. A quick series of discrete items, these custom stipulations are minimally named. The first two items follow directly after and thus are added, grammatically, to the specified rent or the mentioned quarter share due the landowner: "and a pound (*raṭl*) of clarified butter [as] *ʿiwāda* and a laborer (*shāqī*) [as] assistance (*ʿawn*)." Most such contracts specify one pound and one laborer, but the units may be increased for large plots. The former is spoken of as a "gift" to the landlord; the later may be understood as a form of "private" corvée, which usually involved a day's work around the landlord's residence. The additional customary provisions constitute a simple list given in the following sentence. The subject is the tenant; the verb, "is obligated"; and the objects typically include the following: the general upkeep of the property, the use of fertilizer, the avoidance of negligence, the protection of the terrace boundaries, and the delivery of the landlord's share to his place of receipt in Ibb, which usually meant his house. Such further customary stipulations usually conclude with a summary reference to the habitus of proper tenancy: "and everything required of tenants."

As a "lateral" model, my sharecropping contract overrides a great deal of variation. Prior to the advent of the standardizations advocated or required by the nation-state, minor permutations were the norm in

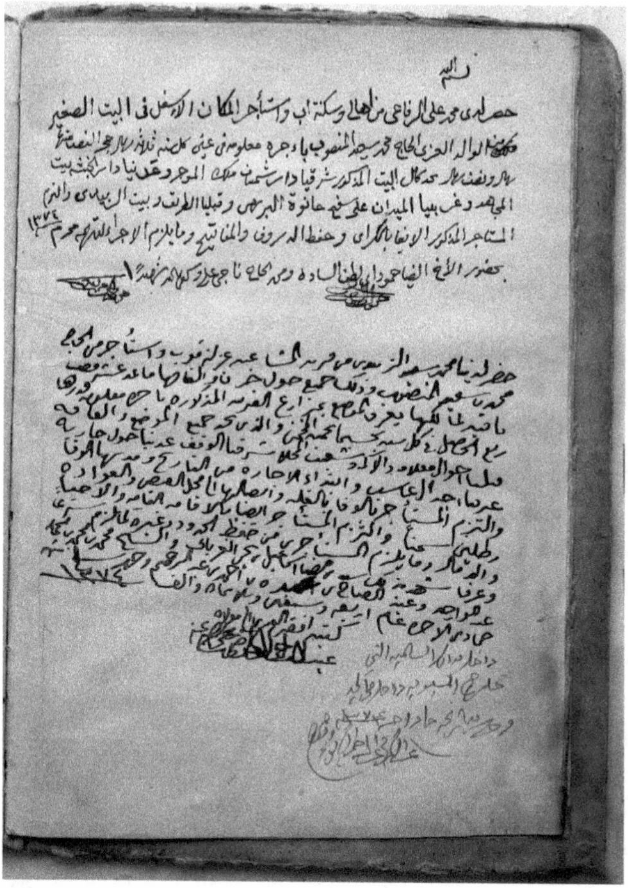

Figure 10.5 Landlord's lease register, sharecropping contract bottom, 1374 AH (1955).

handwritten archival production. In substantive terms, my simplified model text concerns a rain-fed plot and the landlord's share set as one-quarter of the harvest. Actual contracts might include composites of properties, such as a village house and adjoining land, or a mix of terms, such as for a rain-fed and also for an irrigated terrace. Arrangements differed for the main fall harvest, the *ṣarāb*, as opposed to the smaller winter harvest, the *qiyāḍ*. In addition to my male lessee, Ibb women occasionally appear in this role. In the custom "clauses," differences are found instrument to instrument. In addition to such substantive differences, there was a limited amount of variation in overall textual form. While third-person notarial writers prepared most such documents in the "objective" style, one occasionally encounters a first-person or "subjective" text.[58] In addition to *ijāras* there were a few other text-types mixed in the study collection—that is, in the "private" landlord's lease register. An example is an instrument framed as an acknowledgment. This concerns an individual's receipt of money from the landowner to cover the expense of planting greens.[59]

Marriage

> Marriage according to the bourgeois conception was a contract, a transaction, and the most important one of all because it disposed of two human beings, body and mind, for life.
>
> —Frederick Engels, *Origin of the Family*

In the opening of his sixteenth *shurūṭ* treatise section (79–80), which is on the contract of marriage, al-Iryānī sets forth requirements regarding the parties. He also makes explicit a set of further issues that the document writer must consider before setting pen to paper. Complex matters that are given full treatment in two standard chapters in the *Flowers* literature, namely "Marriage" and "Repudiation" (i.e., *ṭalāq*, or unilateral divorce by the husband), are mentioned here in passing, with a pragmatic view toward notarial practice.[60] These include the waiting period (*ʿidda*) that a woman must complete after the termination of her marriage; dissolution (*faskh*) of a marriage contract by a judge; a woman's status as a virgin or a non-virgin prior to the contract; a woman's marriage contract guardian (*walī*) and his guardianship (*wilāya*); the dower (*mahr*); the woman's individual consent (*riḍāʾ*); and, finally, such key features of the contract itself as the "offer and acceptance," derived from the form of the sale contract, and the bilateral consent (*tarāḍīn*) of the contracting parties.

"Then," with these potential circumstances, issues, and prior conditions of the contract properly attended to, "the writer writes." The following translation of al-Iryānī's chapter opens with his checklist section (with paragraphing added) and then presents his model of the marriage contract (set off by indentation):

Chapter Sixteen on Marriage (*nikāḥ*)

It is required of whoever contracts [i.e., presides over] a marriage, whether a judge or his deputy or an officiating party (*muḥakkam*) from among the Muslims, that he knows [i.e., identifies] the husband and his name and his descent (*nasab*), and the woman and her name and her descent. And if he does not know them, it is necessary that they are made known by two just witnesses.

And it is necessary that he ascertains that she is free from any husband [i.e., not married], or of a waiting period [after] any husband; whether she is a virgin or a non-virgin; whether her husband has died and she has completed her waiting period after him, or [whether he] has repudiated her and she has completed her waiting period after him; or whether her [marriage] has been dissolved [contractually] by a judge. The repudiation or dissolution must be valid for the contractor (*al-ʿāqid*) in sharīʿa terms or else he should not engage the contract, because the basic principle (*al-aṣl*) is the continuity of a marriage relation.

And if the woman said, "I was married and he died," or "he repudiated me," or "my marriage was dissolved contractually," then evidence is necessary for this claim. And it is [also] necessary for the contractor to know the guardian of the woman by his name and to validate the establishment of his guardianship by a sharīʿa method, not simply by the statement of the woman that "he is my guardian."

If it is decided that the woman is legally eligible for marriage, and a [verbal] contract occurred between the guardian and the husband, offering and accepting, and the woman having consented, as is required in the sharīʿa, after ascertaining the above from the guardians [*sic*] and [in] the presence of two just witnesses, then the writer writes:

> "There appeared Fulān son of Fulān, guardian of the free woman Fulāna [f.], daughter of Fulān, for himself," or "by representation, according to an agency document from Fulān, and he married Fulāna daughter of Fulān to Fulān son of Fulān by a contract that is valid and complete in its approved sharīʿa stipulations, with the presence of two just witnesses, Fulān and Fulān, with mutual consent (*tarāḍīn*), for a dower of [those] equivalent [to her], the amount of which is such and such, delivered by the husband," if he has delivered it, or, if it remains the husband's financial obligation, he writes, "it remains the financial obligation of the husband." And if her father has received this he [the writer] would say, "Her

father has received this for her benefit, by right of his sharīʿa guardianship, [this] after the establishment of her status as a virgin who deserves interdiction (*ḥajr*)."

He should write all that we have mentioned in three copies, two documents for the spouses, and a [third] document should remain with him to serve as a reference for him in case of need. Caution [is warranted] against negligence in mentioning the amount of the dower, since many are the disputes caused by ambiguity (*al-ibhām*), especially where mention is made of the dower of those equivalent (*mahr al-mithl*), given the differences among the equivalent [women] among the relatives.

(79–81)

According to the preamble to al-Iryānī's model contract, if the notarial writer does not know the prospective parties to a marriage contract, their identities should be established through his inquiries and with the aid of witnesses. In marriage, the envisioned notarial writer, the individual who "writes," is potentially the judge or the judge's delegate, or another individual who officiates. The writer or judge, etc., is somewhat ambiguously identified, beginning in the opening line, as the one who "contracts" and, later, as "the contractor"—that is, the individual who presides over the contract—although he is not a party to it. The potential use of witnesses for purposes of identification represents a distinct step in the evidential process, one that is prior to the later role of witnesses to the contract itself.

In the preparation for the writing of this particular type of archival instrument an emphasis is placed on knowing the woman and her circumstances. Unlike men, women were not so likely to be known to the local face-to-face "public," which typically included the notarial writer. This emphasis on knowing the woman to be married resonates with the fourth of four stipulations for a legal marriage set forth in Zaydī *fiqh*.[61] These are (1) a valid contract made by a legal guardian, (2) the witnessing of two just witnesses, (3) consent by the woman, and (4) "her identification" (*taʿyīnha*).

Commentator al-ʿAnsī elaborates on this last item by stating that it refers to

the identification of the woman at the time of the contract and also the identification of the husband—"I accepted for one of my sons" [for example] is not sufficient. The specification of her can be realized by a [verbal] sign indicating her such as if he [the guardian] says, "I married you to this indicated individual [fem.]" or "the one [fem.] you know," even if she is absent. Or by a description, such as "I married you to my oldest daughter" or "youngest" or "white" or "black" or such like among the designating descriptions for the woman, so that he [the other party, the husband, or his agent] will not confuse her with another. Or she can be identified by name, as Fatima or Zaynab, or such, or [by] *laqab*, such as "I married you to my daughter, 'the Pious,'" or "the Pilgrim," or by a *kunya* for her, like Umm Kalthum or Umm al-Fadl, or such.[62]

In the opening discussion in al-Iryānī's notarial treatise, the further concern prior to the writing of the document is the woman's current legal status and the potential of any impediment in the form of an existing marriage or a required waiting period following a terminated marriage. The several possible legal situations are mentioned together with the underlying rule or operative presumption (*aṣl*): the continuity of any existing legal marriage. A woman's statements, that she is married or repudiated, etc., or that a particular individual is her guardian, must not be taken at face value but must be backed by formal evidence that satisfies the notarial writer. As for the guardian, he, too, must be known, both by name and by the legal terms, the guardianship, on the basis of which he acts on the woman's behalf. The presence of a guardian for the woman is a requirement of this contract, not an option, and it entails a distinct right. The typical case is that the right of guardianship pertains to a father with respect to his daughter. As the model contract notes, an agent may represent the guardian in the contract and, if so, the agency should be verified by a document to this effect. Two forms of representation thus are possible in such contracts: standard agency and the specialized, marriage-contract form of the guardianship, which is not treated as a form of agency. In all such matters, it is the notarial writer's role and responsibility to demand accurate information before writing. His primary sources are the parties, his own knowledge, and, if necessary, two just witnesses. He also could refer to existing documents, including agency or guardianship instruments, or divorce papers and relevant court rulings.

In its basic structure, al-Iryānī's model contract claims, without being more specific, to be "valid and complete in its approved sharīʿa stipulations." In his opening advice we find a conception of a prior verbal contract, witnessed with the notary present. These utterances by the parties satisfy the requirement for an offer and an acceptance, but neither the utterances nor this glossing terminology appear in the model document. According to the doctrine, following the pattern of sale, the appropriate language for this contract also is established in custom.[63]

The marriage contract is underpinned by consent and by structures of intentionality. These are in two parts and in a sequence. There is, first, the individual consent of the woman in question, which is a prior condition of possibility for the contract, and second, the mutual consent of the parties to the contract. Al-Iryānī mentions the first in his opening discussion while the second figures in his model. We note from this further example of the marriage contract that the mutual consent clause of the Zaydī school is a consistent feature across his model contracts. The general absence of such a clause, in contrast, is a characteristic of the spectrum of historical contracts from Ibb.

Marriage Script

My Ibb friend ʿAbd al-Karim al-Akwaʿ, the endowments functionary, wrote out for me what amounts to a script of and for the local marriage contract (*ʿaqd al-zawāj*).[64] In the context of marriage, in which spoken contractual words constitute a formal ritual, the notarial writer, the individual officiating, usually is referred to as the *faqīh*, the "jurist," teacher, or scholar. The setting is a sitting room in a private residence. The woman being married is represented by her guardian. She is not present in the room.

> The *Faqīh* appears.
>
> The *Faqīh* says to the young man, "Say to the father of the young woman, marry me to and give me in marriage your daughter, the free woman *Fulāna* daughter of *Fulān*, according to the precision (*muḥkam*) of the Book of God and the Sunna of His Prophet, and according to [the principle of] 'adherence to what is accepted or release with respect.' "
>
> The father of the girl replies: "I married you to and gave you in marriage my daughter, the free woman *Fulāna* daughter of *Fulān*, according to the precision of the Book of God and the Sunna of His Prophet, and according to [the principle of] 'adherence to what is accepted or release with respect,' for a dower of those equivalent to her, as a virgin."
>
> And the young man says, "I accepted this myself."

Those present say, "May God grant this [marriage] goodness and blessing."
And they recite the *Fātiḥa* [the brief opening *sūra* of the Qurʾan].

And [finally] they scatter raisins over the hands of the young man and the father of the girl.

"And then everyone present grabs some," added ʿAbd al-Karim's son Ahmad, referring to the raisins and to a practice they described as Sunna. In the phrase "adherence to what is accepted or release with respect," the script quotes the Qurʾan (2:229, cf. 2:231, 65:2). This refers to two possibilities: the continuity of the marriage or its termination. If the marriage continues, it should be with proper conduct; if it must be terminated, this should be proper as well. The later part of the phrase concerning "release" implicitly references the husband's right of unilateral repudiation. This citation of Qurʾanic language also occurs in imamic period Ibb marriage contracts but is not found in al-Iryānī's model. Likewise, the script's general invocation of the Book and the Sunna does not appear in the model. Before the scattering of the raisins, the contractual event, which is actually a spoken ceremony, ends with the collective recitation of the *Fātiḥa*.

This written script, a type of model in its own right, offers an expanded account of the offer and acceptance process as an enacted performance. This is depicted as opening with the presence and the prompting words of the Faqīh, the eventual writer. He directs the young man to speak to the father (or other guardian from the male line) of the young woman, and he provides the appropriate words to be repeated or quoted. The young man's words, in the imperative, request the necessary contractual utterance of the offer from the father, whose reply, when uttered, will formally initiate the contract. The script presumes that the young man follows the Faqih's instructions and addresses the young woman's father. The offer and acceptance proper begins with the words of the father, who, in reply, converts the young man's imperative, "marry me," into the required past tense expression, "I married you." Also in his reply, the father adds mention of both the dower and the young woman's status as a virgin. The language of acceptance completes the contract, when the young man states, also in the past tense and referring to the offer, "I accepted this."

Recall here the *Flowers*' doctrinal requirement of "two past expressions" for the offer and acceptance in the sale contract, which also figures in the language of al-Iryānī's model sale document. The Zaydī tradition discussion of the marriage contract holds that the initiating offer, in the past tense, must come, as in the Ibb script, from the bride's side, either from the young woman's father or whoever is acting as her guardian. A special subsection in the doctrinal chapter covers an exchange of words that opens much like the Ibb script. It involves a spoken directive, "Say to *Fulān*," the substance of which is the imperative statement, "Marry me to your daughter." The reply, the offer itself, is of the form "I married."[65]

Ibb Contracts

Al-Iryānī, as noted, encouraged the preparation of three copies of each instrument. However, as opposed to sale and lease documents, numerous examples of which could be found in the hands of a single landowner, marriage contracts do not occur in concentrated private holdings. There also was no institution of a designated public register for such records, although instrument copies occasionally can be found entered in the prerevolutionary court registers.[66]

Unlike family endowment and inheritance instruments, I initially did not think of marriage contracts as integral to my interest in property relations. At the same time, I was reluctant to ask men for such documents since they mentioned the names of their wives. As opposed to my earlier experiences living in Morocco, over the years in Ibb I got to know relatively few wives, as adult women usually did not sit in the room when I was present. When a townsman with a guest called to his wife outside the room, he did so using his son's name. In 1975, in conjunction with the first national census, a skit put on in the town poked intentional fun at the typical rural patriarch (played by my occasional assistant). The old man became enraged when the young census-taker asked for the names of "his women."

I do not remember if I mentioned a difficulty in obtaining marriage contracts when, in 1980, I visited the noted Ibb resident Muhammad Yahya al-Ḥaddād, a former republican cabinet minister at the national level and a published historian of the new generation. Prior to the 1962 Revolution, Muhammad had studied in the Ahmadiyya Madrasa in the former capital, Taʿizz, where he later served as a writer in the *dīwān* of Imam Ahmad. During those years, he also traveled in an international delegation—a photo shows him shaking hands with Mao Zedong.

My first example concerns the marriage contracted on April 30, 1958, between the future historian, representing himself, and one of his male-line relatives. (I use pseudonyms for the first names of the wife and her father, and I add quotation marks for the cited passage from the Qurʾan.)

> In the Name of God.
>
> There occurred the valid sharʿī marriage contract for the free woman Sayyida, daughter of al-Qāḍī Muhammad bin Muhammad al-Ḥaddād, may God protect him, with the one who desires her, the brother, the learned *qāḍī* Muhammad bin Yahya al-Ḥaddād, may God protect him, with the offer from the contractor for her, her guardian, her aforementioned father, according to what God and his Prophet ordered, with "adherence to what is accepted or release with respect," for a dower the amount of which is one hundred riyals, half of which is fifty riyals, and [with] acceptance from the aforementioned desiring one, with the presence of two witnesses, the brother ʿAbd Allah bin Ahmad al-Nujayhī and the brother Muhammad ʿAli al-Najjār. May God grant goodness and blessing in this, amen. 11 Shawwāl, [13]77. [Written by] the lowly (*al-ḥaqīr*) [i.e., the writer], [signature] Muhammad ʿAbd Allah al-Hawthī. [67]

This Ibb contract is for the marriage of male-line cousins, classificatory relatives in this instance, rather than first cousins.[68] As used here (and throughout the highlands), the term *qāḍī* refers, not to a "judge," but to a man from a patriline known for learning.[69] The text contains the same quoted Qurʾanic passage as the local script and, in somewhat different language, also invokes the Book and the Prophet. These features, again, distinguish the local writings from al-Iryānī's marriage contract model. In contrast to the simple adjectival invocation, *sharʿī*, found in this Ibb instrument, the model employs more extensive language concerning the authority of the sharīʿa (viz., "approved sharīʿa stipulations" and "valid and complete"). As opposed to the script, this local marriage contract refers to itself somewhat more formally as a "marriage contract" (*ʿaqd al-nikāḥ*). I note for later reference that the dower of 100 old riyals was a substantial sum.

Unlike the presiding "contractor" of the model, who is the writer, the "contractor" (*al-ʿāqid*) in this historical instrument is the party on the woman's side, who also is identified as her guardian. New to the discussion thus far, but an archival standard, is the paper language figure of the groom as the "one who desires her." This local text is unusual, however, in that there is no statement regarding the woman's virginity or non-virginity, as in other historical documents, the model, and the Ibb script.[70] This local contract gives formal, three-part names while the model and the script give only two-part names. The basic offer and acceptance structure of this historical text is that of the script: the female side opens, the male side follows. While the 1958 contract does not give the parties' spoken words, the script does not use the technical terminology of offer and acceptance. As expected, the Ibb contract elides the initiating role played, in the script, by the notarial writer, the *Faqīh*, as well as his prompting of the male-side statement meant to elicit the offer. The Ibb contract and al-Iryānī's model differ in several important ways, most notably in their respective mention and non-mention of the "offer and acceptance," although, as noted, al-Iryānī refers to these reciprocal statements in his preliminary discussion. Al-Iryānī's discussion leading up to his model also refers to the prior oral contract, which might imply words equivalent to those of the Ibb script. While the Ibb script presents a concretely worded version of an offer and acceptance, it does not reference the various other preliminaries detailed by al-Iryānī. The identities of the parties, the absence of potential impediments, and the consent of the young woman—all would have been ascertained before the Faqīh of the script addressed the young man. In this Ibb document, the writer signs himself using a standard self-effacing term—as the "lowly [before God]."

As was their wont, the jurists dismantled a seemingly unitary event, here a marriage, into clauses and a related chronos. Taken together in relation to this Ibb document, the local script and al-Iryānī's discussion of the preliminaries allow us to isolate and specify the capping work accomplished by writing. The writing of the contract presupposed a series of prior steps, but except for the offer and acceptance structure these are not recapitulated in the instruments. Working backward from the culminating act of writing, we have the oral contract, which is portrayed in the Ibb script. As al-Iryānī says, this must occur before the "writer writes." Prior to the oral contract, however, is the establishment of the woman's consent, "as is required in sharīʿa terms." Together with each of the other elements of this contract type, questions around the consent of the bride-to-be are given expansive treatment in the doctrine, notably including the issues around the interpretation of her possible silence or the meaning of, among other nonverbal acts, her tears.[71] Prior to the consent issue, there are the mentioned inquiries involving various possible impediments to the contract and, at the very beginning, the names and identities of those involved had to be established.

A second Ibb contract is the following instrument dated July 1943, which I give as it is quoted in the litigation record of the local court from 1958 (case 4, see chapter 7). The marriage contract in question involves first cousins, both minors. The parties' names have been changed.

> A valid sharīʿa contract was entered into by Muhammad Naji ʿAli Mustafa for his minor daughter, the free woman Arwā, with his brother's minor son, ʿAziz, son of Ahmad Naji ʿAli Mustafa. The contract was accepted for him [the minor son] by his father, the mentioned Ahmad Naji, according to the precision of the Book of God and the Sunna of His Prophet, with a dower of those equivalent to her (*mahr mithlihā*), as a virgin. Written on its date, Jumada II [no day specified] 1362 AH. [Three named individuals] and others witnessed, and God is sufficient witness. [no signature mentioned]

Al-Iryānī recommended the preparation of a third copy "in case of need," a euphemism for a dispute situation. This contract was one of two instruments presented as evidence in the case involving these cousins. Retrieved during the proceedings from a copy previously entered in a court register, the contract text was transcribed in the minutes of the ongoing litigation, where the writer's name was mentioned.

In the course of the trial, however, it was determined that this particular marriage contract was fraudulent. The notarial writer eventually admitted as much in a statement submitted to the court and entered in the litigation record (see further, chapter 8). False documents such as this contract are interesting not only for the study of the deceitful stratagems they enable but also for the extent to which they mimic standard correctness. This contract, for example, replicates the basic structure of the offer from the female side followed by the acceptance from the male side. Since it specifies the young woman's virginity and also mentions "a dower of those equivalent to her," this historical text, unlike the last, fits the provisions of the Ibb script.

"Even If a Small Sum . . . "

> By Property I must be understood here, as in other places, to mean that Property which Men have in their persons as well as Goods.
>
> —John Locke, *Two Treatises on Civil Government*

The marriage dower is an exceedingly rich topic both in its own right and in terms of its connections with other familial property institutions, and it has been widely studied.[72] Here I want to comment on textual representations of the dower, in both the model and the historical documents, and on how these relate to matters of custom. In so doing I factor in doctrinal and ethnographic views, the latter based on my republican-era research. Concerning the basic textual presence of a dower clause—that is, of language stating that the marriage was agreed to "for a dower," etc.—we have seen that al-Iryānī's contract model, Abd al-Karim's script, and the two period Ibb instruments all point to a regular feature in the local written contract.

At the same time, however, a note of ambiguity marks the place of the dower in the doctrinal conceptualization of marriage as a contract. In considering this doctrine, we must keep in mind the distinction between contracts as the jurists' conceptual objects and the texts of actual written instruments. The summary Zaydī position, conveyed in the *Flowers*, is that "the dower is required for the contract but is not a stipulation [of it]" (*wa-l-mahru lāzimun lil-ʿaqdi lā sharṭun*).[73] Commentator al-ʿAnsī notes that this also is the position of the Ḥanafīs and the Shāfiʿīs. A standard Shāfiʿī formulation is that "specification of the dower is recommended in the contract, but the contract is valid if it is not [specified]."[74] In his verse-form *fiqh* text, Ibn Raslān states that a dower "is Sunna in the contract, even if a small sum," and it "should not be unknown." But in the following line he says, "If it is not specified, the contract is valid." "That is," al-Muftī, his Ibb commentator, concludes, "[i]t is Sunna to specify the dower in the contract of marriage."[75]

The two Ibb contracts I quoted present alternative routes regarding the dower clause: one names a specific cash sum; the other gives the formulation "dower of those equivalent to her," which, again, accords with the Ibb script. This notion of equivalence may be thought of as an intimate or family version of established custom. In this understanding the bride should receive a dower equivalent to the dowers previously received by women like her, which I was told refers to her paternal aunts.[76] In his parenthetical advice on this contract, al-Iryānī advocates "mentioning the amount." In addition to his general caution about the role of "ambiguity" in dowry matters, he raises the specific problem of the potential nonequivalence of the aunts. He consistently prefers specification in contracts, which in this instance challenges the assumption of homogeneity or similarity in intrafamily identity. In his model text, however, al-Iryānī has it both ways. In a nod to prevailing usage, he combines the family custom formulation with specification: "for a dower of [those] equivalent [to her], the amount of which is such and such."

In my republican-era ethnographic experience, in addition to the dower, there lurked a second marriage payment, known as "the *sharṭ*" (a colloquial term that adds a definite article to the formal word for a contract "stipulation"). In contrast to the dower, the *sharṭ* tended to be a very substantial cash amount. In fact, the size of the *sharṭ* became something of a national issue and eventually led to legislation, since the inflation of this type of payment made it impossible for many potential grooms to afford to marry.[77] Unlike the doctrinal status of the dower, the *sharṭ* payment was entirely customary, with no standing in the *fiqh*. When asked about the various payments (including those known as "expenses" and "gifts") in Ibb marriages, the town muftī responded with a fatwā recognizing the dower alone.

While *sharṭ* payments weighed heavily on local marriage negotiations in my day, unlike dowers these sums were not mentioned in written marriage contracts. For the pre-revolutionary period, however, I lack the necessary historical detail concerning the possibility of unrecorded customary transfers such as the *sharṭ*, so I am unable to round out an understanding of the financial terms of marriage in that era. It nevertheless may be noted that the dower and the *sharṭ* differ in their structural implications. The former was the exclusive right of the woman being married while the latter went to her father or another representative of her paternal family, a distinction that had important implications for her personal finances. Together with the basic rule that required her prior consent to the contract, her right to the dower was integral to her overall agency in entering the sharīʿa marriage. Not simply a "gift" to her, the dower was something of ascertainable value, conceivably even a usufruct right, which was "delivered by the husband" and which the wife could accept or refuse, in the latter case possibly also signaling her non-consent to the marriage. According to the doctrine, even when she consented to the marriage and agreed to a specified dower, she could still reject its actual form when she inspected it upon receipt. Under the terms of this type of option (*khiyār*), she could claim, for example, that the actually received form of the dower was defective.[78] While conceptually consistent with the equivalent rights that pertained to other types of transactions such as sale, to my knowledge the exercise of such a technical option did not occur in Ibb.

In his model contract, al-Iryānī takes pains to specify the status of the dower transfer, which meant covering three temporal possibilities. He thus provides wording for the husband having actually "delivered" (*sallama*) the dower to the woman; his still owing it; and his having delivered it to the woman's father. Regarding the last possibility, in the event that the dower was transferred to the father or other marriage guardian, al-Iyrānī's language makes it clear that this individual received the dower only in his capacity as the marriage guardian for the woman being married, it being meant "for her benefit."

The second possibility—that the dower "remained the financial obligation of (*fī dhimma*) the husband"—opens further issues, including the distinction between what is known as the "prompt," as opposed to the "postponed," dower. The "prompt" dower refers to the first situation, that of the dower paid or "delivered," which also conformed with the completed conception of, and the past-tense verbs utilized in, standard contracts. In contrast, the "postponed" dower, as something of specified value owed but not yet paid to the wife, initiated an open-ended future obligation. Technically, a "postponed" dower became due in two eventualities: in a husband-initiated divorce (*ṭalāq*) or with his death. In both situations, the practical implications would depend on the dower in question being something more than a symbolic amount, or "a small sum," as it sometimes was in my day.

I turn now to a brief concluding excursus on the property analytic that underpinned both the marriage contract and a second type of divorce, which was initiated by the wife. Before I do so, however, I want to at least mention the locally documented outcomes associated with a husband's death. A wife's postponed dower represented a claim on the deceased husband's gross estate, to be deducted prior to the division of the net estate into the inheritance shares, which also included a standard share for the surviving wife. Historical documents from Ibb indicate that that such dower deductions were made in the settling of local estates.[79] Another perspective—

although not necessarily an instance of a postponement—is provided by an Ibb *baṣīra* from 1900, which states that the sale object came into possession of the female seller (who is represented by an agent) "by way of dower."[80] For his part, al-Iryānī provides the notarial reader formal directions for this scenario. In such an estate-related dower payment, al-Iryānī breaks the transaction down into a modeled series of documentary steps.[81]

Textual Bodies

The possibility of dower postponement is envisioned in early doctrinal texts, among them the late fourteenth-century *Flowers*.[82] Around 1920, Imam Yahya delivered a "choice" (*ikhtiyār*), an enforceable doctrinal opinion, which takes up the connection of dower postponement to local custom (*ʿurf*). Since an intervention from the imam was necessitated and subsequently generalized for application, it must be assumed that there were conflicts regarding the customary aspects of dowers in that period. I have no information, however, about a particular lawsuit or a pattern of disputes to which this choice responded, or about its subsequent application to other cases. In chapter 4, however, I discussed the origins of choices in the queries posed by appeal court judges to the imam asking for his authoritative and decisive view concerning the relation of *fiqh* issues to the substantive facts of particular hard cases. I also examined how the imam's case-specific responses were converted into applicable imamic choices, which was accomplished by "stripping" the archival details of the originating lawsuit. In reading the result—that is, the edited text of the freestanding choice—it is difficult to reconstruct the instigating claims and arguments. Yet in connection with Imam Yahya's choice on dower postponement, it seems clear enough that the imam directed the questioning judge, and, by extension, through the formally issued "choice," later judges, to rule on the basis of contract language rather than on that of prevailing custom.

Two decades later, commentator al-ʿAnsī located this specific imamic opinion with respect to the doctrinal corpus of the *Flowers* literature. He did so by placing a footnote to connect the specific wording in the *matn*, the text he was commenting on, to the imam's choice, which he reworded slightly in the note. His footnoted version opens by stating that a dower is not to be postponed "only on the [basis of] custom" (*bi-mujarrad al-ʿurf*).[83] The original language of the choice, as reported by Ibb jurist al-Ḥaddād and others, states, with the concision typical of the genre: "No consideration [is to be given] to the custom prevailing in some locales for the postponement of the dower of wives until death or divorce when this postponement is not mentioned expressly"—that is, formally stipulated in the contract.[84] The addressees of this directive—"No consideration . . ."—again, were the imam's appointed sharīʿa court judges of the era.

This choice is among the twenty-three by Imam Yahya that al-Shamāḥī, al-ʿAnsī's contemporary, commented on in his printed booklet of 1937. In restating the position taken regarding the role of custom in dower postponement, al-Shamāḥī highlights the imam's preference for explicit contractual language as opposed to the default authority of unspecified and variable custom. Where the imam's choice gives the formulation "mentioned expressly," al-Shamāḥī employs the term for a formal contractual stipulation, or *sharṭ*. Regarding the contractual force of such explicit and formal stipulations, al-Shamāḥī provides a general principle, one so well known to his readers as to make its identification as a Prophetic *ḥadīth* unnecessary: "The Believers are bound by their stipulations."[85]

Continuing to flesh out the imam's minimally stated view, al-Shamāḥī supplies an additional conceptualization: "Our Master, God support him, chose the non-necessity of a regard for custom, inasmuch as custom has no role in (*lā dakhl lahu fī*) supporting the transactions that are based on a counter-value, like sale." Al-Shamāḥī associates the marriage contract form with that of sale, but the logical tie referenced here takes the relation beyond the shared format of an "offer and acceptance" to include the structural equivalence of the two contracts as property transfers involving a counter-value (*ʿiwaḍ*).

In a sale, as I noted earlier, the transaction may be analyzed, in general terms, as the exchange of two *māl*s, or, somewhat more specifically, as the transfer of something of value for a counter-value. As the sale contract proceeds, this basic relation resolves into an exchange of a sale object for the price money. Finally in the same terminological sequence, with the reciprocal receipt and taking possession of the sale object and of the price, what had been the *milk*, or the individual property of the seller, "became"—in the written enactment of the past-tense verb *ṣār*—the *milk* of the buyer.

In marriage, the equivalent transfer object, from the woman to the man, is the right to intercourse with her, for which the dower, delivered by the man to the woman, represents the counter-value. Al-Shamāḥī quotes the early authority ʿAli bin Abī Ṭālib (d. 661)—for Shīʿīs, the first imam: "A vulva (*farj*) is not made lawful except by a dower." As established in this sharīʿa transaction, licit sexual access to the female body figured among the fundamental property relations of the agrarian age.[86] It did so, however, as a use right rather than as a form of complete ownership. In analytic terms, this feature brings the marriage contract close to the usufruct conception that underpins the lease contract and sharecropping as opposed to the complete ownership that results from the sale contract. As is specified in the doctrine, the right transferred in marriage refers narrowly to the *milk* of intercourse (*waṭʾ*), not to ownership of the woman's substance (*raqaba*), thus constituting the domain-specific analogy to the use right.[87] This use right defined the legitimate issue of the marriage, and therefore inheritance rights, among others.

While it figures prominently in the library jurists' doctrinal analyses, this more abstract property discourse is only latent in written marriage contracts. Yet in certain other archival genres it could turn up explicitly. In the cited court case from 1958, from which I earlier quoted the fraudulent marriage contract, the litigation record also transcribes another type of document, a related agency instrument. In it, using a verb from the same *m-l-k* root as *milk*, the noun of individual property, the young woman (whose father was deceased) is reported to have granted her paternal uncle the right to marry her "and to give her in [conjugal] ownership to his son ʿAziz (*wa-yumliku bi-ha li-ibnihi ʿAziz*)."[88] We learn from the court transcript, however, that this particular paper language act of agency was coerced.

A further textual manifestation of this underlying property conception figures in the wife-initiated divorce, termed *khulʿ*. This type of divorce is based on compensation paid to the husband to get his agreement to repudiate—that is, to get him to exercise his right of divorce. The doctrinal assumption is that the marriage dower (or an equivalent value) figures centrally in this compensation. For example, in a different imamic choice concerning irreconcilable marital differences (quoted in chapter 4), Imam Ahmad states, "The woman must return what she received as dower (*mahr*), and [then] either repudiation by the husband or [contract] dissolution (*faskh*) by the judge." In the notarial model provided for this type of divorce by al-Iryānī, the wife gives up, among other possible rights, that to her dower, if it had been postponed.[89]

At the archival level, a pre-revolutionary *khulʿ* document from Ibb shows the wife giving up her dower (*mahr*), the payment of which evidently had been postponed, and also her maintenance for the waiting period following the divorce (*nafaqat al-ʿidda*).[90] In another such document the wife gives up a series of financial rights, to maintenance, housing, etc., and the text also (like the first) concludes with "repudiation" (*ṭalāq*) pronounced by the husband.[91] The marriage dower is not mentioned, however, as it may not have been postponed. Another possibility is that there was a form of compensation that did not figure in the divorce instrument.

At the republican-era wife-initiated divorce I observed (see introduction), in which the wife also gave up her rights to maintenance, etc., the host slid a stack of money across the narrow rug separating the seated men representing the two sides. This financial inducement from the wife's side was said to be in return for what the husband had spent at the outset of the marriage. Rather than the contractual dower, which had been "a small sum," I was told that this compensation represented a return of "the *sharṭ*," the significant but undocumented customary payment originally made to the wife's family.

According to al-Iryānī and the general doctrine, both Shāfiʿī and Zaydī, in a wife-initiated divorce, the wife "gains ownership of herself" (*tamlīk . . . nafsaha*)—that is, she regains the right of sexual access exchanged in the marriage.[92] In this transfer, the marriage terms are reversed: the wife receives a value, the use right to intercourse (with herself), for a counter-value paid to the husband.

An Analytic

Rather than in the primary archival instruments, this deeper transactional logic of agrarian-age property was formally expressed and elaborated on in other genres of sharīʿa texts. As an example, early in his doctrinal chapter on the sale contract, after introducing the stipulation of an "offer," *Flowers* commentator al-ʿAnsī pauses to provide a one-sentence conceptual overview. In this compact summary he extends the sale paradigm to cover the other two contract types I have discussed in this chapter, along with the just-mentioned wife-initiated divorce. Taken together, these several transactions may be seen as constituting a system of types of exchange. In al-ʿAnsī's structural thinking this set of sharīʿa acts should be both associated with one another and also differentiated. In very succinct language, he indicates that the several acts share the sale contract form of an "offer and acceptance" while at the same time representing different types of property transfers. Each involves a contract-specific exchange of two values, *māl*s, or a value for a counter-value—with the exception of a gift, which he also includes but I have not discussed. Arranging sale, lease, marriage, and the wife-initiated divorce, plus gift, on a continuum of types—and in the process condensing the topical gist of entire doctrinal chapters—al-ʿAnsī follows the earlier jurists of his tradition in stating: "Every offer and acceptance for two *māl*s constitutes a sale; concerning a use right and a *māl*, a lease; concerning a *māl* and a vulva, a marriage; concerning a repudiation and a *māl*, a *khulʿ* divorce; and concerning a single *māl* alone, a gift."[93]

* * *

Were the models provided in the local "stipulations" treatise foundational to the production of notarial instruments in Ibb? Should the doctrinal value or accuracy of the local *baṣīra*, for example, be credited to the existence of the model script? Beyond the basic issue of the local readership of the *shurūṭ* treatise in the period, about which I lack information, I have suggested that two other modeling possibilities ought to be considered. One is that locally available doctrinal books, the works of *fiqh*, provided necessary and sufficient guidance for notarial writers, obviating any intervening need for such a *shurūṭ* work. The other would be to recognize the unremarked on but powerful role of another type of modeling for these complex Ibb instruments. This is the sort of modeling that derived, laterally, from the quiet authority of the existing, already achieved and archived, instruments of the same genres. This informal type of modeling was based on locally available "scripts," which were simply the given and established practices of such writings in the place and time. Notarial writers acquired the necessary knowledge directly, internalizing it in the course of the repeated activity of reading and drafting local instruments, through grounded discursive enactments in the era and realm of a particular formation of sharīʿa texts.

Even if al-Iryānī's "stipulations" treatise were to be considered a purely academic exercise, we learn from it nevertheless. We learn, in particular, about al-Iryānī as a reader—of both the accumulated doctrine of his school and of the documents of his era. We can see that he was influenced by technical juridical concerns and that he was well versed about the on-the-ground circumstances of the writing profession and its products. We learn, in sum, how he thought about sharīʿa theory for the purposes of a sharīʿa practice that he also knew firsthand.

Postscript

THIS BOOK ABOUT a particular past of the sharīʿa has sought to contribute to a general understanding of its premodern history. It also is meant to speak to the present. First, in our era, heinous and criminal acts have been committed in the name of the "sharīʿa," and in that of an "Islamic state." In addition, for chauvinistic political motives, legislatures in states such as Oklahoma have stigmatized the "sharīʿa" and acted to ban (the supposed possibility of) its application in the state courts. In such circumstances, knowledge of the history of the sharīʿa has a contemporary significance and urgency that reaches well beyond, but also informs and motivates, scholarship. Second, I completed this study in a time of war in and upon Yemen, a time of human suffering and devastation. I am ashamed that the United States has been a facilitator of aggression rather than a staunch advocate of peace. May the people of Yemen soon be able to return to building their own futures on the basis of their earlier demonstrated democratic and consultative impulses. As Yemenis are well aware, in the work of political reconstruction, knowledge of history is vital.

Muslim jurists referred to the historical literature of the sharīʿa, or what I term the library, as "an ocean without shores." The documentation associated with its archive is as vast. The practical consequence for me in this project was that I nearly drowned in my source materials. It was only after I decided to postpone other dimensions of the project and to focus on matters of textuality that I was able to bring this book into the harbor. At that juncture, Lila Abu-Lughod provided crucial advice and encouragement. I hope now to turn to two related studies on topics that are foreshadowed in the present book with respect to their textual dimensions—one on "sharīʿa litigation," raising issues of judicial method, truth, evidence, and interpretation, and one on the "agrarian sharīʿa," concerning the relations of landed property, trade, state, and family.

I want to acknowledge the support over the years of my friend Dr. Muhammad Aziz, of Ibb, and Yale University. I am grateful as well for discussions with my friend the public intellectual and scholar Abdullah Hamidaddin, and for the timely infusion of a shipment of books published by the Imam Zayd bin ʿAli Cultural Foundation. Lucine Taminian at one point brought me the four volumes of Shawkānī's *Sayl* from Yemen; Etienne Renaud provided a copy of al-Shamāḥī's *Ṣirāṭ* and access to the original edition of al-ʿAnsī's *Tāj*, both from the collection he brought from Yemen to Rome; John Willis gave me a copy of al-Ḥaddād's *ʿUmdat al-qāriʾ*; and Bernard Haykel lent me his copy of the four volumes of Ibn Muẓaffar's *Bayān*.

As for the archival documents on which this study is equally based, in the preceding pages I have recognized by name the individuals who provided access to the major bodies of these sources. In my time in Yemen, I had the great good fortune to be allowed to photograph or photocopy the sources I sought, and also to be shown writings I did not know existed. People in Ibb and elsewhere in the highlands engaged generously and thoughtfully with my research, and I feel the deep responsibility of their trust in me with these normally guarded materials.

For the support of my long-term research in Yemen, I am grateful to the Social Science Research Council, the Fulbright Program, and the John Simon Guggenheim Foundation, as well as to the University of Michigan and Columbia University.

In my dual intellectual traditions, anthropology and Islamic studies, I have numerous inspiring colleagues on whose efforts I have tried to build. Many of their names are cited in this book. Columbia University has a deep history in both fields of inquiry. At the turn-of-the-twentieth century, Franz Boas built the first modern Department of Anthropology and Richard Gottheil, a student of the sharīʿa, led that known as Oriental Languages. Joseph Schacht was the key mid-century figure in the western study of the sharīʿa, and among his prominent Columbia students from the next generation, Jeanette Wakin warmly welcomed me to the university and Susan

Spectorsky read an early version of this book. My colleague Wael Hallaq arrived at Columbia bearing his just-published *Sharīʿa* (2009) an astonishing scholarly achievement that immediately became the new standard in the field. Najam Haider, my more recent colleague, quickly produced two indispensible books on the sharīʿa and on Shīʿism, both of which include important materials on the Zaydī tradition.

At the center of my Columbia experience in the study of the sharīʿa has been my long-running Anthropology Department seminar on Islamic law, in which I have benefited from the knowledge, ideas, and questions of generations of superb students, some of whom read versions of the chapters in this book. I want to recognize, in particular, Dilyara Agisheva, Sonia Ahsan, Asif Akhtar, Youssef Belal, Caitlyn Bolton, Deniz Duruiz, Omar Farahat, John Halliwell, Sarah Hawas, Ibrahim El Houdaiby, Sohaib Khan, James King, Maya Mikdashi, Ali Moughania, Hélène Quiniou, Yasmina Raiani, Hillel Athias-Robles, Maryam Rutner, Manuel Schwab, Omer Shah, Sophia Stamatopoulou-Robbins, Allia Tamzali, Merve Tezcanli, Ian VanderMeulen, Amin Venjara, Arthur Zárate, Maheen Zaman, Selma Zecevic, and Hengameh Ziai.

Beyond Columbia, I salute the stalwart interlocutors of my decades-long engagement with the sharīʿa, including David Powers, Khalid Masud, Baber Johansen, Norman Calder, Zouhair Ghazzal, Rudolph Peters, Khaled Fahmy, and Beshara Doumani. In recent years, I have learned from the work of Guy Burak, Clark Lombardi, Samera Esmier, Tamer el-Leithy, Ghislaine Lydon, Instisar Rabb, Ahmad El Shamsy, Asad Ahmed, Behnam Sadeghi, and Alexandre Caeiro. For the inspiration I have found in their innovative scholarship, I also thank Setrag Manoukian, Sofian Merabet, Naveeda Khan, Amira Mittermaier, and Fadi Bardawil.

The pair of specialist anthropological communities I have relied on includes those who work on the sharīʿa—especially Lawrence Rosen, Clifford Geertz, Talal Asad, Michael Gilsenan, John Bowen, Ziba Mir-Hosseini, Baudouin Dupret, Léon Buskens, Hussein Agrama, Carolyn Fluehr-Lobban, Michael Peletz, Morgan Clarke, Ido Shahar, Nada Moumtaz, Aria Nakissa, and Matthew Erie—and those who have conducted research in Yemen—including Martha Mundy, Paul Dresch, Steven Caton, Daniel Varisco, Najwa Adra, Lucine Taminian, Anna Würth, Shelagh Weir, Engseng Ho, Ann Meneley, Gabriele vom Bruck, Flagg Miller, Lisa Wedeen, Franck Mermier, and Eirik

Hovden. To these names I would add, as specialists on the Jews of Yemen, S. D. Goitein, whom I am honored to have known, Issac Hollander, Mark Wagner, and Alan Verskin and, as specialists on the history of the region in the late Ottoman period, Jon Mandaville, Isa Blumi, Thomas Kuehn, and John Willis.

Translation, combined with transliteration, is fundamental to the analytic method of this book. I have followed the standard IJMES transliteration system. Only last names are transliterated. Hijrī dates, where mentioned, are followed by the CE date.

For help in preparing the images that appear in this book, I thank Thomas Roma, Kai McBride and Sheryl Crespo. With the exception of figure 4.4, all images were taken and provided by me.

For their careful attention to the publication process, I thank Anne Routon, Miriam Grossman, Kathryn Jorge, and Glenn Perkins of Columbia University Press. And for their astute readings and comments, I thank the two anonymous readers arranged by the press.

I dedicate this work to Karen and to Tyler, Hayley, and Brigitte.

Notes

Abbreviations

EI2 *Encyclopedia of Islam*, 2nd ed., ed. P. Bearman, Th. Bianquis, C. E. Bosworth, E. van Donzel, and W. P. Heinrichs (Leiden: Brill, 2002), http://referenceworks.brillonline.com/browse/encyclopaedia-of-islam-2

EI3 *Encyclopedia of Islam, Three*, ed. Gudrun Krämer, Denis Matringe, John Nawas, and Everett Rowson (Leiden: Brill, 2007–), http://referenceworks.brillonline.com/browse/encyclopaedia-of-islam-3

EQ *Encyclopedia of the Qur'an*, ed. Jane Dammen McAuliffe (Leiden: Brill, 2012–), http://referenceworks.brillonline.com/browse/encyclopaedia-of-the-quran

Introduction

1. Ahmad bin Yahya al-Murtaḍā (Ibn al-Murtaḍā, d. 1437), *Kitāb al-azhār fī fiqh al-a'imma al-aṭhār*, 4th printing (n.p.: n.p., 1972), which I refer to in the text as *The Book of Flowers* or the *Flowers*. The commentary in question is ʿAbd Allah bin Muhammad Ibn Miftāḥ (d. 1472), *al-Muntazaʿ al-mukhtār min al-ghayth al-midrār*, 4 vols. (Cairo: Maṭbaʿa al-dīniyya, 1341 AH [1922]; Ṣanʿā': Maktaba Ghamḍān, 1401 AH [1980]). It is known, and I refer to it, as *The Commentary on the Flowers*, and I cite it as *Sharḥ al-azhār*. (I occasionally also cite a 2003 edition, [Ṣanʿā']: al-Jumhūriyya al-Yamaniyya, Wizārat al-ʿAdl, 2003.) A third principal doctrinal source is a twentieth-century commentary on the *Flowers*: Ahmad bin Qasim al-ʿAnsī (d. 1970), *al-Tāj al-mudhhab li-aḥkām al-madhhab sharḥ matn al-azhār fī fiqh al-a'immat al-aṭhār*, 4 vols. (1938–47; reprint, Ṣanʿā': Dār al-Ḥikma al-Yamāniyya, 1993), which I refer to in the text as the *Gilded Crown*.

2. See Brinkley Messick, *The Calligraphic State* (Berkeley: University of California Press, 1993), chap. 7.

3. Ahmad ibn al-Husayn Ibn Raslān al-Ramlī, *al-Zubad fī fiqh al-Shāfiʿī* (Cairo: ʿĀlam al-Fikr, 1977). This work was commented on by an Ibb jurist known as al-Muftī al-Ḥubayshī al-Ibbī (d. 1866). Muhammad bin ʿAli bin Muḥsin, *Fatḥ al-mannān sharḥ zubad Ibn Raslān*, ed. ʿAbd Allah al-Ḥibshī (Ṣanʿāʾ: Maktab al-Jīl al-Jadīd, 1988).

4. Transcendent and immanent: a founding figure in the study of religion understood these features of the divinity as "complementary." William Robertson Smith, *Lectures on the Religion of the Semites* (New York: Ktav Publishing, 1969 [rpt. of 3rd ed. of 1927; 1st ed., 1894]), 194, 563–64.

5. For discussions of genre by anthropologists, see Karin Barber, *The Anthropology of Texts, Persons and Publics: Oral and Written Culture in Africa and Beyond* (Cambridge: Cambridge University Press, 2007); Charles L. Briggs and Richard Bauman, "Genre, Intertextuality, and Social Power," *Journal of Linguistic Anthropology* 2, no. 2 (1992): 131–72; and John Bowen, *Sumatran Politics and Poetics: Gayo History, 1900–1989* (New Haven: Yale University Press, 1991), 140–43.

6. Hayden V. White, *The Content of the Form: Narrative Discourse and Historical Representation* (Baltimore: Johns Hopkins University Press, 1987), xi.

7. Edward W. Said, *The World, the Text, and the Critic* (Cambridge, MA: Harvard University Press, 1983), 45, referencing Nietzsche.

8. Wilferd Madelung, "Imāma," 3:1163–69, in *EI2*; Dominique Sourdel and Ann K. S. Lambton, "Khalīfa," in *EI2*, 4:937–50. Lambton states that the terms are "broadly interchangeable," although she notes a "preference" for *imām* in the *fiqh* literature. Crone and Hinds remark that the term *khalīfa* also is used among the Shīʿīs, except for the Zaydīs (although, as I note later, this would change in the twentieth century). Patricia Crone and Martin Hinds, *God's Caliph: Religious Authority in the First Centuries of Islam* (Cambridge: Cambridge University Press, 1986), 12–13, 17–18. Cf. the Yemeni commentator on the *Flowers*, Muhammad bin ʿAli al-Shawkānī, *Sayl al-jarrār al-mutadaffiq ʿalā ḥadāʾiq al-azhār*, 4 vols., ed. Maḥmūd Zāyid (Beirut: Dār al-Kutub al-ʿIlmiyya, 1985), 4:506: "The meaning of the caliphate is [the same as] the meaning of the imamate in the custom of the sharīʿa" (*maʿnā al-khilāfa maʿnā al-imāma fī ʿurf al-sharīʿa*).

9. Sunnī examples. The Shāfiʿī jurist Muhiy ad-Dīn Yahya Ibn Sharaf al-Nawawī (d. 1277), *Minhaj al-ṭālibīn* (Cairo: Dār Iḥyāʾ al-Kutub al-ʿArabiyya, [1956]), 120, on the general requirements for becoming an imam; 128, role in the *jizya* tax system; 125–26, 129, in *jihad* and armistice; 138, in the appointment of judges; and 114, 121–24, in capital punishment and the *ḥudūd* punishments. Another Shāfiʿī example, also studied in Ibb, is Ibn Raslān, *Zubad*, which was commented on by the Ibb jurist al-Muftī al-Ḥubayshī, *Fatḥ al-mannān*, 33. A Shīʿī example is the Jaʿfarī (Twelver) jurist Muḥaqqiq al-Ḥillī (d. 1277), *Sharāʾiʿ al-islām fī al-fiqh al-islāmī al-jaʿfarī*, 2 vols. in 1 (Beirut: Maktaba al-Ḥayā, 1930), 1:59, on the role of the *imām al-aṣl* ("the original imam") in prayer; 1:94–97, in the financial institution of the *khums*; 1:146–53, in *jihād*; 1:154–58, in the *jizya*; 1:159–60, in "commanding the right and the forbidding the wrong" and the *ḥudūd* punishments; 2:168–70, in the "enlivening of dead land"; 2:204–7, on the appointment of judges and the imam as judge; 2:247–48, 251, etc., further on the role in the *ḥudūd*. See also such specialized Sunnī juridical

works as ʿAli ibn Muhammad al-Māwardī (d. 1058), *al-Aḥkām al-sulṭāniyya wa-l-wilāyat al-dīniyya* (Cairo: Dār al-Fikr, 1983), and Ahmad ibn Idrīs al-Qarāfī (d. 1285), *al-Iḥkām fī tamyīz al-fatāwā ʿan al-aḥkām wa-taṣarrufāt al-qāḍī wa-l-imām* (Aleppo: Maktab al-Matbūʿāt al-Islāmiyya, 1967).

10. "*Yajibu ʿalā al-muslimīna sharʿan naṣbu imāmin.*" Ibn al-Murtaḍā, *Azhār*, 313. The Shāfiʿī Ibn Raslān, employs the same verb: "*farḍun ʿalā al-nāsi imāmun yunṣabu.*" al-Muftī al-Ḥubayshī, *Fatḥ al-mannān*, 33.

11. Ibn al-Murtaḍā, *Azhār*, 313.

12. See, for example, the short chapter "*Kitāb al-imāma*" by the author of the *Flowers*, Ahmad ibn Yahya al-Murtaḍā (Ibn al-Murtaḍā), in his *Kitāb al-qalāʾid fī taṣḥīḥ al-ʿaqāʾid*, which appears before his *Kitāb al-baḥr al-zakhkhār al-jāmiʿ li-madhāhib ʿulamāʾ al-amṣār* (Beirut: Muʾassasat al-risālah, 1975), intro. vol.: 91–98. For a comparative discussion of theological conceptions regarding Shīʿī imams, including the Zaydīs, see Najam Haider, *Shīʿī Islam: An Introduction* (Cambridge: Cambridge University Press, 2014).

13. E.g., Ibn Miftāḥ, *Sharḥ al-azhār*, 3:1–44, in a section on biographies, sects, and books; 4:518n5. Al-ʿAnsī, *Tāj*, 4:305n2.

14. Ibn al-Murtaḍā, "Kitāb al-imāma," 92.

15. "*Khaṭaʾ al-imām*" and "*qadḥān fī ʿadālat al-imām.*" Al-ʿAnsī, *Tāj*, 4:199, 200, 202, 409; Ibn Miftāḥ, *Sharḥ al-azhār*, 4:325, 329n2, 521. Cf. Haider, *Shīʿī Islam*, 42–43, 46.

16. Émile Tyan, *Institutions du Droit Public Musulman*, 2 vols. (Paris: Recueil Sirey, 1956), 2:485; Madelung, "Imāma," 1166; Bernard Haykel, *Revival and Reform in Islam: The Legacy of Muhammad al-Shawkani* (Cambridge: Cambridge University Press, 2003), 7; Aron Zysow, "Zaydis," *The Princeton Encyclopedia of Islamic Political Thought*, ed. Gerhard Böwering et al. (Princeton: Princeton University Press, 2012), 605–6: with the important exception of the narrow descent requirement, "the qualifications . . . mirror those set down by Sunni jurists for the caliph."

17. Ibn Miftāḥ, *Sharḥ al-azhār*, 4:520n8; cf. Al-ʿAnsī, *Tāj*, 4:407n2.

18. For imamate institutions in adjacent regions in recent times, see, for Oman, John C. Wilkinson, *The Imamate Tradition of Oman* (New York: Cambridge University Press, 1987), and Dale F. Eickelman, "From Theocracy to Monarchy: Authority and Legitimacy in Inner Oman, 1935–1957," *International Journal of Middle East Studies* 17, no. 1 (1985): 3–24; for the early twentieth-century Idrīsī state in ʿAsīr, see Anne K. Bang, *The Idrisi State in ʿAsir, 1906–1934: Politics, Religion and Personal Prestige as State-building Factors in Early Twentieth-Century Arabia* (Bergen: Centre for Middle Eastern and Islamic Studies, 1996).

19. Joseph Schacht, *An Introduction to Islamic Law* (Oxford: Clarendon Press, 1964), 76.

20. Wael B. Hallaq, *Sharīʿa: Theory, Practice, Transformations* (Cambridge: Cambridge University Press, 2009), 369.

21. Schacht, *Introduction*, 210–11; Hallaq, *Sharīʿa*, 362. Hallaq understands this agency of the juridical schools to entail an independent mode of "governance," which he compares and contrasts with that of a modern nation-state inasmuch as both functioned as "lawgivers." Historical Muslim states were stratified into rulers and ruled, and the sharīʿa "governed" the latter, the ordinary population, in a "non-state, community-based, bottom-up jural system" (78, 201, 361, 549). In such historical situations, the "law operated horizontally."

22. Schacht, *Introduction*, chap. 26.

23. Ibid., 2, 199, 209. Schacht devotes a separate chapter to the question of "Theory and Practice," 76–85.

24. Max Weber, *Economy and Society* (Berkeley: University of California Press, 1978), 820-22; Schacht, *Introduction*, 5, 209.

25. In Hallaq's account, Yemen once was a "major center," but became "marginal" to general history "after the third/ninth century." Hallaq, *Sharīʿa*, 44, 183 358, 401. Schacht's principal source for the modern Zaydī imamate appears to have been a book by G. Wyman Bury, an adventurer, bird specimen collector, and British political agent who visited the highlands in 1912 during the last years of Ottoman provincial rule. The gist of what he learned from Bury, who reported the negative remarks made by his soldier-guides, was that the imam "tried to enforce pure Islamic law . . . against the opposition of the people." Schacht, *Introduction*, 88. On Bury himself, see the foreword to the republication of his book, George Wyman Bury, *Arabia Infelix, or, The Turks in Yamen*, Folios Archive Library (Reading: Garnet, 1998).

26. For earlier periods, see Rudolf Strothmann, *Das Staatsrecht Der Zaiditen* (Strassburg: K. J. Trübner, 1912); Cornelis Van Arendonk, *Les débuts de l'imamat Zaidite au Yemen*, trans. Jacques Ryckmans (Leiden: Brill, 1960); and Wilferd Madelung, *Der Imam Al-Qasim Ibn Ibrahim Und Die Glaubenslehre Der Zaiditen* (Berlin: Walter de Gruyter, 1965).

27. For this later period, the key work is Bernard Haykel, *Revival and Reform*, 68–72, 84–85.

28. Shawkānī, *Sayl*, 4:503–12.

29. Al-Hasan bin Yahya Ḥamīd al-Dīn (d. 2003) was governor (*nāʾib* of the imam) in Ibb in the 1940s. He later resided in exile in the United States. On June 13, 1993, I interviewed him at his home in Teaneck, New Jersey, after which he kindly took me out for lunch at a local diner.

30. Among the old rubrics, the silver *riyāl* coin of 1344 AH (1925) identifies Yahya bin Muhammad Ḥamīd al-Dīn as both the *imām* and *amīr al-muʾminīn*, but the same coin also states that it was minted at the *dār al-khilāfa* in Ṣanʿāʾ.

31. Haykel, *Revival and Reform*, 210–12; Paul Dresch, *A History of Modern Yemen* (Cambridge: Cambridge University Press, 2000), 35, 43–44.

32. David Thomas Gochenour III, "The Penetration of Zaydi Islam into Early Medieval Yemen" (PhD thesis, Harvard University, 1984).

33. These appointments of court judges by the ruler and his supervision of their work run counter to the assumption that "Islamic law was never supported by an organized power," Schacht, *Introduction*, 2, and that the "legal profession . . . was generally independent of any state regulation," Wael B. Hallaq, *A History of Islamic Legal Theories: An Introduction to Sunnī uṣūl al-fiqh* (Cambridge: Cambridge University Press, 1997), 208.

34. Among the Ibb *sāda* (sing., *sayyid*), or descendants of the Prophet, the al-ʿIzzī family traces its line to al-Hasan bin al-Qasim; the Mutawakkil family of Ibb and Jibla to Ismaʿil bin al-Qasim . My interlocutors cited the well-known biographical history, Muhammad ʿAli al- Shawkānī, *al-Badr al-ṭāliʿ bi-maḥāsin man baʿd al-qarn sābiʿ*, ed. Muhammad Zabāra, 2 vols. (Cairo: al-Saʿāda, 1348 AH [1929]). For non-*sāda*

jurists, see Messick, *Calligraphic State*, 41n20, 45. I collected the genealogies of some "tribal" families and that of a line of craftsmen, all of whose ancestors were from Upper Yemen.

35. See Thomas Kuehn, *Empire, Islam, and the Politics of Difference: Ottoman Rule in Yemen, 1849–1919* (Leiden: Brill, 2011), esp. 106–16, and John M. Willis, *Unmaking North and South: Cartographies of the Yemeni Past, 1857–1934* (New York: Columbia University Press, 2011), chap. 4–5.

36. Endowed (*waqf*) property, another important category, was created from individually held *milk*.

37. For the Ottoman Levant, see Martha Mundy and Richard Saumarez Smith, *Governing Property, Making the State: Law, Administration and Production in Ottoman Syria* (London: I. B. Tauris, 2007), 13. Referring to *kanun* (also *qānūn*), the non-sharīʿa law promulgated by sultans, they write: "On conquest the [Ottoman] administration confirmed the particular imposts paid by the cultivators in formal *kanuns*, within a thoroughgoing doctrine of treasury ownership of land. The land was known as *miri* (of the ruler) distinct from individual *mulk* [*milk*] land." For Egypt, see Kenneth Cuno, *The Pasha's Peasants: Land, Society and Economy in Lower Egypt, 1740–1858* (Cambridge: Cambridge University Press, 1992), 65: "The *qanuns* also limited the jurisdiction of the sharīʿa over most arable land by defining nearly all of it as *miri*, or state-owned. Not being owned by the peasants, it was not subject to the regulations of the sharīʿa that applied to full property (*milk*) in such areas as sale, bequest, and inheritance."

38. "[S]tudies of ownership and landed property . . . have tended to be framed exclusively in terms of Islamic legal categories that often bear little relationship to actual practice." Roger Owen, introduction to *New Perspectives on Property and Land in the Middle East*, ed. R. Owen (Cambridge, MA: Harvard University Press, 2000), ix.

39. Al-ʿAnsī, *Tāj*.

40. Raymond Williams, *Marxism and Literature* (Oxford: Oxford University Press, 1977), 145–50.

41. Talal Asad, *The Idea of an Anthropology of Islam* (Washington, DC: Occasional Papers Series, Center for Contemporary Arab Studies, Georgetown University, 1986).

42. Whereas "time disappears" for the theorist, "practice is inseparable from temporality." Pierre Bourdieu, *The Logic of Practice* (Stanford: Stanford University Press, 1990), 81.

43. Ibid., 86: "practice has a logic which is not that of the logician."

44. Michel Foucault, "What Is an Author?" in *Language, Counter-Memory, Practice: Selected Essays and Interviews* (Ithaca: Cornell University Press, 1977), 113–38.

45. Ibid., 124.

46. Ibid., 137.

47. Schacht, *Introduction*, 113–14. This is to generalize his notion. His reference is to the arrangement of the "subject-matter" in his principal source, a book of *fiqh*.

48. Bruno Latour, "How to Make a File Ripe for Use," in *The Making of Law: An Ethnography of the Conseil d'Etat*, trans. Marina Brilman and Alain Pottage, revised by the author (Cambridge: Polity Press, 2010), 70–106, esp. 84–87, where the material relation also is visualized in figure 2.7. Finished and bound texts are arranged

vertically on the shelves and the active documents are in folders placed flat on the table. Latour states, "The entire work consists in establishing the relation between these two collections of writings." Cf. Cornelia Vismann, *Files: Law and Media Technology*, trans. Geoffrey Winthrop-Young (Stanford: Stanford University Press, 2008), who studies how "law and files mutually determine each other" (xiii). Charles Hirschkind, *The Ethical Soundscape: Cassette Sermons and Islamic Counterpublics* (New York: Columbia University Press, 2006).

49. On historical paper and watermarks in Yemen, see Anne Regourd, ed., *Catalogue cumulé des manuscrits de bibliothèques privées de Zabid. 1. La bibliothèque de 'Abd al-Rahman al-Hadhrami*, fasc. 1, *Les papiers filigranés* (Ṣanᶜāʾ: CEFAS, FSD, 2008).

50. See Charles Stewart, "Great and Little Traditions," in *Encyclopedia of Social and Cultural Anthropology*, ed. Alan Barnard and Jonathan Spencer (London: Routledge, 1998).

51. Clifford Geertz, *Local Knowledge: Further Essays in Interpretive Anthropology* (New York: Basic Books, 1983).

52. Sheldon Pollock, Homi K. Bhabha, Carol A. Breckenridge, and Dipesh Chakrabarty, "Cosmopolitanisms," *Public Culture* 12, no. 3 (2000): 577–89. See also, Derryl N. MacLean and Sikeena Karmali Ahmed, eds., *Cosmopolitanisms in Muslim Contexts: Perspectives from the Past* (Edinburgh: Edinburgh University Press in association with the Aga Khan University, 2012).

53. Sheldon Pollock, "Cosmopolitan and Vernacular in History," *Public Culture* 12, no. 3 (2000): 591–625, quote at 599.

54. Arjun Appadurai. *Modernity at Large* (Minneapolis: University of Minnesota Press, 1996), chap. 9.

55. Pollock et al., "Cosmopolitanisms," 582.

56. Pollock, "Cosmopolitan and Vernacular in History," 606: "Vernacularization is a new way of doing things with texts, especially written literary texts, in a stay-at-home language. By written, I exclude the oral, even if the written may continue to be performed and received orally; by literary, I exclude the documentary."

57. Pollock et al., "Cosmopolitanisms"; Pollock, "Cosmopolitan and Vernacular in History," 594.

58. Sherman A. Jackson, *Islamic Law and the State: The Constitutional Jurisprudence of Shihāb al-Dīn al-Qarāfī* (Leiden: Brill, 1996) describes the predominance of the Shāfiᶜī school over the Mālikī in Mamlūk-period Egypt. The reverse situation obtained during the Ottoman centuries in the Levant, where the Shāfiᶜī was subordinate to the official Ḥanafī school. Regarding relations between specific Sunnī and Shīᶜī schools, Devin Stewart, *Islamic Legal Orthodoxy: Twelver Shiite Responses to the Sunni Legal System* (Salt Lake City: University of Utah Press, 1998), analyzes interchanges between Shāfiᶜīs and Twelvers among jurists in Iran. Richard Bulliet, *The Patricians of Nishapur* (Cambridge, MA: Harvard University Press, 1972), describes how, in an urban setting in tenth-century Iran, the Ḥanafī and Shāfiᶜī *madhhabs* came to represent opposed political affiliations. For a conceptualization of *madhhab* relations in terms of "legal pluralism," see Iris Agmon and Ido Shahar, "Shifting Perspectives in the Study of Sharīᶜa Courts: Methodologies and Paradigms," *Islamic Law and Society* 15, no. 1 (2008): 1–19.

59. Engseng Ho, *The Graves of Tarim: Genealogy and Mobility Across the Indian Ocean* (Berkeley: University of California Press, 2006), 188–91. Ho refers to the far-flung Ḥaḍramis of the Indian Ocean littoral, a diaspora linked by genealogical texts.

60. For overviews, see G. Libson and Frank Stewart, " ʿUrf," in *EI2*. For extended analyses with specific reference to the sharīʿa, see Baber Johansen, "Coutumes locales et coutumes universelles aux sources des règles juridique en Droit musulman hanéfite," *Annales Islamologiques* 27 (1993): 29–35, and Zouhair Ghazzal, *The Grammars of Adjudication: The Economics of Judicial Decision Making in Fin-de-siècle Ottoman Beirut and Damascus* (Beirut: Institut Français du Proche-Orient, 2007), 35–108.

61. Schacht, *Introduction*, 62.

62. Paul Dresch, *Tribes, Government, and History in Yemen* (Oxford: Clarendon Press, 1989); Dresch, *The Rules of Barat: Tribal Documents from Yemen* (Ṣanʿāʾ: Centre français d'archéologie et des sciences sociales, 2006); Martha Mundy, *Domestic Government: Kinship, Community and Polity in North Yemen* (London: I. B. Tauris, 1995); Shelagh Weir, *A Tribal Order: Politics and Law in the Mountains of Yemen* (Austin: University of Texas Press, 2007).

63. Schacht, *Introduction*, 77.

64. R. B. Serjeant, "The Statute of Ṣanʿāʾ (*Qānūn Ṣanʿāʾ*)," in *Ṣanʿāʾ: An Arabian Islamic City*, by R. B. Serjeant and Ronald Lewcock (London: World of Islam Festival Trust, 1983), 179–240; Franck Mermier, *Le cheikh de la nuit* (Arles: Sinbad/Actes Sud, 1997).

65. Baber Johansen, *Contingency in a Sacred Law: Legal and Ethical Norms in the Muslim Fiqh* (Leiden: Brill, 1999), 42–72, details the genesis of this view, tracing it to the late nineteenth century and the work of the Dutch Orientalist C. Snouck Hurgronje (d. 1936). Johansen remarks that this and related negative views of the sharīʿa later became the "common property," the shared set of assumptions, of subsequent western scholarship. On the "Colonial Sharīʿa," see Messick, *Calligraphic State*, 58–68.

66. Schacht, *Introduction*, v.

67. Ibid., 81, 85n.

68. For a review, see Dror Ze'evi, "The Use of Ottoman Sharīʿa Court Records as a Source for Middle Eastern Social History: A Reappraisal," *Islamic Law and Society* 5, no. 1 (1998): 35–56.

69. Ze'evi identifies "the *sijill* as a text" as one of the "areas in which little work has been done" (ibid., 53). See, however, Boğaç A. Ergene, *Local Court, Provincial Society and Justice in the Ottoman Empire* (Leiden: Brill, 2003), chap. 7.

70. Baber Johansen, *The Islamic Law on Land Tax and Rent* (London: Croom Helm, 1988), 125. Cf. Johansen, *Contingency*, 464.

71. Ghazzal, *Grammars*, 3.

72. Ibid.

73. For a recent advocacy of a "critical philology," see Sheldon Pollock, "Future Philology?: The Fate of a Soft Science in a Hard World," *Critical Inquiry* 35, no. 4 (2009): 931–61. See also Michel Foucault, *The Order of Things: An Archaeology of the Human Sciences* (New York: Pantheon, 1970), xii, 280–307, and Edward Said, *Humanism and Democratic Criticism* (New York: Columbia University Press, 2004).

74. For Islamic epigraphy, see Sheila S. Blair, *Islamic Inscriptions* (Edinburgh: Edinburgh University Press, 1998). On paleography and codicology, see the overview by Jan Just Witkam, "Nuskha," in *EI2*, and the related articles "Daftar" and "Khaṭṭ." See also Yasin Dutton, ed., *The Codicology of Islamic Manuscripts* (London: al-Furqān Islamic Heritage Foundation, 1995). On papyrology, see R. G. Khoury, "Papyrus," in *EI2*, and Petra M. Sijpesteijn and Lennart Sundelin, eds., *Papyrology and the History of Early Islamic Egypt* (Leiden: Brill, 2004). For diplomatic, see W. Björkman, "Diplomatic, i. Classical Arabic," in *EI2*.

75. A recent work edited by Alessandro Bausi et al., *Comparative Oriental Manuscript Studies* (Hamburg: Tredition, 2015), states that the project "does not focus on the contents as such. . . . Contents have been considered only insofar as they were strictly functional, to illustrate issues concerning codicology, principles of text editing, cataloguing, conservation, preservation and restoration. To deal with the contents of the texts would have meant dealing with the unmanageable mass of knowledge." The project "deals with manuscripts as intellectual products of written cultures in the ancient, mediaeval and pre-modern period, before the introduction of printing; it considers manuscripts as products of literary activity, as opposed, as a rule, to purely archival or documentary materials" (1).

76. A foundational work in the first field is Johannes Pederson, *The Arabic Book*, trans. Geoffrey French (1946; reprint, Princeton: Princeton University Press, 1984). See also George N. Atiyeh, ed., *The Book in the Islamic World: The Written Word and Communication in the Middle East* (Albany: State University of New York Press, 1995). On the "history of reading," see Konrad Hirschler, *The Written Word in the Medieval Arabic Lands* (Edinburgh: Edinburgh University Press, 2012). For the second field, see Gregor Schoeler, *The Oral and the Written in Early Islam*, trans. Uwe Vagelpohl (London: Routledge, 2006).

77. Franz Boas, "The History of Anthropology," *Science* 20, no. 512 (1904): 513–24, at 523.

78. George Stocking, *The Ethnographer's Magic and Other Essays in the History of Anthropology* (Madison: University of Wisconsin Press, 1992); James Clifford, "Notes on Fieldnotes," in *Fieldnotes: The Makings of Anthropology*, ed. Roger Sanjek (Ithaca: Cornell University Press, 1990), 47–70; Briggs and Bauman, "Genre," 133; Richard Bauman and Charles L. Briggs, *Voices of Modernity: Language Ideologies and the Politics of Inequality* (Cambridge: Cambridge University Press, 2003), 267–69. See also Williams, *Marxism and Literature*, 26–27. In a brief article, Boas named the connection: Franz Boas, "Some Philological Aspects of Anthropological Research," *Science* 23, no. 591 (1906): 641–45. Malinowski, however, rejected philology categorically.

79. The terms of this break were on display in 1939–40, in a pair of *American Anthropologist* articles by Margaret Mead, Boas's famous student, and Robert Lowie, a prominent old school Boasian. Mead advocated a new method that, not unlike that established two decades earlier by Malinowski, whom she cites, shifts the weight of research activity from the old emphasis on the collection of past-oriented "accurate verbatim texts" and the use of interpreters (a "highly suspect method") to one that is present-oriented and that directly engages the anthropologist in the "recording" of ongoing social life. Unlike Malinowski, Mead specifically rejected what she caustically refers to as linguistic "virtuosity" on the part of the anthropologist—

that is, any more language capacity than the bare minimum necessary for the research task at hand. In response, as opposed to what he refers to as Mead's "streamlined" method, Lowie defends his "horse-and-buggy" mode of ethnography. For Lowie, the basic objective remains to "record as many texts as we can." Margaret Mead, "Native Languages as Field-Work Tools," *American Anthropologist* 41, no. 2 (1939): 189–205; Robert Lowie, "Native Languages as Ethnographic Tools," *American Anthropologist* 42, no. 1 (1940), 81–89.

80. Ian Watt and Jack Goody, "The Consequences of Literacy," *Comparative Studies in Society and History* 5, no. 3 (1963): 304–45; Jack Goody, ed., *Literacy in Traditional Societies* (Cambridge: Cambridge University Press, 1968); Goody, *The Logic of Writing and the Organization of Society* (Cambridge: Cambridge University Press, 1986); Goody, *The Interface Between the Written and the Oral* (Cambridge: Cambridge University Press, 1987); Goody, *The Power of the Written Tradition* (Washington, DC: Smithsonian Institution Press, 2000); Clifford Geertz, *The Interpretation of Cultures* (New York: Basic Books, 1973).

81. Talal Asad, ed., *Anthropology and the Colonial Encounter* (London: Ithaca Press, 1973). His mentor, E. E. Evans-Pritchard, wrote an early work of historical anthropology, *The Sanusi of Cyrenaica* (Oxford: Clarendon Press, 1949).

82. Talal Asad, "The Concept of Cultural Translation in British Social Anthropology," in *Genealogies of Religion: Discipline and Reasons of Power in Christianity and Islam* (Baltimore: Johns Hopkins University Press, 1993), 171–99, originally published in *Writing Culture*, ed. George Marcus and James Clifford (Berkeley: University of California Press, 1986).

83. Ibid., 199.

84. Ibid., 174, emphasis in original. In the same period, Jean and John Comaroff similarly state that this type of anthropological research "must begin by constructing its own archive." John L. Comaroff and Jean Comaroff, *Ethnography and the Historical Imagination* (Boulder: Westview, 1992), 34.

85. Asad, *Anthropology of Islam*. For discussion, see Saba Mahmood, *Politics of Piety: The Islamic Revival and the Feminist Subject* (Princeton: Princeton University Press, 2005), 113–17; David Scott and Charles Hirschkind, *Powers of the Secular Modern: Talal Asad and His Interlocutors* (Stanford: Stanford University Press, 2006), esp. 288–90; Ovamir Anjum, "Islam as a Discursive Tradition: Talal Asad and His Interlocutors," *Comparative Studies of South Asia, Africa and the Middle East* 27, no. 3 (2007): 656–72; Nada Moumtaz, "Refiguring Islam," in *A Companion to the Anthropology of the Middle East*, ed. Soraya Altorki (Hoboken, NJ: Wiley, 2015), 125–50; and Fadi A. Bardawil, "The Solitary Analyst of Doxas: An Interview with Talal Asad," *Comparative Studies of South Asia, Africa and the Middle East* 36, no. 1 (2016): 152–73.

86. Asad, *Anthropology of Islam*, 14.

87. Ibid., 15.

88. Ibid., 14–15: "an *ʿalim*, a *khatib*, a Sufi *shaykh*, or an untutored parent."

89. Talal Asad, "The Limits of Religious Criticism in the Middle East," in *Genealogies of Religion*, 200–236.

90. Ibid., 212.

91. Ibid., 215–19.

92. Ibid., 221.

93. Asad, *Anthropology of Islam*, 17.

94. Asad, "Religious Criticism," 201.

95. Ibid., 232.

96. Talal Asad, "Reconfigurations of Law and Ethics in Colonial Egypt," in Asad, *Formations of the Secular: Christianity, Islam, Modernity* (Stanford: Stanford University Press, 2003), 205–56.

97. Ibid., 209.

98. Ibid., 228–33.

99. On transliteration techniques as an index of disciplinary history, see Brinkley Messick, "Notes on Transliteration," in *Translating Cultures: Perspectives on Translation and Anthropology*, ed. Paula G. Rubel and Abraham Rosman (Oxford: Berg, 2003), 177–196.

100. Asad, "Reconfigurations," 227–32. Asad refers to Foucault on "governmentality," to how the modern state mobilizes "a new knowledge (political economy) and directs it at a new object (population). It is in this context that 'the family' emerges as a category in law."

101. Asad, *Anthropology of Islam*, 17.

102. "Genealogy is not intended here as a substitute for social history ('real history,' as many would put it) but a way of working back from our present to the contingencies that have come together to give us our certainties." Asad, *Formations of the Secular*, 16. On the issue of a contradiction between the approaches of genealogy and tradition, see David Scott, "The Tragic Sensibility of Talal Asad," and Asad's "Response to Scott," in Scott and Hirschkind, *Powers of the Secular Modern*, 137–39, 233–35.

103. Asad, "Religious Criticism," 200.

104. Talal Asad, "Thinking About Religion, Tradition, and Politics in Egypt Today," *Critical Inquiry* 42 (Autumn 2015): 166–214.

105. Hussein Agrama, *Questioning Secularism: Islam, Sovereignty, and the Rule of Law in Modern Egypt* (Chicago: University of Chicago Press, 2012).

106. Asad, "Thinking," 178–80.

107. Ibid., 179. For appraisals of anthropological work on the sharīʿa and "virtue ethics," see Morgan Clarke, "Legalism and the Care of the Self: Sharīʿah Discourse in Contemporary Lebanon," in *Legalism: Rules and Categories*, ed. Paul Dresch and Judith Scheele (Oxford: Oxford University Press, 2015), and Aria Nakissa, "An Ethical Solution to the Problem of Legal Indeterminacy: Sharīʿa Scholarship at Egypt's al-Azhar," *Journal of the Royal Anthropological Institute* (N.S.) 20 (2014): 93–112.

108. See Asad, "Thinking," for important elaborations. For *al-amr bi-l-maʿrūf*, see Michael Cook, *Commanding Right and Forbidding Wrong in Islamic Thought* (Cambridge: Cambridge University Press, 2000); for *ḥisba*, see Cl. Cahen, M. Talbi, R. Mantran, A. K. S. Lambton, and A. S. Bazmee Ansari, "Ḥisba.," in *EI2*.

109. For *naṣīḥa* and *al-amr bi-l-maʿrūf*, see al-ʿAnsī, *Tāj*, 4:413, 468–81; for *ḥisba*, which is mentioned in passing in ʿAnsī, *Tāj*, 4:202, and the treatise by Imam al-Nāṣir li-ʾl-Ḥaqq al-Hasan bin ʿAli al-Uṭrus (d. 917), studied by Robert B. Serjeant, "A Zaidī Manual of Ḥisba of the 3rd Century (H)," *Rivista degli Studi Orientali* 28 (1957): 1–34, reprinted in R. B. Serjeant, *Studies in Arabian History* (London: Variorum, 1981). Cf., infra, chapter 1, n120, on *naṣīḥa* by Ibb Judge Hasan al-Iryānī to Imam Yahya.

110. Asad, *Formations of the Secular*, 226; cf. 209, 225.

111. On the relationship between the Zaydīs and Sufis, see Wilferd Madelung, "Zaydī attitudes to Sufism," in *Islamic Mysticism Contested*, ed. Frederick De Jong and Bernd Radtke (Leiden: Brill, 1999), 124–44, and Muhammad Ali Aziz, *Religion and Mysticism in Early Islam: Theology and Sufism in Yemen* (London: I. B. Tauris, 2011), chap. 8.

112. My attention to rules coincides with a renewed interest among scholars in studies of "legalism." See Paul Dresch, "Introduction to Legalism, Anthropology and History: A View from a Part of Anthropology," in *Legalism: Anthropology and History*, ed. P. Dresch and Hannah Skoda (Oxford: Oxford University Press, 2012). It coincides, more specifically, with the integrated approaches to sharīʿa rules by anthropologists such as Morgan Clarke and Aria Nakissa. Morgan Clarke, "The Judge as Tragic Hero: Judicial Ethics in Lebanon's Shariʿa Courts," *American Ethnologist* 39, no. 1 (2012): 106–21; Aria Nakissa, "An Epistemic Shift in Islamic Law: Educational Reform at al-Azhar and Dār al-ʿUlūm," *Islamic Law and Society* 21 (2014): 209–51.

113. Mikhail M. Bakhtin, *The Dialogic Imagination: Four Essays* (Austin: University of Texas Press, 1981); Valentin N. Voloshinov, *Marxism and the Philosophy of Language* (New York: Seminar Press, 1973), 72; Bakhtin, *Speech Genres and Other Late Essays*, trans. Vern W. McGee (Austin: University of Texas Press, 1986).

114. Annelise Riles, ed., *Documents: Artifacts of Modern Knowledge* (Ann Arbor: University of Michigan Press, 2006). Riles and several of her contributors "focus on questions of form" (18–20). Attention to "form" is also central to innovative work by historical anthropologists on the colonial archive. See Penelope Papailias, *Genres of Recollection: Archival Poetics and Modern Greece* (New York: Palgrave Macmillan, 2005); Ilana Feldman, *Governing Gaza: Bureaucracy, Authority, and the Work of Rule, 1917-1967* (Durham, NC: Duke University Press, 2008); and Ann Laura Stoler, *Along the Archival Grain: Epistemic Anxieties and Colonial Common Sense* (Princeton: Princeton University Press, 2009), 20, 46–53. Issues of both materiality and form are basic to the analysis of written texts in Matthew S. Hull, *Government of Paper: The Materiality of Bureaucracy in Urban Pakistan* (Berkeley: University of California Press, 2012).

115. Williams distinguishes between the "process" of composition and its "result," the finished literary work. He observes that in conventional approaches to "literature" the former dimension typically drops out of the analysis, resulting in "the effective suppression of this process and its circumstances." Williams, *Marxism and Literature*, 46. Bruno Latour, "Steps Toward the Writing of a Compositionist Manifesto," *New Literary History* 41 (2010): 471–90, observes that the term "underlines that things have to be put together (Latin *componere*) while retaining their heterogeneity" (473–74). See also Barber, *Anthropology of Texts*, 214, 222–23, on "assemblage as a mode of composition."

116. Bakhtin, *Dialogic Imagination*, 342–45; Bakhtin, *Speech Genres*, 88.

117. John A. Lucy, ed., *Reflexive Language: Reported Speech and Metapragmatics* (Cambridge: Cambridge University Press, 1993); Kathryn A. Wollard and Bambi B. Schieffelin, "Language Ideology," *Annual Review of Anthropology* 23 (1994): 55–82; Judith T. Irvine and Susan Gal, *Regimes of Language: Ideologies, Politics, and Identities* (Santa Fe: School for Advanced Research, 2000); Bauman and Briggs, *Voices of Modernity*.

Susan Hirsch applies this type of analysis in her work on spoken discourse in a Kenyan sharīʿa court, *Pronouncing and Persevering: Gender and the Discourses of Disputing in an African Islamic Court* (Chicago: University of Chicago Press, 1998).

118. Matthew S. Hull, "The File: Agency, Authority, and Autography in an Islamabad Bureaucracy," *Language & Communication* 23 (2003): 293–94; Hull, *Government of Paper*, 14.

119. Norman Calder, "Nawawī and the Typologies of Fiqh Writing," in *Islamic Jurisprudence in the Classical Era*, ed. Colin Imber (Cambridge: Cambridge University Press, 2010), 74–115; Calder, "Al-Nawawī's Typology of *Muftīs* and Its Significance for a General Theory of Islamic Law," *Islamic Law and Society* 3, no. 2 (1996): 137–64.

120. Franz Boas, *Handbook of American Indian Languages* (Washington, DC: Government Printing Office, 1911), part 1, 63–73. Cf. Boas, "The Ethnological Significance of Esoteric Doctrines," in *Race, Language and Culture* (New York: Free Press, 1966), 312–15. While studying societies "in their own terms" is a hallmark of Boasian anthropology, the data Boas valued most derived their authority from their largely unreflective or fully unconscious character. Linguistic data were especially important because the categories of language "never rise into consciousness." As for other ethnological phenomena, "although the same unconscious origin prevails, these often rise into consciousness, and thus give rise to secondary reasoning and to re-interpretation." Boas generally turned away from what he perceived as the perils of the "secondary explanations" provided by the people studied, although he acknowledged that this sort of information filled fieldworkers' notebooks. For Boas the scientist, the conscious understandings of contemporary natives represented "misleading and disturbing factors," which "generally obscure the real history of the development of ideas."

Across differing theoretical frames, anthropologists of the succeeding generations targeted cultural phenomena that hovered near, or below, the threshold of consciousness. Thus Lévi-Strauss: "history organizes its data in relation to conscious expressions of social life, while anthropology proceeds by examining its unconscious foundations." Claude Lévi-Strauss, *Structural Anthropology*, trans. Claire Jacobson (New York: Basic Books, 1967), 19, 25–26. For Clifford Geertz, "[I]nformants frequently, even habitually, make second order interpretations—what have come to be known as 'native models.' In literate cultures, where 'native' interpretations can proceed to higher levels—in connection with the Maghreb [Northwest Africa], one has only to think of Ibn Khaldun; with the United States, Margaret Mead—these matters become intricate indeed" (*Interpretation of Cultures*, 15n). Geertz does not bring the challenge of this intricacy up from the footnote to be pursued in his main text. He instead held that the proper object of cultural analysis was "the informal logic of actual life" (17). For Pierre Bourdieu, "native theories are dangerous." Bourdieu, *Outline of a Theory of Practice* (Cambridge: Cambridge University Press, 1977), 19; Bourdieu, *Logic of Practice*, 286.

121. *Webster's Third New International Dictionary* (Springfield: Merriam-Webster, 1993).

122. This is to repurpose a pair of concepts first introduced into anthropology by Clifford Geertz, *Interpretation of Cultures*, 93–94, in reference to cultural symbols. The models examined here, however, are specifically written. Writing interrupts and defers a potentially more fluid dialectic. I should note in this connection that

my approach to the library and the archive in terms of modeling relations differs from a study of the wider relation of "law and society." In her study of modern family law in Iran and Morocco, Ziba Mir-Hosseini considers substantive sharīʿa doctrine on the family as a "model" in relation to "existing family patterns." She draws on Sally Falk Moore's conception of law as "both prescriptive and descriptive," as involving a "double image . . . both directing and reflecting social organization." Mir-Hosseini takes a pair of basic questions for her comparative project: "when and under what circumstances does Islamic law direct, and when and under what circumstances does it reflect?" She also sets forth the received wisdom: "In Islam, law is assumed to direct but not reflect the social order." Ziba Mir-Hosseni, *Marriage on Trial: A Study of Islamic Family Law* (London: I. B. Tauris, 1993), 14.

123. Wael B. Hallaq, "From Fatwās to Furūʿ: Growth and Change in Islamic Substantive Law," *Islamic Law and Society* 1, no. 1 (1994): 29–65, at 44; Hallaq, "Model Shurūṭ Works and the Dialectic of Doctrine and Practice," *Islamic Law and Society* 2, no. 2 (1995): 109–34, at 124.

124. Barber, *Anthropology of Texts*, 204, 208, 219, notes the analytic potential of this "bottom-up" perspective and the associated dialectical, "two-way movement between prestigious genres and popular ones."

125. Hull, "The File," 293–94, similarly distinguishes between an "official or normatively standardizing graphic ideology" and an "unofficial graphic ideology," the former contained in administrative manuals, the latter representing an "understanding of artifacts in practice." In *The Calligraphic State*, I describe a "textual habitus" as "[a] set of acquired dispositions concerning writing and the spoken word, and the authoritative conveyance of meaning in texts . . . reproduced in homologous structures and practices across the different genres and institutions. It was the resulting, partly implicit, experience of coherence amid diversity, the reaffirming of basic orientations through multiple forms and sites of expression that enhanced the natural qualities of the dispositions themselves. From domain to domain, the quiet redundancies of discursive routines were mutually confirming" (251).

126. An institution partially theorized by an early jurist, ʿAbd al-Karim bin Muhammad al-Samʿānī (d. 1166), *Adab al-imlāʾ wa-l-istimlāʾ* (Leiden: Brill, 1952). Cf. George Makdisi, "Scholasticism and Humanism in Classical Islam and the Christian West," *Journal of the American Oriental Society* 109, no. 2 (1989): 175–82.

127. Latour, *Making of Law*, 92.

128. Barber, *Anthropology of Texts*, 22–24.

129. D. B. MacDonald and S. A. Bonebakker, "Iḳtibās," in *EI2*; see also W. P. Heinrichs, Julie Scott Meisami, and Paul Starkey, "Rhetorical Figures," *Encyclopedia of Arabic Literature* (New York: Routledge, 1998), 656–62.

130. Voloshinov, *Marxism and the Philosophy of Language*, 115–23; Lucy, *Reflexive Language*; Dennis Tedlock and Bruce Mannheim, *The Dialogic Emergence of Culture* (Urbana: University of Illinois Press, 1995).

131. Bakhtin, *Speech Genres*, 62; Bakhtin, *Dialogic Imagination*, 320–21. Bakhtin's main example was the novel. Hull, "The File," 295–96, likewise extends this concept to the "graphic genres."

132. Thus Julia Kristeva, *Desire in Language* (New York: Columbia University Press, 1980), 66, refers to "absorption and transformation"; Roman Jakobson, cited in

Carlo Ginzburg, *Clues, Myths, and the Historical Method*, trans. John and Anne Tedeschi (Baltimore: Johns Hopkins University Press, 1989), 159, 161, to texts "appropriated and remodeled"; and Jacques Derrida, *Margins of Philosophy*, trans. Alan Bass (Chicago: University of Chicago Press, 1982), 317, 320, to processes of "extraction and grafting" and of "disengagement and citational graft." Among linguistic anthropologists influenced by Bakhtin, Richard Bauman and Charles L. Briggs, "Poetics and Performances as Critical Perspectives on Language and Social Life," *Annual Review of Anthropology* 19, no. 1 (1990): 59–88, at 72 and n2, use the terms "decontextualization and recontextualization"; while Michael Silverstein and Greg Urban, *Natural Histories of Discourse* (Chicago: University of Chicago Press, 1996), 1, refer to "simultaneous processes of entextualization and co(n)textualization."

133. Bakhtin, *Dialogic Imagination*, 255, 324, 330, 341. Cf. Tzevtan Todorov, *Mikhail Bakhtin: The Dialogical Principle* (Manchester: Manchester University Press, 1984), 48.

134. Cf. Bakhtin's integrated time-space concept, the "chronotope," in *Dialogic Imagination*, 84–258.

135. Michel de Certeau, *The Practice of Everyday Life*, trans. Steven Rendall (Berkeley: University of California Press, 1984), 171; cf. Hans-Georg Gadamer, *Truth and Method* (New York: Seabury Press, 1975), 164, who states that a work is "actualized," or "presented," when it is read.

136. Bakhtin, *Dialogic Imagination*, 295–96.

137. Mentioned in an appeal of a finding concerning the dispute by the First Secretary of the Ibb Court, July 1977 (*Murājaʿa*, Digital C095). The term *ḥāʾil* (space) also figures in the doctrine of prayer; see al-ʿAnsī, *Tāj*, 1:92.

138. Thus Derrida: "archivization produces as much as it records the event." Jacques Derrida, *Archive Fever*, trans. E. Prenowitz (Chicago: University of Chicago Press, 1996), 16–17.

1. Books

1. On the *madhhab*, see Peri Bearman, Rudolph Peters, and Frank E. Vogel, eds., *The Islamic School of Law* (Cambridge, MA: Harvard University Press, 2005). For the rise and later consolidation of the Sunnī *madhhab*s between the ninth and eleventh centuries, see Christopher Melchert, *The Formation of the Sunni Schools of Law* (Leiden: Brill, 1997). On the textual consolidation of an official *madhhab*, see Guy Burak, *The Second Formation of Islamic Law: The Ḥanafī School in the Early Modern Ottoman Empire* (New York: Cambridge University Press, 2015).

2. For the state of the broader field, see Sabine Schmidtke, "The History of Zaydī Studies: An Introduction," *Arabica* 59 (2012): 185–99.

3. On the imamic-period madrasa in Ibb, see Messick, *Calligraphic State*, chap. 4.

4. See Haykel, *Revival and Reform*, and Messick, *Calligraphic State*, 42–45, and passim.

5. Messick, *Calligraphic State*, 68–72.

6. Muhammad bin Yahya bin al-Muṭahhar (Ibn al-Muṭahhar), *Aḥkām al-aḥwāl al-shakhṣiyya*, 2 vols. (Cairo: Dār al-Kutub al-Islāmiyya, 1985; Ṣanʿāʾ: Dār al-Fikr, 1989).

A biography of al-Muṭahhar, by Muhammad al-Akwaʿ, in handwritten facsimile, is in 1:5–11.

7. Muhammad Zabāra and Ahmad Zabāra, *Nuzhat al-naẓar fī baʿḍ aʿyān al-qarn al-rābiʿ ʿashar* (MS, 4 vols., Ṣanʿāʾ, n.d.), 4:83–84. This manuscript is based on the father's published book, which has a slightly different title: Muhammad Zabāra, *Nuzhat al-naẓar fī rijāl al-qarn al-rābiʿ ʿashar.* (Ṣanʿāʾ: Markaz al-Dirāsāt wa-l-Abḥāth al-Yamaniyya, 1979). On the genesis of the father-and-son manuscript book, see below.

8. I first saw (and photocopied) this book as a manuscript. It was published posthumously as Muhammad bin ʿAli al-Ghurbānī, *ʿIlm uṣūl al-ḥadīth* (n.p., 2007).

9. On the early Zaydīs in Kūfa, see Najam Haider, *The Origins of the Shīʿa: Identity, Ritual, and Sacred Space in Eighth-Century Kūfa* (Cambridge: Cambridge University Press, 2011).

10. Bernard Haykel and Aron Zysow, "What Makes a *Madhhab* a *Madhhab*: Zaydī Debates on the Structure of Legal Authority," *Arabica* 59 (2012): 32–71.

11. Ibid., 340. I also am grateful to Abdullah Hamidaddin for discussions on this topic.

12. Ibid., 341. The two further generations are known as the *muḥaṣṣilūn* and the *mudhākirūn*.

13. For his biography and a listing of his writings, see Shawkānī, *al-Badr al-ṭāliʿ*, 1:122–26; ʿAbd Allah bin Muhammad al-Ḥibshī, *Maṣādir al-fikr al-Islāmī fī al-Yaman* (Beirut: al-Maktaba al-ʿAṣrīyya, 1988), 634–47.

14. Shawkānī, *al-Badr al-ṭāliʿ*, 1:123.

15. Lit. his "memorized texts" (*maḥfūẓāt*).

16. The Zaydī exegete al-Faqīh Yūsuf (d. 1429) understands this verb to be equivalent to "dictate." Yūsuf bin Ahmad bin Muhammad bin ʿUthmān (al-Thulāʾī), known as al-Faqīh Yūsuf, *Thamarāt al-yāniʿa wa-l-aḥkām al-wāḍiḥa al-qāṭiʿa*, 5 vols. (Saʿda: Maktaba al-turāth al-islāmī, 2002), 2:136.

17. Al-Ḥibshī, *Maṣādir*, 636, quoting the historian Abū al-Rijāl; cf. Husayn bin ʿAbdullah al-ʿAmrī, *The Yemen in the 18th and 19th Centuries* (London: Ithaca Press, 1985), 153, 168, and nn64, 76. A further dimension of the story of the *Flowers* concerns its being based on a monumental prior work, which is currently being brought out in a print edition. See Imam Yahya bin Ḥamza (d. 1344), *al-Intiṣār ʿalā ʿulamāʾ al-amṣār* (Ṣanʿāʾ: Maktaba al-Imām Zayd bin ʿAlī, 2005–), 1:1. Cf. al-Ḥibshī, *Maṣādir*, 635.

18. Roland Barthes, *The Pleasure of the Text*, trans. Richard Miller (New York: Hill and Wang, 1975), 66.

19. The questions and the answer appear in Ibn Miftāḥ, *Sharḥ al-azhār*, 3: 45. The text is reproduced by the republican-era jurist Husayn bin Ahmad al Sayāghī, *al-Madhhab al-zaydī al-yamanī* (Ṣanʿāʾ: Maktaba Ghamḍān, 1984), 28, who states that it was transcribed by ʿAbd al-Wasiʿ bin Yahya al-Wāsiʿī, the twentieth-century Yemeni historian responsible for seeing the *Commentary on the Flowers* into print. For a more complete translation of the questions and answer, see Haykel and Zysow, *Madhhab*, 339–40. A similar question-and-answer set, concerned with the *Commentary on the Flowers* itself, appears in Ibn Miftāḥ, *Sharḥ al-azhār* (2003), 1:11, viz., on the "*madhhab* contained in the *Sharḥ al-azhār.*"

20. "Qawāʿid wa uṣūl." The paired terms *qawāʿid* and *usūl* are repeated by Imam al-Qasim. Haykel and Zysow, 339–40, translate the two, together, as "principles."

See Ahmad bin Muhammad al-Sharafī, "Qawāʿid ahl al-madhhab," included in Ibn Miftāḥ, *Sharḥ al-azhār*, 3:46–8. Sayāghī, *al-Madhhab al-zaydī*, 29–35, gives 89 *qawāʿid* of Faqīh Hasan bin ʿAbd Allah Dalāma. Two such *qawāʿid* concern fatwā-giving; see chapter 4.

Similar concepts occasionally figured at the level of court cases. See Brinkley Messick, "Interpreting Tears: A Marriage Case from Imamic Yemen," in *The Islamic Marriage Contract: Case Studies in Family Law*, ed. Asifa Quraishi and Frank E. Vogel (Cambridge, MA: Harvard University Press, 2008), 175, in which an *aṣl*, cited by a litigant, has to do with assumptions associated with "the contracts of Muslims." In another trial, an *aṣl*, cited by the judge, is the presumption of sanity. In chapter 7, I refer to these as cases 4 and 1.

For recent work on *qawāʿid*, or sharīʿa "maxims," see W. P. Heinrichs, "Ḳawāʿid Fiḳhiyya," in *EI2*; Intisar Rabb, "Islamic Legal Maxims as Substantive Canons of Construction: *Hudud* Avoidance in Cases of Doubt," *Islamic Law and Society* 17 (2010): 63–125; Rabb, "Legal Maxims," *Oxford Encyclopedia of Islam and Law*, ed. Jonathan Brown et al. (Oxford: Oxford University Press, forthcoming); and Necmettin Kizilkaya, "Outline of the Historical Evolution of Qawāʿid Literature in Islamic Law," *American Journal of Islamic Social Sciences* 28, no. 1 (2011): 76–105.

21. Ibn Miftāḥ, *Sharḥ al-azhār*, 3:45.

22. Wilferd Madelung, "Zaydīyya," in *EI2*. Madelung refers to Muhammad bin Ibrahịm al-Wazīr (d. 1439) and to later jurists, up to Muhammad ʿAli al-Shawkānī. Cook, *Commanding Right and Forbidding Wrong*, 247–51, refers to the "Sunnisation of Zaydīsm." Cf. Haykel, *Revival and Reform*, 231.

23. Muhammad bin Ismāʿīl al-Amīr (Ibn al-Amīr al-Ṣanʿānī), *Minḥat al-ghaffār ʿalā ḍawʾ al-nahār*, an extended gloss text printed together with the *Flowers* commentary by Hasan al-Jalāl, *Ḍawʾ al-nahār*, 4 vols. (Ṣanʿāʾ: Majlis al-Qaḍāʾ al-Aʿlā, n.d.); Shawkānī, *Sayl*.

24. Other such labeled sub-genres in this literature include *farʿ*, *fāʾida*, and *ḍabṭ*.

25. *Al-Ghayth al-midrār*, Ibn al-Murtaḍā's commentary on his own work, is not published. On his sister's commentary, see al-Ḥibshī, *Maṣādir*, 220, 635–37; cf. al-ʿAmrī, *The Yemen*, 153; al-ʿAmrī, *Maṣādir turāth al-yamanī fī al-mathaf al-birīṭānī* (Damascus, 1981), 192–217. According to Husayn Ahmad al-Sayāghī, the editor of the *Dawʿ al-nahār* (1:15), al-Jalāl's daughter Fāṭima studied the "sharīʿa sciences" with him. The editor states that he saw her handwriting in a manuscript of the work, which was evidence of her instructional "recitation" (*qirāʾa*) to her father.

26. Ibn Miftāḥ, *Sharḥ al-azhār*. While it is a commentary on the *Flowers*, its title describes this work as a "chosen extract" (*muntazaʿ mukhtār*) from the *Flowers* author's commentary. Another work by a student of Ibn al-Murtaḍā also is authoritative, although it is not a commentary on the *Flowers*: Yahya bin Ahmad bin al-Muẓaffar (Ibn al-Muẓaffar), *Kitāb al-bayān al-shāfī al-muntazaʿ min al-burhān al-kāfī*, 4 vols. (Ṣanʿāʾ: Maktabat Ghamḍān, 1984).

27. Shawkānī, *al-Badr al-ṭāliʿ*, 2:214ff. He mentions the *Flowers* first among his "memorized texts," his *maḥfūẓāt*.

28. Sayāghī, *Madhhab al-zaydī*, 18.

29. Shawkānī, *Sayl*. See al-ʿAmrī, *The Yemen*, 152–64. M. Zabāra, *Nuzhat al-naẓar*, 150n2, says of al-Jalāl's *Dawʾ al-nahār*, the seventeenth-century commentary on the

Flowers, that it is "among the books which criticized *The Book of Flowers* by Imam al-Mahdī [Ahmad] bin Yahya al-Murtaḍā, and Shawkānī relied on it in his book the *Raging Torrent*." Cf. al-Ḥibshī, *Maṣādir*, 635–36, who speaks generally of the "critical commentaries" (*al-shurūḥ al-nāqida*) written by the "Sunnīs."

30. The *Sayl al-jarrār* elicited, in its turn, a heated response from a Hādawī scholar. See Haykel, *Revival and Reform*, 180–82, and al-ʿAmri, *The Yemen*, 129, 138n131.

31. Al-ʿAnsī, *Tāj*.

32. An example is al-ʿAnsī's reduction of a "requirement" to a "recommendation," which necessitated a numbering change in his commentary. Al-ʿAnsī, *Tāj*, 4:187.

33. Cf. Ibn Khaldūn, *The Muqaddimah*, trans. Franz Rosenthal (Princeton: Princeton University Press, 1967), 3:290–91. On the *mukhtaṣar* versus the *mabsūṭ*, see Norman Calder, "Law," in *History of Islamic Philosophy*, ed. Seyyed Hossein Nasr and Oliver Leaman (London: Routledge, 1996), 986, a discussion illustrated by Shawkānī's comments on short and long works of *fiqh* by a Yemeni Shāfiʿī. I should note that there were abbreviations of the *Flowers*, one of which, by Imam Sharaf al-Dīn, is mentioned in chapter 5.

34. Al-ʿAnsī, *Tāj*, 1:45. Internal guillemet quotation marks original.

35. In the first such note, al-ʿAnsī, *Tāj*, 1:13–14n1, explains that he has added the choices of Imam Yahya to complete the value of the *Gilded Crown*. He states that these choices represent the interpretive work of a just *mujtahid* imam for the benefit of the community of Muslims. He also explains that he "attached each choice to its location" in the text. He obtained the choices themselves "from the sharīʿa Appeal Court in Ṣanʿāʾ, Yemen, and from the *Ṣirāṭ al-ʿārifīn ilā idrāk ikhtiyārāt amīr al-muʾminīn*, by their versifier and commentator, the learned Qāḍī ʿAbd Allah bin ʿAbd al-Wahhāb al-Mujāhid al-Shamāḥī." Some of al-ʿAnsī's later footnotes appropriate language from al-Shamāḥī's commentary, e.g., 3:288n1, the first part of which is without attribution from al-Shamāḥī, *Ṣirāṭ*, 44.

36. E.g., from the *Flowers* tradition, the earlier-mentioned Ibn al-Amīr, *Minḥat al-ghaffār*, an extended gloss on *Ḍawʾ al-nahār*, by al-Jalāl. From the Shāfiʿī, a gloss on the principal commentary on the *matn* of Abū Shujāʿ: Ibrāhīm bin Muhammad al-Bājūrī, *Ḥāshiya ʿalā sharḥ Ibn Qasim al-Ghazzī* (Beirut: Dār al-Maʿrifa, 1974).

37. A notice that appears on the title page of Ibn Miftāḥ, *Sharḥ al-azhār*, vol. 1, states that for this print edition the marginal glosses and the explanatory remarks placed between the lines in manuscripts were relocated in a numbered series below the main (*aṣl*) text—that is, below the commentary containing the *matn*.

38. This, too, is explained on the title page of the *Sharḥ al-azhār*, where two types of marks are differentiated. The terms for these marks are *tadhhīb* and *taqrīr*, the latter placed at the end of a line of gloss. *Tadhhīb* marks also appear as superscripts in the commentary text itself. A note concerning the two terms (Ibn Miftāḥ, *Sharḥ al-azhār*, 3:55n) states, "there is no difference between them." The same note also makes an important observation about such marks of doctrinal positions: "a basic principle of *tadhhīb* and *taqrīr* is that neither occurs except with difference (*khilāf*)"—that is, in a situation of conflicting views.

39. Eirik Hovden, "Flowers in Fiqh and Constructions of Validity: Practices and Norms in Yemeni Foundations of Forever Flowing Charity" (PhD thesis, University

of Bergen, 2012), 243–54. Hovden discusses efforts to systematize these marks, and he suggests that they may indicate a *madhhab* authority structure comparable to the *ẓāhir al-riwāya* of the Ḥanafī school. Among the Shāfiʿīs, Nawawī uses the term *madhhab* to indicate the commonly accepted positions of his school, and *naṣṣ* (lit. "text") to indicate the view of al-Shāfiʿī himself. See Messick, *Calligraphic State*, 34–35.

40. Al-ʿAnsī, *Tāj*, 2:3, 2:40, 3:73, 4:81. Mixed references include 4:32: "This is the *madhhab* of al-Qasim and al-Hādī and al-Muʾayyad billah and Abū Ḥanīfa and al-Manṣūr billah, and al-Shāfiʿī."

41. Al-ʿAnsī, *Tāj*, 1:5. *Taqrīr*, again, is another term for *tadhhīb*.

42. Walter J. Ong, *Orality and Literacy: The Technologizing of the Word* (London: Methuen, 1982), 122.

43. Ibn Miftāḥ, *Sharḥ al-azhār*, 3: 43–44, 55–56. For the *rumūz* and *iṣtilāḥāt* in the *matn* of the *Flowers*, see Ibn al-Murtaḍā, *Azhār*, 7.

44. Abbreviations for *aṣḥāb al-Shāfiʿī* and for *ʿan al-Shāfiʿī*, etc.

45. For the *rumūz*, see Ibn al-Murtaḍā, *Baḥr*, intro. vol.: 32–35, and William J. Donaldson, *Sharecropping in the Yemen: A Study of Islamic Theory, Custom and Pragmatism* (Leiden: Brill, 2000), 96–98.

46. Sayāghī, *al-Madhhab al-zaydī*, 8.

47. Rudolf Strothmann, "Al-Zaidīya," *Shorter Encyclopedia of Islam*, ed. H. A. R. Gibb and J. H. Kramers (Leiden: Brill; Ithaca: Cornell University Press, 1965), 651–52.

48. Haykel, *Revival and Reform*, 206–9. Haykel cites the work of R. B. Serjeant and Ismaʿil al-Akwaʿ as examples of how this idea influenced later scholarship.

49. E.g., al-ʿAnsī, *Tāj*, 3:212, lines 2–3 (two *matn* words, *fī al-ikhbār*, are displaced into the *sharḥ* text); 4:84, lines 3–5 (drops two *matn* words); 4:84–85, line 18 (awkward break-up of *matn* word, *al-iqrār*, plus a voweling mistake—*imma* versus the correct *amma*) 4:86, line 3 (an awkward break-up of *matn* language); 4:112, line 20 (mistakenly[?] adds the negative *lā* before the *matn* verb).

50. Al-ʿAnsī, *Tāj*, 4:404n1, explains his reversal of the *matn* word order as an effort to "coordinate the commentary with the *matn* (*li-intiẓām al-sharḥ maʿa al-matn*) in expression and meaning."

51. A detail in the mechanics of quotation related to the *qāla*, or "he said" form, is explained in an editor's note. This concerns the significance of two slightly different formulations used in quoting the *Flowers* author, Imam al-Mahdī al-Murtaḍā. According to the editor's note,

> The difference between the statement of the commentator, "our master, peace upon him, said," and, "he, peace upon him, said," is that if previously in the commentary there had been words of some imams, and if he [the commentator] wants to report the words of Imam al-Mahdī, he says, "our master said," but if there had not previously been words of anyone then he says "he, peace upon him, said."
>
> (Ibn Miftāḥ, *Sharḥ al-azhār*, 3:55)

52. Norman Calder, *Studies in Early Muslim Jurisprudence* (Oxford: Clarendon Press, 1993), 178.

53. Al-ʿAnsī, *Tāj*, 1:340. This is same usage as in the historian's description of the prison genesis of the *Flowers*, cited earlier.

54. The nineteenth-century work is attributed to the earlier al-ʿAnsī and two collaborators. Muhammad Zabāra, *Aʾimmat al-Yaman* (Cairo: Maṭbaʿat al-Salafiyya, 1376 AH [1956]), 22–24, states, "Credited to him [i.e., ʿAbd Allah ʿAli al-ʿAnsī] is the collection known as *The Compilation of al-ʿAnsi* (*Majmūʿ al-ʿAnsī*), [which is] on *fiqh*, in three large, old-size volumes. He was assisted in determining its principles (*qawāʿid*) and what it covered in issues (*masāʾil*) among the chosen opinions (*al-aqwāl al-mukhtāra*) of the Hādawī school by the learned Sayyid ʿAbd al-Wahhāb bin ʿAli al-Warīth and al-Qāḍī Ahmad bin Ahmad al-ʿAnsī from Dhamār." Basing himself on two other histories by Muhammad Zabāra, al-Ḥibshī, *Maṣādir*, 276, states of the *Compilation of al-ʿAnsi* that it, too, is a commentary on the *Flowers*, and he provides location details for extant manuscript copies.

55. Ahmad Husayn Sharaf al-Dīn, *Tārikh al-Fikr al-Islāmī fī al-Yaman* (Cairo: Maṭbaʿat al-Kaylānī, 1968), 213.

56. Muhammad Zabāra and Ahmad Zabāra, *Nuzhat al-naẓar fī baʿḍ aʿyān al-qarn al-rābiʿ ʿashar*, 4 vols. MS (Ṣanʿāʾ, n.d.), 1:112–14. In a post-revolutionary abridgment of the *muʿāmalāt* sections of Zaydī-Hādawī *fiqh* for use in teaching at Ṣanʿāʾ University, Ahmad Zabāra, *Mukhtaṣar al-fiqh al-Zaydī fī al-muʿāmalāt*, MS (Ṣanʿāʾ, n.d.), 33, identifies five sources for his work: "the *Commentary on the Flowers*; the *Bayān* of Ibn Muẓaffar; the *Majmūʿ al-kabīr*, by ʿAbd Allah al-ʿAnsi and his collaborators; *The Gilded Crown*; and the 'new choices' (*ikhtiyārāt jadīda*)," the latter referring to the collective work using the old idiom (see chapter 4) by the early republican Ministry of Justice.

57. *Majmūʿ al-ʿAnsī al-kabīr*. Referred to in Ismaʿil al-Akwaʿ, *Hijar al-ʿilm wa-maʿāqiluhu fī al-Yaman* (Beirut: Dār al-Fikr, 1995), 2317, as *Majmūʿ al-ʿAnsī fī-l-fiqh*. Al-Akwaʿ's massive study is partially translated in *An Introduction to Hijrahs and Other Refuges of Learning in Yemen*, trans. Tim Mackintosh-Smith, Yemen Translation Series 5 (Ardmore: American Institute for Yemeni Studies, 2006).

58. ʿAbd Allah al-Baradūnī, *al-Thaqāfa wa-l-thawra fī al-yaman* (Beirut: Dār al-Thaqāfa, 1993), 145–52.

59. *Intizāʿ*, again, is an old term for textual extraction. From the same root, the title of the book known as the *Sharḥ al-azhār* is *al-Muntazaʿ*.

60. On Husayn al-ʿAmrī see the biography of him and his students in ʿAbd Allah bin ʿAbd al-Karim al-Jirāfī, *Tuḥfat al-ikhwān* (Cairo: Maṭbaʿat al-Salafiyya, 1365 AH [1945]). Al-ʿAnsī is not mentioned among his students.

61. Yemen Arabic Republic, *al-Awqāf wa-l-irshād fī mawkib al-thawra* (Ṣanʿāʾ: Ministry of Endowments, 1987), 252.

62. Al-Akwaʿ, *Hijar al-ʿilm*, does not give a regular biography entry for al-ʿAnsī, but he does mention him (p. 837) in connection with the effort by the conspirators to get coded knowledge of the demise of Imam Yahya.

63. Messick, *Calligraphic State*, 111.

64. The *taqrīẓ* (or *taqrīḍ*) texts were eliminated from my 1993 edition. They originally appeared at the end of vol. 4, in the first edition of 1947, 484–512, following a

note (dated March 31, 1947) by al-ʿAnsī on page 483. Vol. 4 of the 1993 edition ends on p. 482 (with a 1939 note by al-ʿAnsī) and goes immediately to the *fihris*. I consulted Etienne Renaud's copy of the first edition, now at the library of the P.I.S.A.I. (Pontificio Istituto di Studi Arabi ed'Islamistica), Viale di Trastevere, 89, Rome.

Both al-Baradūnī and Zabāra give partial lists of the *taqrīẓ* authors, beginning with the future Imam Ahmad. Al-Baradūnī says Ahmad wrote as the then head of the High Judicial Council, in Ṣanʿāʾ; Zabāra simply says he was the heir to the throne. Al-Baradūnī notes that the future imam's detailed mentioning of the earlier books of the Zaydī fiqh literature that are summarized in *The Gilded Crown* is also meant to demonstrate his own knowledge and so combat the prevailing "suspicion" that he was weak in this area. Al-Baradūnī's list of names also includes ʿAbd al-Karim Muṭahhar, head of the imam's *dīwān*, editor of the imamic newspaper *al-Aymān*, and member of the High Judicial Council; the former Ibb judge Yahya Muhammad al-Iryānī, head of the Appeal Court in Sanʿaʾ; Zayd bin ʿAli al-Daylamī, second to al-Iryrānī at the Appeal Court; ʿAli ʿAbd Allah al-Wazīr, governor of Taʿizz; Yahya Muhammad ʿAbbas al-Mutawakkil, a military commander and future head of the Appeal Court in the 1950s; and poets such as Muhammad Mahmud Zubayrī, the noted nationalist, ʿAli [Ahmad] al-Hagarī, and Husayn al-Waysī. Al-Baradūnī observes that al-ʿAnsī is careful to mention the precise positions occupied by the men who contributed these texts so as to enhance their legitimizing value for his book. Zabāra's list, after the future imam, adds Ahmad ʿAli al-Ansī from Ibb, Yahya bin ʿAli al-Iryānī, ʿAli bin ʿAli al-Iryānī, Muhammad bin Ahmad al-Dhārī, Yahya bin Muhammad bin al-Hadi al-Mudāyrī, and the author's brother Muḥy al-Dīn al-ʿAnsī. Finally, an Egyptian and an Iraqi are listed.

65. See Franz Rosenthal, "'Blurbs' (Taqriz) from Fourteenth-Century Egypt," *Oriens* 27–28 (1981): 177–96.

66. *Taqrīẓ* notes by Egyptian scholars accompanied the printed 1930 edition of Husayn bin Ahmad al-Sayāghī (d. 1806), *al-Rawḍ al-Naḍīr sharḥ majmūʿ al-fiqh al-kabīr* (Cairo: Maṭbaʿat al-Saʿāda, 1347–49 AH [1928–29]). See (republican-era jurist) Husayn bin Ahmad al-Sayāghī, *al-Madhhab al-zaydī*, 9–10.

67. Al-ʿAnsī, *Tāj*, 4:404, uses the modern term at the opening of his commentary chapter on the imamate, saying of the imam that "his *dustūr* is the honored Book of God and the Sunna of His Prophet."

68. Ibid., 4:404. Asad, *Formations of the Secular*, 198n24, points out that the word for "society" (*mujtamaʿ*) "gained currency only in the 1930s."

69. Al-ʿAnsī, *Tāj*, 1:5.

70. Ibid., 4:247n. Cf. 2:376n, where he states that he abbreviated the discussion of the chapter on slave manumission (*al-ʿitq*) since "its issues are rare" (*masāʾilahu nādira*).

71. Ibid., 3:138n1, on leases; 4:244n1, on the customs of the Ṣanʿāʾ market; 4:278n1, on slaughtering an animal at the door of the *awliyāʾ al-dam* in homicide.

72. Ibid., 3:137. Cf. on *waqf*, 3:305, with an in-text reference to prevailing custom; 4:24, on women's wealth.

73. Ibid., *Tāj*, 2:42, *mahr al-mithl* (see chap. 10). In this and other legal domains *al-mithl* indexes a local level of accepted "equivalence."

74. Ibid., 2:309; cf., in the marriage contract, 2:23 (see chap. 10).

75. Al-Sharafī, *Qawāʿid*, 47.

76. *Majalla*, 3rd printing (Istanbul: Maṭbaʿat al-Jawāʾib, 1305 AH [1887]), maxim 43, p. 13. (Cf. maxim 44, concerning merchants, and 45: "What is directed by custom is equivalent to that directed by law [lit. 'text']" [*al-taʿyīn bi-l-ʿurf ka-l-taʿyīn bi-l-naṣṣ*]). Cf. Ghazzal, *Grammars*, 55, 103. See also Johansen, "Coutumes," 30; Haim Gerber, *Islamic Law and Culture 1600–1840* (Leiden: Brill, 1999), 105. A more concise equivalent, cited for example in connection with sharecropping contracts, is "*al-ʿurf ka-l-manṭūq*"; al-ʿAnsī, *Tāj*, 3:137 (see chap. 10).

77. Al-ʿAnsī, *Tāj*, 2:3. Examples of distinctions between "the language," "the sharīʿa," "custom," and "technical uses" are found in the opening lines of Zaydī *fiqh* commentary chapters on marriage, sale, preemption, lease, partnership, and pledge. Al-ʿAnsī, *Tāj*, 2:3 (*lugha* versus *ʿurf al-sharīʿa*); 2:306 (*lugha* versus *ʿurf*, *lugha* versus *sharīʿa*); 3:3, 69 (*lugha* versus *al-iṣtilāḥ*); 172, 226 (*lugha* versus *sharīʿa*). On *ʿurf al-sharīʿa*, cf. Shawkāni, *Sayl*, 4:506.

78. See al-Akwaʿ, *Hijar al-ʿilm*; Wilferd Madelung, "The Origins of the Yemenite Hijra," in *Arabicus Felix: Luminosus Britannicus: Essays in Honour of A. F. L. Beeston on His Eightieth Birthday*, ed. Alan Jones, Oxford Oriental Institute Monographs (Reading: Ithaca Press, 1991); Gerd-R. Puin, "The Yemeni Hijrah Concept of Tribal Protection," in *Land Tenure and Social Transformation in the Middle East*, ed. Tarif Khalidi (Beirut: American University of Beirut, 1984), 483–94; and Gochenour, "The Penetration of Zaydī Islam." Against those who have seen it as a pre-Islamic institution, Madelung argues that the institution was a Zaydī innovation. For comparison with the Hadrami *ḥawṭa*, see R. B. Serjeant, "Ḥaram and Ḥawṭah: The Sacred Enclave in Arabia," in *Mélanges Taha Husain*, ed. 'Abd-ar-Rahhman Badawī and Taha Ḥusain (Miṣr: Dār al-Maʿārif, 1962), and Ho, *The Graves of Tarim*, 53.

79. Madelung, "The Origins of the Yemenite Hijra," 44n109, referring to Ismaʿil al-Akwaʿ, *al-Madāris al-islāmiyya fī al-yaman* (Damascus: Dār al-Fikr, 1980), 7.

80. al-Akwaʿ, *Hijar al-ʿilm*, 126–28.

81. Messick, *Calligraphic State*, 119, 129; Haykel, *Revival and Reform*, 207–8; Hovden, "Flowers of the Fiqh," 242.

82. Messick, *Calligraphic State*, 115–31.

83. Jacques Berque, *Essai sur la méthode juridique maghrebine* (Rabat: Leforestier, 1944), 13–17.

84. Ahmad bin Muhammad bin Luqmān (Ibn Luqmān), *al-Kāshif* (Ṣanʿāʾ: Maṭbaʿat al-Ḥukūma al-Mutawakkiliyya, bi-Dār al-Saʿāda, [1928]). The commentator is a lineal descendant of Imam al-Murtaḍā, the author of the *Flowers*. This printed edition is mentioned by Ettore Rossi, "La stampa nel Yemen," *Oriente Moderno* 18 (1938): 568–80. The Zaydī scholar and later Ibb resident Muhammad ʿAli al-Ghurbānī made his own handwritten copy of this commentary in 1941. I photographed selected pages (Digital H4–9 [1991]).

85. Ibn Luqmān, *Kāshif*, 271–72.

86. Ibid., 274. A hamza is a letter of the Arabic alphabet that may stand alone, or appear on another letter as its "seat." The reference is to seat letters lacking the associated hamza.

87. Cited in A. Demeerseman, "Une étape décisive de la culture et de la psychologie sociale islamique. Les donnés de la controverse autour du problème de l'imprimerie," *IBLA* 16, no. 64 (1954): 123.

88. Ibid., 124–26. In a *firman*, Sultan Aḥmed III named distinguished judges of Istanbul and Saloniqa and a head of a Dervish organization to verify and correct the permitted publications. He ordered them to see that the printed books "do not leave the press, except that they are complete and correct, making sure that not a single mistake slips through." There were equivalent appointments to the typographic presses at Bulaq in Cairo and the l'Imprimerie Officielle in Tunis. Cf. Pederson, *Arabic Book*, 140.

89. Muhsin Mahdī, "From the Manuscript Age to the Age of Printed Books," in Atiyeh, ed., *The Book in the Islamic World*, 10–11. On "correctors" in western printing establishments, see Roger Chartier, *The Order of Books* (Stanford: Stanford University Press, 194), 42.

90. *al-Ḥikma* 3, no. 3 (Muḥarram 1360 AH [January 1941]). I thank Dr. Lucine Taminian for this reference.

91. A note on the front page (vol. 1) of the 1401 AH (1980) print edition of the *Commentary on the Flowers* makes a standard statement reserving the rights of publication and goes on to state that "any copy lacking a seal should be considered stolen."

92. See Messick, *Calligraphic State*, chap. 4–5.

93. Isma^cil bin ^cAli Al-Akwa^c, *al-Madāris al-islāmiyya fī al-yaman* (Damascus: Dār al-Fikr, 1980), 269.

94. See Messick, *Calligraphic State*, 68–72.

95. Qasim bin Ibrāhīm, ʿAbd Allah bin Muhammad al-Saraḥī, and ʿAli bin ʿAbd Allah al-Anisī, *Taysīr al-marām fī masāʾil al-aḥkām li-l-bāḥithīn wa-l-ḥukkām* (Ṣanʿāʾ: al-Maʿhad al-ʿĀlī li-l-Qaḍāʾ, 1986; Beirut: Dār al-Tanwīr, 1986). The facsimile letter referring to Imam Ahmad appears in the Beirut edition, pp. 5–6. See also Rashād al-ʿAlīmī, *al-Taqlīdiyya wa-l-ḥadātha fī al-niẓām al-qānūnī al-yamanī* (Ṣanʿāʾ: Dār al-Kalima, 1989), 129, who explains that this codification circulated but was not issued officially; Anna Würth, *Ash-Shariʿa fi Bab al-Yaman: Recht, Richter und Rechtspraxis an der Familienrechtlichen Kammer des Gerichts Sud-Sanaa (Republik Jemen), 1983–1995* (Berlin: Duncker und Humblot, 2000), 43.

96. Imam Yahya bin Muhammad Ḥamīd al-Dīn, *Taʿlīmāt hayʾatay al-istiʾnāf*, MS (hand copied in a *safīna* register in the possession of Muhammad Yahya al-Muṭahhar, Taʿizz), 237–38, article 12. See chapter 7.

97. A western history remains to be written. For elements of a Zaydī view, see Haykel, *Revival and Reform*, 67–69.

98. The University of Ibb opened in 1996.

99. Ahmad Nuʿmān, quoted in Dresch, *Modern Yemen*, 53–54, translation modified.

100. Messick, *Calligraphic State*, 99–114; cf. Haykel, *Revival and Reform*, 196.

101. See Messick, *Calligraphic State*, chap. 4–5.

102. Work on the medieval madrasa has highlighted this "informal" dimension of Islamic instruction. See Jonathan Berkey, *The Transmission of Knowledge in Cairo: A Social History of Islamic Education* (Princeton: Princeton University Press, 1992), and

Michael Chamberlin, *Knowledge and Social Practice in Medieval Damascus, 1190-1350* (Cambridge: Cambridge University Press, 1994).

103. For a list of books studied in Zabid, see Yahya bin Muhammad al-Hāshimī, *al-Qaḍā' fī al-yaman* (Ṣanʿā': Maktabat Khālid bin Walīd, 2003), 258–66.

104. See Ahmed El Shamsy, "The Ḥashiya in Islamic Law: A Sketch of the Shāfiʿī Literature," *Oriens* 41 (2013): 289–315.

105. al-Muftī al-Ḥubayshī, *Fatḥ al-mannān*. Ibn Raslān also was a noted Sufī, and the *Zubad* contains a "conclusion" on "the Science of Sufism (*tasawwuf*)." For other Yemeni commentaries on the *Zubad*, see Ḥibshī's biographical foreword, p. 10. Another important text, *al-Ḥāwī* by al-Qazwīnī (d. 1266), a work frequently mentioned in biographies of Yemeni Shāfiʿīs, attracted seventeen commentaries or glosses. See H. Algar, "al-Ḳazwīnī," in *EI2*.

106. See also Messick, *Calligraphic State*, 46–49.

107. Quoted in al-Jirāfī, *Tuḥfat al-ikhwān*, 13–25; summarized in M. Zabāra, *Nuzhat al-naẓar*, 265–66.

108. M. Zabāra, *Nuzhat al-naẓar*, 265.

109. Al-Jirāfī, *Tuḥfat al-ikhwān*. Cf. M. Zabāra, *Nuzhat al-naẓar*, 265–66, and I. al-Akwaʿ *Hijar al-ʿilm*, 1459. See also Haykel, *Revival and Reform*, 198–200.

110. For this al-Ḳazwīnī, Khatīb Dimashq (d. 1338), see S. A. Bonebakker, "al-Ḳazwīnī," in *EI2*.

111. Cf. Haykel, *Revival and Reform*, 67.

112. M. and A. Zabāra, *Nuzhat al-naẓar* MS, 4:166. I. al-Akwaʿ, *Hijar al-ʿilm*, 1738, does not give a biography but mentions that al-Ḥaddād wrote a biographical work on Imam Yahya. The biography of his father, ʿAli Naji al-Ḥaddād, is in M. Zabāra, *A'immat al-Yaman*, 149–57.

113. Yahya bin ʿAli al-Ḥaddād, *ʿUmdat al-qāri' fī sīrat imām zamāninā sayf al-bārī* (n.d.), MS, Western Library of the Great Mosque of Ṣanʿā', Tārikh 2594. On the exchange of *ijāzas*, see p. 27. As I learned from Muhammad al-Wahhābī, the Ibb muftī in my day, Yahya bin ʿAli al-Ḥaddād was one of the main teachers in the imamic-period Ibb madrasa.

114. Ibid., 28–33.

115. He studied the *Commentary on the Flowers* among other works, with the 1920s Ibb judge Yahya Muhammad al-Iryānī and also with the father of Judge al-Yamānī. The references are from the biographies of the two teachers, cited below. See Haykel, *Revival and Reform*, 197–200, for further details on the *ijāza* of Ahmad Zabāra.

116. Muhammad bin Yahya bin ʿAli is mentioned at the end of the biography of his grandfather ʿAli Naji al-Ḥaddād in M. Zabāra, *A'immat al-Yaman*, 149–57, as "among the secretaries of the imamic *dīwān* in these days." See also M. Zabāra, *Nuzhat al-naẓar*, 608–9. In 1975 and 1980, I interviewed Muhammad in Ibb.

117. The muftī presented me with photocopies of the unpublished instructional texts he prepared for this teaching, which were written out in his exceptionally clear hand in ordinary school notebooks. One is the previously cited Zabāra, *Mukhtaṣar al-fiqh al-Zaydī fī al-muʿāmalāt*; the other is on inheritance, Ahmad Zabāra, *Mukhtaṣar lil-muḥtāj ilayhi fī al-yaman min ʿilm al-farā'iḍ*, MS (Ṣanʿā', n.d.).

118. A different case of a return to handwriting following print publication is that of the first (1922) print edition of the *Commentary on the Flowers*, which was

heavily annotated by hand and then republished (1980). A third is that of my friend Muhammad al-Ghurbānī who used the 1928 printed text of Luqmān's *Kāshif* (see above, n84) to make a handwritten personal copy, dated 4 Muḥarram [13]60 AH (February 1, 1941), Digital H4–9 (1991).

119. al-Jirāfī, *Tuḥfat al-ikhwān*, 133; M. Zabāra, *Nuzhat al-naẓar*, 635–42; M. and A. Zabāra, *Nuzhat al-naẓar* MS, 4:217–26; al-Akwaʿ, *Hijar al-ʿilm*, 71–77. See also Messick, *Calligraphic State*, 192–93, and Haykel, *Revival and Reform*, 199. On January 3, 2008, in Ṣanʿāʾ, I prepared an al-Iryānī family tree with ʿAbd al-Karim bin ʿAli bin Yahya al-Iryānī, the former prime minister.

120. M. Zabāra, *Nuzhat al-naẓar*, 205–10; M. and A. Zabāra, *Nuzhat al-naẓar* MS, 2:13–17; I. al-Akwaʿ, *Hijar al-ʿilm*, 79–82; and information from his son Muhammad bin Hasan in Ibb. On Hasan bin Ahmad's earlier authorship of a history of the military campaigns of the then heir to the imamate Ahmad bin Yahya Ḥamid al-Dīn against tribal groups, see Willis, *Unmaking North and South*, 130. Al-Iryānī also penned verses of moral "advice" (*naṣīḥa*) to Imam Yahya, warning of the dangers posed by westerners. Among other al-Iryānīs who served in pre-revolutionary Ibb Province judgeships was the later Republican president ʿAbd al-Raḥmān bin Yahya.

121. al-Akwaʿ, *Hijar al-ʿilm*, 77.

122. Yahya bin Muhammad al-Iryānī, *Hidāyat al-mustabṣirīn bi-sharḥ ʿuddat al-ḥiṣn al-ḥaṣīn* (Damascus: Maṭbaʿat al-ʿAlam, 1397 AH [1977]).

123. Al-Jirāfī, *Tuḥfat al-ikhwān*, 68; al-Ḥaddād, *ʿUmdat al-qāriʾ* MS, 98; M. and A. Zabāra, *Nuzhat al-naẓar* MS, 2:32–34.

124. M. and A. Zabāra, *Nuzhat al-naẓar* MS, 1:235; I. al-Akwaʿ, *Hijar al-ʿilm*, 429. For a photo of a Sayāghī *khatm* ceremony, see Messick, *Calligraphic State*, 82. See also Hugh Scott, *In the High Yemen* (London: John Murray, 1942), fig. 53 (facing p. 104), posing with Amir Yahya bin Muhammad bin al-ʿAbbās ibn al-Imām; the judge is to the left. Scott's visit to Ibb was on the "last day of 1937." Individual pictures also are found in I. al-Akwaʿ, *Hijar al-ʿilm*.

125. M. Zabāra, *Nuzhat al-naẓar*, 384; I. al-Akwaʿ, *Madāris*, 309. The Isḥāq register contains case records dated 1954 to 1960, including seventeen judgments and nine *qarārs*. Among the judgments were four *faskh* and five preemption cases. *Daftar* (untitled), Judge ʿAbd Allah bin Muhammad Isḥāq, Ibb, 1954–60, unnumbered photos (roll 13).

126. Also known as al-Yadūmī. As al-Yamānī, see al-Jirāfī, *Tuḥfat al-ikhwān*, 82; M. Zabāra, *Nuzhat al-*naẓar, 378; and M. and A. Zabāra, *Nuzhat al-naẓar* MS, 2:342–44. As al-Yadūmī, see I. al-Akwaʿ, *Hijar al-ʿilm*, 806–8, and *Madāris*, 297. He is referred to as al-Yadūmī in the last of the appended texts to Imam Ahmad's *ikhtiyārāt* (see chapter 4). On his father, see ʿAli bin ʿAli: al-Jirāfī, *Tuḥfat al-ikhwān*, 99–101; M. Zabāra, *Nuzhat al-naẓar*, 438; M. and A. Zabāra, *Nuzhat al-naẓar* MS, 3:81–85; al-Akwaʿ, *Hijar al-ʿilm*, 805–6; and al-Akwaʿ, *al-Madāris*, 297. Al-Akwaʿ gives an oral source for his account of a conflict with Imam Yahya stemming from a *ḥadd* ruling against a highway robber.

127. In another instance of *madhhab* crossing, he also penned a versified appreciation of the Shāfiʿī ʿAbd al-Raḥmān al-Ḥaddād's versification of Imam Yahya's "choices," discussed in chapter 4.

128. Al-Jirāfī, *Tuḥfat al-ikhwān*, 99–101. See Messick, *Calligraphic State*, chap. 4.

129. Shawkānī, *al-Badr al-ṭāliᶜ*, 2:214ff.

130. Haykel, *Revival and Reform*, 199, describes a similar relationship between the imams and members of the al-ᶜAmrī family.

131. M. Zabāra, *Nuzhat al-naẓar*, 440. Al-Akwaᶜ, *Hijar al-ʻilm*, 805, is more specific: he was sent to divide the estate of the wealthy Shaykh ᶜAli bin ᶜAbd Allah Basha. He was unable to resolve the dispute due to the great number of problems associated with endowments for mosques and schools. A local critic is quoted as saying, "Where is the Islam that you are the 'Shaykh' of?"

132. The expertise of the younger al-Yamānī dated back to the Ottoman era, as M. Zabāra, *Nuzhat al-naẓar*, 378, records: "In the year 1911 [at 27]," in an instance of unofficial work, "he went to the region of Yarīm [now in Ibb Province] to resolve some disputes."

133. M. al-Akwaᶜ, biography, in Ibn al-Muṭahhar, *al-Aḥwāl al-shakhṣiyya*, 1: 5–11; M. and A. Zabāra, *Nuzhat al-naẓar* MS, 4:83–84; I. al-Akwaᶜ, *Hijar al-ʻilm*, 1132.

134. M. al-Akwaᶜ, biography, 1:9.

2. Pre-text: Five Sciences

1. Two examples, one providing broad coverage of the Sunnī schools and the second focused on a single jurist of the Shāfiᶜī school, are Wael B. Hallaq, *A History of Islamic Legal Theories: An Introduction to Sunnī Uṣūl al-fiqh* (Cambridge: Cambridge University Press, 1997), and Bernard G. Weiss, *The Search for God's Law: Islamic Jurisprudence in the Writings of Sayf al-Din al-Āmidī* (Salt Lake City: University of Utah Press, 1992).

2. Ibn al-Murtaḍā, *Azhār*, 11–13; Ibn Miftāḥ, *Sharḥ al-azhār*, 1:2–33; al-ᶜAnsī, *Tāj*, 1:6–19.

3. Ahmad bin Yahya Ibn al-Murtaḍā, *Kitāb al-azhār fī fiqh al-aʾimma al-aṭhār* (Cairo: al-Tamaddun, 1332 AH [1913], Hathi Trust Digital Library (University of Michigan).

4. On these commentary works see al-Ḥibshī, *Maṣādir*, 177, 179. An example dating from 938 AH (1532), in the collection of the Yemeni Manuscripts Digitization Initiative, Princeton Digital Library, http://pudl.princeton.edu/objects/vh53wx028#page/1/mode/2up, is *Kitāb talkhīṣ maᶜānī muqaddamat al-azhār.*

5. Shawkānī, *Sayl*, 1:5.

6. Ibn Miftāḥ, *Sharḥ al-azhār*, 1:2.

7. Shawkānī, *Sayl*, 1:4. On Shawkānī's treatment of this passage in the *Flowers*, see the comments of al-ᶜAmrī, *The Yemen*, 154–55.

8. Abdullah Hamidaddin, personal communication, October 9, 2009.

9. Ibn al-Murtaḍā, *Azhār*, 11. In manuscripts the *matn* is not voweled. An example is a c. 1900 codex from the Yemeni Manuscript Digitization Initiative, Princeton Digital Library, http://pudl.princeton.edu/objects/h989r449b, 18, the vowels of the string, *m-q-dd-m*, are not included, although a *fatḥa* may be indicated over the

dāl. The word is written in red ink, as is the word *faṣl*, meaning "part" or "section," indicating a status as a term for a text unit. In the stand-alone commentary cited above (n4), however, on the title page (15) the word is voweled with a *fatḥa*.

10. Botanical metaphors are common in titles. On this particular example, see Messick, *Calligraphic State*, 44. In the "branches" literature of the *fiqh*, a *matn* typically opens with, at most, a few reflexive remarks on the need for an abbreviated work, or concerning the relationship of the present work to a prior text. The same is true also of the "branches" commentaries, exemplified by the opening lines of the *Gilded Crown*, which I quoted and discussed in the last chapter. But there are instances, in both of these "branches" genres, of introductory sections devoted to issues of interpretation. Al-Nawawī (d. 1277), the important Shāfiʿī jurist, states, for example, that his earlier colleague al-Muzanī (d. 878) covers similar topics in the introduction to his *Mukhtaṣar* (see Calder, "Al-Nawawī's Typology," 145). Nawawī refers perhaps to the longer version of the *Mukhtaṣar*, which is lost (cf. W. Heffening, "Muzanī," in *EI2*). A small theoretical treatise on *Adab al-Muftī* is part of the front matter to al-Nawawī's own commentary on al-Shirāzī's *Muhadhdhab* (partial translation in Calder, "Al-Nawawī's Typology," 145). The Zaydī case in question is mentioned in Hallaq, *Impossible State*, 204n74. Among local Shāfiʿīs in Ibb, the nineteenth-century commentary by al-Muftī on Ibn Raslān's *Zubad* opens with a section on "*ʿilm al-uṣūl*," which touches on *uṣūl al-din* matters and *ʿaqīda*, and on the miracles of *awliyāʾ*, before adding "some things from *uṣūl al-fiqh*" (pp. 22–44). Does commentator al-Muftī's discussion of *i* versus *a* vowel marks and his use of the word *muqaddima* or *muqaddama* indicate a *Flowers* tradition influence?

11. Schacht, *Introduction*, 115.

12. Al-Akwaʿ, *Madāris*; Zabāra, *Nuzhat al-naẓar* MS; M. Zabāra and A. Zabāra, *Nuzhat al-naẓar* MS.

13. Ibn Miftāḥ, *Sharḥ al-azhār*, 4:520, 521. The *Baḥr* of Ibn al-Murtaḍā, the *Flowers* author, also has a *dībāja*, with the term explained in a note, intro. vol., 35.

14. Hans Wehr, *A Dictionary of Modern Written Arabic* (Ithaca: Cornell University Press, 1966), s.v. *dabbaja*, 270.

15. See Messick, *Calligraphic State*, chap. 8.

16. The phrasing is formulaic. Al-Ḥibshī, *Maṣādir*, 189, gives examples of other works with titles that are variations on this phrase.

17. A related basic term that covers the legally active person, educated or not, is *mukallaf*, the (male) individual of full adult capacity. One of the related titles that al-Hibshī (ibid.) provides is, "What the *mukallaf* cannot be ignorant of."

18. On the distinction between a *masʾala* in the "branches" of the *fiqh* as opposed to in the "roots" literature, cf. al-Imam al-Muʾayyad Yahya bin Ḥamza, *al-Intiṣār ʿalā ʿulamāʾ al-amṣār* (Ṣanʿāʾ: Muʾassasat al-Imām Zayd bin ʿAlī al-Thaqāfiyya, 1425 AH [2005]), 1:159–61.

19. Al-ʿAnsī, *Tāj*, 1:6. The four modifying adjectives for the indicated type of "cases" are *al-farʿiyya al-ʿamaliyya al-ẓaniyya wa-l-qaṭʿiyya*. *Ẓanniya* is defined by al-ʿAnsī as "that which has a probable indication (*dalīl*)" in the source texts; *qaṭʿiyya* as that "which has a certain indication." A related principle states, "For sharīʿa rulings for which it is possible to arrive at certain knowledge, probable knowledge will not suffice; but when there is no way to attain certain knowledge, then probable knowl-

edge is applied" (*mā kāna mina al-aḥkāmi al-sharʿiyyati yumkinu al-wuṣūlu ilā al-ʿilmi bihi lam yakfi al-ẓannu wa mā kāna fīmā lā sabīla ilā taḥṣīli al-ʿilmi fīhi fa-l-ẓannu maʿmūlun ʿalayhi*). Al-Sharafī, *Qawāʿid*, 47.

20. Referring to the Sunnī schools, Hallaq, *Legal Theories*, 155, writes, "The notion that *ijtihād* is wholly confined to the region of probability is one that legal theory was careful to nurture and promote. In fact, this notion was the linchpin of legal theory." Cf. Asad, *Formations*, 244–45, reading Johansen on probability and contingency.

21. Al-ʿAnsī, *Tāj*, 1:6.

22. Another *qāʿida*, however, holds that "[i]f *ijtihād* is not feasible, *taqlīd* is permitted" (*idhā taʿadhdhara al-ijtihādu jāza al-taqlīdu*). Al-Sharafī, *Qawāʿid*, 47.

23. Wael B. Hallaq, "Was the Gate of Ijtihād Closed?" *International Journal of Middle East Studies* 16, no. 1 (1984): 32–33.

24. Al-ʿAnsī, *Tāj*, 1:7–8; Ibn Miftāḥ, *Sharḥ al-azhār* (2003), 1:129–39.

25. E.g., Hallaq, "Gate of Ijtihād," 6, a list from al-Ghazālī (d. 1111). Examples of modern lists are Mohammad Hashim Kamali, *Principles of Islamic Jurisprudence* (Cambridge: Islamic Texts Society, 2003), 476–80, and Tariq Ramadan, *Western Muslims and the Future of Islam* (Oxford: Oxford University Press, 2004), 47.

26. Muhammad ʿAli al-Shawkānī, *Adab al-ṭalab* (Ṣanʿāʾ: Markaz al-Dirāsāt, 1979), on which see al-ʿAmrī, *The Yemen*, 109–14, and Haykel, *Revival and Reform*, 102–8.

27. Al-Akwaʿ, *Madāris*, 288–89.

28. On the legal content of the Qurʾan, see Wael B. Hallaq, "Law and the Qurʾan," in *EQ*.

29. Al-Akwaʿ, *Madāris*, 288. The first of the four books on this curriculum list is by al-Najrī (d. 1472); it is an abridgement of the third, the much-esteemed *Thamarāt* of al-Faqīh Yūsuf, whose biography is in al-Shawkānī, *al-Badr al-Ṭāliʿ*, 2:350. Second on the curriculum list is a work by a grandson of Imam al-Qasim, Muhammad bin al-Husayn (d. 1657), *Muntahā al-marām fī sharḥ ayāt al-aḥkām* (Dār al-Manāhil: Beirut, 1986). On this work, see al-Ḥibshī, *Maṣādir*, 10, 20, 23, 27, 219. The inter-regionally famous fourth book is Abu al-Qasim Jar Allah Mahmud bin ʿUmar al-Zamakhsharī, *al-Kashshāf ʿan ḥaqāʾiq al-tanzīl wa ʿuyūn al-aqāwīl fī wujūh al-taʾwīl*, 4 vols. (Cairo: al-Bābī al-Ḥalabī, 1966–68). On this work, see Andrew J. Lane, *A Traditional Muʿtazilite Qurʾān Commentary* (Leiden: Brill, 2006), and W. Madelung, "Zamakhsharī," in *EI2*. Al-Zamakhsharī traveled to Yemen, and *al-Kashshāf* was summarized and commented on by a number of Yemeni scholars. See also chapter 5 for a reference to a particular transmission among Yemeni jurist-imams via Zamakhsharī. For the Zaydī *tafsīr* tradition, see also al-ʿAmrī, *The Yemen*, 180–87.

On the twentieth-century shift, elsewhere in the Middle East, from this old-style of *tafsīr musalsal* to a new topical exegesis, or *tafsīr mawḍūʿī*, see Marwa Elshakry, "The Exegesis of Science in Twentieth-Century Arabic Interpretations of the Qurʾān," in *Nature and Scripture in the Abrahamic Religions: 1700–Present*, ed. Jitse M. van der Meer and Scott Mandelbrote (Leiden: Brill, 2008), 2:491–524.

30. Ibn al-Murtaḍā, *Baḥr*, 1:238–308.

31. Al-ʿAnsī, *Tāj*, 1:7n.

32. Ibn al-Murtaḍā, *Baḥr*, 1:238. Cf., again, the related term *al-muntazaʿ* in the formal title of what is known as the *Commentary on the Flowers*.

33. Al-ʿAnsī, *Tāj*, 1:7.

34. Muhammad Zubayr Siddīqī, *Ḥadīth Literature* (Cambridge: Islamic Texts Society, 1993), 12.

35. Abū Dāwūd, *Risāla ilā ahl Makka* (Beirut: al-Maktab al-Islamī, 1997), 81. The printed edition of the *Sunan* contains 5,274 *ḥadīths* arranged in 1,871 "chapters."

36. Al-Iryānī, *Hidāyat al-mustabṣirīn*, 29: "*adhkār al-nabawiyya*" and "*daʿawāt al-muṣṭafawiyya*." Al-Iryānī's work is based based on al-Shawkānī's commentary on a work by al-Jazarī (d. 1429). Cf. al-Akwaʿ, *Hijar al-ʿilm*, 77. Al-ʿAmrī, *The Yemen*, 176, calls it a "truly remarkable new *ḥadīth* work," while also noting that it "depends entirely on Shawkānī." Al-ʿAmrī discusses this work together with a set of four *ḥadīth* works by Shawkānī on topics other than rules. On the Yemeni *ḥadīth* literature, see generally al-Ḥibshī, *Maṣādir*, 35–87.

37. Ibn Miftāḥ, *Sharḥ al-Azhār* (2003), 1:131n3.

38. Christopher Melchert, "Abū Dāwūd al-Sijistānī," in *EI3*.

39. Ibn Miftāḥ, *Sharḥ al-azhār* (2003), 1:131.

40. Ibn Khaldūn also did not recognize Ibn Māja. Cf. J. Robson, "*Ḥadīth*," in *EI2*, and Jonathan Brown, *The Canonization of al-Bukhārī and Muslim: The Formation and Function of the Sunnī Ḥadīth Canon* (Leiden: Brill, 2007), 8–10.

41. This final phrase links to still another gloss that provides three additional titles of Zaydī-school specific *ḥadīth* works: (1) Imam al-Mutawakkil Ahmad bin Sulaymān (d. 1170), *Uṣūl al-aḥkām*, 2 vols. (Ṣanʿāʾ: Muʾassasat Imām Zayd, 2003), which al-Ḥibshī, *Maṣādir*, 588–91, describes as containing more than 3,000 rule-*ḥadīths*, arranged according to *fiqh* chapters; (2) the *Amālī* of Ahmad bin ʿĪsā, cf. Haykel *Revival and Reform*, 9; and, the gloss concludes, (3) "Some of our ʿulamāʾ said, *Sharḥ al-nukat* by al-Qāḍī Jaʿfar is sufficient for the *mujtahid*." On this last, which is by Jaʿfar bin Ahmad bin ʿAbd al-Salam (d. 1177), see al-Ḥibshī, *Maṣādir*, 41, 106–8. For a listing of the major Zaydī *ḥadīth* works, see ʿAbd Allah bin Mahmud al-ʿIzzī,*ʿUlūm al-ḥadīth ʿinda al-Zaydīyya wal-l-muḥaddithīn* (Amman: Muʾassasat al-Imām Zayd bin ʿAlī al-Thaqāfiyya, 2001), 275–86.

42. Al-Husayn bin Badr al-Dīn, *Shifāʾ al-uwām fī aḥādīth al-aḥkām*, 3 vols. (N.p.: Jamʿiyyat ʿUlamāʾ al-Yaman, 1996). An indicator of the significance of this work is that the author is given his own abbreviation (*al-Amīr Ḥ*) in the *Commentary on the Flowers* (see chapter 1, on the *rumūz*). Cf. al-Ḥibshī, *Maṣādir*, 44; Al-ʿIzzī, *ʿUlūm al-ḥadīth ʿinda al-Zaydīyya*, 285–86; and Haider, *Origins of the Shīʿa*, 38.

43. Haykel, *Revival and Reform*.

44. Muhammad bin Ismāʿīl al-Amīr (Ibn al-Amīr al-Ṣanʿānī), *Subul al-salām sharḥ Bulūgh al-marām*, 4 vols. (Beirut: Dār al-Kitāb al-ʿArabī, 1987).

45. Brown, *Canonization*, 314–18, quote at 316.

46. Al-Akwaʿ, *Madāris*, 289. On its use in Indonesia, see Martin van Bruinessen, "Kitab Kuning: Books in Arabic Script Used in the Pesantren Milieu," *Bijdagen tot de Taal-, Land en Volkenkunde* 146 (1990): 255. In Nigeria, the same work was cited in a recent criminal case, with the author given as al-Kaḥlanī (i.e., "*thumma al-Sanʿānī*"). Rudolph Peters, "The Re-Islamization of Criminal Law in Northern Nigeria and the Judiciary: The Safiyyatu Hussaini Case," in *Dispensing Justice in Islam: Qadis and Their Judgments*, ed. M. K. Masud, R. Peters, and D. S. Powers (Leiden: Brill, 2006), 232–33. On Ibn Ḥajar al-ʿAsqalānī, who also visited Yemen, see F. Rosenthal, "Ibn Hadjar," in *EI2*.

47. Muhammad bin ʿAli al-Shawkānī, *Nayl al-awṭār fī sharḥ muntaqā al-akhbār* (Cairo: Sharikat al-Quds li-l-Tijāra, 2008). On Shawkānī's oeuvre in *ḥadīth*, see al-ʿAmri, *The Yemen*, chap. 8, and Haykel, *Revival and Reform*. On the influence of Shawkānī's work in South Asia, see Claudia Preckel, "Ahl-i Ḥadīth," *EI3*.

48. Al-Akwaʿ, *Madāris*, 11. The Zaydīs of Upper Yemen during the same month carried out the ritualized recitation and study of their works on inheritance.

49. Messick, *Calligraphic State*, 272n27.

50. M. al-Akwaʿ, author biography, in Ibn al-Muṭahhar, *Aḥwāl al-shakhṣiyya*, 1:9.

51. Muhammad bin ʿAli al-Shawkānī, *Wābl al-ghamām ʿalā shifāʾ al-uwām*, ed. M. Hallaq, 2 vols. (Cairo: Maktabat Ibn Taymiyya, 1416 AH [1996]).

52. N. Cottart, "Mālikiyya," in *EI2*. See also Ignaz Goldziher, *Muslim Studies*, trans. S. Stern (Chicago: Aldine, 1967), 2:197–204; Siddīqī, *Ḥadīth Literature*, 7–8; and Yasin Dutton, *The Origins of Islamic Law: The Qurʾan, the Muwaṭṭaʾ and Madinan ʿAmal* (London: Curzon, New York, 1999).

53. Schacht, "Mālik b. Anas," in *EI2*; elsewhere, in "Fiḳh," in *EI2*, 2:889, Schacht says the "*Majmūʿ* . . . though of an early date, is not authentic." Cf. Schacht, *The Origins of Muhammadan Jurisprudence* (Oxford: Clarendon Press, 1950), 262.

54. G.-H. Bousquet and J. Berque, *Recueil de la loi musulmane de Zaid ben ʿAli* (Alger: La Maison des Livres, 1941), 9, citing earlier studies by Griffini (1919) and Santillana (1919–20).

55. Bousquet and Berque, *Recueil*, 11n, 13, 14.

56. Al-Sayāghī, *al-Rawḍ al-Naḍīr*. Commentator Sayāghī's intellectual biography, by Muhammad Zabāra, opens as follows: "He memorized the *matn* of the *Flowers* by heart, and he studied all of its commentaries and its glosses with his father" (2). See also the "completion" of this commentary work, by the author's great grandson, Ahmad bin Ahmad bin Muhammad bin Husayn al-Sayāghī (d. 1981), *al-Minhāj al-munīr tatimmat al-rawḍ al-naḍīr*, 5 vols. (Ṣanʿāʾ: Muʾassasat al-Imām Zayd bin ʿAlī, 2005).

57. Ibn Miftāḥ, *Sharḥ al-azhār*, 1:135.

58. Cf. Johansen, *Contingency*, 31, on views of its "reduced authority."

59. Cf., again, al-ʿAnsī, *Tāj*, 1:6, and Imam Yahya bin Ḥamza, *al-Intiṣār*, 1:159.

60. See chapter 1 for his biography and chapter 7 for the cases.

61. Muhammad bin Yahya Bahrān, *Matn al-Kāfil* (Ṣanʿāʾ: Muʾassasāt Dār al-Turāth al-Yamanī, 1991), 39–42. At the end of this handwritten lithograph is the following old-style statement: "With praise to God, the transcription [*naql*] of *Matn al-Kāfil* was completed on the date Jumādā II, 1407, in the handwriting [*khaṭṭ*] of . . . may God forgive him, from an authoritative copy [*nuskha muʿtamada*] in the handwriting and checking [*ḍabṭ*] of . . . may God forgive him and his parents, and it has been compared with a number of copies and commentaries, and God is the bringer of good fortune."

62. Al-Akwaʿ, *Madāris*, 288. The first of the six (referenced in the preceding note), *al-Kāfil* of Muhammad bin Yahya Bahrān (d. 1550), was studied three ways: in a versification and in two different commentaries. One of these commentaries was *al-Kāshif*, by Ibn Luqmān, the printed work discussed in chapter 1. The other works on the madrasa curriculum include Muhammad ʿAli al-Shawkānī, *Irshād al-faḥūl*, and Ibn al-Murtaḍā, *Miʿyār al-ʿuqūl*, which appears among the pre-texts located

before the main texts of his *Sea* (Ibn al-Murtaḍā, *Baḥr*, intro. vol.:159–204). The *Miʿyār* was to be studied with *al-Minhāj* (a work that al-Ḥibshī, *Maṣādir*, 179, describes as a commentary by Luqmān on another of Ibn al-Murtaḍā's *uṣūl* treatises). Finally on this list is *al-Ghāya*, by al-Husayn bin al-Qasim (d. 1640), the prominent son of the famous imam, studied in an unidentified commentary. For a general discussion of Yemeni *uṣūl* works, see al-ʿAmri, *The Yemen*, 140–52; for further discussion and bibliography, see al-Ḥibshī, *Maṣādir*, 169–85.

63. Ibn al-Ḥājib, *Mukhtaṣar al-Muntahā* (Cairo: Būlāq, 1316–19 AH [1898–1901]) This work was studied in the highlands and elsewhere in the Muslim world in the commentary by ʿAḍud al-Din al-Ijī, a text known as *al-ʿAḍudiyya*. Cf. H. Fleisch, "Ibn al-Ḥādjib," in *EI2*, 3:781.

64. See al-Ḥibshī, *Maṣādir*, 170, 176.

65. See Yasin Dutton, "The Introduction to Ibn Rushd's *Bidayat al-Mujtahid*," *Islamic Law and Society* 1, no. 2 (1994): 188–205, and references cited. In 2008 in Yemen, a recent graduate told me that *Bidayat al-mujtahid* appears on the curriculum of the Islamist-oriented al-Imān University, in Ṣanʿāʾ.

66. Al-ʿAnsī, *Tāj*, 1:8; Ibn Miftāḥ, *Sharḥ al-azhār* (2003), 1:135–37.

67. For the same terms in Sunnī *uṣūl*, see Hallaq, *Legal Theories*, index: *ʿāmm, khāṣṣ; mujmal, mubayyan; naskh; amr, nahy; ijmāʿ, qiyās*. Only the two minor terms *takrār* and *fawr*, which are treated in the section on "commanding and forbidding," are not familiar.

68. Al-ʿAnsī here mentions the sciences of *al-jarḥ wa-l-taʿdīl* and *uṣūl al-dīn*.

69. See the discussion of logocentrism in Messick, *Calligraphic State*.

70. Harald Motzki, "The Collection of the Qurʾan: A Reconsideration of Western Views in Light of Recent Methodological Developments," *Der Islam* 78 (2001): 1–34.

71. Messick, *Calligraphic State*, 24.

72. Michael Cook, "The Opponents of the Writing of Tradition in Early Islam," *Arabica* 44 (1997): 437–530; Paul L. Heck, "The Epistemological Problem of Writing in Islamic Civilization: al-Khaṭīb al-Baghdādī's (d. 463 [1071]) 'Taqyīd al-ʿilm,'" *Studia Islamica* 94 (2002): 85–114; and Gregor Schoeler, *The Oral and the Written in Early Islam*, trans. Uwe Vagelpohl, ed. James E. Montgomery (London: Routledge, 2006). See also J. Robson, "*Ḥadīth*," in *EI2*, who mentions opposed *ḥadīths* on the topic cited by Abū Dāwūd.

73. Al-Ghurbānī, *ʿIlm uṣūl al-ḥadīth*, 24–27. Al-Ghurbānī also cites early evidence in favor of writing.

74. Shawkānī, *al-Badr al-ṭāliʿ*, 2:331; 1:122. Similar statements were made by biographers about such twentieth-century figures as Husayn al-ʿAmrī, Yahya bin Muhammad al-Iryānī, and ʿAli al-Yamānī (Yadūmī).

75. In his *Thamarāt*, 1:91, Faqīh Yūsuf reflects on his decision to arrange the verses by their *sura* order rather than by *fiqh* chapters. He explains that a single verse can contain multiple rules that would pertain to different *fiqh* chapters, and that it would have been necessary to mention the same verse in each of them. He also mentions (1:32) the *fiqh* ordering (*tartīb*) of the earlier work on which his book is based.

76. See the section, "Law" in *Arabic Language and Islam: Oxford Online Research Guide*, ed. Mustafa Shah, http://www.oxfordbibliographies.com/view/document/obo-9780195390155/obo-9780195390155-0009.xml, for citations to M. G. Carter

and others. Cf. Nakissa, "Epistemic Shift," for the rule-orientation of the two disciplines.

77. Ibn al-Muẓaffar, *Bayān*.

78. Al-Akwaʿ, *Madāris*, 288.

79. George Makdisi, *The Rise of Colleges. Institutions of Learning in Islam and the West* (Ediburgh: Edinburgh University Press, 1981), xiii, 12. Cf. Norman Calder, "Law," 983; Hallaq, *Sharīʿa*, 413, referring to "the queen of all sciences."

80. Ibn Miftāḥ, *Sharḥ al-azhār* (2003), 1:138n4.

81. Muhammad ʿAli al-Shawkānī, *Matn al-durar al-bahiyya* (N.p., n.d., [1964]); Shawkānī, *Darārī al-muḍiyya sharḥ al-durar al-bahiyya* (Beirut: Dār al-Jīl, 1987).

82. Ibn Miftāḥ, *Sharḥ al-azhār*, 4:520n8; cf. Al-ʿAnsī, *Tāj*, 4:407n2.

83. For a nuanced study of *taqlīd*, see Wael B. Hallaq, *Authority, Continuity and Change in Islamic Law* (Cambridge: Cambridge University Press, 2001).

84. Al-ʿAnsī, *Tāj*, 1:10.

85. The relevant formula is *al-ʿāmmī lā madhhab lahu*. Ibn Miftāḥ, *Sharḥ al-azhār*, 3:51–54.

86. Compare the notion of the "initiators of discursive practice" who are differentiated by Foucault from the "great" authors. Foucault, "What Is an Author?," 131.

87. Among the Sunnīs, this would be termed *ijtihād fī'l-madhhab*. Cf. Calder, "Al-Nawawī's Typology."

88. On theorizing *madhhab* boundaries, see Lutz Wiederhold, "Legal Doctrines in Conflict: The Relevance of *Madhhab* Boundaries to Legal Reasoning in the Light of an Unpublished Treatise on *Taqlīd* and *Ijtihād*," *Islamic Law and Society* 3, no. 2 (1996): 234–304.

89. Ho, *Graves of Tarim*.

90. Yahya bin Abū al-Khayr bin Sālim al-ʿImrānī (d. 1162/1163). Al-Ḥibshī, *Maṣādir*, 192–93; al-Akwaʿ, *Introduction*, 44.

91. Al-Ḥibshī, *Maṣādir*, 189–285.

92. Al-Muftī, *Fatḥ al-Mannān*.

93. Al-Ḥibshī, *Maṣādir*, 271.

94. Messick, *Calligraphic State*, 15–16.

95. Cf. Hallaq, *Legal Theories*, 118: it is not necessary for *mujtahid* to be just.

96. Cf. Ibn al-Muẓaffar, *Bayan*, 1:22.

97. This is standard terminology. Nawawī's usage is translated as "affiliation" by Calder, "Al-Nawawī's Typology," 149. See also the related usage of Ibn ʿĀbidīn, *Manṣūban li-l-fatwā*, translated by Ghazzal, *Grammars*, 128, as "dedicated to fatwas."

98. Al-ʿAnsī, *Tāj*, 1:8.

99. Ibid. On the terms, and their implications for Zaydī-Shāfiʿī relations, see Haykel, *Revival and Reform*, 38.

100. Schacht, "Khaṭaʾ," in *EI2*.

101. Al-ʿAnsī, *Tāj*, 1:9.

102. Ibn Miftāḥ, *Sharḥ al-azhār*, 1:144n4; 145n2 (quoting *al-Miʿyār*).

103. Ibid., 145n1.

104. Hallaq, *Sharīʿa*, 368.

105. Al-ʿAnsī, *Tāj*, 1:9; cf. Ibn Bahrān, *al-Kāfil*, 41. For the opposite view, see Ibn Miftāḥ, *Sharḥ al-azhār* (2003), 1:169–74, on the acceptance of transmission from the

dead; and Sayāghī, *al-Madhhab al-zaydī*, 30, *qāʿida* number 4: "*al-taqlīd lil-mayt yajuwzu mutlaqan.*" See also Hallaq, "From Fatwās to Furūʿ," 49–50.

106. Shawkānī, *al-Badr al-ṭāliʿ*, 1:3.

107. As Haykel, *Revival and Reform*, 6, 150, among others, has noted. In Ibb, the sons of some regional shaykhs were held as "hostages" by the imamic state. Their instructors taught this line, together with its counterpart, the requirement of obedience.

3. Commentaries: "Write It Down"

1. Faqīh Yūsuf, *al-Thamarāt*, 2:134–49; Zamakhsharī, *Kashshāf*, 1:402–6; Muhammad bin ʿAli al-Shawkānī, *Fatḥ al-qadīr al-jāmiʿ bayna fannay al-riwāya waʾl-dirāya min ʿilm al-tafsīr*, 5 vols. (Cairo: Muṣṭafā al-Bābī al-Ḥalabī, 1349 AH [1930]), 1:269–70. (This last work, which I consulted from the holdings of Columbia University Library, is the former personal copy of Arthur Jeffrey).

2. In *The Koran Interpreted*, trans. Arthur J. Arberry (London: Oxford University Press, 1964), 70–71.

3. Faqīh Yūsuf, *al-Thamarāt*, 2:136.

4. Zamakhsharī, *Kashshāf*, 2:402, "*wa-l-amr lil-nadb*"; Faqīh Yūsuf, *al-Thamarāt*, 2:134, "*al-amr lil-nadb wa-l-irshād*," cf. 135–36, on *wujūb* regarding the second order to the writer to write, which also is specified as a *farḍ kifāya*, among the collective duties. Writing four centuries later, Shawkānī, *Fatḥ al-qadīr*, 1:270, states, "*wa-ẓāhir al-amr al-wujūb*," although it is unclear whether this reference is to the second order or to both the first and second; he also mentions the alternative *al-amr lil-nadb* opinion. ʿAbd Allah bin ʿUmar al-Bayḍāwī, *Tafsīr al-Bayḍāwī* (Beirut: Muʾassasat al-Aʿlamī, 1990–), 230, 232, gives the equivalent term as *istiḥbāb*.

5. ʿAli bin ʿAbd Allah al-Iryānī, *Najāḥ al-ṭālib fī ṣifat mā yaktubu al-kātib*, MS (1343 AH [1923]), Western Library of the Great Mosque of Ṣanʿāʾ, 64 Fiqh, p. 54: "*qad naṣṣa fī muḥkam kitābihi ʿalā wujūb kitābat al-dayn wa qīss bihi ghayrahu min al-muʿāmalāt.*"

6. Leah Kinberg, "Ambiguous," in *EQ*.

7. Faqīh Yūsuf, *al-Thamarāt*, 2:136. Shawkānī, *Fatḥ al-qadīr*, 1:270, identifies the two kinship groups of speakers.

8. Shawkānī, *Fatḥ al-qadīr*, 1:270.

9. On the association with *ribāʾ* and with the *salam* contract, see Faqīh Yūsuf, *al-Thamarāt*, 2:135, and Zamakhsharī, *Kashshāf*, 2:402. On substantive timing, using the harvest (*al-ḥaṣād*) and the pilgrimage schedule, Faqīh Yūsuf permits; Zamakhsharī and al-Bayḍāwī do not.

10. The Zaydīs accepted other customary language in contracts. Thus the "offer" in a sale contract may be expressed "according to custom" (*ḥasaba al-ʿurfi*). Ibn al-Murtadā, *Kitāb al-azhār*, 143.

11. "*Adfaʿ li-l-nizāʿ wa aqṭaʿ li-l-khilāf.*" Shawkānī, *Fatḥ al-qadīr*, 1:270. The first part of this phrase also appears in early *tafsīr* writings, e.g., al-Bayḍāwī (d. 1286), *Tafsīr al-Bayḍāwī*, 1:230.

12. Certeau, *Practice of Everyday Life*, 171.

13. On these two distinct moments, cf. Matthias Radscheit, "Witnessing and Testifying," in *EQ*.

14. Zamakhsharī, *Kashshāf*, 1:402.

15. Shawkānī, *Fatḥ al-qadīr*, 1:270.

16. Faqīh Yūsuf, *al-Thamarāt*, 2:143.

17. Shawkānī, *Badr al-ṭāliʿ*, 2: 350.

18. For a reading of the Zaydī chapter on "evidence" in the *Flowers*, see Brinkley Messick, "Evidence: From Memory to Archive," *Islamic Law and Society* 9, no. 2 (2002): 1–40.

19. Ibn Miftāḥ, *Sharḥ al-azhār*, 4:185. The second cited Qurʾanic verse is from *sūra* 65:2.

20. Having taken down the teacher's oral "dictation" of the lesson text in his own writing, a student would "orally read" back his just transcribed text "to" the listening teacher.

21. Al-ʿAnsī, *Tāj*, 4:104–5. Cf., in the 1950s codification, Qasim bin Ibrāhīm et al., *Taysīr al-marām*, art. 1038.

22. The term is a minor one in American legal practice.

23. Wael B. Hallaq, "Qāḍīs Communicating: Legal Change and the Law of Documentary Evidence," *Al-Qanṭara* 20 (1999): 437–66.

24. Al-ʿAnsī, *Tāj*, 4:195–96.

25. Messick, *Calligraphic State*, 210. "Mobile witnesses, who travel with the text (and whose probity must be so manifest, so little context-dependent, as to be apparent even in districts where they are not known), are the ultimate conveyers of truth." That the judge is the reader is made explicit in the 1950s codification, Qasim bin Ibrāhīm et al., *Taysīr al-marām*, art. 1038.

26. Al-ʿAnsī, *Tāj*, 4:196. See a similar model text provided in a Shāfiʿī law book, quoted in Messick, *Calligraphic State*, 210.

27. Al-ʿAnsī, *Tāj*, 4:196.

28. Shawkānī, *Sayl*, 4:294.

29. A theme that has interested many. See, e.g., Derrida, *Archive Fever*. My thanks to Mohammad Fadel for sharing the reference to the *Federal Rules of Evidence*.

30. "*in lam yadhkur.*"

31. Al-ʿAnsī, *Tāj*, 4:110–11, "*bi-mujarrad ma wajada fī dīwānihi.*" Cf. Ibn al-Murtaḍā, *Azhār*, 268.

32. Using the symbols *Abī Ḥ* and *Sh*. Ibn Miftāḥ, *Sharḥ al-azhār*, 4:233. Schacht, *Introduction*, 82–83, differentiates the Sunnī schools in terms of their recognitions of written documents. He writes that this occurred among "the Mālikīs to the widest extent, the Ḥanafīis and the Ḥanbalis with some hesitation, whereas the Shāfiʿīs continued to regard them strictly as accessories." An early Ḥanafī school treatise by al-Khaṣṣāf (d. 875) separately discusses the judge and the witness. Aḥmad bin ʿUmar al-Khaṣṣāf, *Kitāb adab al-qāḍī*, ed. Farhat Ziyada (Cairo: American University in Cairo Press, 1978). The first (section 382, pp. 335–38) concerns a judge who "finds in his archive (*dīwān*) something he does not remember (lit. 'memorize')." Abū Hanīfa is quoted by al-Khaṣṣaf as holding the same position, expressed in the same language, as Ibn al-Murtaḍā in the *Flowers*: "The judge is not permitted to rule on the basis of what he finds in his archive if he does not remember it." This

was the case even if the archive had remained securely in his possession. For his disciples Abū Yūsuf and Muhammad Shaybānī, however, the fact of this form of archival security led to the reverse position. See also Baber Johansen, "Formes de langage et fonctions publiques: Stéréotypes, témoins et offices dans la preuve par l'écrit en droit musulman," *Arabica* 44 (1997): 349 and n100, where he observes that the doctrine of Abū Ḥanīfa did not prevail in the Ḥanafī school. As for the witness (al-Khaṣṣāf, section 830, pp. 702–3), the issue concerns a "man who sees his name and his script and his seal in a writing (*kitāb*) and does not remember the witnessing"—that is, the prior witnessing act set down in the written instrument in question. The rule is that "it is not permitted for a man to testify about something without knowing its veracity, [that is, simply] on the basis of his script, name and seal in a document (*sakk*)."

33. See Johansen, "Formes," 347–57, and Wael B. Hallaq, "The Qāḍī's Dīwān (*Sijill*) Before the Ottomans," *Bulletin of the School of Oriental and African Studies* 61, no. 3 (1998): 415–36.

34. In early Muslim history, the term referred to the register of military personnel compiled during the conquests. Later, it indicated a number of institutional organs of premodern government, notably including the state chancellery. See the articles "Dīwān" and "Dīwān-I Humayun" in *EI2*.

35. H. Inalcik and Carter Findley, "Maḥkama, 2: The Ottoman Empire," in *EI2*.

36. Interview, Ṣanʿāʾ, September 21, 1995.

37. Under Imam Yahya, the Appeal Court sometimes was referred to as the *dīwān al-istiʾnāf*, e.g., in al-Jirāfī, *Tuḥfat al-ikhwān*, 132.

38. Al-ʿAnsī, *Tāj*, 4:111n1. Cf. the 1950s code, Qasim bin Ibrāhīm et al., *Taysīr al-marām*, art. 1048, which glosses the term *dīwān* as "his register (*daftar*) or the handwriting of his secretary."

39. Ibn Miftāḥ, *Sharḥ al-azhār*, 4:233n10.

40. Ibid., n12. *ʿAlāma* may also mean "seal." The use of personal seals declined in the twentieth-century highlands, except among the ruling imams.

41. Al-Jalāl, *Dawʾ al-nahār*, 4:212–13.

42. Shawkanī, *Sayl*, 4:213–14.

43. Al-ʿAnsī, *Tāj*, 4:104. These concepts also came into play in other legal discussions. For their use in the analysis of intent, see Brinkley Messick, "Indexing the Self: Wording and Intentionality in Legal Acts," *Islamic Law and Society* 8, no. 2 (2001): 151–78.

44. Al-ʿAnsī, *Tāj*, 4:110–11.

45. The term "document" (*wathīqa*) appears in the last line of the *Flowers* chapter on "claims." Al-ʿAnsī, *Tāj*, 4:38–39, cf. 35.

46. In the "Repudiation" (*ṭalāq*) chapter these include "the joker," the "coerced speaker," and the "sleeper who murmurs his dreams aloud." See Messick, "Indexing the Self," 169.

47. Al-ʿAnsī, *Tāj*, 4:115; Ibn al-Murtaḍā, *Azhār*, 269; cf. in the 1950s codification, Qasim bin Ibrāhīm et al., *Taysīr al-marām*, art. 1055.

48. Al-ʿAnsī, *Tāj*, 4:116.

49. Ibid., 115–16; Ibn Miftāḥ, *Sharḥ al-azhār*, 4:237–38n8.

50. See the extended discussion of the marriage contract in chapter 10.
51. Derrida, *Archive Fever*, 26–34.
52. Al-ʿAnsī, *Tāj*, 2:122.
53. Johansen, "Formes," 357.
54. Derrida, *Archive Fever*, 100.
55. Al-ʿAnsī, *Tāj*, 2:122.
56. Hallaq, *Legal Theories*, 42, cf. 100.
57. Jalāl, *Dawʾ al-nahār*, 3:905–6, cf. G. E. von Grunebaum, "Bayān," in *EI2*.
58. Al-ʿAnsī, *Tāj*, 2:26.
59. Writing per se also figured in analogies. In the analysis of a planting contract, for example, the issue in question may be considered to be "like the thread of the tailor, the dye of the dyer, and the ink of the copiest" (*ka-khayt al-khayyāt wa sabgh al-sabbāgh wa midād al-nāsikh*). Ibn al-Murtaḍā, *Bahr*, 4:68.

4. Opinions

1. I adapt Max Weber's question that opens his section "Emergence and Creation of Legal Norms" in his "Sociology of Law": "How do new legal rules arise?" Max Weber, *Economy and Society* (Berkeley: University of California Press, 1978), 753. Cf. Dresch, "Introduction to Legalism"; Clarke, "Judge as Tragic Hero"; and Nakissa, "Epistemic Shift." Ghazzal, *Grammars*, 82, also poses the question of the "new" opinion. On the wider history of the "opinion," see Jeanette Wakin and Aron Zysow, "*Raʾy*," in *The Encyclopedia of Islam*, vol. 12 (suppl.) (Leiden: Brill, 1965–86).
2. Al-ʿAnsī, *Tāj*, 2:306–521.
3. Hallaq, "Fatwās to Furūʿ."
4. Cf. Brinkley Messick, "The Muftī, the Text and the World: Legal Interpretation in Yemen," *Man*, n.s., 21 (1986): 102–19; Messick, *Calligraphic State*, chap. 7.
5. Brinkley Messick, "Media Muftīs: Radio Fatwās in Yemen," in *Islamic Legal Interpretation*, ed. K. Masud, B. Messick, and D. Powers (Cambridge, MA: Harvard University Press, 1996), 310–20. In substantive terms, there was a marked shift away from the "legal" (centered mainly on *muʿāmalāt* issues) and toward the "religious" (centered on the *ʿibādāt*, and also on Qurʾan exegesis, *tafsīr*); in terms of the identities of the questioners, while women had posed questions through men in Ibb, many of al-Ghurbānī's direct questioners now were women; as for the textual medium, while the earlier Ibb fatwā had been issued on a one-by-one basis and was written out on paper, professional broadcasters read al-Ghurbānī's texts to mass radio audience listeners; and, finally, in comparison with the Ibb muftī's relatively cryptic and technical answers, which often had to be explicated for the recipient, al-Ghurbānī consciously composed his fatwā-responses in a newly accessible, more literary style. Selections of his fatwās have published (together with fatwās by Ahmad Muhammad Zabāra and Muhammad Yahya al-Muṭahhar) in ʿIzz al-dīn Hasan Taqī, ed., *al-Fatāwā al-sharʿiyya wa-l-ʿilmiyya wa-l-diniyya li-ʿulamāʾ al-diyār al-yamaniyya* (Ṣanʿāʾ: Maktaba al-Irshād, n.d.).

6. Khalid Muhammad Masud, Brinkley Messick and David S. Powers, eds., *Islamic Legal Interpretation: Muftīs and Their Fatwās* (Cambridge, MA: Harvard University Press, 1996).

7. Abu Zakariyya Yahya bin Sharaf al-Nawawī, *Adab al-fatwā wa-l-muftī wa-l-mustaftī* (Damascus: Dār al-Fikr, 1988), which is a chapter extract from his *Majmūᶜ*, a commentary on al-Shirāz's *al-Muhadhdhab*. For a detailed study of the *adab al-muftī* literature, see Masud, Messick, and Powers, "Muftīs, Fatwās, and Islamic Legal Interpretation," in Masud, Messick and Powers, *Islamic Legal Interpretation*, 15–26, and Calder, "Al-Nawawī's Typology."

8. ᶜAbd al-Rahman bin ᶜAli al-Ḥaddād, *al-Intiṣārāt naẓm al-ikhtiyārāt* (c. 1920), Dar al-Makhṭūṭāt Collection, Sanᶜaʾ, 48:81–86. The verse list (pp. 81–84) gives thirteen choices; the accompanying prose list (85–86), fifteen.

9. ᶜAbd Allah bin ᶜAbd al-Wahhāb al-Shamāḥī, *Ṣirāṭ al-ᶜārifīn ilā idrāk ikhtiyārāt amīr al-muʾminīn* (Ṣanᶜāʾ: Maṭbaᶜat al-Maᶜārif, 1356 AH [1937]).

10. Rashād al-ᶜAlīmī, *al-Taqlīdiyya wa-l-ḥadātha fī al-niẓām al-qānūnī al-yamanī* (Ṣanᶜāʾ: Dār al-Kalima, 1989), 258–60; Bernard Haykel, "Order and Righteousness: Muhammad ᶜAli al-Shawkānī and the Nature of the Islamic State in Yemen" (PhD thesis, Oxford University, 1997), 380–82. Bernard kindly provided me a copy of the handwritten text.

11. Yemen Arabic Republic, *Qarārāt Wizārat al-ᶜAdl* (Ṣanᶜāʾ: Ministry of Justice, 1971); *Majallat al-Buḥūth wa-l-aḥkām al-qaḍāʾiya al-yamaniyya*, vol. 1, no. 1 (Ṣanᶜāʾ: Maᶜhad al-ᶜālī li-l-qaḍāʾ, 1980); Muhammad Ismāᶜīl al-ᶜImrānī, *Niẓām al-qaḍāʾ fī al-islām* (Ṣanᶜāʾ: Dār al-Jīl, 1984), 227–32.

12. Imam Yahya bin Muhammad Ḥamīd al-Dīn, *Ikhtiyārāt* (MS copy by Muhammad Yahya al-Muṭahhar, Taᶜizz, October 1995).

13. Imam Ahmad bin Yahya Ḥamīd al-Dīn, *Ikhtiyārāt* (c. 1950, MS copy of ᶜAbd al-Qādir bin ᶜAbd Allah, Ṣanᶜāʾ, September 1995). This list differs slightly from that in the Haykel thesis. ᶜAbd al-Qādir also provided me the earlier-mentioned versification by al-ᶜĀmuwa. For a biography of ᶜAbd al-Qādir bin ᶜAbd Allah, see M. Zabāra, *Nuzhat al-naẓar*, 382–83; M. and A. Zabāra, *Nuzhat al-naẓar* MS, 2:373–75. See also Gabriele vom Bruck, *Islam, Memory, and Morality in Yemen: Ruling Families in Transition* (New York: Palgrave Macmillan, 2005), 114–19.

14. See chapter 7.

15. Dr. Aziz gave alternative language in the Ibb dialect: "*maqā ṭārinsh al-mukhtārāt*" or "*mā qā ṭārtsh al-mukhtārāt*." Personal communication, April 24, 2010.

16. Masud, Messick, and Powers, *Islamic Legal Interpretation*. See also Jakob Skovgaard-Petersen, *Defining Islam for the Egyptian State: Muftīs and Fatwās of the Dār al-Iftāʾ* (Leiden: Brill, 1997); cf. Brinkley Messick, "Fatwā: Process and Function," *The Oxford Encyclopedia of the Modern Islamic World*, ed. John Esposito (New York: Oxford University Press, 1995) 2:10–13; Messick, "Fatwā, Modern," in *EI3*.

17. Al-ᶜAnsī, *Tāj*, 4:200; cf. Masud, Messick, and Powers, "Muftīs, Fatwās, and Islamic Legal Interpretation," 19–20.

18. Shawkānī, *Sayl*, 4:273.

19. Ibn al-Murtaḍā, *Azhār*, 283; al-ᶜAnsī, *Tāj*, 4:192. Ghazzal, *Grammars*, 129, states, reading Ibn ᶜĀbidīn, that the judge was permitted to issue fatwās to non-litigants.

20. Ibn al-Murtaḍā, *Azhār*, 283; al-ᶜAnsī, *Tāj*, 4:192.

21. According to Ibn Miftāḥ, *Sharḥ al-azhār*, 4:318, the key issue is to avoid giving judgment where there is a "presumption of suspicion," but the super-commentary (318n6), states that what is actually "intended" by this rule—that is, what is forbidden by it—"is if he [the judge] rules for the questioner (*al-mustaftī*, i.e., the previous fatwā-seeker)." Another view, however, which is said to represent the "manifest meaning of the *Flowers*" (*ẓāhir al-az*, using the symbol for the book title), is that such an act of giving judgment is forbidden even if the judge rules against the former questioner.

22. Known as a *muḥtasib*. Al-ʿAnsī, *Tāj*, 4:408, 418 (cf. 407n1, on the conception of a *muqallid* imam); Haykel, *Revival and Reform*, 83.

23. Haykel, *Revival and Reform*, 66, 67, 69.

24. The case, which involved a preemption claim concerning a house in Ṣanʿāʾ, was handled by Judge Ahmad bin Ahmad al-Jirāfī. See I. al-Akwaʿ, *Hijar al-ʿilm*, 366; M. and A. Zabāra, *Nuzhat al-naẓar* MS, 2:274–75.

25. Haim Gerber, *State, Society, and Law in Islam: Ottoman Law in Comparative Perspective* (Albany: State University of New York Press, 1994), 23; David Powers, *Law, Society, and Culture in the Maghrib, 1300–1500* (Cambridge: Cambridge University Press, 2002); cf. Emile Tyan, *Histoire de l'organisation judiciaire en pays d'Islam* (Leiden: Brill, 1960), 219–30.

26. As in the Sunnī schools, Zaydī doctrine urges the judge to have scholars present in court for consultation. Al-ʿAnsī, *Tāj*, 4:191. At al-Ghurbānī's residence one afternoon, I watched as Judge Yahya al-ʿAnsī discussed the issues of his decision with his friend prior to writing his ruling at the foot of a court judgment document.

27. Again, in the typical historical state, the law "operated horizontally." Hallaq, *Sharīʿa*, 362. Cf. Schacht, *Introduction*, 210–211.

28. Hallaq, "Fatwās to Furūʿ," 44–45. Particular terms (*tajrīd*, *talkhīṣ*, and *tanqīḥ*) refer to such transformative editorial interventions.

29. Hallaq, "Shurūṭ Works," 124.

30. Al-Sharafī, *Qawāʿid*, in Ibn Miftāḥ, *Sharḥ al-azhār*, 3:47. Cf. supra, chapter 1, n20.

31. Powers, *Law, Society, and Culture*, 232, refers to questions posed to muftīs by judges about court cases: "[W]hen a qāḍī asked a muftī for advice, he customarily translated the names of the litigants and their stories into the abstract and impersonal language of the law, and the resulting fatwā was equally abstract." That is, the editorial stripping, the move from the proper name to *fulān*, from the archive to the library, began in formulating the question.

32. Cf. Geertz, "Local Knowledge," 173: "legal facts are made not born, are socially constructed."

33. See Masud, Messick, and Powers, "Muftīs, Fatwās, and Islamic Legal Interpretation," 20–26. An exception that has been noted is that of the Ottoman Shaykh al-Islam where the questions were reformulated to elicit a simple yes or no response.

34. On the provincial muftī in the Ottoman Empire, see Uriel Heyd, "Some Aspects of the Ottoman Fetvā," *BSOAS* 32 (1969): 54.

35. Cited in Messick, *Calligraphic State*, 130.

36. Masud, Messick, and Powers, "Muftīs, Fatwās, and Islamic Legal Interpretation," 1–8.

37. Author's field notes, 1980.

38. For details and discussion, see ibid., 16–17, and Calder, "Al-Nawawī's Typology."

39. Al-Sharafī, "*Qawāʿid*," in Ibn Miftāḥ, *Sharḥ al-azhār*, 3:47. The same principle appears as number 23 in the list attributed to Hasan bin ʿAbd Allah Dalāma, which is included in al-Sayāghī, *Madhhab al-zaydī*, 31. As I noted in chapter 2, and according to Ibn Muẓaffar, *Bayān*, 1:22, the *mustaftī* may be treated as equivalent to the *muqallid*.

40. Ḥussein Ali Agrama, "Ethics, Tradition, Authority: Toward an Anthropology of the Fatwā," *American Ethnologist* 37, no. 1 (2010): 2–18.

41. Messick, *Calligraphic State*, 149.

42. Wiederhold, "*Madhhab* Boundaries," 242, 272, 291.

43. Hallaq, "Fatwās to Furūʿ," 50, 54.

44. Calder, "Al-Nawawī's Typology" 143, 148, 159.

45. Norman Calder, *Islamic Jurisprudence*, 169.

46. In this connection one may cite a *qāʿida:* "The juridical differences of opinion behind an issue do not benefit the ignorant" (*al-khilāfu fī warāʾi al-masʾalati lā yufīdu al-jāhila*). Al-Sharafī, *Qawāʿid*, 46.

47. "*Al-ʿammī lā madhhab lahu.*" Cf. the related discussions in Ibn Miftāḥ, *Sharḥ al-azhār*, 3:51–54.

48. As far as I know, the post was attained by intellectual stature rather than by formal appointment. The Ottoman district accounts of 1916 give a salary entry for one of the uncles, Abū Bakr, but without mention of a title. For the deeper history of Shāfiʿī muftīs in the Ibb region, see, for example, the manuscript volume of fatwās organized in *fiqh* chapters by the seventeenth-century jurist al-Hubayshī, *Fatāwī al-Ḥubayshī*, MS (c. 17th century), Vatican Library, Arab 1353.

49. Hallaq, *Sharīʿa*, 219.

50. Four examples: (1) Imam al-Mansur billāh ʿAbd Allah bin Hamza (d. 1217) (see al-Ḥibshī, *Maṣādir*, 592–600, and Haykel, *Revival and Reform*, 202); (2) *Ikhtiyārāt al-muʾayyadiya* of al-Muʾayyad billāh Yahya bin Hamza bin ʿAli bin Ibrahīm bin Rasūl Allah (d. 1346) (see Berlin MS Glaser 164, cited in C. Brockelmann, *Geschichte der Arabischen Litteratur*, 2nd ed. [Leiden: Brill, 1943–49], 237, and Shawkānī, *al-Badr al-ṭāliʿ*, 2:331; cf. al-Ḥibshī, *Maṣādir*, 616–23); (3) *Ikhtiyārāt* of Imam al-Muʾayyad billāh Muhammad bin al-Qasim (d. 1644) (referred to in R. B. Serjeant and Ronald Lewcock, *Ṣanʿāʾ: An Arabian Islamic City* [London: World of Islam Festival Trust, 1983], 79; (4) *al-Masāʾil al-murtaḍāt fīmā yaʿtamiduhu al-quḍāt* by Imam al-Mutawakkil Ismāʿil bin al-Qasim (d. 1776), a photocopied and transcribed text of which was provided to me by the High Judicial Institute, Ṣanʿāʾ, in 1993 (cf. Haykel, *Revival and Reform*, 202–3).

51. A post-revolutionary Yemeni jurist characterized the imamic *ikhtiyārāt* as issued in areas of the law where "the Zaydī school does not give a text and where the author of the *Flowers* does not exercise a choice." Al-ʿImrānī, *Niẓām al-qaḍāʾ*, 227.

52. "In most cases," Schacht, *Introduction*, 202, 204, states, the "*ikhtiyār* is limited to the elimination of differences of opinion among earlier authorities," and "it of-

ten amounts merely to making a choice between the several opinions." Although "a very limited scope" existed for such an *ikhtiyār*, it nevertheless represented a significant mechanism for the legal framing of "new developments." See also Hallaq, *Authority*, 162–64.

53. Al-Ḥaddād, *al-Intiṣārāt*, a versified list and an accompanying prose list; Imam Yahya, *Ikhtiyārāt* (al-Muṭahhar MS); al-ʿAlīmī, *al-Taqlīdiyya*, 258–60.

54. *Majallat al-Buhūth*.

55. In comparison with the Imam Ahmad, *Ikhtiyārāt* (ʿAbd al-Qadir bin ʿAbd Allah MS), see the slightly different versions of Imam Ahmad's set of early choices in *Majallat al-Buḥūth*.

56. "*Al-ikhityarāt tataghayyar bi mā yatanāsab maʿa al-ʿaṣr, wa la takhtalif maʿa al-sharīʿa*." Author's field notes, Ṣanʿāʾ, 1993.

57. See Sayyid Mustafa Sālim, *Wathāʾiq yamaniyya*, 2nd printing (Cairo: al-Maṭbaʿat al-Fanniyya, 1985), 202–4, for a document (no. 24), dated 1909, during Ottoman rule, which Sālim describes as "equivalent to a fatwā from the imam." It is unlike the Ibb fatwā of 1924 in that it contains only the response, the fatwā alone, without the question text, which is referred to as "your letter." It is on "the transactions of commoners" (*taṣarrufāt al-ʿawāmm*), a topic that figured in an Ibb court case (see below n77; chapter 7, case 2).

58. Document number 55, Burayhī-ʿAzīz MS Collection, Ibb.

59. The term *marjiʿ* is also used by Shawkānī as his technical characterization of the first of four types of students of knowledge. Shawkānī, *Adab al-ṭalab*, cited in Haykel, *Revival and Reform*, 103, cf. 59, 114.

60. Ahmad Jābir ʿAfīf, *al-Ḥarakat al-waṭaniyya fī al-yaman* (Damascus: Dār al-Fikr, 1982), 258–59, 261, 264. For a translation of one such letter and further references, see Haykel, *Revival and Reform*, 203. I thank Ms. Arwa Ahmad ʿAbd Allah al-Khattābī, a Yemeni student in Berlin, for sharing with me her father's appointment letter dated 1364 AH (1944).

61. Imam Yahya, *Taʿlīmāt* (1937), MS copy in a *safīna* register in the possession of Muhammad Yahya al-Muṭahhar, Taʿizz, art. 8, p. 234.

62. Al-ʿAlīmī, *al-Taqlīdiyya*, 258–60; Muhammad Yahya Muṭahhar, personal communication, 1995. A republican-era collection of imamic choices (without attribution to the imams) gives a retrospective view of how they were archived. In his introduction to a collection prepared by an Egyptian adviser, the minister of justice states, "The choices were scattered about in the pages of registers and in folders, which lacked indexes or tables of contents, making it difficult for the student to gain access to what was being looked for. . . . But now they [the choices] are before you, in a single volume, distinct and clear in method and meaning, divided in chapters and indexed." *Majallat al-buḥūth*, 1.

63. *Daftar qayd al-qarārāt, Al-hayʾa al-sharʿiyya* (appellate rulings register), Taʿizz, 1380 AH (1960), register in the possession of ʿAli Sharaf al-Dīn, an employee of the Taʿizz (Province) Appeal Court. This organ also was known as *al-hayʾa al-ʿilmiyya*.

64. Lucine Taminian, "Playing with Words: The Ethnography of Poetic Genres in Yemen" (PhD thesis, University of Michigan, 2001), refers to this scholarly branch of Yemeni verbal art as "*fiqhī* poetry."

65. This flexibility is related to a general attitude toward such language. Imam Yahya's choice no. 5 concerns the non-necessity of specific contractual "expressions" to constitute a sale. As I noted earlier, a basic conceptual distinction between "expression" (*lafẓ*) and "meaning" (*maʿnā*) figured in the jurists' analyses of contractual language and its relation to intention or consent. See Messick, "Indexing the Self," and infra, chapter 10.

66. Al-Ḥaddād, *al-Intiṣārāt*.

67. Ibid., 83.

68. Commentary on choices also occurred in the past. See Haykel, *Revival and Reform*, 202–3n48.

69. My copy of this versification is from ʿAbd al-Qadir bin ʿAbd Allah. It is ninety-nine lines long in the photocopy I was provided, but a last line or two may have been cut off. Cf. Ahmad Muhammad al-Shāmī, *Imām al-Yaman Ahmad Ḥamīd al-Dīn* (Beirut: Dār al-Kitāb al-Jadīd, 1965), 139.

70. Dated 12 al-Qaʿda [13]69. His work of derivation was referred to as *istikhrāj*. Author's digital image B-669. Also quoted in Messick, *Calligraphic State*, 272n30. Judge al-Ḥaddād did not have a copy of the commentary letter he sent to the imam.

71. In chapter 7, this is case 1.

72. Judge of Ibb Province, Ismaʿil ʿAbd al-Raḥman al-Manṣūr (see chapters 1, 7), decided 28 Rabīʿ II 1379 AH (1959), with an appellate ruling citing accordance with "the honored choice." *Al-daftar al-khāmis ʿashr min al-dafātir al-maḥkamat al-liwāʾ ibb*, 1379–80 AH (1959–60), 56–58.

73. In chapter 7, this is case 4.

74. In chapter 7, this is case 2.

75. Case 2. I am reading from the original rolled judgment (*ḥukm*) held by one of the litigant parties, lines 70–71, 71–75, 85–87. For an earlier treatment of this case, see Brinkley Messick, "Textual Properties: Writing and Wealth in a Sharīʿa Case," *Anthropological Quarterly* 68, no. 3 (1995): 157–70.

76. Al-ʿAlīmī, *al-Taqlīdiyya*, 259, nos. 1, 2; al-Ḥaddād, *al-Intiṣārāt*, nos. 1, 2; Imam Yahya, *Ikhtiyārāt* (al-Muṭahhar MS), nos. 1, 2.

77. I will merely mention that the doctrine on bequests to an heir is an instance in which the Hadawī position of the *Flowers* is close to that of the Jaʿfarī or Twelver Shīʿī school. The opposed position, taken by highland "Sunnīs" such as al-Shawkānī, and by regular Sunnīs, is also that of the twentieth-century imamic choices. See Shawkānī, *Sayl*, 4:496–99, and al-ʿAnsī, *Tāj*, 4:403, who mentions the choices of Imam Yahya on this topic and says they are "opposed to the [Hādawī] *madhhab* and represent current practice in the sharīʿa courts."

78. Al-ʿAlīmī, *al-Taqlīdiyya*, 259, no. 22; Imam Yahya, *Ikhtiyārāt* (al-Muṭahhar MS), no. 21. Cf. al-Shamāḥī, *Ṣirāṭ*, 44–45. This choice holds that commoners intend such transactions for postmortem implementation, which means that they may be retracted inter-vivos. In case 2, line 23, the patriarch-endower is found to be among the commoners (*fī silk al-ʿawāmm*), and what had been termed a *waqfiyya* was recategorized as a *waṣiyya*.

79. These three questions appear as the first, fifth, and sixth appended and unnumbered texts in Imam Aḥmad, *Ikhtiyārāt* (ʿAbd al-Qādir bin ʿAbd Allah MS).

80. Ibid., appended text three, which has a title: "Dissolution [of marriage contract] for Extreme Hatred and Timidity."

81. Thābit bin Qays was a Companion of the Prophet. His wife, Ḥabība bint Sahl, told the Prophet that they were not compatible. The Prophet told her to compensate Thābit in return for the dissolution of the marriage, and in one version of this story she returned a garden Thābit had given her. See Susan Spectorsky, *Chapters on Marriage and Divorce: Responses of Ibn Ḥanbal and Ibn Rāhwayh* (Austin: University of Texas Press, 1993), 50, cf. 108. See my discussion of this type of divorce in chapter 10.

82. In chapter 7, this is case 4.

83. Case 4, lines 295–98.

84. "*Lā nufūdh laha*." Haykel, "Order and Righteousness," 380, has "are invalid (*bāṭil*)." This is one of six minor differences in comparison with the ʿAbd al-Qādir bin ʿAbd Allah MS, which has the same text as that quoted in *Majallat al-buhūth*, 13, in the section titled "Sale."

85. Imam Aḥmad, *Ikhtiyārāt* (ʿAbd al-Qādir bin ʿAbd Allah MS).

86. Of the total of eight appended texts in the manuscript, numbers 2 and 4 are explicitly identified as "choices," even though the rules in question remain associated with specific court case materials; 3 (the quoted marriage dissolution case and rule) and 7 are not identified as choices and also contain court materials, but they are identified elsewhere as choices; 1, 5, and 6 are the earlier referenced examples of queries to the imam about existing choices; and 8 concerns a court case and an appellate court ruling that has no explicit connection with the imam but is said to relate to "discussions of the people of the school" (*kalām ahl al-madhhab*). There also is an additional choice entered in the margins next to original choice number 2.

87. Hallaq, "Fatwās to Furūʿ," 57.

5. "Practice with Writing"

1. Al-Shamāḥī, *Sirāṭ*, 31–33. I draw here on Messick, *Calligraphic State*, 211–16.

2. Ahmad bin Zayd al-Kibsī, "Baḥth fī al-ʿamal bi-l-khaṭṭ," in *Dhakhāʾir ʿulamāʾ al-yaman*, ed. ʿAbd Allah bin ʿAbd al-Karīm al-Jirāfī (Beirut: Muʾassasat Dār al-Kitāb al-Ḥadīth, 1991), 329–36.

3. "*Al-ʿamal biʾl-khaṭt muʿtabar idhā ʿurifa al-khaṭṭ wa kāna kātibuhu maʿrūfan biʾl-ʿadāla*." Twentieth-century *Flowers* commentator al-ʿAnsī, *Tāj*, 4:115n1, using slightly different wording and a footnote, positions the imam's opinion in the chapter titled "Testimonies," specifically at the earlier cited (chapter 3) phrase, "sufficient for the forgettor, where he knows the general but is in doubt about the detail, is writing."

4. "*Khaṭṭ ʿadlin qad ʿarafnā yuqbalu / dalīlahu muʿanʿanun musalsalu*."

5. The imam's choice resonates with a principle established in the late nineteenth-century Ottoman *Majalla*, 250–51, art. 1736: "Writing and seals are not to be relied upon in and of themselves, but if they are [determined to be] free from suspicion of forgery and fabrication, they may be relied upon, that is, they may be

the determining element (*madār*) of the judgment without requiring support of another type." For the role of the analytic term *madār* among *ḥadīth* specialists, see G. H. A. Juynboll, "Tawātur," in *EI2*.

6. For a biography of al-Kibsī, see Muhammad Zabāra, *Nayl al-waṭar*, 2 vols. (Cairo: Matba'at al-Salafiyya, 1348 and 1350 AH [1929 and 1931]), 1:101–4.

7. I made a draft translation and then had opportunities to read sections with Abdullah Hamidaddin (New York, October 8, 2009) and Dr. Muhammad Aziz (New Haven, May 26, 2010). I am grateful to both men. Neither is responsible for the result.

8. Mary Carruthers, *The Book of Memory* (Cambridge: Cambridge University Press, 1990), 6.

9. This last view was related via the famous exegete al-Zamakhsharī (d. 1144). On the extensive writings of these four imams, see al-Ḥibshī, *Maṣādir* (1988), 592–600, 616–23, 588–91, 613–15.

10. Al-Faqīh ʿAbd Allah bin Zayd, *al-Durar al-maṣūna*, which I do not have.

11. In relation to the *Flowers* rule discussed in chapter 3 and below, cf. Nawawī's statement: "[I]f he [the judge] sees a document containing his judgment or his certificate . . . he should not implement it . . . until he remembers." *Minhāj al-ṭālibīn*. Cf. Messick, *Calligraphic State*, 210.

12. A. J. Arberry, *The Koran Interpreted*, 70–71.

13. Ibn al-Murtaḍā, *Bahr*, intro. vol.: 251–52.

14. Cf. Schoeler, *The Oral and the Written*, 82–83n507.

15. Yemeni exegetes, again, speak in the plural of "orders" (*awāmir*) to write documents (cf. chapter 3).

16. Mentioned in passing in Muhammad bin Yahya Bahrān, *Kitāb jawāhir al-akhbār wa-al-āthār al-mustakhraja min lughat al-Baḥr al-zakhkhār*, a super-commentary printed in Ibn al-Murtaḍā, *Bahr*, 5:127.

17. Joseph Schacht, "Fiḳh," in *EI2*. Ibn Musayyib was "one of the first specialists in religious law whose activity can be regarded as historical," individuals whose "reasoning represents the beginning of Islamic jurisprudence."

18. J. Robson, "Ḥadīth," in *EI2*: in comparison to *saḥīḥ*, or "sound" traditions, "*Ḥasan* traditions are not considered quite so strong, but they are necessary for establishing points of law. Indeed, most of the legal traditions are of this type."

19. Imam al-Muʾayyad Billāh Ahmad bin al-Husayn, *Sharḥ al-tajrīd* (Ṣanʿāʾ: Markaz al-Turāth wa-l-Buḥūth al-Yamanī, 2006), 6:242–44.

20. On these early writings, including other references to the sword and sheath as an archival site, see Gregor Schoeler, *The Genesis of Literature in Islam: From the Aural to the Read*, rev. ed., trans. Shawkat M. Toorawa (Edinburgh: Edinburgh University Press, 2009), 17. Cf. Schoeler, *The Oral and the Written*, 64–65.

21. The *ḥadīth* of ʿAbd Allah bin ʿAkīm.

22. This paraphrases Qurʾan 4:29.

23. Al-Ghurbānī, *ʿIlm uṣūl al-ḥadīth*, 25.

24. Brown, *Canonization*, 53. *Mutawātir* is the typical version of the term.

25. On *ẓann* among *ḥadīth* specialists, see Brown, *Canonization*, s.v.

26. Al-Ḥibshī, *Maṣādir* (2004), 201.

27. Al-Jalāl, *Ḍawʾ al-nahār,* 4:2123. The passage appears as follows (*Flowers* language in italics): "*and* [it is] *not* permitted for the judge to judge *on the basis of what he found in his archive* written in his handwriting or the handwriting of his secretary whom he does not disavow *if he does not remember* the circumstance of the writings."

28. The text reads "*al-Ithmār.*"

29. Imam al-Mutawakkil Sharaf al-Dīn Yahya bin Shams al-Dīn, *al-Athmār fī fiqh al-aʾimmat al-aṭhār,* which I do not have. Cf. al-Husaynī, *Muʾallafāt al-Zaydīyya,* 1:44.

30. See chapter 3. For Ḥanafī usage, see Guy Burak, "Evidentiary Truth Claims, Imperial Registers, and the Ottoman Archive: Contending Legal Views of Archival and Record-Keeping Practices in Ottoman Greater Syria (Seventeenth–Nineteenth Centuries)," *Bulletin of the School of Oriental and African Studies* (2016): 11, 12.

31. The term *sijill* means "document," but in the Ottoman tradition it also referred to the court register, also known as a *daftar.* Al-Kibsī uses the term in the sense of "register."

32. Cf. Ibn Muẓaffar, *Bayān,* 4:178–79.

33. For a late Ḥanafī view, see Gerber, *Islamic Law and Culture,* 107, who quotes Ibn ʿĀbidīn to the effect that "the discourse of the [jurists] on the question of the acceptance (*fī masʾalat al-ʿamal*) of writing is confused."

34. Cf. Jalāl, *Ḍawʾ al-nahār,* 4:2123, where Abū Yusuf and Muhammad are mentioned as permitting the judge to judge without remembering.

35. Al-Muʾayyad Billāh, *Sharḥ al-tajrīd,* 6: 242–43.

36. In an alternative practice, witnesses were named in a document but did not sign. This possibility is made explicit in a law book passage cited in chapter 3, which refers to a witness whose "witnessing [act] is written in his writing or in the writing of one trusted by a judge." Al-ʿAnsī, *Tāj,* 4:115.

37. Al-Kibsī, "Baḥth," 233: "*yatadhakkara al-shahādata wa-yatayqqanahā.*"

38. Cf. chapter 3.

39. Johansen, "Formes," 362–633, quotes Sarakhsī's use of the related term *muḥtamil,* which he translates as "ambiguous."

40. Al-Shamāḥī, *Ṣirāṭ,* 31–32; cf. Messick, *Calligraphic State,* 214, where I translated it as "potentiality."

41. "*Al-khaṭṭ al-ladhī huwa min al-ghayr al-mawthūq bihi.*"

42. Muhammad bin Yahya Bahrān, *Taftīḥ al-qulūb wa-l-abṣār lil-ihtidāʾ ilā iqtiṭāf athmār al-azhār,* 4 vols. I do not have this work. Cf. Ahmad al-Husaynī, *Muʾallafat al-Zaydīyya* (Qom: Maṭbaʿat al-Ismāʿīliyyan, 1413 AH [1993]), 1:301. Ibn Bahrān also is known as the author of the earlier discussed basic *uṣūl al-fiqh* treatise *al-Kāfil,* which was printed in the twentieth century (see chapter 1), and of the super-commentary on Ibn al-Murtaḍā, *Baḥr,* cited above, n16.

43. A well-known analytic distinction that may be compared to that of "expression" versus "meaning," *lafẓ* versus *maʿnā,* cited in chapter 3.

44. The ellipsis is meant to translate al-Kibsī's words, "until the end of what he mentioned" (*ilā ākhir mā dhakarahu*).

45. Al-Kibsī, "Baḥth," 335.

46. Cf. al-Muʾayyad Billāh, *Sharḥ al-tajrīd,* 6:244; Ibn al-Murtaḍā, *Baḥr,* 5:127, "Writings and seals are similar [to one another]"; Ibn Muẓaffar, *al-Bayān,* 179n30 (quoting

al-Bustān), "writing is not a route to knowledge (*ʿilm*) because writings may be similiar." In the related, rule-oriented *ḥadīth* literature, see the refutation by Shawkānī, *Wabl al-ghamām*, 2:316, of a passage from the commented-on work, the *Shifāʾ al-uwām*. Schoeler, *The Oral and the Written*, 83, translates *al-kitab yushbihu ʿl-kitab* as "one piece of writing resembles another piece of writing (so that they easily become confused)."

47. See further chapter 7, final section.

48. Cf. the Shāfiʿī jurist Nawawī's notion of a "protected document" (*waraqa maṣūna*), cited and discussed in Messick, *Calligraphic State*, 211.

49. The early juristic generation of the *muḥaṣṣilūn* was "headed by" these two brothers. Haykel and Zysow, "Madhhab," 342.

50. "Common meaning" or, more technically, "*ratio legis*." See Hallaq, *Legal Theories*, 20, passim.

6. Intermission

1. Gayatri Chakravorty Spivak, *A Critique of Postcolonial Reason: Toward a History of the Vanishing Present* (Cambridge, MA: Harvard University Press, 1999), 205: "Literature and archives seem complicit in that they are both a crosshatching of condensations, a traffic in telescoped symbols, that can only too easily be read as each other's repetition-with-a-displacement."

2. An "art" (*fann*). Cf. Jacques Berque, "ʿamal," in *EI2*: "*Fiḳh* [*fiqh*] is above all an 'art' in the service of orthodoxy and of urban economy."

3. Bakhtin, *Dialogic Imagination*, 320, 323. He also refers to the incorporating texts as "secondary" genres, which typically are written texts. Cf. M. Bakhtin, *Speech Genres and Other Late Essays*, trans. Vern W. McGee (Austin: University of Texas Press, 1986), 62.

4. Max Weber opens his "Sociology of Law" as follows: "One of the most important distinctions in modern legal theory and practice is that between 'public' and 'private' law." Weber, *Economy and Society*, 641. The "public" responsibilities of a ruling imam are defined in terms of concepts such as *al-ʿāmma*. See al-ʿAnsī, *Tāj*, 4:426.

5. See Feldman, *Governing Gaza*; Matthew Hull, "The File"; Hull, *Government of Paper*; Vismann, *Files*; Bruno Latour, "How to Make a File Ripe for Use," in *The Making of Law*, trans. M. Brilman and A. Pottage (Cambridge: Polity Press, 2010), 70–106; and Messick, *Calligraphic State*, chap. 12, and further references cited there.

6. Riles, *Documents*.

7. The question of the "central archive" figures in comparative thinking. Thus, W. Björkman, "Diplomatic," in *EI2*, 2:304: "There is no evidence of the existence of a central archive, as there was in Greek times."

8. Wael B. Hallaq, "The *Qāḍī's Dīwān* (*Sijill*) Before the Ottomans," *Bulletin of the School of Oriental and African Studies* 61, no. 3 (1998): 418, 435.

9. Cf. Schacht, *Introduction*, 83.

10. Martha Mundy, "Women's Inheritance of Land in Highland Yemen," *Arabian Studies* 5 (1979): 174; Paul Dresch, *A History of Modern Yemen*, 65.

11. S. D. Goitein, "Portrait of a Yemenite Weavers' Village," *Jewish Social Studies* 17, no. 1 (1955): 3–26; Isaac Hollander, *Jews and Muslims in Lower Yemen: A Study of Protection and Restraint 1918-1949* (Leiden: Brill, 2005).

12. Dresch, *Tribes, Government, and History*; Dresch, *The Rules of Baraṭ*; Martha Mundy, *Domestic Government*; Shelagh Weir, *A Tribal Order.*

13. Mundy, *Domestic Government*, 63, 64. Note Mundy's argument in chapter 3, "Law in the Locality," 50–58.

14. Weir, *A Tribal Order*, 17, 321.

15. According to a "Progress report" dated April 1980 (copy in author's files), the Ottoman court records Mandaville and Muhammad al-Shuʿaybī collected from Hodeidah, Bājil, al-Zaydiyyah, Kamarān, and Turbah were deposited at the Ministry of Justice Library in Ṣanʿāʾ. The ministry has since moved, and the fate of these records is unknown. Cf. Jon E. Mandaville, "The Ottoman Court Records of Syria and Jordan," *Journal of the American Oriental Society* 86 (1966): 311–19.

16. Sālim, *Wathāʾiq yamaniyya.*

17. Jacques Berque, *Structures sociales du Haut-Atlas* (Paris: Presses Universitaires de France, 1955), 62, my translation.

18. Ahmed Akgündüz, "Shariʿah Courts and Shariʿah Records: The Application of Islamic Law in the Ottoman State," *Islamic Law and Society* 16 (2009): 202–30. For Egypt in the same period, see Rudolph Peters, "The Violent Schoolmaster: The 'Normalization' of the Dossier of a Nineteenth-Century Egyptian Legal Case," in *Narratives of Truth in Islamic Law*, ed. Baudouin Dupret et al. (London: I. B. Tauris, 2008), 69.

19. The transformation of property relations began with the 1858 Land Code. For the courts, the changes involved: (1) the mid-century addition to the Ottoman (and Egyptian) sharīʿa court systems of the parallel/superior jurisdiction of the "councils" (*majālis*), and (2) the late-century restriction of the jurisdiction of the sharīʿa courts to matters of personal status. Comparison with the highland instance is further hampered by the role in the handling of property disputes of the Ottoman institution of *qānūn* (Turkish, *kanun*), the parallel body of law promulgated by the sultan. For Ottoman legal changes in the nineteenth and twentieth centuries, see C. V. Findley, "Maḥkama, ii. The Reform era (ca. 1789–1922)," *EI2*, 6:5–11; Iris Agmon, *Family and Court: Legal Culture and Modernity in Late Ottoman Palestine* (Syracuse: Syracuse University Press, 2006); and Avi Rubin, *Ottoman Nizamiye Courts: Law and Modernity* (New York: Palgrave Macmillan, 2011). For Egypt, see Rudolph Peters, "Murder on the Nile: Homicide Trials in 19th Century Egyptian Shariʿa Courts," *Die Welt des Islams*, n.s., 30, no. 1 (1990): 98–116, and Khaled Fahmy, "Anatomy of Justice: Forensic Medicine and Criminal Law in Nineteenth-Century Egypt," *Islamic Law and Society* 6, no. 2 (1999): 224–71.

20. Ghazzal, *Grammars*, 12, 16, 138n30, 164–67, 323–24, 391–92.

21. Ibid., 29; cf. 324: "[An] analysis of Ḥanafī texts on land tenure reveals how much the Ottoman mīrī system was deliberately ignored by the jurists, even though the courts for their part had to impose their arbitration on a growing number of land disputes."

22. For the late Ottoman *tapu*, see Anton Minkov, "Ottoman *Tapu* Title Deeds in the Eighteenth and Nineteenth Centuries: Origins, Typology and Diplomatics,"

Islamic Law and Society 7, no. 1 (2000): 1–29. For both *tapu* documents and *ijāra* contracts, see Ghazzal, *Grammars*, s.v. "contract: lease, sharecropping," and Mundy and Saumarez Smith, *Governing Property*, s.v. *tapu*, *ijara*.

23. Schacht, *Introduction*, 2.

24. Cf. the reverse as an assumption; e.g., Ghazzal, *Grammars*, 18.

25. Beshara Doumani, *Rediscovering Palestine: Merchants and Peasants in Jabal Nablus, 1700–1900* (Berkeley: University of California Press, 1995), 9–12, 249–51.

26. For a corpus similar in some respects to privately held archival documents from Ibb, see Geoffrey Khan, *Bills, Letters and Deeds: Arabic Papyri of the 7th to 11th Centuries* (London: Nour Foundation, Oxford University Press, 1992). For the Geniza, see Geoffrey Khan, *Arabic Legal and Administrative Documents in the Cambridge Genizah Collections* (Cambridge: Cambridge University Press, 1993), 173–89.

27. Rudolph Peters, *Wathāʾiq madīnat al-Qaṣr bi-l-wāḥāt al-Dākhila maṣdarān li-tārīkh Miṣr fī l-ʿaṣr al-ʿuthmānī* (Cairo: Maṭbaʿat al-ʿĀmma li-Dār al-Kutub wa-l-Wathāʾiq al-Qawmiyya, 2011).

28. Mikhail Rodionov and Hanne Schönig, *The Hadramawt Documents, 1904–51: Family Life and Social Customs Under the Last Sultans* (Beirut: Ergon Verlag, 2011).

29. Al-ʿAnsī, *Tāj*, 4:111n1. Cf. the 1950s code, Qasim bin Ibrāhīm et al., *Taysīr al-marām*, 213, art. 1048, which glosses the term *dīwān* as "his register (*daftar*) or the handwriting of his secretary."

30. Ze'evi, "Ottoman Sharīʿa Court Records," considers both litigation documentation and instruments such as estate inventories.

31. Burak, "Evidentiary Truth Claims," 10. Concerning the integrity of the imperial register, Burak quotes the Ḥanafī jurist al-Haskafī: "Whoever [seeks] to rely [on the register] follows this [register] knowing with great [certainty] that it is impossible that [the bureaucrats] would connive at the slightest neglect [of the registers], let alone their forgery, out of fear of the authority of the sultan—may God grant him victory."

32. Ibid. 11, 12, 16, 18. Cf. supra, chapter 5.

33. Johansen, "Formes," 367–75. Cf. Burak, "Evidentiary Truth Claims," 9–12.

34. This little-known choice was turned up by an Egyptian adviser attached to the Ministry of Justice and published in 1980 in *Majallat al-buḥūth*, 1:6–7, together with his comments relating it to republican legislation. Cf. Al-ʿAnsī, *Tāj*, 4:37, a passing example, "*daftar al-ḥisāb*." Al-ʿImrānī, *Niẓam al-qaḍāʾ*, 232, gives the following rendition.

35. Case 3 (1956) in chapter 7, lines 84, 102.

36. See also Messick, *Calligraphic State*, 187–92 ("court order"), 237–41 ("scribal registers").

37. See the employee list translated in Messick, *Calligraphic State*, 187.

38. For the legal dimension, see Kuehn, *Empire*, 106–16.

39. In the activities of certain of these offices there were direct sharīʿa implications. The major example is the collection of the agrarian tithe (*wājibāt*; cf. *zakāt*, *ʿushr*) and the distribution of charity (*sadaqa*), both of which were under the auspices of the local Office of the Treasury (*al-māliyya*), where part of the accounting was in-kind in a central register for daily grain revenues and disbursements (*yawmiyyāt*

al-ḥubūb); see Brinkley Messick, "Transactions in Ibb: Economy and Society in a Yemeni Highland Town" (PhD thesis, Princeton University, 1978).

Other types of official work necessitate a qualification of my earlier schema. Administrations also issued and retained certain types of sharīʿa instruments. An example is the *kafāla,* the personal bond, a primary genre backed by its own chapter in the *Flowers*-tradition law books (e.g., al-ʿAnsī, *Tāj*, 4:138–50). Written under the aegis of, and then kept by, an administration such the Municipality or the Gendarme Office, *kafāla*s had a quasi-"public" character. Those from the municipality bore the signature of the *kafīl*, the "private" individual providing the guarantee, and the affirming signatures and seals of the functionaries. Such instruments guaranteed the good conduct of craftsmen and others active in the town marketplace, including both Muslims and Jews. While the Ottoman-era Ibb office produced these written guarantees as separate documents, which it then retained, in the following imamic period, the equivalent texts, without the signatures and seals, were entered informally in a notebook. At the Gendarme Office, a small register contained *kafāla*s for the individual gendarmes. I have examples of both Ottoman- and imamic-period *baladiyya kafāla*s and imamic gendarme *kafāla*s.

With its recognized "religious" (*dīniyya*) character, the Endowments Office existed in an administrative realm neither exactly "public" nor "private." Endowments registers held various genres of sharīʿa texts. One type of register, known as *takrīs*, contained copies of both court judgments and various types of primary instruments. All of these pertained, as supporting documentation, to particular endowed properties under office supervision. A different type of endowments register contained leases (sing. *ijāra*) for the administered endowed properties, mainly cultivated terraces but also some urban real estate properties, including the town bath (*hammām*) and some of the warehouses (sing. *khān*).

40. I have examples of wholesale commercial documentation in such forms as an early twentieth-century order addressed by an Ibb trader to his agent (*wakīl*) in Aden and a very comprehensive personal will (*waṣiyya*) from the same period that includes detailed sections on the disposition of commercial goods in hand.

41. See Messick, *Calligraphic State*, 218–19.

42. Donald P. Little, *A Catalogue of the Islamic Documents from the al-Ḥaram ash-Sharīf in Jerusalem* (Beirut: Beiruter Texte und Studien, 1984).

43. Ibid., 13.

44. Christian Müller, "The Ḥaram al-Sharīf Collection of Arabic Legal Documents in Jerusalem: A Mamlūk Court Archive?" *Al-Qantara* 32, no. 2 (2011): 435–59. See also Müller, *Der Kadi und seine Zeugen: Studie der mamlukischen Haram-Dokumente aus Jerusalem* (Wiesbaden: Harrassowitz, 2013).

45. Müller, "The Ḥaram al-Sharīf Collection," 446, 448.

46. The physical movement of certain genres of archival writings within a region or between related regions was envisioned doctrinally, however, in the theory of judge-to-judge written communications and also in that of a judge's appointment letter from the imam, both of which doctrines stipulated that, in their travels, the writings be accompanied by witnesses. See Messick, *Calligraphic State*, 210, referring to Shāfiʿī doctrine.

47. Hallaq, *Sharīʿa*, 15–16. Cf. Hallaq, *Impossible State*, 2.

48. Hallaq, *Sharīʿa*, 15.

49. Ibid., 16, italics original.

50. Johansen, "Formes," 344–48, French translations mine; Hallaq, "*Qāḍī*'s *Dīwān*."

51. Hallaq's approach is "dialectical" in conception. Hallaq, "*Qāḍī*'s *Dīwān*," 431.

52. Al-Khaṣṣāf, *Adab al-qāḍī*.

53. Johansen, "Formes," 348. Hallaq, "*Qāḍī*'s *Dīwān*," 420–21, starts with the two basic types of registers associated with litigation and then lists the range of instruments as the first of eight further types of court writings.

54. Johansen, "Formes," 347.

55. Tyan, *Organisation*, 245. Cf. note 407, supra.

56. Geertz, "Local Knowledge," 190–95; Lawrence Rosen, *The Anthropology of Justice: Law as Culture in Islamic Society* (Cambridge: Cambridge University Press, 1989); Rosen, *The Justice of Islam: Comparative Perspectives on Islamic Law and Society* (Oxford: Oxford University Press, 2000). For an Ottomanist view, see Gerber, *State, Society, and Law*, 37–39.

57. Johansen, "Formes," 344n52, n57, notes that the petition is a rough equivalent to the *ruqʿa*, and that the latter is not a "universal" practice.

58. "*Yuḥaḍḍirū fulān li-inṣāf al-shākī*." This was the action of *al-infādh*, or the judge's dispatch of a soldier-retainer to bring in the adversary.

59. Johansen, "Formes," 344, 347.

60. On this key prior step, which is not mentioned in the records of the following litigations, see Messick, "Evidence," 233–34.

61. See Messick, "Evidence," 244–45.

62. Johansen, "Formes," 345.

63. Ibid., 346.

64. Ibid., 347.

65. Christian Müller, "Judging with God's Law on Earth: Judicial Powers of the Qāḍī al-Jamāʿa of Cordoba in the Fifth/Eleventh Century," *Islamic Law and Society* 7, no. 2 (2000): 167–68.

66. Cf. Schacht, *Introduction*, 83.

67. Johansen, "Formes," 342; cf. 348, 358–59.

68. Hallaq, "*Qāḍī*'s *Dīwān*," 3.

69. Jeanette Wakin, *The Function of Documents in Islamic Law: The Chapters on Sales from Ṭaḥāwī's Kitāb al-shurūṭ al-kabīr* (Albany: State University of New York Press, 1972), 42.

70. Lit. "the custom of the merchants" (*ʿurf al-tujjār*). See case 3 in chapter 7.

71. It usually is assumed that *ʿurf* was unwritten. This is associated with the assumption that, while often established and authoritative as such, custom was variable and subject to change. In Yemen, however, both customary rules and specific customary settlements often were documented. While this mainly concerned the phenomenon of "tribal custom," there also are limited examples (see chapter 10) of explicit stipulations within the sharīʿa archive. Regarding other places in the world, Hallaq, *Sharīʿa*, 384–98, writes that a feature of colonial modernity involved

the writing down of previously unwritten custom, causing the fixing of this previously flexible supplement.

72. Hollander, *Jews and Muslims*, 280–83. The text is countersigned with a note from Ibb sharīʿa court judge al-Manṣur (cf. chapter 7, cases 3, 4) in which he distinguishes the result from a sharīʿa judgment (*ḥukm sharʿī*).

7. Judgments

1. This and related usage also occurred in writing. Thus, with the article retained, "*Baynī wa baynak, al-sharīʿa*" (lit. "Between me and you, the sharīʿa"). The reported speaker was Imam Yahya and he was addressing his eventual litigation adversary in a preemption case. M. Zabāra and A. Zabāra, *Nuzhat al-naẓar* MS, 2:375. In a marriage case (case 4, line 326), a litigant stated that, in the past, "he feared that they [his adversaries] would cause them trouble and sharīʿa."

2. Muhsin Jasim al-Musawi, *The Postcolonial Arabic Novel: Debating Ambivalence* (Boston: Brill, 2003). 7.

3. I particularly want to acknowledge ʿAli Hasan Ṣāliḥ, a former advocate (*wakīl*) in Ibb; ʿAli Ismaʿil Bā Salāma, a town-based shaykh and the son of the noted former Ibb district officer (*qāʾim maqām*, *ʿāmil*) in the final years of the Ottoman Empire and the first decade under Imam Yahya; Qasim al-Manṣūb, a leading Ibb businessman; and Mansur al-Ṣabāḥī, who led his siblings against their older brother in a major case that started in the period of Imam Yahya's rule and concluded in the time of Imam Ahmad.

4. The four registers cover the years 1955–58, al-Manṣūr, Judge of the Province; 1959–60, al-Manṣūr; 1955–57, al-Iryānī, Judge of the Maqām; and 1961–63, al-Iryānī, Judge of the Maqām, then of the Province. On January 6, 2008, Dr. Muhammad Aziz and I made an inventory of the twenty mid-century registers in this collection.

5. Another usage was as a "scrapbook of poetry." Mark S. Wagner, *Like Joseph in Beauty: Yemeni Vernacular Poetry and Arab-Jewish Symbiosis* (Leiden: Brill, 2009), 39.

6. These *Taʿlīmāt*, as they are termed, were published by Rashād al-ʿAlīmī, *al-Taqlīdiyya wa-l-ḥadātha fī al-Niẓam al-qānūnī al-yamanī* (Ṣanʿāʾ: Dār al-Kalima, 1989), 265–68, but without identifying this *safīna* (233–39) as the source. Al-Muṭahhar writes in the *safīna* that he copied this text on "the evening of the 10th of al-Ḥijja, 1359 [January 8, 1941], in my room in the Taʿizz Government Building."

7. The well-known brand name was *abū shubbāk*. The watermarks of the paper rolls of cases 4 and 5 read, in part, "*bayāḍ abū shubbāk isṭambūlī*." Cf. Regourd, *Catalogue*, 176, 184.

8. The etymological ancestor of the term "volume." See D. C. Greetham, *Textual Scholarship: An Introduction* (New York: Garland, 1992), 59. For the history of the shift from the volumen to the codex form, see Chartier, *Order of Books*, 18, 91, and references cited. The more specific ancestor to rolled Yemeni documents is the also vertically rolled *rotulus*. See François Déroche et al., *Islamic Codicology: An Introduction to*

the Study of Manuscripts in Arabic Script, trans. D. Dusinberre and D. Radzinowicz (London: Al-Furqān Foundation, 2005), 12–13.

9. Cf. Tamer El-Leithy, "Living Documents, Dying Archives: Towards a Historical Anthropology of Medieval Arabic Archives," *Al-Qanṭara* 32, no. 2 (2011): 389–434.

10. Unpublished. Choice cited: on the permissibility of sales by a fiduciary in a situation of "urgent need" (i.e., in times of drought and famine), lines 224–25, 271. I cite these original case rolls by line number.

11. Messick, "Textual Properties." Choice cited: on disinheriting heirs, line 65ff.

12. Brinkley Messick, "Commercial Litigation in a Sharīʿa Court," in *Dispensing Justice in Islam: Qādīs and Their Judgments*, ed. Muhammad Khalid Masud, Rudolph Peters, and David S. Powers (Leiden: Brill, 2006), 195–218.

13. Messick, "Interpreting Tears." Choices cited: "hatred" (*karāha*) in marriage, line 296; "central issue" (*jawhar*) in litigation, line 304.

14. Brinkley Messick, "L'écriture en procès: Les récits d'un meurtre devant un tribunal *sharʿī*," *Droit et Société* 39 (1998): 237–56.

15. The litigation process was "exhaustive" by classical design, which could result in extended records of testimony and litigant statements. As opposed to the well-known Ottoman tradition of recording brief summaries, it seems that by the late nineteenth century court records elsewhere in the empire had become fuller. Hallaq, *Sharīʿa*, 415–16, attributes the advent of more expansive judgment records to the introduction of the new institution of the appeal court. Oral history in Ibb held that the Ottomans around the turn of the century were of the same mind as the Egyptian advisers in the republican courts in my day in that they sought to reform the local tendency to great length in such records by introducing new standards for concision.

16. *Al-Qisṭās* 22 (April 2000). The phrase *al-qisṭās al-mustaqīm*, the "balanced scale," is from the Qurʾan (17:35; 26:182) and is cited as such within the title design. See Brinkley Messick, "Cover Stories: A Genealogy of the Legal-Public Sphere in Yemen," in *Religion, Social Practice, and Contested Hegemonies: Reconstructing the Public Sphere in Muslim Majority Societies*, ed. Armando Salvatore and Mark Levine (New York: Palgrave Macmillan, 2005), 207–29.

17. Cf. Müller, "Ḥaram al-Sharīf Collection," 437.

18. E.g., cases 4, 5. There also was some use of *intihāʾ*, or *alif hāʾ*, or simply the letter *hāʾ*, to signal the end of a quotation from a written document. *Hāʾ* alone, written as a nucleated circle, sometimes is used as a blank space filler at the end of a line, as in written instruments.

19. E.g., case 5, lines 123–24: "He [the defendant] undertook to bring in the further evidence he had within a period of a week from the date 6 Rajab 1380, and he was given an appointment."

20. The terminology involved—date of writing issue (*taḥrīr*) and recording date (*qayd*)—is the same as that of the late Ottoman period. See Brigitte Marino and Tomoki Okawara, *Dalīl sijillāt al-maḥākim al-sharʿīyya al-ʿUthmāniyya* (Damascus: Insitut français de Damas, 1999), 55–56.

21. In the period in question, only the lunar *hijrī* calendar was used. The related time reckoning system also was in use, as in the reference in case 5, line 7, to "six o'clock, that is noon."

22. One of the photocopied rolls left behind at Judge al-Haddad's house (following his move in June 1980) was marked, "People (*ahl*) of . . . ," a reference to a named rural village. The outer flaps of some judgment rolls identified the litigants: e.g., "Sharīʿa judgment (*ḥukm sharʿī*) in the possession (*bi-yad*) of [litigant name], and one like it is in the possession of [litigant name]."

23. Including that known as the "triumph of white over black." See Chartier, *Order of Books*, 11. On the significance of western spacing conventions and punctuation see, Paul Saenger, *Space Between Words: The Origins of Silent Reading* (Stanford: Stanford University Press, 1997), and Malcolm Parkes, *Pause and Effect: An Introduction to the History of Punctuation in the West* (Berkeley: University of California Press, 1993).

24. In case 4, line 305: "*akhdh wa radd.*"

25. Also *khuṣūma*, *mukhāṣama*.

26. The dictionary meaning includes "cutting off" (*qatʿ*) and "resolution" or "decision." In grammar, *jazm* refers to the imperative or jussive, which fits the discursive shift to the first-person form of "dictation," on which see the concluding section of this chapter.

27. Ghazzal, *Grammars*, 668, speaks of *dafʿ* as a "strategy of counter-arguments."

28. Case 5, lines 412–14.

29. Leslie Peirce likewise found her early Ottoman judges to be "textually silent." Leslie Peirce, *Morality Tales: Law and Gender in the Ottoman Court of Aintab* (Berkeley: University of California Press, 2003), 93.

30. The language of such notes refers to acts of copy-inscription using verbs for "to record" and "to enter" (*ḍabaṭa*, *qayyada*, *dawwana*, *sajjala*).

31. See Messick, "Evidence."

32. Al-Ḥibshī, *Maṣādir*, 258, lists an example. The *qaḍāʾ* chapters have an internal section on *adab al-qāḍī*, however. Cf. Irene Schneider, *Das Bild des Richters in der "Adab al-Qāḍī" Literatur* (Frankfurt am Main: Peter Lang, 1990).

33. Cf. Hallaq, "*Qāḍī*'s *Dīwān*," 426–27, 435n118, presents evidence for a practice of copying the judge's archive. In Ibb, the registers were simply transferred to the new judge.

34. Al-Khaṣṣāf, *Adab al-qāḍī*, 59.

35. Jeanette Wakin, "The Qāḍī's Archives: The Public Aspect of Notarial Literature" (unpublished draft paper in author's possession, n.d.), 2.

36. For a highly elaborated seventeenth-century work on this topic in a different genre, also Ḥanafī, see al-Shaykh al-Niẓām et al., *al-Fatāwā al-hindiyya*, 6 vols. (Peshawar: Nūrānī Kutub Khānah, [197-?]), 6:160–248. Cf. Masud, Messick, and Powers, *Islamic Legal Interpretation*, 14–15.

37. Imam Yahya, *Taʿlīmāt* MS. ʿAlīmī, *al-Taqlīdiyya*, 265–68, states that the text represents a "mixture" of Ottoman regulations with selections from the *adab al-qāḍī* literature. The opening reads: "This is a copy of the honored *taʿlīmāt* printed at the [government] press of the capital of Yemen, Ṣanʿāʾ." I have not seen the printed text. ʿAlīmī states, incorrectly, that the text has sixteen articles. Actually there are three texts, the first two of which he reproduces. The first is the *taʿlīmāt* for the regular courts, which has twenty-four articles. It was "written" in 1354 AH (1935), issued by the imam in 1355 AH (1937), and copied by al-Muṭahhar on "the evening of the 10th of al-Ḥijja, 1359 (January 9, 1941)." This text is followed by the *taʿlīmāt*

for the two Appeal Panels (*hayʾatay al-istiʾnāf*), also dated 1354 AH, which has sixteen articles. Finally, third, is a further set of *taʿlīmāt*, with four articles, dated 1349 AH, concerning the organization of salaries.

An Ottoman example for the sharīʿa courts of Damascus is the *taʿlīmāt* of 1884, which comprises twenty-five articles. According to Marino and Okawara, *Dalīl sijillāt*, 56n79, these Ottoman "Instructions" concern, among other things, the types of court registers to be kept. Another example is the *taʿlīmāt* of 1878, referred to by Akgūndūz, "Shariʿah Courts and Shariʿah Records," 206, 217.

Taʿlīmāt existed in Yemen for other organizational units. Ms. Arwā al-Khattābī, a Yemeni student at the Free University of Berlin, has a copy of the *taʿlīmāt* for the *māliyya*, or treasury office, of al-Ḥudayda. An equivalent text is referred to in a quoted administrative document in case 3, line 95.

38. Al-ʿAnsī, *Tāj*, 4:193.

39. The Ibb list, from a 1916 local Ottoman accounting document, is quoted in Messick, *Calligraphic State*, 187.

40. Article 4 concerns "[t]he writing (*taḥrīr*) of litigations and the written work associated with them, in entering claims and responses and evidence, and whatever else, [goes] in the register named the 'entering register' (*daftar al-ḍabṭ*). For the writing of a judgment-record (*raqm*) of the conflict for the two parties and the recording of the [judgment] record itself, [this is] in the register named the 'recording register' (*daftar al-qayd*)." Article 4 goes on to say that judges and court secretaries are not permitted to charge fees for any of this recording work, and that they must limit themselves to their treasury salaries. Article 5 states, "The court shall have a register named the 'entering register,' which records the litigations from beginning to end, and the number of its [viz., the register's] pages should be known, such that if others are added they should form an appendix. The second register is the 'recording register' for terminal [judgment] documents (*al-marāqim*), in a numbered series, leaving a wide space for the transcribing of final appeal rulings and for the contents of what [communications] occurred between the judge and the Appeal Court surrounding the entering of the appeal if it [the Appeal Court] ordered completion or correction [of the judge's ruling] prior to the issuance of the final ruling from the Appeal Court." "These two registers (*daftarān*)," article 5 continues, "are the two important ones among the registers (*sijillāt*) of the courts."

41. Wakin, *Function*, 11: "[T]he *maḥāḍir* were the written records of the proceedings before the qāḍī, the minutes of the court, and the *sijillāt* were the written judgments containing the qāḍī's decisions." Cf., Donald P. Little, "sidjill," in *EI2*, 9:539, and Hallaq, "*Qāḍī*'s *Dīwān*," 420.

42. In the late nineteenth-century Ottoman Empire, there was a related distinction between two types of registers, the *jarīda* and the *sijill*. Marino and Okawara, *Dalīl sijillāt*, 54, cf. 56. Introduced in the nineteenth century, the *jarīda*, in which the minutes were recorded, and which was sometimes also known as the register of *ḍabṭ*, as in Imam Yahya's "Instructions," "recorded all stages of cases which went to trial and which were subsequently recorded in the *sijills*." According to Marino and Okawara, the identities of these court registers are specified in the Ottoman-era "Instructions" (*taʿlīmāt*), as they were in the "Instructions" issued by Imam Yahya in Yemen.

43. Nawawī, *Minhāj al-ṭālibīn*, 158.

44. The term *raqm* sometimes can be used interchangeably with *hukm* to refer to the final judgment record document. It is used this way, for example, in the collation note at the top of the copied 1960 judgment document of case 5. Judge of the Province al-Manṣūr, who wrote the note, affirms that the *raqm*, the rolled copy of the judgment document he is annotating, is an exact copy of the original, which was issued and signed by Judge al-Iryānī. Having been compared to, and found to agree with, the original, "letter for letter," the copy has "the authority (*ḥukm*) of the original." However, according to an Ibb jurist (author's field notes, April 23, 1980), *raqm* is a more general term for a written court document, one with less strength than a *ḥukm*. In this view, whereas a *ḥukm* contains an opinion, a *raqm* is merely a record. In case 4, lines 125–26, there is mention of a document written by one of the litigants that is called a *raqm*, which I translate as "memorandum." A common (if irregular) plural of *raqm* is *marāqim*, as in the *taʿlīmāt* texts.

45. As opposed to "copy," which is how I translate *ṣūra*. As noted earlier, Yemeni court registers of the period clearly indicate the "copy" status of register-recorded judgments, with the issued rolls being considered "original" (*aṣl*) documents.

46. The term has a range related usages in different genres. It refers, among the *ḥadīth* specialists, to the authoritative process of locating and then excerpting texts; among the jurists, to the logical process of deduction from source texts. On *takhrīj*, as "extrapolation," see Jackson, *Islamic Law and the State*, 91–96.

47. Ibn Miftāḥ, *Sharḥ al-azhār* (chapter: *Bāb al-qaḍāʾ*), 4:315n11; al-ʿAnsī, *Tāj*, 4:189. According to modern Yemeni law, "judicial rulings are issued with the form (*ṣīgha*) stipulated by the code." Republic of Yemen, *al-Sulṭa al-qaḍāʾiyya* (Law 1 of 1991), *al-Jarīda al-Rasmiyya* (1991), art. 4 (p. 3).

48. Letter number 1 (dated 1917), in Saʿīd Ahmad Janāḥī, *al-Ḥaraka al-waṭaniyya fī al-yaman* (Ṣanʿāʾ: Markaz al-Amal lil-Dirāsāt wa al-Nashr, [1992?]), 258.

49. Author's field notes, March 4, 1980: a court *kātib* prepares a *daʿwā* for an individual unable to pay to have a proper claim drafted. Frank E. Vogel, *Islamic Law and Legal System: Studies of Saudi Arabia* (Leiden: Brill, 2000), 152, writes that the modern Saudi court record typically opens with the parties' statements: "After each party's oral statement, the qāḍī will dictate the statement into the record, but distilled greatly into concise briefs of the party's position."

50. Author's field notes, March 28, 1980.

51. For cases 3 and 5, I photographed both an original roll and the associated copy in the second type of court register.

52. See Jacques Derrida, "Signature Event Context," in *Margins of Philosophy*, trans. Alan Bass (Chicago: University of Chicago Press, 1982), 328.

53. On imamic seals, see Messick, *Calligraphic State*, 241–46.

54. Al-ʿAnsī, *Tāj*, 4:189.

55. Using *raqm* here for the issued record to distinguish it from the included ruling, also *ḥukm*. Modern republican court judgments are to be pronounced in a public session: Republic of Yemen, *al-Sulṭa al-qaḍāʾiyya*, art. 5, section a (p. 3).

56. Cf. Messick, *Calligraphic State*, 171–76, where I note that the petition was a key text in the *maẓālim* institution.

57. In a case concerning a property conflict between two Ibb families: Judge al-Yamānī (al-Yadūmī), Taʿizz, 1378 AH (1958), line 13, photos Ibb111–18.

58. From al-Sayāghī family sources in Ibb, I photocopied a set of ninety handwritten petitions sent by mail in 1946 to Governor al-Sayāghī. A secretary received and annotated each petition and the governor then responded, but for an unknown reason the petitions were not returned. See also a reference to such documents in Sālim, *Wathāʾiq yamaniyya*, 17, although he does not include any examples. I also obtained a summary of 260 categorized petitions received by the governor of Ibb in the months of April and May 1980.

59. Cf. Bakhtin, *Dialogic Imagination*, 289.

60. Author's field notes, July 28, 1993, Ṣanʿāʾ.

61. Cf. Hallaq, *Authority*, 90 and n16, on the *aṣḥāb al-imlāʾ*, the students who copied down jurists' lectures.

8. Minutes

1. Jeremy Bentham, *Rationale of Judicial Evidence, Specially Applied to English Practice*, 5 vols. (London: Hunt and Clarke, 1827), 3:115, 117.

2. Ibid., 121.

3. Judge Hasan Ahmad al-Iryānī, *Ḥukm*, Ibb, 1380 AH (1961), line 86 (hereafter case 5). This suggests that the report was copied into the minutes without being oralized. This "investigation" was not police-modern in form. The Ibb governor was educated in a madrasa curriculum rather than in forensic pathology. He examined the wounds on the corpse and wrote his report using the standard "injuries" (*urūsh*) terminology associated with "sharīʿa medicine" (*ṭibb al-sharʿī*) and the *fiqh*.

4. Acting Judge Yahya bin ʿAli al-Ḥaddād, *Ḥukm*, Ibb, 1349 AH (1931), lines 195–97, 216–17 (hereafter case 1).

5. Judge Ismaʿil ʿAbd al-Rahman al-Manṣūr, *Ḥukm*, Ibb, 1378 AH (1958), line 255 (hereafter case 4).

6. Ibid., lines 125–26.

7. Case 1, lines 195, 216, 264 ("dictation" of a text); Judge Abd Allāh bin ʿAli al-Yamānī (al-Yadūmī), *Ḥukm*, Taʿizz, 1366 AH (1947), line 3 ("*muḥaṣṣal al-shijārāt*," with the first word written with marked vowels) (hereafter case 2); case 4, lines 166, 168, 175 ("*mulakhkhaṣ*"), line 255 ("*wa lamā samaʿa . . . mā amlāʾ ʿalayhi min al-mulakhkhaṣ*"), line 310 ("*mulakhkhaṣ al-shijār*"); case 5, line 124 ("*imlāʾ al-muḥaṣṣal*"), line 161 ("*al-muḥaṣṣal*"). Cf. Peters, "The Violent Schoolmaster," 72, on the "minutes" of a new type of mid-nineteenth-century Egyptian court separate from the first-instance sharīʿa court.

8. Bentham, *Judicial Evidence*, 3:89–107.

9. Technically, the former is "notation *ipsissimis verbis*." Bentham, ibid., 6:470, also glosses the term as "*verbatim et literatim*."

10. E.g., case 2, lines 57–58. This concerns a prior ruling in the case, mentioning the "rebuke (*qadḥ*) of the judge for violation of his justness (*ʿadāla*)."

11. In case 5, lines 12–13, after the opening claim, the judge's simple procedural directives are reported as follows: "And the question [was posed] to the defendant. He answered with a denial and it was required of the claimant to provide evidence." About three decades earlier, in case 1, lines 26–28, a different judge provides detailed instructions to each side concerning their evidence requirements.

12. Bentham, *Judicial Evidence*, 4:460.

13. On the Zaydī evidence doctrine, see Messick, "Evidence."

14. Bentham, *Judicial Evidence*, 2:438.

15. Bentham also notes a downside to the use of writing; ibid., 440–43. Abuses may stem from the recording of "irrelevant matter" and from the time and opportunities writing may open for "mendacious invention." "The grand abuse," which he describes as the "perverted application" of judicial writing, which is associated with "factitious delay, vexation, and expense," involves "pages of surplusage, oftentimes without truth, sometimes without meaning, and always without use. This excrementitious matter has been made up into all the forms that the conjunct industry of the demon of mendacity, seconded by the genius of nonsense, could contrive to give it."

16. Ibid., 3:107; cf. 101n.

17. A. F. L. Beeston, *Arabic Nomenclature* (Oxford: Oriental Institute, 1971); Annemarie Schimmel, *Islamic Names: An Introduction* (Edinburgh: Edinburgh University Press, 1989).

18. A limited number of passports were issued by the imamic state to diplomats, students studying abroad, and some merchants, such as those who regularly traveled to Aden or to the Ḥijāz.

19. See Messick, *Calligraphic State*, 187–92, 237–41.

20. I obtained lists of names for twenty-five Ibb town quarters as of 1962 from ʿAbd al-Karim al-Akwaʿ, formerly the responsible functionary in this section of the old Treasury (*bayt al-māl*) Administration. See Messick, "Transactions in Ibb," 463–66, discussion at 223–33.

21. The same census also attempted to ascertain approximate birth dates, which were not ordinarily known (much less celebrated). To this end people were asked if they were born before or after certain key local historical events listed as prompts on the census form.

22. Case 5, lines 1–5. I use pseudonyms.

23. This is my general term, which stands for a specific indicated location in Upper Yemen.

24. See Anna Würth, "A Sanaʿa Court: The Family and the Ability to Negotiate," *Islamic Law and Society* 2, no. 3 (1995): 320–40, and Würth, *Ash-Sharīʿa fī Bāb al-Yaman*.

25. Sometimes referred to as *taʿrīf* witnesses. Of these four identifiers, two were listed by simple, two-part names, one with a two-part name plus a *nisba* and the other by a preceding honorific (*al-faqīh*, lit. "the jurist"). Case 5, lines 22–23.

26. Cf. Rudolph Peters, "Murder on the Nile," on *ism thulāthī*.

27. Case 5, lines 248–49.

28. Case 1, line 24. Cf. Natalie Davis, *The Return of Martin Guerre* (Cambridge, MA: Harvard University Press, 1983).

29. On *muwājaha*, see Messick, *Calligraphic State*, 168–71.

30. Case 5, lines 38, 126, 267.

31. W. Robertson Smith, *Kinship and Marriage in Early Arabia* (Cambridge: Cambridge University Press, 1885). For an excellent recent study, see Morgan Clarke, *Islam and New Kinship: Reproductive Technology and the Shariah in Lebanon* (New York: Berghahn Books, 2009).

32. Case 5, lines 93–94.

33. Case 4, lines 110–12.

34. Case 5, lines 13–22.

35. Messick, "Evidence," 245–48.

36. Bakhtin, *Dialogic Imagination*, 342f.

37. Case 4, lines 313–15.

38. Judge Ismāʿīl ʿAbd al-Raḥman al-Manṣūr, *Ḥukm*, Ibb, 1376 AH (1956), lines 3–26 (hereafter case 3).

39. Case 1, lines 3–19.

40. The opening *ijāba* was required in the sense that, following the *daʿwā*, the court turned to the defendant for a response. As noted earlier, some individuals were unable to respond while others declined to respond. When a person refused to appear, this was referred to as *tamarrad ʿan al-maḥkama* or *ʿan al-sharʿ*. Al-ʿAnsī, *Tāj*, 4:15. An example is Judge al-Yamānī, *Ḥukm* (regarding an Ibb property case), Taʿizz, 1378 AH (1958), line 16: "*tamarrad ʿan al-ḥuḍūr.*" Cf. author's field notes, April 12, 1980.

41. My terms. See Messick, "Evidence," 244–54.

42. Case 3, lines 26–27.

43. Case 5, line 35.

44. The linguistic phenomenon in question seems to have been the persistence of a northern plateau dialect among individuals resident in Lower Yemen who trace their ancestry to places in Upper Yemen. A story told about the Ottoman era in Ibb is that a newly appointed district officer asked how he could distinguish the Zaydīs resident in the area from the indigenous Shāfiʿīs. He was told that all he had to do was to ask an individual to pronounce the word "cow"—in Upper Yemen, *bagara* and in Lower Yemen, *baqara*.

45. For more on the *wakīl* and other forms of representation in court, see Messick, "Evidence," 241. The pioneering research is by R. C. Jennings, "The Office of Vekil," *Studia Islamica* 42 (1975): 147–69. H. Inalcik, "Maḥkama, 2. The Ottoman Empire, 1. The Earlier Centuries," in *EI2*, 6:5, writes, "In principle, the Islamic judicial system does not recognize the institution of attorney" and "the system of legal representation by *wakīls*, widely used in Islamic *maḥkamas*, including those of the Ottoman Empire, . . . cannot be equated with attorneyship."

46. The revolutionary-period text is translated in Messick, *Calligraphic State*, 196–97.

47. See Messick, "Prosecution in Yemen: The Introduction of the Niyāba," *International Journal of Middle East Studies* 15 (1983): 507–18.

48. These cases are in the register of Judge Isḥāq, which was left behind in his former residence when Judge al-Ḥaddād moved out.

49. In my day, al-Muṣannif, still very fiesty, could be seen in court pursuing petty neighborhood grievances with one of the judges over, in one instance, a drainage ditch between their houses. He regularly recited his poems at local celebrations such as school graduations. His father, Ghālib bin ʿAbbās, was a teacher (*shaykh*) at the Madrasa of the Great Mosque in Ibb. See Messick, *Calligraphic State*, 297n3.

50. Case 1, line 231: "*Al-muthabbat muqaddam ʿalā al-nāfī.*" Cf. Messick, "Evidence," 250–51, 259–60.

51. Judge al-Yamānī, *Ḥukm*, 1378 AH (1958), lines 108–9.

52. Case 4, lines 147–51. Again, the notion of "unitary" testimonies refers to the evidence doctrine regarding "difference" in such testimonies.

53. Case 2, lines 21, 24, 34 ("*ḥāṣil*"); Judge al-Yamānī, *Ḥukm*, 1378 AH (1958), line 15. *Ḥ-k-ā*—case 1, lines 119, 126, 136; case 2, lines 20, 26, 29; Judge al-Yamānī, *Ḥukm*, 1378 AH (1958), lines 19, 22, 25, 27, 32.

54. Case 5, lines 126–27.

55. Case 3, line 31.

56. Judge al-Yamānī, *Ḥukm*, 1378 AH (1958), lines 29–31.

57. Case 3, lines 73–74.

58. Case 4, lines, 360–62.

59. Case 2, lines, 41–42.

60. Case 2, lines, 31–32.

61. *Ḥurrir*, "it was written."

62. Case 4, line 13.

63. For formal examples, see Messick, "Evidence."

64. Case 4, lines 166–68.

65. Case 2, lines 33–41

66. Cf. Hiroyuki Yanagihashi, "The Doctrinal Development of 'Maraḍ al-Mawt' in the Formative Period of Islamic Law," *Islamic Law and Society* 5, no. 2 (1998): 326–58; Yanagihashi, *A History of the Early Islamic Law of Property: Reconstructing the Legal Development, 7th-9th Centuries* (Leiden: Brill, 2004), 141.

67. Case 2, lines 42–46.

68. Case 2, lines 46–51.

69. I also encountered instances in my fieldwork, one of which I discuss in Messick, *Calligraphic State*, 223.

70. Case 4, line 47.

71. Case 4, line 65; also referred to as an *ʿahd*, line 162.

72. Al-ʿAnsī, *Tāj*, 4:71

73. Case 4, lines 70–77.

74. Case 4, line 77.

75. Case 4, lines 99–103.

76. Case 5, lines 220–25.

77. Clifford Geertz, "Common Sense as a Cultural System," in *Local Knowledge* (New York: Basic Books, 1983), 76; Peter Seitel, "Haya Metaphors for Speech," *Language in Society*, 3, no. 1 (1974): 51–67.

78. Mark S. Wagner, *Jews and Islamic Law in Early 20th Century Yemen* (Bloomington: Indiana University Press, 2015).

79. Ismāʿīl al-Akwaʿ, who resided for a time in Ibb, published *Al-Amthāl al-yamaniyya*, 2 vols. (1968; reprint, Ṣanʿāʾ: Maktab Jīl al-Jadīd, 1984). My friend al-ʿIzzī Fahmī al-Ṣabāḥī, the court secretary, whom I occasionally sat with in his marketplace shop late in the afternoon, kept a personal list of local proverbs in an unpublished notebook. In his characteristic humor, he referred to his explanatory proverb commentary in stilted terms as his *tafsīr.*

80. Case 4, lines 79–88.

81. This "proverb" is known in the northern highlands as well. Cf. Weir, *A Tribal Order*, 206.

82. Case 4, lines 350–58.

83. Al-ʿAnsī, *Tāj*, 4:70.

84. Christian Lange, *Justice, Punishment and the Medieval Muslim Imagination* (Cambridge: Cambridge University Press, 2008), 223–26.

9. Moral Stipulations

1. *Kātib*, "writer," is also the term for the court secretary and, generally, for the old-style, unspecialized functionary in an administration (Messick, *Calligraphic State*, 189). This included the powerful individuals in the circle, the *dīwān*, of the ruling imam or the provincial governor. Still another type was the man who set up a box-top desk outside an official residence to write petitions (see figure 7.9). On the notarial writer, see also the discussion in ibid., 224–26.

2. Weber, *Economy and Society*, 805n33, contrasts the American type of notary public "whose primary function is that of authenticating signatures and thus creating official evidence of genuineness," with the Continental type, "who is also a specialist in legal drafting." Cf. ibid., 792–94, 681–83, and 740n54.

3. See Messick, *Calligraphic State*, 225.

4. For references, see ibid., 45, 272n27.

5. "*Aghlā min māʾ al-dhahab, qalam Ṣāliḥ al-ʿAnsī.*"

6. Other general terms for a legal document are *wathīqa* (pl. *wathāʾiq*); *waraqa* (pl. *awrāq*); *ḥujja* (pl. *ḥujāj*); and, technically, as "documentary proof," *mustanad* (pl. *mustanadāt*).

7. Muhammad Zabāra, *Nashr al-ʿArf li-nubalāʾ al-yaman baʿd al-alf*, vol. 2 (Cairo: Maṭbaʿa al-Salafiyya, 1377 AH [1958]), 875–77.

8. *Niyāba*, Ibb, 1979, case notes in author's files. Cf. Messick, "Prosecution in Yemen."

9. According to my 2008 inventory, of the twenty mid-century registers held by Judge Muhammad Hasan al-Iryānī, one was of this designated third type for entering documents. But seven registers of the second type also contained instrument copies mixed in with final judgments. Cf. supra, chapter 7, n7.

10. Judge Ismāʿīl ʿAbd al-Raḥman al-Manṣūr, *Ḥukm*, Ibb, 1378 AH (1958) (case 4), line 30: "*ṣūrat waraqat al-ʿaqd naqlan ʿan daftar al-qayd fī maḥkamat al-liwāʾ.*"

11. "*maktūba ʿinda al-nās.*" Al-ʿAnsī, *Tāj*, 4:37. Cf. the earlier cited notions of the "public" responsibilities of a ruling imam, ibid., 4:426.

12. See Messick, "Indexing the Self," for a discussion of how the jurists theorized the role of speech and human presences in the conveyance of intent. Intent, or consent, provides the ultimate authority for sharīʿa acts, but it originates internally—that is, in the "self."

13. As was a recording fee (lit. "the right of the signature," *ḥaqq al-imḍāʾ*). See W. Björkman, "Diplomatic, i. Classical Arabic," in *EI2*.

14. Mundy and Saumarez Smith, *Governing Property*.

15. Capt. F. M Hunter, *An Account of the British Settlement of Aden in Arabia* (1877; reprint, London: Frank Cass, 1968), 131, 134.

16. Messick, *Calligraphic State*, 215–16, 230.

17. For the fully blank first type, see the 1991 Ibb document reproduced in Messick, *Calligraphic State*, 236. For the second, which has the standardized legal language printed, I have a sharīʿa marriage contract (*ʿaqd nikāḥ sharʿī*) from the same year, issued by the Ṣanʿāʾ-South Court, on a form produced by the Ministry of Justice, Office of *al-tawthīq wa-l-tasjīl*. The Ministry of Endowments uses a similar type of form for its leases, *ʿaqd ijār ʿaqār*. An example of a typed agency contract, on letterhead and dated 1974, is that between an Ibb businessman and the Yemen Weaving & Textile Corporation, in author's files.

18. Adolph Grohmann, *Arabic Papyri in the Egyptian Library*, vol. 2 (Cairo: Egyptian Library Press, 1936) 3–10; Geoffrey Khan, *Arabic Papyri: Selected Material from the Khalili Collection* (London: Nour Foundation and Oxford University Press, 1992), 140–41.

19. See W. Björkman, "Diplomatic, i. Classical Arabic," in *EI2*.

20. In the late 1920s, Schacht published an edition of sections of the early *shurūṭ* work by al-Ṭaḥāwī (d. 933). See the bibliography in Schacht, *Introduction*, 243–44.

21. Hallaq, "From Fatwās to Furūʿ"; Hallaq, "Model Shurūṭ Works," 128, emphasis in original.

22. Two other differences of approach should be noted. Where Hallaq, "Model Shurūṭ Works," 111, maintains that the *shurūṭ* works "structurally and organically constitute an integral part of the *furūʿ* and *adab al-qāḍī* manuals," I place emphasis on distinctions of genre and sub-genre. Second, the connection of document production with the judge and the sharīʿa court, which is a background assumption of Hallaq's discussion (e.g., 114–15), did not obtain in the Ibb context.

23. Al-Muftī, *Fatḥ al-mannān sharḥ Zubad bin Raslān*.

24. ʿAli bin ʿAbd Allah al-Iryānī, *Najāḥ al-ṭālib fī ṣifat mā yaktubu al-kātib* (MS, 1343 AH [1923]), Western Library of the Great Mosque of Ṣanʿāʾ, 64 Fiqh.

25. For biographies, see ʿAbd Allah al-Ḥibshī, *Maṣādir al-fikr al-Islāmī fī al-Yaman* (Beirut: al-Maktaba al-ʿAṣrīyya, 1988), 278; al-Ḥibshī, *Maṣādir al-fikr al-islāmī fī al-yaman* (Abū Ẓabbī: al-Majmaʿ al-Thaqāfī, 2004), 42, 168, 295–96, 543; M. Zabāra and A. Zabāra, *Nuzhat al-naẓar* MS, 3:71–80. He was the paternal uncle of Yahya bin Muhammad bin ʿAbd Allah, the first judge appointed in Ibb by Imam Yahya in the 1920s (see chapter 1).

26. ʿAli bin ʿAbd Allah al-Iryānī, *Sīrat al-Imām Muhammad bin Yahya Ḥamīd al-Din*, 2 vols., ed. Muhammad ʿIsa al-Ṣāliḥiyya (Amman: Dār al-Bashīr, 1996). Cf. Willis, *Unmaking North and South*, 112.

27. Other such formularies also open with a "theoretical discussion of the uses of documents." El-Leithy, "Living Documents," 393.

28. *Taḥayyulāt*, from the same root as *ḥīla* (i.e., "legal stratagems"). See also al-Iryānī, *Najāḥ al-ṭālib* MS, 87.

29. He mentions by name Muhammad bin ʿAbd al-Rahman al-Makhzūmī (ibid., 56).

30. Arberry, *The Koran Interpreted*, 70–71.

31. A summary of this "logic":

Dictates	Keeps document
"Against whom . . ."	"For whom . . ."
Debtor	Lender
Seller	Buyer

32. On these topics, cf. Schacht, *Introduction*, 144–47.

33. For an instance of a complex notebook of notarial activities, see El-Leithy, "Living Documents," 412.

34. "*Wahaba wa nadhara wa taṣaddaqa wa mallaka.*"

35. Al-ʿAnsī, *Tāj*, 2:308–9, cf. Messick, "Indexing the Self."

36. Cf. introduction, esp. n115.

37. See the section on the marriage contract in chapter 10.

38. Clause-by-clause approaches are characteristic of western scholarship concerning both the early Arabic papyri from Egypt and the later Arabic documents from the Cairo Geniza. For example, Wakin, *Function*, 39–40, adapted her approach to the order and types of sale contract clauses from Adolph Grohmann, whose method was that of European diplomatics.

10. Contracts

1. Émile Durkheim, *The Division of Labor in Society*, trans. George Simpson (New York: Free Press, 1933), 211–25.

2. Hallaq, "Model Shurūṭ Works."

3. This refers to shaykly (tribal), imamic, or other *sayyid* families and leading *qāḍī* families. For background on northern tribal holdings in Lower Yemen, see Dresch, *Tribes, Government, and History*, chap. 6. An example of interregional property holding by a *sayyid* is the inheritance document (*faṣl*) of an individual resident in Ṣanʿāʾ. This instrument shows itemized properties in "Lower Yemen" (*al-yaman al-asfal*), including both coffee cultivations and sections of houses in Ibb town, specifically mentioning a room in Dār al-Bayḍāʾ, a large old residence east of the Great Mosque. *Faṣl*, section on "Lower Yemen" *sayyid* family, Ṣanʿāʾ, n.d., Digital B387–89.

4. E. P. Thompson, *Whigs and Hunters: The Origin of the Black Act* (New York: Pantheon, 1975), 261.

5. Dresch, *Rules of Barat*, 50.

6. On the word "context" having the "etymological meaning" of "co-texts," see Latour, *Making of Law*, 94. Among linguistic anthropologists, see Alessandro Durant

and Charles Goodwin, eds., *Rethinking Context: Language as an Interactive Phenomenon* (Cambridge: Cambridge University Press, 1992).

7. Al-ʿAnsī, *Tāj*, 2:306–521.

8. Wakin, *Function*.

9. Al-Iryānī, *Najāḥ al-ṭālib* MS, 62–72.

10. Al-ʿAnsī, *Tāj*, 2:309.

11. "*Lafẓayn māḍīyayn*." Al-ʿAnsī, *Tāj*, 2:306, 308–9, 311–12.

12. See Messick, "Indexing the Self," 157–62. I have no information on either the genesis of this "choice" in a specific case or its subsequent application.

13. Wakin, *Function*, 32ff, discusses how Ṭaḥāwī's model documents accounted for the differences of opinion (*ikhtilāf*) among the academic jurists of his school.

14. Ibb *baṣīra* documents QMi (1358 AH [1939]), QMh (1360 AH [1941]), QMc (1376 AH [1957]), and QMb (1377 AH [1958])—see the bibliography for digital archive details. My larger study corpus consists of of forty original *baṣīras*, dating 1649 to 1991, from private archives in Ibb. Two are seventeenth century, although one of these may be a forgery; four are eighteenth; nineteen are nineteenth; fifteen are twentieth, with four of these from after the 1962 Revolution. A further corpus is among the documents in the Burayhī-ʿAzīz Collection, Ibb. Many other copies of *baṣīras* appear in the local court registers I have photocopied, and there are excerpts of such instruments in the litigation records.

15. Compare the analysis of Geniza documents of sale by Khan, *Cambridge Genizas*, 7–140. See also the translation of "a typical contract of sale," dated 1803, which concerns a house in Damascus, in Ghazzal, *Grammars*, 201.

16. In contrast, under his stamped title, name, and address, a printed-form marriage contract from 1991 is signed by the modern instrument writer, the *amīn taḥrīr ʿuqūd*, whose numbered identity card issued by the Ministry of Justice, is mentioned in the contract. Cf. chapter 9, n17.

17. A few begin, "This is what . . ." (*hadhā mā . . .*). The 1941 *baṣīra* is unusual in both its signature clause, which is at the end, and in its opening, which does not use the verb "bought." It instead states, "[T]here occurred the issuance (*ṣudūr*) of a valid sharīʿa sale object (*mabīʿ*)." A later "subjective" *baṣīra* from 1980 states, "I sold."

18. Al-Iryānī, *Najāḥ al-ṭālib* MS, 56, in his first section on debt acknowledgment, states that the latter language should appear in all instruments.

19. Agency is the subject of a chapter in the law books; e.g., al-ʿAnsī, *Tāj*, 4:117–154, and al-Iryānī, *Najāḥ al-ṭālib* MS, 82.

20. Al-ʿAnsī, *Tāj*, 2:306. Cf. Schacht, *Introduction*, 145.

21. Sergeant refers to a judge canceling (*taʿtīl*) a *baṣīra* for a house. An Ibb document (Ibb 506) states that a prior document was read by the notarial writer, and then "became canceled (*ṣārat ʿaṭilan*) in the possession of the buyer." Serjeant did not see any documents, as the house owners were "generally loath to produce them for the perusal of strangers." Ronald Lewcock and R. B. Serjeant, "The Houses of Ṣanʿāʾ," in *Ṣanʿāʾ: An Arabian City*, ed. R. B. Serjeant and Ronald Lewcock (London: World of Islam Festival Trust, 1983), 487 and n42. On forms of archival cancellation in western legal history, see Vismann, *Files*, chap. 1–2.

22. Cf. al-ʿAnsī, *Tāj*, 2:340.

23. Cf. Hollander, *Jews and Muslims*, xxii. One local document I have seen includes a specification of the size of the *qaṣaba* in question. *Baṣīra*, Ibb, 1324 AH (1906), photo Ibb323.

24. Al-Iryānī, *Najāḥ al-ṭālib* MS, 76.

25. *Baṣīra* QMi, line 13, directly echoes the formulary text when it states, "these boundaries are distinguishing boundaries with respect to similarities to other than it."

26. *Baṣīra*, Ibb, 2 Dhi al-Qaʿda 1375 AH (June 11, 1956).

27. *Baṣīras* QMh, QMb, QMf 1202 AH (1788), QMg 1267 AH (1851).

28. *Baṣīra* QMe, 1331 AH (1913).

29. Also, in some pre-Ottoman Ibb documents, e.g., QMg.

30. In addition to the *madhhab* specificity of Johansen's study, the agrarian property regimes addressed by the jurists he reads for the Mamluk and later Ottoman periods mainly involved "state lands"—that is, *mīrī* and related forms—whereas in the highlands, a *milk* regime of "private" ownership predominated. Johansen, *Land Tax and Rent*.

31. William J. Donaldson, *Sharecropping in the Yemen: A Study of Islamic Theory, Custom and Pragmatism* (Leiden: Brill, 2000). Donaldson combines a careful survey of the "source" texts, the *ḥadīth*s on the topic, and the treatments in Shāfiʿī and Zaydī doctrine, with the results of his on-the-ground interviews conducted in 1992–93 in a number of highland locales. Regarding the doctrinal materials, on the Shāfiʿī side, I additionally refer to the nineteenth-century commentary by Ibb jurist al-Muftī, commenting on Ibn Raslān; on the Zaydī side, I concentrate on the *Flowers* literature, including al-ʿAnsī's twentieth-century commentary. In a manner related to my juxtaposition of models from the Zaydī *shurūṭ* treatise by al-Iryānī with historical instruments, Donaldson juxtaposes late nineteenth-century Shāfiʿī model texts from the Hadramawt (studied by R. B. Serjeant) with three republican-era (1986) documents from a district west of Ibb town. The latter are very different from the corpus of imamic-era instruments discussed here.

32. I photographed a landlord's register in its entirety. The contents are divided into Series A (44 leases, 1961–64, 1969), Series B (70 leases, 1952–58), and Series C (43 leases, 1959–61, 1965). See bibliography for digital archive information. The endowments documents from *Maktab al-awqāf*, Ibb, are in a register of leases for properties endowed for the Great Mosque (*waqf al-kabīr*) and other town mosques (*waqf al-masājid*): 25 leases dated 1948–60.

33. In *Ijāra* Series B, 38 documents are for cultivable land, and 33 are for buildings (three rooms, eight floors, six houses, seven shops, eight small warehouses [sing. *samsara*], and one storeroom). The equivalent breakdown of lease types for the land is given below.

34. The old relationship was said to have fundamentally changed, such that whereas "the landlord was prince, these days the sharecropper is prince." Quoted in Richard Tutwiler and Sheila Carapico, *Yemenī Agriculture and Economic Change* (Ṣanʿāʾ: American Institute for Yemenī Studies, 1981), 60. The old relationship also involved mutual support. In their evidence doctrine, the Zaydī jurists considered the "affection" between the master and the tenant to be an obstacle in accepting related testimony. Al-ʿAnsī, *Tāj*, 4:76. In my day, when their landlord, an Ibb-based

shaykh, got into a scrape, an armed group of his tenants immediately showed up in town. And if an individual tenant ran afoul of the police, his landlord might be found at the station, petitioning or providing a guarantee for his release. Tenants in town expected to be provided lunch at the landlord's house. Some townspeople spoke of "our village," which generally referred to a concentration of agricultural holdings and thus of locally resident tenants. Imamic period leases show that, in addition to cultivable land near a tenant's village, some landlords owned the tenant's house. In such a village, a landlord could take refuge in times of trouble in the town, such as in 1948 and 1962. Documents were apt to be destroyed if a house in town was pillaged (e.g., 1948), so some people took the precaution of sending their documents to villages for safekeeping.

35. Frederick Engels, *The Origin of the Family, Private Property and the State* (New York: International Publishers, 1972), 136, emphasis in original. Cf. Karl Marx, *Pre-Capitalist Economic Formations*, trans. Jack Cohen (New York: International Publishers, 1965), 107, on "the simple and 'just' laws of the exchange of equivalents."

36. The first type was common in endowment holdings; an example of the latter is Judge al-Yamānī, *Ḥukm*, 1378 AH (1958).

37. Reading the eleventh-century Ḥanafī jurist Sarakhsī, Johansen argues that the usufruct, or use right, either of the productive capacity of land or of the labor power of the laborer, was "commodified," in a preindustrial sense. Unlike the commodities transacted for in the sharīʿa sale, the use rights that are the objects of *ijāras* do not preexist the contract but are brought into existence by it. Johansen also notes the early resistance to viewing use rights as commodities, a view anchored in the general conceptual world, in the religious, moral and practical concerns of a largely subsistence economy, which included several types of non-remunerated mutual-aid exchanges that are characteristic of peasant societies. In elaborating their systems of law, however, the early jurists coordinated their doctrines, including the *ijāra* contract, with reference to different dictates, specifically those of commodity exchange and a pre-modern market economy. Johansen, *Land Tax and Rent*, 28–32, 52–53.

38. On local weights and measures, see also Hollander, *Jews and Muslims*, xxii.

39. Al-ʿAnsī, *Tāj*, 3:68–69. It is "a contract with an offer and an acceptance, undertaken like sale contractors, concerning a thing (*ʿayn*) for [its] usufruct. It is [classified as] indifferent (*mubāḥ*), It must have a specified duration, and a specified rent." For Schacht, *Introduction*, 151–52, sale is a "model." Johansen, *Land Tax and Rent*, 30, explains, however, that *ijāra* "contradicts the basic rule of the contract of sale according to which nothing may be legally sold that is not in existence and in the disposal of the seller at the time of sale."

40. Schacht, *Introduction*, 146ff; Donaldson, *Sharecropping*, 34–35.

41. Al-Muftī, *Fatḥ al-Mannān*, 299, cites additional *ḥadīths*; cf. Donaldson, *Sharecropping*, 52, 56, on the negative *ḥadīths*. Abū Hanīfa opposed the contract on the same grounds, as Sarakhsī reports. See Johansen, *Land Tax and Rent*, 27.

42. For citations and comments on the *ḥadīth* of the Jews of Khaybar, see *Flowers* commentator Shawkānī, *Sayl*, 3:220.

43. Al-Muftī, *Fatḥ al-mannān*, 297, 298, 299. See below, n53, for a similar array of principles in the Ḥanafī school.

44. Al-Muftī, *Fatḥ al-mannān*, 299.

45. The Shāfiʿīs present the contract they refer to as the *qirāḍ* in the chapter preceding the three contracts related to sharecropping; the Zaydīs treat the *muḍāraba*, their term for same contract, in the final section of their chapter on the *ijāra* (al-ʿAnsī, *Tāj*, 3:149–71). Al-Muftī, *Fatḥ al-mannān*, 297, 298, makes the analogy explicit. For the Ḥanafīs, see Johansen, *Land Tax and Rent*, 76n61. For a historical anthropological study touching on the commenda, see Clifford Geertz, "Suq, the Bazaar Economy in Sefrou," in *Meaning and Order in Moroccan Society*, ed. C. Geertz, Hildred Geertz, and Lawrence Rosen (Cambridge: Cambridge University Press, 1979), 123–313.

46. Ibn al-Murtaḍā, *Azhār*, 189–90.

47. Al-ʿAnsī, *Tāj*, 3:134–42.

48. Ibid., 134–35.

49. Ibid., 136–37. Al-ʿAnsī had years of administrative experience in Lower Yemen prior to the Revolution of 1962.

50. Ibn al-Murtaḍā, *Azhār*, 189 (section on the sharecropping contract). Cf. al-ʿAnsī, *Tāj*, 3:137.

51. "*. . . ilā mā kānat muḥarrama fī nafsihā*." Shawkānī, *Sayl*, 3:222.

52. Johansen, *Land Tax and Rent*, 30–31, 54.

53. Noting the early rejection of the sharecropping contract (*muzāraʿa*) by the school's eponym, Abu Ḥanīfa, Yanagihashi explains its later acceptance by the jurists of the school as being based on (1) the analogy with the commercial *muḍāraba* and (2) the existence of the "source" text concerning the Jews of Khaybar, together with (3) the broader factor of "social need" and (4) the role of custom. Hiroyuki Yanagihashi, *A History of the Early Islamic Law of Property: Reconstructing the Legal Development, 7th–9th Centuries* (Leiden: Brill, 2004), 272–73. The Ḥanafīs also elaborated distinct notions of locally specific custom (*ʿurf khāṣṣ*) versus interregional or general custom (*ʿurf ʿāmm*), and the latter applied to sharecropping. See Johansen, *Land Tax and Rent*, 54, where he notes that the "main argument" for *istiḥsān* was the fact that the contract is the "recognized custom of people in all countries" (*ʿurfun ẓāhirun fī jamīʿi l-buldān*); cf. Johansen, *Contingency*, 163–71.

54. "*al-ʿurf ka-l-manṭūq bihi*." Al-ʿAnsī, *Tāj*, 3:137.

55. Cf. Robert B. Serjeant, "The Cultivation of Cereals in Medieval Yemen," *Arabian Studies* 1 (1974): 29, notes that for the same reason most "*ijāra*" contracts in the Hadramawt are "illegal." See also Mundy, *Domestic Government*, 69; cf. 219n2, on the "so-called '*waraqat al-ijāra*,' rental document—something of a misnomer, as people point out. This is in principle renewed every year. By their nature these contracts tend to be long-term."

56. M. Piamenta, *Dictionary of Post-Classical Yemenī Arabic*, vol. 2 (Leiden: Brill, 1991), 345, defines *ʿiwadah* as "cash payment to a private landlord." Spelled slightly differently in the Ibb contracts, it refers to a payment in kind, usually, as here, in clarified butter.

57. One lease (*Ijāra* Series B 31a, dated 1373 AH [1953]), after the terms of the *ujra* are stated, adds "and this is based on the consent (*riḍāʾ*) of the lessee."

58. *Ijāra* Series B 1, dated Ramaḍān, 1378 AH (1959): "I leased . . ."

59. *Ijāra* Series A 11b, dated Jumad I, 1381 AH (1961).

60. E.g., al-ʿAnsī, *Tāj*, 3:3–117; 118–305. Cf. supra, chapter 3. For studies of the Islamic marriage contract, see Asifa Quraishi and Frank E. Vogel, eds., *The Islamic Marriage Contract: Case Studies in Family Law* (Cambridge, MA: Harvard University Press, 2008). My chapter in that volume, "Interpreting Tears," includes some material presented in this section. See also Léon Buskens, "Tales According to the Book: Professional Witnesses (*ʿudūl*) as Cultural Brokers in Morocco," in Dupret et al., *Narratives of Truth*, 143–60, on the modern Moroccan marriage contract, which was entered on a printed form.

61. Al-ʿAnsī, *Tāj*, 2:22–36.

62. Ibid., 2:35.

63. "*Ḥasaba al-ʿurfi*." Ibn al-Murtaḍā, *Azhār*, 102; al-ʿAnsī, *Tāj*, 2:23.

64. Author's field notes, Ibb, March 1975.

65. Al-ʿAnsī, *Tāj*, 2:26. This subsection refers to the special circumstances involving a messenger.

66. Tucker notes that the entering of marriage contracts in Ottoman court registers was a "common practice in eighteenth-century Jerusalem, but less often the case in Damascus or Nablus, where we find only the occasional marriage contract." She also translates an example of such "standard" contracts, a document that has no "offer and acceptance." Judith E. Tucker, *In the House of the Law: Gender and Islamic Law in Ottoman Syria and Palestine* (Berkeley: University of California Press, 1998), 39.

67. Marriage contract, al-Ḥaddād, Ibb, 11 Shawwāl 1377 AH (May 1, 1958).

68. I have the supporting al-Ḥaddād family kinship data.

69. Again, a patriline other than those of descendants of the Prophet (the *sāda*, sing. *sayyid*).

70. A republican-era marriage contract for a woman's second marriage (for which she does not need a guardian), written by Muhammad al-Ghurbānī and dated October 10, 1975, is translated in Messick, "Transactions in Ibb," 397–98.

71. Al-ʿAnsī, *Tāj*, 2:33–34.

72. See Kecia Ali, *Sexual Ethics and Islam: Feminist Reflections on Qurʾan, Hadith, and Jurisprudence* (Oxford: Oneworld, 2006), chap. 1; Ali, "Marriage in Classical Islamic Jurisprudence: A Survey of Doctrines," in Quraishi and Vogel, *Islamic Marriage Contract*, 19–21; and Judith Tucker, *Women, Family, and Gender in Islamic Law* (Cambridge: Cambridge University Press, 2008), s.v. "*mahr* (dower)." For an anthropological analysis, see Annelies Moors, "Part II: The Dower," in *Women, Property and Islam: Palestinian Experiences, 1920–1990* (Cambridge: Cambridge University Press, 1995). In the same context, see the important study by Lynn Welchman, *Beyond the Code: Muslim Family Law and the Sharʿi Judiciary in the Palestinian West Bank* (The Hague: Kluwer Law International, 2000). The western term "dower" is misleading, however. Susan Spectorsky, *Women in Classical Islamic Law* (Leiden: Brill, 2010), 1n1, suggests "marriage portion."

73. Ibn al-Murtaḍā, *Azhār*, 104; al-ʿAnsī, *Tāj*, 2:40.

74. Abū Shujāʿ, *Matn Abī Shujāʿ* (Beirut: Muʾassasat al-Kutub al-Thaqāfiyya, 1985), 42.

75. Al-Muftī, *Fatḥ al-mannān*, 351.

76. The conception of *mahr al-mithl* also figures in the *Flowers*, where the standard for equivalence is, first, women on the father's side, then the mother's, then in the locale (*balad*). Ibn al-Murtaḍā, *Azhār*, 105–7.

77. Yemen Arab Republic, Law no. 127 of 1976, on "The Facilitation of Marriage," *Tashrīʿāt* 4:16–18. The preamble speaks of this law as arising from "the necessity of protection of the essence of Yemeni society, in beliefs, formation and morals." This "facilitation of marriage" law has the "aim of solving the [indicated] social problems." Article 1 limits the dower to four gold guineas (in equivalent riyals). Article 2 similarly limits what is paid to the marriage guardian as the "marriage expenses" or "what is known as '*sharṭ*.'" Other colloquially named transfers, some described as "custom" (*ʿurf*) are similarly limited, or abolished. Cf. Yemen Arab Republic, Law no. 87 of 1976, *Tashrīʿāt* 4:37–39. On republican-era marriage and divorce, see Anna Würth, "A Sanaʿa Court," with the *sharṭ* mentioned at 329n30, and Würth, *Ash-Sharīʿa*. A backdrop for *sharṭ* inflation was a huge rise in immigrant Yemeni workers' remittances from Saudi Arabia and the Gulf.

78. Al-ʿAnsī, *Tāj*, 2:43.

79. E.g., an Ibb estate settled in 1265 AH (1849) mentions deductions from the gross estate for the *mahrs* of two wives (*farz*, photo Ibb2); a large estate settled in 1322 AH (1904) indicates a deduction for the "*mahr* of the wife" of one thousand riyals, while her one-eighth inheritance share as the wife of the deceased amounted to 12,013 (*ḥaṣr* register, photo Ibb 214); an estate settled in 1338 AH (1919), shows *mahr* deductions for two wives (*tarkīz*, photo Ibb96). A related inheritance document, also dated 1338 AH (1919), differentiates the deducted *mahr* of a wife married as a virgin (*bikr*) from that of a previously married (*thayyib*) wife (*farz*, photo Ibb67).

80. "*bi-ṭarīqi al-mahri*." *Baṣīra*, Ibb, 1317 AH (1899), photo Ibb174.

81. Al-Iryānī, *Najāḥ al-ṭālib* MS, 71–72.

82. Ibn al-Murtaḍā, *Azhār*, 107.

83. Al-ʿAnsī, *Tāj*, 2:57n1. The choice is versified and commented upon in Shamāḥī, *Ṣirāṭ*, 52–53. It also is glossed by the republican author al-ʿImrānī, *al-Qaḍāʾ*, 227 (*jim*).

84. "*Lā ʿibrata bi-l-ʿurfi al-jārī fī baʿḍi al-jihāti bi-taʾjīli mahri al-zawjāti ilā al-mawti aw al-ṭalāqi mā lam yudhkaru al-taʾjīlu lafẓan*." Al-Ḥaddād, *Intiṣārāt*, prose section, 84, no. 15; al-ʿAlīmī, *Taqlīdiyya*, 258, item 15; Imam Yahya, *Ikhtiyārāt* (al-Muṭahhar MS), no. 14. In terms of its familial political economy, this "choice" may be connected to two others, also issued circa 1920, mentioned in chapter 4, on legacies, endowments, and inheritance.

85. "*Al-muʾminūn ʿinda shurūṭihim*." Cf. Qurʾan 5:1, which some consider the *ḥadīth* to be a comment upon. The *ḥadīth* is more commonly given as "*al-muslimūn ʿinda shurūtihim*."

86. Cf. Ghazzal, *Grammars*, 13.

87. Al-ʿAnsī, *Tāj*, 2:3. This is in contrast to rights in the slave woman, which are both. Ali, *Sexual Ethics*, 12, notes that the husband "obtained a legitimate (but non-transferable) proprietary interest over his wife's sexual capacity through the marriage contract, incurring the obligation to pay dower in exchange."

88. Judge Ismaʿil ʿAbd al-Rahman al-Manṣūr, *Ḥukm*, Ibb, 1378 AH (1958), line 17 (case 4).

89. Using the closely related term *mukhālaʿa* for this type of divorce, al-Iryānī, *Najāḥ al-ṭālib* MS, 81, gives the following option: "or on the basis of her freeing him from his obligation regarding the dower" (*aw ʿalā an tabarraʾahu ʿan al-mahr al-ladhī fī dhimmatihi*).

90. Copy of a divorce document dated 1 Jumād I, 1379 AH (November 2, 1959), entered in *al-Daftar al-khāmis ʿashr min al-dafātir maḥkamat al-liwāʾ ibb*, Ibb Province Court Register 15, Judge al-Manṣūr, 1379–80 AH (1959–60), p. 46.

91. Divorce document, Ibb, 1333 AH (1915). This document includes a clause in which the wife frees her husband of "waiting period maintenance, expenses, clothes, and the rent of a house, and all of the conjugal rights" (*nafaqatu al-ʿiddati wa-l-maṣrūfi wa-l-kiswati wa kirā*[ʾ]*i al-maskani wa jamīʿi al-ḥuqūqi al-zawjiyyati*). Presumably, there was no postponed dower. Known in Ibb as a *baraʾa wa ṭalāq*, this type of instrument also ends by indicating that the husband pronounced a *ṭalāq*.

92. Al-Iryānī, *Najāḥ al-ṭālib* MS, 82: "*mallakat al-marʾata bi-dhalik nafsahā*"; al-Muftī, *Fatḥ al-mannān*, 359: "*tamliku nafsahā bihi*"; al-ʿAnsī, *Tāj*, 2:175 (see also the many following pages), third *sharṭ*: that the *khulʿ* be contracted "for a financial counter-value" (*ʿalā ʿiwadin māl*).

93. Al-ʿAnsī, *Tāj*, 2:308. Taken from Ibn Miftāḥ, *Sharḥ al-Azhār*, 2:3n1, which was taken from still another source.

Manuscripts and Archival Materials

With the exception of the indicated library holdings and a few originals, the following sources are either photocopies or 35mm photos. A subset of the photos has been digitized.

Manuscripts

Ahmad bin Yahya Ḥamīd al-Dīn (Imam). *Ikhtiyārāt*. N.d. (c. 1950). MS copy in the possession of ʿAbd al-Qādir bin ʿAbd Allāh, Ṣanʿāʾ, September 1995, 10 pp. Photocopy.

——. Letter to Mufti Ahmad Muhammad al-Ḥaddād, Ibb, 12 al-Qaʿda [13]69 AH (1950). Imamic seal. Digital B669.

al-Akwaʿ, ʿAbd al-Karim. *ʿAqd al-zawāj* (script for marriage contract). Ibb, March 1975. Handwritten on notebook paper.

al-Ḥaddād, ʿAbd al-Rahman bin ʿAli. *Al-intiṣārāt naẓm al-ikhtiyārāt* (versified list and an accompanying prose list of *ikhtiyārāt* of Imam Yaḥyā Ḥamīd al-Dīn). N.d. (c. 1920). MS, Dār al-Makhṭūṭāt Collection, Sanʿaʾ, 48:81–86. Photocopy.

al-Ḥaddād, Yahya bin ʿAli. *ʿUmdat al-qāriʾ fī sīrat imām zamāninā sayf al-bārī*. N.d. MS, Western Library of the Great Mosque of Ṣanʿāʾ, Tārikh 2594.

al-Ḥubayshī. *Fatāwī al-Ḥubayshī*. Shāfiʿī school, n.d. (c. 17th century; author details unknown). MS, Vatican Library, Arab 1353. Photocopy.

Ibn Luqmān, Ahmad bin Muhammad. *Al-Kāshif*. Ibb, 4 Muḥarram [13]60 AH (February 1941). MS copy of printed book by Muhammad ʿAli al-Ghurbānī. Selected pages, Digital H4–9 (summer 1991).

Ibn al-Murtaḍā, Ahmad bin Yahya. *Matn al-Azhār.* Yemeni Manuscript Digitization Initiative (ymdi_03_33), Princeton University Library, http://pudl.princeton.edu/objects/h989r449b#page/111/mode/2up.

al-Iryānī, ʿAlī bin ʿAbd Allāh. *Najāḥ al-ṭālib fī ṣifat mā yaktubu al-kātib.* 1343 AH (1923). MS, Western Library of the Great Mosque of Ṣanʿāʾ, 64 Fiqh. Photocopy. (*Shurūṭ* treatise, pp. 50–91.)

Majmūʿa ʿAzīz. Ibb, n.d. MS, text miscellanea, leather bound, including Ibn Raslān, *Zubad.*

Yahya bin Muhammad Ḥamīd al-Dīn (Imam). Fatwā, 1342 AH (1924). Burayhī-ʿAzīz Document Collection, no. 25. Photocopy.

—. *Ikhtiyārāt.* MS copy by Muhammad Yahya Muṭahhar, Taʿizz, October 1995.

—. *Taʿlīmāt.* 1937. MS copy in a *safīna* register (pp. 233–39), in the possession of Muhammad Yahya Muṭahhar, Taʿizz. Photocopy.

—. *Taʿlīmāt hayʾatay al-istiʾnāf.* 1937. MS copy in a *safīna* register (pp. 237–38), in the possession of Muhammad Yahya Muṭahhar, Taʿizz. Photocopy.

Zabāra, Ahmad bin Muhammad. *Mukhtaṣar fiqh al-zaydī fī al-muʿāmalāt.* Ṣanʿāʾ, n.d. (c. 1970). MS, 213 pp. Photocopy.

—. *Mukhtaṣar lil-muḥtāj ilayhi fī al-yaman min ʿilm al-farāʾiḍ.* Ṣanʿāʾ, n.d. (c. 1970). MS, 47 pp. Photocopy.

Zabāra, Muhammad, and Ahmad Zabāra. *Nuzhat al-naẓar fī baʿḍ aʿyān al-qarn al-rābiʿ ʿashar.* Ṣanʿāʾ, n.d. (c. 1993). MS, 4 vols. Photocopy.

Archival Documents

Ḥukm—*Court Judgment*

Case numbers refer to five judgments outlined at the beginning of chapter 7.

* * *

al-Ḥaddād, Yahya bin ʿAli, First Secretary, Acting Judge. *Ḥukm*, Ibb, 1349 AH (1931). Urban real estate (case 1). Original roll.

al-Iryānī, Judge Hasan Ahmad. *Ḥukm*, Ibb, 1380 AH (1961). Murder (case 5). Original roll.

al-Manṣūr, Ismaʿil ʿAbd al-Rahman, Judge of Ibb province. *Ḥukm*, Ibb, 1376 AH (1956). Commercial sale contract (case 3). Original roll. Photos Ibb101–10 (rolls 6, 7).

—. *Ḥukm*, Ibb, 1378 AH (1958). Marriage contract (case 4). Original roll.

—. *Ḥukm*, Ibb, 1379 AH (1959). Damages due to operation of a mill in Ibb. Copy, with an appellate ruling, entered in *al-Daftar al-khāmis ʿashr*, Ibb Province Court Register 15 (see below), pp. 56–58. Photocopy.

al-Yamānī (al-Yadūmī), ʿAbd Allāh bin ʿAli, Judge of the Provincial Seat. *Ḥukm*, Taʿizz, 1366 AH (1947). Ibb inheritance and family waqf, including two later documents, a *tafwīḍ* and an associated settlement (case 2). Photos Ibb294–306 (roll 13).

—. *Ḥukm*, Taʿizz, 1378 AH (1958). Ibb case, property in cultivated land. Original roll, photos Ibb111–18 (roll 7).

Daftar—*Court Register*

Daftar (untitled). Court register. Judge ʿAbd Allah bin Muhammad Isḥāq, Ibb, 1954–60. Unnumbered photos.

Daftar (untitled). Judge Hasan Ahmad al-Iryānī (*ḥākim al-maqām*), Ibb, 1375–77 AH (1955–57). Photocopy.

al-Daftar al-ḥādī ʿashr min dafātir qayd bi-Ibb bi-l-aḥkām wa-l-baṣāʾir bi-maḥkamat. Ibb court records, judgments, and land sale documents, Register 11. Judge al-Manṣūr, 1374–77 AH (1955–58). Photocopy.

al-Daftar al-khāmis ʿashr min al-dafātir maḥkamat al-liwāʾ ibb. Ibb Province Court Register 15. Judge al-Manṣūr, 1379–80 AH (1959–60). Photocopy.

al-Daftar al-thālith. Al-Aḥkām li-maḥkamat liwāʾ Ibb. Ibb Province judgment records, Register 3. Judge Hasan Ahmad al-Iryānī, 1381–83 AH (1961–63). Photocopy.

Daftar qayd al-qarārāt. Al-hayʾa al-sharʿiyya. Appellate rulings register. Taʿizz, 1380 AH (1960). Unnumbered photos.

Shakwā—*Petition*

Shakāwā. Collection of 90 petitions, 1946. Sayāghī family, Ibb. Photocopies.

Shakāwā. Summary of 260 petitions received by the Governor of Ibb, April–May 1980.

Wathīqa—*Instrument*

BAṢĪRA—LAND SALE CONTRACT

Baṣīra. Ibb, 1287 AH (1870). Photos Ibb506 (roll 21).
Baṣīra. Ibb, 1317 AH (1899). Photos Ibb174–77 (roll 10).
Baṣīra. Ibb, 1324 AH (1906). Photos Ibb323–24 (roll 13).
Baṣīra. Ibb, 1375 AH (1956). Photos Ibb86–87 (roll 5).
Baṣīra QMb. Ibb, 1377 AH (1958). Digital H16–17 (1991).
Baṣīra QMc. Ibb, 1376 AH (1957). Digital H14–15 (1991).
Baṣīra QMe. Ibb, 1331 AH (1913). Digital H12 (strip 11, 005).
Baṣīra QMf. Ibb, 1202 AH (1788). Digital H12 (strip 11, 006).
Baṣīra QMg. Ibb, 1267 AH (1851). Digital H12 (strip 11, 007).
Baṣīra QMh. Ibb, 1360 AH (1941). Digital H12 (strip 11).
Baṣīra QMi. Ibb, 1358 AH (1939). Digital H22–24 (1991).

IJĀRA (LANDLORD'S REGISTER)—AGRARIAN LEASE

Series A. 45 documents, mostly 1381–84 AH (1961–64). Digital E4–30.
Series B. 70 documents, 1372–78 AH (1952–58). Digital F1–36.
Series C. 46 documents, 1379–81, 1385 AH (1959–61, 1965). Digital B1–25, G1–23.

IJĀRA (*AWQĀF* REGISTER)—AGRARIAN LEASE, INSTITUTIONAL

Daftar ajāʾir waqf al-kabīr ibb wa masājid nāḥiyat ibb. Maktab al-Awqāf, Ibb, 1368–80 AH (1948–60). 25 leases. Photos Ibb128–31 (roll 8); Digital B175–86.
Daftar, waqf al-kabīr, ibb. Harvest revenue for 1343 AH (1924), receipts for 1344 AH (1925). 9pp. Handwritten original.

ʿAQD AL-NIKĀḤ—MARRIAGE CONTRACT

Marriage contract. Ibb, 1333 AH (1915). Digital C182.
Marriage contract. Ibb, 1362 AH (1943). Quoted in court record as evidence, in Judge al-Manṣūr, *ḥukm*, 1378 AH (1958), lines 40–43.
Marriage contract, al-Ḥaddād. Ibb, 11 Shawwāl 1377 AH (May 1, 1958). Photo Ibb114 (roll 5).
Marriage contract, copy. Ibb, 1379 AH (1959). Entered in *al-Daftar al-khāmis ʿashr*, Ibb Province Court Register 15 (see above), p. 46. Photocopy.
Marriage contract (*ʿaqd nikāḥ sharʿī*). Issued by the Ṣanʿāʾ-South Court, on a form produced by the Ministry of Justice, Office of *al-tawthīq wa-l-tasjīl*, 1991.
Divorce document (*ibrāʾa* or *baraʾa wa ṭalāq*). Ibb, 1333 AH (1915). Unnumbered photo.
Divorce document, copy. Ibb, 1 Jumād I 1379 AH (November 2, 1959). Entered in *al-Daftar al-khāmis ʿashr*, Ibb Province Court Register 15 (see above), p. 46

Inheritance Documents

Farz (or *faṣl*). Ibb, 1265 AH (1849). Photos Ibb2–4 (roll 1).
Farz. Ibb, 1338 AH (1919). Photos Ibb67–69 (roll 4).
Faṣl, section on "Lower Yemen," *sayyid* family. Ṣanʿāʾ, n.d. Digital B387–89.
Ḥaṣr (register). Ibb, 1322 AH (1904). Photos Ibb181–215 (rolls 9, 10).
Tarkīz. Ibb, 1338 AH (1919). Photos Ibb94–100 (roll 6).

Miscellaneous Documents

Burayhī-ʿAzīz Document Collection, Ibb. 112 documents. Photocopies.
Murājaʿa (appeal of a settlement finding in a dispute). Ibb, Shaʿban 1397 AH (July 1977). Digital C095.

Bibliography

Abū Dāwūd. *Risāla ilā ahl Makka*. Beirut: al-Maktab al-Islamī, 1997.

Abū Shujāʿ, Ahmad. *Matn Abī Shujāʿ*. Beirut: Muʾassasat al-Kutub al-Thaqāfiyya, 1985.

Afīf, Ahmad Jabir. *al-Ḥarakat al-waṭaniyya fī al-yaman*. Damascus: Dār al-Fikr, 1982.

Agmon, Iris. *Family and Court: Legal Culture and Modernity in Late Ottoman Palestine*. Syracuse: Syracuse University Press, 2006.

Agmon, Iris, and Ido Shahar. "Shifting Perspectives in the Study of Sharīʿa Courts: Methodologies and Paradigms." Theme issue, *Islamic Law and Society* 15, no. 1 (2008).

Agrama, Hussein Ali. "Ethics, Tradition, Authority: Toward an Anthropology of the Fatwā." *American Ethnologist* 37, no. 1 (2010): 2–18.

——. *Questioning Secularism: Islam, Sovereignty, and the Rule of Law in Modern Egypt*. Chicago: University of Chicago Press, 2012.

Akgündüz, Ahmed. "Shariʿah Courts and Shariʿah Records: The Application of Islamic Law in the Ottoman State." *Islamic Law and Society* 16 (2009): 202–30.

al-Akwaʿ, Ismaʿil bin ʿAli. *al-Madāris al-islāmiyya fī al-yaman*. Damascus: Dār al-Fikr, 1980.

——. *al-Amthāl al-yamaniyya*, 2 vols. 1968. Reprint, Ṣanʿāʾ: Maktab Jīl al-Jadīd, 1984.

——. *Hijar al-ʿilm wa-maʿāqiluhu fī al-Yaman*. Beirut: Dār al-Fikr, 1995.

——. *An Introduction to Hijrahs and Other Refuges of Learning in Yemen*. Translated by Tim Mackintosh-Smith. Yemen Translation Series 5. Ardmore: American Institute for Yemeni Studies, 2006.

Ali, Kecia. *Sexual Ethics and Islam: Feminist Reflections on Qurʾan, Hadith, and Jurisprudence*. Oxford: Oneworld, 2006.

——. "Marriage in Classical Islamic Jurisprudence: A Survey of Doctrines." In Quraishi and Vogel, *The Islamic Marriage Contract*, 11-45.

al-ʿAlīmī, Rashad. *al-Taqlīdiyya wa-l-ḥadātha fī al-niẓām al-qānūnī al-yamanī*. Ṣanʿāʾ: Dār al-Kalima, 1989.

al-ʿAmrī, Husayn ʿAbd Allah. *The Yemen in the Eighteenth and Nineteenth Centuries.* London: Ithaca Press, 1985.

Anjum, Ovamir. "Islam as a Discursive Tradition: Talal Asad and His Interlocutors." *Comparative Studies of South Asia, Africa and the Middle East* 27, no. 3 (2007): 656–72.

al-ʿAnsī, Ahmad bin Qasim. *al-Tāj al-mudhhab li-aḥkām al-madhhab sharḥ matn al-azhār fī fiqh al-aʾimmat al-aṭhār.* Ṣanʿāʾ: Dār al-Ḥikma al-Yamāniyya, 1993.

Appadurai, Arjun. *Modernity at Large.* Minneapolis: University of Minnesota Press, 1996.

Arberry, Arthur J. *The Koran Interpreted.* London: Oxford University Press, 1964.

Asad, Talal, ed. *Anthropology and the Colonial Encounter.* London: Ithaca Press, 1973.

——. *The Idea of an Anthropology of Islam.* Washington, D.C.: Center for Contemporary Arab Studies, Georgetown University, 1986.

——. *Genealogies of Religion: Discipline and Reasons of Power in Christianity and Islam.* Baltimore: Johns Hopkins University Press, 1993.

——. *Formations of the Secular: Christianity, Islam, Modernity.* Stanford: Stanford University Press, 2003.

——. "Thinking About Religion, Tradition, and Politics in Egypt Today." *Critical Inquiry* 42 (2015): 166–241.

Atiyeh, George N., ed. *The Book in the Islamic World: The Written Word and Communication in the Middle East.* Albany: State University of New York Press, 1995.

Aziz, Muhammad Ali. *Religion and Mysticism in Early Islam: Theology and Sufism in Yemen.* London: I. B. Tauris, 2011.

al-Bājūrī, Ibrahim bin Muhammad. *Ḥāshiya ʿalā sharḥ Ibn Qāsim al-Ghazzī.* Beirut: Dār al-Maʿrifa, 1974.

Bakhtin, Mikhail M. *The Dialogic Imagination: Four Essays.* Translated by Michael Holquist. Austin: University of Texas Press, 1981.

——. *Problems of Dostoevsky's Poetics.* Translated by Caryl Emerson. Minneapolis: University of Minnesota, 1984.

——. *Speech Genres and Other Late Essays.* Translated by Vern W. McGee. Austin: University of Texas Press, 1986.

Bang, Anne K. *The Idrisi State in ʿAsir 1906–1934: Politics, Religion and Personal Prestige as Statebuilding Factors in Early Twentieth-Century Arabia.* Bergen: Centre for Middle Eastern and Islamic Studies, 1996.

al-Baradūnī, ʿAbd Allah. *al-Thaqāfa wa-l-thawra fī al-yaman.* Beirut: Dār al-Thaqāfa, 1993.

Barber, Karin. *The Anthropology of Texts, Persons and Publics: Oral and Written Culture in Africa and Beyond.* Cambridge: Cambridge University Press, 2007.

Bardawil, Fadi A. "The Solitary Analyst of Doxas: An Interview with Talal Asad." *Comparative Studies of South Asia, Africa and the Middle East* 36, no. 1 (2016): 152–173.

Barthes, Roland. *The Pleasure of the Text.* Translated by Richard Miller. New York: Hill and Wang, 1975.

Bauman, Richard, and Charles L. Briggs. "Poetics and Performances as Critical Perspectives on Language and Social Life." *Annual Review of Anthropology* 19, no. 1 (1990): 59–88.

——. *Voices of Modernity: Language Ideologies and the Politics of Inequality.* Cambridge: Cambridge University Press, 2003.

Bausi, Alessandro, et al., eds. *Comparative Oriental Manuscript Studies*. Hamburg: Tredition, 2015.

al-Bayḍāwī, ʿAbd Allah bin ʿUmar. *Tafsīr al-Bayḍāwī*. Beirut: Muʾassasat al-Aʿlamī, 1990.

Bearman, P., Th. Bianquis, C. E. Bosworth, E. van Donzel, and W. P. Heinrichs, eds. *Encyclopedia of Islam*. 2nd ed. Leiden: Brill, 2002.

Bearman, Peri, Rudolph Peters, and Frank E. Vogel, eds. *The Islamic School of Law*. Cambridge, MA: Harvard University Press, 2005.

Beeston, A. F. L. *Arabic Nomenclature*. Oxford: Oriental Institute, 1971.

Bentham, Jeremy. *Rationale of Judicial Evidence, Specially Applied to English Practice*. 5 vols. London: Hunt and Clarke, 1827.

Berkey, Jonathan. *The Transmission of Knowledge in Cairo: A Social History of Islamic Education*. Princeton: Princeton University Press, 1992.

Berque, Jacques. *Essai sur la méthode juridique maghrébine*. Rabat: Leforestier, 1944.

——. *Structures sociales du haut-atlas*. Paris: Presses Universitaires de France, 1955.

Björkman, W. "Diplomatic, i. Classical Arabic." In Bearman et al., *Encyclopedia of Islam*, 2nd ed.

Blair, Sheila S. *Islamic Inscriptions*. Edinburgh: Edinburgh University Press, 1998.

Boas, Franz. "The History of Anthropology." *Science* 20, no. 512 (1904): 513–524.

——. "Some Philological Aspects of Anthropological Research." *Science* 23, no. 591 (1906): 641–45.

——. *Handbook of American Indian Languages*. Washington, D.C.: Government Printing Office, 1911.

——. *Race, Language and Culture*. New York: Free Press, 1966.

Borges, Jorge Luis. *The Aleph and Other Stories, 1933–1969*. New York: E. P. Dutton, 1978.

Bourdieu, Pierre. *Outline of a Theory of Practice*. Cambridge: Cambridge University Press, 1977.

——. *The Logic of Practice*. Stanford: Stanford University Press, 1990.

Bousquet, G.-H., and J. Berque. *Recueil de la Loi Musulmane de Zaid ben ʿAlī*. Alger: La Maison des Livres, 1941.

Bowen, John. *Sumatran Politics and Poetics: Gayo History, 1900–1989*. New Haven: Yale University Press, 1991.

Briggs, Charles L., and Richard Bauman. "Genre, Intertextuality, and Social Power." *Journal of Linguistic Anthropology* 2, no. 2 (1992): 131–72.

Brockelmann, C. *Geschichte der Arabischen Litteratur*. 2nd edition. Leiden: Brill, 1943–49.

Brown, Jonathan. *The Canonization of al-Bukhārī and Muslim: The Formation and Function of the Sunnī Ḥadīth Canon*. Leiden: Brill, 2007.

Bulliet, Richard. *The Patricians of Nishapur*. Cambridge, MA: Harvard University Press, 1972.

Burak, Guy. "Evidentiary Truth Claims, Imperial Registers, and the Ottoman Archive: Contending Legal Views of Archival and Record-Keeping Practices in Ottoman Greater Syria (Seventeenth–Nineteenth Centuries)." *Bulletin of the School of Oriental and African Studies* 79, no. 2 (2016): 1–22.

Bury, George Wyman. *Arabia Infelix; or, The Turks in Yamen*. Folios Archive Library. Reading: Garnet, 1998.

Calder, Norman. *Studies in Early Muslim Jurisprudence*. Oxford: Clarendon Press, 1993.

——. "Law." In *History of Islamic Philosophy*, edited by Seyyed Hossein Nasr and Oliver Leaman. London: Routledge, 1996.
——. "Al-Nawawī's Typology of *Muftīs* and Its Significance for a General Theory of Islamic Law." *Islamic Law and Society* 3, no. 2 (1996): 137–64.
——. *Islamic Jurisprudence in the Classical Era*. Edited by Colin Imber. Cambridge: Cambridge University Press, 2010.
Carruthers, Mary. *The Book of Memory*. Cambridge: Cambridge University Press, 1990.
Certeau, Michel de. *The Practice of Everyday Life*. Translated by Steven Rendall. Berkeley: University of California Press, 1984.
Chamberlin, Michael. *Knowledge and Social Practice in Medieval Damascus, 1190–1350*. Cambridge: Cambridge University Press, 1994.
Chartier, Roger. *The Order of Books*. Stanford: Stanford University Press, 1994.
Clarke, Morgan. *Islam and New Kinship: Reproductive Technology and the Shariah in Lebanon*. New York: Berghahn, 2009.
——. "The Judge as Tragic Hero: Judicial Ethics in Lebanon's Shariʿa Courts." *American Ethnologist* 39, no. 1 (2012): 106–21.
Comaroff, John L., and Jean Comaroff. *Ethnography and the Historical Imagination*. Boulder: Westview, 1992.
Cook, Michael. "The Opponents of the Writing of Tradition in Early Islam." *Arabica* 44 (1997): 437–530.
——. *Commanding Right and Forbidding Wrong in Islamic Thought*. Cambridge: Cambridge University Press, 2000.
Crone, Patricia, and Martin Hinds. *God's Caliph: Religious Authority in the First Centuries of Islam*. Cambridge: Cambridge University Press, 1986.
Cuno, Kenneth. *The Pasha's Peasants: Land, Society and Economy in Lower Egypt, 1740–1858*. Cambridge: Cambridge University Press, 1992.
Demeerseman, A. "Une étape décisive de la culture et de la psychologie sociale islamique. Les donnés de la controverse autour du problème de l'imprimerie." *Institut des Belles Lettres Arabes* 16, no. 64 (1954): 113–40.
Déroche, François, et al. *Islamic Codicology: An Introduction to the Study of Manuscripts in Arabic Script*. Translated by D. Dusinberre and D. Radzinowicz. London: Al-Furqān Foundation, 2005.
Derrida, Jacques. *Margins of Philosophy*. Translated by Alan Bass. Chicago: University of Chicago Press, 1982.
——. *Archive Fever*. Translated by E. Prenowitz. Chicago: University of Chicago Press, 1996.
Donaldson, William J. *Sharecropping in the Yemen: A Study of Islamic Theory, Custom and Pragmatism*. Leiden: Brill, 2000.
Doumani, Beshara. *Rediscovering Palestine: Merchants and Peasants in Jabal Nablus, 1700–1900*. Berkeley: University of California Press, 1995.
Dresch, Paul. *Tribes, Government, and History in Yemen*. Oxford: Clarendon Press, 1989.
——. *A History of Modern Yemen*. Cambridge: Cambridge University Press, 2000.
——. *The Rules of Barat: Tribal Documents from Yemen*. Ṣanʿāʾ: Centre français d'archéologieet des sciences sociales, 2006.

——. "Introduction to Legalism, Anthropology and History: A View from Anthropology." In *Legalism: Anthropology and History*, edited by P. Dresch and Hannah Skoda, 1–37. Oxford: Oxford University Press, 2012.

Dupret, Baudouin, et al., eds. *Narratives of Truth in Islamic Law.* London: I. B. Tauris, 2008.

Durant, Alessandro, and Charles Goodwin. *Rethinking Context: Language as an Interactive Phenomenon.* Cambridge: Cambridge University Press, 1992.

Durkheim, Émile. *The Division of Labor in Society.* Translated by George Simpson. New York: Free Press, 1933.

Dutton, Yasin. "The Introduction to Ibn Rushd's Bidayat al-Mujtahid." *Islamic Law and Society* 1, no. 2 (1994): 188–205.

——. *The Codicology of Islamic Manuscripts.* London: al-Furqān Islamic Heritage Foundation, 1995.

——. *The Origins of Islamic Law: The Qurʾan, the Muwaṭṭaʾ and Madinan ʿAmal.* London: Curzon, 1999.

Eickelman, Dale F. "From Theocracy to Monarchy: Authority and Legitimacy in Inner Oman, 1935–1957." *International Journal of Middle East Studies* 17, no. 1 (1985): 3–24.

El-Leithy, Tamer. "Living Documents, Dying Archives: Towards a Historical Anthropology of Medieval Arabic Archives." *Al-Qanṭara* 32, no. 2 (2011): 389–434.

Elshakry, Marwa. "The Exegesis of Science in Twentieth-Century Arabic Interpretations of the Qurʾān," In *Nature and Scripture in the Abrahamic Religions*, vol. 2, *1700–Present*, edited by Jitse M. van der Meer and Scott Mandelbrote, 491–524. Leiden: Brill, 2008.

El Shamsy, Ahmed. "The Ḥashiya in Islamic Law: A Sketch of the Shāfiʿī Literature." *Oriens* 41 (2013): 289–315.

Engels, Frederick. *The Origin of the Family, Private Property and the State.* New York: International Publishers, 1972.

Ergene, Boğaç A. *Local Court, Provincial Society and Justice in the Ottoman Empire.* Leiden: Brill, 2003.

Fahmy, Khaled. "Anatomy of Justice: Forensic Medicine and Criminal Law in Nineteenth-Century Egypt." *Islamic Law and Society* 6, no. 2 (1999): 224–71.

al-Faqīh Yūsuf, Yusuf bin Ahmad bin Muhammad bin ʿUthman. *Thamarāt al-yāniʿa wa-l-aḥkām al-wāḍiḥa al-qāṭiʿa.* Saʿda: Maktaba al-turāth al-islāmī, 2002.

Feldman, Ilana. *Governing Gaza: Bureaucracy, Authority, and the Work of Rule, 1917-1967.* Durham: Duke University Press, 2008.

Foucault, Michel. *The Order of Things: An Archaeology of the Human Sciences.* New York: Pantheon Books, 1970.

——. *The Archaeology of Knowledge.* Translated by A. M. Sheridan Smith. New York: Harper, 1972.

——. "What Is an Author?" In *Language, Counter-Memory, Practice: Selected Essays and Interviews by Michel Foucault*, edited by D. F. Bouchard, 113–38. Ithaca: Cornell University Press, 1977.

Gadamer, Hans-Georg. *Truth and Method.* New York: Seabury Press, 1975.

Geertz, Clifford. *The Interpretation of Cultures.* New York: Basic Books, 1973.

——. "Suq, the Bazaar Economy in Sefrou." In *Meaning and Order in Moroccan Society*, edited by C. Geertz, Hildred Geertz, and Lawrence Rosen, 123–313. Cambridge: Cambridge University Press, 1979.

——. *Local Knowledge: Further Essays in Interpretive Anthropology*. New York: Basic Books, 1983.

Gerber, Haim. *State, Society, and Law in Islam: Ottoman Law in Comparative Perspective*. Albany: State University of New York Press, 1994.

——. *Islamic Law and Culture, 1600–1840*. Leiden: Brill, 1999.

Ghazzal, Zouhair. *The Grammars of Adjudication: The Economics of Judicial Decision Making in Fin-de-siècle Ottoman Beirut and Damascus*. Beirut: Institut Français du Proche-Orient, 2007.

al-Ghurbānī, Muḥammad bin ʿAlī. *ʿIlm uṣūl al-ḥadīth*. N.p.: n.p., 2007.

Ginzburg, Carlo. *Clues, Myths, and the Historical Method*. Translated by J. and A. Tedeschi. Baltimore: Johns Hopkins University Press, 1989.

Gochenour, David Thomas, III. "The Penetration of Zaydi Islam Into Early Medieval Yemen." PhD thesis, Harvard University, 1984.

Goitein, S. D. "Portrait of a Yemenite Weavers' Village." *Jewish Social Studies* (1955): 3–26.

Goldziher, Ignaz. *Muslim Studies*. Translated by S. Stern. Chicago: Aldine, 1967.

Goody, Jack. *Literacy in Traditional Societies*. Cambridge: Cambridge University Press, 1968.

——. *The Logic of Writing and the Organization of Society*. Cambridge: Cambridge University Press, 1986.

——. *The Interface Between the Written and the Oral*. Cambridge: Cambridge University Press, 1987.

——. *The Power of the Written Tradition*. Washington, D.C.: Smithsonian Institution Press, 2000.

Greetham, D. C. *Textual Scholarship: An Introduction*. New York: Garland, 1992.

Grewal, J. S. *In the By-Lanes of History: Some Persian Documents from a Punjab Town*. Simla: India Institute of Advanced Study, 1975.

Grohmann, Adolph. *Arabic Papyri in the Egyptian Library*. Volume 2. Cairo: Egyptian Library Press, 1936.

Haider, Najam. *The Origins of the Shīʿa: Identity, Ritual, and Sacred Space in Eighth-Century Kūfa*. Cambridge: Cambridge University Press, 2011.

——. *Shīʿī Islam: An Introduction*. Cambridge: Cambridge University Press, 2014.

Hallaq, Wael B. "Was the Gate of Ijtihād Closed?" *International Journal of Middle East Studies* 16, no. 1 (1984): 3–41.

——. "From Fatwās to Furūʿ: Growth and Change in Islamic Substantive Law." *Islamic Law and Society* 1, no. 1 (1994): 29–65.

——. "Model Shurūṭ Works and the Dialectic of Doctrine and Practice." *Islamic Law and Society* 2, no. 2 (1995): 109–34.

——. *A History of Islamic Legal Theories: An Introduction to Sunnī Uṣūl al-fiqh*. Cambridge: Cambridge University Press, 1997.

——. "The Qāḍī's Dīwān (*Sijill*) Before the Ottomans." *Bulletin of the School of Oriental and African Studies* 61, no. 3 (1998): 415–36.

——. "Qāḍīs Communicating: Legal Change and the Law of Documentary Evidence." *al-Qanṭara* 20 (1999): 437–66.

——. *Authority, Continuity and Change in Islamic Law.* Cambridge: Cambridge University Press, 2001.

——. *Sharīʿa: Theory, Practice, Transformations.* Cambridge: Cambridge University Press, 2009.

al-Hāshimī, Yahya bin Muhammad. *al-Qaḍāʾ fī al-yaman.* Ṣanʿāʾ: Maktabat Khālid bin Walīd, 2003.

Haykel, Bernard. "Order and Righteousness: Muḥammad ʿAlī al-Shawkānī and the Nature of the Islamic State in Yemen." PhD thesis, Oxford University, 1997.

——. *Revival and Reform in Islam: The Legacy of Muhammad al-Shawkani.* Cambridge: Cambridge University Press, 2003.

Haykel, Bernard, and Aron Zysow. "What Makes a Madhhab a Madhhab: Zaydī Debates on the Structure of Legal Authority." *Arabica* 59 (2012): 32–71.

Heck, Paul L. "The Epistemological Problem of Writing in Islamic Civilization: al-Khaṭīb al-Baghdādī's (d. 463/1071) 'Taqyīd al-ʿilm.'" *Studia Islamica* 94 (2002): 85–114.

Heinrichs, W. P. "Ḳawāʿid Fiḳhiyya." In Bearman et al., *Encyclopedia of Islam*, 2nd ed.

Heinrichs, W. P., Julie Scott Meisami, and Paul Starkey. "Rhetorical Figures." *Encyclopedia of Arabic Literature.* New York and London: Routledge, 1998.

Heyd, Uriel. "Some Aspects of the Ottoman Fetvā." *Bulletin of the School of Oriental and African Studies* 32 (1969): 35–56.

al-Ḥibshī, ʿAbd Allah bin Muhammad. *Maṣādir al-fikr al-Islāmī fī al-Yaman.* Beirut: al-Maktaba al-ʿAṣrīyya, 1988.

——. *Maṣādir al-fikr al-Islāmī fī al-Yaman.* Abū Ẓabī: al-Majmaʿ al-Thaqāfī, 2004.

al-Ḥillī, Muḥaqqiq. *Sharāʾiʿ al-islām fī al-fiqh al-islāmī al-jaʿfarī.* 2 vols. in 1. Beirut: Maktaba al-Ḥayā, 1930.

Hirsch, Susan. *Pronouncing and Persevering: Gender and the Discourses of Disputing in an African Islamic Court.* Chicago: University of Chicago Press, 1998.

Hirschkind, Charles. *The Ethical Soundscape: Cassette Sermons and Islamic Counterpublics.* New York: Columbia University Press, 2006.

Hirschler, Konrad. *The Written Word in the Medieval Arabic Lands.* Edinburgh: Edinburgh University Press, 2012.

Ho, Engseng. *The Graves of Tarim: Genealogy and Mobility Across the Indian Ocean.* Berkeley: University of California Press, 2006.

Hollander, Isaac. *Jews and Muslims in Lower Yemen: A Study of Protection and Restraint, 1918–1949.* Leiden: Brill, 2005.

Hovden, Eirik. "Flowers in Fiqh and Constructions of Validity: Practices and Norms in Yemeni Foundations of Forever Flowing Charity." PhD thesis, University of Bergen, 2012.

Hull, Matthew S. "The File: Agency, Authority, and Autography in an Islamabad Bureaucracy." *Language & Communication* 23 (2003): 287–314.

——. *Government of Paper: The Materiality of Bureaucracy in Urban Pakistan.* Berkeley: University of California Press, 2012.

Hunter, Capt. F. M. *An Account of the British Settlement of Aden in Arabia.* 1877. Reprint, London: Frank Cass, 1968.

al-Ḥusayn bin Badr al-Dīn. *Shifāʾ al-uwām fī aḥādīth al-aḥkām.* Jamʿiyyat ʿUlamāʾ al-Yaman, 1996.

al-Ḥusaynī, Ahmad. *Muʾallafāt al-Zaydīyya*. 3 vols. Qom: Maṭbaʿat al-Ismāʿīliyyan, 1413 AH (1993).
Ibrāhīm, Qasim, ʿAli bin ʿAbd Allah al-Anisī, and ʿAbd Allah bin Muhammad al-Saraḥī. *Taysīr al-marām fī masāʾil al-aḥkām li-l-bāḥithīn wa-l-ḥukkām*. Ṣanʿāʾ: al-Maʿhad al-ʿĀlī li-l-Qaḍāʾ; Beirut: Dār al-Tanwīr, 1986.
Ibn Bahrān, Muhammad bin Yahya. *Matn al-Kāfil*. Ṣanʿāʾ: Muʾassasāt Dār al-Turāth al-Yamanī, 1991.
Ibn al-Ḥājib, Jamal al-Din Abu ʿAmr ʿUthman. *Mukhtaṣar al-Muntahā*. Cairo: Būlāq, 1316–19 AH (1898–1901).
Ibn Ḥamza, Yahya (Imam). *al-Intiṣār ʿalā ʿulamāʾ al-amṣār*. Ṣanʿāʾ: Maktaba al-Imām Zayd bin ʿAlī, 2005.
Ibn Khaldūn. *The Muqaddimah*. 3 vols. Translated by Franz Rosenthal. Princeton: Princeton University Press, 1967.
Ibn Luqmān, Ahmad bin Muhammad bin Luqman. *al-Kāshif*. Ṣanʿāʾ: Maṭbaʿat al-Ḥukūma al-Mutawakkiliyya, bi-Dār al-Saʿāda, 1346 AH (1927).
Ibn Miftāḥ, Abd Allah bin Muhammad. *al-Muntazaʿ al-mukhtār min al-Ghayth al-midrār* [*Sharḥ al-Azhār*]. 4 vols. Cairo: Maṭbaʿa al-dīniyya, 1341 AH (1922); Ṣanʿāʾ: Maktaba Ghamḍān, 1401 AH (1980).
——. *al-Muntazaʿ al-mukhtār min al-Ghayth al-midrār* [*Sharḥ al-Azhār* (2003)]. 4 vols. [Ṣanʿāʾ]: al-Jumhūriyya al-Yamaniyya, Wizārat al-ʿAdl, 2003.
Ibn al-Murtaḍā, Ahmad bin Yahya. *Kitāb al-azhār fī fiqh al-aʾimma al-aṭhār*. 4th printing. N.p.: n.p., 1972.
——. *Kitāb al-azhār fī fiqh al-aʾimma al-aṭhār*. Cairo: al-Tamaddun, 1332 AH (1913). Hathi Trust Digital Library (University of Michigan).
——. *Kitāb al-baḥr al-zakhkhār al-jāmiʿ li-madhāhib ʿulamāʾ al-amṣār*. Beirut: Muʾassasat al-Risālah, 1975.
Ibn al-Muṭahhar, Muhammad bin Yahya. *Aḥkām al-aḥwāl al-shakhṣiyya*. 2 vols. Cairo: Dār al-Kutub al-Islāmiyya, 1985; Ṣanʿāʾ: Dār al-Fikr, 1989.
Ibn Muẓaffar, Yahya bin Ahmad. *Kitāb al-bayān al-shāfī al-muntazaʿ min al-burhān al-kāfī*. 4 vols. Ṣanʿāʾ: Maktabat Ghamḍān, 1984.
Ibn Raslān al-Ramlī, Ahmad ibn al-Husayn. *al-Zubad fī fiqh al-Shāfiʿī*. Cairo: ʿĀlam al-Fikr, 1977.
al-ʿImrānī, Muhammad Ismaʿil. *Niẓām al-qaḍāʾ fī al-islām*. Ṣanʿāʾ: Dār al-Jīl, 1984.
Irvine, Judith T., and Susan Gal. *Regimes of Language: Ideologies, Politics, and Identities*. Santa Fe: School for Advanced Research, 2000.
al-Iryānī, ʿAli bin ʿAbd Allah. *Sīrat al-Imām Muḥammad bin Yaḥyā Ḥamīd al-Din*. Amman: Dār al-Bashīr, 1996.
al-Iryānī, Yahya bin Muhammad. *Hidāyat al-mustabṣirīn bi-sharḥ ʿuddat al-ḥiṣn al-ḥaṣīn*. Damascus: Maṭbaʿat al-ʿAlam, 1397AH.
al-ʿIzzī, ʿAbd Allah bin Mahmud.*ʿUlūm al-ḥadīth ʿinda al-Zaydīyya wal-l-muḥaddithīn*. Amman: Muʾassasat al-Imam Zayd bin ʿAlī al-Thaqāfiyya, 2001.
Jackson, Sherman A. *Islamic Law and the State: The Constitutional Jurisprudence of Shihāb Al-Dīn Al-Qarāfī*. Leiden: Brill, 1996.
Janāḥī, Saʿid Ahmad. *al-Ḥaraka al-waṭaniyya fī al-yaman*. Ṣanʿāʾ: Markaz al-Amal lil-Dirāsāt wa al-Nashr, 1992.
Jennings, R. C. "The Office of Vekil." *Studia Islamica* 42 (1975): 147–69.

al-Jirāfī, ʿAbd Allah bin ʿAbd al-Karim. *Dhakhāʾir ʿulamāʾ al-yaman*. Beirut: Muʾassasat Dār al-Kitāb al-Ḥadīth, 1991.
——. *Tuḥfat al-ikhwān*. Cairo: Maṭbaʿat al-Salafiyya, 1365 AH (1945).
Johansen, Baber. *The Islamic Law on Land Tax and Rent*. London: Croom Helm, 1988.
——. "Coutumes locales et coutumes universelles aux sources des règles juridique en droit musulman hanéfite." *Annales Islamologiques* 27 (1993): 29–35.
——. "Formes de langage et fonctions publiques: Stéréotypes, témoins at offices dans la preuve par l'écrit en droit musulman." *Arabica* 44 (1997): 333–76.
——. *Contingency in a Sacred Law: Legal and Ethical Norms in the Muslim Fiqh*. Leiden: Brill, 1999.
Juynboll, G. H. A. "Tawātur." In Bearman et al., *Encyclopedia of Islam*, 2nd ed.
Kamali, Mohammad Hashim. *Principles of Islamic Jurisprudence*. Cambridge: Islamic Texts Society, 2003.
Khan, Geoffrey. *Arabic Papyri: Selected Material from the Khalili Collection*. London: Nour Foundation and Oxford University Press, 1992.
——. *Bills, Letters and Deeds: Arabic Papyri of the 7th to 11th Centuries*. London: Nour Foundation, Oxford University Press, 1992.
——. *Arabic Legal and Administrative Documents in the Cambridge Genizah Collections*. Cambridge: Cambridge University Press, 1993.
al-Khaṣṣāf, Ahmad bin ʿUmar. *Kitāb adab al-qāḍī*. Edited by Farhat Ziyada. Cairo: American University in Cairo Press, 1978.
al-Kibsī, Ahmad bin Zayd. "Baḥth fī al-ʿamal bi-l-khaṭṭ." In *Dhakhāʾir ʿulamāʾ al-yaman*, edited by ʿAbd Allah bin ʿAbd al-Karim al-Jirāfī, 329–36. Beirut: Muʾassasat Dār al-Kitāb al-Ḥadīth, 1991.
Kinberg, Leah. "Ambiguous." In *Encyclopaedia of the Qurʾān*, edited by Jane Dammen McAuliffe. Leiden: Brill, 2012–.
Kizilkaya, Necmettin. "Outline of the Historical Evolution of Qawāʿid Literature in Islamic Law." *American Journal of Islamic Social Sciences* 28, no. 1 (2011): 76–105.
Kristeva, Julia. *Desire in Language*. New York: Columbia University Press, 1980.
Kuehn, Thomas. *Empire, Islam, and the Politics of Difference: Ottoman Rule in Yemen, 1849-1919*. Leiden: Brill, 2011.
Lane, Andrew J. *A Traditional Muʿtazilite Qurʾān Commentary*. Leiden: Brill, 2006.
Lange, Christian. *Justice, Punishment and the Medieval Muslim Imagination*. Cambridge: Cambridge University Press, 2008.
Latour, Bruno. *The Making of Law: An Ethnography of the Conseil d'État*. Translated by Marina Brilman and Alain Pottage. Cambridge: Polity Press, 2010.
——. "Steps Toward the Writing of a Compositionist Manifesto." *New Literary History* 41 (2010): 471–90.
El-Leithy, Tamer. "Living Documents, Dying Archives: Towards a Historical Anthropology of Medieval Arabic Archives." *Al-Qanṭara* 32, no. 2 (2011): 389–434.
Lévi-Strauss, Claude. *Structural Anthropology*. Translated by Claire Jacobson. New York: Basic Books, 1967.
Little, Donald P. *A Catalogue of the Islamic Documents from the al-Ḥaram ash-Sharīf in Jerusalem*. Beirut: Beiruter Texte und Studien, 1984.
Locke, John. *Two Treatises on Civil Government*. London: Routledge, 1884.

Lowie, Robert. "Native Languages as Ethnographic Tools." *American Anthropologist* 42, no. 1 (1940): 81–89.
Lowry, Heath W. *Studies in Defterology: Ottoman Society in the Fifteenth and Sixteenth Centuries.* Istanbul: Isis Press, 1992.
Lucy, John A. *Reflexive Language: Reported Speech and Metapragmatics.* Cambridge: Cambridge University Press, 1993.
MacLean, Derryl N., and Sikeena Karmali Ahmed, eds. *Cosmopolitanisms in Muslim Contexts: Perspectives from the Past.* Edinburgh: Edinburgh University, 2012.
Madelung, Wilferd. "Imāma." In Bearman et al., *Encyclopedia of Islam*, 2nd ed.
Madelung, Wilferd. *Der Imam Al-Qasim Ibn Ibrahim und die Glaubenslehre der Zaiditen.* Berlin: Walter de Gruyter, 1965.
—. "The Origins of the Yemenite Hijra." In *Arabicus Felix: Luminosus Britannicus: Essays in Honour of A. F. L. Beeston on His Eightieth Birthday*, edited by Alan Jones. Reading: Ithaca Press, 1991.
—. "Zaydī Attitudes to Sufism," In *Islamic Mysticism Contested*, edited by Frederick De Jong and Bernd Radtke, 124–44. Leiden: Brill, 1999.
Mahdī, Muhsin. "From the Manuscript Age to the Age of Printed Books." In *The Book in the Islamic World*, ed. George N. Atiyeh, 10–11. Albany: State University of New York Press, 1995.
Mahmood, Saba. *Politics of Piety: The Islamic Revival and the Feminist Subject.* Princeton: Princeton University Press, 2005.
Majalla. 3rd printing. Istanbul: Maṭbaʿat al-Jawāʾib, 1305 AH [1887].
Majallat al-Buḥūth wa-l-aḥkām al-qaḍāʾiya al-yamaniyya. Vol. 1, no. 1. Ṣanʿāʾ: Maʿhad al-ʿālī li-l-qaḍāʾ, 1980.
Makdisi, George. *The Rise of Colleges. Institutions of Learning in Islam and the West.* Ediburgh: Edinburgh University Press, 1981.
—. "Scholasticism and Humanism in Classical Islam and the Christian West." *Journal of the American Oriental Society* 109, no. 2 (1989): 175–82.
Mandaville, Jon E. "The Ottoman Court Records of Syria and Jordan." *Journal of the American Oriental Society* 86 (1966): 311–19.
Marino, Brigitte, and Tomoki Okawara. *Dalīl sijillāt al-maḥākim al-sharʿīyya al-ʿUthmāniyya.* Damascus: Insitut Français de Damas, 1999.
Marx, Karl. *Pre-capitalist Economic Formations.* Translated by Jack Cohen. New York: International Publishers, 1965.
Masud, Muhammad Khalid, Brinkley Messick, and David S. Powers. *Islamic Legal Interpretation: Muftīs and Their Fatwās.* Cambridge, MA: Harvard University Press, 1996.
Masud, Muhammad Khalid, Rudolph Peters, and David S. Powers. *Dispensing Justice in Islam: Qadis and Their Judgments.* Leiden: Brill, 2006.
al-Māwardī, ʿAli bin Muhammad. *al-Aḥkām al-sulṭāniyya wa-l-wilāyat al-dīniyya.* Cairo: Dār al-Fikr, 1983.
Mead, Margaret. "Native Languages as Field-Work Tools." *American Anthropologist* 41, no. 2 (1939): 189–205.
Melchert, Christopher. *The Formation of the Sunni Schools of Law.* Leiden: Brill, 1997.
—. "Abū Dāwūd al-Sijistānī." In *Encyclopedia of Islam 3*, edited by Gudrun Krämer, Denis Matringe, John Nawas, and Everett Rowson. Leiden: Brill, 2007–.
Mermier, Franck. *Le cheikh de la nuit.* Arles: Sinbad/Actes Sud, 1997.

Messick, Brinkley. *The Calligraphic State*. Berkeley: University of California Press, 1993.

——. "Cover Stories: A Genealogy of the Legal-Public Sphere in Yemen." In *Religion, Social Practice, and Contested Hegemonies: Reconstructing the Public Sphere in Muslim Majority Societies*, edited by A. Salvatore and M. Levine, 207–29. New York: Palgrave Macmillan, 2005.

——. "L'Écriture en procès: Les récits d'un meurtre devant un tribunal sharʿī." *Droit et Société* 39 (1998): 237–56.

——. "Evidence: From Memory to Archive." *Islamic Law and Society* 9, no. 2 (2002): 231–70.

——. "Fatwā, Modern." In *Encyclopedia of Islam* 3, edited by Gudrun Krämer, Denis Matringe, John Nawas, and Everett Rowson. Leiden: Brill, 2007–.

——. "Fatwā: Process and Function." In *The Oxford Encyclopedia of the Modern Islamic World*, edited by John Esposito, 2:10–13. New York: Oxford University Press, 1995.

——. "Indexing the Self: Wording and Intentionality in Legal Acts." *Islamic Law and Society* 8, no. 2 (2001): 151–78.

——. "Interpreting Tears: A Marriage Case from Imamic Yemen." In Quraishi and Vogel, *The Islamic Marriage Contract*, 156–79.

——. "Islamic Texts: The Anthropologist as Reader." In *Islamic Studies in the Twenty-first Century*, edited by Léon Buskens and Annemarie van Sandwijk, 29–46. Amsterdam: Amsterdam University Press, 2016.

——. "Media Muftīs: Radio Fatwās in Yemen." In *Islamic Legal Interpretation*, edited by K. M. Masud, B. Messick and D. S. Powers, 310–20. Cambridge, MA: Harvard University Press, 1996.

——. "The Muftī, the Text and the World: Legal Interpretation in Yemen." *Man*, n.s., 21 (1986): 102–19.

——. "Textual Properties: Writing and Wealth in a Sharīʿa Case." *Anthropological Quarterly* 68, no. 3 (1995): 157–70.

——. "Notes on Transliteration." In *Translating Cultures: Perspectives on Translation and Anthropology*, edited by Paula G. Rubel and Abraham Rosman, 177–96. Oxford: Berg, 2003.

——. "Prosecution in Yemen: The Introduction of the Niyāba." *International Journal of Middle East Studies* 15 (1983): 507–18.

——. "Transactions in Ibb: Economy and Society in a Yemeni Highland Town." PhD thesis, Princeton University, 1978.

Minkov, Anton. "Ottoman Tapu Title Deeds in the Eighteenth and Nineteenth Centuries: Origins, Typology and Diplomatics." *Islamic Law and Society* 7, no. 1 (2000): 1–29.

Mir-Hosseini, Ziba. *Marriage on Trial: A Study of Islamic Family Law*. London: I. B. Tauris, 1993.

Moors, Annelies. *Women, Property and Islam: Palestinian Experiences, 1920–1990*. Cambridge: Cambridge University Press, 1995.

Motzki, Harald. "The Collection of the Quran: A Reconsideration of Western Views in Light of Recent Methodological Developments." *Der Islam* 78 (2001): 1–34.

Moumtaz, Nada. "Refiguring Islam." In *A Companion to the Anthropology of the Middle East*, edited by Soraya Altorki, 125–50. Hoboken, NJ: John Wiley and Sons, 2015.

al-Muʾayyad Ahmad bin al-Husayn (Imam). *Sharḥ al-tajrīd*. Ṣanʿāʾ: Markaz al-Turāth wa-l-Buḥūth al-Yamanī, 2006.

al-Muʾayyad Yahya bin Ḥamza (Imam). *al-Intiṣār ʿalā ʿulamāʾ al-amṣār*. Ṣanʿāʾ: Muʾassasat al-Imām Zayd bin ʿAlī al-Thaqāfiyya, 1425 AH (2005).

al-Muftī al-Ḥubayshī al-Ibbī, Muhammad bin ʿAli bin Muhsin. *Fatḥ al-mannān sharḥ zubad Ibn Raslān*, ed. ʿAbd Allah al-Ḥibshī. Ṣanʿāʾ: Maktab al-Jīl al-Jadīd, 1988.

Muhammad bin al-Ḥusayn. *Muntahā al-marām fī sharḥ ayāt al-aḥkām*. Dār al-Manāhil: Beirut, 1986.

al-Mutawakkil Ahmad bin Sulaymān (Imam). *Uṣūl al-aḥkām*. Ṣanʿāʾ: Muʾassasat Imam Zayd, 2003.

Müller, Christian. "Judging with God's Law on Earth: Judicial Powers of the Qāḍī al-Jamāʿa of Cordoba in the Fifth/Eleventh Century." *Islamic Law and Society* 7, no. 2 (2000): 159–86.

——. "The Ḥaram al-Sharīf Collection of Arabic Legal Documents in Jerusalem: A Mamlūk Court Archive?" *Al-Qantara* 32, no. 2 (2011): 435–59.

——. *Der Kadi und seine Zeugen: Studie der mamlukischen Haram-Dokumente aus Jerusalem*. Wiesbaden: Harrassowitz, 2013.

Mundy, Martha. *Domestic Government: Kinship, Community and Polity in North Yemen, Society and Culture in the Modern Middle East*. London: I. B. Tauris, 1995.

——. "Women's Inheritance of Land in Highland Yemen." *Arabian Studies* 5 (1979): 161–78.

Mundy, Martha, and Richard Saumarez Smith. *Governing Property, Making the State: Law, Administration and Production in Ottoman Syria*. London: I. B. Tauris, 2007.

al-Musawi, Muhsin Jasim. *The Postcolonial Arabic Novel: Debating Ambivalence*. Boston: Brill, 2003.

Nakissa, Aria. "An Epistemic Shift in Islamic Law: Educational Reform at al-Azhar and Dār al-ʿUlūm." *Islamic Law and Society* 21 (2014): 209–51.

——. "An Ethical Solution to the Problem of Legal Indeterminacy: Sharīʿa Scholarship at Egypt's al-Azhar." *Journal of the Royal Anthropological Institute* 20 (2014): 93–112.

al-Nawawī, Abu Zakariyya Yahya bin Sharaf. *Minhaj al-ṭālibīn*. Cairo: Dār Iḥyāʾ al-Kutub al-ʿArabiyya, 1956.

——. *Adab al-fatwā wa-l-muftī wa-l-mustaftī* . Damascus: Dār al-Fikr, 1988.

Ong, Walter J. *Orality and Literacy: The Technologizing of the Word*. London: Methuen, 1982.

Owen, Roger, ed. *New Perspectives on Property and Land in the Middle East*. Cambridge, MA: Harvard University Press, 2000.

Papailias, Penelope. *Genres of Recollection: Archival Poetics and Modern Greece*. New York: Palgrave Macmillan, 2005.

Parkes, Malcolm. *Pause and Effect: An Introduction to the History of Punctuation in the West*. Berkeley: University of California Press, 1993.

Pederson, Johannes. *The Arabic Book*. Translated by Geoffrey French. Princeton: Princeton University Press, 1984.

Peters, Rudolph. "Murder on the Nile: Homicide Trials in 19th Century Egyptian Sharīʿa Courts." *Die Welt des Islams* 30, no. 1 (1990): 98–116.

——. "The Re-Islamization of Criminal Law in Northern Nigeria and the Judiciary: The Safiyyatu Hussaini Case." In *Dispensing Justice in Islam: Qadis and Their Judgments*, edited by M. K. Masud, R. Peters, and D. S. Powers, 219–41. Leiden: Brill, 2006.

——. "The Violent Schoolmaster: The 'Normalization' of the Dossier of a Nineteenth-Century Egyptian Legal Case." In *Narratives of Truth in Islamic Law*, edited by Baudouin Dupret et al., 69–82. London: I. B. Tauris, 2008.

——. *Wathāʾiq madīnat al-Qaṣr bi-l-wāḥāt al-Dākhila maṣdarān li-tārīkh Miṣr fī l-ʿaṣr al-ʿuthmānī*. Cairo: Maṭbaʿat al-ʿĀmma li-Dār al-Kutub wa-l-Wathāʾiq al-Qawmiyya, 2011.

Piamenta, M. *Dictionary of Post-Classical Yemenī Arabic*. Leiden: Brill, 1991.

Pierce, Leslie. *Morality Tales: Law and Gender in the Ottoman Court of Aintab*. Berkeley: University of California Press, 2003.

Pollock, Sheldon. "Cosmopolitan and Vernacular in History." *Public Culture* 12, no. 3 (2000): 591–625.

——. "Future Philology? The Fate of a Soft Science in a Hard World." *Critical Inquiry* 35, no. 4 (2009): 931–61.

Pollock, Sheldon, Homi K. Bhabha, Carol A. Breckenridge, and Dipesh Chakrabarty. "Cosmopolitanisms." *Public Culture* 12, no. 3 (2000): 577–89.

Powers, David S. *Law, Society, and Culture in the Maghrib, 1300–1500*. Cambridge: Cambridge University Press, 2002.

Puin, Gerd-R. "The Yemeni Hijrah Concept of Tribal Protection." In *Land Tenure and Social Transformation in the Middle East*, edited by Tarif Khalidi, 483–94. Beirut: American University of Beirut, 1984.

al-Qarāfī, Ahmad bin Idris. *al-Iḥkām fī tamyīz al-fatāwā ʿan al-aḥkām wa-taṣarrufāt al-qāḍī wa-l-imām*. Aleppo: Maktab al-Matbūʿāt al-Islāmiyya, 1967.

al-Qurʾān. Translated by Ahmed Ali. Princeton: Princeton University Press, 1984.

Quraishi, Asifa, and Frank E. Vogel, eds. *The Islamic Marriage Contract: Case Studies in Family Law*. Cambridge, MA: Harvard University Press, 2008.

Rabb, Intisar. "Islamic Legal Maxims as Substantive Canons of Construction: Hudud Avoidance in Cases of Doubt." *Islamic Law and Society* 17 (2010): 63–125.

——. "Legal Maxims." In *The Oxford Encyclopedia of Islam and Law*, edited by Jonathan Brown et al. Oxford: Oxford University Press, forthcoming.

Radscheit, Matthias. "Witnessing and Testifying." In *Encyclopaedia of the Qurʾān*, edited by Jane Dammen McAuliffe. Leiden: Brill, 2012–.

Ramadan, Tariq. *Western Muslims and the Future of Islam*. Oxford: Oxford University Press, 2004.

Regourd, Anne. *Catalogue cumulé des manuscrits de bibliothèques privées de Zabid / La bibliothèque de ʾAbd al-Rahman al-Hadhrami, fasc. 1, Les papiers filigranés*. Ṣanʿāʾ: Centre Français d'Archéologie et de Sciences Sociales de Sanaa (CEFAS), 2006.

Riles, Annelise, ed. *Documents: Artifacts of Modern Knowledge*. Ann Arbor: University of Michigan Press, 2006.

Robson, James. "Ḥadīth." In Bearman et al., *Encyclopedia of Islam*, 2nd ed.

Rodionov, Mikhail, and Hanne Schönig. *The Hadramawt Documents, 1904–51: Family Life and Social Customs Under the Last Sultans*. Beirut: Ergon Verlag, 2011.

Rosen, Lawrence. *The Anthropology of Justice: Law as Culture in Islamic Society.* Cambridge: Cambridge University Press, 1989.

——. *The Justice of Islam: Comparative Perspectives on Islamic Law and Society.* Oxford: Oxford University Press, 2000.

Rosenthal, Franz. " 'Blurbs': Taqriz. From Fourteenth Century Egypt." *Oriens* 27–28 (1981): 177–96.

——. "Ibn Hadjar." In Bearman et al., *Encyclopedia of Islam*, 2nd ed.

Rossi, Ettore. "La stampa nel Yemen." *Oriente Moderno* 18 (1938): 568–80.

Rubin, Avi. *Ottoman Nizamiye Courts: Law and Modernity.* New York: Palgrave Macmillan, 2011.

Saenger, Paul. *Space Between Words: The Origins of Silent Reading.* Stanford: Stanford University Press, 1997.

Said, Edward. *The World, the Text, and the Critic.* Cambridge, MA: Harvard University Press, 1983.

——. *Humanism and Democratic Criticism.* New York: Columbia University Press, 2004.

Sālim, Sayyid Musṭafa. *Wathāʾiq yamaniyya.* 2nd printing. Cairo: al-Maṭbaʿat al-Fanniyya, 1985.

al-Samʿānī, ʿAbd al-Karim bin Muhammad. *Adab al-imlāʾ wa-l-istimlāʾ.* Leiden: Brill, 1952.

al-Ṣanʿānī, Muḥammad bin Ismāʿīl Ibn al-Amīr. *Subul al-salām sharḥ Bulūgh al-marām.* Beirut: Dār al-Kitāb al-ʿArabī, 1987.

Sanjek, Roger, ed. *Fieldnotes: The Makings of Anthropology.* Ithaca: Cornell University Press, 1990.

Sanni, Amidu. *The Arabic Theory of Prosification and Versification.* Beirut: In Kommission bei Steiner Verlag, 1998.

al-Sayāghī, Ahmad bin Ahmad bin Muhammad bin Husayn. *al-Minhāj al-munīr tatimmat al-rawḍ al-naḍīr.* Ṣanʿāʾ: Muʾassasat al-Imām Zayd bin ʿAlī, 2005.

al-Sayāghī, Husayn bin Ahmad. *al-Rawḍ al-Naḍīr sharḥ majmūʿ al-fiqh al-kabīr.* Cairo: Maṭbaʿat al-Saʿāda, 1347–49 AH [1928–30].

al-Sayāghī, Husayn bin Ahmad. *al-Madhhab al-zaydī al-yamanī.* Ṣanʿāʾ: Maktaba Ghamḍān, 1984.

Schacht, Joseph. *An Introduction to Islamic Law.* Oxford: Clarendon Press, 1964.

Schimmel, Annemarie. *Islamic Names: An Introduction.* Edinburgh: Edinburgh University Press, 1989.

Schmidtke, Sabine. "The History of Zaydī Studies: An Introduction." *Arabica* 59 (2012): 185–99.

Schneider, Irene. *Das Bild des Richters in der "Adab al-Qāḍī" Literatur.* Frankfurt am Main: Peter Lang, 1990.

Schoeler, Gregor. *The Oral and the Written in Early Islam.* Translated by Uwe Vagelpohl. Edited by James E. Montgomery. London: Routledge, 2006.

——. *The Genesis of Literature in Islam: From the Aural to the Read.* Revised ed. Translated by Shawkat M. Toorawa. Edinburgh: Edinburgh University Press, 2009.

Scott, David, and Charles Hirschkind, eds. *Powers of the Secular Modern: Talal Asad and His Interlocutors.* Stanford: Stanford University Press, 2006.

Scott, Hugh. *In the High Yemen.* London: John Murray, 1942.

Seitel, Peter. "Haya Metaphors for Speech." *Language in Society* 3, no. 1 (1974): 51–67.

Serjeant, Robert B. "A Zaidī Manual of Ḥisba of the 3rd Century. H." *Rivista degli Studi Orientali* 28 (1957): 1–34.
——. "Ḥaram and Ḥawṭah: The Sacred Enclave in Arabia." In *Mélanges Taha Husain*, edited by 'Abd-ar-Raḥmān Badawī and Ṭāhā Ḥusain. Miṣr: Dār al-Maʿārif, 1962.
——. "The Cultivation of Cereals in Medieval Yemen." *Arabian Studies* 1 (1974).
Serjeant, R. B., and Ronald Lewcock. *Ṣanʿāʾ: An Arabian Islamic City*. London: World of Islam Festival Trust, 1983.
Shah, Mustafa, ed., *Arabic Language and Islam: Oxford Bibliographies Online Research Guide*. Oxford: Oxford University Press, 2011.
al-Shamāḥī, ʿAbd Allah bin ʿAbd al-Wahhab. *Ṣirāṭ al-ʿārifīn ilā idrāk ikhtiyārāt amīr al-muʾminīn*. Ṣanʿāʾ: Maṭbaʿat al-Maʿārif, 1356 AH (1937).
al-Shāmī, Ahmad Muhammad. *Imām al-Yaman Ahmad Ḥamīd al-Dīn*. Beirut: Dār al-Kitāb al-Jadīd, 1965.
Sharaf al-Dīn, Ahmad Husayn. *Tārikh al-Fikr al-Islāmī fī al-Yaman*. Cairo: Maṭbaʿat al-Kaylānī, 1968.
al-Sharafī, Ahmad bin Muhammad. "Qawāʿid ahl al-madhhab." In *al-Muntazaʿ al-mukhtār min al-Ghayth al-midrār* [*Sharḥ al-Azhār*], by Abd Allāh bin Muḥammad Ibn Miftāḥ, 3:46–48. Cairo: Maṭbaʿa al-dīniyya, 1341 AH (1922); Ṣanʿāʾ: Maktaba Ghamḍān, 1401 AH (1980).
al-Shawkānī, Muhammad ʿAli. *Adab al-ṭalab*. Ṣanʿāʾ: Markaz al-Dirāsāt al-Yamaniyya, 1979.
——. *Darārī al-muḍiyya sharḥ al-durar al-bahiyya*. Beirut: Dār al-Jīl, 1987.
——. *Fatḥ al-qadīr al-jāmiʿ bayna fannay al-riwāya waʾl-dirāya min ʿilm al-tafsīr*. Cairo: Muṣṭafā al-Bābī al-Ḥalabī, 1349 AH (1930).
——. *Matn al-durar al-bahiyya*. N.p.: n.p., [1964].
——. *Nayl al-awṭār fī sharḥ muntaqā al-akhbār*. Cairo: Sharikat al-Quds li-l-Tijāra, 2008.
——. *Sayl al-jarrār al-mutadaffiq ʿalā ḥadāʾiq al-azhār*. Beirut: Dār al-Kutub al-ʿIlmiyya, 1985.
——. *Wābl al-ghamām ʿalā shifāʾ al-uwām*. Edited by M. Hallaq. 2 vols. Cairo: Maktabat Ibn Taymiyya, 1416 AH (1995).
al-Shaykh al-Niẓām, et al. *al-Fatāwā al-hindiyya*. Vol. 6. Peshawar: Nūrānī Kutub Khānah, [197-?].
Siddīqī, Muhammad Zubayr. *Ḥadīth Literature*. Cambridge: Islamic Texts Society, 1993.
Sijpesteijn, Petra M., and Lennart Sundelin, eds. *Papyrology and the History of Early Islamic Egypt*. Leiden: Brill, 2004.
Silverstein, Michael, and Greg Urban, eds. *Natural Histories of Discourse*. Chicago: University of Chicago Press, 1996.
Skovgaard-Petersen, Jakob. *Defining Islam for the Egyptian State: Muftīs and Fatwās of the Dār al-Iftāʾ*. Leiden: Brill, 1997.
Smith, William Robertson. *Kinship and Marriage in Early Arabia*. Cambridge: Cambridge University Press, 1885.
——. *Lectures on the Religion of the Semites*. New York: Ktav Publishing, 1969.
Spectorsky, Susan. *Chapters on Marriage and Divorce: Responses of Ibn Ḥanbal and Ibn Rāhwayh*. Austin: University of Texas Press, 1993.
——. *Women in Classical Islamic Law*. Leiden: Brill, 2010.

Spivak, Gayatri Chakravorty. *A Critique of Postcolonial Reason: Toward a History of the Vanishing Present*. Cambridge, MA: Harvard University Press, 1999.

Stewart, Charles. "Great and Little Traditions." In *Encyclopedia of Social and Cultural Anthropology*, edited by Alan Barnard and Jonathan Spencer. London: Routledge, 1998.

Stewart, Devin. *Islamic Legal Orthodoxy: Twelver Shiite Responses to the Sunni Legal System*. Salt Lake City: University of Utah Press, 1998.

Stocking, George. *The Ethnographer's Magic and Other Essays in the History of Anthropology*. Madison: University of Wisconsin Press, 1992.

Stoler, Ann Laura. *Along the Archival Grain: Epistemic Anxieties and Colonial Common Sense*. Princeton: Princeton University Press, 2009.

Strothmann, Rudolf. *Das Staatsrecht der Zaiditen*. Strassburg: K. J. Trübner, 1912.

—. "Al-Zaidīya." In *Shorter Encyclopedia of Islam*, edited by H. A. R. Gibb and J. H. Kramers, 651–52. Leiden: Brill; Ithaca: Cornell University Press, 1965.

Taminian, Lucine. "Playing with Words: The Ethnography of Poetic Genres in Yemen." PhD thesis, University of Michigan, 2001.

Taqī, ʿIzz al-din Hasan, ed. *al-Fatāwā al-sharʿiyya wa-l-ʿilmiyya wa-l-diniyya li-ʿulamāʾ al-diyār al-yamaniyya*. Ṣanʿāʾ: Maktaba al-Irshād, n.d.

Tedlock, Dennis, and Bruce Mannheim, eds. *The Dialogic Emergence of Culture*. Urbana: University of Illinois Press, 1995.

Thompson, E. P. *Whigs and Hunters: The Origin of the Black Act*. New York: Pantheon, 1975.

Todorov, Tzevtan. *Mikhail Bakhtin: The Dialogical Principle*. Manchester: Manchester University Press, 1984.

Tucker, Judith E. *In the House of the Law: Gender and Islamic Law in Ottoman Syria and Palestine*. Berkeley: California, 1998.

—. *Women, Family, and Gender in Islamic Law*. Cambridge: Cambridge University Press, 2008.

Tutwiler, Richard, and Sheila Carapico. *Yemenī Agriculture and Economic Change*. Ṣanʿāʾ: American Institute for Yemenī Studies, 1981.

Tyan, Émile. *Institutions du Droit Public Musulman*. 2 vols. Paris: Recueil Sirey, 1956.

—. *Histoire de l'organisation judiciaire en pays d'Islam*. Leiden: Brill, 1960.

Van Arendonk, Cornelis. *Les débuts de l'imamat zaidite au Yemen*. Translated by Jacques Ryckmans. Leiden: E. J. Brill, 1960.

van Bruinessen, Martin. "Kitab Kuning: Books in Arabic Script Used in the Pesantren Milieu." *Bijdagen tot de Taal-, Land en Volkenkunde* 146 (1990): 226–69.

Vismann, Cornelia. *Files: Law and Media Technology*. Translated by Geoffrey Winthrop-Young. Stanford: Stanford University Press, 2008.

Vogel, Frank E. *Islamic Law and Legal System: Studies of Saudi Arabia*. Leiden: Brill, 2000.

Voloshinov, Valentin N. *Marxism and the Philosophy of Language*. New York: Seminar Press, 1973.

vom Bruck, Gabriele. *Islam, Memory, and Morality in Yemen: Ruling Families in Transition*. New York: Palgrave Macmillan, 2005.

Wagner, Mark S. *Like Joseph in Beauty: Yemeni Vernacular Poetry and Arab-Jewish Symbiosis*. Leiden: Brill, 2009.

——. *Jews and Islamic Law in Early 20th Century Yemen*. Bloomington: Indiana University Press, 2015.

Wakin, Jeanette. *The Function of Documents in Islamic Law: The Chapters on Sales from Ṭaḥāwī's Kitāb al-shurūṭ al-kabīr*. Albany: State University of New York Press, 1972.

Wakin, Jeanette, and Aron Zysow. "*Raʾy*." In *The Encyclopedia of Islam*, 12 (supplement). Leiden: Brill, 1965–86.

Walz, Terence. *Family Archives in Egypt: New Light on Nineteenth-Century Provincial Trade*. L'Egypte au XIXe siècle. Paris: Editions du CNRS, 1982.

Watt, Ian, and Jack Goody. "The Consequences of Literacy." *Comparative Studies in Society and History* 5, no. 3 (1963): 304–45.

Weber, Max. *Economy and Society*. Berkeley: University of California Press, 1978.

Wehr, Hans. *A Dictionary of Modern Written Arabic*. Ithaca: Cornell University Press, 1966.

Weir, Shelagh. *A Tribal Order: Politics and Law in the Mountains of Yemen*. Austin: University of Texas Press, 2007.

Weiss, Bernard G. *The Search for God's Law: Islamic Jurisprudence in the Writings of Sayf al-Din al-Āmidī*. Salt Lake City: University of Utah Press, 1992.

Welchman, Lynn. *Beyond the Code: Muslim Family Law and the Sharʿi Judiciary in the Palestinian West Bank*. The Hague: Kluwer Law International, 2000.

White, Hayden V. *The Content of the Form: Narrative Discourse and Historical Representation*. Baltimore: Johns Hopkins University Press, 1987.

White, James Boyd. *The Legal Imagination: Studies in the Nature of Legal Thought and Expression*. Chicago: University of Chicago Press, 1985.

Wiederhold, Lutz. "Legal Doctrines in Conflict: The Relevance of Madhhab Boundaries to Legal Reasoning in the Light of an Unpublished Treatise on Taqlīd and Ijtihād." *Islamic Law and Society* 3, no. 2 (1996): 234–304.

Wilkinson, John C. *The Imamate Tradition of Oman*. Cambridge: Cambridge University Press, 1987.

Williams, Raymond. *Marxism and Literature*. Oxford: Oxford University Press, 1977.

Williams, Tennessee. *Camino Real*. New York: New Directions, 1953.

Willis, John M. *Unmaking North and South: Cartographies of the Yemeni Past, 1857–1934*. New York: Columbia University Press, 2011.

Witkam, Jan Just. "Nuskha." In Bearman et al., *Encyclopedia of Islam*, 2nd ed.

Wollard, Kathryn A., and Bambi B. Schieffelin. "Language Ideology." *Annual Review of Anthropology* 23 (1994): 55–82.

Würth, Anna. "A Sanaʿa Court: The Family and the Ability to Negotiate." *Islamic Law and Society* 2, no. 3 (1995): 320–40.

——. *Ash-Shariʿa fi Bab al-Yaman: Recht, Richter und Rechtspraxis an der Familienrechtlichen Kammer des Gerichts Sud-Sanaa*. Republik Jemen, 1983–1995. Berlin: Duncker and Humblot, 2000.

Yanagihashi, Hiroyuki. "The Doctrinal Development of "Maraḍ al-Mawt" in the Formative Period of Islamic Law." *Islamic Law and Society* 5, no. 2 (1998): 326–58.

——. *A History of the Early Islamic Law of Property: Reconstructing the Legal Development, 7th–9th Centuries*. Leiden: Brill, 2004.

Yemen Arab Republic. *al-Awqāf wa-l-irshād fī mawkib al-thawra*. Ṣanʿāʾ: Ministry of Endowments, 1987.

——. *Qarārāt Wizārat al-ʿAdl*. Ṣanʿāʾ: Ministry of Justice, 1971.
——. Law no. 87 of 1976. *Tashrīʿāt* 4:37–39.
——. Law no. 127 of 1976 (on "The Facilitation of Marriage"). *Tashrīʿāt* 4:16–18.
——. *Qarārāt Wizārat al-ʿAdl*. Ṣanʿāʾ: Ministry of Justice, 1971.
Yemen, Republic of. *Al-sulṭa al-qaḍāʾiyya* (Law 1 of 1991). *Al-Jarīda al-Rasmiyya* (1991).
Zabāra, Muḥammad. *Nayl al-waṭar.* 2 vols. Cairo: Matbaʾat al-Salafiyya, 1348 and 1350 AH (1929 and 1931).
——. *Nashr al-ʿarf li-nubalāʾ al-yaman baʿd al-alf.* Vol. 2. Cairo: Maṭbaʿa al-Salafiyya, 1958.
——. *Nuzhat al-naẓar fī rijāl al-qarn al-rābiʿ ʿashar.* Ṣanʿāʾ: Markaz al-Dirāsāt wa-l-Abḥāth al-Yamaniyya, 1979.
al-Zamakhsharī, Abual-Qasim Jar Allah Mahmud bin ʿUmar. *al-Kashshāf ʿan ḥaqāʾiq al-tanzīl wa ʿuyūn al-aqāwīl fī wujūh al-taʾwīl.* 4 vols. Cairo: al-Bābī al-Ḥalabī, 1966–68.
Ze'evi, Dror. "The Use of Ottoman Sharīʿa Court Records as a Source for Middle Eastern Social History: A Reappraisal." *Islamic Law and Society* 5, no. 1 (1998): 35–56.

Index

al-Akwaʿ, ʿAbd al-Karim, 276, 326, 389; at Ibb Endowments Office, 4–6, *5*; local fatwās and, 173–74
al-Akwaʿ, Ismāʿīl, 89, 98, 103, 123
ʿalāma. See signature
ʿalayhi al-ḥaqq (individual against whom is the right), 336
alfāẓ (expressions), 333, 340, 342, 357–59, 448*n*65
ʿAli bin Abī Ṭālib, 11–12, 115, 204, 213, 400
al-ʿAlimī, Rashād, 163, 457*n*6
al-ʿamal bi-l-khaṭṭ. See practice with writing
amīn taḥrīr ʿuqūd (modern instrument writer), 469*n*16
al-Amīr ʿAli bin al-Husayn, 207
amr (divine order), 136–38
al-amr bi-l-maʿrūf wa-l-nahy ʿan al-munkar (commanding right and forbidding wrong), 40
al-ʿAmrī, Husayn, 80, 93–95, 113, 115, 118
analytic underpinning of a matter, issue, or case (*ʿilla*), 214
and if (*wa in, wa idhā*), 344, 346, 355–57
announcement (*iʿlān*), 89
al-ʿAnsī, Ahmad bin Qasim, 69, 78, 93, 124; career of, 80–81, 98, 217–18; on contracts, 151, 353, 358, 378–80; *dīwān* defined by, 147–48, 233, 442*n*38; on expression, 153–54; on judgments, 274, 279–80; on material trace, 152; on memory, 146–51; on oral reading, 142–46; on pre-text, 101–2, 106–12, 114, 116, 119, 130–31. See also *Gilded Crown, The*
al-ʿAnsī, Yahya, 161, *163*, 253–54, 275; consultation with, 445*n*26; as mufti, 161, *163*; as notarial writer, 324–25
al-ʿAnsī family, 78, 113–14
anthropologist: common sense and, 317; disciplinary orientations of, 343; kinship studies by, 296; linguistic, 43–44, 420*n*120; native theory and, 44, 343, 420*n*120; as reader, 33–52, 416*n*79
Appeal Court (*dīwān al-istiʾnāf*), 91, 178, 180, 187, 398, 460*n*40; introduction of, 458*n*15; name of, 442*n*37
appellate ruling, 227
ʿaqd al-nikāḥ. See marriage contract
ʿaqd al-zawāj (local marriage contract), 389
al-ʿāqid (contractor), 189, 386–87, 392–93
Arabic language: academic subfields, 108; dialects, 138, 302–3, 464*n*44; vernacularization of, 27–28
arbāb al-tazwīr (practitioners of forgery), 309
Archaeology of Knowledge, The (Foucault), 57
archive (*dīwān*): access to, 405; articulations within, 37; central, 227, 452*n*7; commentary and, 134–44, 146–49, 151–52; as contingent, 25, 27; defined, 147–48, 233, 442*n*38; elementary forms of, 221–25; ethnographic sourcing and, 227–29; evidential status of, 195–99, 234–35; fatwā in, 25, 171–72; formal language in, 43; genres, 23, 28, 222, 455*n*46; interregional cosmopolitanism in, 352; introduction to, 20–33, 52–54; of judges, 236–38, 240–45, 256, 459*n*33; library and, 21–27, 41, 43–46, 217–21, 332, 348; literature and, 452*n*1; local texts, 26–30; memory and, 146–51, 155, 322, 441*n*32; modeling and, 44–46; proper names in, 252, 291–92, 296; roles of, 140; specificity of, 219, 229–37; *tafsīr* and, 110; text building in, 219–22, 252; textual architecture of, 21–33; textual surrounds of, 53, 225–27; theories of practice of, 229, 237–46, 343, 403; uncertainty of, 210, 213–14; written custom of, 246–48. *See also* contracts; judgment; minutes; notarial documents; practice with writing; stipulations
art (*fann*), 452*n*2

branches (*furūʿ*), of jurisprudence, 98, 102–3, 106, 434*n*10
Brown, Jonathan, 113
Bulūgh al-marām (Ibn Ḥajar), 113
Burak, Guy, 234, 454*n*31
Bury, G. Wyman, 412*n*25
buyer (*al-mushtarī*), 362, 364–67, 369

Calder, Norman, 44, 77
calendar, 458*n*21
caliph (*khalīfa*), 11, 15, 410*n*8
Calligraphic State, The (Messick), 33, 38, 163, 254, 421*n*125
canceling annotation (*tanbīh*), 363–64
case. See *mas'ala*
case law, 159, 250
cases, 257
census, 293, 391, 463*n*21
central archive, 227, 452*n*7
charity (*ṣadaqa*) lists, 292–94, 454*n*39
choice, of a ruling imam (*ikhtiyār*), 25, 446*nn*51–52; of Ahmad, 159, 164–65, 177–78, 181–85, 187–92, *192*, 235, 449*n*86; application of, 184–88, 448*n*77; archiving of, 447*n*62; on commercial registers, 235; contracts and, 353, 359; defined, 176–77; fatwā compared with, 179–80; finished, 191–93, 192*f*; *The Gilded Crown* and, 177, 425*n*35; interpretive community and, 181–84; introduction to, 157–60; judges and, 177–78, 180–81, 185–91, 193–94, 198, 251, 257; in *madhhab*, 177, 183; al-Muṭahhar and, 164–65, 177, 182, 187; practice with writing and, 195–99, 244, 309, 322; as precedent, 16; quotations and, 186–88, 190, 305; Schacht on, 446*n*52; al-Shamāḥī and, 163, 183, 196–98, 399; as source, 7; sourcing of, 161–67; stripping of, 160, 165, 188–94, *192*, 251, 398; versification of, 181–83, 196; of Yahya, 53, 73, 159, 163–65, *165*, 177–79, 182–87, 196–99, 244, 309, 322, 359, 399, 425*n*35, 448*n*65
clause-by-clause approaches, 135, 350, 382, 468*n*38
codification, 90–91
colonialism, 17–18, 83, 328, 456*n*71
commanding right and forbidding wrong (*al-amr bi-l-maʿrūf wa-l-nahy ʿan al-munkar*), 40
commas, 345–46
commenda, 378–79
commentary (*sharḥ*): abridged, 71, 75, 77; archive and, 134–44, 146–49, 151–52; *fiqh* and, 142–56; issues not brought up in, 124; *mas'ala* in, 66–67; *tafsīr* as, 135–42; witnessing in, 138–40, 142–47, 149–51. *See also specific works*
Commentary on the Flowers (Ibn Miftāḥ), 67, 70–71, 92, 93, 425*n*38; authority of, 114, 123; cross-citations, 75; al-Ghurbānī and, 67, *68*; *The Gilded Crown* on, 73–74, 114; inquiry and, 204, 208; on interpreter's role, 124–25; on judgment, 275; on memory, 147; as modeling text, 331; pre-text and, 101–2, 104–5, 112, 116, 119; on testimonies, 142
commercial documentation, lack of, 355, 455*n*40
commercial registers, 234–36
commercial sale contract case: introduction to, 257; al-Manṣūr, I., hearing, 257; al-Muṣannif in, 304; quotation in, 302, 304–5; as simple proceeding, 302
common law, 54, 190, 250–51
common sense, 317
Compilation of al-ʿAnsī, The, 78, 427*n*54
complaint. *See* petition
complex proceedings, 302
composition: of contracts, 349–50; of court records, 252; first-person, 300, 327, 385, 459*n*26; organization of, 261; as performance, 221; process of, 42, 419*n*115; reading and, 40–45, 47, 49–50, 52; sources in, 42–43; spacing in, 71, *72*, 261, 459*n*23; standards, 218

ʿ*ilm al-shurūṭ* (Science of the Stipulations), 334
imam (jurist-leader): in *The Book of Flowers*, 11; caretaker, 169; conflict resolution by, 15–16, 85, 176–77, 184–85; defined, 11, 410*n*8; fatwās and, 176, 178–80; justness of, 104, 129–33; role of, 15–16, 157–60, 163–67, 169, 218. *See also* choice, of a ruling imam
imamate (*imāma*), 11–13, 40
imlāʾ. *See* dictation
immanent, 6, 410*n*4
incorporative genres, 48
independent sharīʿa reasoning and interpretation. See *ijtihād*
individual against whom is the right (ʿ*alayhi al-ḥaqq*), 336
individual opinion or statement. See *qawl*
individual ownership. See *milk*
inheritance case. *See* endowment and inheritance case
inheritance instruments (*fuṣūl*, sing. *faṣl*; *furūz*, sing. *farz*), *6, 201, 211, 246, 325, 346, 362, 468n*3, 480
initial response of defendant (*ijāba*), 301–2, 464*n*40
inquiry (*baḥth*): *The Book of Flowers* and, 206–10, 214; *Commentary on the Flowers* and, 204, 208; fatwā and, 195, 199–201; *fiqh* and, 206–14; by al-Kibsī, 199–214; *masʾala* and, 206, 212, 214; practice with writing and, 195, 199–201; quotation in, 201–2; Qurʾan and, 201–3; Shāfiʿī school and, 200; Sunna and, 203–6; Zaydī school and, 200
"Instructions" (*taʿlīmāt*) (Yahya, Imam), 224, 256, 348; on dictation, 278; doctrine in, 269; judgment and, 54, 218, 267–72, *268*, *271*, 275–76, 278, 329; on minutes, 272, 287, 290, 329; motivations in issuing, 267; sourcing, 256; stipulations compared with, 329–30; on unscrupulous legal representatives, 303–4
interdisciplinarity, 121–22
interest taking, 337, 339
interpreter. See *mujtahid*
"In the Name of God" (*Basmala*), 101, 179, *259*, 329, 361, 369
intizāʿ (textual extraction), 79, 427*n*59
invocation of God, 338, 361. See also *Basmala*; *Ḥamdala*
Iran, 61, 204, 414*n*58, 420*n*122
irrigated land, 372–73
al-Iryānī, ʿAli ʿAbd Allah, 137, 332; on contracts, 336–38, 343–46, 350, 352–53, 355–59, *358*, 364–67, 370–71, 374–77, 380–83, 385–88, 401–3, 474*n*89; as reader, 403. See also *Success of the Student in the Description of What the Writer Writes*
al-Iryānī, Hasan bin Ahmad, 97–98; murder case heard by, 255, 257
al-Iryānī, Muhammad bin Hasan: registers of, 253–54, 466*n*9
al-Iryānī, Yahya bin Muhammad, 96–97, 111, 118, 436*n*36
ishtarā (bought), 361–62
Islamic law: nature of, 14; Schacht on, 13–14, 29–31, 103, 114–15, 131, 246, 412*n*25, 446*n*52, 467*n*20; studies, 30–33; textual forms of, 158–59; will-to-power and, 13. *See also* sharīʿa
Islamic mysticism (*tasawwuf*), 40
issue. See *masʾala*
istikhrāj (extraction), 274
iṣṭilāḥāt (technical uses), 84, 154, 340
iʿtimād (authentication), 245
al-ʿIzzī family, 412*n*34
al-ʿIzzī (Muhammad) Fihmī al-Ṣabāḥī, 254, 275, 466*n*79

al-Jabrī scholars, 85
al-Jalāl, al-Hasan bin Ahmad, 65, 148–49, 207, 424*n*25, 424*n*29
jarḥ wa-l-taʿdīl (negative and positive evaluation), 122, 288–89, 309

CPSIA information can be obtained
at www.ICGtesting.com
Printed in the USA
JSHW022259250722
28419JS00010B/25

9 780231 178754